MYTHS AND MYTHOLOGIES

Critical Categories in the Study of Religion

Series Editor: Russell T. McCutcheon, Professor, Department of Religious Studies, University of Alabama

Critical Categories in the Study of Religion aims to present the pivotal articles that best represent the most important trends in how scholars have gone about the task of describing, interpreting, and explaining the place of religion in human life. The series focuses on the development of categories and the terminology of scholarship that make possible knowledge about human beliefs, behaviors, and institutions. Each volume in the series is intended as both an introductory survey of the issues that surround the use of various key terms as well as an opportunity for a thorough retooling of the concept under study, making clear to readers that the cognitive categories of scholarship are themselves historical artefacts that change over time.

Published:

Syncretism in Religion
A Reader
Edited by Anita M. Leopold and Jeppe Sinding Jensen

Ritual and Religious Belief
A Reader
Edited by Graham Harvey

Defining Hinduism
A Reader
Edited by J.E. Llewellyn

Religion and Cognition
A Reader
Edited by D. Jason Slone

Mircea Eliade
A Critical Reader
Edited by Bryan Rennie

Defining Buddhisms
A Reader
Edited by Karen Derris and Natalie Gummer

Defining Islam
A Reader
Edited by Andrew Rippin

Forthcoming:

Readings in the Theory of Religion
Map, Text, Body
Edited by Scott S. Elliott and Matthew Waggoner

Defining Religion
A Reader
Edited by Tim Murphy

Religious Experience
A Reader
Edited by Russell T. McCutcheon and Leslie Smith

Missions, Management and Effects
A Reader in Religion and Colonialism
Edited by Mark Elmore and Caleb Elfenbein

What is Religious Studies?
A Reader in Disciplinary Formation
Edited by Steven J. Sutcliffe

Defining Judaism
A Reader
Edited by Aaron W. Hughes

Defining Shinto
A Reader
Edited by Okuyama Michiaki and Mark MacWilliams

MYTHS AND MYTHOLOGIES

A READER

Edited by

Jeppe Sinding Jensen

LONDON   OAKVILLE

Published by
UK: Equinox Publishing Ltd., Unit 6, The Village, 101 Amies St., London SW11 2JW
USA: DBBC, 28 Main Street, Oakville, CT 06779

www.equinoxpub.com

First published 2009

British Library Cataloguing-in-Publication Data
A catalogue record for this book is available from the British Library.

Library of Congress Cataloging-in-Publication Data
Myths and mythologies : a reader / edited by Jeppe Sinding Jensen.
        p. cm. — (Critical categories in the study of religion)
    Includes bibliographical references and index.
    ISBN 1-904768-08-3 (hb) —
    ISBN 1-904768-09-1 (pb) 1. Myth. 2.
    Mythology. I. Jensen, Jeppe Sinding, 1951- II. Series.
    BL304.M929 2009
    201'.3—dc22
    2006010168

ISBN-13   978 1 904768 08 1 (hardback)
          978 1 904768 09 8 (paperback)

Typeset by S.J.I. Services, New Delhi
Printed and bound in Great Britain by Antony Rowe, Chippenham, Wiltshire

CONTENTS

Contents

PREFACE

The study of myth is a vast field – in the study of religion, in anthropology, in literature, in semiotics and other subjects as well. It is not a study to approach without some hesitation. There is an incredible amount of literature and no one can read and master it all. That may also explain why there are few volumes of this kind around. You can do it but you are most likely to fail in some – or more – respects. Thus, my own embarkation on this project was very much due to the encouragement and support from the editor of the series "Critical Categories in the Study of Religion," Russell McCutcheon from the University of Alabama, Tuscaloosa. As we have both been working with the formations, transformations and criticism of theories in the study of religion, Russell contacted me and asked if I could help in pointing to a possible editor for a volume on "Myth" as one of those crucial, but critical categories in the study of religion. I suggested several possible scholars who might undertake this and he then replied that he had already contacted the same people and that they had declined. Then what? After some hesitation I realized that I should perhaps take up the challenge. After all, I had written a draft of an unpublished small book on mythology in the mid 1980s when I was a young assistant professor in the Department of Philosophy at the University of Southern Denmark and I had taught courses and seminars on this for students from departments across the faculty of humanities. The old reading-packages were still on my shelves and other materials had been collected since. So, the enthusiasm and interest that my students then afforded the subject gave me confidence that the idea of studying myth was not in vain. I do now thank them for that. Later, I took up a position at the University of Aarhus, Denmark, in the Department for the Study of Religion and have since then offered a few undergraduate courses on myth as well as graduate courses on such topics as discourse analysis, structuralism, semiotics and, later, cognitive theory based studies of culture, religion, narrativity and myth.

Sometimes a scholar dreams of a university without students, but that is only when we are too busy and squeezed between deadlines, funding cuts and so on. I could not have undertaken or produced this work without the collaboration of my students. To wit, the draft manuscript of this volume has been used twice in courses and seminars and I have benefited so much from my students' suggestions, comments and questions, in order to make the volume more clear and accessible. To the extent that I have not succeeded in this, it remains my liability and certainly not theirs. Besides my friend and colleague Russell McCutcheon, whom I first met when I was a visiting lecturer and he was a doctoral student at the then Center for Advanced Studies in Religion, the University of Toronto, I wish to thank another friend and colleague from the University of Alabama, Tim Murphy, who, like I, has taken an indelible interest in semiotics and thus kept me confident that this was indeed a way for religious studies to go. In that corner of the academic field I wish to extend my most gracious thanks to my colleagues at my current faculty, Hans Jørgen Lundager Jensen, Ole Davidsen and Jens Peter Schjødt for sharing with me the immense erudition they have in their respective studies on myth and myths: Ancient Israelite, early Christian and Old Norse. My colleague Armin W. Geertz's work on Hopi mythology and his subsequent work on the cognitive science of religion, as well as our close collaboration for decades, have been invaluable sources of inspiration. Further afield, one of my greatest inspirations has come from Hans H. Penner, of Dartmouth College, who made me think very differently about language and myth. Among other sources of inspiration are many great and friendly scholars whom I have met and exchanged views with, perhaps not directly on myth, but they have nevertheless contributed importantly to the composition of this project: Luther H. Martin, Willam E. Paden, Donald Wiebe, E. Thomas Lawson, Merlin Donald, Terrence Deacon, Edwin Hutchins, Bradd Shore, Robert A. Segal, Chris Sinha, Per Aage Brandt, Nancy Frankenberry, Benson Saler, Tom Sjöblom, Ilkka Pyysiäinen and, not least, my close friend Alan V. Williams. Also, my thanks go to Janet Joyce and Valerie Hall of Equinox who both very patiently and receptively waited for me to finish the project and supported it all along in this arduous process. Finally, Sarah Norman's assistance in editing the manuscript and her help in turning it into this volume has been most constructive.

Since antiquity, the Western history of ideas has demonstrated a troubled relation between imagination and rationality. There have always, and probably always will be, myth as well as criticism of "it." It is my sincere hope that this publication will aid us in understanding this aspect of human nature and culture. We would not have human culture and all that has come with it were it not for our ability to imagine things and so mythmaking is in all likelihood an ineradicable aspect of our nature. I have striven to present just such a picture of humanity, myth and mythology. Whether I have succeeded is up to the readers to judge, but I have delighted much in the making of this presentation. Myth is a wondrous and fascinating subject.

Jeppe Sinding Jensen
Aarhus, August 2008

SOURCES

Part I. Philosophical Approaches

Lévy-Bruhl, Lucien. 1987. "The Transition to the Higher Mental Types." In idem, *How Natives Think*. Chapter IX, 361–385. Princeton: Princeton University Press.

Langer, Susanne K. 1951. "Life-Symbols: The Roots of Myth." In idem, *Philosophy in a New Key: A Study in the Symbolism of Reason, Rite and Art* [orig. 1942], 148–174. Cambridge, MA: Harvard University Press. Copyright © 1942, 1951, 1957 by the President and Fellows of Harvard College. Renewed 1970, 1979 by Susanne K. Langer, 1985 by Leonard C.R. Langer.

Cassirer, Ernst. 1946. "The Place of Language and Myth in the Pattern of Human Culture." In idem, *Language and Myth*, 1–17. Mineola, NY: Dover Publications.

Popper, Karl R. 1982. "The Worlds 1, 2, and 3" from "Indeterminism is Not Enough: An Afterword." In idem, *The Open Universe: An Argument for Indeterminism*, 114–130. London: Routledge.

Searle, John R. 1995. "Language and Social Reality." In idem, *The Construction of Social Reality*, 59–78. New York: The Free Press. Reprinted by permission of Simon & Schuster Adult Publishing Group and Penguin Group UK.

Part II. Psychological Approaches

Max Müller, Friedrich. 1856. *Comparative Mythology.* (20 p. edited excerpts, 6-178) [Arno Press 1977, reprint of George Routledge & Sons 1909 ed.]

Malinowski, Bronislaw. 1951. "Myth in Primitive Psychology." In idem, *Magic, Science and Religion*, 96–101. New York: Doubleday [orig. 1925].

Freud, Sigmund. 1950. Extract from *Introductory Lectures on Psycho-Analysis*, 195–208. (transl. James Strachey). London: Routledge. Reprinted by permission of Taylor & Francis Books Ltd.

Eliade, Mircea. 1969. "Cosmogonic Myth and 'Sacred History'." In idem, *The Quest: History and Meaning in Religion*, 72–87. Chicago: University of Chicago Press. Copyright © 1969 The University of Chicago Press. Reprinted by permission of The University of Chicago Press and the Literary Executor, The Estate of Mircea Eliade.

Part III. Sociological Approaches

Durkheim, Émile and Marcel Mauss. 1963. "Conclusion." In idem, *Primitive Classification*, 81–88. (transl., ed. and intro. Rodney Needham) Chicago: University of Chicago Press. (orig. in *Année Sociologique*, vol. VI (1901–2), 1–72). Copyright © 1963 The University of Chicago Press. Reprinted by permission of The University of Chicago Press.

Dumézil, Georges. 1977. "The Gods: Æsir and Vanir." In idem (and Einar Haugen, ed.), *Gods of the Ancient Northmen*, 1–25. Berkeley: University of California Press. © 1977 The Regents of the University of California.

Douglas, Mary. 1984. "Primitive Worlds." In idem, *Purity and Danger: An Analysis of the Concepts of Pollution and Taboo*, 74–94. London: Routledge. Reprinted by permission of Taylor & Francis Books Ltd.

Clastres, Pierre. 1977. "What Makes Indians Laugh." In idem, *Society Against the State*, 108–127. Oxford: Blackwell. Reprinted by permission of Blackwell Publishing.

Part IV. Semiological Approaches

Lévi-Strauss, Claude. 1986. "Overture." In idem, *The Raw and the Cooked: Introduction to a Science of Mythology*, 1–14. Harmondsworth: Penguin. (1st. English ed. publ. 1970 by Jonathan Cape, London.) Reprinted by permission of The Random House Group Ltd.

Détienne, Marcel. 1981. "The Myth of 'Honeyed Orpheus.'" In R.L. Gordon, ed., *Myth, Religion & Society*, 95–109. Cambridge: Cambridge University Press. (Orig. 'Orphée au Miel', *Faire de l'histoire III: Nouveaux objets*). Copyright © Editions Gallimard, 1974. Reprinted by permission of Gallimard.

Barthes, Roland. 1994. "Introduction to the Structural Analysis of Narratives." In idem, *The Semiotic Challenge*, 95–120. (orig. 1966). Berkeley: University of California Press. Copyright © 1994 The Regents of the University of California.

Wagner, Roy. 1978. "The Theory of Symbolic Obviation." In idem, *Lethal Speech: Daribi Myth as Symbolic Obviation*, 19–38. Ithaca: Cornell University Press. Copyright © 1978 by Cornell University. Used by permission of the publisher, Cornell University Press.

Part V. Cognitivist Approaches

Hutchins, Edwin. 1987. "Myth and Experience in the Trobriand Islands." In Dorothy Holland and Naomi Quinn, eds., *Cultural Models in Language and Thought*, 269–289. Cambridge: Cambridge University Press. Copyright © Cambridge University Press, reproduced with permission of the author and publisher.

Shore, Bradd. 1996. "Dreamtime Learning, Inside-Out: The Narrative of the Wawilak Sisters." In idem, *Culture in Mind: Cognition, Culture, and the Problem of Meaning*, 207–235. New York: Oxford University Press. Copyright © 1996 by Oxford University Press, Inc. Used by permission of Oxford University Press, Inc.

Bruner, Jerome. 1986. "The Transactional Self." In idem, *Actual Minds, Possible Worlds*, 57–69. Cambridge, MA: Harvard University Press. Copyright © 1986 by the President and Fellows of Harvard College.

Clark, Andy. 1997. "Language. The Ultimate Artifact." Chapter 10 in idem, *Being There: Putting Brain, Body, and World Together Again*, 193–218. © 1996 Massachusetts Institute of Technology, by permission of the MIT Press.

GENERAL INTRODUCTION: MYTHS AND MYTHOLOGIES

Why This Volume?

As part of a series of volumes on *Critical Categories in the Study of Religion*, the need for a volume on "myths" and "mythologies" hardly needs to be justified. "Myth" *is* a critical category in the study of religion – one that is referred to with much uncertainty. Not least the current use of the term "myth" in public discourse as synonymous to "false belief" or "lie" suggests that some clarification could be called for. "Myth" carries negative connotations in modern standard usage in the Western world and represents, in most public opinion, the opposite of science and rationality and something better avoided. This attitude of "mythoclasm" – the debunking and destruction of myth – is an intellectual attitude of criticism and irreverence that has been known since antiquity. The story of the study of myth is very much the history and study of the criticism of myth and related issues in traditional worldviews.

Myth is not a uniform concept, nor is "mythology." It means either collections of myths, as in "Greek mythology" or "Hindu mythology," or the scholarly study of myths and mythologies. In this volume, which focuses predominantly on methods and theories in the study of myth, it is the latter meaning of the term that prevails.

Recently, myth has been "rehabilitated," but in two (at least) very different ways. One is the "New Age" use of the concept and the view of myths as actual pathways to the sacred, the metaphysical world "beyond." In this view myth is universally "deep" and existentially true. However interesting, this view goes beyond the realm of scholarly

1

inquiry and it may rather be classified as a new object for the *study* of myth. The other trend in "rehabilitation" came with narrative and structuralist theory. Especially in anthropology these theories demonstrated that "how the natives think" was not just a survival from the childhood of humanity or a neurotic attempt at wish-fulfilment, but modes of thought that reflected indigenous cosmologies and that there was some kind of logic in myth. This theoretical and methodological shift has been important and influential and, with later elaborations, it is the one that underlies many of the thoughts behind this volume. Here, myths are viewed as traditional stories about gods and other superhuman agents and as vehicles in the transmission of religious traditions and worldviews. The stories may have lost their credibility as realistic explanations of the world but the "stuff" of myths live on, in art, literature and not least in the entertainment industry where myths are the materials and templates upon which many new tales are spun.

To the question: "Who is the book for?" – the answer is simply that it is for anyone with an interest in myths and mythologies. Obviously, the readers may have very different experiences with the many aspects involved in this study. What to one is banal is new to the other. This is unavoidable, but as I also wish to present an historian of religions' point of view to others with very different backgrounds this is how it must be. In certain places, I explain things that may be evident to some, and perhaps not even do it in an adequate manner according to their judgment but I have aimed at a very inclusive perspective. That is also because myth is "in itself" a phenomenon that cuts across the borders of literature, philosophy, sociology, anthropology, semiotics, narratology, linguistics, psychology, cognitive science and even more. Over many years I have taught myth and mythology to students coming from many fields and that has given me both inspiration and taken me to critical reflections on what I was doing. It was also obvious that colleagues in other disciplines took an interest in this subject, and they are most welcome to join in this pursuit. Thus, this volume has been conceived primarily as a reader for students of religion but with a keen eye to its probable use for scholars and students from other fields who take an interest in myth and the study of it as it may be carried out in the manner suggested in this volume.

Confessions of the Author

First, a few brief and somewhat personal notes on the perspectives of this volume are in order. When I "grew up" as a student around 1980, myth and mythologies were considered plainly intrinsic to the study of religion and quite unproblematic as well. Myths were the stories of all religious traditions, large and small; myths were "sacred narratives" which demonstrated the values and beliefs of traditions and cultures and presented the ideas by which humans ordered their lives. In short, this was a rather idealist picture of things, one where myths were causes and human behaviour the effects and in this it was also a form of literalist, and perhaps even theological, interpretation based on an inheritance of what normative texts could or should do.

There were variations of course, but in the history of religions the view of myth was generally a positive and sometimes even a quite nostalgic one.[1] There was also a range of more critical anthropological and sociological studies emphasizing the aspects of conflict, power and ideology related to myths, but by historians of religions such studies were seen mostly as functionalist studies about the role of myth in society and thus not about myth "as such."

In the last decades of the twentieth century, the academic worlds of the arts and humanities and, in part, the social sciences were hit by a wave of post-modern tendencies towards an increasing "incredulity" in great narratives and a de-legitimization of claims to disinterred knowledge. This meant that knowledge produced in many academic contexts was seen not as scholarly achievements but as political products in the service of various interest, that were not in themselves scholarly. Scholarly produced knowledge was in the end no different from mythological discourse; it had become "myth" in itself. Thus, science and scholarship were but "language games": ways of using language and knowledge in such ways as to sustain certain social formations and thus political domination. In the end, any discourse about anything could be seen as an attempt to construct and control knowledge over any social object, be it ethnic, national, religious, economic, political, etc. In such a perspective, where every action becomes an instance of the will to dominate and control, power is both the means and the end. As history proves that may certainly be true. Power-issues are closely linked to the analysis of discourse, and thus also to the study of myth. As we shall see, myths are often the means of making and upholding cosmologies as well as the social hierarchies and privileges and thus they are frequently the charters behind human inequality.

As important as the analysis of power is in relation to myth, even so is it for the *study* of myths and mythologies. If that study is not itself going to alter itself into another myth, as some earlier studies of myth have, there is nothing but relentless self-critical reflexivity, which may prevent such a change. We are all, and that includes editors of anthologies on myth, the products of our own time and place and although this may be demanding to overcome, then, in this case, as in many others, some critical awareness is better than none.

The "power"-driven approaches to myth, discourse and social realities presuppose that myths really do have a power over minds, that is, over individuals' cognitive and emotional processing of information. How that may be achieved is a vexed problem, the answer to which I consider to be of the utmost importance in the study of human culture and society.[2] We are in a position where we acknowledge that there is no final answer to everything – for such is the condition of modernity and post-modernity, but it does not mean that we know nothing, on the contrary. The "totalizing" ambition of traditional religious and mythical discourse waned in the Western world when science gradually came to replace religion as the authoritative voice on the nature of the world. Scientific progress has secularized and "de-mythologized" the world. This process of "disenchantment" and increasing rationalization was acutely diagnosed by the German sociologist Max Weber. In contrast to pre-modern societies where myths were entertainment as well as literature and authoritative socio-cultural voices, these functions have been segregated into quite different domains with their own characters and properties in modern society. This development enables us to view myths as something outside us, as an external object, instead of forming the invisible structures that make up our universe. Through the loss of mythical "innocence," or "the disenchantment of the world," we have greater insights into the workings of language and discourse and thus of myth. This does not mean, however, that now we see the world in an un-mediated fashion – as "it really is" – for that is but another (empiricist) myth produced by scientific ideology itself. We rely as much upon culturally established codes and patterns of thought and language as we ever did; all human knowledge – from the Homeric gods to sub-particle physics – consists of "cultural posits." The difference is above all one of reflexive complexity; that we ourselves recognize what we are doing.

In my view, myths are narrative and discursive products that are rooted in language and culture and which influence humans in their complex social behaviour. An important point is that myths mostly work subconsciously, as when Claude Lévi-Strauss studied "not how men think in myths, but how myths operate in men's minds without their being aware of the fact" (1969, 12). In myths, the relations between minds, imaginations, language, culture, society, and the "real" world of practical survival unite. This makes the study of the human achievement "myth" so undeniably interesting if we want to know more about our species and its history. So, I suggest that we simply do the best we can. If the result is lacking, there will surely be others to remedy that. The inter-subjective character of the scholarly venture ensures that what were once considered virtues may turn out to be vices and the other way round as well.

Confusions

The study of myth has abounded in confusions. A few examples serve to demonstrate those confusions. Embarking upon the study of myths and mythologies will bring out such designations as "nature mythology," the "myth and ritual school," "charter myths," "myths and archetypes," "symbolism in religious language," "syntagmatic narratology" and many more. The field of myths and mythologies is immense and it has a rather complicated history. The range of theoretical agendas of, as well the attitudes to, myth in scholarship contribute to the confusion. Generally, one may say that the more favourable the view of myth is, the less theoretical it mostly is. Positive proponents replicate the idea that myth is important in a human, existential perspective and so become "caretakers" more than critics. Critical studies have also come in a very broad range and not always equally composed. The two general attitudes to myth are (1) A positive attitude associated with the legacy from Antiquity, the Romantic era and its celebration of human artistic creativity, in nationalist movements, carrying over into depth psychology, and now into New Age worldviews. (2) A critical attitude proceeds

4

from the Enlightenment, over the philosophical critique of religion, into positivism and empiricism, then into the critiques of ideology in general and it is now found in many forms ranging from the Frankfurt School to postmodernism.[3] The history of research shows us that the ideas about "myth" as an object of academic studies have ranged from that of the scandal to one of rehabilitation. Now, the more recent rehabilitation of myth as an academic object is not the same as a rehabilitation of myth as being true about its subject matter, but as a subject that may tell us something important about humanity in its historical, social, cultural and mental life. Some have rehabilitated myth more than current academic standards allow, for example the Italian historian of religions, Raffaele Pettazoni, who put forward the somewhat euphoric view on the science of myth that: "It must be livened by the spirit of humanism, by an attitude of sympathy towards the myth as a mark and a document of our human estate" (1954, 36). Thus, the present collection aims at presenting and discussing the extensive range of opinions, ideas, sentiments and scholarly debates on the issue of myth. I have chosen to do so both in an historical or "archaeological" way so as to portray the antecedents of current positions and then present perspectives as to how theories and methods may develop the study of myths and mythologies.

Criteria for the Selection and Compilation of this Volume

In brief outline, I shall explain the layout of the volume. The criteria for the selection of the essays in the volume are clear concerning some and more vague concerning others – especially the contributions in the last sections of the volume. Some chapters do not include "myth" in their title and perhaps not even much in the text itself, but they have been chosen because they are "good to read" in connection with more theoretically oriented study of myths and mythologies. The problems and solutions they contain may point to advantageous use of the same theories and methods in the study of myth. The reason for dividing the volume into sections by approach is that I consider the concept of "approach" one that covers the aspect of theory as well as of method.

On the more traditional criteria for selecting the contributions, I have considered their virtual importance relative to a comprehension of the development of the study of myth. The study of myth has had a fate rather similar to that of religion when it comes to the philosophical reflections on myth, its origin, function and meaning. I have not attempted any thorough exposition of the "question" of myth in philosophy but focused on a selection of contributions that I deem seminal for an understanding of subsequent developments. Most important are the questions concerning the human construction of meaning, of social realities, and their concomitant ontology. In that connection, the importance of language as the *sine qua non* of social formations must be taken into account. In the section on psychological approaches, some contributions may seem not to belong there. The point is that the contributions here need not be produced by psychologists, but rather that the arguments presented by these scholars proceed from psychological premises, in the sense that they theorize on the basis of assumptions about the mental life of humans as the primary basis for the production of myth. The section on sociological approaches is relatively short because this dimension of the study of myth is copiously treated elsewhere and the relevant theoretical points are neither difficult nor controversial. The sociological approaches obviously tap into the philosophical discussions on the constructions of social formations and realities. The specifically social has to do with the more holistic views of society and of social architectures as likely means to social cohesion and control. "Semiological approaches" is the designation chosen to refer to a section of some theoretical diversity. On the other hand, they would all have been unthinkable without the foundations laid in structural linguistics, from Ferdinand de Saussure onwards, as they view myth as a cultural phenomenon that is language-like and thus closely connected with the study of narrativity. Hence, they may also have been characterized as "structuralist" but although this is certainly to the point for some, it would have been a too narrow classification for others. "Semiotic" would have been another option, but that designation carries quite specific connotations of technical analyses of sign-systems, hence "semiological" as a more neutral, and in some sense, more classical term. The last part, "Cognitivist approaches" is a section that (as far as I know) is new to a volume on the study of myth. The contributions are not many but the main points of the theoretical positions involved may be demonstrated through what is presented here. It is quite obvious that myth is "fabricated" by humans and that they therefore depend on the human mental apparatus, that is, the boundary conditions are set by cognitive constraints. There are two dimensions here. The first tells us how myth and other things socio-cultural depend on and are caused, to some extent, by cognitive properties and mechanisms. The second dimension informs us about how important the socio-cultural realm is for the formation of individuals and groups, that is, the influence on individuals and groups of explicit cultural knowledge such as that presented in myths. In the final section, I bring together some aspects of all these approaches as I consider them all to contain something of importance for inclusion in the practising mythologist's "toolbox." In that section I also set forward some more personal ideas on how to study myths in the (post-)modern world. Myths never disappeared. They changed forms so that they are now "disguised" in art, music, film, TV, advertising and – not least – in politics. If the study of myth has something to offer today, it is not only interesting stories about ideas that once were, but precisely because what we have learnt from the study of myths that once were can now be employed in a study of contemporary ideological production. If myths are economies of signs they may be suspected to be closely related to other forms of economies as well.

"Myth" as a Critical Category

It should, by now, already be clear why "myth" is a critical category in the study of religion. There is just so much scholarly politics, ideas about progress and academic and popular polemics, which act as the background for attitudes to "myth." The debate over myth was always reflective of the interests of the scholars embarking on it. Some did study myths as their subject matter, but the theoretical object, that which they *really* wanted to study, was something else, such as the human psyche or political discursive domination.[4] This divide between subject matter and theoretical object often obscures the issues and does not make it easier to evaluate the scholars' intentions. No wonder then, that the borders have been drawn sharply between the different theories about myth and mythologies. Here are some examples of myth definitions as attitudinal vectors, which illustrate how prominent scholars have dealt with myths for very different reasons and in very diverse manners.

For example, Friedrich Max Müller, one of the main proponents of the school of "Nature mythology," was also keenly interested in the origin and history of language: "Mythology is only a dialect, an ancient form of language. Mythology, though chiefly concerned with nature, and here again mostly with those manifestations which bear the character of law, order, power, and wisdom impressed on them, was applicable to all things" (1856, 178).[5] Nevertheless, to Müller myth was a product of the childhood of humankind and of the "disease of language" through which words such as "dawn" and "moon" became personified and deified. Myth was thus poetic and metaphoric. Likewise, the grandfather of anthropology, E. B. Tylor, in the view afforded by his own animistic theory expressed the common evolutionist conviction that: "To the human intellect in its early childlike state may be assigned the origin and first development of myth," because the "primitives," like children, believe that all things may be animated (1873, I, 284). Tylor's view of myth was highly intellectualist, i.e. that myths literally explain things in the world – that is, to those that adhere to them. But Tylor also stated that the basis of myth "is not to be narrowed down to poetic fancy and transformed metaphor. They rest upon a broad philosophy of nature, early and crude indeed, but thoughtful, consistent, and quite really and seriously meant" (1873, I, 285).[6] Tylor's real interest, his theoretical object, was the evolution of culture. Another great name from the early history of anthropology, namely Sir James George Frazer, held a very different view of myths, which to him and subsequently many others, were closely related to and explained rituals. Myths were primarily metaphorical, i.e., the myth about the dying and reviving god Adonis was *really* about the seasons of cultivated vegetations. To the "inventor" of modern fieldwork-based anthropology, Bronislaw Malinowski, the study of myth was one avenue into the study of the psychology and sociology of small-scale "primitive" societies, and the ways in which myths functioned primarily as legitimizing social institutions and conventions; myths were, in his words, "charters" for social reality as well as psychological factors in collective, social adaptation to nature. Carl G. Jung, the creator of "analytic" or "depth" psychology, is quite well known for his studies on myth, but these are more often than not about analogies between motives of myths and his own theory of archetypes (or "primordial images"), and here the materials of myths function as support for the theory about the "collective unconscious." To the historian of religions Mircea Eliade, myth were important, non-political, self-evident truths about the human condition, and as such he used the study of myth in pursuit of a religious existentialist agenda. A completely different manner of is exemplified by E. Thomas Lawson, who proposed that "Rather than identifying myth as a species of language having the special properties of a semantic system, we now have the means for identifying myths as a species of knowledge, i.e., having the special properties of a cognitive system. Therein lies its power" (1978, 521). Myths also have obvious political and worldview-sustaining (or critical potential), for example, in the view of Roland Barthes and elaborated on by McCutcheon of "Myth as What-Goes-Without-Saying" (2000, 201–202). Biblical scholar Burton Mack states that mythmaking is something that turns: "the collective agreements of a people into truths held to be self-evident" (1994, 301). That is as true today as it once was, in Antiquity, for instance. The many ways of using myths as the subject matter in the pursuit of very different theoretical objects is not over. Is it at all possible then to answer the question "What are myths?" Well, one can do as the Finnish historian of religions Lauri Honko did and present a comprehensive account of most of the relevant aspects that could go into a generalized interpretation:

> Myth, a story of the gods, a religious account of the beginning of the world, the creation, fundamental events, the exemplary deeds of the gods as a result of which the world, nature and culture were created together with all the parts thereof and given their order, which still obtains. A myth expresses and confirms society's religious values and norms, it provides patterns of behaviour to be imitated, testifies to the efficacy of ritual with its practical ends and establishes the sanctity of cult. The true milieu of myth is to be found in religious rites and ceremonial. The ritual acting out of myth implies the defence of the world order; by imitating sacred exemplars the world is prevented from being brought to chaos. The re-enactment of a creative event, for example, the healing wrought by a god in the beginning of time, is the common aim of myth and ritual. In this way the event is transferred to the present and its result, i.e. the healing of a sick person, can be achieved once more here and now. In this way, too, the world order, which was created in the primeval era and which is reflected in myths, preserves its value as an exemplar and model for the people of today. The events recounted in myths have true validity for a religious person. For this reason the use of the term myth in everyday language is from the scholarly point of view inexact (in ordinary language myth is often used expressly for something untrue, utopian, misguided, etc.). The *point de départ*, then, is criticism directed towards religious groups and traditions from outside and this criticism has always existed. Nowadays attempts have often been made to brand non-religious ideas, political ideas, economic teaching, etc., as myth. (1984, 49)

This is fairly much the standard sort of conception among most scholars of religion and quite a few others.

Myths and Other Kinds of Narratives

As myths are conventionally defined in the study of religion, they are narratives, they are stories. As for the contents of myth it is often held that they are stories about gods, spirits, heroes, ancestors and so on. This is a criterion based on content, on what the stories are literally *about*. In this context, the difference between myths and legends becomes relational in that the legends are about *humans*, however unhistorical the narrative may be. This was already noted by the German scholar on myth, Fr. Creuzer, in 1810 in his work *Symbolik und Mythologie der alten Vôlker* ("Symbolism and Mythology of the Ancient Nations"). It is a classification which clearly comes to the fore in a quite common and meticulous – and therefore telling – description of what is considered myth according to the historian of religions Åke Hultkrantz:

> The *myth* is an epic narrative dealing with figures belonging to the supernatural sphere: cosmic beings, gods and spirits. The action of the narrative takes place in a remote prehistoric period, but in principle the once consummated course of event is still of topical interest: timeless and eternal as the course of the planets. The scene of the drama is as a rule (but not always) another world than our own: heaven, the underworld or an unknown country. The myth gives instruction concerning the world of the gods, and therewith concerning the cosmic order; it confirms the social order and the cultural values obtaining in it and it is in itself sacred. It is therefore self-evident that it is intended to be embraced with belief and reverence. (1957, 12–13)

Myths are often distinguished from legends and other stories not only by the aspect of "belief and reverence" but also by the timeframe, that is, when myths relate to and about the "time before time" legends pretend to be about matters taking place in historical time.[7] Both myths and legends may be aetiolocigal, that is, they "present answers to questions" and may also have edifying points to present. Fairytales normally come as entertainment and perhaps with moralizing twists, but their "once upon a time" is rarely about the creation of the world. A now classic distinction between genres was offered by William Bascom in 1965:

> Definitions: *Myths* are prose narratives which, in the society in which they are told, are considered to be truthful accounts of what happened in the remote past. *Legends* are prose narratives which, like myths, are regarded as true by the narrator and his audience, but they are set in a period considered less remote, when the world was much as it is today. *Folktales* are prose narratives which are regarded as fiction.

Historical narrative, in turn, pretends to be the plain truth about what happened and without (mostly) the intervention of super-human forces or agents. As generally understood today, historical narratives are (presumably) without moral or edifying points, although that presumption very often seems to be contradicted by both the texts and contexts of historical narratives. As it readily appears, the distinctions along these criteria concerning the form, contents and referents of the different genres of narratives are not easy to draw. The genres should be seen *only* as ideal types, as models *about* genres, as the scholars understand them, which may direct our attention to some features rather than others. Other criteria for distinction besides form, contents and referents could be function and context. The functions of myth could be, for example, social and political, so that myths mirror and sustain the order of the world and the privileges of some over others. This function would hardly be held by fairytales, and historical narratives could be questioned because they do not come with the inbuilt immunity that myths seem to have because of their relations to transcendent realms. Myths could also have psychological and cognitive functions, which they may share with other genres, but myths then often seem to hold more prestige in the sense that they are considered more foundational. When myths have such functions they are partly responsible for the ways in which humans think and feel as the cultural component in socialization, where myths are *the* tales about the world that are used to narrativize our place in it. We learn to think *with* the stories and *in* and *through* the stories. To a large extent we are what the stories make us.[8]

Another criterion for the distinction between myths and other genres is that of ritual context. The myth-ritual debate is old and tried and not to be rehearsed here. Suffice it to say that some myths in some traditions enjoy a position of prominence in ritual and many others do not feature directly, but they may, nevertheless, be part of a pool of stories that can be activated in specific situations. Narratives with such an "activation-potential" belong to the cosmology (worldview) of a given tradition, religion or culture (these may overlap) and they are different from other kinds of stories because they are validated by the cosmology. In the end, these definitorial exercises should not be taken for literal depictions of *things real*; these *concepts* are the means by which scholars make sense of the myriad narratives recorded. The concepts are maps and the world of narratives in the territory in which we navigate is assisted by the maps.

My own definition, because such "a thing" the author must have in order that readers know where we stand in the discussions that follow, could be formulated in this way: "Myths are traditional, authoritative narratives referring to transcendent referents, and which fuse the lived-in world with the thought-of world in such a manner that this seems the only plausible version." This is not merely a definition of religious myths – it goes for many narratives in ideological and cultural formations as well – but an addition to "transcendent referent" could make the difference: "such as superhuman beings." Notice that I omit an otherwise common element in a definition of myth, namely the temporal dimension that points to "origins" or "the beginning of things." Although these may be important in the making of the authority of myths, I do consider it somewhat treacherous to focus too much on this dimension, as it may lead us to perpetuate the verities of the myths themselves and disregard the flexibility and manufactured nature of the mythical narratives under study.

There are many kinds of myths. In addition, in the available literature a certain amount of definitorial individualism is clearly discernable, as is understandable from the state of affairs. Keeping the above-mentioned criteria in mind a more traditional catalogue looks somewhat like this: Cosmogonic myths about the creation of the world, anthropogonic myths about the origin of humankind, theogonic myths about the origin of the god(s), myths about animals, fire, agriculture, cooking, sexual and gender relations, song and dance, sacred kingship and social hierarchy, myths of floods and droughts, ancestors and demons, rituals and special religious (professional) roles. In short, anything that can or has been of importance to humans in this world may become the subject of myth – it is as simple as that.

Thus it is understandable that in the course of the history of the study of myths, many catalogues and inventories, classifications and typologies of myth have been suggested.[9] Most of these focus on specific contents or functions of myths. It is, however, not always the case that the stories that many scholars have called "myths" are actually full-fledged narratives, as they may rather be loose compositions of motifs. The question as to how much emphasis must be placed on the necessity of myth having a clearly definable narrative structure and order is one of definitional and theoretical decision. It is obvious that most of the myths we have from ancient or primal societies are presented to us in perfected narrative shape, but closer inspection sometimes discloses the editorial dexterity of field-workers, translators, compilers and editors, just to mention some of those who "tamper with texts." The actual situation where the myth "was alive" could very well have been one of competition among the "managers" of fragmentary versions, constant revisions, tribal privileges and so on. This is just a note of caution so that we do not without suspicious perpetuate a mystique about grand and magnificently composed epics. A closer look at a Christian Bible in Greek with a critical apparatus also tells us that *this* was never *one* book, a fact unknown to the general public and one which generally seems to shock first-year students of religion.

Taxonomy and Classification

To some it seems to be almost a cause for despair that "myth" is such a broad concept – and referring to a multi-faceted set of phenomena. If myth is so difficult to define then perhaps we should better avoid it or if the phenomena supposedly referred to are so elusive, then perhaps we should give up the term "myth" altogether. However, these conditions and circumstances are no different from the attempts to define so many other "things" in the human and social sciences. If we keep in mind that one could consider a definition to be a theory expressed in its shortest form, then it becomes clear why it is that we have these difficulties. It is because we are not simply looking at physical objects "in the world," but at phenomena that to a large extent have been created by the very categories, definitions and theories which we have and employ. This does not imply, as some sceptics imagine, the non-existence of the subject matters of study. Myths are socio-cultural facts and the study of them is another set of socio-cultural fact, but the former only become visible as belonging to the category "myth" because we have concepts. The sceptic may then argue that the category "myth" is an academic concoction, something that has been invented, for the sake of scholarship and ideological domination.[10] That argument may, however, turn out to be not quite adequate, for some "local" traditions actually *do* have concepts and classifications of their own stories (cf. Malinowski below).

Certainly, categories and generalities may always be said "not to exist" – it all depends upon what we mean by "exist." A lot of things that we think of and work with do not "exist" or they are "inventions." One could say that literature does not exist; only books or that "traffic" is an invention. My favourite answer to students' worries about these issues is that we can say that is also true about the metric system. We even know its "inventers" by name (check any encyclopaedia) but that does not detract one bit from its usefulness or reality. Thus, it is clear that although precarious conditions hold for "myth" then this is no cause for intellectual paralysis. The best we can to do is to reflect on what it is we do with our categories and what we do when we use a concept such as "myth." The cure against such methodological anxiety is to know the history of research and what the many different theories may contribute (or not) to our descriptions, explanations and interpretations of myths. Increased scholarly reflexivity and historical awareness is the only way out of the conundrum. It should be noted that there have been many discussions recently about and *for* the "dissolution" of various concepts in the study of religion (and of other subjects) and we should openly recognize that the problems concerning the "term" are the same problems, no more no less, that pertain to other definitions, concepts and models employed in all other human and social sciences. On the other hand, it could equally be a cause for optimism that experience tells us that it not at all impossible to become wiser and, as Émile Durkheim and Marcel Mauss once observed: "the history of scientific classification is, in the last analysis, the history of the stages by which this element of social affinity has progressively weakened, leaving more and more room for the reflexive thought of individuals" (1963, 88).

Methodological Outlooks

On the ways in which myth may and can be studied in contemporary scholarship, there are many voices. They differ profoundly in their theoretical and methodological outlooks, but, for the most part, they do have something in common. Russell McCutcheon has summed up the main trends in previous scholarship:

> Common to all these approaches is the assumption that "myth" is the product, the effect or an evidentiary trace of some absent, forgotten, distant – that is, not immediately apparent – phenomenon or human intention. Thus the mission of myth scholarship has generally been construed as a reconstructive and hermeneutic labor bent on ferreting out the truth or falsity of myth, on decoding and then recovering obscured meanings. In short, common to all these approaches has been the view that myths are signs of such personal or interior

causes and intentions as (1) a mentality, (2) an emotional or psychological "experience," (3) a universal human "estate" such as Human Nature. (2000, 199)

Thus the study of myth has mostly been an exercise in recovering something "hidden" and then in the form of interpretive, hermeneutic attempts of understanding the deeper, or true, "meanings" of the myths. "Meaning" is one of the more elusive terms in the English language, but translating it does not really help. Let us only note that it may refer to intention, purpose, semantics content – and even reference (e.g. Jensen 2004). For the sake of simplicity, let us content ourselves with an exploratory solution: the meaning of myths is what they "are about," whether it be on a narrative surface level or on an underlying level of semantic and cognitive operations. As an example, we all know that the fairytale "The Ugly Duckling" is not a discourse on zoology.[11] The explicit questions and demonstrations concerning methods, their applications and the results they generate will be left aside for now as there will be more concrete and comprehensive discussions about methodological issues in the sections below. As the sections are distinguished by "approaches" the division into parts is clearly done on both theoretical and methodological grounds.

Myths, Cognition and Culture

Myths are the building blocks of culture if by culture we mean something like "common orientations," "common ideas and values" in a given human population. The borders between societies and cultures may be difficult to draw, as they have fuzzy edges, overlap or simply are quite messy. However, for human communication to function, there must be a measure of common, and often tacit knowledge, which forms the basis of the communication, the "backdrop," so to speak. This is where myths come in as a medium for acquiring, maintaining and reproducing socially adaptive mechanisms. Although mythical narratives may be very elusive as to their "meaning" they are always the stories "we" tell and they thereby function as common virtual experiences. The stories may more or less plausibly, more or less humorously, exploit the limits of the realms of the collective imagination. Myths may also be the storehouse of socially relevant information and what is socially relevant will mostly also be individually relevant. Myth may help order the lived-in world, not least through the role of myth in taxonomies, "world-making," where "mythmaking" is part and parcel of the "making of worlds." Myth may thus be seen generally as a mode of understanding the world, but also of a form of expression of a certain conception of the world and thereby constitutive of that world. If we want to make ourselves understood we must organize our speech, actions and emotions along the cultural models familiar to others. By so doing we align our cognitive ways of processing much of the information we get as well as produce.[12]

Typically, a narrated, mythical, religious world consist of three domains: the first world and factual world in which humans live, a second world and ideal world in which the sacred is located, and a third domain of the communicative activities that ensure the relations between the human and the superhuman, ideal world.[13] The mythical, narrative creation of the second world is the necessary condition for this cosmology. The really interesting aspect, however, is how the present world – seen as an ontological fact in a given culture based on religious tradition – is that the protagonists of the second world are responsible for the ways in which the first world is constructed. It is *through* the construction of the thought-of second world that religious groups conceive of and understand the first world. This is a curious fact and one that has puzzled philosophers and others. Why is it that humans conceive of imaginary realities which they then endow with more "reality" and power than the physical world in which they live? The answer is blowing in the wind.

Myths, Social Reflexivity and Narrativity

Narrativity in general is always linked to a semantic universe: a story that is not told in language or about some world we know, be it real or imaginary, is simply not a story. Stories, fairytales, poetry and myths always come with a background of shared information, distributed knowledge, norms for communication, history, or language that may serve as a vehicle for "transmitting" conceptions from one mind to others. As noted, narrative is not only a practical means for communication or gathering knowledge about the world. More recent research has demonstrated how important narration and narratives are in the construction and maintenance of human individual and social identity (Donald 2001). This accords well with the traditional view from the perspective of theories of projection: when humans tell myths about the gods, spirits ancestors, etc. they do in fact communicate stories that are indirectly about themselves. The importance of myth in social and cultural reproduction can hardly be overestimated. Myth has served as an external memory system for so many peoples over such a long time that it must be seen as one of the prime devices (ritual is another) by which humanity has been able to invent and maintain itself (Rappaport 1999). Individual identity is also held together, joined, by the narratives available to the person in the course of socialization. It should be stressed that this does not necessitate the post-modernist conclusions, that identities are free-floating options and signs without reference, and that anyone can create her own identity as she pleases. Especially when speaking of traditional societies, it is apparent that there are severe cultural, social, economic, political and thus religious constraints on the "making of selves," because religion is the sacred canopy suspended over the totality of human life. What goes into the creation of the person is determined by the discourses and classifications that make up any given society's ideal world, the one to be emulated in practice. Tradition ensures that although "You are what your stories tell you" then this is a story to be told from the basis of a very specific stock of elements. Although cultures and religious tradition are no longer quite the neat systematic entities they were once thought to be, there is no doubt that the repertoires and inventories of human "worlds" certainly do differ. Being brought up as a Maori or an Inuit, a Japanese

Buddhist or a Mexican Roman Catholic, a Swedish Lutheran or a Yemenite Muslim does certainly not imply quite the same.[14] The options available for humans in their "worlds" are posited and maintained in respect to mythical authority.

Religious Language and the Semantics of Myth

Scholars working from theological or philosophical perspectives may use the term "myth" not only to refer to certain kinds of narrative, but rather to a more comprehensive mode of understanding the world in existential terms, say, in mythical and religious conceptions of the world.[15] It is obvious, however, that any such conception or understanding is made possible only through language, and then again, not in just any kind of language, but in religious language, of which myth is a large part. As the religious conception of the world has its special characteristics, the same applies to religious language as a general category. Certainly, there are various kinds of religious language: dogmas, moral and ethical teachings, sermons, dietary rules, etc. This could lead to the conclusion that the language of religion is quite ordinary; there are prescriptions, imperatives and prohibitions and other grammatical and syntactical forms known from ordinary language. In general, religious language is thus normative but that is not all there is to it. The most important feature of the religious linguistic universe is that, although it uses ordinary everyday language as its basis, it is also foundational. Religious language is related to the foundation of the cosmos it refers to, and this foundation is mostly encountered in myths. There are two peculiarities here. The first is that even though myths relate forwards, from the beginnings until later, perhaps the present human condition, they are "scripted" backwards, because they are narrated by humans from the perspective of the present condition. That present condition is not necessarily the present time: The story about the disobedience of Adam and Eve informs us about the origin of the human condition as seen in the Abrahamic monotheistic traditions and what then happened and the consequences this had for all humans – a somewhat different fate resulted from this original "crime" in each of the traditions, because the stories are different.

The second peculiarity is that religious language, especially in the mythical form, *hides* the fact that humans produce it. The world is made by myth and the myth tells us how the world is. This is evidently circular, but that is a formal characteristic of myth as well as of religious language. Thus myth, and religious language as an extension of myth, set up a world. "Our" world is always a world mediated by language and we would not know the world as *our* world if not through language. It is for this reason we see that the mythical and religious language, as perceived from within the traditional universe, lay the foundations for all that follows. This also means that such a universe founded in and by myth cannot be measured by rational standards of truth, at least from the internal view of the tradition, as the mythical discourse is the very standard by which *other* forms of language have to be measured. They set their own rationality, for it is also a characteristic of myths and the cosmologies expressed in religious language and worldviews that they are not just non-rational; they do have their own sets of rules of compositions and regulations – otherwise they would be impossible for humans to operate in (Jensen and Martin 2002).

The world does not "speak" of itself, but humankind has made it speak – primarily in myth. Therefore, myth became the "language of the world," but one that quotes itself endlessly. Contingency and critique is ruled out. Mythical and religious language may diminish the complexities of life, because they each represent one "way" of existence, but that also means that they also reduce the spectrum of what can and may be said. Evidently, the gap between religious, mythically constructed worlds and the modern, scientific worldview is thus both immense and mutually incompatible.

Types and Structures of Discourse

Most often, religious myths about the origins of things have a narrator who is more than human, an authority that must be trusted and obeyed. This need not be in the form of a superior godhead, but it may be the ancestors, a set of ritual prescriptions, or the universe itself. Characteristic of religious and ideological discourse is that its authority is not to be questioned. The structure of the cosmos in which such a discourse unfolds is generally a threefold construction. If imagined as consisting of layers, the top will be the level of "the immutable," of eternal beings and verities, of transcendent axiomatic statements, or the "ultimate sacred postulates" as they have aptly been designated (Rappaport 1999, 263–5).[16] This level is where ancestors dwell, where gods reside, where inviolable cosmic principles are located and from whence the ordered world ensues. This realm, the second world, is beyond human intervention: things are as they are and we humans are not to tamper with them. The middle layer is the mediating, "go-between layer" of the activities of both humans and super-humans because this is the realm of communication, of interpretations and interpreters. It consists of revelations, diviners, prophets, angels, laws and rituals, hymns and prayers and much more in dialectic, mutual, reciprocal exchange and the interaction between this and the "other world." The bottom layer consists of all that belongs to common, daily life, and is that of the "participants." Note, however, that this is a model of sacral communication in the ordered universe and not a static description of all religious or mythical universes: In many traditions is it quite possible for participants to go in and out of one and the other sphere and move about in the entire universe, for instance in rituals. This, in fact, often seems to be the whole point of having a complete cosmology that includes all levels. Where myths mediate "downwards" as the statements about what the world is, where it comes from and who was involved in the process, rituals are responses to this founding and the existential conditions that arose from it. Thus, through gifts to the ancestors, food for the gods, sacrifices, prayers, pilgrimages and so on we are in a position to master various features of the physical world, of the mental world, of the social world, and even – and this is the real "trick" of religion – of the supernatural world. Without myths "all this" would not have been there.

The History of the Study of Myth and Mythology

The study of myth and the history of that study are both very extensive. They have been undertaken by many different kinds of scholars with many different interests and agendas. As the study of religion (as well as anthropology) is a relative newcomer to the academic world, previous studies of myths have been pursued by scholars in many other fields and here I think primarily of classics, literature and philosophy. The history of the study of myth is an immense subject in itself and in here I shall limit the presentation to a very brief overview and include references to further study. Briefly, from Plato, Aristotle and onwards the history of the search for the "meaning of myth" is also a history of the "scandal" of myth and the search for its causes. The scandal would not go away but the causes were hard to find – and scholars have not yet reached any agreement on that subject. This does not make it any less interesting. General histories are presented by Lincoln (1999), Detienne (1986), Dubuisson (2003), Bietenholz (1994). An interesting contribution to the more recent history is Strenski (1987). A general bibliographical overview is offered by Sienkewicz (1997).

Antiquity

As used here, "Antiquity" refers to the time and domain of the Classical Western world, that is, primarily to the myths and mythologies of the ancient Greeks and Romans. This may be a restricted, perhaps even Eurocentric view, but if I am to recount the story about the inception and growth of the study of mythology into an academic field that is how it must be.[17]

The myths of Antiquity, especially in Greece, were no uniform collection of stories. The traditions of Homer and Hesiod were the two largest collections, dating back approximately to the sixth century BC. These were tales that in all probability had a fairly long oral tradition behind them and in their written form they became the general cultural property of all the Greek-speaking world in Classical time (fifth to fourth centuries BC). Later, in Hellenistic and Roman times, they became the models for other editors and compilers, "mythographers" as they were called. Much of the mythological material was also used by the classical authors and play-writers, as the stock of mythological motifs was enormous. It was a universe of imaginations that writers, orators, politicians and philosophers could refer to. In current idiom, one could say that the mythological inventory was a web of significations from which it was possible to "download" materials for communication. Among the consumers of myth, the philosophers went their own way and from the time of Xenophanes' criticism of Homer and Hesiod the term *muthos* (Greek for "myth") became increasingly applied to the stories about gods, heroes, daemons, fairies, etc., that is, to stories that were not to be *trusted* in the ordinary sense.[18] Before the philosophical critique, the word *muthos* plainly referred to the spoken word, belonging to the general category of *logos*, "that which is said." Now, with the philosophical critique, *logos* became the word for speech that referred to rational arguments and truths. Thus, myth, as the opposite, was turned into a term for untrue stories and associated with irrationality. There was a further development, as Zaidman and Pantel explain:

> The emergence of writing helped to precipitate and sharpen this conceptual dichotomy. With the transition from a purely oral tradition to various types of written literature, a new way of thinking became established that is attested from the last quarter of the fifth century onwards in medical treatises, historical narratives, forensic orations and philosophical tracts (1992, 143–4)

Accordingly, historians, such as Herodotus and Thucydides, avoided the mythical in their quest for historical truth, and the philosopher Plato spoke about myths as acceptable for poets but not for "more true discourse" such as that of the sciences and philosophy that now became possible through the arts of writing and reading (Havelock 1982).[19] Without much hesitation, we can say that this ancient distinction has lived on till today. Myth "lost its innocence" and since then it has been driven out, displaced in time as belonging to an era past, or in space as surviving among the "primitives" or something that resides in or springs from the depths of the psyche of humankind.

Thus, already in Antiquity, we find scepticism concerning myths and as it was realized that they could not be understood literally, numerous attempts were presented so as to explain what myths could then *really* be about. The general idea was that there *had* to be some kind of explanation for the creation and existence of myth. A concise catalogue of such efforts has been compiled by Lauri Honko (1984). It is interesting in order to demonstrate how ideas that are more than 2000 years old are still used in common discourse. Honko lists the following 10 forms of myth-interpretation in Antiquity: (1) Mythographic interpretations used by poets who believed in and transmitted the myths in their works; (2) Philosophical criticisms of various kinds, where the rejection of myth was often quite harsh; (3) The pre-scientific interpretations where the mythical lived on along with early scientific speculation; (4) Allegorical "nature"-interpretation where Apollo is fire, Poseidon water, Artemis the moon, etc.; (5) Allegorical interpretation based on spiritual qualities where Aphrodite is desire, Athena wisdom, Hermes the intellect, etc.; (6) Etymological interpretations trying to make sense of the names of the gods by tracing an original meaning: "the secret of the gods lay in their names and epithets" (1984, 45); (7) Historical interpretation, amply found in Herodotus, where gods are borrowed from other cultures or the idea that myths "really" refer to historical events; (8) Euhemeristic interpretations as a variation on this: the gods were originally remarkable humans who had then been deified;[20] (9) "Sociological" interpretations as in e.g. Critias who "taught that the gods had been invented to maintain social order" (1984, 46) and (10) Psychological interpretations where the belief in gods, etc. is seen as the outcome of fear and anxiety.

These criticisms of mythology were the products of learned interests and a growing attention to investigations into the physical nature of the world. The logic of the critical argument was that as myths could not be taken to be true on face value, then one must recount for their meaning with reference to something *outside* myth. That critical idea was set in motion in Antiquity and has persisted during the history of the study of myth, as we shall see.

Myths and Mythologies in Medieval Era

After the formation of Christianity as Roman state religion in the late fourth century AD, the position of both scholarship and myth changed. The churches increasingly exerted influence over the development of scholarship and philosophy, which both came to be controlled by and subordinated to religious and political powers. The "scandal of myth" was changed, from an epistemic to a moral one, as the church considered the traditional myths of antiquity to be heathen and immoral. The myths did live on, not least, in the growing genre of romance in literature. To the extent that classical myths and their constituent motifs were studied and interpreted, they were often reformulated as allegorical, that is, figurative and symbolic. It is interesting to note that the myths were transmitted with large amounts of commentary added to them:

> When medieval poets and clerks encountered mythological narratives by such classical authors as Vergil, Ovid, or Statius, they not only read the narrative themselves but layer upon layer of commentary and interpretation. Woven into the very fabric of the text, filling every available square inch of the margin, or appended to the text itself, the interpretive tradition constantly insinuated itself into the act of reading. (Blumenfeld-Kosinski 1997, 1)

The question was then how to use the classical and highly fascinating, "pagan" materials in such a way that it did not affront the religious authorities. One way was to use only those parts that were beneficial, seen from a Christian point of view. Most authors and commentators reckoned that parts of the stock of classical myths could have great didactic and educational value. The classical literature, and thus many "pagan" myths, lived on because all stages of education were based on learning Latin and every educated, literate person knew large parts of the classical literature.

However, there was also the methodological question of *how* to read and use the myths. To this purpose, allegorical reading proved to be one of the dominant solutions.[21] Hellenized Jews had used allegorical methods already in the first century AD in their exegesis of the Hebrew scriptures. In late Antiquity philosophical interpreters transformed myths into allegories concerning moral principles or into stories about the true hidden nature of the world and about the soul's journey through cosmos.[22] A system of interpretation evolved in which four main principles are at work in the reading of scriptures and myths. Thus, according to the "Fourfold method":

the Exodus can be simultaneously understood 1) "literally" or "historically," as the departure of the Israelites from Egypt to the Promised Land; 2) "allegorically" (with special reference to the typological fulfilment of Old Testament figures in Christ or in the Church), as the redemption of Christ; 3) "morally," as the conversion of the soul to grace; and 4) "anagogically" ("leading up" to the other world) as the passage of the soul to eternal glory. (Whitman 2000, 10)

Every motif can thus have multiple "meanings" – not so much in their original context but in the context in which they are interpreted and although this is a basic condition for all interpretation, there is always a point where the scale tips, when myths and elements become part of interpretive activities so creative that the mythographer becomes mythmaker. One of the criteria for myth-interpretation was that of usefulness, that is, when a myth or any of its motifs could contribute to modes of behaviour, to morality and piety, and when the readers' needs become the driving force in the process of interpretation, almost anything can happen. Commentators and interpreters were thus increasingly taking the texts apart and analysing single elements in an atomistic fashion according to which interpretation would best suit their own purposes.

A related phenomenon of analysis and reading was that of "unveiling" so as to bring out the "hidden meaning," that is, the true meaning of the text. The consequences of this way of reading were very important for the interpretation of myths, because it opened to the door to a Christian interpretation of each and every text. The interpretation could in principle start from anywhere, for: "this mode of interpretation requires no direct interpretive index (an explicit invitation to interpretation within the text)... the pagan author was considered to have been unaware of the hidden meaning of his text. It was up to the interpreter to decide whether and what to interpret" (Blumenfeld-Kosinski 1997, 7). One of the consequences of these methods was that myths were reduced to mere catalogues of motif and examples, mostly of moral and ethical virtues and vices.[23]

The Renaissance – a Transitional Period

The term "Renaissance" specifically refers to a renewed and intensified interest in the intellectual and artistic heritage from Antiquity – a "re-birth." The renaissance began in northern Italy where city-states opted for independence from the church, both politically and ideologically. The renewed interest in the classical pre-Christian culture offered a way of looking at the world with humankind as its focus. Old texts were re-discovered, some were translated from (for example) Arabic, many were re-edited and, most importantly, books could now be printed and made available to a wider audience.[24] Many learned writers used the classical mythological materials as a way to demonstrate their intellectual prowess and create allegories that were didactical and moral.[25] The classical myths could thus also be used as a symbolic medium to support the Christian worldview as well as offer critiques of it. As for the continuation of interpretive programmes after the late medieval period it is interesting how the code-centred, "crypto-logical" approach gradually changes into a more historical way of thinking. Jon Whitman has summed up this move concisely:

> Allegorical interpretation continues to flourish in the Renaissance treatment of ancient mythology, culminating in the vast, mid-sixteenth century mythographic encyclopedias of Giraldi, Conti, and Cantari. This interpretive movement overlaps with iconographic programs for displaying and decoding conspicuously allusive images, ranging from the enigmatic pictograms of hieroglyphics to the intricate designs of emblems. Even in the treatment of non-sacred texts and images, however, counterstrains are developing. The sixteenth-century humanist revival of Aristotle's *Poetics* increasingly inclines critical theorists to seek the organizing principles of imaginary plots not in "allegory," but in "credibility"... Efforts in the sixteenth and seventeenth centuries to specify the ancient origins of myths, either by Euhemerist methods or by the argument that Hebrew scripture is the source of pagan stories, gradually encourage an early "historicist" approach to mythology. (2000, 12)

This quote gives us an indication of the roots of some contemporary (in modern times) speculations about the existence of deep and "hidden," eternal and universal meanings of myth, which it is possible for us to decipher and "live by." Perhaps there is a human, cognitively anchored tendency for over-interpretation that makes us think that deep mysteries dwell where extraordinary appearances abound.

The Enlightenment and the Critique of Religion and Myth

The "Enlightenment" is a term that covers a rather variegated set of philosophical, ideological and political trends. It covers such diverse developments as the founding of the first modern scientific academies, a quest for reason in social affairs, the great political upheavals and revolution in France and the United States. The philosophical development was largely French in origin but in many ways it accorded well with the increasing empiricist philosophies of the English-speaking world. Below these diverse manifestations lay an increased pursuit towards reason in all spheres of human life and this has profound consequences for the ways in which most Western societies changed. With Reason as master, the fate of myth as something humanly valuable was clear: myth was superstition and unreason and thus to be banished. On the other hand, there was an interest in "the irrational," but then mostly because this interest was linked to contacts with many "savage" nations. These new contacts could be seen as providing information about humankind in its "infancy" and this was important, if only to demonstrate how far the human race had progressed.[26] This may appear a conceited attitude, so it must also be emphasized that a basic element in Enlightenment thought is its persistent humanism: what is human is the measure of all things and humankind is one. This conviction also lay beneath the ideas of equality, ranging from matters of citizenship and education to the abolition of slavery. However, like other modes of thought or mentalities, this is also a complex, if not contradictory one at points, for it was also assumed that there is basically just one "Culture" – the one proposed by the Enlightenment thinkers themselves and it is therefore not only about reason but it is also ideological. Thus, one could say that the Enlightenment to a certain degree exiled myths from its own world but at the same time it helped create another great myth, the one about human reason and progress.[27]

The Enlightenment attitude to traditional Christian religion and the hegemony of the churches was a very critical one. Philosophers and other writers increasingly wrote with fervour about the origin and function of religion. If religion should be awarded a role in contemporary society, it had to be as a warrant of public morality and social stability. This may sound trivial today, but it was a revolution in the true sense of the word: a "turning around." For millennia, religion had ruled over the minds of humans and their societies; religion was the "sacred canopy" suspended over all spheres of human life. However, now it was the other way round and religion was accorded, at most, a particular place and role to play. Therefore, the Enlightenment period may be seen as the birth of modern society and thought. The critique of religion, and thus the mythical worldview, was pursued by many thinkers and writers, first and foremost among these are Ludwig Feuerbach and Karl Marx who extensively investigated and wrote about myth and religion as human projections and imaginations that were to be exposed and done away with. It was generally agreed in critical circles that religion would disappear as science and technology increased in size and scope. Later in the nineteenth century, it led to very aggressive confrontations in many European countries between proponents of religion, mostly the churches, and secular, ideological social powers.

The Romantic Movement

A reaction could be expected to the reign of reason. It arose in the form of the Romantic Movement in the late eighteenth and early nineteenth centuries, especially in the Germanic speaking artistic and intellectual milieus of continental Europe. It emphasized emotion, passion, love, in-born virtue, individuality, self-expression and the spiritual superiority of art, literature and music. One of the most remarkable rehabilitations of myth is to be found in that Romantic Movement. Myth now came to be seen as a genuine expression of human creativity, in stories that tell us about a specific form of a world, that of the imagination, about dreams and hopes. In short, about all that is important for humans as feeling and sensing beings. On this note Romanticism was quite an optimistic way of thinking. However, Romanticism was also a sentimental and nostalgic movement, which in many countries coincided with the growing nationalism in Europe. The idea of a "nation" now became intimately tied to language, as the romanticists were convinced that languages express particular cultural orientations towards the world. Languages, cultures and peoples had their own character, their own personality and tone, thus it was an essentialist view. Thus, in opposition to the Enlightenment thinkers' (many French) single human culture, the Romanticists (many of them German) posited a multitude cultures, so that the romanticists were, to some degree, also cultural relativists. Romanticists in all nations looked to the past to find inspiration for their nation building, and Celts, Italians, Germans, Danes, Scotsmen and many others found their heroes in the vestiges of their ancient mythologies. In the case that none was to be found, they could be invented.[28] In Denmark, for instance, this led to massive regenerations and reformulations of the myths of the ancient Norsemen, with Viking associations being not the least important aspect in this project of nationalist cultural self-aggrandisement. The names associated with Romanticism are primarily German: Johann Gottfried Herder, Friedrich Schlegel, Friedrich W. J. von Schelling. Herder said that various nations had myths so diverse that they would not understand each other's stories, stories that were hereditary and the passing on of a communal soul. Myths were also considered spiritual, as when Schlegel pronounced that "Mythology has a great advantage. What otherwise escapes consciousness, is here to be seen as spiritual meaning...and grasped as the soul in its body." To him "Mythology is such an artwork of nature" and he deplored the lack of knowledge about the world's many other mythologies: "But the other mythologies must again be awakened in accordance with their profundity, their beauty and their formation so that we may quicken the instigation of the new mythology. If only the treasures of the Orient were as accessible as those of Antiquity."[29] Thus, with Romanticism came the desire to probe into the depths of the folklore traditions and popular mythologies of the various "peoples" in Europe but also an ardent interest in the myths of distant lands.

Evidently, this movement was in many ways a counter-reaction to the reign of reason propagated by Enlightenment thinkers, and not least in what concerns the status and role of myth. Romanticism did not disappear – it survived well in many areas and is "alive" today. Romantic modes of thought entered the Western mind and never lost hold of some parts of that "mind." As a consequence for the study of myth, we can see that since the early romantic era, there have been two parallel trends in the Western attitude to myth. One is the critical heritage from the Enlightenment and the other is the positive attitude, inspired by Romanticism, which has been noticeable in parts of the study of religion, but otherwise more in the arts, in literature and very strongly in the modern popular media.

Comparative Mythology

"Comparative mythology" is a term that is pre-eminently associated with the names Friedrich Max Müller (1823–1900) and James George Frazer (1854–1941). Many others followed their ideas, which were in fact quite simple: Find "things" that look comparable and then "distil" the essence or sift the kernels from the chaff and then this will disclose the meaning of the myth, of the ritual or of any other social and cultural phenomenon. The intention behind the "comparative mythology" programme was to find as many commonalities as could be amassed – or imagined. The earlier comparativist ideas of Max Müller were initially very heavily influenced by Romanticism and these ideas were imported into "Nature mythology" according to which the "meaning" of a myth was to be found in the natural phenomenon that it referred to, as when Apollo becomes the sun or Zeus is the lightning in the sky. All of this was because of the human awe and inspiration over against nature. Some developed the idea into "Astral mythology" where, again, the "true" referents were the elements in the sky. James G. Frazer, originally a classical scholar, set out to explain a strange ritual from Roman antiquity about a priest being considered "King of the Woods." As the mythical materials provided very little in way of explanation, he embarked upon a true Odyssey that spanned the world in search for evidence that could explain the ritual. He gathered so much information that the work came to a dozen (!) volumes, but fortunately also in an abridged version. Frazer's method was simply to assemble and resemble. In so doing, he of course also extracted his materials from their contexts and it therefore becomes very difficult to ascertain what they mean and how they function. The method is thus "atomistic" and anecdotal, but the worst methodological "sin" lies in the confusion of form with content, so that things that look alike are considered identical and that they therefore have the "same meaning."[30] Comparative mythology waned towards the middle of the twentieth century, but it lingers on in more popular forms in, for example, the entertainment and tourism industries. Comparisons of all things have a strong hold on the human mind, as it is an integral part of our cognitive constitution.

Historicism and Empiricism

The beginning of the last part of the nineteenth century, of the German "History of religions school" in theology and the historical critical methodology introduced by this school had profound consequences not only for Lutheran theology, but it was also to become paramount to the study of religion in general and also in the study of myth. As far as this orientation was "historical" it stressed the importance of studying its subject matters (text mostly) in their proper and original historical context in order to explain and understand them. It was critical in the sense that the accepted religious and dogmatic "truths" were not allowed as evidence in a scholarly discussion. Thus, the Holy Book was no longer a "Holy Book" but a historical document that did not point to any divine revelation, but only to human beliefs about revelations. This was, of course, a grave attack on the established privileges of the churches. However, it was a necessary theological corrective to and acceptance of the premises of the earlier philosophical criticism of religion – theology simply had to turn away from fundamentalist discourse if it wanted to retain some credibility in the academy and in the surrounding culture. Biblical exegesis, in this line of inquiry, was profoundly transformed and this also had consequences for the history of religions which was then in its formative years, not least because many of its earliest professionals had a background in Christian theologies. On the issue of myth, however, theology and the history of religions parted ways: the latter was keen on the study of myth whereas the former tended to marginalize or downplay the role of the mythical elements in the Bible.

The introduction and influence of historical methods in the study of religion and myth had further consequences. The all-encompassing generalizations of comparative mythology were met with suspicion by historians and philologists especially in the continental European tradition. The ideal of erudition now became detailed and piecemeal (and often pedantic) studies of particulars. Greek mythology, for instance, came to be seen as a random collection of very specific, local elements. Most of this research focused on meticulous reconstruction of particular cults and myths and with a great emphasis on origins and tracing historical circumstances and developments. This trend in research produced a disparate and heterogenous picture of Greek myths. The meaning of a myth could lay buried in the historical causes, often as a result of migrations of peoples, or "influences." Some scholars found such influences in the cultural contacts between the Near Eastern traditions and their Greek counterparts (Kirk 1970). Another, more concrete historicist idea was to search for, or reconstruct, "real" historical events as the background for a myth. This may have worked in the discovery of Troy, but it certainly does not always work, which the many attempts to locate Atlantis or the "lost kingdom of Mu" have abundantly demonstrated.[31]

In a certain number of religious and cultural traditions, myth has become history – at least when seen from the tradition's own perspective. This happened in ancient Israel where a complex amount of earlier mythological and legendary traditions later became integrated in a single, progressive narrative of salvation history. In ancient Rome, the typical motifs and structures of mythology, as known from other Indo-European peoples, were transformed into and rewritten as foundational history with divine legitimation. These two transformations of the mythical into a narrated history in turn set the tone for both Christianity and Islam as founded, in their own self-understanding, on specific historical events.[32]

Later during the mid twentieth century, the historical-critical mode of research began posing problems for biblical exegesis. Greater insight was gained on the historical Jesus, the first congregations and into the conceptual and historical contexts of the formation of the New Testament. At the same time, however, this estranged the message of the scripture from believers in the modern age. How could it be relevant when so strongly tied to the semantic universe of their time in the ancient world? The research into the background and foundations of the Christian teachings threatened to render the teachings irrelevant. The German theologian Rudolf Bultmann launched the method of "de-mythologization" as a way in which to preserve the *kerygma* (Greek: "proclamation") of the church. The suggestion was that as the worldview of the New Testament is mythological then it presents the message of salvation in mythical terms. However, this does not fit with the modern scientifically based worldview, which makes the myth seem implausible and anachronistic and thus render Christianity obsolete. In order to remedy this difficulty Bultmann held that Christians should "de-mythologize" the scripture; that is to interpret the essential messages of the New Testament from the basis of an existential philosophy, which presumes that the existential situation, that is, being human, has not changed. Thus, through "existential interpretation" it becomes possible to disclose or "translate" and by emphasizing intentions more than actual wordings, access is gained to the existential message about being human that is contained in the worldview of the scripture.[33]

The "Myth and Ritual School"

Particular, but brief, mention must be made of the "Myth and Ritual School" in the study of myth; others have already admirably synthesized this intellectual movement (Segal 1998). Sometimes also called the "Cambridge School" because some of its most ardent proponents worked there, this "school" proceeded from the premise that the proper way to account for the meanings of myths was to find or reconstruct the rituals they were associated with or originated from. The general thesis was that ritual is more important than myth, because rituals endure (also called "cult continuity") whereas myth is secondary and may be altered without major changes in the forms of rituals and thus myths become an explanatory narrative that provides the ritual and the community with a story that makes the ritual understandable.[34] In all probability, ritual behaviour *is* a very old feature of human behaviour, as also opined by much later theorists, but that does not entail that this applies across the board to the relations between myths and rituals in historical time. One of the main advocates of that school, the classical philologist Jane Harrison (1912), set out to explain a corpus of ancient Greek myths by linking them to corresponding rituals. The exercise was no success as the relations between ancient Greek rituals and myths are quite dim, but the Myth-ritual hypothesis was subsequently quite broadly applied in the studies of ancient Near Eastern religions, such as the Mesopotamian and also in Old Testament studies where it held a position of some tenacity for several decades. The Myth-ritual hypothesis is now largely abandoned and it is easily traceable in the older scholarly literature. As a concluding note, we may say that of course myths and rituals are related in any given tradition and of course ritual action may be given diverging explanations and "local exegesis" but the relations are not simple causal ones. Rather, we may say that rituals and myths relate by being parts of larger webs of worldviews, norms and attitudes – in what we conventionally call culture.[35]

And... Later Developments

Much has happened in the study of myth. After the trends introduced here came functionalism, structuralism and other later developments, but as these "-isms" are logically related to the contributions in the sections below introductions and analyses will be left until then. This is certainly not the first book about myths and mythologies (e.g. Doty 1986). It does differ somewhat, however, in kind, contents and scope from others. As this volume is intended as a general reader on the problems related to the study of myth primarily in a perspective from the study of religions, it is obvious that many other publications may present other views from other disciplines and be much more detailed on some issues that have only been touched upon here. This only indicates the richness of the field and it is not to be deplored in any way. The bibliography below contains publications that may be an aid in further studies. The bibliographies and references in the sections below also indicate relevant literature.

As a final editorial remark I must note that I have striven to reproduce the contributions as close to the originals as possible. Some of them have been published in styles and formats very different from that of the present series, so a certain amount of editing has been inevitable, but the wording should be exactly as in the original. This also means that many of the contributions are written in non-inclusive language, that is, they are not gender neutral and so use the terms "man" and "mankind" instead of "human" and "humankind" and so on. Also, today no one writes about "primitives," but as this collection also concerns the history of the study of myths and mythologies I think it would be worse if we tampered with the sources. In that sense this volume is also a documentation of the changes in academic discourse, rhetoric and style.

Notes

1. It should be noted, especially to the benefit of the "disciplinary outsider" that the scholarly study of religion was largely impervious to the political trends/turmoil at that time. The philosophical history of criticism of religion as launched by Feuerbach, Marx, Nietzsche et al. was considered irrelevant as these had not "really" (that is philologically) studied religion but only tried to explain it "away" – as "learned despisers" are wont to.

2. It is for this reason that the present anthology has two sections that are unusual to anthologies about myths: one is on the cognitive approaches and the other is the final section on the "myth today" question.

3. This overview is very brief and probably quite bewildering, but the issues and their history will be dealt with in more detail below, also in the introduction to the separate sections.

4. This distinction between "subject matter" and "theoretical object" is common in the philosophy of science and I shall use it below as a standard analytical tool.

5. In E. E. Evans-Pritchard's rendition: "The nature-myth school was predominantly a German school, and it was mostly concerned with Indo-European religions, its thesis being that the gods of antiquity, and by implication god anywhere and at all times, were no more than personified natural phenomena: sun, moon, stars, dawn, the spring renewal, mighty rivers etc." (1965, 20).

6. On Tylor's view of myth, see Segal (1999, 7–18).

7. Admittedly, this is not a very convincing formal criterion, because it relies entirely on a given tradition or culture's sense of time and in many instances the distinction is not at all clear. It seems to work best for scriptural traditions.

8. This constructionist view of the function of myth in culture and cognition will be expanded in Part VI.
9. One example among many is Rogerson (1974) who lists 12 different kinds – not all sensible though.
10. See e.g. Detienne (1986) for such a perspective.
11. The relations between narrative, semantics and cognition will be take up in the sections below, but think of how children, until a certain age, will recount the *sequence of the elements* of a narrative when asked what the story "is about."
12. Obviously, our cognitive apparatus is also pan-human or universal.
13. This exposition is a very brief summary of points already made by Emile Durkheim and later by Mircea Eliade and, in my rendition, especially by Edmund Leach (1976).
14. At this point it should be noted that I consider the widely promoted concept of "globalization" to be quite ideological in (subconscious) orientation and intention and one that serves as a master narrative promoting certain kinds of, mostly Western, values: global trade and capitalism, secularization, democracy. "Globalization" is thus an example of modern myth in disguise; that is, it is not (yet) narratively organized.
15. Mention should be made here of philosophers and scholars Hans Blumenberg, and Hans Jonas; see e.g. Segal (1999) the chapter "Does myth have a future," 19–35 and "Hans Blumenberg as theorist of myth," 143–52.
16. This is a model, not a description: some cosmologies are vertical "top-down"; some are horizontal or combinations of both.
17. The "Eastern civilizations" (admittedly a clumsy term) have also witnessed scepticism and criticism of the traditional tales about how the world and how the ensuing cosmology e.g. Indian, Buddhist, and Chinese philosophies, came into existence.
18. Besides being the first known criticism of religion, Xenophanes' view was quite humorous and ironic: He said that all peoples had gods that looked remarkably like themselves, so that if horses has gods these would most likely look like horses etc. This is obviously a psychological theory of projection.
19. The reference to Plato's view of myth is generally from his work *The Republic*. Analyses of the complicated story about logos and mythos may be found in Lincoln (1999), Graf (1993), Buxton (1994).
20. Euhemerus (from Messene in Greece) lived in the fourth to third century BC, wrote of fantastic travels to utopian lands and promoted the interpretation that many gods were originally kings and other great figures who were then deified. This view was popular in the Hellenistic era, not least among the rulers.
21. For more comprehensive accounts of these issues, see e.g. Whitman (2000) and Blumenfeld-Kosinski (1997).
22. The trend towards allegorical and mystical interpretations of scripture also flourished in Judaism and Islam in the same era.
23. See Brumble (1998), *Dictionary of Allegorical Meanings*, concerning later uses of classical myths.
24. Text as diverse as, for example, the Roman historian Tacitus' work on "Germania," which was later to feature prominently in German nationalism, and the gnostic "Poimandres" from the Corpus Hermeticum, a mystical text about the libration of the soul which was to become very influential in the Renaissance.

25. Art from this period amply demonstrates how motifs as well as symbols were used allegorically and very extensively. The "language of flowers," for example, was used in paintings as symbols for moral and religious vices and virtue.

26. Some other nations were very favourably valued. There was a great veneration, for instance, for the Chinese civilization as this was seen (through the writings of Confucius) as non-mythical, practical and borne by reason.

27. See comprehensive collection of materials on the study of myth in this period in Feldman and Richardson (1972).

28. The "invention of tradition" is amply demonstrated in, e.g., the three-volume forgery (1760–3) by James Macpherson (1736–96) of poetry supposedly composed by the blind third-century bard Ossian.

29. Excerpt translated by this editor from *Rede über die Mythologie*, first published 1800.

30. In more technical terms: analogous properties or relations are taken as homological properties or relations. But "not all that glitters is gold" – which is also an important lesson for comparative studies.

31. See Vernant (1980, 186–242) for a succinct history of the study of Greek myths.

32. General introductions to or handbooks on Judaism, Christianity, and Islam do not normally have "myth" as a topic or an entry. This is remarkable and in turn demonstrates the "problem with myth." In the present author's view, Judaism, Christianity, and Islam as practised traditions are full of mythological materials.

33. As Bultmann is not directly represented in the sections below, I include this paragraph because of the immense influence of his thoughts on "de-mythologization" in Christian theology and because the term must be represented in a volume on the study of myth. There are also indications that other traditions based on authoritative ancient scriptures face similar problems vis-à-vis modernity and that Bultmann's proposal of a solution could prove influential.

34. Therefore, this theory is sometimes also referred to as the "libretto theory" – libretto being Italian for the "little book" that the audience receives because the style of singing makes it difficult to discern the words of the opera-text.

35. This is not the place to discuss problems "with culture," for although some maintain that it is difficult to define culture clearly there is much to recommend for its continued use. Thus I use the concept quite loosely in general and then specify when needed.

References

Bascom, William R. 1965. "The Forms of Folklore: Prose Narratives." *Journal of American Folklore* 78: 3–20.

Bietenholz, Peter. 1994. *"Historia" and "Fabula": Myths and Legends in Historical Thought from Antiquity to the Modern Age*. Leiden: Brill.

Blumenfeld-Kosinski, Renate. 1997. *Reading Myth: Classical Mythology and its Interpretations in Medieval French Literature*. Stanford, CA: Stanford University Press.

Brumble, H. David. 1998. *Classical Myths and Legends in the Middle Ages and Renaissance: A Dictionary of Allegorical Meanings*. London: Routledge.

Buxton, Richard G. A. 1994. *Imaginary Greece: The Contexts of Mythology*. Cambridge: Cambridge University Press.

Detienne, Marcel. 1986. *The Creation of Mythology*. Chicago: University of Chicago Press. (orig.: *L'Invention de la mythologie*. Paris: Gallimard).

Donald, Merlin. 2001. *A Mind so Rare: The Evolution of Human Consciousness*. New York: W.W. Norton.

Doty, William G. 1986. *Mythography: The Study of Myths and Rituals*. Tuscaloosa: University of Alabama Press.

Dubuisson, Daniel. 2003. *The Western Construction of Religion: Myths, Knowledge and Ideology*. Baltimore: Johns Hopkins University Press.

Durkheim, Émile and Marcel Mauss. 1963. *Primitive Classification*. Chicago: University of Chicago Press. (orig. in *L'Année Sociologique*, vol. VI, 1901–1902, Paris 1903, 1–72).

Evans-Pritchard, E. E. 1965. *Theories of Primitive Religion*. Oxford: Oxford University Press.

Feldman, Burton and Robert D. Richardson, eds. 1972. *The Rise of Modern Mythology 1680–1860: A Critical History with Documents*. Bloomington: Indiana University Press.

Graf, Fritz. 1993. *Greek Mythology: An Introduction*. Baltimore: Johns Hopkins University Press.

Harrison, Jane. 1912. *Themis*. Cambridge: Cambridge University Press.

Havelock, E. A 1982. *The Literate Revolution in Greece and its Cultural Consequences*. Princeton: Princeton University Press.

Honko, Lauri. 1984. "The Problem of Defining Myth." In *Sacred Narrative: Readings in the Theory of Myth*, ed. Alan Dundes, 41–52. Berkeley: University of California Press.

Hultkrantz, Åke. 1957. *The North American Indian Orpheus Tradition: A Contribution to Comparative Religion*. Stockholm: The Ethnographical Museum.

Jensen, Jeppe S. 2004. "Semantics in the Study of Religion." In *New Approaches to the Study of Religion*, ed. Peter Antes, R. Warne and A. W. Geertz, 219–52. Berlin and New York: Walter de Gruyter.

Jensen, Jeppe S. and Luther H. Martin, eds. 2002. *Rationality and the Study of Religion*. London: Routledge.

Kirk, G. S. 1970. *Myth: Its Meaning and Function in Ancient and Other Cultures*. Cambridge: Cambridge University Press.

Lawson, E. Thomas. 1978. "The Explanation of Myth and Myth as Explanation." *Journal of the American Academy of Religion*, XLVI: 507–523.

Leach, Edmund. 1976. *Culture and Communication*. Cambridge: Cambridge University Press.

Lévi-Strauss, Claude. 1969. *The Raw and the Cooked: Introduction to a Science of Mythology*, vol. I (orig. 1964). Harmondsworth: Penguin.

Lincoln, Bruce. 1999. *Theorizing Myth: Narrative, Ideology, and Scholarship*. Chicago: University of Chicago Press.

Mack, Burton. 1994. *Who Wrote the New Testament? The Making of the Christian Myth*. New York: HarperOne.

McCutcheon, Russell T. 2000. "Myth." In *Guide to the Study of Religion*, ed. Willi Braun and R. T. McCutcheon, 190–208. London: Cassell.

Müller, Friedrich Max. 1856. *Comparative Mythology*. Oxford.

Pettazzoni, Raffaele. 1954. *Essays on the History of Religions*. Leiden: Brill.

Rappaport, Roy. 1999. *Religion and Ritual in the Making of Humankind*. Cambridge: Cambridge University Press.

Rogerson, J. W. 1974. *Myth in Old Testament Interpretation*. Berlin: Walter de Gruyter.

Segal, Robert. 1998. *The Myth and Ritual Theory*. Oxford: Blackwell.

_____1999. *Theorizing about Myth*. Amherst: University of Massachusetts Press.

Sienkewicz, Thomas J. 1997. *Theories of Myth: An Annotated Bibliography*. Lanham: Scarecrow Press.

Strenski, Ivan. 1987. *Four Theories of Myth in Twentieth-Century History: Cassirer, Eliade, Lévi-Strauss, and Malinowski*. Iowa City: University of Iowa Press.

Tylor, Edward Burnett. 1873. *Primitive Culture*. London: Murray.

Vernant, Jean-Pierre. 1980. *Myth and Society in Ancient Greece*. London: Methuen.

Whitman, Jon, ed. 2000. *Interpretation and Allegory: Antiquity to the Modern Period*. Leiden: Brill.

Zaidman, Louise Bruit and Pauline Schmitt Pantel. 1992. *Religion in the Ancient Greek City*. Cambridge: Cambridge University Press.

PART I

PHILOSOPHICAL APPROACHES

INTRODUCTION TO PART I

J udging from the historical sketch of the history of the study of myth in the "General Introduction," above, many philosophers have had their say on myths and mythologies. It should be remembered, however, that disciplinary boundaries have not always been what they are now. There were times when any learned person was to some degree a philosopher and when studying philosophy was an integral part of becoming learned. What follows is but a brief outline of the development of philosophical orientations and paradigms with relevance to the study of myth and mythologies and reference to some philosophers who have taken an interest in myth but who are not contributors to this volume. Next is a review of certain philosophical issues that concern the study of myth more specifically. These include, for example, the debates over the validity of science and religion as worldviews, questions in analytic philosophy concerning the meaning of words and the differences between descriptive versus prescriptive uses of language.

The history of philosophy is not straightforwardly cumulative, for it may also be read as a history of intellectual disagreement. Although there have been periods in intellectual history of relative stability and agreement, it seems that today one can be a philosopher of one of many different persuasions. Therefore, there is little sense in trying to search for universal concord or consensus here and, instead, I have chosen to represent some aspects of the history of philosophy and some current views that may be helpful in our understanding of the fate of the study of myths and mythologies and how we may go about these studies. The criteria applied to the selection are thus primarily instrumental, epistemic and methodological.

Philosophical Orientations: An Historical Sketch

The development of general trends in the Western history of philosophy and ideas – and with a bearing on our subject – has been quite concisely described by French philosopher Jean-Francois Lyotard (1924–98) in his history of "forms of knowledge." Before the modern age, knowledge was mainly presented in narrative form. Traditional narratives, for example myths, consist of many kinds of language: they are simultaneously entertaining, descriptions of the world and the supernatural, prescriptive as to human action and behaviour and many more things. They are "multivocal" and quite often contradictory, inconsistent and messy.[1] Traditional tales, such as religious narratives, set roles and positions for the listener or the reader in a cosmology legitimated by its own self-evidence. It is no longer so in modern society, according to Lyotard, but there is also no reason to be nostalgic about this condition, because the tradition's inclusion of the reader also limited her freedom. Over time, beginning with the Renaissance, a more sceptical view of myth was introduced. The contradictions and inconsistencies of narrative knowledge were met with an emancipating incredulity based on emerging scientific worldviews. From the era of the Enlightenment and even more so in modernity, the authorities and institutions based on traditional forms of narrative knowledge eroded. However, the technologically useful and logically consistent modes of knowledge that dominate in a modern scientific worldview raise problems. For, where traditional narrative knowledge came with its own legitimation, scientific knowledge cannot legitimate itself, because it is supposedly and in principle value-free. It needs legitimation from somewhere else and so modernity, surprisingly, created its own mythology. The legitimating "myths" of modernity are the narratives of reason, of progress, of the supremacy of the scientific worldview – and, not least, of those who govern it. In its core, this orientation is also remarkably protestant, anti-mythological, anti-ritualist, hygienic, and focuses on the control of minds and bodies. It is a religious worldview transformed, with a post-protestant zeal and as a mission it is a plan to save the world. One of the ways in which to accomplish this is to make it seem that reason rules. This mode of thought began with the Enlightenment and it has been dominant ever since in the Western world.

In his insistence on the supremacy of reason and rationality, the philosopher Immanuel Kant was outright suspicious of myth as a "survival" from the past, which may, at the most, have some didactic value for the uneducated. In his grand philosophy of the evolution of the human spirit, Georg W. F. Hegel presented a triumphalist history of the evolution of Western civilization as humanity "growing up." This view also harboured some nationalist and political implications, as this maturation should end with a strong Prussian nation. Interesting in Hegel's thought, in the context of myth analysis, is his reposition of human self-knowledge from subjective mind to a more objective form of "spirit" – as in the "Spirit of the Age" ("Zeitgeist"). This move entails that we only have access to knowledge of ourselves through media that are intersubjective and public, such as symbols and language. And this also leaves some space for myth because they display the work of the human "spirit."

Later in the nineteenth century, the general intellectual climate changed into one of empiricism, one that denounced myth as falsehood and error. According to this point of view myth belonged to the past or to the worlds of "savages." This rationalizing expansion reached a provisional zenith in "Positivism," the philosophical theory of history developed by Auguste Comte, which consisted of three stages: the first is the stage of Religion and superstition from the childhood of humanity until the second stage of Philosophy, in which rational argument and reason reign and then lastly comes the third stage of Science. Thus, first the priests rule, then the philosophers and finally, the scientists. No longer was there any room for myth. As the philosopher Georges Bataille has noted much later, the "absence of myth" had become the very myth of the modern world.

Myth, in the More Positive Perspective

It is interesting that about the same time as the Enlightenment there was also a growing interest in mythology, especially in comparative studies of language, religion and culture; but these studies were now not the trade of philosophers. The modern university with its division of disciplines was taking shape with a growing compartmentalization of intellectual life. Scholars from many areas (Classics, linguistics, etc.) were attracted to the study of myth, but as these other disciplines will be treated separately in the sections below, I shall restrict the perspective to philosophy here.

As noted in the "General Introduction" above, these affirmative ideas on myths and mythologies were offered by the romanticists. Prominent among them was the philosopher Friedrich Schelling (1775–1854) who even imagined the possibility of a genuine "philosophy of mythology." Romanticism held a positive view of myth because it was seen as a characteristic of a creative, artistic phase in the history of humankind; one that could and should be revived because it is a vital dimension of human existence. Thus, myths were not to be considered an old and forgotten phenomenon, but a force to be taken into account, not least because myths were deemed important to humans in their expression of their own identity. The theologian and philosopher Johann Gottfried Herder (1744–1803) used his romanticist interests in myth in a manner not so innocent. He developed these views in a large work, *Ideas on the Philosophy of the History of Mankind*, in which he saw the identities of peoples determined by climate and language. In 1770 he even won a prize for an essay on the origin of language (a very hot topic then). Myths were important in his view of the history of humankind, because they conferred collective identity and because of their conservative nature they play a role in the reproduction of collective memory and the differences between groups. Herder was repeatedly theorizing about the "Volksgeist," the spirit of the people, and such ideas were warmly welcomed by romanticist thinkers and used by them in their critique of Enlightenment views and values. Myths were now becoming identified and classified according to the social, ethnic or political groups they "belonged to," say "Greek myths," "Celtic myths," etc., as if there was a self-evident and natural bond between the social or ethnic groups and their myths. In mythical nationalist identity-construction the myths provided the undiluted essence of the people in question as old, genuine, and authentic. Myths contained primordial foundations for nation-building. This view is still in wide circulation.[2] As Bruce Lincoln concludes on Herder:

> his ideas have been highly influential well beyond romantic and nationalist circles and arise whenever myths and peoples are understood as mutually – and unproblematically – constitutive. It is not always the case that myths are the product and reflection of a people who tell stories in which they effectively narrate themselves. At times, myths are stories which some people narrate others, and at times the existence of those others is itself the product of mythic discourse. (1999, 211)

Ludwig Feuerbach (1804–72), who otherwise kept a very sober and critical mind in his analysis of religion as a human projection, was negatively influenced by the romantic discourse of ethnic differentiation and mentalities in his polemics against Jews. Mythical narratives could be employed for good or bad, but in his case, the romantic ideas about the unity of myth, homeland, "Volk"-identity and mentality were turned into a programme of marginalization and persecution: The Jews were considered as not being a "proper" people or nation because they did not have a homeland or a language of their own.

Friedrich Schlegel (1772–1829) wrote extensively about philosophy, poetry and myths and their mutual relations. In his view the goal of the theoretical and hermeneutical efforts of the scholars was not to approach the ancient myths in interpretations of them but scholars should rather use the myths in an effort to make their own new mythology. To wit, the work with mythology was "intoxicating" and spiritually stimulating. To get an idea of this romantic spirit, witness one of Schlegel's many praises of myth:

> Mythology has a great advantage. That which would otherwise eternally escape consciousness, is here to be perceived in the spiritual sense and kept hold of as the soul surrounded by love, through which it shines before our eyes and speaks to our ears. Mythology is such an artwork of nature. In it weavings the highest is really given form, all is relation and alteration, formed and changed, and this forming and changing is its peculiar procedure, its inner life, its method if I am allowed to say so.

Schlegel's work was quite creative in itself. In 1808 he published *On the Language and Wisdom of the Indians*, a work that included a theory about India as the Aryan homeland. This hypothesis started a long speculative obsession with ancient India in the Germanic-speaking world. The ideas about the unity of language and race also had a reverse side, and again with the Jews as the victims: As Jews were not of Aryan descent, they were a danger to the peoples among whom they settled. However, many romantics also – positively – suggested that the Jews ought to have a homeland of their own like any other ethnic group. These configurations of thought really are prime examples of essentialism and the use of pollution-metaphors.

Friedrich Nietzsche (1844–1900) entertained some quite particular views on myth. From his studies on myths he derived certain opinions that appear rather heinous according to later standards. In his many writings he often reverted to the question of the use of myth, and he was consistently praising "the blond, that is Aryan, conqueror races" and the nature of the Germanic peoples. Today all this stands out as tenaciously racist. He used one kind of mythology that was known from history and used that to create another new one, one that was simultaneously nostalgic and highly politicized, a myth that set the Germanic ideals above all else. The Germanic spirit was to be restored in all its glory and purged of all foreign elements and he proclaimed: "that this spirit must begin its fight with the elimination of everything Romanic" (Lincoln 1999, 63). This statement fell, however, just after the French-German war and was thus an ideological contribution to the unification of the German state. He even went so far as to proclaim that non-blond Germans were pre-Aryan. These examples may remind us how philosophers' views of myth may be deeply entrenched in political predicaments.[3] The new European nationalists of the nineteenth century were avid myth-"consumers" as well as myth producers in their constructions of privileged ancestries and the ideological uses of myth were rampant in nationalist and racist formations of thought and ideology. Not surprisingly, all of the nations' histories turned out as having been glorious at some point.

After World War I, the entire vision changed. The self-evident certainties about European culture as the pinnacle of civilization were shattered; after the evolutionary optimism of the preceding decades a Zeitgeist of uncertainty and doubt now appeared. Intellectuals, artists and philosophers now turned to the "primitives" and the roots of the symbolic life of humankind – which includes myth. In that revised perspective myth is not so much considered an erroneous narrative about the world, but rather, and indirectly, a mode of narration about the human existence that could even be relevant to modern humans if only deciphered and understood in the right manner. Thus, we witness the arrival of surrealism and primitive art, psychoanalysis and the positive view of madness as a countermove against bourgeois high-culture with all its restrictions, frustrations and regulations. Philosophers such as Georges Bataille or Roger Caillois held sympathetic views of myths as human expressions that contained an appropriate amount of "madness." Up until World War II many used myths and mythologies in their nationalist and ideological propagandas but that issue does not so much belong here, in the history of philosophical interests in myth, but rather to historical, social and political analyses. The experience of World War II, however, strongly influenced philosophers such as Hans Jonas (1903–93) and Hans Blumenberg (1920–96) who became later protagonists of more positive and de-politicized existential views of myth as a human attempt to make sense in a world of contingency and apparent meaninglessness. To them, myth is a human mode of expression comparable to art, music or literature. Now, these modes have not been disallowed in spite of growing secularization and the supremacy of the rational and scientific in most spheres of life in modern society, so neither should myth be exorcised, for it holds a legitimate place in human existence. We could say that myth now finds a place in a kind of parallel universe.

General Philosophical Issues as They Concern the Study of Myth More Specifically

Analytic philosophy was probably *the* most important movement in twentieth-century Anglo-American philosophy. The primary occupation of its proponents was the analysis of language and concepts and so it was intensely concerned with the relations between language and reality, between word and object, and between meaning and reference. The question about meaning and reference, that is, of the relation between word and object, has a very long and complicated history. It is not simple, nor has it really yet been solved. This problem, also called the "res-verbum" argument, goes back all the way to the discussions between Socratic philosophers and Sophist rhetorical scholars in the fifth and fourth centuries BC. The Socratics held that language is a medium for discovering more basic truth and reality whereas the Sophists regard language as the ultimate human creative achievement and that truth is a fiction based on human beliefs. Consequently, the first (Socratic) attitude was hostile to myth as non-realist and imaginative and the second (Sophist) viewed myth as a creative expression of the power of words and language. This conflict later proved to be of great concern to the humanists in the Renaissance where it marked the beginning of the later division between philosophy and literary studies. The divide has remained ever since and it is evident that this conflict has had implications for the study of myth through history. Today the division surfaces in the differences of opinion between those who hold that science can tell us all we need to know and others who are convinced that the arts and other creative activities are what make us human. The debate also concerns the distinction between descriptive versus prescriptive (normative) language and the decision of which should have priority. The first, descriptive language contains models *of* the world and the second, prescriptive language contains models *for* the world. As regards myths it is clear that although they are generally descriptive in the sense that they are stories *about* something, then it is also evident that they are prescriptive and normative, that is: they are about how the world *should* be and also frequently about why it is that matters could not be any other way than they are. In that perspective a major function of myth is one that is equivalent to symbolism more generally and to questions relating to the nature and function of aesthetics and art.

Thus, the old and obstinate battle over "Science versus religion" becomes more explicable and manageable. If you pardon the old-fashioned way of expression we could say that the "Human Spirit" may manifest itself in many ways: in thought and action, in politics, economics, art, religion and even myth. The compartmentalization and segregation of modern society and modes of thought has made it quite acceptable and understandable that there are different views on myths and mythologies. No longer does any *one* philosophy seem responsible for *all* attitudes that we may hold towards myth. In critical scientific realism, there is certainly not much space for myth as a way of describing the natural world, but in other equally critical and scholarly pursuits, the study of myth becomes one that informs us about what it means to be human and about the developments of cultural and social history. The social history of ideas has demonstrated that "mentalities," as socially distributed configurations of thought, are quite long-lived undercurrents in human constructions of meaningful communication and action. Philosophical questions are not only about logic, science and epistemology, but also about questions that concern existence, self, understanding, and "lifeworlds." This notion has been put forward, for example, by Jürgen Habermas (1987) in his theory about the modern world as consisting in a dialectic between the system of rationality, money and power on the one hand and the normative "lifeworld" on the other: a sphere of life which is integrated through human symbolic communicative action, such as language, art, literature, religion and, therefore, even myth.

The Philosophy of Language

The philosophy of language – closely related to analytic philosophy mentioned above – has been very much concerned with the "problem of meaning." Meaning is a notoriously difficult word in English as it may have denotations as varied as purpose, intention, reference, and semantic content. The question about the "meaning of life" is not quite the same as that about the meaning of a word, concept or sentence. In this context, it is sensible to restrict the use of "meaning" to denote semantic contents. Some philosophers, not least Ludwig Wittgenstein, have pointed out that the meanings of words, sentences and concepts are disclosed by the ways in which we *use* them and in what contexts they appear reasonable to speakers. This has proved to be a constructive move, because we know that although words may denote something specific (their reference) then they may also change their meaning over time and between groups of people, not least because the referents themselves change. This is especially evident in the case of abstract referents, say concepts such as social equality, childhood, love and justice. Such conditions seem to support a relativism of meaning. Humans "are not led by the same physical evidence to the same picture of the universe, unless their linguistic backgrounds are similar" said Benjamin Whorf (1956, 214). Or, as Wittgenstein framed it: "A whole mythology is deposited in our language" (1979, 10e).

Language is only partially referential about the world and often not so in any straightforwardly empirical manner. There are many kinds of "language-games" and language use comes in many forms and modes: it may express, seduce, prescribe, prohibit, command, encourage, etc. In this philosophy of language perspective, we see parallels to myths, because they are about so many different things and employ such different kinds of language and discourse.[4] Religious language, and thus also mythic language, is sometimes held to be of a different nature, one that does not respect or need the same kinds of reference and truth conditions as do ordinary or scientific language. Thus, even if one accepts the epistemic superiority of scientific language in cognitive matters, then some claim that myth and religious language may be superior as means to grasp the exigencies of human existence. As a further consequence it could be said that these different forms of language are incommensurable, i.e., there is no single or common yardstick for measuring, which is the more true or correct. This view is often called the "two-level theory of truth." For all its attractiveness to some, such a theory about two or more levels of truth does not seem plausible to others, who hold that religious language is simply just language and that it is false (e.g. Frankenberry 2002). It is, however, undeniable that language comes in different modes that are used for different purposes and that language may be much more than descriptive and empirical about matters that can be verified or falsified. It could also be argued that the condition by which to judge myth (for example) is not one of verification or truth but rather by its being meaningful or by bringing something about.

The term "speech act theory" was coined by the philosopher J. L. Austin and it refers to his theory about language as much more than reporting or describing. Language can also *do*; it can change things or create them, that is, language can be "performative." When we say things, we may also be *doing* something at the same time, the classical example is that when I say "I promise" I also *make* a promise, as part of a contractual relationship. This is especially apparent in rituals, for example when the bride and groom are "pronounced husband and wife" – because from that moment on they *are* husband and wife. One does not ask whether this is *really* true, because the ritual and performative uses of language posit their own conditions by which they are judged. Instead of asking if a performative is "true" one may ask whether it is correctly applied or done, if it is performed according to the rules and so, hopefully, accomplishes what it had set out to do. Austin used the term "felicity conditions" to designate the circumstances under which a performative utterance can be said to be successful. This has consequences for how we may view the role of language in religion and myth as well. From the "believer's point of view," religious language is not judged by its veridical relations to the world, for it is the world that is judged by religious language. Religious language shapes the world and consequently the world must conform to it, to the myth – or it is the world that is wrong. In this different perspective, we notice the creative and world-constituting aspects of religious language, rituals and myths without endorsing the myths' own perspectives (there is a limit to how many cosmologies one can believe in). Myths are creative and performative narratives more than they are descriptive. They often *pretend* to describe a world, but what they really do is to set it up. Among others, the philosopher Paul Ricoeur (1913–2005) repeatedly pointed out how fiction is used to create meaning systems in which humans can socially and culturally operate (e.g. Ricoeur 1991). It is an important point in his hermeneutic theory that humans have no direct access to their own subjectivity; there is always some symbolic mediation as the basis of self-knowledge. That knowledge is, again, linked to given cultural understandings of the world, the sum total of which we may call a "lifeworld." Thus, Ricoeur also sees meaningful action as text, because most of the forms of actions that humans are engaged in are actions that can be "read" against the backdrop of the lifeworld.

To this I would add the idea that there are close connections between the narrative interpretability of action and the forms and functions of other socio-cultural institutions, because institutions also come as stories – they are stories in disguise. This is not as strange as it may sound. Cultural institutions, say marriage, are only what they are because they contain a certain message and practice; they carry a certain kind of institutional intentionality. Institutions are "about something" and myths have always been full of stories about such institutions. In more concrete terms, this means that we get an idea of who we are by saying and doing things that are meaningful to ourselves and others. Ultimately, if we had no symbolic media such as language, we would not know our own thoughts and our own existential situation. Myths and mythologies have always been active forces in these processes.

A more recent direction in the philosophy of language is "semantic holism." The theory has diverse sources, among them the philosophers Ludwig Wittgenstein and W. v. O. Quine. Semantic holism is a technical term for a theory that views meanings as inextricable from context, as it is the whole system of meanings that counts as a background. For instance, if one refutes a proposition, then it is in some measure a refutation of the complete theory or worldview from which the proposition is stated. Meanings of word, concepts and utterances are not given in a direct one-to-one relation with things in the world; words, concepts or sentences language does not "mirror" or "picture" the world in any direct way. Nothing in the world causes a statement to be true or meaningful. That is because the world does not speak; only humans do. For any proposition to be meaningful it must be part of a larger complex of meanings and references and so it must relate to a great many other beliefs, propositions and theories. That is why the theory is termed "holist" – it is the wholeness that counts. This position is fundamentally important in "post-analytic philosophy." One of its main proponents was Donald Davidson (1917–2003) who championed the "principle of charity," which says that however different and mutually disagreeing human conceptualizations might appear on the surface there must be massive agreements underneath the diversity and we must proceed from the assumption that the other speaker is a rational creature like us. Disagreement is only meaningful against the assumption of a shared world. Take an example: religious groups may differ on the issue of eating pork, but they don't disagree on what counts as pork meat. In accordance with this precept, his theory states that the notion of incommensurablity and untranslatability of languages or conceptual schemes is simply a misunderstanding. In this context concerning the analysis of myth, the holist semantic theory provides a rationale for the notion that we can, *in fact*, understand even the strangest of myths, for as long as they have been made by humans and stated in a human language they are accessible to us. It may involve hard work, but that is another matter.

World-making and Social Constructionism

Immanuel Kant (1724–1804) forcefully formulated the ideas of humans as perceiving the world indirectly through the forms and categories of the mind. Without these, we would not be able to form empirical knowledge or even synthesize our thoughts in general. This idea has become known as the "framework model."[5] In Kant's view, frameworks rely on some basic philosophical and epistemological preconditions for our perception of the world. They are the "transcendental forms" of space and time and the "transcendental categories" of, for example, matter, causation, existence, possibility, reality and negation. In later philosophical developments this idea of the framework was expanded in two directions. The first direction was more socially oriented, in the sense that frameworks and categories were seen as conditions for human culture as shared social activity. This orientation became known as "Neo-Kantian" and later represented, among others, by Ernst Cassirer (see contribution below). In Cassirer's philosophy, the notion of culture emerges as sets of opinions, norms, values, etc. that constitute a specific outlook on life and the world. In the second direction, which followed much later and more in psychology and anthropology than in philosophy, the framework became "naturalized," that is, not seen as transcendental conditions, but as innate human cognitive capacities with which we are all endowed. The first direction is relativist in inclination and the second is universalist and materialist. The degree to which each point of view is more salient is not the issue here; rather the point is that both ideas have something to offer for our views of myth. It is evident that varying cultures tap into certain reservoirs of ideas, models and stories and we may call this a framework. It is also evident that the human mind has certain characteristics, capacities and competences. With the help of both we "make our worlds" (e.g. Lyotard 1984). Nelson Goodman is a philosopher who has offered some relevant points in his theories of "world-making." According to Goodman (1978) it is perfectly possible to be a pluralist who "takes the sciences at full value" and yet also hold that there are many ways of describing and understanding the world, for example in poetry or watercolours. Goodman opens his book by reflecting upon the reception of the work of Ernst Cassirer:

> Countless worlds made from nothing but the use of symbols – so might a satirist summarize some major themes in the work of Ernst Cassirer. These themes – the multiplicity of worlds, the speciousness of 'the given', the creative power of the understanding, the variety and formative function of symbols – are also integral to my own thinking. Sometimes, though, I forget how eloquently they have been set forth by Cassirer, partly perhaps because his emphasis on myth, his concern with the comparative study of cultures, and his talk of the human spirit

have been mistakenly associated with current trends toward mystical obscurantism, anti-intellectual intuitionism, or anti-scientific humanism. Actually these attitudes are as alien to Cassirer as to my own sceptical, analytic, constructionalist orientation. (1978, 1)

From there, Goodman goes on to explore the philosophical problems involved in a theory of "world-making." That we need not pursue here, but just note that myth is a very potent world-making tool. Part of the meaning of myth is, I think, to be found in its utility in this respect. Our impressions and perceptions of the world "as it is" are always undetermined – there is no theory for the interpretation of the world that comes with the impressions and perceptions, and therefore the theory we supply and which governs our interpretation takes precedence. That is how myth becomes more "real" than reality and why myths will in all probability never disappear. They may change shapes and functions, from traditional to post-modern cultural settings. But that is another matter (and one I shall take up in the last chapter of this volume).

A brief note on the number of contributions in this section: Some may consider the philosophical approaches to be overrepresented. Historians of religions, ethnologists and anthropologists are the disciplines who have worked most closely with and on myths and mythologies and most often without too much involvement of philosophy and philosophers. I do hope, however, that the above introduction and the subsequent contributions will convince the sceptical reader that the philosophical aspects and foundations are important in the study of myth not only in understanding past historical developments and trends but even more so in the pursuit of future studies in a constructive and reflexive vein.

Contributions

Lucien Lévy-Bruhl

Lucien Lévy-Bruhl (1857–1939) was born in Paris, where he studied psychology and philosophy and lived most of his life, from 1896, as professor of Modern Philosophy at the Sorbonne. Until the outbreak of World War I, this period around the turn of the century was one of unusual intellectual and scientific activity, as most of the great and founding names brought out their seminal works around that time.[6] Lévy-Bruhl belongs there. His main interest, as it developed over the years, was "primitive mentality," particularly in relation to myth and religion "among the natives." There he found patterns of thought, which he called "pre-logical" as evidence of the "primitive mentality," that is mainly characterized by not obeying the established canons of Aristotelian logic. The "primitives" or "natives" associate matters by means of a "law of participation" where the categories and classifications may blend and fuse in manners that may seem confusing to the outside observer. To the immediate successors, especially among anthropologists, his ideas came to represent all the worst in evolutionist conjectural "armchair" scholarship and it seemed to imply normative scales of cultural evolution and an ethnocentric hierarchy in support of colonialism. This was not entirely fair and to a large extent the result of misapprehensions. Lévy-Bruhl's idea of "mentality" is not a phenomenon of individual psychology, but a term for the patterns of thought in a society; it is rather akin to "public opinion." Lévy-Bruhl's numerous works on the myths and classifications systems also show his Neo-Kantian inspiration. In the introduction to "How Natives Think" he discloses himself as a keen adherent to the sociology of Émile Durkheim and the "French school." This is very clear, for example, in the critique of Tylor and Frazer on the theory of animism when he states that: "Collective representations are social phenomena, like the institutions for which they account… Consequently, any attempt to 'explain' collective representations solely by the function of mental representations in the individual (the association of ideas, the naïve application of the theory of causality, and so on), is foredoomed to failure" (1987, 23). Lévy-Bruhl's work has been widely rehabilitated long after his death. It turned out, for example, that the "law of participation" was not restricted to primitive mentality, but that it is an inherent feature of religious thought and discourse.[7]

Susanne K. Langer

Susanne K. Langer (1895–1985) grew up in a cultured and intellectual German immigrant family in New York City. She studied at Radcliffe College until 1920, married in 1921, and travelled with her husband to Vienna where she studied for a few years, returned to Radcliffe and then finished her doctorate in philosophy at Harvard in 1926. Subsequently, she taught at a number of colleges, raised two sons, divorced in 1942, the year that the work which made her famous appeared. From 1945 she worked at Harvard and Connecticut College, from which she retired in 1962. Langer's philosophical interests were, from early on, inspired first by Alfred North Whitehead in logic and the philosophy of science and his theory of science as expressed in different symbolic modes, then by Karl Jaspers' work on the symbolic nature of language and inquiry. The philosophy of Ernst Cassirer was also to prove a major motivation for her work on linguistic and symbolic creativity and she translated Cassirer's *Language and Myth* from German into English. Langer published studies of myth and fantasy as well as more philosophical volumes before the publication of *Philosophy in a New Key: A Study in the Symbolism of Reason, Rite and Art*, the book that proved to be an all-time bestseller in philosophy with the sale of more than 500,000 copies. In the book she set out to demonstrate, as a philosopher of aesthetics, that art and music are as important as are philosophy, logic, and science and that they are meaningful human expressions and actions. Her philosophy in a "new key" was an explicit challenge to the highly empirical orientation at the time and the book has takes on discourse and meaning that seem very modern – almost strangely ahead of her time. For many years that book was used extensively in and across many disciplines, not least because of its ability to present difficult matters in an accessible manner. In

1953 Susanne Langer published *Feeling and Form*, where she further elaborated on the distinction between the articulations and expressions of non-discursive symbols in music and art and the discursive forms of scientific language. Her last major publication was the ambitious three-volume work *Mind: An Essay on Human Feeling* about the history of the mind. According to Langer, myth is an unintentional product of the imagination, which has its primary roots in dreams. However, myths are serious, collective, and shared narratives that take into account the conflicts and desires of human life and these are often expressed in archetypical figures and structures. Myths are lessons about life and bear witness to human intellectual and artistic creativity.

Ernst Cassirer

Ernst Cassirer (1874–1945) was a very versatile scholar. He studied law, language, literature, philosophy, and mathematics at the University of Marburg. He became professor of philosophy in Hamburg, left Germany in 1933, then taught at Oxford and Yale. Cassirer is associated with "Neo-Kantianism," an influential German philosophical movement that was critical of all metaphysics and saw the epistemology and the philosophy of science as primary tasks of philosophy. In contrast to the preceding currents of metaphysics and idealism with influence, for example from Hegel, the Neo-Kantians urged a return to Kant's critical investigation of the conditions for human knowledge, but in an even stricter fashion than Kant himself. For the critics, the very idea of "the thing in itself" was suspect, and they thus turned to investigations of the foundations of consciousness and knowledge. Cassirer turned Kant's ideas of the universality of the transcendental forms as conditions for human knowledge into a more relative framework depending upon time and place. Human consciousness determines what we see and know; this in turn depends on the symbolic forms or systems at our disposal and a philosophy of symbolic forms therefore becomes a necessary examination. However, it need not be restricted only to scientific modes of conception, for the modalities of human understanding of the world are many, unique and distinct. Language and myth are among these modalities or dimensions that make up the "unity of cultural consciousness" through which we make our worlds. Cassirer is thus a philosopher with a positive view of myth in an era when positivism and materialism were the most prominent philosophical "worldviews."

Karl Popper

Karl Popper (1902–94) studied philosophy in Vienna, when logical positivism was the ruling thought. He escaped from Austria in 1937, lived in New Zealand until 1945 and from 1946 to 1969 was professor at the London School of Economics. Popper's name is primarily associated with his work as a philosopher of science, famous for the idea that scientific hypotheses and theories are validated, not by verification, but by their ability to resist falsification. Popper also applied his critical realism and rationalism to political issues where he was vehemently against all kinds of totalitarian politics and dictatorship. It may seem strange to choose a contribution by Popper for a volume on myth. The reason for this is his elaboration on the notion of a "third realm" or "world 3." Popper is not the inventor of the idea, but he gave it precision and utility. The proposal is that in addition to the two conventionally accepted worlds of (1) the physical and (2) the mental, there is also a world "3" consisting of the objective products of human meaning making, "objective knowledge." Examples of such knowledge are, for example, the rules of chess, the symphonies of Beethoven, the periodic table or mathematics. Once such "objective knowledge" has been produced it may be used by all others who have the ability to use it. There is good reason to include myths in the category of matters pertaining to "world 3" – in traditional societies, especially pre-literate, myths and mythologies are collections, "archives" of objective knowledge, that is, conventional knowledge that is available to the society as its objectified and collective memory.

John R. Searle

John R. Searle (b. 1932) is professor at the University of California, Berkeley and one of the world's most influential philosophers. He has worked extensively in the philosophy of language, on problems of meaning and intentionality, and on consciousness. One of his main areas of reflection is the construction of human and social reality. In the philosophy of language he advanced J. L. Austin's theory of speech acts ("doing things with words") and took this further as the idea about how human lived-in reality is a result of social constructions through language as the primary medium. The human social realities (say, religion, law, economy, etc.) are not only regulated by rules, but they are also constituted by rules; he therefore distinguishes between "constitutive rules" and "regulatory rules." Constitutive rules are rules for "what counts as what" – e.g. paper counts as money, because *we* as humans have rules for just that. Searle's ideas are interesting in relation to the study of myth because they inform us of the creative potentials of human worldmaking through the construction of realities, "institutional facts," that are mediated in language and symbols. The theories also tell us that such "realities" are not any less real than the many other conventions we simply take for granted in social life. As he says on the difference of classes of "facts": "Symbols do not create cats and dogs and evening stars; they create only the possibility of referring to cats, dogs and evening stars in publicly accessible ways. But symbolization creates the very ontological categories of money, property, points scored in games and political offices as well as the categories of words and speech acts." By extension we see how myth can be a mode of symbolization involved in the processes that create ontological categories.

Notes

1. From my own teaching, I am very well aware of the problems that most contemporary students have with religious and mythical narratives and discourse. The students are more modern than they think.
2. Being Danish I know how references to Vikings – "a glorious past" – are uncritically taken to represent something about who "we really are." These ideas circulate in the educational system, in the media, public discourse and thus acquire the status of self-evident truth.
3. For a thorough analysis of this side of Nietzsche's work, see Lincoln 1999, ch. 5 "Nietzsche's 'Blond Beast,'" 101–20.
4. Religious language holds certain peculiarities, e.g. in ritual contexts, see Keane 1997 for a more anthropological discussion and Stiver 1996 for a more theological and philosophical presentation. Quinn and Taliaferro (1996) contain conspicuously little on mythology. Hale and Wright (1997) have very little on religious language. Frankenberry and Penner (eds.) 1999 is to be recommended.
5. See Godlove 1997. His solution to the framework problem is as simple as it is elegant and convincing: Instead of viewing frameworks as having epistemic priority and constituting radically different worlds (incommensurable and untranslatable) he considers them to have interpretive priority only. The example concerning pork meat explains this.
6. Just to mention some: Boas, Curie, Durkheim, Einstein, Frazer, Freud, Heisenberg, Husserl, Pareto, Picasso, Russell, Saussure, Simmel, Weber, Whitehead – and many more might be included.
7. See the introduction to the section in this volume on "cognitive approaches."

References

Cassirer, Ernst. 1955. *The Philosophy of Symbolic Forms. Vol II: Mythical Thought.* New Haven: Yale University Press.

Frankenberry, Nancy. 2002. "Religion as a 'Mobile Army of Metaphors.'" In idem, ed., *Radical Interpretation in Religion*, 171–87. Cambridge: Cambridge University Press.

Frankenberry, Nancy and Hans. H. Penner, eds. 1999. *Language, Truth, and Religious Belief.* Atlanta: Scholars Press.

Godlove, Terry F., Jr. 1997. *Religion, Interpretation and Diversity of Belief: The Framework Model from Kant to Durheim to Davidson.* Macon, GA: Mercer University Press.

Goodman, Nelson. 1978. *Ways of Worldmaking.* Hassocks, Sussex: The Harvester Press.

Habermas, Jürgen. 1987. *The Theory of Communicative Action.* Vol. 1: *Lifeworld and System: A Critique of Functionalist Reason.* Boston: Beacon Press & Cambridge: Polity Press in association with Basil Blackwell, Oxford.

Hale, Bob and Crispin Wright, eds. 1997. *A Companion to the Philosophy of Language.* Oxford: Blackwell.

Keane, Webb. 1997. "Religious Language." *Annual Review of Anthropology*, 26: 47–71.

Langer, Susanne K. 1951. "Life-symbols: The Roots of Myth." In idem, *Philosophy in a New Key: A Study in the Symbolism of Reason, Rite and Art* [orig. 1942], 148–74. New York: A Mentor Book.

Lévy-Bruhl, Lucien. 1987. *How Natives Think* (with a new introduction by C. Scott Littleton). Princeton: Princeton University Press.

Lincoln, Bruce. 1999. *Theorizing Myth: Narrative, Ideology, and Scholarship*. Chicago: University of Chicago Press.

Lyotard, Jean-Francois. 1984 [orig. 1979]. *The Postmodern Condition*. Manchester: Manchester University Press.

Popper, Karl R. 1982. *The Open Universe: An Argument for Indeterminism*. London: Routledge.

Quinn, Philip L. and Charles Taliaferro, eds. 1996. *A Companion to the Philosophy of Religion*. Oxford: Blackwell.

Ricoeur, Paul. 1991. "The Function of Fiction in Shaping Reality." In *A Ricoeur Reader: Reflection and Imagination*, ed. Mario. J. Valdés, 117–36. Hemel Hempstead: Harvester Wheatsheaf. [Orig., in *Man and His World* 12, no.2, 1979, 123–41.]

Searle, John R. 1995. "Language and Social Reality." In idem, *The Construction of Social Reality*, 59–78. New York: The Free Press.

Stiver, Dan. 1996. *The Philosophy of Religious Language: Sign, Symbol, and Story*. Oxford: Blackwell.

Whorf, Benjamin Lee. 1956. *Language, Thought, and Reality*. Cambridge, MA: MIT Press.

Wittgenstein, Ludwig. 1979. *Remarks on Frazer's Golden Bough* (ed. and rev. Rush Rhees). Retford: Brymill.

The Transition to the Higher Mental Types

Lucien Lévy-Bruhl

III

When we consider myths in their relation to the mentality of the social groups in which they originate, we are led to similar conclusions. Where the participation of the individual in the social group is still directly felt, where the participation of the group with surrounding groups is actually lived – that is, as long as the period of mystic symbiosis lasts – myths are meagre in number and of poor quality. This is the case with the Australian aborigines and the Indians of Northern and Central Brazil, etc. Where the aggregates are of a more advanced type, as, for instance, the Zuñis, Iroquois, Melanesians, and others, there is, on the contrary, an increasingly luxuriant outgrowth of mythology. Can myths then likewise be the products of primitive mentality which appear when this mentality is endeavouring to realize a participation no longer directly felt – when it has recourse to intermediaries, and vehicles designed to secure a communion which has ceased to be a living reality? Such a hypothesis may seem to be a bold one, but we view myths with other eyes than those of the human beings whose mentality they reflect. We see in them that which they do not perceive, and that which they imagine there we no longer realize. For example, when we read a Maori or Zuñi or any other myth, we read it translated into our own language, and this very translation is a betrayal. To say nothing of the construction of the sentences, which is bound to be affected by our customary habits of thought, if only in the very order of the words, to primitives, the words themselves have an atmosphere – which is wholly mystic, whilst in our minds they chiefly evoke associations having their origin in experience. We speak, as we think, by means of concepts. Words, especially those expressive of group-ideas, portrayed in myths, are to the primitive mystic realities, each of which determines a *champ de force*. From the emotional point of view, the mere listening to the myth is to them something quite different from what it is to us. What they hear in it awakens a whole gamut of harmonics which do not exist for us.

Moreover, in a myth of which we take note, that which mainly interests us, that which we seek to understand and interpret, is the actual tenor of the recital, the linking-up of facts, the occurrence of episodes, the thread of the story, the adventures of the hero or mythical animal, and so forth. Hence the theories, momentarily regarded as classic, which see in myths a symbolic presentment of certain natural phenomena, or else the result of a "disease of language"; hence the classifications (like that of Andrew Lang, for instance) which arrange myths in categories according to their content.[1] But this is overlooking the fact that the prelogical, mystic mentality is oriented differently from our own. It is undoubtedly not indifferent to the doings and adventures and vicissitudes related in myths; it is even certain that these interest and intrigue the primitive's mind. But it is not the positive content of the myth that primarily appeals to him. He does not consider it as a thing apart; he undoubtedly sees it no more than we see the bony framework beneath the flesh of a living animal, although we know very well that it is there. That which appeals to him, arouses his attention and evokes his emotion is the mystic element which surrounds the positive content of the story. This element alone gives myth and legend their value and social importance and, I might almost add, their power.

It is not easy to make such a trait felt nowadays, precisely because these mystic elements have disappeared as far as we are concerned, and what we call a myth is but the inanimate corpse which remains after the vital spark has fled. Yet if the perception of beings and objects in nature is wholly mystic to the mind of the primitive, would not the presentation of these same beings and objects in myths be so likewise? Is not the orientation in both cases necessarily the same? To make use of a comparison, though but an imperfect one, let us hark back to the time when in Europe, some centuries ago, the only history taught was sacred history. Whence came the supreme value and importance of that history, both to those who taught and those who learnt? Did it lie in the actual facts, in the knowledge of the sequence of judges, kings or prophets, of the misfortunes of the Israelites during their strife with the neighbouring tribes? Most certainly not. It is not from the historical, but from the sacred, point of view that the Biblical narrative was of incomparable interest. It is because the true God, perpetually intervening in the story, makes His presence manifest at all times and, to the Christian idea, causes the coming of His Son to be anticipated. In short, it is the mystic atmosphere which surrounds the facts and prevents them from being ordinary battles, massacres or revolutions. Finally it is because Christendom finds in it a witness, itself divine, of its communion with its God.

Myths are, in due proportion, the Biblical narrative of primitive peoples. The preponderance of mystic elements, however, in the group ideas of myths, is even greater than in our sacred history. At the same time, since the law of participation still predominates in the primitive mind, the myth is accompanied by a very intense feeling of communion with the mystic reality it interprets. When the adventures, exploits, noble deeds, death and resurrection of a beneficent and civilizing hero are recounted in a myth, for instance, it is not the fact of his having given his tribe the idea of making a fire or of cultivating mealies that of itself interests and especially appeals to the listeners. It is here as in the Biblical narrative, the participation of the social group in its own past, it is the feeling that the group is, as it were, actually living in that epoch, that there is a kind of mystic communion with that which has made it what it is. In short, to the mind of the primitive, myths are both an expression of the solidarity of the social group with itself in its own epoch and in the past and with the groups of beings surrounding it, and a means of maintaining and reviving this feeling of solidarity.

Such considerations, it may be urged, might apply to myths in which the human or semi-human ancestors of the social group, its civilizing or its protecting heroes, figure; but are they valid in the case of myths relating to sun, moon, stars, thunder, the sea, the rivers, winds, cardinal points, etc.? It is only to an intellect such as ours that the objection appears a serious one. The primitive's mind works along the lines that are peculiar to it. The mystic elements in his ideas matter considerably more to him than the objective features which, in our view, determine and classify beings of all kinds, and as a consequence the classifications which we regard as most clearly evident escape his attention. Others, which to us are inconceivable, however, claim it. Thus the relationship and communion of the social group with a certain animal or vegetable species, with natural phenomena like the wind or the rain, with a constellation, appear quite as simple to him as his communion with an ancestor or a legendary hero. To give but one instance, the aborigines studied by Spencer and Gillen regard the sun as a Panunga woman, belonging to a definite sub-class, and consequently bound by the ties of relationship to all the other clans of the tribe. Let us refer again to the analogy indicated above. In the sacred history of primitives natural history forms a part.

If this view of the chief significance of myths and of their characteristic function in aggregates of a certain mental type be correct, several consequences of some importance will ensue. This view does not render the careful and detailed study of myths superfluous. It provides neither a theory for classifying them in genera and species, nor an exact method of interpreting them, nor does it throw positive light upon their relations with religious observances. But it does enable us to avoid certain definite errors, and at any rate it permits of our stating the problem in terms which do not falsify the solution beforehand. It provides a general method of procedure, and this is to mistrust "explanatory" hypotheses which would account for the genesis of myths by a psychological and intellectual activity similar to our own, even while assuming it to be childish and unreflecting.

The myths which have long been considered the easiest to explain, for instance, those regarded as absolutely lucid, such as the Indian nature-myths, are on the contrary the most intriguing. As long as one could see in them the spontaneous product of a naïve imagination impressed by the great natural phenomena, the interpretation of them was in fact self-evident. But if we have once granted that the mentality which generates myths is differently oriented from ours, and that its collective representations obey their own laws, the chief of which is the law of participation, the very intelligibility of these myths propounds a fresh problem. We are led to believe that, far from being primitive, these myths, in the form in which they have reached us, are something absolutely artificial, that they have been very highly and consciously elaborated, and this to such an extent that their original form is almost entirely lost. On the other hand, the myths which may possibly seem the easiest to explain are those which most directly express the sense of the social group's relationship, whether it be with its legendary members and those no longer living, or with the groups of beings which surround it. For such myths appear to be the most primitive in the sense that they are most readily allied with the peculiar prelogical, mystic mentality of the least civilized aggregates. Such, among others, are the totemic myths.

If, however, the aggregates belong to a type even slightly more advanced, the interpretation of their myths very soon becomes risky and perhaps impossible. In the first place, their increasing complexity diminishes our chances of correctly following up the successive operations of the mentality which produces these myths. This mentality not only refuses to be bound by the law of contradiction – a feature which most myths reveal at first sight, so to speak – but it neither abstracts nor associates, and accordingly it does not symbolize as our thought does. Our most ingenious conjectures, therefore, always risk going astray.

If Cushing had not obtained the interpretation of their myths from the Zuñis themselves, would any modern intellect have ever succeeded in finding a clue to this prehistoric labyrinth? The true exposition of myths which are somewhat complicated involves a reconstruction of the mentality which has produced them. This is a result which our habits of thought would scarcely allow us to hope for, unless, like Cushing, a savant were exceptionally capable of creating a "primitive" mentality for himself, and of faithfully transcribing the confidences of his adopted compatriots.

Moreover, even in the most favourable conditions, the state in which the myths are when we collect them may suffice to render them unintelligible and make any coherent interpretation impossible. Very frequently we have no means of knowing how far back they date. If they are not a recent product, who is our authority for assuming that some fragments at any rate have not disappeared, or, on the other hand, may not myths which were originally quite distinct, have been mingled in one incongruous whole? The mystic elements which were the predominant feature at the time when the myth originated may have lost some of their importance if the mentality of the social group has evolved at the same time as their institutions and their relations with neighbouring groups. May not the myth which has gradually come to be a mystery to this altered mentality have been mutilated, added to, transformed, to bring it into line with the new collective representations which dominate the group? May not this adaptation have been performed in a contrary sense, without regard to the participations which the myth originally expressed? Let us assume – an assumption by no means unreasonable – that it has undergone several successive transformations of this kind: by what analysis can we hope ever to retrace the evolution which has been accomplished, to find once more the elements which have disappeared, to correct the misconceptions grafted upon one another? The same problem occurs with respect to rites and customs which are often perpetuated throughout the ages, even while they are being distorted, completed in a contrary sense, or acquiring a new significance to replace that which is no longer understood.

IV

When the participations which matter most to the social group are secured by means of intermediaries or "vehicles," instead of being felt and realized in more direct fashion, the change reacts upon the mentality of the group itself. If, for instance, a certain family or a certain person, a chief, a medicineman in any tribe is represented as "presiding" over the sequence of the seasons, the regularity of the rainfall, the conservation of species which are advantageous – in short, the periodic recurrence of the phenomena upon which the existence of the tribe depends – the group-idea will be peculiarly mystic, and it will preserve the characteristic features proper to prelogical mentality to a very high degree. Participation, concentrated, as it were, upon the beings who are its media, its chosen vessels, thus itself becomes ideological. By force of contrast, other families, other individuals of the social group, the neighbouring groups not interested in this participation, are represented in a more indifferent and impartial way, a fashion less mystic and therefore more objective. This means that a more and more definite and permanent distinction tends to be established between sacred beings and objects on the one hand, and profane beings and objects on the other. The former, inasmuch as they are the necessary vehicles of participation, are essentially and eternally sacred. The latter only become so intermittently by virtue of their communion with the former, and in the intervening periods they present no more than faint, derivative mystic features.

This leads to two connected consequences. In the first place, since the beings and the objects among which the social group lives are no longer felt to be in direct communion with it, the original classifications by which this communion was expressed tend to become obliterated, and there is a redistribution of less mystic nature, founded upon something other than the ramifications of the social group. Ideas of animal and plant life, the stars, etc., are doubtless still impregnated with mystic elements, but not all of them to the same extent. Some of them are markedly so, others to a far lesser degree, and this difference brings about fresh classifications. The beings and the objects represented as "containers" of mystic virtue, the vehicles of participation, are inevitably differentiated from those which do not possess this supreme interest for the social group. The latter are beginning to be ranged according to an interest of another order; their distinguishing features are less mystic, but more objective. In other words, the collective representations of these beings and objects is beginning to tend towards that which we call "concept." It is still remote from this, but the process which is to bring it nearer has already begun.

Moreover, the perception of these entities at the same time loses some of its mystic character. The attributes we term objective, by which we define and classify entities of all kinds, are to the primitive enveloped in a complex of other elements much more important, elements exacting almost exclusive attention, at any rate to the extent allowed by the necessities of life. But if this complex becomes simpler and the mystic elements lose their predominance, the objective attributes *ipso facto* readily attract and retain the attention. The part played by perception proper is increased to the extent in which that of the mystic collective representations diminishes. Such a modification is favourable to the change of classification of which we have spoken, and in its turn this change reacts upon the method of perceiving, as an inducted stream reacts upon the main current.

Thus, as by degrees the participations are less directly felt, the collective representations more nearly approach that which we properly call "idea" – that is, the intellectual, cognitive factor occupies more and more space in it. It tends to free itself from the affective and motor elements in which it was at first enveloped, and thus arrives at differentiating itself. Primitive mentality, as a consequence, is again modified in another respect. In aggregates in which it is least impaired, in which its predominance is at its maximum, we have found it impervious to experience. The potency of the collective representations and their interconnections is such that the most direct evidence of the senses cannot counteract it, whilst the interdependence of the most extraordinary kind between phenomena is a matter of unwavering faith. But when perception becomes less mystic, and the preconnections no longer impose the same sovereign authority, surrounding nature is seen with less prejudiced eyes and the collective representations which are evolving begin to feel the effect of experience. Not all at the same time, nor to the same extent: on the contrary, it is certain that these are unequally modified, in accordance with a good many diverse circumstances, and especially with the degree of interest felt by the social group in the object. It is on the points in which participation has become weakest that the mystic preconnections most quickly yield, and the objective relations first rise to the surface.

At the time when the mentality of primitive peoples grows more accessible to experience, it becomes, too, more alive to the law of contradiction. Formerly this was almost entirely a matter of indifference, and the primitive's mind, oriented according to the law of participation, perceived no difficulty at all in statements which to us are absolutely contradictory. A person is himself and at the same time another being; he is in one place and he is also somewhere else; he is individual as well as collective (as when the individual identifies himself with his group), and so on. The prelogical mind found such statements quite satisfactory, because it did more than perceive and understand them to be true. By virtue of that which I have called a mystic symbiosis, it felt, and lived, the truth of them. When, however, the intensity of this feeling in the collective representations diminishes, the logical difficulty in its turn begins to make its presence felt. Then by degrees the intermediaries, the vehicles of participation, appear. They render it *representable* by the most varied methods – transmission, contact, transference of mystic qualities – they secure that communion of substance and of life which was formerly sensed in a direct way, but which runs the risk of appearing unintelligible as soon as it is no longer lived.

Properly speaking, the absurdities to which the primitive mind remains insensible are of two kinds, undoubtedly closely connected with each other, but yet appearing very different to our way of thinking. Some, like those we have just instanced, arise out of what seems to us an infringement of the logical law of contradiction. These manifest themselves gradually, as the participations formerly felt are "precipitated" in the form of definite statements. Whilst the feeling of participation remains a lively one, language conceals these absurdities, but it betrays them when the feeling loses some of its intensity. Others have their source in the preconnections which the collective representations establish between persons, things, occurrences. But these preconnections are only absurd through their incompatibility with the definitely fixed terms for these persons, things, occurrences – terms which the prelogical mind has not at its command in the beginning. It is only when such a mind has grown more cognizant of the lessons taught by experience, when the attributes we term "objective" get the better of the mystic elements in the collective representations, that an interdependent relation between occurrences or entities can be rejected as impossible or absurd.

In the earlier stage the dictum deduced from Hume's argument, that "anything may produce anything," might have served as a motto for primitive mentality. There is no metamorphosis, no generating cause, no remote influence too strange or inconceivable for such a mentality to accept. A human being may be born of a boulder, stones may speak, fire possesses no power to burn, and the dead may be alive. *We* should refuse to believe that a woman may be delivered of a snake or a crocodile, for the idea would be irreconcilable with the laws of nature which govern the birth even of monstrosities. But the primitive mind, which believes in a close connection between a human social group and a snake or crocodile social group would find no more difficulty in this than in conceiving of the identity of the larva with the insect, or the chrysalis with the butterfly. Moreover, it is just as incompatible with "the laws of nature" that a corpse, whose tissues have become chemically incapable of sustaining life, should arise again; nevertheless, there are millions of cultivated persons who believe implicitly in the resurrection of Lazarus. It is enough that their representation of the Son of God involves His having the power to effect miracles. To the primitive mind, however, everything is a miracle, or rather, nothing is; and therefore everything is credible, and there is nothing either impossible or absurd.

As a matter of fact, however – and in this sense the dictum is only partially applicable to the prelogical mind – the preconnections involved in its collective representations are not as arbitrary as they appear. While indifferent to that which we call the real and objective relations between entities and manifestations, they express others much more important to such a mind, to wit, the mystic participating relations. It is these relations, and no others, which are realized in the preconnections, for these are the only ones about which the primitive mind troubles. Suggest to a primitive that there are other relations, imaginary or actual, between persons, things and occurrences: he will set them aside and reject them as untrue or insignificant or absurd. He will pay no attention to them, because he has his own experience to guide him, a mystic experience against which, as long as it continues to exist, actual experience is powerless. It is not only therefore because, in itself and in the abstract, any relation whatever between entities and occurrences is just as acceptable as any other; it is above all because the law of participation admits of mystic preconnections that the mind of the primitive seems undeterred by any physical impossibility.

But, granted that in a certain community the mentality evolves at the same rate as the institutions, that these preconnections grow weaker and cease to obtrude themselves – other relations between persons and things will be perceived, representations will tend to take on the form of general, abstract concepts, and at the same time a feeling, an idea of that which is physically possible or impossible will become more definite. It is the same then with a physical as with a logical absurdity, for the same causes render the prelogical mind insensible to both. Therefore the same changes and the same process of evolution cause it to be alive to the impossibility of affirming two contradictory statements at the same time, and the impossibility of believing in relations which are incompatible with experience.

Such a concomitance cannot be merely adventitious. In both cases the impossibility is felt only in a condition common to both: it is necessary, and it is enough, that the collective representations tend towards conceptual form. On the one hand, in fact, participations expressed in such a form can only be preserved, as we have already seen, by transforming themselves in order to avoid contradiction. And, on the other hand, it is when sufficiently definite concepts of beings and objects have been formed that the absurdity of certain mystic preconnections is first felt to obtrude. When the essential features of stone are, as it were, registered and fixed in the concept "stone," which itself forms one among other concepts of natural objects differing from stone by properties no less definite and constant than its own, it becomes inconceivable that stones should speak or boulders move of their own accord or procreate human beings, etc. The more the concepts are determined, fixed and arranged in classes, the more contradictory do the statements which take no account of such relations appear. Thus the logical demand made by the intellect grows with the definition and determination of concepts, and it is an essential condition of such definition and determination that the mystic preconnections of the collective representations become impaired. It grows then simultaneously with the knowledge acquired by experience. The progress of the one helps the other and vice versa, and we cannot say which is cause and which effect.

V

The process which is going on does not necessarily present itself as progressive, however. In the course of their evolution concepts do not submit to a kind of "finalité interne" which directs them for the best. The weakening of the mystic preconnections and elements is not inevitable nor always continuous. The mentality of primitive peoples, even whilst becoming less impervious to the teaching of experience, long remains prelogical, and most of its ideas preserve a mystic imprint. Moreover, there is nothing to prevent abstract and general concepts, once formed, retaining elements which are still recognizable as vestiges of an earlier stage. Preconnections, which experience has been unable to dissolve, still remain; mystic properties are yet inherent in beings and objects. Even in aggregates of the most advanced type, a concept which is free of all admixture of this kind is exceptional, and it is therefore scarcely to be met with in any others. The concept is a sort of logical "precipitate" of the collective representations which have preceded it, and this precipitate nearly always brings with it more or less of a residuum of mystic elements.

How can it be otherwise? Even in social aggregates of a fairly low type abstract concepts are being formed, and while not in all respects comparable with our own, they are nevertheless concepts. Must they not follow the general direction of the mentality which gives rise to them? They too, then, are prelogical and mystic, and it is only by very slow degrees that they cease to be so. It may even happen that after having been an aid to progress, they constitute an obstacle. For if the determination of the concept provides the rational activity of the mind with a lever which it did not find in collective representations subject to the law of participation; if the mind inures itself to reject as impossible statements which are incompatible with the definition of the concepts, it very often pays dearly for the privilege when it grows used to regarding, as adequate to reality, conceptual ideas and relations which are very far removed from it. If progress is not to find itself arrested, concepts of entities of all kinds must remain plastic and be continually modified, enlarged, confined within fixed limits, transformed, disintegrated and reunited by the teaching of experience. If these concepts crystallize and become fixed, forming themselves into a system which claims to be self-sufficing, the mental activity applied to them will exert itself indefinitely without any contact with the reality they claim to represent. They will become the subject of fantastical and frivolous argument, and the starting-point of exaggerated infatuation.

Chinese scientific knowledge affords a striking example of this arrested development. It has produced immense encyclopaedias of astronomy, physics, chemistry, physiology, pathology, therapeutics and the like, and to our minds all this is nothing but balderdash. How can so much effort and skill have been expended in the long course of ages, and their product be absolutely nil? This is due to a variety of causes, no doubt, but above all to the fact that the foundation of each of these so-called sciences rests upon crystallized concepts, concepts which have never really been submitted to the test of experience, and which contain scarcely anything beyond vague and unverifiable notions with mystic preconnections. The abstract, general form in which these concepts are clothed allows of a double process of analysis and synthesis which is apparently logical, and this process, always futile yet ever self-satisfied, is carried on to infinity. Those who are best acquainted with the Chinese mentality – like De Groot, for instance – almost despair of seeing it free itself from its shackles and cease revolving on its own axis. Its habit of thought has become too rigid, and the need it has begotten is too imperious. It would be as difficult to put Europe out of conceit with her savants as to make China give up her physicians and doctors and *Fung-shui* professors.

India has known forms of intellectual activity more akin to our own. She has had her grammarians, mathematicians, logicians and metaphysicians. Why, however, has she produced nothing resembling our natural sciences? Undoubtedly, among other reasons, because there, too, concepts as a rule have retained a very considerable proportion of the mystic elements of the collective representations whence they are derived, and at the same time they have become crystallized. Thus they have remained unable to take advantage of any later evolution which would gradually have freed them from such elements, as in similar circumstances Greek thought fortunately did. From that time, even in becoming conceptual, their ideas were no less destined to remain chiefly mystic, and only with difficulty pervious to the teaching of experience. If they furnished matter for scientific knowledge, the sciences could only be either of a symbolical and imaginative kind, or else argumentative and purely abstract. In peoples of a less advanced type, even although already fairly civilized, such as in Egypt or Mexico, for instance, even the collective representations which have been "precipitated" as concepts have distinctly retained their prelogical, mystic features.

Finally let us consider the most favourable case, that of peoples among whom logical thought still continues its progress, whose concepts remain plastic and capable of continual modification under the influence of experience. Even in such circumstances logical thought will not entirely supersede prelogical mentality. There are various reasons for the persistence of the latter. Firstly, in a large number of concepts there are indelible traces which still remain. It is far from being *all* the concepts in current use, for instance, which express the objective features and relations of entities – and of phenomena solely. Such a characteristic is true of a very small number only, and these are made use of in scientific theorizing. Again, these concepts are, as a rule, highly abstract, and only express certain properties of phenomena and certain of their relations. Others, that is our most familiar concepts, nearly always retain some vestiges of the corresponding collective representations in prelogical mentality. Suppose, for example, that we are analysing the concepts of soul, life, death, society, order, fatherhood, beauty or anything else you like. If the analysis be complete it will undoubtedly comprise some relations dependent upon the law of participation which have not yet entirely disappeared.

Secondly, even supposing that the mystic, prelogical elements *are* finally eliminated from most concepts, the total disappearance of mystic, prelogical mentality does not necessarily follow. As a matter of fact the logical thinking which tends to realize itself through the purely conceptual and the intellectual treatment of pure concepts is not coextensive with the mentality which expressed itself in the earlier representations. The latter, as we know, does not consist of one function merely, or of a system of functions which are exclusively intellectual. It undoubtedly does comprise these functions but as still undifferentiated elements of a more complex whole in which cognition is blended with motor and above all emotional elements. If, then, in the course of evolution the cognitive function tends to differentiate itself and be separated from the other elements implied in collective representations, it thereby achieves some kind of independence, but it does not provide the equivalent of the functions it excludes. A certain portion of these elements, therefore, will subsist indefinitely outside and side by side with it.

The characteristic features of logical thought are so clearly differentiated from those of prelogical mentality that the progress of the one seems, *ipso facto*, to involve the retrogression of the other. We are tempted to conclude that in the long run, when logical thought imposes its laws on all mental operations, prelogical mentality will have entirely disappeared. This conclusion is both hasty and unwarranted, however. Undoubtedly the stronger and more habitual the claims of reason, the less tolerant it is of the contradictions and absurdities which can be proved as such. In this sense it is quite true to say that the greater the advance made by logical thought, the more seriously does it wage war upon ideas which, formed under the dominance of the law of participation, contain implied contradictions or express preconceptions which are incompatible with experience. Sooner or later such ideas are threatened with extinction, that is, they must be dissolved. But this intolerance is not reciprocal. If logical thought does not permit contradiction, and endeavours to suppress it as soon as it perceives it, prelogical, mystic mentality is on the contrary indifferent to the claims of reason. It does not seek that which is contradictory, nor yet does it avoid it. Even the proximity of a system of concepts strictly in accordance with the laws of logic exerts little or no influence upon it. Consequently logical thought can never be heir to the whole inheritance of prelogical mentality. Collective representations which express a participation intensely felt and lived, of which it would always be impossible to demonstrate either the logical contradiction or the physical impossibility, will ever be maintained. In a great many cases, even, they will be maintained, sometimes for a long time, *in spite of* such a demonstration. The vivid inner sentiment of participation may be equal to, and even exceed, the power of the intellectual claim. Such, in all aggregates known to us, are the collective representations upon which many institutions are founded, especially many of those which involve our beliefs and our moral and religious customs.

The unlimited persistence of these collective representations and of the type of mind of which they are the witness, among peoples in whom logical thought is most advanced, enables us to comprehend why the satisfaction which is derived from the most finished sciences (exclusive of those which are purely abstract) is always incomplete. Compared with ignorance – at least, conscious ignorance – knowledge undoubtedly means a possession of its object; but compared with the participation which prelogical mentality realizes, this possession is never anything but imperfect, incomplete, and, as it were, external. To know, in general, is to objectify; and to objectify is to project beyond oneself, as something which is foreign to oneself, that which is to be known. How intimate, on the contrary, is the communion between entities participating of each other, which the collective representations of prelogical mentality assures! It is of the very essence of participation that all idea of duality is effaced, and that in spite of the law of contradiction the subject is at the same time himself and the being in whom he participates. To appreciate the extent to which this intimate possession differs from the objectifying apprehension in which cognition, properly so called, consists, we do not even need to compare the collective representations of primitive peoples with the content of our positive sciences. It will be sufficient to consider one object of thought – God, for instance, sought after by the logical thought of advanced peoples, and at the same time assumed in the collective representations of another order. Any rational attempt to know God seems both to unite the thinking subject with God and at the same time to remove Him to a distance. The necessity of conforming with the claims of logic is opposed to a participation between man and God which is not to be represented without contradiction. Thus knowledge is reduced to a very small matter. But what need is there of this rational knowledge to the believer who feels himself at one with his God? Does not the consciousness which he possesses of his participation in the Divine essence procure him an assurance of faith, at the price of which logical certainty would always be something colourless and cold and almost a matter of indifference?

This experience of intimate and entire possession of the object, a more complete possession than any which originates in intellectual activity, may be the source and undoubtedly is the mainspring of the doctrines termed anti-intellectual. Such doctrines reappear periodically, and on each reappearance they find fresh favour. This is because they promise that which neither a purely positive science nor any theory of philosophy can hope to attain: a direct and intimate contact with the essence of being, by intuition, interpenetration, the mutual communion of subject and object, full participation and immanence in short, that which Plotinus has described as ecstasy. They teach that knowledge subjected to logical formulas is powerless to overcome duality, that it is not a veritable possession, but remain merely superficial. Now the need of participation assuredly remains something more imperious and more intense, even among peoples like ourselves, than the thirst for knowledge and the desire for conformity with the claims of reason. It lies deeper within us and its source is more remote. During the long prehistoric ages, when the claims of reason were scarcely realized or even perceived, it was no doubt all-powerful in all human aggregates. Even today the mental activity which, by virtue of an intimate participation, possesses its object, gives it life and lives through it, aspires to nothing more, and finds entire satisfaction in this possession. But actual knowledge in conformity with the claims of reason is always unachieved. It always appeals to a knowledge that protracts it yet further, and yet it seems as if the soul aspires to something deeper than mere knowledge, which shall encompass and perfect it.

Between the theories of the "intellectualists" and their opponents the dialectic strife may be indefinitely prolonged, with alternating victories and defeats. The study of the mystic, prelogical mentality of undeveloped peoples may enable us to see an end to it, by proving that the problems which divide the two parties are problems which are badly couched. For lack of proceeding by a comparative method, philosophers, psychologists and logicians have all granted one common postulate. They have taken as the starting-point of their investigations the human mind always and everywhere homogeneous, that is, a single type of thinker, and one whose mental operations obey psychological and intellectual laws which are everywhere identical. The differences between institutions and beliefs must be explained, therefore, by the more childish and ignorant use which is made of principles common to all aggregates. Accordingly a reflective self-analysis carried out by a single individual ought to suffice to discover the laws of mental activity, since all subjects are assumed to be constituted alike, as far as the mind is concerned.

Now such a postulate does not tally with the facts revealed by a comparative study of the mentality of the various human aggregates. This teaches us that the mentality of primitive peoples is essentially mystic and prelogical in character; that it takes a different direction from our own – that is, that its collective representations are regulated by the law of participation and are consequently indifferent to the law of contradiction, and united, the one to the other, by connections and preconnections which prove disconcerting to our reason.

It throws light, too, upon our own mental activity. It leads us to recognize that the rational unity of the thinking being, which is taken for granted by most philosophers, is a *desideratum*, not a fact. Even among peoples like ourselves, ideas and relations between ideas governed by the law of participation are far from having disappeared. They exist, more or less independently, more or less impaired, but yet ineradicable, side by side with those subject to the laws of reasoning. Understanding, properly so called, tends towards logical unity and proclaims its necessity; but as a matter of fact our mental activity is both rational and irrational. The prelogical and the mystic are co-existent with the logical.

On the one hand, the claims of reason desire to impose themselves on all that is imagined and thought. On the other hand, the collective representations of the social group, even when clearly prelogical and mystic by nature, tend to subsist indefinitely, like the religious and political institutions of which they are the expression, and, in another sense, the bases. Hence arise mental conflicts, as acute, and sometimes as tragic, as the conflict between rival duties. They, too, proceed from a struggle between collective habits, some time-worn and others more recent, differently oriented, which dispute the ascendancy of the mind, as differing moral claims rend the conscience. Undoubtedly it is thus that we should account for the so-called struggle of reason with itself, and for that which is real in its antinomies. And if it be true that our mentality is both logical and prelogical, the history of religious dogmas and systems of philosophy may henceforth be explained in a new light.

Note

1. "Mythology," in *Encylopedia Britannica* (9th ed.), vol. XVII, 156–7.

Life-Symbols: The Roots of Myth

Susanne K. Langer

While religion grows from the blind worship of Life and magic "aversion" of Death to a definite totem-cult or other sacramentalism, another sort of "life-symbol" develops in its own way, starting also in quite unintentional processes, and culminating in permanent significant forms. This medium is myth. Although we generally associate mythology with religion, it really cannot be traced, like ritual, to an origin in anything like a "religious feeling," either of dread, mystic veneration, or even festal excitement. Ritual begins in motor attitudes, which, however personal, are at once externalized and so made public. Myth begins in fantasy, which may remain tacit for a long time; for the primary form of fantasy is the entirely subjective and private phenomenon of *dream*.

The lowest form of story is not much more than a dream-narrative. It has no regard whatever for coherence or even consistency of action, for possibility or common sense; in fact, the existence of such yarns as, for instance, the Papuans tell, in a society which is after all intelligent enough to gauge the physical properties of clubs and arrows, fire and water, and the ways of animals and men, shows that primitive story has some other than literal significance. It is made essentially of dream-material; the images in it are taken from life, they are things and creatures, but their behavior follows some entirely unempirical law; by realistic standards it is simply inappropriate to them.

Roland Dixon, in his *Oceanic Mythology* (1916) cites a story from Melanesia, in which two disputants, a buffalo and a crocodile, agree to ask "the next to come down the river" to arbitrate their quarrel; their request for a judgment is refused successively by a leaf-plate, a rice-mortar, and a mat, before the Mouse-Deer finally acts as judge

(Dixon 1916, 198). There is another tale which begins: "One day an egg, a snake, a centipede, an ant, and a piece of dung set out on a head-hunting expedition. . . " (202). In yet another narrative, "while two women were sleeping in a house, a *tapa*-beater transformed itself into a woman resembling one of the pair, and waking the other, said to her, 'Come, it is time for us to go fishing.' So the woman arose, and they took torches and went out to sea in a canoe. After a while she saw an island of driftwood, and as the dawn came on, perceived that her companion had turned into a *tapa*-beater, whereupon she said: 'Oh, the *tapa*-beater has deceived me. While we were talking in the evening it stood in the corner and heard us, and in the night it came and deceived me.' Landing her on the island, the *tapa*-beater paddled away and abandoned her . . ." After a miraculous rescue and return, ". . .the woman told her parents how the *tapa*-beater had deceived and kidnapped her; and her father was angry, and building a great fire, he threw the *tapa*-beater into it and burned it up" (141–2).

In these stories we have certainly a very low stage of human imagination; one cannot call them "myths," let alone "religious myths." For the leaf-plate which refused to arbitrate a quarrel (it was peeved, by the way, because it had been thrown out when it was still perfectly good), the equally unobliging mortar and mat, the piece of dung that went headhunting, and the deceitful *tapa*-beater, are not "persons" in a strange disguise; despite their humanoid activities they are just domestic articles. In fact, the *tapa*-beater is in disguise when it resembles a woman, and when the rising sun breaks the spell it must return to its *real* form. But even as a *tapa*-beater it has no trouble in paddling the canoe home, and returning alone to the house.

No sane human being, however simple, could really "suppose" such events to occur; and clearly, in enjoying this sort of story nobody is trying to "suppose" anything. To imagine the assorted hunting-party really on its way through the jungle is perhaps just as impossible for a Papuan as for us. The only explanation of such stories is, then, that nobody cares whether their *dramatis personae* act in character or not. The act is not really proper to its agent, but to *someone its agent represents*; and even the action in the story may merely *represent* the deeds of such a symbolized personality. In other words, the psychological basis of this remarkable form of nonsense lies in the fact that the story is a fabrication out of subjective symbols, not out of observed folkways and nature-ways. The psychoanalysts, who have found such unconscious metaphor to be the rationale of our otherwise inexplicable dreams, can give us ample illustration of this sort of fantasy. It is entirely bound to feelings and wishes of its author, cast in its bizarre or monstrous mold by his unavowed fears and reticences, formulated and told and retold as a means of *self-expression*. As we meet it in these Melanesian stories, it is really only a cut above genuine dream. But even so, the story is an improvement on mere dream, because the very telling of it requires a little more coherence than our nightmares usually have. There must be a thread of logic; a *tapa*-beater who is *also* a woman must, in one capacity or the other, be "in disguise"; the head-hunting dung, egg, and animals must set out together, and – though the head-hunt is forgotten before the end of the story – they must either do *something* together or get separated. Characters have to be generally accounted for, which is more than we do in dreaming.

So long as a story is told to a very uncritical audience by the person who made it up, it may be ever so silly without giving offense. Anyone who has heard young children telling yarns to each other can corroborate this. But as soon as the story goes abroad, it meets with more rigorous demands for significance. If it survives in a larger sphere, it undergoes various modifications, in the interests of coherence and public appeal. Its purely personal symbols are replaced by more universal ones; animals, ghosts, and witches take the place of *tapa*-beaters and suchlike in the villain's role. Just as sacra change their form, and become gradually personified with the growth of ritual action, so the development and integration of story-action makes the symbols of fantasy take on more and more reasonable outward form to fit the role in which they are cast. A higher fictional mode emerges – the animal fable, the trickster story, or the orthodox ghost story.[1] Often the theme is quite ephemeral – merely the homecoming of a strayed person, the theft of a cocoanut, or somebody's meeting with a cannibalistic ghoul in the bush – but such simple plots grow, with the advancing arts of life and social organization, into the well-known *genre* of fairytale.

Here we have a literary product belonging to the civilized races of Europe just as much as to the savage cultures of darker continents. Aristocratic beings, chiefs or princes, now play the leading role; dragons and ogres and wicked kings, or beautiful witches of great power, replace the monkeys, crocodiles, angry dead men, or local cannibals of the older tradition. The wishful imagination of man has been disciplined, by public exposure and realistic reflection, into a genuine art-form, as far removed from personal dreaming as the ritual dance from self-expressive bouncing and shouting.

Yet this high development of fantasy has brought us nowhere in the direction of mythology. For although fairy story is probably an older form than myth, the latter is not simply a higher development of the former. It, too, goes back to primitive fantasy, but the point of its origin from that source lies far back in cultural history, long before the evolution of our modern fairytale – of *Kunstmärchen*, as the Germans say, or even *Volksmärchen*. It required not a higher stage of story-telling, but a *thematic shift*, to initiate what Miss Harrison called "the myth-making instinct."

The difference between the two fictional modes – many scholars to the contrary notwithstanding[2] – is a crucial one. For the fairytale is irresponsible; it is frankly imaginary, and its purpose is to gratify wishes, "as a dream doth flatter." Its heroes and heroines, though of delightfully high station, wealth, beauty, etc., are simply individuals; "a certain prince," "a lovely princess." The end of the story is always satisfying, though by no means always moral; the hero's heroism may be slyness or luck quite as readily as integrity or valor. The theme is generally the triumph of an unfortunate one – an enchanted maiden, a youngest son, a poor Cinderella, an alleged fool – over his or her superiors, whether these be kings, bad fairies, strong animals (e.g. Red Riding Hood's wolf), stepmothers, or elder brothers. In short, the fairytale is a form of "wishful thinking," and the Freudian analysis of it fully explains why it is perennially attractive, yet never believed by adults even in the telling.

Myth, on the other hand, whether literally believed or not, is taken with religious seriousness, either as historic fact or as a "mystic" truth. Its typical theme is tragic, not utopian; and its personages tend to fuse into stable *personalities* of supernatural character. Two divinities of somewhat similar type – perhaps miraculously born, prodigious in strength, heroically defeated and slain – become identified; they are one god under two names. Even those names may become mere epithets linking the god to different cults.

This sets the hero of myth strikingly apart from the fairytale hero. No matter how closely the Prince Charming of Snow White's story resembles the gentleman who wakens Sleeping Beauty, the two characters do not become identified. No one think that the trickster "Little Claus" is the little tailor who slew "seven at a stroke," or that the giant whom Jack killed was in any way related to the ogre defeated by Puss in Boots, or that he figured elsewhere as Bluebeard. Fairy stories bear no relation to each other. Myths, on the other hand, become more and more closely woven into one fabric, they form cycles, their *dramatis personae* tend to be intimately connected if not identified. Their stage is the actual world – the Vale of Tempe, Mount Olympus, the sea, or the sky – and not some ungeographical fairyland.

Such radical dissimilarities between two kinds of story lead one to suspect that they have fundamentally different functions. And myth has, indeed, a more difficult and more serious purpose than fairytale. The elements of both are much alike, but they are put to quite different uses. Fairytale is a personal gratification, the expression of desires and of their imaginary fulfillment a compensation for the shortcomings of real life, an escape from actual frustration and conflict. Because its function is subjective, the hero is strictly individual and human; for, although he may have magic powers, he is never regarded as divine; though he may be an oddity like Tom Thumb, he is not considered supernatural. For the same reason – namely that his mission is merely to represent the "self" in a day-dream – he is not a savior or helper of mankind. If he is good, his goodness is a personal asset, for which he is richly rewarded. But his humanitarian role is not the point of the story; it is at best the setting for his complete social triumph. The beneficiary of his clever acts, his prowess, or his virtue is he himself, not mankind forever after. And because an individual history is what the fairytale fancies, its interest is exhausted with the "happy ending" of each finished story. There is no more mutual reference between the adventures of Cinderella and those of Rapunzel than between two separate dreams.

Myth, on the other hand, at least at its best, is a recognition of natural conflicts, of human desire frustrated by nonhuman powers, hostile oppression, or contrary desires; it is a story of the birth, passion, and defeat by death which is man's common fate. Its ultimate end is not wishful distortion of the world, but serious envisagement of its fundamental truths; moral orientation, not escape. That is why it does not exhaust its whole function in the telling, and why separate myths cannot be left entirely unrelated to any others. Because it presents, however metaphorically, a world-picture, an insight into life generally, not a personal imaginary biography, myth tends to become systematized; figures with the same poetic meaning are blended into one, and characters of quite separate origin enter into definite relations with each other. Moreover, because the mythical hero is not the subject of an egocentric day-dream, but a subject greater than any individual, he is always felt to be superhuman, even if not quite divine. He is at least a descendant of the gods, something more than a man. His sphere of activity is the real world, because what he symbolizes belongs to the real world, no matter how fantastic its expression may be (this is exactly contrary to the fairytale technique, which transports a natural individual to a fairyland outside reality).

The material of myth is, indeed, just the familiar symbolism of dream-image and fantasy. No wonder psychologists have discovered that it is the same material as that of fairytale; that both have symbols for father and son, maiden and wife and mother, possession and passion, birth and death.[3] The difference is in the two respective *uses* of that material: the one, primarily for supplying vicarious experience, the other essentially for understanding actual experiences.[4] Both interests may be served in one and the same fiction; their complete separation belongs only to classic cases. Semi-mythical motives occur in sheer day-dream and even night-dream, and an element of compensation – fantasy may persist in the most universalized, perfected myths. That is inevitable, because the latter type has grown at some point out of the former, as all realistic thinking springs from self-centered fancy. There is no clean dividing line. Yet the two are as distinct as summer and winter, night and day, or any other extremes that have no exact zero-point between them.

We do not know just where, in the evolution of human thought, myth-making begins, but it begins somewhere with the recognition of *realistic significance* in a story. In every fantasy, no matter how utopian, there are elements that represent real human relations, real needs and fears, the quandaries and conflicts which the "happy ending" resolves. Even if the real situation is symbolized rather than stated (a shocking condition may well be disguised, or a mysterious one strangely conceived), a certain importance, an emotional interest, attaches to those elements. The ogre, the dragon, the witch, are intriguing figures in fairy lore. Unlike the hero, they are usually ancient beings that have troubled the land for many generations. They have their castles or caves or hermitages, their magic cook-pots and sorcerer's wands; they have evil deeds laid up against them, and extremely bad habits, usually of a cannibalistic turn. Their records are merely suggested in the story, which hastens to get on with the fortunes of the hero; but the suggestion is enough to activate a mind which is, after all, committed to some interests besides dream-spinning. Because they represent the realistic setting from which the dream starts its fanciful escape, they command a serious sort of contemplation.

It is significant that people who refuse to tell their children fairytales do not fear that the children will believe in princes and princesses, but that they will believe in witches and bogeys. Prince or princess, to whom the wish-fulfillment happens, we find in ourselves, and need not seek in the outer world; their reference is subjective, their history is our dream, and we know well enough that it is "make-believe." But the incidental figures are material for superstition, because their meanings are in the real world. They represent those same powers that are conceived, first perhaps through "dreadful" objects like corpses or skulls or hideous idols, as ghosts, keres, hoodoos, and similar spooks. The ogres of literature and the ghouls of popular conception embody the same mysterious Powers; therefore the fairytale, which even most children will not credit as a narrative, may carry with it a whole cargo of ideas, purely secondary to its own purpose, that are most convincing elements for superstition. The awful ancestor in the grave goes abroad as the goblin of story: that is the god of superstition. The world-picture of spook-religion is a reflection of fairytale, a dream whose nightmare elements become attached to visible cult objects and thus taken seriously.

There is nothing cosmological about the being such a symbol can embody. Deities in the classical sense cannot be born of tales whose significance is personal, because the setting of such tales is necessarily a *genre* picture, a local, temporal, human environment, no matter how distorted and disguised. The forces that play into an individual's dream are social forces, not world-powers. So long as the hero is the self, the metaphorical dragons he slays are his elders, his rivals, or his personal enemies; their projection into the real world as sacred beings can yield only ancestors, cave-monsters, manitos, and capricious demigods.

It is noteworthy that when these secondary characters of day-dream or story are incorporated into our picture of the external world as objects of superstition, they represent a generalized, heightened conception of the social forces in question: not a man's father, but his *fathers*, the paternal power in all generations, may be seen in the fabulous animal-ancestor he reveres; not his brother, but a "Great Brother," in the manito-bear that is his familiar of the forest. The process of symbolization, while it often obscures the origin of our ideas, enhances their conceptual form. The demon, therefore, presents to us not a specific person, but the human estate of such a person, by virtue of which we are oppressed, challenged, tempted, or triumphant. Though he is born of a purely self-centered imagination, he is super-personal; a product not only of particular experience, but of *social insight*. He is the envisagement of a vital factor in life; that is why he is projected into reality by the symbolism of religion.

The great step from fairytale to myth is taken when not only social forces – persons, customs, laws, traditions – but also cosmic forces surrounding mankind, are expressed in the story; when not only relationships of an individual to society, but of mankind to nature, are conceived through the spontaneous metaphor of poetic fantasy.

Perhaps this transition from subjectively oriented stories, separate and self-contained, to the organized and permanent envisagement of a world-drama could never be made if creative thought were not helped by the presence of permanent, obvious symbols, supplied by nature: the heavenly bodies, the changes of day and night, the seasons, and the tides. Just as the social framework of personal life, first conceived in dream-like, inchoate forms, is gradually given enduring recognition through religious symbols, so the cosmic setting of man's existence is imponderable, or at best a mere nightmare, until the sun and the moon, the procession of stars, the winds and waters of earth, exhibit a divine rule, and define the realm of human activity. When these gods arrive, whose names connote heavenly powers and natural processes, the deities of local caves and groves become mere vassals and lesser lights.

It has often been asked, not without justification, how men of sane observant minds – however unschooled or innocent – can be led to identify sun, moon, or stars with the anthropomorphic agents of sacred story. Yet the interpretation of gods and heroes as nature-symbols is very ancient; it has been variously accepted and rejected, disputed, exploded, and re-established, by Hellenic philosophers, medieval scholars, modern philologists, archeologists, and theologians, over a period of twenty-five hundred years. Mystifying as it is to psychology, it challenges us as a fact. Demeter was certainly an earth-goddess, and the identity of Olympian Zeus with the heavens, Apollo with the sun, Artemis with the moon, etc., is so authentic that it has long been considered a truism to declare these gods "personifications" of the corresponding natural phenomena. Yet such a process of personification seems like an unnatural flight of fancy. It is a fairly safe rule not to impute to the savage mind processes that never even threaten to arise in our own minds. The difference between savage and civilized mentality is, after all, one of naïve versus critical thinking; bizarre and monstrous imagery pops into our heads, too, but is rejected almost instantly by disciplined reason. But I do not think that either in dream or in childhood we are prone to think of the sun as a man. As for the stars, it takes a sophisticated literary tradition to make them people, or even Lady Moon's sheep.

How then did heroic adventures become attached to these most impersonal actors, as they almost universally did? The process, I believe, is a natural phase of the evolution of mythology from fairy story, and indeed, represents a potent factor in that development. The change is a gradual one, and has necessarily its intermediate steps; one of these is marked by the introduction of the first cosmic symbols. This transitional stage between the egocentric interest of folktale, focused on a human hero, and the emergence of full-fledged nature mythology dealing with divine characters of highly general import, is the so-called *legend*, which produces the "culture-hero."

This widely represented fictional character is a hybrid of subjective and objective thinking; he is derived from the hero of folktale, representing an individual psyche, and consequently retains many of that personage's traits. But the symbolic character of the other beings in the fairytale has infected him, too, with a certain supernaturalism; he is more than an individual wrestling with powers of society. Just what else he is must be gathered from his personality as it reveals itself in the legendary mode.

He is half god, half giant-killer. Like the latter, he is often a Youngest Son, the only clever one among his stupid brothers. He is born of high parentage, but kidnapped, or exposed and rescued, or magically enslaved, in his infancy. Unlike the dream-subject of fairytale, however, his deeds only begin with his escape from thraldom; they go on to benefit mankind. He gives men fire, territory, game, teaches them agriculture, ship-building, perhaps even language; he "makes" the land, finds the sun (in a cave, in an egg, or in a foreign country), and sets it in the sky, and controls wind and rain. But despite his greatness he slips back frequently into his role of folktale hero, and plays the trickster, outwitting human enemies, local ghosts, or even a venerable ancestor just for mischief.

The status of the culture-hero is thus very complex. His activities lie in the real world, and their effects are felt by real men forever after; he therefore has a somewhat vague, yet unmistakable historical relation to living men, and a tie to the locality on which he has left his mark. This alone would suffice to distinguish him from the hero of fairyland, whose acts are bound up entirely with a story, so that he can be dispensed with at the end of it, and a new hero introduced for the next story. The historical and local attachments of the culture-hero give his being a certain permanence. Stories gather round him, as they gather round real heroes of history whose deeds have become legendary, such as Charlemagne, Arthur, or Kubla Khan. But whereas these princes are credited with enhanced and exaggerated human acts, the primitive culture-hero interferes with the doings of nature rather than of men; his opponents are not Saracens or barbarians, but sun and moon, earth and heaven.

A perfect example of such a demigod is the Indian Manabozho or Michabo, also known as Hiawatha.[5] He is at once a supernatural being, and a very human character. The fact that he is a manito who can take whole mountain ranges at a couple of strides, that he chastises his father the West Wind for the indignities inflicted on his moon-descended mother, does not put him above feeling the pinch of hunger in winter, or getting stung in robbing a bee-tree.

Brinton, one of the earliest systematic collectors of Indian folk-lore, looking for "natural theology" in the Red Man, was baffled and distressed by the character of Manabozho; for "He is full of pranks and wiles, but often at a loss for a meal of victuals; ever itching to try his magic arts on great beasts and often meeting ludicrous failure therein; envious of the powers of others, and constantly striving to outdo them in what they do best; in short, little more than a malicious buffoon delighting in practical jokes, and abusing his superhuman powers for selfish and ignoble ends." At the same time, "From a grain of sand brought from the bottom of the primaeval ocean he fashioned the habitable land and set it floating on the waters... One of his footsteps measured eight leagues, the Great Lakes were the beaver dams he built, and when the cataracts impeded his progress he tore them away with his hands" (Brinton 1896, 194–5). He invented picture writing and made the first fishing-nets. Obviously he is a deity; yet his name, in every dialect that varies or translates it, means "Great Hare" or "Spirit Hare." Brinton was convinced that the popular stories about him are "a low, modern, and corrupt version," and that his name rests on a philological mistake which the Indians made, confusing *wabo*, "hare," with *wapa*, "the dawn"; that his various names originally designated a sun-god, but led to his representation as a hare, by an accident of language.[6]

Manabozho is in all likelihood not a degraded Supreme God, but an enhanced, exalted fictional hero. He still bears the marks of his human origin, though he has established relations to the great forces which encompass human life, the heavens, the seasons, and the winds. His superhuman deeds have raised him to a comradeship with these powers; and his pseudo-historic relation to mankind leads to his identification with the totem-animal, the mystic ancestor of his people. Therefore he is at once the son of the West Wind, grandson of the Moon, etc., and the Great Hare;

and at the same time the clever trickster, the great chief, the canoe-builder, and the superman.

We meet the culture-hero again, in all his glory, as Maui, the Polynesian demigod.[7] He, too, combines the buffoon, trickster, or naughty boy with heroic and even divine qualities. Like Manabozho, he is of cosmological descent, though his normal shape is human. Maui is too widely claimed to bear the marks of any totem, but can change himself into fish, bird, or beast at will. He is, indeed, everything from a troll to a deity, because he belongs to all stages of culture – he is known as a prankster in Papuan fairytale, the fire-stealer and dragon-killer ("hero" in a classical sense) in more advanced legends, the demiurge who shapes earth and sky in Hawaiian cosmology, and in the mythology of New Zealand he actually becomes a benevolent patron of humanity, self-sacrificed in an attempt to bestow immortality on men.

Yet Maui, like Manabozho, is not worshiped. He has no cult, his name is not sacred, nor do men feel or fear his power as a factor in current events. He has died, or gone west, or otherwise ended his local career; one may see his footprints in the lava, his handiwork in the arrangements of heaven and earth, but he no longer presides over these. His old adversary the Sun still runs the course Maui bade him follow; his ancestress and murderess, the Moon, still vaunts her immortality in one resurrection after another. These are visible powers, deities to be entreated or honored. Why is their son, grandson, conqueror, or playmate, the culture-hero, not an eternal god, set as a star in the sky, or imagined as a king of the sea?

Because he is not as seriously "believed in" as gods and spirits are. Like the hero of fairytale, the culture-hero is a vehicle of human wishes. His adventures are fantasies. But, whereas the story-hero is an individual overcoming personal opponents – father, master, brothers, or rivals – *the culture-hero is Man, overcoming the superior forces that threaten him*. A tribe, not a single inventor, is unconsciously identified with him. The setting of his drama is cosmic; storm and night are his foes, deluge and death his ordeals. These are the realities that inspire his dream of deliverance. His task is the control of nature – of earth and sky, vegetation, rivers, season – and the conquest of death.

Just as the fairytale served to clarify a personal environment and human relations in its secondary characters, its kings, witches, ghosts, and fairies (which were often identified with real beings and so abstracted from the mere tale), so the culture-hero's story furnishes symbols of a less personal encircling reality. The hero's exploits are largely make-believe even to their inventors; but the forces that challenge him are apt to be taken seriously. They belong to the real world, and their symbols mean something beyond the pipe dream in which they were formulated. Maui is a superman, a wishful version of human power, skill, and importance; but his place among the forces of nature is Man's own place. Where did he come from? From nature, from heaven and earth and sea. In cosmic terms, he came "out of the Night." In human terms he came out of Woman. In his myth, therefore, he is descended from Hine-nui-te-po, Great Woman of Night.[8]

The Polynesian word "Hine" (variants "Hina," "Ina") has an interesting etymology. By itself, it seems to be always either a proper noun or an adjective connoting either light (e.g. white, pale, glimmering) or falling, declining; in composite words it usually refers to woman.[9] As a name, it denotes the woman or maiden of such-and-such character, somewhat like the Greek *Korê*. The mixture of common and proper meaning gives the word a *generalizing* function; therefore it applies with special aptness to supernatural beings which, as we have seen, are generalized personalities.[10] But when several personages bear the same name because they have essentially the same symbolic value, they naturally tend to merge. Since every "Great Woman," "Mountain Maid," "Mother," or "She" is Woman, we find a great confusion of Hinas.

In Polynesian mythologies the various Hina characters are developed mainly as secondary figures in the story of Maui. They appear as his mother, sister, grandmother, or very first ancestress. As few English readers are familiar with the legend, I will sketch briefly the most important tales of this powerful, mischievous, and brilliant hero.

The Quest of Fire

Maui was the youngest of four or five brothers, all named Maui with various epithets. The Mauis were all stupid except this youngest son, who was miraculous from his infancy. He had been prematurely born, and his mother Hina, not interested in such a weakling, threw him into the sea. But a jellyfish nursed him, and the elements returned him to his home, where consequently he was received as a foundling. He was full of power and mischief, always in trouble with his brothers and his elders.

Maui's mother slept in a hut with her children, like any Polynesian mother. But when the first dawn light appeared she would depart, and keep herself in some mysterious retreat all day. Young Maui, determined to find her out, blocked all the chinks and window-holes of the hut, so that no ray of light wakened her until it was full day; then, when she woke and hastily fled, he followed her, and discovered the path she took to the Underworld, where she was wont to spend the day with her dead ancestors. Maui, in the form of a bird, joined this company of chthonic gods, who gave him his first taste of cooked food. Here he found the ancestress in whose custody was the precious secret of fire.

There are many versions of his Promethean exploit. In one of these, the ancestress gives him one of her fingers, in which the principle of fire dwells; sometimes he wrests it from her, and sometimes he learns the secret of fire-making from the Alae, "the bird of Hina," a mud-hen sacred to that ancestral fire-woman. But in every case, an ancient Hina, living in a volcano, in a cave, or simply in the earth, possesses the treasure, and Maui obtains it by trickery, cajoling, or violence.

The Magic Fish-hook

This story, current in New Zealand, tells how Maui was sent to take food to one of his aged progenitors; "but when he came to his ancestress he found her very ill, one half of her body being already dead, whereupon he wrenched off her lower jaw, made from it a fish-hook, which he concealed about him, and then returned to his home" (Dixon 1916, 43ff.). With this hook he went fishing, and drew up a huge fish, which proved to be the dry land. Had his foolish brothers who were in the canoe with him not cut up the fish, there would have been a continent; as it was, the land fell apart into several islands.

The Hina of Hilo, and Maui's Deed of Snaring the Sun[11]

The Wailuku river, which flows through the town of Hilo, has its own peculiar and weird beauty. For miles it is a series of waterfalls and rapids.... By the side of this river Hina's son Maui had his lands. In the very bed of the river, in a cave under one of the largest falls, Hina made her home.... By the side of this river, the legends say, she pounded her tapa, and prepared her food.... The days were very short and there was no time for rest while making tapa-cloth.... Although Hina was a goddess and had a family possessing miraculous power, it never entered the mind of the Hawaiian legend tellers to endow her with ease in producing wonderful results....

The Hina of Hilo was grieved as she toiled because after she had pounded the sheets out so thin that they were ready to be dried, she found it almost impossible to secure the necessary aid of the sun in the drying process.... The sun always hurried so fast that the sheets could not dry.... Hina found her incantations had no influence with the sun. She could not prevail upon him to go slower and give her more time for the completion of her task. Then she called on her powerful son, Maui-ki-i-ki-i, for aid.

... He took ropes made from the fibre of trees and vines (in another version, his sister Ina-Ika's hair)[12] and lassoed the sun while it climbed the side of the mountain and entered the great crater which hollows out the summit. The sun came through a large gap in the eastern side of the crater, rushing along as rapidly as possible. Then Maui threw his lassoes one after the other over the sun's legs (the rays of light), holding him fast and breaking off some of them. With a magic club Maui struck the face of the sun again and again. At last, wounded and weary, and also limping on its broken legs, the sun promised Maui to go slower forevermore.

The Death of Maui

This story belongs to New Zealand, and has a tragic, ethical ring that really suggests a more epic phase of mythology than the Oceanic. For here the mischievous, wily hero appears in a serious mood, contemplating the unhappy fate of mankind, whereby every man must sooner or later go through the gate of death, and never return. Maui, in the pride of his magic power, tries to undo this fate, to find life beyond death and bring it to men on earth.

Maui, after his many successful exploits, came home to his parents in high spirits. His father, though duly admiring the hero's feats, warned him that there was one who might yet overcome him.

When Maui asked incredulously by whom he could be overcome, "His father answered him, 'By your great ancestress, by Hine-nui-te-po, who, if you look, you may see flashing, and as it were, opening and shutting there, where the horizon meets the sky.... What you see yonder shining so brightly are her eyes, and her teeth are as sharp and hard as volcanic glass; her body is like that of man, and as for the pupils of her eyes, they are jasper; and her hair is like the tangles of long seaweed, and her mouth is like that of a barracouta.' "[13]

Maui, despite all warnings, set forth to find the dreadful ancestress Hina, and to creep through her gaping mouth into her belly, where Eternal Life was hidden in her womb. He took his friends the little birds with him – presumably for moral support, since they certainly offered no other aid – on his way down the shining path to the horizon; and he adjured them to make no noise that might wake the monster before he was safely out of her mouth again. Then he crept into her, past her obsidian teeth that were the gates of death. He found the treasure of Eternal Life, and started to make his escape. But just as he was between the sharp gates once more, one of the silly small birds could no longer contain itself at the sight of his undignified exit, and burst into loud, chirping laughter. Hine-nui-te-po awoke, and Maui was bitten in two. So his great ancestress conquered him, as she conquers all men – for through her jaws they must all go in the end.

*

Maui is the same person in various poses throughout these stories; but it is certainly bewildering to find so many strange females bearing the name of Hina, and claiming to be Maui's mother, grandmother, first begotten ancestress, first divine ancestress, sister, or other relative. Between his mother who lived in a hut, and threw him away for a useless weakling – a very true Polynesian lady, we may assume – and the terrible giantess Hine-nui-te-po, there seems to be little likeness. Why do all these mythical women merge their weird personalities in one name?

The mystery lightens when we consider that *Hina also means the moon.*[14] In the various Hinas of Polynesian myth we have just so many stages of "personification" of the moon, from the luminous, hollow woman on the horizon at the end of the shining path, to the mother who spends the nights with her children but goes down beneath the earth by day. The ancestress who is alive on one side and dead on the other, who appears to be the same Hina that owned the fire-secret, is clearly a lunar deity (Dixon 1916, 43; Westervelt 1910, 220ff.); the Hina of Hilo, emerging from a cave to spread her *tapa*-cloth, seems to be a transitional figure.

If the gods of mythology really arose by a process of "personification," then Maui's mother who threw him away and later re-adopted him must be regarded as the end-result of a process beginning with a mere animistic conception of the moon. But in view of the fairytale character of all primitive story, the complete lack of cosmic interest in the truly savage mind, and the clear nature-symbolism in the higher mythologies, I believe the process of development to be exactly the contrary: Hina is not a symbol of the moon, but *the moon is a symbol of Hina, Woman.*

The moon, by reason of its spectacular changes, is a very expressive, adaptable, and striking symbol – far more so than the sun, with its simple career and unvarying form. A little contemplation shows quite clearly why the moon is so apt a feminine symbol, and why its meanings are so diverse that it may present many women at once – Hina in many, often incompatible forms, mother and maid and crone, young and old. The human mind has an uncanny power of recognizing symbolic forms; and most readily, of course, will it seize upon those which are presented again and again without aberration. The eternal regularities of nature, the heavenly motions, the alternation of night and day on earth, the tides of the ocean, are the most insistent repetitious forms outside our own behavior-patterns (the symbolic value of which was discussed in the previous chapter). They are the most obvious metaphors to convey the dawning concepts of life-functions – birth, growth, decadence, and death.

Woman is, to primitive reflection, one of the basic mysteries of nature. In her, life originates; only the more enlightened societies know that sexual union initiates it. To naive observation, her body simply waxes and wanes with it for a certain length of years. She is the Great Mother, the symbol as well as the instrument of life.

But the actual process of human conception and gestation is too slow to exhibit a pattern for easy apprehension. One needs a symbol, to think coherently about it. Long before discursive thought could frame propositions to this purpose, men's minds probably recognized that natural symbol of womanhood, the waxing and waning moon.

It is a characteristic of presentational symbolism that many concepts may be telescoped into one total expression, without being severally presented by its constituent parts. The psychoanalysts, who discovered this trait in dream-symbolism, call it "condensation." The moon is a typical "condensed" symbol. It expresses the whole mystery of womankind, not only in its phases, but in its inferiority to the sun, its apparent nearness to the clouds that veil it like garments; perhaps the element of mystery that moonlight invariably creates, and the complicated time-cycle of its complete withdrawal (women, in tribal society, have elaborate schedules of taboo and ritual, of which a man cannot keep track), are not to be underestimated as symbolical factors.

But just as life grows to completeness with every waxing phase, so in the waning period one can see the old moon take possession, gradually, of the brilliant parts; life is swallowed by death in a graphic process, and the swallowing monster was ancestor to the life that dies. The significance of the moon is irresistible. Ages of repetition hold the picture of life and death before our eyes. No wonder if men learn to contemplate it, to form their notions of an individual life on the model of that cycle, and conceive death as a work of ghostly forbears, the same who gave life – Hina the ancestress is image of them all; nor that notions of resurrection or reincarnation should arise from such contemplation.

All this may explain why the name Hina should be bestowed on the moon, and why that luminary should be deified. But since savage ideation does not require human form to embody a power, why should this Hina be personified?

It is a generally accepted doctrine, almost a truism, that a savage thinks everything that acts on him must be a person like himself, and attributes human forms, needs, and motives to inanimate objects because he cannot explain their activities in any other way. Again and again we read how primitive men, the makers of mythology, believed the sun, moon, and stars to be people like themselves, with houses and families, because the untutored mind could not distinguish between heavenly bodies and human bodies, or between their respective habits. Almost any book on primitive myth that one picks up repeats this credo, expounded long ago in the classic work of Tylor: "To the lower tribes of man, sun and stars, trees and rivers, winds and clouds, become personal animate creatures, leading lives conformed to human or animal analogies, and performing their special functions with the aid of limbs like beasts or of artificial instruments like men" (1871, I, 285). Or, in the words of Andrew Lang: "The savage draws no hard and fast line between himself and the things in the world.... He assigns human speech and feelings to sun and moon and stars and wind, no less than to beasts, birds and fishes" (Lang 1887, I, 47).

Now, there is no doubt that Maui was said to have cut off the sun's legs, (Westervelt 1910, 46) and that the god Tane saw daylight under the armpit of his father Rangi, the sky (Shortland 1882, 20); these natural elements were certainly anthropomorphized in their full-fledged myths. What I do not believe, however, is that savages originally and spontaneously see the sun as a man, the moon as a woman, etc., else cosmological fantasy would be found much lower in the scale of human mentality than it is; nor do I think that nature-myths are originally attempts to explain astronomical or meteorological events. Nature-myths are originally stories of a superman hero, Maui, Hiawatha, Balder, or Prometheus, who is a superman because he is felt to be more than a man – he is Mankind in a single human figure. He battles with the forces of nature, the very same forces that made him and still sustain him. His relation to them is both filial and social; and *it is his incarnation that leads his elemental ancestors, brethren, and opponents to be personified.* In his story, he has a mother who is human enough; but, as he is Man, so she is Woman. Now the symbol of womanhood is the moon; and as a myth-making mentality does not keep symbol and meaning apart, the moon not only *represents*, but *presents*, Woman, the mother of Maui. Not personification of the moon, but a lunarization of Hina, gives rise to Polynesian cosmology.

Here we have the genesis of myth from legend. The savage does not, in his innocence, "think" the moon is a woman because he cannot tell the difference; he "thinks" it is a round fire, a shining disk; but he sees Woman in it, and names it Woman, and all its acts and relationships that interest him are those which carry out that significance. The connection of the culture-hero with the moon helps to humanize and define the functions of that deity, because the culture-hero is unequivocally human; so the lunar changes of light and form and place, nameless and difficult as mere empirical facts, acquire importance and obviousness from their analogy to human relations and functions: conceiving, bearing, loving, and hating, devouring and being devoured. The moon lends itself particularly to such interpretations, because it can present so many phases of womanhood. A host of different Hinas are lunar deities. Yet the unity of the underlying symbol reacts on the theological conception, to make the various distinct Hinas *all of one blood*, the "mother" with her "daughters." This calls for mythological elaboration, and gives rise to genuine nature-myths.

The apparently irrational genealogies of gods and demigods spring from the fact that family relationships in myth may represent many different physical or logical relationships in nature and in human society. Night "gives birth" to Hanging Night, Drifting Night, Moaning Night; Morn, by a different logic, to Abiding Day, Bright Day, and Space (Shortland 1882, 12). And Man, in yet a different sense, is descended from the family of all these Powers (Dixon 1916, 26–7). The moon's "daughters" owe their filial status to a very different source than Maui his sonship, yet they are, by reason of both relations, unquestionably his sisters. Thus it is that one may find a personage who is clearly a moon-goddess taking part in one of Maui's fishing adventures (Westervelt 1910, 156).

I have dwelled so long on the personification of the moon because it is, in the first place, the most convincing example of myth-making, and in the second place it may well have been the original inspiration to that age-long and world-wide process. There is a school of mythologists who maintain that not only the first, but *all*, mythology is moon-mythology.[15] I doubt whether this sweeping assumption is justified, since analogous treatment would most naturally be accorded the sun, stars, earth, sea, etc., as soon as human mentality advanced to the conception of an anthropomorphic lunar deity. Such an epoch-making stride of creative imagination could hardly have been limited to one subject or one symbol. Once we envisage Man's status in nature as that of a hero among cosmic gods, we cannot fail to see a host of gods all round us; one would naturally expect, at this point, a "vegetative period" of religious fantasy.

The term "*religious* fantasy" is deliberately used here, although many mythologists quite explicitly reject it. Lessmann, of the afore-mentioned school, points out as a peculiar fact that "Greek mythology creates an impression as though religion and mythology were two closely related phenomena" (1907, 7), and explains the origin of that deceptive appearance through a confusion of Greek mythological gods with the

Babylonian cultus-gods. The gods of ritual are related to ancestral spooks, devils, and local deities; but "at bottom," he says, "demonology is nothing but a low state of religion, and has no more than the latter to do with mythology" (7). I have tried to show how this "confusion" is the normal meeting point of ritual gods and story gods, how the harvest sheaf who becomes a harvest maid takes over the story of some maiden of mythology, whereby the story becomes theology, and enters into genuine religious thought.

In a book called *La genèse des mythes*, A. H. Krappe declares categorically that myths are made up out of whole cloth by poets, are purely aesthetic productions, and are not believed unless they happen to be incorporated in some sacred book (1938, 23ff.). But this is to confuse the myth-making stage of thought with the literal stage. Belief and doubt belong essentially to the latter; the myth-making consciousness knows only the appeal of ideas and uses or forgets them. Only the development of literal-mindedness throws doubt upon them and raises the question of religious *belief.* Those great conceptions which can only dawn on us in a vast poetic symbolism are not propositions, to which one says yea or nay; but neither are they literary toys of a mind that "knows better." The Homeric Greeks probably did not "believe in" Apollo as an American fundamentalist "believes in" Jonah and the whale, yet Apollo was not a literary fancy, a pure figment, to Homer, as he was to Milton. He was one of the prime realities – the Sun, the God, the Spirit from which men received inspirations. Whether anyone "believed" in all his deeds and amours does not matter; they were expressions of his character and seemed perfectly rational. Surely the Greeks believed in their gods just as we believe in ours; but they had no dogma concerning those gods, because in the average mind no matter-of-fact doubts of divine story had yet arisen, to cloud the significance of those remote or invisible beings. Common sense had never asserted itself *against* such stories, to make them look like fairytales or suggest that they were figures of speech. They were *figures of thought*, and the only figures that really bold and creative thought knew.

Yet there is something to be said for the contention that mythology is made by the epic poets. The great dreams of mankind, like the dreams of every individual man, are protean, vague, inconsistent, and so embarrassed with the riches of symbolic conception that every fantasy is apt to have a hundred versions. We see this in the numberless variants in which legends are handed down by peoples who have no literature. One identical hero has quite incompatible adventures, or one and the same adventure is ascribed to several heroes, gods, or ogres. Sometimes one cannot tell a maiden from a bird, or from her own mother, whose "attributive animal" may be that same bird; and this bird-mother-daughter may be the Earth-Goddess and the Moon and the First Woman. Mythological figures in their pristine stages have no fixity, either of form or meaning; they are very much like dream images, elusive, over-determined, their stories condensations of numberless ideas, their names often the only evidence of any self-identity.[16] As soon as their imaginative growth is accomplished, traditions become meaningless and corrupt. Disconnected fragments of great primitive world-concepts survive in superstitions or in magic formulae, which the skilled mythologist may recognize as echoes of a more ancient system of thought, but which the average intelligent mortal can only view as bizarre and surprising forms of foolishness.

The great mythologies which have survived both the overgrowth of mystic fable and the corruption of popular tradition are those that have become fixed in national poems, such as the Iliad, the Eddas, the Ramayana, the Kalevala. For an epic may be fantastic, but it cannot be entirely inconsistent; it is a narrative, its incidents have temporal order, its world is geographical and its characters personal. Just as the introduction of nature-symbols gave fantasy a certain dominant pattern by seeing its monsters and personages exemplified in the behavior of sun and moon and stars, so the great vehicle of mythological tradition, the epic, places its peculiar restrictions on the rampant imagination and disciplines it further into consistency and coherence. For it demands not only personification, not only some sort of rise and fall in heroic action, but *poetic form*, a unity above the separate incidents, a beginning, climax, and solution of the entire mythical drama. Such formulation requires a radical handling of the story-material which tradition is apt to supply in prodigal quantities and utter confusion; therefore the principle of poetic form is a powerful agent in the refashioning of human ideas. This has given rise to the belief, stated in somewhat doctrinaire and exaggerated terms by Krappe, that mythology is *essentially* the work of epic poets. "Without the epic, no mythology. Homer is the author of the Hellenic mythology, the Norwegian and Icelandic Skalds have created the mythology of Scandinavia. The same phenomenon may be seen in India, in Ireland, and in Japan" (1938, 57).

Indeed, the mythologies of Hellas and of the Eddas seem very remote from the crazy dreamlike yarns of savages. For the great epics may move against a background of divine powers and cosmic events, but their heroes are human, not mystical, and the most wonderful deeds are logically motivated and accomplished. Ulysses or Siegfried or Beowulf sets out on a definite quest, and the story ends with its success or frustration; the whole structure presents the career of a superhuman personage, a representative of the race in its strength and pride, definitely oriented in a world of grand forces and conflicts, challenges, and destinies. When we look from these perfected cosmic and social conceptions in the great epics to the fantasies of Iroquois and South Sea Islanders, we may well be tempted to say that savages have no mythology worthy of the name, and that the poets are the creators of that vast symbolic form.

Yet this is not true. The "making" of mythology by creative bards is only a metamorphosis of world-old and universal ideas. In the finished works of Homer and Hesiod we may see only what looks like free invention for the sake of the story, but in the poetry of ruder tribes the popular, religious origin of myth is still clearly apparent despite the formative influence of a poetic structure.

The Finnish *Kalevala* is a classic example of the transition from mystical nature-theology and immemorial legend, to a national treasure of philosophical beliefs and historical traditions embodied in permanent poetic form. It is probably the most primitive – though by no means the oldest – of all epics; and it is quite obviously a transcript of savage mythology, more concerned with cosmic origins, conflicts of nature-deities, incantations, feats and contests of magic, than with the exploits of brave men and the good or evil ways of women. It knows no Trojan wars, no planned campaigns of vengeance; neither lifelong quests, nor founding of cities and temples. In its first "rune," or canto, the Water-Mother swims in the sea for seven hundred years; at last she lets the blue teal nest on her lifted knee, until from the fragments of its broken eggs the land, the shallows, the deeps and the sky are fashioned; after this creation she carries the hero in her womb for thirty years, whereupon he is born an old man full of magic. The Queen of Night supplies him with Rainbow Maidens and Air Princesses for unwilling ladyloves whom he never actually manages to marry. Wainamoinen, this strangely old and unsuccessful hero, plants forests and fells them, supervises the creation of grain, invents the steam bath, builds boats by sheer magic, and makes the first harp. He is no fairytale prince beloved of women, but is purely a culture-hero. When he conquers an adversary he does so by magic songs, and his rash young enemies and rivals challenge him not to armed combat, but to singing-contests.

The whole story really reads more like Polynesian mythology than like European epic poetry. Animals are men's messengers or servants, heroes are custodians of sun, moon, fire and water, maidens go to live with fishes, their mothers are Night Queens and their brothers Frost Giants. *Kalevala* is essentially a string of magic fishings and plantings and strange encounters, like a told dream, patched together with such human episodes as sledge-building, broom-binding, and the Finns' inevitable baths, to hold heroes and spirits somehow to the local scene. How far a call to Helen and Menelaus and Paris, the Achaean armies encamped, the death of Hector, the sorrow of Andromache!

Yet there are culture-heroes in Greek legend, too, who steal fire from the gods, and youths who would contend with the sun; and in the *Kalevala* there are sudden passages of human import set in its strange mystical frame. When ancient Wainamoinen seeks the Rainbow Maid, the daughter of the Night Woman, that very real and lovely little girl throws herself into a lake rather than give herself to the weird magician who was old when he was born. The maiden Aino is too childlike, too human for him. She sits on a rock above the water, bewailing her youth and freedom and the cruel decree of her parents. Her plight is realistic and touching, and her suicide quite naturally taboos the lake for the family, the tribe, and the unhappy lover.

There is nothing in Polynesian or Indian mythology that comes as near to real life as the lament and desperate act of the Rainbow Maiden Aino. Every nature mythology treats the rainbow as an elusive maiden, but it requires the thoughtful formulation of poetry to see the rainbow's ephemeral beauty in a girl too wayward and beautiful for her aged lover, to put the human story first and incorporate the heavenly phenomenon merely in her symbolic name. Here is the beginning of that higher mythology wherein the world is essentially the stage for human life, the setting of the true epic, which is human and social. This development in fantasy depends on the clarifying and unifying medium of conscious composition, the discipline of the compact metrical verse, which inevitably sets up standards of coherence and continuity such as the fragmentary dream-mode does not know or require.

The effect of this poetic influence is incomplete in the *Kalevala*, but it is there, and lets us see the process by which mythology is "made" in the epic. The embodiment of mythology in poetry is simply its perfected and final form; because it has no subsequent higher phases, we regard this formulation as the "true" mythical imagination. And because the symbolic forms stand forth so clearly as pure articulations of fantasy, we see them only as fictions, not as the supreme concepts of life which they really represent, and by which men orient themselves religiously in the cosmos.

It is a peculiar fact that every major advance in thinking, every epoch-making new insight, springs from a new type of symbolic transformation. A higher level of thought is primarily a new activity; its course is opened up by a new departure in semantic. The step from mere sign-using to symbol-using marked the crossing of the line between animal and man; this initiated the natural growth of language. The birth of symbolic gesture from emotional and practical movement probably begot the whole order of ritual, as well as the discursive mode of pantomime. The recognition of vague, vital meanings in physical forms – perhaps the first dawn of symbolism – gave us our idols, emblems, and totems; the primitive function of dream permits our first envisagement of events. The momentous discovery of nature-symbolism, of the pattern of life reflected in natural phenomena, produced the first universal insights. Every mode of thought is bestowed on us, like a gift, with some new principle of symbolic expression. It has a logical development, which is simply the exploitation of all the uses to which that symbolism lends itself; and when these uses are exhausted, the mental activity in question has found its limit. Either it serves its purpose and becomes truistic, like our orientation in "Euclidean space" or our appreciation of objects and their accidents (on the pattern of language-structure, significantly called "logic"); or it is superseded by some more powerful symbolic mode which opens new avenues of thought.

The origin of myth is dynamic, but its purpose is philosophical. It is the primitive phase of metaphysical thought, the first embodiment of *general* ideas. It can do no more than initiate and present them; for it is a non-discursive symbolism, it does not lend itself to analytic and genuinely abstractive techniques. The highest development of which myth is capable is the exhibition of human life and cosmic order that epic poetry reveals. We cannot abstract and manipulate its concepts any further *within the mythical mode*. When this mode is exhausted, natural religion is superseded by a discursive and more literal form of thought, namely philosophy.

Language, in its literal capacity, is a stiff and conventional medium, unadapted to the expression of genuinely new ideas, which usually have to break in upon the mind through some great and bewildering metaphor. But bare denotative language is a most excellent instrument of exact reason; it is, in fact, the only general precision instrument the human brain has ever evolved.[17] Ideas first adumbrated in fantastic form become real intellectual property only when discursive language rises to their expression. That is why myth is the indispensable forerunner of metaphysics; and metaphysics is the literal formulation of basic abstractions, on which our comprehension of sober facts is based. All detail of knowledge, all exact distinction, measure, and practical manipulation, are possible only on a basis of truly abstract concepts, and a framework of such concepts constitutes a philosophy of nature, literal, denotative, and systematic. Only language has the power to effect such an analysis of experience, such a rationalization of knowledge. But it is only where experience is already presented – through some other formative medium, some vehicle of apprehension and memory – that the canons of literal thought have any application. We must have ideas before we can make literal analyses of them; and really new ideas have their own modes of appearance in the unpredictable creative mind.

The first inquiry as to the literal truth of a myth marks the change from poetic to discursive thinking. As soon as the interest in factual values awakes, the mythical mode of world-envisagement is on the wane. But emotional attitudes that have long centered on a myth are not easily broken; the vital ideas embodied in it cannot be repudiated because someone discovers that the myth does not constitute a *fact*. Poetic significance and factual reference, which are two entirely different relations in the general symbol-and-meaning pattern, become identified under the one name of "truth." People who discover the obvious discrepancy between fantasy and fact deny that myths are true; those who recognize the truth of myths claim that they register facts. There is the silly conflict of religion and science, in which science must triumph, not because what it says about religion is just, but because religion rests on a young and provisional form of thought, to which philosophy of nature – proudly called "science," or "knowledge" – must succeed if thinking is to go on. There must be a rationalistic period from this point onward. Some day when the vision is totally rationalized, the ideas exploited and exhausted, there will be another vision, a new mythology.

The gods have their twilight, the heroes are forgotten; but though mythology has been a passing phase in man's mental history, the epic lives on, side by side with philosophy and science and all the higher forms of thought. Why? What is the epic, the apotheosis of myth, to those who have repudiated that metaphorical view of life?

The epic is the first flower – or one of the first, let us say – of a new symbolic mode, the mode of art. It is not merely a receptacle of old symbols, namely those of myth, but is itself a new symbolic form, great with possibilities, ready to take meanings and express ideas that have had no vehicle before. What these new ideas are to which art gives us our first, and perhaps our only, access, may be gathered from an analysis of that perfectly familiar yet cryptic notion, "musical significance," to which we proceed in the next chapter.

Notes

1. It must be borne in mind here that the primitive animal fable has no conscious allegorical import, as Aesop's or La Fontaine's fables have, and that the ghost story has no naturalistic "explanation," because ghosts are accepted beings in the savage's cosmos.
2. See especially Ehrenreich 1910; Mudrak 1939 and Rank 1922.

3. Cf. *Collected Papers*, vol. IV (1925), Essay ix (pp. 173–83), "The Relation of the Poet to Day-Dreaming"; also Rank 1922, esp. essays VI "Das Brüdermärchen" (119–45) and VII "Mythus und Märchen" (146–84).

4. This distinction was made fairly long ago by E. Bethe, in his monograph (1905) in which he writes: "Myth, legend, and fairytale differ from one another in origin and purpose. Myth is primitive philosophy, the simplest presentational (*anschauliche*) form of thought, a series of attempts to understand the world, to explain life and death, fate and nature, gods and cults. Legend is primitive history, naively formulated in terms of love and hate, unconsciously transformed and simplified. But fairytale has sprung from, and serves, no motive but entertainment." Cf. also Thimme 1909.

5. The first printed source of the Hiawatha legend seems to be Clark's *History of Onondaga* (1849), from which Longfellow drew the materials for his version. Schoolcraft's *The Myth of Hiawatha* (1856) is fuller and more coherent, but less authentic.

6. Brinton 1896, 194ff. On Brinton's theory, one might suppose that the Sacred Cod of Massachusetts, enshrined in the State House, and sometimes pictured, totem-like, on Massachusetts number-plates, had originated through a little confusion in the Puritan mind between "Cod" and "God." The Indian is no more likely than the white man to mistake even exact homonyms for each other where their meanings are so diverse that their interchange is patently absurd. The same objection holds against every attempt to rest mythology on verbal errors or garbled versions of fact, as Max Müller and Herbert Spencer proposed to do. We do not learn religious thinking on the one hand, nor on the other turn gospel into bed-time stories, just by mistake – by reading "son" for "sun," or confusing Simon called Peter with Peter Rabbit; and presumably right-minded Indians don't, either.

7. See Dixon 1916; Shortland 1882; Andersen 1907; Westervelt 1910.

8. See Dixon 1916, 52; Shortland 1882, 23; Westervelt 1910, 133; for complete genealogy see Andersen 1907, 182.

9. The general word for "woman" is "wahine." See Hitchcock 1887; Tregear 1891; Andrews 1865.

10. Shortland (1882, chap. ii) gives the following translations:
    Hine-ahu-one – the Earth-formed Maid (first created woman).
    Hine-a-tauira – the Pattern Maid (first begotten woman).
    Hine-tu-a-maunga – the Mountain Maid.
    Hine-nui-te-po – Great Woman of Night.

11. An excerpt from Westervelt 1910, 140–5.

12. Westervelt 1910, 54. Ina-Ika is another "Hina," for "Ina" = "Hina."

13. From Sir George Grey, *Polynesian Mythology and Ancient Traditional History of the New Zealand Race, as Furnished by their Priests and Chiefs*, quoted by Dixon (1916, 52).

14. Cf. Westervelt 1910, 165; Beckwith 1940, 220ff.

15. *Gesellschaft für vergleichende Mythenforschung.*

16. Miss Harrison has given recognition to this fact, and it was this very insight which led her to find the primitive sources of religion behind the civilized forms of Greek antiquity which she knew as a scholar. "Our minds are imbued with classical mythology," she says, "our imagination peopled with the vivid personalities, the clear-cut outlines of Olympian gods; it is only by a severe mental effort that we realize ... that *there were no gods at all*, ... but only conceptions of the human mind, shifting and changing colour with every

human mind that conceived them. Art which makes the image, literature which crystallizes attributes and functions, arrest and fix this shifting kaleidoscope; but, until the coming of art and literature and to some extent after, the formulary of theology is 'all things are in flux'" (1903, 164; original italics).

17. I regard mathematical symbolism as a linguistic form of expression.

References

Andersen, Johannes C. 1907. *Maori Life in Ao-tea*. Christchurch: Whitcombe and Tombs.

Andrews, Lorrin. 1865. *Dictionary of the Hawaiian Language*. Honolulu: H. M. Whitney.

Beckwith, Martha. 1940. *Hawaiian Mythology*. New Haven: Yale University Press.

Bethe, E. 1905. *Mythus – Sage – Märchen*. Leipzig: Quelle & Meyer.

Brinton, Daniel G. 1896. *The Myths of the New World*. Philadelphia: D. McKay.

Clark, J. V. H. 1849. *History of Onondaga*. Syracuse, NY: Stoddard and Babcock.

Dixon, Roland. 1916. *Oceanic Mythology*. In the series *The Mythology of All Races*, ed. L. H. Gray and John A. MacCullock. [no publisher]

Ehrenreich, Paul. 1910. *Die allgemeine Mythologie und ihre ethnologischen Grundlagen*. Leipzig.

Freud, Sigmund. 1925. "The Relation of the Poet to Day-Dreaming." In idem, *Collected Papers*, vol. IV, 173–83. London: Hogarth Press.

Harrison, Jane. 1903. *Prolegomena to the Study of Greek Religion*. Cambridge.

Hitchcock, Harvey R. 1887. *An English-Hawaiian Dictionary*. San Francisco: Bancroft.

Krappe, A. H. 1938. *La génèse des mythes*. Paris: Payot.

Lang, Andrew. 1887. *Myth, Ritual, and Religion*. 2 vols. London.

Lessmann, Heinrich. 1907. *Aufgaben und Ziele der vergleichenden Mythenforschung*. Leipzig.

Mudrak, Edmund. 1939. "Die deutsche Heldensage." *Jahrbuch für historische Volkskunde*, VII.

Rank, Otto. 1922. *Psychoanalytische Beiträge zur Mythenforschung*. Zürich: Internationale Psychoanalytische Verlag.

Schoolcraft, H. R. 1856. *The Myth of Hiawatha*. Philadephia: Lippincott & Co; London: Trübner & Co.

Shortland, Edward. 1882. *Maori Religion and Mythology*. London: Longmans & Co.

Thimme, Adolf. 1909. *Das Märchen*. Leipzig.

Tregear, Edward. 1891. *The Maori-Polynesian Comparative Dictionary*. Wellington: Lyon & Blair.

Tylor, Edward B. 1871. *Primitive Culture: Researches into the Development of Mythology, Philosophy, Religion, Language, Art and Custom*. 2 vols. London.

Westervelt, William D. 1910. *Legends of Maui, a Demigod of Polynesia, and of his Mother Hina*. Honolulu: Hawaiian Gazette.

The Place of Language and Myth in the Pattern of Human Culture

Ernst Cassirer

The opening passage of the Platonic dialogue Phaedrus describes how Socrates lets Phaedrus, whom he encounters, lure him beyond the gates of the city to the banks of Ilissus. Plato has pictured the setting of this scene in nicest detail, and there lies over it a glamour and fragrance well-nigh unequalled in classical descriptions of nature. In the shade of a tall plane tree, at the brink of a cool spring, Socrates and Phaedrus lie down; the summer breeze is mild and sweet and full of the cicada's song. In the midst of this landscape Phaedrus raises the question whether this be not the place where, according to a myth, Boreas carried off the fair Orithyia; for the water is clear and translucent here, fitting for maidens to sport in and bathe. Socrates, when pressed with questions as to whether he believes this tale, this "mythologemen," replies that, although he cannot be said to believe it, yet he is not at a loss as to its significance. "For," he says, "then I could proceed as do the learned, and say by way of clever interpretation, that Orithyia, while playing with her companion Pharmacia had been borne over yonder cliffs by Boreas the Northwind, and because of this manner of her death she was said to have been carried off by the god Boreas.... But I," he adds, "for my part, Phaedrus, I find that sort of thing pretty enough, yet consider such interpretations rather an artificial and tedious business, and do not envy him who indulges in it. For he will necessarily have to account for centaurs and the chimaera, too, and will find himself overwhelmed by a very multitude of such creatures, gorgons and pegasuses and countless other strange monsters. And whoever discredits all these wonderful beings and tackles them with the intention of reducing them each to some probability, will have to devote a great deal of time to this bootless sort of wisdom. But I have no leisure at all for such pastimes, and the reason, my dear friend, is that as yet I cannot, as the Delphic precept has it, know myself. So it seems absurd to me that, as long as I am in ignorance of myself, I should concern myself about extraneous matters. Therefore I let all such things be as they may, and think not of them, but of myself – whether I be, indeed, a creature more complex and monstrous than Typhon, or whether perchance I be a gentler and simpler animal, whose nature contains a divine and noble essence" (Phaedrus, 229D ff.).

This sort of myth interpretation, which the Sophists and Rhetoricians of the time held in high repute as the flower of polite learning and the height of the urbane spirit, seemed to Plato the very opposite of this spirit; but although he denounced it as such, calling it a rustic science (àgroikos sophía), his judgment did not prevent the learned from indulging in this sort of wisdom for centuries to come. As the Sophists and Rhetoricians vied with each other at this intellectual sport in Plato's day, so the Stoics and Neoplatonists did in the Hellenistic period. And it was ever and always the science of language, of etymology, that served as a vehicle for such research. Here in the realm of spooks and daemons, as well as in the higher reaches of mythology, the Faustian word seemed ever to hold good: here it was always assumed that the essence of each mythical figure could be directly learned from its name. The notion that name and essence bear a necessary and internal relation to each other, that the name does not merely denote but actually *is* the essence of its object, that the potency of the real thing is contained in the name – that is one of the fundamental assumptions of the mythmaking consciousness itself. Philosophical and scientific mythology, too, seemed to accept this assumption. What in the spirit of myth itself functions as a living and immediate conviction becomes a postulate of reflective procedure for the science of mythology; the doctrine of the intimate relation between names and essences, and of their latent identity, is here set up as a methodological principle.

Among the philosophers it was especially Herbert Spencer who tried to prove the thesis that the mythico-religious veneration of natural phenomena, as, for instance, the sun and the moon, has its ultimate origin in nothing more than a misinterpretation of the names which men have applied to these objects. Among the philologists, Max Müller has taken the method of philological analysis not only as a means to reveal the nature of certain mythical beings, especially in the context of Vedic religion, but also as a point of departure for his general theory of the connection between language and myth. For him, myth is neither a transformation of history into fabulous legend nor is it fable accepted as history; and just as certainly it does not spring directly from the contemplation of the great forms and powers of nature. What we call myth is, for him, something conditioned and negotiated by the agency of language; it is, in fact, the product of a basic shortcoming, an inherent weakness of language. All linguistic denotation is essentially ambiguous – and in this ambiguity, this "paronymia" of words lies the source of all myths. The examples by which Max Müller supports this theory are characteristic of his approach. He cites, as one instance, the legend of

Deucalion and Pyrrha, who, after Zeus had rescued them from the great flood which destroyed mankind, became the ancestors of a new race by taking up stones and casting them over their shoulders, whereupon the stones became men. This origin of human beings from stones is simply absurd and seems to defy all interpretation – but is it not immediately clarified as we recall the fact that in Greek men and stones are denoted by identical or at least similar sounding names, that the words (laoí) and (lâas) are assonant? Or take the myth of Daphne, who is saved from Apollo's embraces by the fact that her mother, the Earth, transforms her into a laurel tree. Again it is only the history of language that can make this myth "comprehensible," and give it any sort of sense. Who was Daphne? In order to answer this question we must resort to etymology, that is to say, we must investigate the history of the word. "Daphne" can be traced back to the Sanskrit *Ahanâ*, and *Ahanâ* means in Sanskrit the redness of dawn. As soon as we know this, the whole matter becomes clear. The story of Phoebus and Daphne is nothing but a description of what one may observe every day: first, the appearance of the dawnlight in the eastern sky, then the rising of the sun-god who hastens after his bride, then the gradual fading of the red dawn at the touch of the fiery rays, and finally its death or disappearance in the bosom of Mother Earth. So the decisive condition for the development of the myth was not the natural phenomenon itself, but rather the circumstance that the Greek word for the laurel (dáphne) and the Sanskrit word for the dawn are related; this entails with a sort of logical necessity the identification of the beings they denote. This, therefore, is his conclusion:

> Mythology is inevitable, it is natural, it is an inherent necessity of language, if we recognize in language the outward form and manifestation of thought; it is in fact the dark shadow which language throws upon thought, and which can never disappear till language becomes entirely commensurate with thought, which it never will. Mythology, no doubt, breaks out more fiercely during the early periods of the history of human thought, but it never disappears altogether. Depend upon it, there is mythology now as there was in the time of Homer, only we do not perceive it, because we ourselves live in the very shadow of it, and because we all shrink from the full meridian light of truth.... Mythology, in the highest sense, is the power exercised by language on thought in every possible sphere of mental activity (Müller 1873, 353–5).

It might seem an idle pursuit to hark back to such points of view, which have long been abandoned by the etymology and comparative mythological research of today, were it not for the fact that this standpoint represents a typical attitude which is ever recurrent in all related fields, in mythology as in linguistic studies, in theory of art as well as in theory of knowledge. For Max Müller the mythical world is essentially a world of illusion – but an illusion that finds its explanation whenever the original, necessary self-deception of the mind, from which the error arises, is discovered. This self-deception is rooted in language, which is forever making game of the human mind, ever ensnaring it in that iridescent play of meanings that is its own heritage. And this notion that myth does not rest upon a positive *power* of formulation and creation, but rather upon a mental *defect* – that we find in it a "pathological" influence of speech – this notion has its proponents even in modern ethnological literature (e.g. Brinton 1907, 115ff.).

But when we reduce it to its philosophical lowest terms, this attitude turns out to be simply the logical result of that naïve realism which regards the reality of objects as something directly and unequivocally given, literally something tangible – àprix taîu kheroin, as Plato says. If reality is conceived in this manner, then of course everything which has not this solid sort of reality dissolves into mere fraud and illusion. This illusion may be ever so finely wrought, and flit about us in the gayest and loveliest colors; the fact remains that this image has no independent content, no intrinsic meaning. It does indeed reflect a reality – but a reality to which it can never measure up, and which it can never adequately portray. From this point of view all artistic creation becomes a mere imitation, which must always fall short of the original. Not only simple imitation of a sensibly presented model, but also what is known as idealization, manner, or style, must finally succumb to this verdict; for measured by the naked "truth" of the object to be depicted, idealization itself is nothing but subjective misconception and falsification. And it seems that all other processes of mental gestation involve the same sort of outrageous distortion, the same departure from objective reality and the immediate data of experience. For all mental processes fail to grasp reality itself, and in order to represent it, to hold it at all, they are driven to the use of symbols. But all symbolism harbors the curse of mediacy; it is bound to obscure what it seeks to reveal. Thus the sound of speech strives to "express" subjective and objective happening, the "inner" and the "outer" world; but what of this it can retain is not the life and individual fullness of existence, but only a dead abbreviation of it. All that "denotation" to which the spoken word lays claim is really nothing more than mere suggestion; a "suggestion" which, in face of the concrete variegation and totality of actual experience, must always appear a poor and empty shell. That is true of the external as well as the inner world: "When *speaks* the soul, alas, the *soul* no longer speaks!"

From this point it is but a single step to the conclusion which the modern skeptical critics of language have drawn: the complete dissolution of any alleged truth content of language, and the realization that this content is nothing but a sort of phantasmagoria of the spirit. Moreover, from this standpoint, not only myth, art, and language, but even theoretical knowledge itself becomes a phantasmagoria; for even knowledge can never reproduce the true nature of things as they are, but must frame their essence in "concepts." But what are concepts save formulations and creations of thought which, instead of giving us the true forms of objects, show us rather the forms of thought itself? Consequently all schemata which science evolves in order to classify, organize, and summarize the phenomena of the real world turn out to be nothing but arbitrary schemes – airy fabrics of the mind, which express not the nature of things, but the nature of mind. So knowledge, as well as myth, language, and art, has been reduced to a kind of fiction – to a fiction that recommends itself by its usefulness, but must not be measured by any strict standard of truth, if it is not to melt away into nothingness.

Against this self-dissolution of the spirit there is only one remedy: to accept in all seriousness what Kant calls his "Copernican revolution." Instead of measuring the content, meaning, and truth of intellectual forms by something extraneous which is supposed to be reproduced in them, we must find in these forms themselves the measure and criterion for their truth and intrinsic meaning. Instead of taking them as mere copies of something else, we must see in each of these spiritual forms a spontaneous law of generation; an original way and tendency of expression which is more than a mere record of something initially given in fixed categories of real existence. From this point of view, myth, art, language and science appear as symbols; not in the sense of mere figures which refer to some given reality by means of suggestion and allegorical renderings, but in the sense of forces each of which produces and posits a world of its own. In these realms the spirit exhibits itself in that inwardly determined dialectic by virtue of which alone there is any reality, any organized and definite Being at all. Thus the special symbolic forms are not imitations, but *organs* of reality, since it is solely by their agency that anything real becomes an object for intellectual apprehension, and as such is made visible to us. The question as to what reality is apart from these forms, and what are its independent attributes, becomes irrelevant here. For the mind, only that can be visible which has some definite form; but every form of existence has its source in some peculiar way of seeing, some intellectual formulation and intuition of meaning. Once language, myth, art and science are recognized as such ideational forms, the basic philosophical question is no longer that of their relation to an absolute reality which forms, so to speak, their solid and substantial substratum; the central problem now is that of their mutual limitation and supplementation. Though they all function organically together in the construction of spiritual reality, yet each of these organs has its individual assignment.

From this angle, the relation between language and myth also appears in a new light. It is no longer a matter of simply deriving one of these phenomena from the other, of "explaining" it in terms of the other – for that would be to level them both, to rob them of their characteristic features. If myth be really, as Max Müller's theory has it, nothing but the darkening shadow which language throws upon thought, it is mystifying indeed that this shadow should appear ever as in an aura of its own light, should evolve a positive vitality and activity of its own, which tends to eclipse what we commonly call the immediate reality of *things*, so that even the wealth of empirical, sensuous experience pales before it. As Wilhelm von Humboldt has said in connection with the language problem:

> Man lives with his objects chiefly – in fact, since his feeling and acting depends on his perceptions, one may say exclusively – as language presents them to him. By the same process whereby he spins language out of his own being, he ensnares himself in it; and each language draws a magic circle round the people to which it belongs, a circle from which there is no escape save by stepping out of it into another. (Humboldt, 60)

This holds, perhaps, even more for the basic mythical conceptions of mankind than for language. Such conceptions are not culled from a ready-made world of Being, they are not mere products of fantasy which vapor off from fixed, empirical, realistic existence, to float above the actual world like a bright mist; to primitive consciousness they present the *totality* of Being. The mythical form of conception is not something superadded to certain definite *elements* of empirical existence; instead, the primary "experience" itself is steeped in the imagery of myth and saturated with its atmosphere. Man lives with *objects* only in so far as he lives with these *forms*; he reveals reality to himself, and himself to reality, in that he lets himself and the environment enter into this plastic medium, in which the two do not merely make contact, but fuse with each other.

Consequently all those theories which propose to find the roots of myth by exploring the realm of experience, of *objects*, which are supposed to have given rise to it, and from which it then allegedly grew and spread, must always remain one-sided and inadequate. There are, as is well known, a multitude of such explanations – a great variety of doctrines about the ultimate origin and real kernel of mythmaking, hardly less motley than the world of objects itself. Now it is found in certain psychical conditions and experiences, especially the phenomenon of dreaming, now in the contemplation of natural events, and among the latter it is further limited to the observation of natural objects such as the sun, the moon, the stars, or else to that of great occurrences such as storms, lightning and thunder, etc. Thus the attempt is made again and again to make soul mythology or nature mythology, sun or moon or thunder mythology the basis of mythology as such.

But even if one of these attempts should prove successful, this would not solve the real problem which mythology presents to philosophy, but at best would push it back one step. For mythical formulation as such cannot be understood and appreciated simply by determining the *object* on which it is immediately and originally centered. It is, and remains, the same miracle of the spirit and the same mystery, no matter whether it covers this or that realistic matter, whether it deals with the interpretation and articulation of psychical processes or physical things, and in the latter case, just what particular things these may be. Even though it were possible to resolve all mythology to a basic astral mythology – what the mythical consciousness derives from contemplation of the stars, what it sees in them directly, would still be something radically different from the view they present to empirical observation or the way they figure in theoretical speculation and scientific "explanations" of natural phenomena. Descartes said that theoretical science remains the same in its essence no matter what object it deals with – just as the sun's light is the same no matter what wealth and variety of things it may illuminate. The same may be said of any symbolic form, of language, art, or myth, in that each of these is a particular way of seeing, and carries within itself its particular and proper source of light. The function of envisagement, the dawn of a conceptual enlightenment can never be realistically derived from things themselves or understood through the nature of its objective contents. For it is not a question of what we see in a certain perspective, but of the perspective itself. If we conceive the problem in this way, it is certainly clear that a reduction of all myth to one subject matter brings us no nearer to the solution, in fact it removes us further than ever from any hope of a real answer. For now we see in language, art and mythology so many archetypal phenomena of human mentality which can be indicated as such, but are not capable of any further "explanation" in terms of something else. The realists always assume, as their solid basis for all such explanations, the so-called "given," which is thought to have some definite form, some inherent structure of its own. They accept this reality as an integrated whole of causes and effects, things and attributes, states and processes, of objects at rest and of motions, and the only question for them is which of these elements a particular mental product such as myth, language or art originally embodied. If, for instance, the phenomenon in question is language, their natural line of inquiry must be whether names for things preceded names for conditions or actions, or vice versa – whether, in other words, nouns or verbs were the first "roots" of speech. But this problem itself appears spurious as soon as we realize that the distinctions which here are taken for granted, the analysis of reality in terms of things and processes, permanent and transitory aspects, objects and actions, do not precede language as a substratum of given fact but that language itself is what initiates such articulations, and develops them in its own sphere. Then it turns out that language could not begin with any phase of "noun concepts" or "verb concepts," but is the very agency that produces the distinction between these forms, that introduces the great spiritual "crisis" in which the permanent is opposed to the transient, and Being is made the contrary of Becoming. So the linguistic fundamental concepts must be realized as something prior to these distinctions, forms which lie between the sphere of noun conception and that of verb conception, between thinghood and eventuality, in a state of indifference, a peculiar balance of feeling.

A similar ambiguity seems to characterize the earliest phases to which we can trace back the development of mythical and religious thought. It seems only natural to us that the world should present itself to our inspection and observation as a pattern of definite forms, each with its own perfectly determinate spatial limits that give it its specific individuality. If we see it as a whole, this whole nevertheless consists of clearly distinguishable units, which do not melt into each other, but preserve their identity that sets them definitely apart from the identity of all the others. But for the mythmaking consciousness these separate elements are not thus separately given, but have to be originally and gradually derived from the whole; the process of culling and sorting out individual forms has yet to be gone through. For this reason the mythic state of mind has been called the "complex" state, to distinguish it from our abstract analytic attitude. Preuss, who coined this expression, points out, for instance, that in the mythology of the Cora Indians, which he has studied exhaustively, the conception of the nocturnal heaven and the diurnal heaven must have preceded that of the sun, the moon, and the separate constellations. The first mythical impulse, he claims, was not toward making a sun-god or a lunar deity, but a community of stars:

> The sun-god does indeed hold first rank in the hierarchy of the gods, but ... the various astral deities can stand proxy for him. They precede him in time, he is

created by them, by somebody's jumping into a fire or being thrown into it; his power is influenced by theirs, and he is artificially kept alive by feeding on the hearts of sacrificed victims, i.e., the stars. The starry night sky is the necessary condition for the existence of the sun; that is the central idea in the whole religious ideation of the Coras and of the ancient Mexicans, and must be regarded as a principal factor in the further development of their religion.[1]

The same function here attributed to the nocturnal heavens seems to be imputed by the Indo-Germanic races to the daylit sky. Their religions show many traces of the fact that the worship of light as an undifferentiated, total experience preceded that of the individual heavenly bodies, which figure only as its media, its particular manifestations. In the Avesta, for instance, Mithra is not a sun-god, as he is for later ages; he is the spirit of heavenly light. He appears on the mountaintops *before* the sun rises, to mount his chariot which, drawn by four white horses, runs the course of heaven during the day; when night comes, he the unsleeping still lights the face of earth with a vague glimmering light. We are explicitly told that he is neither the sun, nor the moon, nor any or all of the stars, but through them, his thousand ears and ten thousand eyes, he perceives everything and keeps watch over the world.[2]

Here we see in a concrete instance how mythic conception originally grasps only the great, fundamental, qualitative contrast of light and darkness, and how it treats them as *one* essence, one complex whole, out of which definite characters only gradually emerge. Like the spirit of language, the mythmaking genius "has" separate and individualized forms only in so far as it "posits" them, as it carves them out of the undifferentiated whole of its pristine vision.

This insight into the determining and discriminating function, which myth as well as language performs in the mental construction of our world of "things," seems to be all that a "philosophy of symbolic forms" can teach us. Philosophy as such can go no further; it cannot presume to present to us, *in concreto*, the great process of emergence, and to distinguish its phases for us. But if pure philosophy is necessarily restricted to a general, theoretical picture of such an evolution, it may be that philology and comparative mythology can fill in the outline and draw with firm, clear strokes what philosophical speculation could only suggestively sketch. An initial and portentous step in this direction has been taken by Usener in his work on divine names. "An Essay toward a Science of Religious Conception" (1896) is the subtitle he has given to his book, which brings it definitely into the realm of philosophical problems and systematic treatment. To trace the history of the divinities, their successive appearance and development among the several tribes of man, he tells us, is not an attainable goal; only a history of mythic ideas can be reconstructed. Such ideas, no matter how manifold, how varied, how heterogeneous they may appear at first sight, have their own inner lawfulness; they do not arise from a boundless caprice of the imagination, but move in definite avenues of feeling and creative thought. This intrinsic law is what mythology seeks to establish. Mythology is the science (logos) of myth, or the science of the forms of religious conception. His findings in this field may certainly give pause to philosophers, who tend to regard the human mind as endowed *ab initio* with logical categories. "There have been long periods in mental evolution," he observes:

> ...when the human mind was slowly laboring toward thought and conception and was following quite different laws of ideation and speech. Our epistemology will not have any real foundation until philology and mythology have revealed the processes of involuntary and unconscious conception. The chasm between specific perception and general concepts is far greater than our academic notions, and a language which does our thinking for us, lead us to suppose. It is so great that I cannot imagine how it could have been bridged, had not language itself, without man's conscious awareness, prepared and induced the process. It is language that causes the multitude of casual, individual expressions to yield up one which extends its denotation over more and more special cases, until it comes to denote them all, and assumes the power of expressing a class concept. (Usener 1896, 321)

Here, then, it is the philologist, the student of language and religion, who confronts philosophy with a new question, which emerges from his own investigations. And Usener has not merely indicated a new approach; he has resolutely followed it up, employing to this end all the clues which the history of language, the precise analysis of words, and especially that of divine names provided. The question naturally arises whether philosophy, not commanding any such materials, can handle this problem which the humanistic sciences have presented to it, and what intellectual resources it can tap to meet such a challenge. Is there any other line than the actual *history* of language and of religion that could lead us closer to the origin of primary linguistic and religious concepts? Or is it, at this point, one and the same thing to know the genesis of such ideas and to know their ultimate meanings and functions? This is the issue I propose to decide in the following pages. I shall take up Usener's problem in exactly the form in which he has cast it; but I shall attempt to tackle it on other grounds than linguistic and philological considerations. Usener himself has indicated the propriety, in fact the necessity of such an approach, in that he formulated the main issue as not merely a matter of linguistic and intellectual history, but also of logic and epistemology. This presupposes that the latter disciplines, too, can handle the problem of semantic and mythic conception from their own standpoint, and treat it by their own methodological principles and procedures. Through this expansion, this apparent overstepping of the usual boundaries of logical inquiry, the science of logic really comes into its own, and the realm of pure theoretical reason becomes actually defined and distinguished from other spheres of intellectual being and development.

Notes

1. Preuss 1912. Cf. further Preuss 1914, 9.

2. Yasht X, 145; Yasna I, ii, 35 [old Iranian religious texts, ed.]; cf. Cumont 1899, I, 225.

References

Brinton, Daniel G. 1907. *Religions of Primitive Peoples*. New York and London.

Cumont, F. 1899. *Textes et monuments figurés relatifs aux mystères de Mithra*. Brussels.

Humboldt, Wilhelm von. 1836–9. "Einleitung zum Kawi-werk." In idem, *Über die Kawi-Sprache auf der Insel Java*. S.W. (Coll. ed.), VII, 60. Berlin.

Müller, Max Fr. 1873. "The Philosophy of Mythology." In idem, *Introduction to the Science of Religion*. London.

Preuss, Konrad Th. 1912. *Die Nayarit-Expedition I: Die Religion der Cora Indianer in Texten nebst Wörterbuch*. Leipzig.

_____1914. *Die geistige Kultur der Naturvölker*. Leipzig and Berlin: Teubner.

Usener, Herman. 1896. *Götternamen. Versuch einer Lehre von der religiösen Begriffsbildungen*. Bonn.

The Worlds 1, 2, and 3

Karl R. Popper

By "World 1" I mean what is usually called the world of physics: of rocks, and trees and physical fields of forces. I also mean to include here the worlds of chemistry and biology. By "World 2" I mean the psychological world. It is studied by students of the human mind, but also of the minds of animals. It is the world of feelings of fear and of hope, of dispositions to act, and of all kinds of subjective experiences, including subconscious and unconscious experiences. Thus the terms "World 1" and "World 2" are both easily explained. The explanation of what I call "World 3" is a little more difficult. By "World 3" I mean the world of the products of the human mind. Although I include works of art in World 3 and also ethical values and social institutions (and thus, one might say, societies), I shall confine myself largely to the world of scientific libraries, to books, to scientific problems, and to theories, including mistaken theories.

Books, journals, and libraries belong to both World 1 and World 3. They are physical objects, and as such belong to World 1: they are subject to the physical restrictions or physical laws of World 1. For example, though two copies of the same book may be physically altogether similar, they cannot take up the same part of physical space; thus they are two different World 1 objects. But they belong not only to World 1: they also belong to World 3. *Two* very similar copies of the same book are *different* as World 1 objects; but if the *contents* of two physically similar (or dissimilar) books are the same, then as World 3 objects, the two books are identical: they are different copies of *one* World 3 object. Moreover, this one World 3 object is subject to the restrictions and the valuations of World 3; it can, for instance, be examined for its logical consistency, and evaluated for its informative content.

The *content* of a book, or of a theory, is something abstract. All *concrete* physical bodies, such as rocks, trees, animals and human bodies, belong to World 1; and all psychological states, whether conscious or subconscious, belong to World 2. But *abstract* things, such as problems, theories and arguments, including mistaken ones, belong to World 3. (Also inconsistent arguments and theories. This does not, of course, make World 3 inconsistent, for World 3 is neither a theory nor an assertion nor an argument: it is a class of things, a universe of discourse.) Moreover, unless we choose to introduce for works of art, say, a new term such as "World 4," a play like *Hamlet* and a symphony like Schubert's "Unfinished" also belong to World 3; and just as an individual copy of a book belongs *both* to World 1 and to World 3, so particular performances of *Hamlet* and of Schubert's Unfinished Symphony belong both to World 1 and to World 3. They belong to World 1 in so far as they consist of complex physical events; but they belong to World 3 in so far as they have a content, a message, or a meaning.

The terms "World 1," "World 2," and "World 3" are consciously chosen as being colourless and arbitrary. But there is a historical reason for numbering them 1, 2, and 3: it seems that the physical world existed before the world of animal feelings; and I conjecture that World 3 begins only with the evolution of a specifically human language. I will take the world of *linguistically formulated human knowledge* as being most characteristic of World 3. It is the world of problems, theories and arguments; and I shall also include those problems, theories and arguments which have not yet been linguistically formulated. I will also assume that World 3 has a history – that certain problems, theories and arguments were discovered, or perhaps refuted, at certain dates, while others were at those dates still undiscovered, or unrefuted.

The Reality of the Three Worlds

It is, I think, good common sense to accept the reality or existence of the World 1 of physical bodies. As Dr Johnson's famous refutation of Berkeley shows, a physical body such as a rock can be said to exist because it can be *kicked*; and if you kick a rock hard enough, you will feel that it can kick back. Following Alfred Landé, I propose to say that something exists, or is real, if and only if it can be kicked and can, in principle, kick back; to put it a little more generally, I propose to say that something exists, or is real, if and only if it can *interact* with members of World 1, with hard, physical bodies.

Thus, World 1, or the physical world, may be taken as the standard example of reality or of existence. However, I believe in the insignificance of questions of terminology or of the usage or meaning of words. Thus I regard the usage of words like "real" or "existing" as not very important; especially if compared with questions about the *truth* of theoretical assertions or propositions.

The proposition the truth of which I wish to defend and which seems to me to go a little beyond common sense is that not only are the physical World 1 and the psychological World 2 real but so also is the abstract World 3; *real* in exactly that sense in which the physical World 1 of rocks and trees is real: the objects of World 2 and of World 3 can kick each other, as well as the physical objects of World 1; and they can also be kicked back.

The Reality of Worlds 1 and 2

Although I propose, with Dr Johnson, Alfred Landé, and other commonsense realists, to regard World 1 as the very standard of reality, I am not a monist but a pluralist.[1] A monistic immaterialism or phenomenalism that denies the existence of World 1 and admits only experiences as existing, thus only World 2, was fairly fashionable until quite recently. At present, the opposite view is much more fashionable. I mean the view that *only* World 1 exists. This view is called monistic materialism or physicalism or philosophical behaviourism. More recently this theory has also been called the "identity theory," because it asserts that mental experiences are, in reality, identical with brain processes.

The various forms of monism will be replaced here by a pluralism: the thesis of the three worlds. This pluralism can be supported by two very different lines of argument. First, to show the reality of World 2 one can appeal to common sense, and to the failure of the physicalists to produce telling arguments against the commonsense view that a bad toothache can be very real indeed.

However, my second and main argument proceeds very differently. It starts from the assertion that World 3 objects, such as theories, do in fact strongly interact with the physical World 1. The simplest examples are the ways in which we make changes in World 1 when building, say, nuclear reactors or atom bombs or skyscrapers or airfields, in accordance with World 3 plans and with theories that are often highly abstract.

My main argument for the existence of the World 2 of subjective experiences is that we must normally grasp or understand a World 3 theory before we can use it to act upon World 1; but grasping or understanding a theory is a mental affair, a World 2 process: World 3 usually interacts with World 1 via the mental World 2. An example is the planning, construction and use of bulldozers for the building of airfields. There is, first, an interaction between the World 2 planning by the human mind and the internal restrictions of both World 1 and World 3 which limit the planning of the machinery. Secondly, we have an interaction between World 2 and the World 1 of the human brain, which in turn acts upon our limbs which steer the bulldozers.

The effectiveness of this argument clearly depends on World 3. If World 3 exists and is at least in part autonomous, and if, further, plans in World 3 do affect World 1, then it seems to me inescapable that there also exists a World 2. In this way my main argument for the existence of World 2 has led us back to the problem of whether World 3 exists; and further to the problem of whether World 3 is, in part, autonomous.

The Reality and Partial Autonomy of World 3

Human language and human thought evolve together, in mutual interaction. Human language, admittedly, expresses human thought processes, that is, World 2 objects. But it makes a very great difference to these subjective World 2 objects when they are formulated in an objective human language: there is a powerful feedback effect between human language and the human mind.

This is mainly because a thought, once it is formulated in language, becomes an *object* outside ourselves. Such an object can then be inter-subjectively *criticized* – criticized by others as well as by ourselves. Intersubjective or objective criticism in this sense only emerges with human language; and with it emerges the human World 3, the world of objective standards and of the contents of our subjective thought processes.

Thus it makes a great difference whether we merely *think* some thought or whether we *formulate* it in a language (or still better, write it down, or get it printed). As long as we merely think the thought it cannot be objectively criticized. It is part of ourselves. To be criticizable it must be formulated in a human language, and become an object: a World 3 object. Linguistically formulated thoughts belong to World 3. They can be *logically* criticized, for example by showing that they have certain unwelcome or even absurd logical consequences. Only *thought contents* belonging to World 3 can stand in logical relationships, such as equivalence, deducibility, or contradiction.

Thus we must clearly distinguish between the subjective *thought processes*, which belong to World 2, and the objective *contents* of thoughts, the contents in themselves, as it were, which constitute World 3.

In order to make the point quite clear, take two mathematicians who, by making some mistakes, both arrive at a false theorem – for example, at the theorem that $5 + 7 = 13$. Their thought processes, which belong to World 2, can either be similar or entirely different. But the *content* of their thoughts, which belongs to World 3, is one and the same, and can be criticized. The two mathematicians can be kicked back by the logical structure of World 3, which shows that their alleged theorem *contradicts* the objectively *true* statement "$5 + 7 = 12$," and that it therefore must be objectively *false*. The two mathematicians are kicked; not by other people, but by the laws of arithmetic itself.

Most people are dualists: it is part of common sense to believe in the Worlds 1 and 2. But it is not easy for most people to accept the existence of World 3. They will of course admit that a very special part of World 1 exists which consists of printed books, or of acoustical language noises; and they will admit brain processes, and subjective thought processes. But they will assert that what distinguishes books from other physical bodies like trees, or human language from other noises like the howling of wolves, is only the fact that they help us to have certain special kinds of World 2 experiences, namely thought processes of a special kind (perhaps running parallel with brain processes) which are correlated with just these books or these linguistic noises.

I regard this view as totally insufficient. I shall try to show that we ought to admit the existence of an autonomous part of World 3; a part which consists of objective *thought contents* which are *independent of*, and clearly distinct from, the subjective or personal *thought processes* by which they are grasped, and whose grasp they can causally influence. I thus assert that there exist autonomous World 3 objects which have not yet taken up either World 1 shape or World 2 shape, but which, nevertheless, interact with our thought processes. In fact, they influence our thought processes decisively.

Let us take an example from elementary arithmetic. The infinite sequence of natural numbers, 0, 1, 2, 3, 4, 5, 6, and so on, is a human invention, a product of the human mind. As such it may be said *not* to be autonomous, but to depend on World 2 thought processes. But now take the even numbers, or the prime numbers. These are not invented by us, but *discovered* or found. We *discover* that the sequence of natural numbers consists of even numbers and of odd numbers and, whatever we may think about it, no thought process can alter this fact of World 3. The sequence of natural numbers is a result of our learning to count – that is, it is an invention within the human language. But it has its unalterable inner laws or restrictions or regularities which are the *unintended consequences* of the manmade sequence of natural numbers; that is, the unintended consequences of some product of the human mind.

The same may be said about the prime numbers. It was found that the higher you proceed in the sequence of natural numbers (say, first to the numbers from 100 to 200, and then from 1100 to 1200) the rarer becomes the occurrence of prime numbers: this is an *autonomous property* of World 3. Now this discovery leads us to a new autonomous problem in World 3; a problem that is discovered, as simply being there, like the prime numbers themselves. It is the following interesting problem: if we proceed to greater and greater numbers, to 10 million, for example, do the prime numbers die out in the end, or are there *always* new prime numbers to come, even if they become rarer and rarer? Or in the terminology of Euclid, does there exist one greatest prime number or is the sequence of prime numbers infinite, like the sequence of natural numbers itself?

This is an objective and autonomous problem: either there exists a greatest prime number, or the sequence of prime numbers goes on and on, to infinity. Euclid, who may even have discovered the problem, solved it. He showed that the assumption that there exists a greatest prime number leads to an absurdity.

Thus he gave a proof, an indirect proof, of the objective fact that no greatest prime number exists but that there is always a greater one: the sequence of prime numbers is infinite, just as is that of natural numbers. And this fact is an objective, autonomous, fact of World 3. It is a World 3 theorem, an autonomous World 3 object. We can discover it, we can prove it, but we can do nothing to alter it.

The discovery of prime numbers has led to many difficult problems, some of which have been solved, and many of which are still open. These problems are discovered by us in the new field which we have created, in the sequence of natural numbers. They are discovered as being there, independently of whether anybody has thought of them before. Thus we have constructions in mathematics which are the products of the human mind, and problems and theories which are the objective and perhaps never thought of consequences of these constructions. This shows that the world of mathematics contains an autonomous part: an autonomous part of World 3.

My next point is that this autonomous part of World 3 is "*real*" in the sense that it can interact with World 2 and also, via World 2, with World 1. If some men or many men seek for a solution of an as yet unsolved mathematical problem, then they are all, possibly in many different ways, influenced by this problem. The success of their attempts to solve it will depend, at least partly, upon the existence or non-existence, in World 3, of a solution to the problem, and partly upon whether or not they are led by their thought processes to objectively true thought contents. This shows that the autonomous World 3 objects can have a strong causal influence upon World 2 processes. And if a newly discovered World 3 problem, with or without a solution, is published, then the causal influence extends even into World 1, by helping to set in motion the fingers of typesetters and even the wheels of printing machines.

For simple reasons such as these, I hold not only that World 3 is partly autonomous, but that its autonomous part is real, since it can act upon World 1, at least via World 2. The situation is fundamentally the same for every scientific discovery and every technical invention. In all these cases, World 3 problems and theories play a major role. The problems may be discovered, and though the theories (which are, say, about World 1) may be products of the human mind, they are *not merely* our constructs; for their truth or falsity depends entirely upon their relation to World 1, a relation which, in all important cases, we cannot alter. Their truth or falsity depends both upon the inner structure of World 3 (especially language) and upon World 1, the latter of which, as I have suggested, is the very standard of reality.

The Human Situation and the Natural World

The origin of life may be, for all we know at present, a unique occurrence in the universe. We cannot explain it and it comes very near to what David Hume would have called, grudgingly, a miracle. The emergence of a World 2 of animal consciousness, of feelings of joy and of pain, seems to be a second such miracle.

It seems reasonable to regard the emergence of consciousness and previously that of life as two comparatively recent events in the evolution of the universe; as events which, like the beginning of the universe, are at present, and perhaps for ever, beyond our scientific understanding. This modest approach admits freely the existence of open problems, and thereby does not close the way to discovering more about them – about their character and perhaps even about the ways to a possible solution, or at least to a partial solution.

A third great miracle is the emergence of the human brain, and of the human mind and of human reason. This third miracle may be less far removed than the others from an explanation, at least in evolutionary terms. Man is an animal. He appears to stand much nearer to the other animals than these stand to inanimate matter. But this is not to belittle the gulf which separates the human brain from the animal brain, and human language from all other animal languages – from the dispositions which most higher animals possess to *express* their inner states and to *communicate* with other animals.

Man has created human language, with its *descriptive* function and the value of truth, and with its *argumentative* function and the value of the validity of arguments, thus transcending animal languages with their merely expressive and communicative functions.[2] With it man has created the objective World 3, something for which there are only fairly remote analogues in the animal kingdom. And with this, he has produced a new world of civilization, of learning, of non-genetic growth – of growth that is not transmitted by the genetic code; of growth which depends not so much on natural selection as on selection based upon rational criticism.

It is, therefore, to the role of human language and of World 3 that we should look when we are trying to explain this third great miracle: the emergence of the human brain and of the human mind; of human reason and of human freedom.

Determinism and Indeterminism in Physics

The title of this essay is "Indeterminism is Not Enough"; that is, not enough for human freedom. But I have yet to give at least a sketch of classical determinism (or physical determinism, or World 1 determinism), and of that indeterminism which is its opposite. Moreover, I have yet to show why these two ideas are insufficient for a discussion of human freedom.

Classical determinism, or World 1 determinism, is a very old idea which was most sharply formulated by Laplace, on the basis of Newton's mechanics.

Laplace's thesis of determinism can be stated in the following way. Assume we are given the exact masses, positions and velocities of all material particles in the universe at some moment of time; then we can in principle calculate, with the help of Newtonian mechanics, all that has ever happened in the past and all that will ever happen in the future. This would include all the physical movements of all men, and therefore all spoken or written words, all poetry, and all the music that will ever be written. The calculation can be done by a machine. It need *only* be programmed with Newton's laws of motion and the existing initial conditions. It can be stone deaf, and unaware of the problems of musical composition. But it will be able to predict what black marks would be placed on white music paper by any given composer in the past or in the future.

I personally find Laplacean determinism a most unconvincing and unattractive view; and it is a doubtful argument, for the calculator may have greatly to exceed the universe in complexity, as was pointed out (first, I think) by F. A. Hayek.[3] But it is, perhaps, worth stressing that Laplace does draw the correct conclusions from his idea of a causally closed and deterministic World 1. If we accept Laplace's view, then we must not argue (as many philosophers do) that we are nevertheless endowed with genuine human freedom and creativity.

However, Laplacean determinism had to be modified upon the collapse of some attempts of Maxwell's to reduce electricity and magnetism to Newtonian mechanics by a mechanical model of the ether. With these attempts collapsed also the thesis of the closedness of Newton's mechanical World 1: it became open towards the electromagnetic part of World 1. Nevertheless, Einstein, for example, remained a determinist. He believed, almost to the end of his life, that a unified and closed deterministic theory was possible, comprising mechanics, gravitation, and electricity. In fact, most physicists are inclined to regard a causally open (and therefore indeterministic) physical universe – say, a physical universe that is open to the influence of World 2 – as a typical superstition, upheld only perhaps by some spiritualist members of the Society for Psychical Research. Few physicists of repute would take it seriously.

But another form of indeterminism became part of the official creed of physics. The new indeterminism was introduced by quantum mechanics, which assumes the possibility of elementary chance events that are causally irreducible.

There are, it appears, two kinds of chance events. One kind is due to the independence of two causal chains which happen, accidentally, to interfere at some place and time, and so combine in bringing about the chance event. A typical example consists of two causal chains, one of which loosens a brick while the other independent causal chain makes a man take up a position where he will be hit by the brick. This kind of chance event (whose theory was developed by Laplace himself, in his work on probability) is perfectly compatible with Laplacean determinism: anybody furnished in advance with sufficiently full information about the relevant events could have predicted what was bound to happen. It was only *the incompleteness of our knowledge* which gave rise to this kind of chance.

Quantum mechanics, however, introduced chance events of a second, and much more radical kind: absolute chance. According to quantum mechanics, there are elementary physical processes which are not further analysable in terms of causal chains, but which consist of so-called "quantum jumps"; and a quantum jump is supposed to be an absolutely unpredictable event which is controlled neither by causal laws nor by the coincidence of causal laws, but by probabilistic laws alone.[4] Thus quantum mechanics introduced, in spite of the protests of Einstein, what he described as "the dice-playing God." Quantum mechanics regards these absolute chance events as the basic events of World 1. The various particular results of these chance events, such as the disintegration of an atom with consequent radioactive emission, are not predetermined and therefore cannot be predicted however great our knowledge of all relevant conditions prior to the event may be. But we can make testable statistical predictions about such processes.

Although I do not believe that quantum mechanics will remain the last word in physics, I happen to believe that its indeterminism is fundamentally sound. I believe that even classical Newtonian mechanics is in principle indeterministic. This becomes clear if we introduce into it physical models of human knowledge – for example, computers.[5] The introduction of objective human knowledge into our universe – the introduction of a World 3 (we must not forget that computers, even though inhuman, are manmade) – allows us to prove not only the indeterministic character of this universe, but its essential openness or incompleteness.

Returning now to quantum mechanics, I want to point out that the indeterminism of a dice-playing God, or of probabilistic laws, fails to make room for human freedom. For what we want to understand is not only how we may act *unpredictably and in a chancelike fashion*, but how we can act *deliberately and rationally*. The famous probabilistic constancy of such chance events as the posting of letters bearing no address may be an interesting curiosity, but it has no similarity whatever to the problem of the freedom to write a piece of poetry, good or bad, or to advance a new hypothesis concerning, say, the origin of the genetic code.

It must be admitted that if quantum mechanics is right, then Laplacean determinism is wrong and that arguments from physics can no longer be used to combat the doctrine of indeterminism. But indeterminism is not enough.

Indeterminism Is Not Enough

Let us take the physical world to be partially but not completely determined. That is to say, let us assume that events follow each other according to physical laws, but that there is sometimes a certain *looseness* in their connection, filled in by unpredictable and perhaps probabilistic sequences similar to those we know from roulette or from dicing or from tossing a coin or from quantum mechanics. Thus we would have an indeterministic World 1, as indeed I have suggested that we have. *But nothing is gained for us if this World 1 is causally closed towards World 2 and World 3*. Such an indeterministic World 1 would be unpredictable; yet World 2, and with it World 3, could not have any influence upon it. A *closed* indeterministic World 1 would go on as before, whatever our feelings or wishes are, with the sole difference from Laplace's world that we could not predict it, even if we *knew* all about its present state: it would be a world ruled, if only partly, by chance.

Thus indeterminism is *necessary but insufficient* to allow for human freedom and especially for creativity. What we really need is the thesis that World 1 is incomplete; that it can be influenced by World 2; that it can interact with World 2; or that it is causally open towards World 2, and hence, further, towards World 3.

We thus come back to our central point: we must demand that World 1 is not self-contained or "closed," but open towards World 2; that it can be influenced by World 2, just as World 2 can be influenced by World 3 and, of course, also by World 1.

Determinism and Naturalism

There can be little doubt that the fundamental philosophical motive in favour of a Laplacean determinism and the theory that World 1 is causally closed is the realization that man is an animal, and the wish to see ourselves as part of nature. I believe that the motive is right; if nature were fully deterministic then so would be the realm of human actions; in fact there would be no actions, but at most the appearance of actions.

But the argument can be turned around. If man is free, at least in part free, then so is nature; and the physical World 1 is open. And there is every reason to regard man as at least partly free. The opposite view – that of Laplace – leads to predestination. It leads to the view that billions of years ago, the elementary particles of World 1 contained the poetry of Homer, the philosophy of Plato, and the symphonies of Beethoven as a seed contains a plant; that human history is predestined, and with it all acts of human creativity. And the quantum theoretical version of the view is just as bad. If it has any bearing on human creativity, then it makes human creativity a matter of sheer chance. No doubt there is an element of chance in it. *Yet the theory that the creation of works of art or music can, in the last instance, be explained in terms of chemistry or physics seems to me absurd.* So far as the creation of music can be explained, it has to be explained at least partly in terms of the influence of other music (which also stimulates the creativity of the musician); and, most important, in terms of the inner structure, the internal laws and restrictions, which play such a role in music and in all other World 3 phenomena – laws and restrictions whose absorption (and whose occasional defiance) are immensely important for the musician's creativity.

Thus our freedom and especially our freedom to create stand, clearly, under the restrictions of all three worlds. Had Beethoven, by some misfortune, been deaf from birth, he would hardly have become a composer. As a composer he freely subordinated his freedom to the structural restrictions of World 3. The autonomous World 3 was the world in which he made his great and genuine discoveries, being free to choose his path like a discoverer in the Himalayas, but being restrained by the path so far chosen and by the restrictions of the world he was discovering. (Similar remarks could be made about Gödel.)

The Open Universe

Thus we are led back to assert that there is interaction between the Worlds 1, 2, and 3.

There is no doubt in my mind that Worlds 2 and 3 do interact. If we try to grasp or understand a theory, or to remember a symphony, then our minds are causally influenced; not merely by the memory of noises stored in our brains, but at least in part by the work of the composer, by the autonomous inner structures of the World 3 object which we try to grasp.

All this means that World 3 can act upon the World 2 of our minds. But if so, there is no doubt that, when a mathematician *writes down* his World 3 results on (physical) paper, his mind – his World 2 – acts upon the physical World 1. Thus World 1 is open towards World 2, just as World 2 is open towards World 3.

This is of fundamental importance; for it shows that nature, or the universe to which we belong, and which contains as parts the Worlds 1, 2, and 3, is itself open; it contains World 3, and World 3 can be shown to be *intrinsically open*.

One aspect of the openness of World 3 is a consequence of Gödel's theorem that axiomatized arithmetic is not completable. Yet the incompletability and openness of the universe is perhaps best illustrated by a version of the well-known story of the man who draws a map of his room, including in his map the map which he is drawing. His task defies completion, for he has to take account, within his map, of his latest entry.

The story of the map is a trivial case compared with World 3 theories and their impact upon World 1, although it illustrates in a simple way the incompleteness of a universe that contains World 3 objects of knowledge. But so far it does not yet illustrate indeterminism. For each of the different "last" strokes actually entered into the map determines, within the infinite sequence of entries to be made, a determined entry. However, this determinacy of the strokes holds only if we do not consider the fallibility of all human knowledge (a fallibility which plays a considerable role in the problems, theories and mistakes of World 3). Taking this into account, each of these "last" strokes entered into our map constitutes for the draughtsman a new *problem*, the problem of entering a *further* stroke which depicts the "last" stroke *precisely*. Because of the fallibility that characterizes all human knowledge, this problem cannot possibly be solved by the draughtsman with absolute precision; and the smaller the strokes to which the draughtsman proceeds, the greater will be the relative imprecision which will in principle be unpredictable and indeterminate, and which will constantly increase. In this way, the story of the map shows how the fallibility which affects objective human knowledge contributes to the essential indeterminism and openness of a universe that contains human knowledge as a part of itself.

The universe is thus bound to be open if it contains human knowledge; papers, and books, like the present one, which are on the one hand physical World I objects, and, on the other, World 3 objects that fallibly try to state or to describe fallible human knowledge.

Thus we live in an open universe. We could not make this discovery before there was human knowledge. But once we have made it there is no reason to think that the openness depends exclusively upon the existence of human knowledge. It is much more reasonable to reject all views of a closed universe – that of a causally as well as that of a probabilistically closed universe; thus rejecting the closed universe envisaged by Laplace, as well as the one envisaged by wave mechanics. Our universe is partly causal, partly probabilistic, and partly open: it is emergent. The opposite view results from mistaking the character of our manmade World 3 theories about World 1 –

especially their characteristic oversimplifications – for the character of World 1 itself. We might have known better.

No good reason has been offered so far against the openness of our universe, or against the fact that radically new things are constantly emerging from it; and no good reasons have been offered so far that shed doubt upon human freedom and creativity, a creativity which is restricted as well as inspired by the inner structure of World 3.

Man is certainly part of nature, but, in creating World 3, he has transcended himself *and* nature, as it existed before him. And human freedom is indeed part of nature, but it transcends nature – at least as it existed before the emergence of human language and of critical thought, and of human knowledge.

Indeterminism is not enough: to understand human freedom we need more; we need the openness of World 1 towards World 2, and of World 2 towards World 3, and the autonomous and intrinsic openness of World 3, the world of the products of the human mind and, especially, of human knowledge.

Notes

NB. The editorial remarks in [...] are by W. W. Bartley III.

1. See *The Self and its Brain*, chapters P3 and P5.
2. [For Popper's account of the functions of language, see his discussions in *Conjectures and Refutations*, chapters 4, 12; *Objective Knowledge*, chapters 2, 3, 4, 6; *Unended Quest*, section 15; and *The Self and its Brain*, section 17, with particular reference to his discussion and amplification of Bühler's account. Ed.]
3. von Hayek 1952, chapter 8, section 6.
4. [Popper may seem at this place to concede that there are quantum jumps while elsewhere agreeing with Schrödinger that there are not (see *Quantum Theory and the Schism in Physics*, Vol. III of this *Postscript*, section 13). Questioned about this, he said that, while upholding the impossibility of predicting the jumps other than probabilistically, he agrees with Schrödinger that it is an open problem whether we must adopt an interpretation of the formalism that makes the quantum jumps instantaneous. Ed.]
5. [See Popper's discussions in *The Poverty of Historicism*, "Preface"; "Indeterminism in Quantum Physics and in Classical Physics," *British Journal for the Philosophy of Science* 1, no. 2: 117–33, and no. 3: 173–95; and sections 20–22 of this volume of the *Postscript*. Ed.]

References

Hayek, F. A. von. 1952. *The Sensory Order: An Inquiry into the Foundations of Theoretical Psychology*. Chicago: University of Chicago Press.

Popper, Karl R. 1957. *The Poverty of Historicism*. London: Routledge & Kegan Paul.

_____1963. *Conjectures and Refutations*. London: Routledge & Kegan Paul.

_____1972. *Objective Knowledge.* Oxford: Oxford University Press.

_____1983. *The Self and its Brain.* (orig. Berlin and Heidelberg: Springer-Verlag). London: Routledge.

_____1992. *Unended Quest.* London: Routledge. (orig. *Autobiography of Karl Popper.* LaSalle, IL: Open Court Publishing).

LANGUAGE AND SOCIAL REALITY

John R. Searle

The primary aim of this chapter is to explain and justify my claim that language is essentially constitutive of institutional reality. I have made this claim in general terms but I now want to make fully explicit what I mean by it, and to present arguments for it. At the end of the chapter I will mention some other functions of language in institutional facts.

I said in the last chapter that it seems impossible to have institutional structures such as money, marriage, governments, and property without some form of language because, in some weird sense I have not yet explained, the words or other symbols are partly constitutive of the facts. But this will seem puzzling when we reflect that social facts in general do not require language. Prelinguistic animals can have all sorts of cooperative behavior, and human infants are clearly capable of interacting socially in quite complex ways without any words. Furthermore, if we are going to say that institutional reality requires language, what about language itself? If institutional facts require language and language is itself an institution, then it seems language must require language, and we have either infinite regress or circularity.

There is a weaker and a stronger version of my claim. The weaker is that in order to have institutional facts at all, a society must have at least a primitive form of a language, that in this sense the institution of language is logically prior to other institutions. On this view language is the basic social institution in the sense that all others presuppose language, but language does not presuppose the others: you can have language without money and marriage, but not the converse. The stronger claim is that each institution requires linguistic elements of the facts within that very institution. I believe both claims are true, and I will be arguing for the stronger claim. The stronger claim implies the weaker.

Language-Dependent Thoughts and Language-Dependent Facts

To explain the issues and the arguments I will be presenting, I need to make, if only briefly, certain elementary clarifications and distinctions. I need to make explicit which features of language are relevant to this issue. I will not attempt to define "language" here, and many features that are essential to full-blown natural languages – such as infinite generative capacity, the presence of illocutionary force indicating devices, quantifiers, and logical connectives – are irrelevant to this discussion. The feature of language essential for the constitution of institutional facts is the existence of symbolic devices, such as words, that by convention *mean* or *represent* or *symbolize* something beyond themselves. So when I say that language is partly constitutive of institutional facts, I do not mean that institutional facts require full-blown natural languages like French, German, or English. My claim that language is partly constitutive of institutional facts amounts to the claim that institutional facts essentially contain some symbolic elements in this sense of "symbolic": there are words, symbols, or other *conventional* devices that *mean* something or express something or represent or symbolize something beyond themselves, *in a way that is publicly understandable*. I want that to sound very vague and general at this point, because it is, so far, designed only to specify the feature of language that I want to claim has a constitutive role in institutional reality.

Language, as I am using the notion here, essentially contains entities that symbolize; and in language, as opposed to prelinguistic intentional states, such intentionalistic capacities are not intrinsic to the entities but are imposed by or derived from the intrinsic intentionality of humans. Thus the sentence "I am hungry" is part of language because it has representational or symbolic capacities by convention. But the actual feeling of hunger is not part of language because it represents its conditions of satisfaction intrinsically. You do not need language or any other sorts of conventions to feel hungry.

We need first to distinguish between *language-independent facts*, such as the fact that Mt. Everest has snow and ice at the summit, and *language-dependent facts* such as the fact that "Mt. Everest has snow and ice at the summit" is a sentence of English. Though there are no doubt marginal cases, the principle is clear enough – a fact is language independent if that very fact requires no linguistic elements for its existence. Take away all language and Mt. Everest still has snow and ice near the summit; take away all language and you have taken away the fact that "Mt. Everest has snow and ice at the summit" is a sentence of English.

A second distinction we need is between *language-dependent thoughts* and *language-independent thoughts*. Some thoughts are language dependent in the sense that an animal could not have that very thought if the animal did not have words or some other linguistic devices for thinking that very thought, but some thoughts are language independent in the sense that an animal can have those thoughts without having words or any other linguistic devices. An obvious case of a language-dependent thought is the thought that "Mt. Everest has snow and ice at the summit" is a sentence of English. A being that did not have a language could not think that thought. The most obvious cases of language-independent thoughts are noninstitutional, primitive, biological inclinations and cognitions not requiring any linguistic devices. For example, an animal can have conscious feelings of hunger and thirst and each of these is a form of desire. Hunger is a desire to eat and thirst a desire to drink, and desires are intentional states with full intentional contents; in the contemporary jargon, they are "propositional attitudes." Furthermore, an animal can have prelinguistic perceptions and prelinguistic beliefs derived from these perceptions. My dog can see and smell a cat run up a tree and form the belief that the cat is up the tree. He can even correct the belief and form a new belief when he sees and smells that the cat has run into the neighbor's yard. Other cases of prelinguistic thoughts are emotions such as fear and rage. We ought to allow ourselves to be struck both by the fact that animals can have prelinguistic thoughts and by the fact that some thoughts are language dependent and cannot be had by prelinguistic beings.

With these distinctions in mind, let us restate the thesis we are trying to examine. I have argued that some facts that do not on the surface appear to be language dependent – facts about money and property, for example – are in fact language dependent. But how could they be language dependent since, unlike English sentences, money and property are not words nor are they composed of words?

It is a sufficient condition for a *fact* to be language dependent that two conditions be met. First, mental representations, such as thoughts, must be partly constitutive of the fact; and second, the representations in question must be language dependent. It follows immediately from the structure of constitutive rules that the first of these conditions is met by institutional facts. From the fact that the status function specified by the Y term can be fulfilled only if it is recognized, accepted, acknowledged, or otherwise believed in, it follows that the institutional fact in question can exist only if it is represented as existing. Ask yourself what must be the case in order that it be true that the piece of paper in my hand is a twenty dollar bill or that Tom owns a house, and you will see that there must be mental representations as partly constitutive of these facts. These facts can exist only if people have certain sorts of beliefs and other mental attitudes. This is what I was driving at earlier when I said that a type of thing is money only if people believe it is money; something is property only if people believe it is property. All institutional facts are, in this sense, ontologically subjective, even though in general they are epistemically objective.

But what about the second condition? Must the representations in question be language dependent? The satisfaction of the first condition does not by itself entail the satisfaction of the second. A fact could contain mental states as constitutive features and still not be linguistic. For example, suppose we arbitrarily create a word "dogbone" to mean a bone desired by at least one dog. Then the fact that such and such is a dogbone is in part constituted by some canine mental state. But there is nothing necessarily linguistic about such mental states, because dogs can desire bones without any language in which to express the desire.

So what is the difference between dogbones and money, for example? Why does the belief that something is money require language for its very existence in the way that the desire for a bone does not? What exactly must happen in order for me to think, "This is money"? We saw in Chapter 2 that I do not need the word "money" itself, so the word does not have to figure in its own definition. But why do I still have to have some words or wordlike elements to think the thoughts? This is not a trivial question. The answer to it can derive only from the character of the move from X to Y when we count some X as having the status function named by the Y term. The answer, in short, must come from an understanding of the nature of status functions. The answer I will give, to anticipate a bit, is that the move from X to Y is *eo ipso* a linguistic move, even in cases that apparently have nothing to do with language.

Why Are Any Thoughts Language Dependent?

Our original thesis, that institutional facts are language dependent, boils down to the thesis that the thoughts that are constitutive of institutional facts are language dependent. But why? What is the argument? Let's begin by asking, why are *any* thoughts, other than thoughts about linguistic elements themselves, language dependent? There are different sorts of cases.

First, some thoughts are of such complexity that it would be *empirically impossible* to think them without being in possession of symbols. Mathematical thoughts, for example, require a system of symbols. It would be extremely difficult and probably impossible for a prelinguistic beast to think even such a simple arithmetical thought as that

$$371 + 248 = 619.$$

But these are cases of empirical difficulty. Because of the way we are constituted, complex abstract thoughts require words and symbols. I see no *logical* impossibility in thinking such a thought without language. It is easy to imagine that the course of evolution might produce beings who can think of complex arithmetical relations without using symbols.

Another sort of case involves language as a matter of *logical necessity*, because the linguistic expression of the thought is essential to its being the thought that it is. For example, consider the thought "Today is Tuesday the 26th of October." Such a thought requires a quite definite set of words or their synonyms in English and other languages because the content of the thought locates a day in relation to a specific verbal system for identifying days and months. That is why my dog cannot think "Today is Tuesday the 26th of October."

We who are in possession of the relevant vocabulary can translate the expression "Tuesday the 26th of October" into French but not into another radically different calendar, such as the Mayan. The Mayans, using their system, could have identified an actual day we call "Tuesday the 26th of October," but their thought does not translate into "Tuesday the 26th of October." Same reference, different sense.

The thought is language dependent because the corresponding fact is language dependent. There is no fact of the matter about its being Tuesday the 26th of October except the fact that it occupies a position relative to a verbal system. "But," one might say, "exactly the same is true of, for example, dogs and cats. Something is correctly called a 'dog' or a 'cat' only relative to a linguistic system. Something is a dog only relative to a system for identifying animals and objects generally." There is this crucial difference: The features that an object has *in virtue of which the word "dog" is true of it, i.e., the features in virtue of which it is a dog, are features that exist independently of language.* And to the extent that one can think of those features independently of a language, one can have that thought independently of language. But the features in virtue of which today is Tuesday the 26th of October cannot exist independently of a verbal system, because its being Tuesday the 26th of October is a matter of its relation to a verbal system. If there were no verbal system, there would be no such fact, even though this day remains the day that it is regardless of what anybody thinks or says. In short, this thought is language dependent because part of the content of the thought is that this day satisfies conditions that exist only relative to words.

The fact that today is Tuesday the 26th of October is not an institutional fact because, though the day is institutionally identified as such, no new status function is carried by the label.* Now let us consider institutional facts. I am claiming that the thoughts that this is a twenty dollar bill and that this is my property require a language as a matter of conceptual necessity. I am claiming that such thoughts are like thoughts about today's date in that they are essentially language dependent. Why?

Games and Institutional Reality

To argue for this claim, I want to begin by considering some fairly simple facts regarding games, because they illustrate the points I want to make. Consider the case of points scored in a game such as football. We say "a touchdown counts six points." Now, that is not a thought that anyone could have without linguistic symbols. But, to repeat, why? Because points can exist only relative to a linguistic system for representing and counting points, and thus we can think about points only if we are in possession of the linguistic apparatus necessary for such a system. But that pushes the question further back. Why can points exist only relative to such a linguistic system? The answer, to put it simply, is that if you take away all the symbolic devices for representing points, there is nothing else there. There is just the system for representing and counting points. That would be misleading if it gave us the impression that points are just words. That is not right. The words have consequences. People try desperately hard to score points in a way they would not try for mere words, because the points determine victory and defeat, and thus are the occasion of emotions ranging from ecstasy to despair. Mere words, it seems, could not be the focus of such deep feelings. But there is no thought independent of the words or other symbols to the effect that we have scored six points. The points might be represented by some symbolic devices other than actual words, for example, we might count points by assembling piles of stones, one stone for each point. But then the stones would be as much linguistic symbols as would any others. They would have the three essential features of linguistic symbols: they *symbolize* something beyond themselves, they do so by *convention*, and they are *public*.

There are no prelinguistic perceptions of points, nor prelinguistic beliefs about points, because there is nothing there to perceive or have beliefs about except the relevant symbolic devices. The animal cannot prelinguistically see points the way it can see the cat up the tree, nor can it prelinguistically desire points the way it desires food.

But why could an animal not just be born with a prelinguistic desire to score points in football games as animals are born with prelinguistic desires to drink their mother's milk? The answer is that the desire to score points has no content independently of a socially accepted system of representing and counting points. Take away all symbolic systems for counting points and you have taken away all possible beliefs, desires, and thoughts generally about points. Later I will argue that what is true of points in football games is true of money, property, and other institutional phenomena.

Our difficulty in seeing these facts derives in part from a certain model we have of how language works. The model works for a large number of cases and therefore we think it must work in all cases. Here is the model: There are words and other expressions, these have senses or meanings, and in virtue of these senses they have referents. For example, there is an expression "The Evening Star"; it has a sense or meaning; in virtue of that meaning, when we think or utter the expression we refer to or think about the language-independent object, the Evening Star. On this model, if you can think the sense or meaning without the words, then you can think of the referent without the words. All you have to do is detach the sense or meaning from the expression and just think the sense or meaning. And it seems we must *always* be able to detach the meaning because we can translate the expression into other languages, and this translatability seems to prove that there is a detachable, thinkable sense that can attach now to English now to German words, etc. The model gives us the impression that there are no such things as thoughts that are necessarily language dependent, because it seems any expression in any language can be translated into other languages, and this seems to imply that the thinkable sense is always detachable from the speakable or writable expression.

Whatever its other limitations, this model does not work for institutional facts. In the case of scoring points in games, we can see clearly why it does not work. Even if we don't have words for "man," "line," "ball," etc., we can see that man cross that line carrying that ball, and thus we can think a thought without words, which thought we would report in the words "The man crossed the line carrying the ball." But we cannot in addition see the man score six points because there is nothing in addition to see. The expression "six points" does not refer to some language-independent objects in the way that the expressions "the man," "the ball," "the line," and "The Evening Star" refer to language-independent objects. Points are not "out there" in the way that planets, men, balls, and lines are out there.

I hope the reader shares my intuitions so far, because I now want to state the general principle that underlies them. At the lowest level, the shift from the X to the Y in the move that creates institutional facts is a move from a brute level to an institutional level. That shift, as I have emphasized over and over, can exist only if it is represented as existing. But there can be no prelinguistic way to represent the Y element because there is nothing there prelinguistically that one can perceive or otherwise attend to in addition to the X element, and there is nothing there prelinguistically to be the target of desire or inclination in addition to the X element. Without a language, we can see the man cross a white line holding a ball, and without language we can want a man to cross a white line holding a ball. But we cannot see the man score six points or want the man to score six points without language, because points are not something that can be thought of or that can exist independently of words or other sorts of markers. And what is true of points in games is true of money, governments, private property, etc., as we will see.

The lessons from this example can now be extended to institutional facts in general. The very design of status functions is such that they both are partly constituted by thoughts and that prelinguistic forms of thought are inadequate to do the job. The reason is that they exist only by way of collective agreement, and there can be no prelinguistic way of formulating the content of the agreement, because there is no prelinguistic natural phenomenon there. The Y term creates a status that is additional to the physical features of the X term, and that status has to provide reasons for action that are independent of our natural inclinations. The status exists only if people believe it exists, and the reasons function only if people accept them as reasons. Therefore, the agent must have some way to represent the new status. He cannot do it in terms of prelinguistic brute features of the X term. He can't get from thoughts just about the color and the shape of the dollar bill to the status "money" any more than he can get from thoughts just about the movement of the man with the ball to the status "touchdown, six points." Because the new status exists only by convention, there must be some conventional way to represent the status or the system will not work. "But why couldn't the X term itself be the conventional way to represent the new status?" The answer is that it could, *but to assign that role to the X term is precisely to assign it a symbolizing or linguistic status.*

Notice that status functions differ from causal agentive functions in regard to their language dependency. One can think that this is a screwdriver without any words or other linguistic devices because one can just think that this thing is used to screw in these other things. No words at all are logically necessary to treat and use an object as a screwdriver because its ability to so function is a matter of its brute physical structure.

But in the case of status functions, there is no structural feature of the X element sufficient by itself to determine the Y function. Physically X and Y are exactly the same thing. The only difference is that we have imposed a status on the X element, and this new status needs *markers*, because, empirically speaking, there isn't anything else there.

To summarize: Because the Y level of the shift from X to Y in the creation of institutional facts has no existence apart from its representation, we need some way of representing it. But there is no natural prelinguistic way to represent it, because the Y element has no natural prelinguistic features in addition to the X element that would provide the means of representation. So we have to have words or other symbolic means to perform the shift from the X to the Y status.

I believe these points can be made clearer by calling attention to the deontic status of institutional phenomena. Animals running in a pack can have all the consciousness and collective intentionality they need. They can even have hierarchies and a dominant male; they can cooperate in the hunt, share their food, and even have pair bonding. But they cannot have marriages, property or money. Why not? Because all these create institutional forms of powers, rights, obligations, duties, etc., and it is characteristic of such phenomena that they create reasons for action that are independent of what you or I or anyone else is otherwise inclined to do. Suppose I train my dog to chase dollar bills and bring them back to me in return for food. He still is not buying the food and the bills are not money to him. Why not? Because he cannot represent to himself the relevant deontic phenomena. He might be able to think "If I give him this he will give me that food." But he cannot think, for example, now I have the *right to buy* things and when someone else has this, he will also have the right to buy things.

Furthermore, such deontic phenomena are not reducible to something more primitive and simple. We cannot analyze or eliminate them in favor of dispositions to behave or fears of negative consequences of not doing something. Famously, Hume and many others have tried to make such eliminations, but without success.

I have argued in this chapter that institutional facts in general require language because the language is partly constitutive of the facts. But let us turn the question around. Could there be any institutional facts that are not language dependent, genuine facts satisfying our formula, X counts as Y, where the Y term imposes a new status by collective intentionality, but where the intentionality in question is not language dependent? Well, what about our first example of the physical barrier, the wall, that decays into a purely symbolic barrier, the line of stones? Isn't that an example of an institutional fact without language? This depends on how the tribe regards the line of stones. If, just as a matter of fact, they are not disposed to cross the line but just avoid crossing it out of habit, then they do not need a language for such a disposition. Prelinguistic animals, for example, can be trained not to cross certain boundaries, and many species of animals have natural ways, amazingly various, of marking territorial boundaries. As Broom writes, "The demarcation of a territory may be visual as in cleaner fish and other reef fish, auditory as in many birds, olfactory as in scent marking by many mammals, or electrical as in electric fish" (1981, 196–7). If our imagined tribe just is not disposed to cross the boundaries as a matter of inclination, they do not in our sense have an institutional fact. They simply have a disposition to behave in certain ways, and their behavior is just like the case of animals marking the limits of their territory. There is nothing deontic about such markings. The animals simply behave in such and such ways, and "behave" here means they simply move their bodies in specific ways.

But if we suppose that the members of the tribe recognize that the line of stones creates rights and obligations, that they are *forbidden* to cross the line, that they are *not supposed to* cross it, then we have symbolization. The stones now symbolize something beyond themselves; they function like words. I do not think there is a sharp dividing line between either the institutional and the non-institutional or the linguistic and the prelinguistic, but to the extent that we think the phenomena are genuinely institutional facts, and not just conditioned forms of habitual behavior, to that very extent we must think of language as constitutive of the phenomena, because the move that imposes the Y function on the X object is a symbolizing move.

Does Language Require Language?

The account so far, however, seems to leave us in a fix. I have said that institutional facts require language because language is constitutive of the facts. But linguistic facts are also institutional facts. So it looks as if language requires language. Does this not lead to an infinite regress or another form of circularity? We got out of the first charge of circularity – the apparent circularity that defining institutional concepts such as "money" seemed to require those very concepts in the definition – by widening the circle to include other institutional concepts. How do we get out of this charge of circularity?

The short, but unsatisfactory-sounding, answer to this question is that language does not need language because it already is language. Now, let me explain what that means. The requirement that there be linguistic markers for institutional facts is the requirement that there be some conventional way for the participants in the institution to mark the fact that the X element now has the Y status. Since there is nothing in the physics of the X element that gives it the Y function, since the status is only by collective agreement, and since the status confers deontic properties that are not physical properties, the status cannot exist without markers. Those markers are now partly constitutive of the status. There needs to be some way to mark the fact that the man holding the ball has scored a touchdown, and that a touchdown counts six points. There is nothing in the physics of the situation that makes it apparent. And this is not an epistemic but an ontological point. Similarly, there is nothing in the physical relations between me and a piece of land that makes it my property. There is nothing in the chemical composition of this piece of paper that makes it a twenty dollar bill. So we have to have some symbolic devices for marking these institutional facts. But now, what about the symbolic devices themselves? How are they to be marked as symbolic? If it is true, as it surely is, that there is nothing in the physical structure of the piece of paper that makes it a five dollar bill, nothing in the physical structure of the piece of land that makes it my property, then it is also true that there is nothing in the acoustics of the sounds that come out of my mouth or the physics of the marks that I make on paper that makes them into words or other sorts of symbols.

The solution to our puzzle is to see that language is precisely designed to be a self-identifying category of institutional facts. The child is brought up in a culture where she learns to treat the sounds that come out of her own and others' mouths as standing for, or meaning something, or representing something. And this is what I was driving at when I said that language doesn't require language in order to be language because it already is language. But doesn't this only force our question back further? Why can't all institutional facts have this self-identifying character of language? Why can't the child just be brought up to regard this as so-and-so's private property, or this physical object as money? The answer is, she can. But precisely to the extent that she does, she is treating the object as symbolizing something beyond itself; she is treating it as at least partly linguistic in character.

The move from the brute to the institutional status is *eo ipso* a linguistic move, because the X term now symbolizes something beyond itself. But that symbolic move requires thoughts. In order to think the thought that constitutes the move from the X term to the Y status, there must be a vehicle of the thought. You have to have something to think with. The physical features of the X term are insufficient for the content of the thought, but any object whatever that can be conventionally used and thought of as the bearer of that content can be used to think the thought. The best objects to think with are words, because that is part of what words are for. Indeed, it is a condition for something to be a word that it be thinkable. But strictly speaking, any conventional marker will do. Though it is easy to think in words, it is hard to think in people, mountains, etc., because they have too many irrelevant features and they are too unmanageable. So we use real words or we can use wordlike markers as vehicles of thought. Using words, we say, "That is my property," "He is the chairman," etc. But words like "property" and "chairman" don't stand for prelinguistic objects in the way that "The Evening Star" stands for The Evening Star. Sometimes we put labels or symbols on the X element itself. The labels say, e.g., "This note is legal tender for all debts public and private." But that representation is now, at least in part, a declaration: it creates the institutional status by representing it as existing. It does not represent some prelinguistic natural phenomenon.

We can treat the X object itself as having the Y status by convention, as we can treat coins as money, or the line of stones as a boundary, but to do that is already to assign a linguistic status, because the objects now are conventional public symbols of something beyond themselves; they symbolize a deontic status beyond the physics. And all the cases I can think of where the X term is in this way self-identifying have the essential features of words: the type-token distinction applies, the X elements are readily recognizable, they are easily thinkable, and we see them as symbolizing the Y status by convention.

From the time of preliterate societies to the present, there have been lots of conventional markers that are not words but function just like words. Here are half a dozen examples: In the Middle Ages felons had their right palms branded to identify them as such. This is why we have to raise our right hand while taking an oath in court, so everybody can see that we are not felons. Priests had a bald spot shaved at the top of their head to mark the fact that they were priests. Kings wore crowns, husbands and wives wear wedding rings, cattle are branded, and lots of people wear uniforms as markers of their status.

The entire argument of this chapter has produced a strange result. I am not entirely comfortable with it, but here it is. The move from X to Y is already linguistic in nature because once the function is imposed on the X element, it now symbolizes something else, the Y function. This move can exist only if it is collectively represented as existing. The collective representation is public and conventional, and it requires some vehicle. Just scrutinizing or imaging the features of the X element will not do the job. So we need words, such as "money," "property," etc., or we need wordlike symbols, such as those we just considered, or in the limiting case we treat the X elements themselves as *conventional representations* of the Y function. To the extent we can do that, they must be either words or symbols themselves or enough like words to be *both* bearers of the Y function and representations of the move from X to Y.

The account also has this consequence: the capacity to attach a sense, a symbolic function, to an object that does not have that sense intrinsically is the precondition not only of language but of all institutional reality. The preinstitutional capacity to symbolize is the condition of possibility of the creation of all human institutions. In certain contexts, uttering the sounds "the cat is on the mat" counts as making the statement that the cat is on the mat, and in certain contexts crossing the line while holding the ball counts as scoring a touchdown. Both are cases of the creation of institutional facts according to the formula. The difference in the two cases is that the creation of a speech act is the creation of something with further representational capacities, but in that sense points scored in games do not stand for something beyond themselves. Statements can be true or false, but touchdowns do not in that way have semantic properties.

Typically the "stands for" relation requires the existence of some object that exists independently of the symbol that stands for it, but in the case of institutional reality at the lowest level, the practice of attaching a sense to an object according to the constitutive rules creates the very category of potential referents. Symbols do not create cats and dogs and evening stars; they create only the possibility of referring to cats, dogs, and evening stars in a publicly accessible way. But symbolization creates the very ontological categories of money, property, points scored in games and political offices, as well as the categories of words, and speech acts. Once the categories are created, we can have the same sense/reference distinctions that we have for evening stars, etc.

Thus we can refer or fail to refer to "the touchdown we scored at the end of the fourth quarter" or "the President of the United States" in the same way we can succeed or fail to refer to "The Evening Star," but the difference is that the creation of the category of touchdowns and presidents is already achieved by the structures according to which we attach status functions to the X terms, because the existence of these features is created by attachment of the status functions.

Think of it this way: What stands to the sound "cat" as its meaning is what stands to the piece of paper as its function as a dollar bill. However, the sound "cat" has a *referential* function that the piece of paper does not have. For example, the sound can occur in sentences where the speaker in uttering the sentence refers to a cat. Pieces of paper, even pieces of paper construed as dollar bills, are not in that way used to refer. But the practice of using pieces of paper as dollar bills creates a class of entities that cannot exist without the practice. It creates the class of entities: dollar bills. In order that the practice should exist, people must be able to think the thought "This piece of paper is a dollar bill," and that is a thought they cannot think without words or other symbols, even if the only symbol in question is the object itself.

Other Functions of Language in Institutional Facts

This discussion has been very abstract and has concerned the conditions of the possibility of the creation of institutional reality, linguistic or otherwise. But if we consider actual natural languages such as French or German and the actual complexity of social institutions, we can see several other reasons why institutional facts require language.

First, language is epistemically indispensable.

I said that in the structure of institutional facts we impose a Y status function on the X term, which it does not perform solely in virtue of its physical constitution. But now how are we to tell which entities have this status function imposed on them? For many causal agentive functions – not all – it is reasonably easy to tell which objects are chairs, tables, hammers, and screwdrivers because you can read off the function from the physical structure. But when it comes to money, husbands, university professors, and privately owned real estate, you cannot read off the function or status from the physics. You need labels. In order that we can *recognize* bits of paper as money, for example, we must have some linguistic or symbolic way of representing the newly created facts about functions, because they cannot be read off from the physics of the objects themselves. The recognition of the fact that something is money requires that it be linguistically or symbolically represented. I will have more to say about this feature in the next chapter, when we discuss what I call "status indicators."

Second, the facts in question, being inherently social, must be communicable.

If the systems are to function, then the newly created facts must be communicable from one person to another, even when invisible to the naked eye. You must be able to tell people that you are married, that you are the chairman, that the meeting is adjourned if the system is to function. Even in simple cases of institutional facts, this communicability requires a means of public communication, a language.

Third, in real life the phenomena in question are extremely complex, and the representation of such complex information requires language.

Even the most apparently simple act of buying and selling has great complexity, as we saw in our example of ordering beer in a cafe at the beginning of the book. Because the structure of the facts exists only to the extent that it is represented, complex facts require a complex system of representation for their existence; and such complex systems of representation are languages.

Fourth, the facts in question persist through time independently of the duration of the urges and inclinations of the participants in the institution.

This continued existence requires a means of representation of the facts that is independent of the more primitive prelinguistic psychological states of the participants, and such representations are linguistic.

Note

* Some names for dates are labels for status functions, for example, "Christmas," or "Thanksgiving." Such labels do more than identify a day relative to a verbal system; they also assign a status to which functions attach.

Reference

Broom, Donald M. 1981. *The Biology of Behavior: Mechanisms, Functions and Applications.* Cambridge: Cambridge University Press.

PART II

PSYCHOLOGICAL APPROACHES

INTRODUCTION TO PART II

Psychological approaches interpret or explain myths in terms that concern the mental world of the human individual. They strive to "make sense" of myth through psychological methods or theories, that is, by appealing to the human psyche as the locus of origin of myths. Psychological approaches have been undertaken not only by psychologists, but also by many others who employ psychological methods or theories, or just appeal to the human psyche as the origin and location of myth. "Where else?" might one ask. But the main characteristic of a psychological approach is that it interprets and explains myth from the perspective of the individual *only*, that is, it applies an individualist methodology. A rather broad range of approaches can be termed psychological, because any attempt to understand myth that points to the human "mind," human "intuition," "emotion," etc. as its foundation is a psychological approach. Not surprising, an individualist methodology proceeds from what can be said based on the study of the individual. What is more important to note, in a philosophy of science perspective, is that the relevant theoretical terms and modes of explanation are restricted to what concerns and refers to individuals *only*. Thus, in a strict individualist methodology, sociological and cultural levels of explanation are not only considered irrelevant, but they may even be seen as disturbing factors to be eliminated in order to sort out the purely individual. This demonstrates how critical the border between psychological and sociological approaches may be when seen in a strict theoretical perspective. Theories are like languages – you can only speak one at a time. However, you may also create new hybrid languages and new complex methods. Many divisions between disciplines and methodologies are now being bridged as may be seen in the last chapter of this volume. From a more moderated point of view it is obvious that most things human are many-faceted and that the study of them needs a well-stocked toolbox. This goes for myth as well as for religion, culture or society.[1] It is not always easy to classify an approach in a decisive and singular manner. Some of the contributions in this volume could have been placed in several sections simultaneously, but as this would indeed make strange reading I had to make some decisions that were not always easy, nor perhaps entirely beyond the range of suspicion and correction.

In a broad sense, one could view most of the history of the study of myth as psychologically oriented, for it is only recently that other approaches have appeared. In antiquity, most of the approaches to and interpretations of myth were of a psychological nature. Certainly, some were metaphorical and allegorical, but these were also often linked to psychological explanations, because they dealt with human moral and mental behaviour, with feelings and experiences. From antiquity to the late nineteenth century, the study of myth was parallel to that of the study of religion in general in terms of methodology.[2] Some of the major contributors to the development of the modern academic study of religion, e.g. Fr. Max Müller, Herbert Spencer, Edward B. Tylor and James G. Frazer, were clearly concerned with myth and in a psychological perspective. The main components of the "spirit of the age" were historicism, evolutionism and comparativism and this meant that scholars worked on questions concerning origins, developments and comparison. Their primary method in research was comparison, for by applying contemporary conceptions of the "savages" scholars produced their theories about the origins of humankind. The "primitives" or the "savages" were imagined to represent the childhood of humanity and from there on, the stages of cultural and social evolution could be envisioned. Much of their scholarship was conjectural and the sweeping generalizations that were put before the audiences were often based on introspective speculation. As E. E. Evans-Pritchard stated – on Herbert Spencer's idea that the origin of religion was ancestor-worship: "The argument is *a priori* speculation, sprinkled with some illustrations, and is specious. It is a fine example of the introspectionist psychologist's, or 'if I were a horse', fallacy, to which I shall have to make frequent reference" (1965, 24). The main reason for classifying these early theorists of myth and religion as representing psychological approaches – when they were overtly working with cultural traits, etymologies and comparative studies – is that they uniformly focused on, or took their departure from beliefs, imaginations, and other workings of the individual minds of their imagined early humans.

In this context, some scholars deserve mention for setting the stage for a more comprehensive grasp of the ideas presented in the contributions below. Originally trained as a doctor and later regarded as one of the founders of ethnography, Adolf Bastian (1826–1905) developed the psychological concept of "Elementargedanken" – elementary ideas, conceived as imaginary extensions of the body and common to all humans. Bastian travelled extensively around the globe and wrote a number of books on issues that also touch upon mythologies (e.g. Polynesian). In contrast to the general climate of thought, his main thesis was not evolutionist; it proceeded from the principle of the psychic unity of all humankind and with the environment as responsible for the outcome of cultural differences and how elementary thoughts were expressed.

Another prominent scholar in the history of psychologically based interpretations of culture, religion and myth was Wilhelm Wundt (1832–1920). Later recognized as the founder of experimental psychology he wrote the monumental work *Völkerpsychologie* (1904) in which he also took up language, religion and myth as specific subjects. His views deserve mention not only because they were typical of his time but also because they influenced a whole generation of other scholars. In Wundt's perspective, the mythical fantasy images are fixed in the cult and thus they become norms in the collective life. Wundt's romantic inspiration drove him to consider myth on a par with poetry and art. Myth was collective and involuntary whereas art was individual and voluntary. The myths of the "primitives" belong to the domain of imagination and to the realm of play, which he considered an expression of a childish mentality, as well as innate and individually based. Emblematic of his time, he overlooked the social nature of the phenomena he addressed. This is interesting as he explicitly took on what would later be seen as a collective phenomenon: "Völkerpsychologie" – the psychology of "peoples." In Wundt's view, a collective was composed of individuals who were all endowed with a general fantasy aptitude and this sufficed to explain myth as a human phenomenon. He never addressed why individual "fantasies" would converge and become more stable and socially distributed representations.

Sir James George Frazer, a classicist turned anthropologist, was a genuine spokesman of the comparative and psychological approach to mythology. Whereas the comparative aspects of his work are easily detected – comparisons abound everywhere – the psychological theorizing remains implicit, but it is thoroughly based on the then current psychological views on how "primitive man" thinks. Much of his argument depends on how myths, to their audience, represent or associate the fate of gods with fertility, the cycles of agriculture or the movements of celestial bodies. But perhaps the savages and the primitives were not quite so backwards. In 1930 Ludwig Wittgenstein said: "Frazer is much more savage than most of his savages, for these savages will not be so far from any understanding of spiritual matter as an Englishman of the twentieth century. His explanations of the primitive observances are much cruder than the sense of the observances themselves" (1979, 8e).

Sigmund Freud (1856–1939) occupies a very special position in the study of myth. As can be seen in the contribution below, Freud held a critical view on myth and religion, and many scholars in the history of religions and anthropology have been sceptical about the validity of Freud's theories as well as of the use of psychoanalytic methods in the study of cultural, social and religious matters. They were unconvinced because Freud's theory is "culture-blind" and because the method seems to provide circular confirmations of the premises of the theory. The key feature in Freud's view of myth is his analysis of symbolism in dreams, with which myths are compared. Dreams as well as myths present symbols and distorted images that express unconscious and repressed wishes. These images and symbols are primarily related to sexuality as Freud opined that the entire humanity was oppressed by its sexual needs. Thus, many myths are to be seen as covert messages about castration, homosexuality, and penis envy and, above all, the Oedipus complex. Psychoanalysis thus provides a method for deciphering those hidden messages as if they are uttered in a forgotten language. The parallels between psychological and socio-cultural phenomena were crafted with no small degree of conviction, as noted in William Doty's remarks on the work of the anthropologist Géza Róheim:

> Cultural elements such as myths and rites are to be understood as being based upon the same sorts of psychological mechanisms that underlie the various types of personal neuroses, and Róheim notes approvingly Freud's threefold comparison of paranoia to philosophy, compulsion neurosis to religion, and hysteria to art. (1986, 145)

To what should we then compare psychoanalysis? Its proponents were convinced that they were nothing but scientific, whereas philosophers such as Karl Popper deemed psychoanalysis an example of "pseudo-science" (along with Marxism). In spite of the interpretive excesses it must be noted that Freud's psychoanalytic work, as well as that of his followers, have had an immense influence upon the twentieth century (and later) convictions and the ways in which "we think now," not only about persons and their feelings and motives, but also about myths and mythologies.[3] With the advent of psychoanalysis and the "invention of the subconscious," a whole new discourse was born about humanity, a discourse characterized by a "hermeneutics of suspicion" for things were no longer what they had seemed to be. There are things hidden in this world, not least in the depth of the human psyche. There was a "new," hidden "language" to be discovered, remnants of some original human condition, which could now be recovered in dream analysis. This, however, demands shrewdness on the part of the analyst and so Freud, as also indicated in the text below, resorts to profoundly semiotic and hermeneutic exercises in his attempts to unlock the secrets of the unconscious. Most of the materials of dream-analysis turned out to be about sex – in Freud's time and in the European bourgeois culture all this was outrageous. Freud is included in this collection not least in order to address the ramifications of that new and different understanding and explanation of the workings of the human psyche and myth. To a certain extent most modern, public ("folk-psychology") discourse is so saturated with Freudian assumptions about the human mental life that a closer look at Freud's position has merit in the service of unravelling these hidden assumptions of our own. Although Freud was deeply concerned with origins (that betrays his nineteenth-century heritage) the psychoanalytic perspective can be more fruitfully drawn on in the study or analysis of the psychodynamics of the groups where the myths are alive and reproduced over the generations (see e.g. Clastres and Hutchins, this volume). In that perspective, psychological analyses can supplement the sociological and anthropological in that they address different aspects of complex phenomena.

Rudolf Otto (1869–1937) was, among his many other activities, engaged in a theologically motivated psychological study of religious belief. He did not write much on myth but his apologetic views of religion and individual religiosity has been influential during decades and surface repeatedly among scholars such as Mircea Eliade. Although the psychologist Carl Gustav Jung explicitly worked on myth(s), his work is not represented in this volume in the form of a contribution. The main reason for this omission is that there is ample literature on Jung and his views on symbols and myths; they are comprehensively and competently dealt with by others in detailed studies.[4] He began as a follower of Freud but he did not share Freud's obsession with sexuality and developed a positive view on religion and mythology as important means of human self-understanding and with a positive potential in therapeutic practice. However, a fair part of the literature on Jung and myth have applied his ideas constructively and so contributed to the therapeutic project more than to the study of myth *per se*. A psychological approach to myth may not only take its point of departure in the psyche, but it may also have the psyche so clearly as its theoretical object that it says much less about myth than about, as in Jung's case, matters pertaining to depth psychology, or "analytic psychology" as it is also called. Among Jung's major concepts are the two well known of the "collective unconsciousness" and "archetypes," both revealed in dreams and in myths; they, and others, display the structure and function of the human psyche, the "objective psyche" of humanity in contrast to the individual or subjective psyche. The theory is thoroughly universalist, that is, symbols and signs mean the same everywhere; the archetypes are transhistorical and transpersonal. They are found all over the world because they represent common psychic phenomena and Jung's theory holds the key (Jung 1964). At times, the analyses presented were stranger than the stories analysed. However, Jung's work and its effective history also represent a case of modern mythmaking in itself.

The work of Mircea Eliade is commonly perceived as belonging to the history of religions or to the phenomenology of religion but rarely as psychological. The reason for including his work in the present category is that Eliade's *theory* is thoroughly psychological however obliquely this may emerge. Although he never clearly defined religion, he did speak of it as "a structure in the human consciousness," and his works are replete with observations, explanations and interpretations in psychological terms and modes. In several contexts Eliade noted how "depth psychology" has paved the way for the comparative and general study of religion and freed the historians of religion of their last hesitations towards comparative studies. For Eliade it is the unity of the human psyche that makes it all possible.

The psychology of religion is an established academic discipline, but the focus of research is rarely on myth. Therefore, the contribution from that discipline is – somewhat unfortunately – scarce. Some of the contributions to the section on "Cognitive approaches" might equally have been termed psychological, as cognitive studies are closely related to and in a large measure spring from psychology. However, none of these contributions are supplied by psychologists of religion.

Contributions

Friedrich Max Müller

Fr. Max Müller (1823–1900) was born in Germany in a deeply Romanticist milieu with all the passion for emotion, for nature, for the ancients in mythology and history, as well as for the exotic. Müller studied philology, specializing in Sanskrit, in Berlin and Paris before moving to England in 1847 where he later became the first professor of comparative philology at Oxford in 1868. All his interests converged in the many works (about one hundred in all!) on language, myth, religion and Ancient India. He was fascinated with origins and developments – but not an evolutionist in Darwinian terms. As many others at the time, his method of making wild comparisons have to this day stamped the comparative study of religion and myth as problematic. For Müller, mythology is primarily about nature, and his approach was consequently termed "Nature mythology" (e.g. Evans-Pritchard 1965, 20–23). Solar mythology was awarded a special position, so much that a colleague jokingly wrote an introduction where he "proved" that Müller himself was but a solar myth(!). His theory of the origin of mythology is peculiar. It is often referred to as the "disease of language" hypothesis as the idea is that "the ancients" at some point began to personify and then deify natural phenomena, so that out of "nomina" (words) they made "numina" (sacred entities). The key to myth was, then, to trace that disease backwards and discover that Zeus "really" was thunder and Apollo "really" is the sun etc. and so etymology becomes the royal method. The names were thought to have singular, traceable referents and once that reference is found, the mystery is solved. This did, of course, lead to eccentric interpretations and conclusions (Müller 1856). Müller is often credited as being the founder of the history of religions as an academic discipline, but this is an erroneous assumption (Masuzawa 1993, 58–59). His slogan for comparative religion was "He who knows one, knows none" and this did mark a break from the study of religion as almost exclusively about Christianity on to a much broader history of religions, a new academic field that attracted immense popular attention.[5] To Müller's merits also counts his editorship of the massive series (50 volumes) *The Sacred Books of the East*, where large collections of religious scriptures in many and difficult Oriental languages were made available to an eager Western audience. Among the later criticisms of his work are not those that concern his sweeping comparisons, generalizations and conjectures about origins. More troubling are the racist ideas implicit in his work (and in those of many of his contemporaries) on the relations between languages and mentalities. The ancient Aryans were held to be especially creative and imaginative in poetry and myth because of the structure of Indo-European languages – in contrast to the Semitic languages which influenced their speakers to become more partial to ritual and monotheism (Lincoln 1999, 66–71). Müller's theories did not survive him, and as Masuzawa says "he is truly fossil, dead beyond controversy" (1993, 59) – but anyone with an interest in the history of the study of myth must know about Müller and "Nature mythology." Finally, I should clarify the reason for placing Müller in the section on "psychological approaches." Müller is normally credited for saying that language creates the gods, but this has to be modified, for in his theory language mirrors experience, and thus mythology reflects the mind such when he stated: "Let us now return to mythology in the narrower sense of the word. One of the earliest objects that would strike and stir the mind of man, and for which a sign or a name would soon be wanted, is surely the Sun."[6] As Masuzawa aptly sums up this overlooked aspect: "It is therefore no longer a matter of language generating a mythical being; on the contrary language takes a secondary, derivative position. A sign or a name merely follows and satisfies a psychological demand which precedes it" (1993, 74). Thus, philology becomes psychology.

Bronislaw Malinowski

Bronislaw Malinowski (1884–1942) grew up in an academic family in Krakow. His father was professor of Slavic philology who studied Polish dialects and folklore. The young Malinowski mostly lived with his mother who travelled much in the Mediterranean area but returned to Krakow where he received his doctorate in philosophy at the age in 1908 – a time when Poland did not yet exist as an independent nation. Then, for two years he studied at Leipzig where he was influenced by the folk psychology of Wilhelm Wundt and the then new discipline of anthropology. From 1910 he studied at the London School of Economics and in 1914 he went to pursue anthropological studies in Papua New Guinea (which subsequently earned him the DSc degree at LSE in 1916). In 1915 he moved to the Trobriand Islands to do more fieldwork but had to remain there, somewhat under duress, because as a national of the Austrian-Hungarian empire, he formally had enemy status. In 1922 he did a PhD in social anthropology and the book *Argonauts of the Western Pacific* was published and earned him instant fame. In 1927 he became the first professor of anthropology at the London School of Economics. The people he studied – the Trobrianders – were later to become "famous" among anthropologists and the general public, not least due to his marketing skills, such as when he published a book about kinship patterns and titled it *The Sexual Life of the Savages* or when he promoted social anthropology as an indispensable tool for the British colonial administration. Later he took up a position at Yale University and remained there until his death. It has been suggested that Malinowski's Romanticist ideas about the collective, cultural identities of nations and peoples are due to the fate of his homeland when he grew up (e.g. Lincoln 1999, 71–72). Malinowski did not invent anthropological fieldwork, as is sometimes asserted, but he made it the trademark of "modern anthropology" after Frazer. The present contribution might as well have been included in the section on sociological approaches, as Malinowski's views of myth equally focus on social aspects and functions of myth.[7] For instance, he coined the term "charter myth" as the designation for social myths that authorize and legitimate legal, political and economical rights and duties. For Malinowski, myth "is not an idle rhapsody…but a hard-working cultural force." It is so, not least because myth has a cognitive function in guiding humans in their lives, but also because it is an important element in the collective memory of the group. To Malinowski, myth, ritual and religion – as part of the total culture and society – serve to fulfil human needs. His perspective is clearly functionalist, of a psychological persuasion, because the needs he concentrates on are those of the individual, primarily emotional and cognitive. It is a central functionalist tenet that any cultural and social element must be considered in its relation to others, to the larger context. As we see, Malinowski is not content with reading myths as texts because the pragmatic aspects of the tale are "manifested as much in its enactment, embodiment, and context relations as in the text." This is the holistic perspective of later social anthropology taking shape; everything must be studied in its proper setting. On the other hand, this principle has as its corollary that comparison becomes fraught with difficulties, if not outright discredited. Malinowski's views on myth have lived on in large measure. As an anthropologist of repute he has (of course) been subjected to much criticism, but it is difficult not to recognize him as a creator of a new mode of myth analysis and one that set new methodological standards.

Sigmund Freud

Sigmund Freud (1856–1939) was first a medical doctor and later he became the originator of psychoanalysis. Whatever history has proved about the merits of his theory and therapeutic practice it cannot be denied that he was the founder of a new discourse about humanity. Many of his terms and concepts have entered ordinary public language in most of modern Western culture. From the outset Freud compared religion (and myth) to neurosis and he became more and more anti-religious. The contribution below is a sample of how the psychoanalytic method is applied to dreams as well as to narratives (Freud 1966). The anthropologist de Waal Malefijt explains the method: "The story is fragmented into its components: the key words ('symbols') are replaced by the appropriate sexual terms; and a new story emerges bearing the 'real' meaning of the original myth." She also gives a condensed example of an analysis of the well-known folk-tale, "Little Red Riding Hood" by one of Freud's followers, Erich Fromm as exemplary:

> Little Red-Cap is a maiden who has become sexually mature (red = menstruation), but she has had no sexual experience (she carries an unbroken bottle of wine to her grandmother = virginity). She meets a wolf (man) in the forest (trees = phalli). The wolf eventually eats her (aggressive intercourse), and, later on, he is punished by Red-Cap, who put stones (sterility) in his belly. He dies. The story symbolizes "the triumph of man-hating women, ending with their victory." (Malefijt 1968, 175)

The works of Freud and his followers and their "monolithic hermeneutic" represent, in their own way, a case of modern mythmaking. As far as the study of myth goes,

Freudian theories and methods of analysis belong mostly to the history of research. First, the theories have appeared starkly euro- and ethnocentric to many anthropologists and others working cross-culturally and, second, the catalogue of (mainly sexual) symbolic meanings with their direct one-to-one references is peculiarly problematic. This does not mean, however, that all psychoanalytic perspectives are irrelevant for an understanding of myth in context, when this is done with adequate cultural sensitivity – see e.g. Hutchins, this volume. That psychoanalytic theories are popular outside academic discourse only proves their myth-like qualities.

Mircea Eliade

Mircea Eliade (1907–86) was born in Romania. She graduated in philosophy and then (1928–32) went to Calcutta, India to study the Yogic tradition. After a complicated period before and during World War II, in various exiles (England, France, Portugal) and then associated with the Sorbonne in Paris (1946–55) Eliade ended (1957–87) as professor at the University of Chicago in the History of Religions, which was then a rather new field of study in the US. At Chicago he became responsible for training almost an entire generation of North American historians of religions. His life and work has been greatly, and at times hotly, debated. Few scholars have been so admired by some, controversial by others and therefore he and his work deeply divided opinions among fellow academics.[8] His personal life and political leanings towards the right have also been a topic of criticism. In terms of theory Eliade's perspective is decidedly universalist, the variations in religions and religious thought and practice are but different expressions of the same underlying essence. Analogously, his method is primarily comparative. His approach was encyclopaedic and it was only fitting that he became the general editor of the multi-volume *Encyclopedia of Religion* (2nd rev. ed. 2005). Eliade envisions religion as a genuine element of the human psyche in its natural state and therefore humankind has a drive towards life in a religious mode. Modern humans, who are not religious, are thus imperfect humans and they should long for or return to the original state. Eliade is thus both nostalgic and existentially normative. He was, however, theologically elusive – his view of religiosity seems at least to rest on a blend of elements from Gnosticism, orthodox Christianity and Indian Vedanta cosmology. One of his many catchphrases is a "New Humanism" by which he means a second Renaissance where the modern world would become spiritually enriched by inspiration from the East. In a sense Eliade is a forebear of later New Age spirituality. Eliade was not theoretically rigorous and never really defined religion but his general idea is that religion is a "structure in human consciousness." He views religion and mythology in terms of the individual and existentially, thus the reason for presenting his views in this section. The contribution is also chosen for the way in which it demonstrates his method: comparisons, analyses of symbols and the existential lesson he wishes to draw from the analysis of e.g. cosmogonies. It also highlights his passion for the rejection of history and the persistence of myth as humanly more valuable.

Notes

1. A good example to use in teaching is "food" as an item that anyone can refer to. It is a material phenomenon of nutrition, agriculture, fishing etc. and of economy, but it is also culturally defined and individually appreciated just to name some of the relevant aspects.
2. See Feldman and Richardson (2000) for a copious volume on the study of myth in the early modern period.
3. On Freudian myth analysis and his intellectual legacy in the study of religion see e.g. Doty 1986.
4. The literature on Jung is extensive: see e.g., on Jung and myth, the works by Robert Segal (1998 and 1999) and Doty (1986).
5. The fascination with comparative religion was an aspect of the Spirit of the Age that reigned around the beginning of the twentieth century. The public interest in this new and "emancipated" study of religion was remarkable in many European countries, not least in Germany, France and the UK.
6. Quote in Masuzawa (1993, 74) with a reference to his lecture "Philosophy of Mythology" from 1871.
7. For both Malinowski and Eliade on myth see Strenski (1987), and the review by Grottanelli (1990).
8. Rennie (1996) sums up most of the points of the debate on Eliade.

References

Doty, William G. 1986. *Mythography: The Study of Myths and Rituals.* Tuscaloosa: University of Alabama Press.

Evans-Pritchard, E. E. 1965. *Theories of Primitive Religion.* Oxford: Oxford University Press.

Feldman, Burton and Robert D. Richardson, eds. 2000 (orig. 1972). *The Rise of Modern Mythology, 1680–1860.* Indiana: Indiana University Press

Freud, Sigmund. 1966 (orig. 1916–17). *Introductory Lectures on Psychoanalysis* (trans. J. Strachey, intro. P. Gay). New York and London: W.W. Norton & Company.

Grottanelli, Christiano. 1990. "Discussing Theories of Myth." *History of Religions* 30/2: 197–203.

Jung, Carl G., ed. 1964. *Man and his Symbols.* London: Aldus Books.

Lincoln, Bruce. 1999. *Theorizing Myth: Narrative, Ideology, and Scholarship.* Chicago: University of Chicago Press.

Malefijt, Annemarie de Waal. 1968. *Religion and Culture: An Introduction to Anthropology of Religion.* New York: Macmillan.

Masuzawa, Tomoko. 1993. *In Search of Dreamtime: The Quest for the Origin of Religion.* Chicago: Chicago University Press.

Müller, Friedrich Max. 1856. *Comparative Mythology.* London. (reproduced from the 1909 edition "Edited, with additional notes and an introductory preface on solar mythology, by

A. Smythe Palmer, D.D.," London: George Routledge and Sons). Reprinted 1977 by the Arno Press, New York.

Rennie, Bryan. 1996. *Reconstructing Eliade: Making Sense of Religion.* Albany: State University of New York Press.

Segal, Robert A., ed. 1998. *Jung on Mythology.* Princeton: Princeton University Press.

_____1999. *Theorizing About Myth.* Amherst: University of Massachusetts Press.

Strenski, Ivan. 1987. *Four Theories of Myth in Twentieth-Century History: Cassirer, Eliade, Lévi-Strauss and Malinowski.* London: Macmillan.

Wittgenstein, Ludwig. 1979. *Remarks on Frazer's Golden Bough* (ed. and rev. Rush Rhees). Retford: Brymill.

COMPARATIVE MYTHOLOGY

Friedrich Max Müller

The history of the world, or, as it is called, "Universal History," has laid open new avenues of thought, and it has enriched our language with a word which never passed the lips of Sokrates, or Plato, or Aristotle – *man-kind*. Where the Greek saw barbarians, we see brethren; where the Greek saw heroes and demi-gods, we see our parents and ancestors; where the Greek saw nations (èthne) we see mankind, toiling and suffering, separated by oceans, divided by language, and severed by national enmity – yet evermore tending, under a divine control, towards the fulfilment of that inscrutable purpose for which the world was created, and man placed in it, bearing the image of God. History, therefore, with its dusty and mouldering pages, is to us as sacred a volume as the book of nature. In both we read, or we try to read, the reflex of the laws and thoughts of a Divine Wisdom. As we acknowledge no longer in nature the working of demons or the manifestation of an evil principle, so we deny in history an atomistic conglomerate of chances, or the despotic rule of a mute fate. We believe that there is nothing irrational in history and nature, and that the human mind is called upon to read and to revere in both the manifestations of a Divine Power. Hence, even the most ancient and shattered pages of traditions are dear, to us, nay dearer, perhaps, than the more copious chapters of modern times. The history of those distant ages and distant men – apparently so foreign to our modern interests – assumes a new charm as soon as we know that it tells us the story of our own race, of our own family – nay, of our own selves.

*

As far as we can trace back the footsteps of man, even on the lowest strata of history, we see that the divine gift of a sound and sober intellect belonged to him from the very first; and the idea of a humanity emerging slowly from the depths of an animal brutality can never be maintained again. The earliest work of art wrought by the human mind – more ancient than any literary document, and prior even to the first whisperings of tradition – the *human language,* forms an uninterrupted chain from the first dawn of history down to our own times. We still speak the language of the first ancestors of our race; and this language, with its wonderful structure, bears witness against such unhallowed imputations.

The formation of language, the composition of roots, the gradual discrimination of meanings, the systematic elaboration of grammatical forms – all this working which we can still see under the surface of our own speech – attests from the very first the presence of a rational mind of an artist as great, at least, as his work. This period, during which expressions were coined for the most necessary ideas – such as pronouns, prepositions, numerals, and the household words of the simplest life – a period to which we must assign the first beginnings of a free and simply agglutinative grammar – grammar not impressed as yet with any individual or national peculiarities, yet containing the germs of all the Turanian,[1] as well as the Arian[2] and Semitic forms of speech – this period forms the first in the history of man – the first, at least, to which even the keenest eye of the antiquarian and the philosopher can reach – and we call it the *Rhematic Period.*

This is succeeded by a second period, during which we must suppose that at least two families of language left the simply agglutinative, or nomadic stage of grammar, and received, once for all, that peculiar impress of their formative system which we still find in all the dialects and national idioms comprised under the names of *Semitic* and *Aryan,* as distinguished from the *Turanian,* the latter retaining to a much later period, and in some instances to the present day, that agglutinative reproductiveness which has rendered a traditional and metamorphic system of grammar impossible, or has at least considerably limited its extent. Hence we do not find in the nomadic or Turanian languages scattered from China to the Pyrenees, from Cape Comorin, across the Caucasus, to Lapland, that traditional family likeness which enables us to treat the Teutonic, Celtic, Windic, Italic, Hellenic, Iranic, and Indic languages on one side, and the Arabian, Aramean, and Hebrew dialects on the other, as mere varieties of two specific forms of speech, in which, at a very early period, and through influences decidedly political, if not individual and personal, the floating elements of grammar have been arrested and made to assume an amalgamated, instead of a merely agglutinative character. This second is called the *Dialectical Period.*

Now, after these two periods, but before the appearance of the first traces of any national literature, there is a period, represented everywhere by the same characteristic features – a kind of Eocene period, commonly called the *Mythological* or *Mythopoeic Age.* It is a period in the history of the human mind, perhaps the most difficult to understand, and the most likely to shake our faith in the regular progress of the human intellect. We can form a tolerably clear idea of the origin of language, of the gradual formation of grammar, and the unavoidable divergence of dialects and languages. We can understand, again, the earliest concentrations of political societies, the establishment of laws and customs, and the first beginnings of religion and poetry. But between the two there is a gulf which it seems impossible for any philosophy to bridge over. We call it the *Mythic Period*, and we have accustomed ourselves to believe that the Greeks, for instance, such as we find them represented to us in the Homeric poems, far advanced in the fine arts, acquainted with the refinements and comforts of life, such as we see at the palaces of Menelaos and Alkinoos, with public meetings and elaborate pleadings, with the mature wisdom of a Nestor and the cunning enterprise of an Odysseus, with the dignity of a Helena and the loveliness of a Nausikaa, could have been preceded by a race of men whose chief amusement consisted in inventing absurd tales about gods and other nondescript beings.

*

Although later poets may have given to some of these fables a charm of beauty, and led us to accept them as imaginative compositions, it is impossible to conceal the fact that, taken by themselves, and in their literal meaning, most of these ancient myths are absurd and irrational, and frequently opposed to the principles of thought, religion, and morality which guided the Greeks as soon as they appear to us in the twilight of traditional history. By whom, then, were these stories invented? – stories, we must say at once, identical in form and character, whether we find them on Indian, Persian, Greek, Italian, Slavonic, or Teutonic soil. Was there a period of temporary insanity, through which the human mind had to pass, and was it a madness identically the same in the south of India and in the north of Iceland?

*

There *was* an age which produced these myths – an age half-way between the Dialectical Period – presenting the human race gradually diverging into different families and languages, and the National Period – exhibiting to us the earliest traces of nationalized language, and a nationalized literature in India, Persia, Greece, Italy, and Germany. The fact is there, and we must either explain it, or admit in the gradual growth of the human mind, as in the formation of the earth, some violent revolutions, which broke the regularity of the early strata of thought, and convulsed the human mind, like volcanoes and earthquakes arising from some unknown cause, below the surface of history.

Much, however, will be gained if, without being driven to adopt so violent and repugnant a theory, we are able to account in a more intelligible manner for the creation of myths. Their propagation and subsistence in later times, though strange in many respects, is yet a much less intricate problem. The human mind has an inborn reverence for the past, and the religious piety of the man flows from the same natural spring as the filial piety of the child. Even though the traditions of past ages may appear strange, wild, and sometimes immoral, or impossible, each generation accepts them, and fashions them so that they can be borne with again, and even made to disclose a true and deeper meaning.

＊

We find frequent indications in ancient history that the Greeks themselves were shocked by the stories told of their gods; yet as even in our own times faith with most men is not faith in God or in truth, but faith in the faith of others, we may understand why even men like Sokrates were unwilling to renounce their belief in what had been believed by their fathers. As their idea of the Godhead became purer, they also felt that the idea of perfection, involved in the idea of a divine being, excluded the possibility of immoral gods. Pindar, as pointed out by Otfried Müller,[3] changes many myths because they are not in harmony with his purer conceptions of the dignity of gods and heroes; and because, according to his opinion, they *must be false*. Plato[4] argues in a similar spirit when he examines the different traditions about Eros, and in the *Symposium* we see how each speaker maintains that myth of Eros to be the only true one which agrees best with his own ideas of the nature of this god – Phaedrus[5] calling him the oldest, Agathon the youngest of the gods; yet each appealing to the authority of an ancient myth.

＊

The past has its charms, and Tradition has a powerful friend in Language. We still speak of the sun rising and setting, of rainbows, of thunderbolts, because Language has sanctioned these expressions. We use them, though we do not believe in them. The difficulty is how at first the human mind was led to such imaginings – how the names and tales arose, and unless this question can be answered, our belief in a regular and consistent progress of the human intellect, through all ages and in all countries, must be given up as a false theory.

Nor can it be said that we know absolutely nothing of this period during which the as yet undivided Aryan nations – for it is chiefly of them that we are now speaking – formed their myths. Even if we saw only the deep shadow which lies on the Greek mind from the very beginning of its political and literary history, we should be able to infer from it something of the real character of that age which must have preceded the earliest dawn of the national literature of Greece. Otfried Müller, though he was unacquainted with the new light which comparative philology has shed on this primitive Aryan period, says, "The mythic form of expression which changes all beings into persons, all relations into actions, is something so peculiar that we must admit for its growth *a distinct period* in the civilisation of a people" (1825, 78; original italics). But comparative philology has since brought this whole period within the pale of documentary history. It has placed in our hands a telescope of such power that, where formerly we could see but nebulous clouds, we now discover distinct forms and outlines; nay, it has given us what we may call contemporary evidence, exhibiting to us the state of thought, language, religion, and civilization at a period when Sanskrit was not yet Sanskrit, Greek not yet Greek, but when both, together with Latin, German, and other Aryan dialects, existed as yet as *one* undivided language, in the same manner as French, Italian, and Spanish may be said to have at one time existed as *one* undivided language, in the form of Latin.

●

All the common Aryan words which we have hitherto examined referred to definite objects. They are all substantives, in so far as expressing something substantial, something open to sensuous perception. Nor is it in the power of language to express originally anything except objects as nouns, and qualities as verbs. Hence, the only definition we can give of language during that early state is that it is the conscious expression in sound, of impressions received by all the senses.

To us, abstract nouns are so familiar that we can hardly appreciate the difficulty which men experienced in forming them. We can scarcely imagine a language without abstract nouns. There are, however, dialects spoken at the present day which have no abstract nouns, and the more we go back in the history of languages, the smaller we find the number of these useful expressions. As far as language is concerned, an abstract word is nothing but an adjective raised into a substantive; but in thought the conception of a quality as a subject is a matter of extreme difficulty, and, in strict logical parlance, impossible. If we say, "I love virtue," we seldom connect any definite notion with virtue. Virtue is not a being, however unsubstantial; it is nothing individual, personal, active; nothing that could by itself produce an expressible impression on our mind. The word virtue is only a short-hand expression, and when men said for the first time "I love virtue," what they meant by it originally was "I love all things that are virtuous."

But there are other words, which we hardly call abstract, but which nevertheless were so originally, and are so still, in form; I mean words like day and night, spring and winter, dawn and twilight, storm and thunder. For what do we mean if we speak of day and night, or of spring and winter? We may answer, a season, or any other portion of time. But what is time, in our conceptions? It is nothing substantial, nothing individual; it is a quality raised by language into a substance. Therefore if we say "the day dawns," "the night approaches," we predicate actions of things that cannot act, we affirm a proposition which, if analysed logically, would have no definable subject.

The same applies to collective words, such as sky and earth, dew and rain – even to rivers and mountains. For if we say, "the earth nourishes man," we do not mean any tangible portion of soil, but the earth, conceived as a whole; nor do we mean by the sky the small horizon which our eye can scan. We imagine something which does not fall under our senses, but whether we call it a whole, a power, or an idea, in speaking of it we change it unawares into something individual.

Now in ancient languages every one of these words had necessarily a termination expressive of gender, and this naturally produced in the mind the corresponding idea of sex, so that these names received not only an individual, but a sexual character. There was no substantive which was not either masculine or feminine; neuters being of later growth, and distinguishable chiefly in the nominative.

What must have been the result of this? As long as people thought in language, it was simply impossible to speak of morning or evening, of spring and winter, without giving to these conceptions something of an individual, active, sexual, and at last, personal character. They were either nothings, as they are nothings to our withered thought, or they were something; and then they could not be conceived as mere powers, but as beings powerful. Even in our time, though we have the conception of nature as a power, what do we mean by power, except something powerful? Now, in early language, nature was *Natura*, a mere adjective made substantive; she was the Mother always "going to bring forth." Was this not a more definite idea than that which we connect with nature? And let us look to our poets, who still think and feel in language – that is, who use no word without having really enlivened it in their mind, who do not trifle with language, and may in this sense be called *muthologoi*. Can they speak of nature and similar things as neutral powers, without doing violence to their feelings?

＊

Why then, if we ourselves, in speaking of the Sun or the Storms, of Sleep and Death, of Earth and Dawn, connect either no distinct idea at all with these names, or allow them to cast over our mind the fleeting shadows of the poetry of old; why, if we, when speaking with the warmth which is natural to the human heart, call upon the Winds and the Sun, the Ocean and the Sky, as if they would still hear us; why, if plastic thought cannot represent any one of these beings or powers, without giving them, if not a human form, at least human life and human feeling – why should we wonder at the ancients, with their language throbbing with life and revelling in colour, if instead of the grey outlines of our modern thought, they threw out those living forms of nature, endowed with human powers, nay, with powers more than human, inasmuch as the light of the Sun was brighter than the light of a human eye, and the roaring of the Storms louder than the shouts of the human voice. We may be able to account for the origin of rain and dew, of storm and thunder; yet, to the great majority of mankind, all these things, unless they are mere names, are still what they were to Homer, only perhaps less beautiful, less poetical, less real, and less living.

So much for that peculiar difficulty which the human mind experiences in speaking of collective or abstract ideas – a difficulty which, as we shall see, will explain many of the difficulties of Mythology.

*

The mythology of the *Veda* is to comparative mythology what Sanskrit has been to comparative grammar. There is, fortunately, no system of religion or mythology in the *Veda*. Names are used in one hymn as appellatives, in another as names of gods. The same god is sometimes represented as supreme, sometimes as equal, sometimes as inferior to others. The whole nature of these so-called gods is still transparent; their first conception, in many cases, clearly perceptible. There are as yet no genealogies, no settled marriages between gods and goddesses. The father is sometimes the son, the brother is the husband, and she who in one hymn is the mother, is in another the wife. As the conceptions of the poet varied, so varied the nature of these gods. Nowhere is the wide distance which separates the ancient poems of India from the most ancient literature of Greece more clearly felt than when we compare the growing myths of the *Veda* with the full-grown and decayed myths on which the poetry of Homer is founded. The *Veda* is the real Theogony of the Aryan races, while that of Hesiod is a distorted caricature of the original image. If we want to know whither the human mind, though endowed with the natural consciousness of a divine power, is driven necessarily and inevitably by the irresistible force of language as applied to supernatural and abstract ideas, we must read the *Veda*; and if we want to tell the Hindus what they are worshipping – mere names of natural phenomena, gradually obscured, personified, and deified – we must make them read the *Veda*. It was a mistake of the early Fathers to treat the Heathen gods[6] as demons or evil spirits, and we must take care not to commit the same error with regard to the Hindu god. Their gods have no more right to any substantive existence than Eos or Hemera – than Nyx or Apatê. They are masks without an actor – the creations of man, not his creators; they are nomina, not numina; names without being, not beings without names.

In some instances, no doubt, it happens that a Greek, or a Latin, or a Teutonic myth, may be explained, from the resources which each of these languages still possesses, as there are many words in Greek which can be explained etymologically without any reference to Sanskrit or Gothic. We shall begin with some of these myths, and then proceed to the more difficult, which must receive light from more distant regions, whether from the snowy rocks of Iceland and the songs of the *Edda*, or from the borders of the "Seven Rivers," and the hymns of the *Veda*.

The rich imagination, the quick perception, the intellectual vivacity, and ever-varying fancy of the Greek nation, make it easy to understand that, after the separation of the Aryan race, no language was richer, no mythology more varied, than that of the

Greeks. Words were created with wonderful facility, and were forgotten again with that carelessness which the consciousness of inexhaustible power imparts to men of genius. The creation of every word was originally a poem, embodying a bold metaphor or a bright conception.[7] But, like the popular poetry of Greece, these words, if they were adopted by tradition, and lived on in the language of a family, of a city, of a tribe, in the dialects, or in the national speech of Greece, soon forgot the father that had given them birth, or the poet to whom they owed their existence. Their genealogical descent and native character were unknown to the Greeks themselves, and their etymological meaning would have baffled the most ingenious antiquarian.

*

If Hegel calls the discovery of the common origin of Greek and Sanskrit the discovery of a new world, the same may be said with regard to the common origin of Greek and Sanskrit mythology. The discovery is made, and the science of comparative mythology will soon rise to the same importance as comparative philology. I have here explained but a few myths, but they all belong to one small cycle, and many more names might have been added. I may refer those who take an interest in the geology of language to the *Journal of Comparative Philology*, published by my learned friend, Dr. Kuhn, at Berlin, who, in his periodical, has very properly admitted comparative mythology as an integral part of comparative philology, and who has himself discovered some striking parallelisms between the traditions of the *Veda* and the mythological names of the other Aryan nations. The very "Hippokentaurs and the Chimæra, the Gorgons and Pegasos, and other monstrous creatures," have been set right; and though I do not hold Dr. Kuhn's views on many points, and particularly with regard to the elementary character of the gods, which he, like Lauer, the lamented author of the *System of Greek Mythology*, connects too exclusively with the fleeting phenomena of clouds, and storms, and thunder, while I believe their original conception to have been almost always solar, yet there is much to be learnt from both, even where we cannot agree with their conclusions. Much, no doubt, remains to be done, and even with the assistance of the *Veda*, the whole of Greek mythology will never be deciphered and translated. But can this be urged as an objection? There are many Greek words of which we cannot find a satisfactory etymology, even by the help of Sanskrit. Are we therefore to say that the whole Greek language has no etymological organization? If we find a rational principle in the formation of but a small portion of Greek words, we are justified in inferring that the same principle which manifests itself in part governed the organic growth of the whole; and though we cannot explain the etymological origin of all words, we should never say that language had no etymological origin, or that etymology "treats of a past which was never present." That the later Greeks, such as Homer and Hesiod, ignored the *lógos* of their *múthoi* I fully admit, but they equally ignored the real origin *tò étymon* of their words. What applies to etymology, therefore, applies with equal force to mythology. It has been proved by comparative philology that there is nothing irregular in language, and what was formerly considered as irregular in declension and conjugation is now recognized as the most regular and primitive formation of grammar. The same, we hope, may be accomplished in mythology, and instead of deriving it, as heretofore, "ab ingenii humani imbecillitate et a dictionis egestate," it will obtain its truer solution, "ab ingenii humani sapientia et a dictionis abundantia." Mythology is only a dialect, an ancient form of language. Mythology, though chiefly concerned with nature, and here again mostly with those manifestations which bear the character of law, order, power, and wisdom impressed on them, was applicable to all things. Nothing is excluded from mythological expression; neither morals nor philosophy, neither history nor religion, have escaped the spell of that ancient sibyl. But mythology is neither philosophy, nor history, nor religion, nor ethics. It is, if we may use a scholastic expression, a *quale*, not a *quid* – something formal, not something substantial, and, like poetry, sculpture, and painting, applicable to nearly all that the ancient world could admire or adore.

Notes

[Editor's comment: the notes were added in the 1909 edition by Palmer, cf. bibliography in the introduction to this section, 'Psychological Approaches']

1. Turanian means virtually non-Aryan, being originally applied to the nomad races of Asia as swift (*Tura*) horsemen. See Müller (1864, I, 277, 334); Whitney (1874, 243).
2. The author afterwards abandoned this spelling for the more correct "Aryan," Sanskrit *Arya*, the tillers, or land-owners, which is adopted from this point.
3. See O. Müller's excellent work (1825, 87).
4. *Phaedrus*, 242 E.
5. *Symp*. 178 C; 195 A. [I have omitted the copious Greek quotations in this note – no one understands them anyway.]
6. Aristotle has given an opinion of the Greek gods in a passage of the *Metaphysics*. He is attacking the Platonic ideas, and tries to show their contradictory character, calling them *aïsthetà aídia* eternal uneternals, *i.e.* things that cannot have any real existence; as men, he adds, maintain that there are gods, but give them a human form, thus making them really "immortal mortals," *i.e.* non-entities.
7. So Archbishop Trench: "Language is fossil poetry; in other words, we are not to look for the poetry which a people may possess only in its poems, or its poetical customs, traditions, and beliefs. Many a single word also is itself a concentrated poem, having stores of poetical thought and imagery laid up in it" (1859, 5). And Carlyle: "For every word we have there was a man and poet. The coldest word was once a glowing new metaphor, and bold questionable originality"(1843, ch. xvii).

References

(as supplied by Palmer in the 1909 edition)

Carlyle, Thomas. 1843. *Past and Present*. London.

Müller, Fr. Max. 1864. *Lectures on the Science of Language*. London.

Müller, K. Otfried. 1825. *Prolegomena zu einer wissenschaftlichen Mythologie*. Göttingen.

Trench, Richard Chevenix. 1859. *On the Study of Words*. London: Routledge.

Whitney, W. D. 1874. *Oriental and Linguistic Studies*. New York: Scribner, Armstrong.

Myth in Primitive Psychology

Bronislaw Malinowski

Dedication to Sir James Frazer

If I had the power of evoking the past, I should like to lead you back some twenty years to an old Slavonic university town – I mean the town of Cracow, the ancient capital of Poland and the seat of the oldest university in eastern Europe. I could then show you a student leaving the medieval college buildings, obviously in some distress of mind, hugging, however, under his arm, as the only solace of his troubles, three green volumes with the well-known golden imprint, a beautiful conventionalized design of mistletoe – the symbol of *The Golden Bough*.

I had just then been ordered to abandon for a time my physical and chemical research because of ill-health, but I was allowed to follow up a favorite side line of study, and I decided to make my first attempt to read an English masterpiece in the original. Perhaps my mental distress would have been lessened, had I been allowed to look into the future and to foresee the present occasion, on which I have the great privilege of delivering an address in honor of Sir James Frazer to a distinguished audience, in the language of *The Golden Bough* itself.

For no sooner had I begun to read this great work, than I became immersed in it and enslaved by it. I realized then that anthropology, as presented by Sir James Frazer, is a great science, worthy of as much devotion as any of her elder and more exact sister studies, and I became bound to the service of Frazerian anthropology.

We are gathered here to celebrate the annual totemic festival of *The Golden Bough*; to revive and strengthen the bonds of anthropological union; to commune with the

146

source and symbol of our anthropological interest and affection. I am but your humble spokesman, in expressing our joint admiration to the great writer and his classical works; *The Golden Bough*, *Totemism and Exogamy*, *Folklore in the Old Testament*, *Psyche's Task*, and *The Belief in Immortality*. As a true officiating magician in a savage tribe would have to do, I have to recite the whole list, so that the spirit of the works (their "mana") may dwell among us.

In all this, my task is pleasant and in a way easy, for implicit in whatever I may say is a tribute to him, whom I have always regarded as the "Master." On the other hand this very circumstance also makes my task difficult, for having received so much, I fear I may not have enough to show in return. I have therefore decided to keep my peace even while I am addressing you – to let another one speak through my mouth, another one who has been to Sir James Frazer an inspiration and a lifelong friend, as Sir James has been to us. This other one, I need hardly tell you, is the modern representative of primitive man, the contemporary savage, whose thoughts, whose feelings, whose very life breath pervades all that Frazer has written.

In other words, I shall not try to serve up any theories of my own, but instead I shall lay before you some results of my anthropological field work, carried out in northwest Melanesia. I shall restrict myself, moreover, to a subject upon which Sir James Frazer has not directly concentrated his attention, but in which, as I shall try to show you, his influence is as fruitful as in those many subjects that he has made his own.

(The above formed the opening passages of an address delivered in honor of Sir James Frazer at the University of Liverpool, in November, 1925.)

The Role of Myth in Life

By the examination of a typical Melanesian culture and by a survey of the opinions, traditions, and behavior of these natives, I propose to show how deeply the sacred tradition, the myth, enters into their pursuits, and how strongly it controls their moral and social behavior. In other words, the thesis of the present work is that an intimate connection exists between the word, the mythos, the sacred tales of a tribe, on the one hand, and their ritual acts, their moral deeds, their social organization, and even their practical activities, on the other.

In order to gain a background for our description of the Melanesian facts, I shall briefly summarize the present state of the science of mythology. Even a superficial survey of the literature would reveal that there is no monotony to complain of as regards the variety of opinions or the acrimony of polemics. To take only the recent up-to-date theories advanced in explanation of the nature of myth, legend, and fairy tale, we should have to head the list, at least as regards output and self-assertion, by the so-called school of Nature-mythology which flourishes mainly in Germany. The writers of this school maintain that primitive man is highly interested in natural phenomena, and that his interest is predominantly of a theoretical, contemplative, and poetical character. In trying to express and interpret the phases of the moon, or the regular and yet changing path of the sun across the skies, primitive man constructs symbolic personified rhapsodies. To writers of this school every myth possesses as its kernel or ultimate reality some natural phenomenon or other, elaborately woven into a tale to an extent which sometimes almost masks and obliterates it. There is not much agreement among these students as to what type of natural phenomenon lies at the bottom of most mythological productions. There are extreme lunar mythologists so completely moonstruck with their idea that they will not admit that any other phenomenon could lend itself to a savage rhapsodic interpretation except that of earth's nocturnal satellite. The Society for the Comparative Study of Myth, founded in Berlin in 1906, and counting among its supporters such famous scholars as Ehrenreich, Siecke, Winckler, and many others, carried on their business under the sign of the moon. Others, like Frobenius for instance, regard the sun as the only subject around which primitive man has spun his symbolic tales. Then there is the school of meteorological interpreters who regard wind, weather, and colors of the skies as the essence of myth. To this belonged such well-known writers of the older generation as Max Müller and Kuhn. Some of these departmental mythologists fight fiercely for their heavenly body or principle; others have a more catholic taste, and prepare to agree that primeval man has made his mythological brew from all the heavenly bodies taken together.

I have tried to state fairly and plausibly this naturalistic interpretation of myths, but as a matter of fact this theory seems to me to be one of the most extravagant views ever advanced by an anthropologist or humanist – and that means a great deal. It has received an absolutely destructive criticism from the great psychologist Wundt and appears absolutely untenable in the light of any of Sir James Frazer's writings. From my own study of living myths among savages, I should say that primitive man has to a very limited extent the purely artistic or scientific interest in nature; there is but little room for symbolism in his ideas and tales; and myth, in fact, is not an idle rhapsody, not an aimless outpouring of vain imaginings, but a hard-working, extremely important cultural force. Besides ignoring the cultural function of myth, this theory imputes to primitive man a number of imaginary interests, and it confuses several clearly distinguishable types of story, the fairy tale, the legend, the saga, and the sacred tale or myth.

In strong contrast to this theory which makes myth naturalistic, symbolic, and imaginary, stands the theory which regards a sacred tale as a true historical record of the past. This view, recently supported by the so-called Historical School in Germany and America, and represented in England by Dr. Rivers, covers but part of the truth. There is no denying that history, as well as natural environment, must have left a profound imprint on all cultural achievements, hence also on myths. But to take all mythology as mere chronicle is as incorrect as to regard it as the primitive naturalist's musings. It also endows primitive man with a sort of scientific impulse and desire for knowledge. Although the savage has something of the antiquarian as well as of the naturalist in his composition, he is, above all, actively engaged in a number of practical pursuits, and has to struggle with various difficulties; all his interests are tuned up to this general pragmatic outlook. Mythology, the sacred lore of the tribe, is, as we shall see, a powerful means of assisting primitive man, of allowing him to make the two ends of his cultural patrimony meet. We shall see, moreover, that the immense services to primitive culture performed by myth are done in connection with religious ritual, moral influence, and sociological principle. Now religion and morals draw only to a very limited extent upon an interest in science or in past history, and myth is thus based upon an entirely different mental attitude.

The close connection between religion and myth which has been overlooked by many students has been recognized by others. Psychologists like Wundt, sociologists like Durkheim, Hubert, and Mauss, anthropologists like Crawley, classical scholars like Miss Jane Harrison have all understood the intimate association between myth and ritual, between sacred tradition and the norms of social structure. All of these writers have been to a greater or lesser extent influenced by the work of Sir James Frazer. In spite of the fact that the great British anthropologist, as well as most of his followers, have a clear vision of the sociological and ritual importance of myth, the facts which I shall present will allow us to clarify and formulate more precisely the main principles of a sociological theory of myth.

I might present an even more extensive survey of the opinions, divisions, and controversies of learned mythologists. The science of mythology has been the meeting point of various scholarships: the classical humanist must decide for himself whether Zeus is the moon, or the sun, or a strictly historical personality; and whether his ox-eyed spouse is the morning star, or a cow, or a personification of the wind – the loquacity of wives being proverbial. Then all these questions have to be rediscussed upon the stage of mythology by the various tribes of archaeologists, Chaldean and Egyptian, Indian and Chinese, Peruvian and Mayan. The historian and the sociologist, the student of literature, the grammarian, the Germanist and the Romanist, the Celtic scholar and the Slavist discuss, each little crowd among themselves. Nor is mythology quite safe from logicians and psychologists, from the metaphysician and the epistemologist – to say nothing of such visitors as the theosophist, the modern astrologist, and the Christian Scientist. Finally, we have the psychoanalyst who has come at last to teach us that the myth is a daydream of the race, and that we can only explain it by turning our back upon nature, history, and culture, and diving deep into the dark pools of the subconscious, where at the bottom there lie the usual paraphernalia and symbols of psychoanalytic exegesis. So that when at last the poor anthropologist and student of folklore come to the feast, there are hardly any crumbs left for them!

If I have conveyed an impression of chaos and confusion, if I have inspired a sinking feeling towards the incredible mythological controversy with all the dust and din which it raises, I have achieved exactly what I wanted. For I shall invite my readers to step outside the closed study of the theorist into the open air of the anthropological field, and to follow me in my mental flight back to the years which I spent among a Melanesian tribe of New Guinea. There, paddling on the lagoon, watching the natives under the blazing sun at their garden work, following them through the patches of jungle, and on the winding beaches and reefs, we shall learn about their life. And again, observing their ceremonies in the cool of the afternoon or in the shadows of the evening, sharing their meals round their fires, we shall be able to listen to their stories.

For the anthropologist – one and only among the many participants in the mythological contest – has the unique advantage of being able to step back behind the savage whenever he feels that his theories become involved and the flow of his argumentative eloquence runs dry. The anthropologist is not bound to the scanty remnants of culture, broken tablets, tarnished texts, or fragmentary inscriptions. He need not fill out immense gaps with voluminous, but conjectural, comments. The anthropologist has the myth-maker at his elbow. Not only can he take down as full a text as exists, with all its variations, and control it over and over; he has also a host of authentic commentators to draw upon; still more he has the fullness of life itself from which the myth has been born. And as we shall see, in this live context there is as much to be learned about the myth as in the narrative itself.

Myth as it exists in a savage community, that is, in its living primitive form, is not merely a story told but a reality lived. It is not of the nature of fiction, such as we read today in a novel, but it is a living reality, believed to have once happened in primeval times, and continuing ever since to influence the world and human destinies. This myth is to the savage what, to a fully believing Christian, is the Biblical story of Creation, of the Fall, of the Redemption by Christ's Sacrifice on the Cross. As our sacred story lives in our ritual, in our morality, as it governs our faith and controls our conduct, even so does his myth for the savage.

The limitation of the study of myth to the mere examination of texts has been fatal to a proper understanding of its nature. The forms of myth which come to us from classical antiquity and from the ancient sacred books of the East and other similar sources have come down to us without the context of living faith, without the possibility of obtaining comments from true believers, without the concomitant knowledge of their social organization, their practiced morals, and their popular customs – at least without the full information which the modern fieldworker can easily obtain. Moreover, there is no doubt that in their present literary form these tales have suffered a very considerable transformation at the hands of scribes, commentators, learned priests, and theologians. It is necessary to go back to primitive mythology in order to learn the secret of its life in the study of a myth which is still alive – before, mummified in priestly wisdom, it has been enshrined in the indestructible but lifeless repository of dead religions.

Studied alive, myth, as we shall see, is not symbolic, but a direct expression of its subject matter; it is not an explanation in satisfaction of a scientific interest, but a narrative resurrection of a primeval reality, told in satisfaction of deep religious wants, moral cravings, social submissions, assertions, even practical requirements. Myth fulfills in primitive culture an indispensable function: it expresses, enhances, and codifies belief; it safeguards and enforces morality; it vouches for the efficiency of ritual and contains practical rules for the guidance of man. Myth is thus a vital ingredient of human civilization; it is not an idle tale, but a hard-worked active force; it is not an intellectual explanation or an artistic imagery, but a pragmatic charter of primitive faith and moral wisdom.

I shall try to prove all these contentions by the study of various myths; but to make our analysis conclusive it will first be necessary to give an account not merely of myth, but also of fairy tale, legend, and historical record.

Let us then float over in spirit to the shores of a Trobriand[1] lagoon, and penetrate into the life of the natives – see them at work, see them at play, and listen to their stories. Late in November the wet weather is setting in. There is little to do in the gardens, the fishing season is not in full swing as yet, overseas sailing looms ahead in the future, while the festive mood still lingers after the harvest dancing and feasting. Sociability is in the air, time lies on their hands, while bad weather keeps them often at home. Let us step through the twilight of the approaching evening into one of their villages and sit at the fireside, where the flickering light draws more and more people as the evening falls and the conversation brightens. Sooner or later a man will be asked to tell a story, for this is the season of *fairy tales*. If he is a good reciter, he will soon provoke laughter, rejoinders, and interruptions, and his tale will develop into a regular performance.

At this time of the year folk tales of a special type called *kukwanebu* are habitually recited in the villages. There is a vague belief, not very seriously taken, that their recital has a beneficial influence on the new crops recently planted in the gardens. In order to produce this effect, a short ditty in which an allusion is made to some very fertile wild plants, the *kasiyena*, must always be recited at the end.

Every story is "owned" by a member of the community. Each story, though known by many, may be recited only by the "owner"; he may, however, present it to someone else by teaching that person and authorizing him to retell it. But not all the "owners" know how to thrill and to raise a hearty laugh, which is one of the main ends of such stories. A good raconteur has to change his voice in the dialogue, chant the ditties with due temperament, gesticulate, and in general play to the gallery. Some of these tales are certainly "smoking-room" stories; of others I will give one or two examples.

Thus there is the maiden in distress and the heroic rescue. Two women go out in search of birds' eggs. One discovers a nest under a tree, the other warns her: "These are eggs of a snake, don't touch them." "Oh, no! They are eggs of a bird," she replies and carries them away. The mother snake comes back, and finding the nest empty starts in search of the eggs. She enters the nearest village and sings a ditty:

"I wend my way as I wriggle along,
The eggs of a bird it is licit to eat;
The eggs of a friend are forbidden to touch."

This journey lasts long, for the snake is traced from one village to the other and everywhere has to sing her ditty. Finally, entering the village of the two women, she sees the culprit roasting the eggs, coils around her, and enters her body. The victim is laid down helpless and ailing. But the hero is nigh; a man from a neighboring village dreams of the dramatic situation, arrives on the spot, pulls out the snake, cuts it to pieces, and marries both women, thus carrying off a double prize for his prowess.

In another story we learn of a happy family, a father and two daughters, who sail from their home in the northern coral archipelagoes, and run to the southwest till they come to the wild steep slopes of the rock island Gumasila. The father lies down on a platform and falls asleep. An ogre comes out of the jungle, eats the father, captures and ravishes one of the daughters, while the other succeeds in escaping. The sister from the woods supplies the captive one with a piece of lawyer cane, and when the ogre lies down and falls asleep they cut him in half and escape.

A woman lives in the village of Okopukopu at the head of a creek with her five children. A monstrously big stingaree paddles up the creek, flops across the village, enters the hut, and to the tune of a ditty cuts off the woman's finger. One son tries to kill the monster and fails. Every day the same performance is repeated till on the fifth day the youngest son succeeds in killing the giant fish.

A louse and a butterfly embark on a bit of aviation, the louse as a passenger, the butterfly as aeroplane and pilot. In the middle of the performance, while flying overseas just between the beach of Wawela and the island of Kitava, the louse emits a loud shriek, the butterfly is shaken, and the louse falls off and is drowned.

A man whose mother-in-law is a cannibal is sufficiently careless to go away and leave her in charge of his three children. Naturally she tries to eat them; they escape in time, however, climb a palm, and keep her (through a somewhat lengthy story) at bay, until the father arrives and kills her. There is another story about a visit to the Sun, another about an ogre devastating gardens, another about a woman who was so greedy that she stole all food at funeral distributions, and many similar ones.

In this place, however, we are not so much concentrating our attention on the text of the narratives, as on their sociological reference. The text, of course, is extremely important, but without the context it remains lifeless. As we have seen, the interest of the story is vastly enhanced and it is given its proper character by the manner in which it is told. The whole nature of the performance, the voice and the mimicry, the stimulus and the response of the audience mean as much to the natives as the text; and the sociologist should take his cue from the natives. The performance, again, has to be placed in its proper time setting – the hour of the day, and the season, with the background of the sprouting gardens awaiting future work, and slightly influenced by the magic of the fairy tales. We must also bear in mind the sociological context of private ownership, the sociable function and the cultural role of amusing fiction. All these elements are equally relevant; and must be studied as well as the text. The stories live in native life and not on paper, and when a scholar jots them down without being able to evoke the atmosphere in which they flourish he has given us but a mutilated bit of reality.

I pass now to another class of stories. These have no special season, there is no stereotyped way of telling them, and the recital has not the character of a performance, nor has it any magical effect. And yet these tales are more important than the foregoing class; for they are believed to be true, and the information which they contain is both more valuable and more relevant than that of the *kukwanebu*. When a party goes on a distant visit or sails on an expedition, the younger members, keenly interested in the landscape, in new communities, in new people, and perhaps even new customs, will express their wonder and make inquiries. The older and more experienced will supply them with information and comment, and this always takes the form of a concrete narrative. An old man will perhaps tell his own experiences about fights and expeditions, about famous magic and extraordinary economic achievements. With this he may mix the reminiscences of his father, hearsay tales and legends, which have passed through many generations. Thus memories of great droughts and devastating famines are conserved for many years, together with the descriptions of the hardships, struggles, and crimes of the exasperated population.

A number of stories about sailors driven out of their course and landing among cannibals and hostile tribes are remembered, some of them set to song, others formed into historic legends. A famous subject for song and story is the charm, skill, and performance of famous dancers. There are tales about distant volcanic islands; about hot springs in which once a party of unwary bathers were boiled to death; about mysterious countries inhabited by entirely different men or women; about strange adventures which have happened to sailors in distant seas; monstrous fish and octopi, jumping rocks and disguised sorcerers. Stories again are told, some recent, some ancient, about seers and visitors to the land of the dead, enumerating their most famous and significant exploits. There are also stories associated with natural phenomena; a petrified canoe, a man changed into a rock, and a red patch on the coral rock left by a party who ate too much betel nut.

We have here a variety of tales which might be subdivided into *historical accounts* directly witnessed by the narrator, or at least vouched for by someone within living memory, *legends*, in which the continuity of testimony is broken, but which fall within the range of things ordinarily experienced by the tribesmen, and *hearsay tales* about distant countries and ancient happenings of a time which falls outside the range of present-day culture. To the natives, however, all these classes imperceptibly shade into each other, they are designated by the same name, *libwogwo*; they are all regarded as true; they are not recited as a performance, nor told for amusement at a special season. Their subject matter also shows a substantial unity. They all refer to subjects intensely stimulating to the natives; they all are connected with activities such as economic pursuits, warfare, adventure, success in dancing and in ceremonial exchange. Moreover, since they record singularly great achievements in all such pursuits, they redound to the credit of some individual and his descendants or of a whole community; and hence they are kept alive by the ambition of those whose ancestry they glorify. The stories told in explanation of peculiarities of features of the landscape frequently have a sociological context, that is, they enumerate whose clan or family performed the deed. When this is not the case, they are isolated fragmentary comments upon some natural feature, clinging to it as an obvious survival.

In all this it is once more clear that we can neither fully grasp the meaning of the text, nor the sociological nature of the story, nor the natives' attitude towards it and interest in it, if we study the narrative on paper. These tales live in the memory of man, in the way in which they are told, and even more in the complex interest which keeps them alive, which makes the narrator recite with pride or regret, which makes the listener follow eagerly, wistfully, with hopes and ambitions roused. Thus the essence of a *legend*, even more than that of a *fairy tale*, is not to be found in a mere perusal of the story, but in the combined study of the narrative and its context in the social and cultural life of the natives.

But it is only when we pass to the third and most important class of tales, the *sacred tales* or *myths*, and contrast them with the legends, that the nature of all three classes comes into relief. This third class is called by the natives *liliu*, and I want to emphasize that I am reproducing prima facie the natives' own classification and nomenclature, and limiting myself to a few comments on its accuracy. The third class of stories stands very much apart from the other two. If the first are told for amusement, the second to make a serious statement and satisfy social ambition, the third are regarded, not merely as true, but as venerable and sacred, and they play a highly important cultural part. The *folk tale*, as we know, is a seasonal performance and an act of sociability. The *legend*, provoked by contact with unusual reality, opens up past historical vistas. The *myth* comes into play when rite, ceremony, or a social or moral rule demands justification, warrant of antiquity, reality, and sanctity.

In the subsequent chapters of this book we will examine a number of myths in detail, but for the moment let us glance at the subjects of some typical myths. Take, for instance, the annual feast of the return of the dead. Elaborate arrangements are made for it, especially an enormous display of food. When this feast approaches, tales are told of how death began to chastise man, and how the power of eternal rejuvenation was lost. It is told why the spirits have to leave the village and do not remain at the fireside, finally why they return once in a year. Again, at certain seasons in preparation for an overseas expedition, canoes are overhauled and new ones built to the accompaniment of a special magic. In this there are mythological allusions in the spells, and even the sacred acts contain elements which are only comprehensible when the story of the flying canoe, its ritual, and its magic are told. In connection with ceremonial trading, the rules, the magic, even the geographical routes are associated with corresponding mythology. There is no important magic, no ceremony, no ritual without belief; and the belief is spun out into accounts of concrete precedent. The union is very intimate, for myth is not only looked upon as a commentary of additional information, but it is a warrant, a charter, and often even a practical guide to the activities with which it is connected. On the other hand the rituals, ceremonies, customs, and social organization contain at times direct references to myth, and they are regarded as the results of mythical event. The cultural fact is a monument in which the myth is embodied; while the myth is believed to be the real cause which has brought about the moral rule, the social grouping, the rite, or the custom. Thus these stories form an integral part of culture. Their existence and influence not merely transcend the act of telling the narrative, not only do they draw their substance from life and its interest – they govern and control many cultural features, they form the dogmatic backbone of primitive civilization.

This is perhaps the most important point of the thesis which I am urging: I maintain that there exists a special class of stories, regarded as sacred, embodied in ritual, morals, and social organization, and which form an integral and active part of primitive culture. These stories live not by idle interest, not as fictitious or even as true narratives; but are to the natives a statement of a primeval, greater, and more relevant reality, by which the present life, fates, and activities of mankind are determined, the knowledge of which supplies man with the motive for ritual and moral actions, as well as with indications as to how to perform them.

In order to make the point at issue quite clear, let us once more compare our conclusions with the current views of modern anthropology, not in order idly to criticize other opinions, but so that we may link our results to the present state of knowledge, give due acknowledgment for what we have received, and state where we have to differ clearly and precisely.

It will be best to quote a condensed and authoritative statement, and I shall choose for this purpose of definition an analysis given in *Notes and Queries on Anthropology*, by the late Miss C. S. Burne and Professor J. L. Myres. Under the heading "Stories, Sayings, and Songs," we are informed that "this section includes many *intellectual* efforts of peoples" which "represent the earliest attempt to exercise reason, imagination, and memory." With some apprehension we ask where is left the emotion, the interest, and ambition, the social role of all the stories, and the deep connection with cultural values of the more serious ones? After a brief classification of stories in the usual manner we read about the sacred tales: "*Myths* are stories which, however marvelous and improbable to us, are nevertheless related in all good faith, because they are intended, or believed by the teller, to explain by means of something concrete and intelligible an abstract idea or such vague and difficult conceptions as Creation, Death, distinctions of race or animal species, the different occupations of men and women; the origins of rites and customs, or striking natural objects or prehistoric monuments; the meaning, of the names of persons or places. Such stories are sometimes described as *etiological*, because their purpose is to explain why something exists or happens."[2]

Here we have in a nutshell all that modern science at its best has to say upon the subject. Would our Melanesians agree, however, with this opinion? Certainly not. They do not want to "explain," to make "intelligible" anything which happens in their myths – above all not an abstract idea. Of that there can be found to my knowledge no instance either in Melanesia or in any other savage community. The few abstract ideas which the natives possess carry their concrete commentary in the very word which expresses them. When being is described by verbs to lie, to sit, to stand, when cause and effect are expressed by words signifying foundation and the past standing upon it, when various concrete nouns tend towards the meaning of space, the word and the relation to concrete reality make the abstract idea sufficiently "intelligible." Nor would a Trobriander or any other native agree with the view that "Creation, Death, distinctions of race or animal species, the different occupations of men and women" are "vague and difficult conceptions." Nothing is more familiar to the native than the different occupations of the male and female sex; there is nothing to be *explained* about it. But though familiar, such differences are at times irksome, unpleasant, or at least limiting, and there is the need to justify them, to vouch for their antiquity and reality, in short to buttress their validity. Death, alas, is not vague, or abstract, or difficult to grasp for any human being. It is only too hauntingly real, too concrete, too easy to comprehend for anyone who has had an experience affecting his near relatives or a personal foreboding. If it were vague or unreal, man would have no desire so much as to mention it; but the idea of death is fraught with horror, with a desire to remove its threat, with the vague hope that it may be, not explained, but rather explained away, made unreal, and actually denied. Myth, warranting the belief in immortality, in eternal youth, in a life beyond the grave, is not an intellectual reaction upon a puzzle, but an explicit act of faith born from the innermost instinctive and emotional reaction to the most formidable and haunting idea. Nor are the stories about "the origins of rites and customs" told in mere explanation of them. They never explain in any sense of the word; they always state a precedent which constitutes an ideal and a warrant for its continuance, and sometimes practical directions for the procedure.

We have, therefore, to disagree on every point with this excellent though concise statement of present-day mythological opinion. This definition would create an imaginary, non-existent class of narrative, the etiological myth, corresponding to a non-existent desire to explain, leading a futile existence as an "intellectual effort," and remaining outside native culture and social organization with their pragmatic interests. The whole treatment appears to us faulty, because myths are treated as mere stories, because they are regarded as a primitive intellectual armchair occupation, because they are torn out of their life context, and studied from what they look like on paper, and not from what they do in life. Such a definition would make it impossible either to see clearly the nature of myth or to reach a satisfactory classification of folk tales. In fact we would also have to disagree with the definition of legend and of fairy tale given subsequently by the writers in *Notes and Queries on Anthropology*.

But above all, this point of view would be fatal to efficient field work, for it would make the observer satisfied with the mere writing down of narratives. The intellectual nature of a story is exhausted with its text, but the functional, cultural, and pragmatic aspect of any native tale is manifested as much in its enactment, embodiment, and contextual relations as in the text. It is easier to write down the story than to observe the diffuse, complex ways in which it enters into life, or to study its function by the observation of the vast social and cultural realities into which it enters. And this is the reason why we have so many texts and why we know so little about the very nature of myth.

We may, therefore, learn an important lesson from the Trobrianders, and to them let us now return. We will survey some of their myths in detail, so that we can confirm our conclusions inductively, yet precisely.

Notes

1. The Trobriand Islands are a coral archipelago lying to the northeast of New Guinea. The natives belong to the Papuo-Melanesian race, and in their physical appearance, mental equipment and social organization they show a combination of Oceanic characteristics mixed with some features of the more backward Papuan culture from the mainland of New Guinea.

   For a full account of the Northern Massim, of which the Trobrianders form a section, see the classical treatise of Professor C. G. Seligman (1910). This book shows also the relation of the Trobrianders to the other races and cultures on and around New Guinea. A short account will also be found in *Argonauts of the Western Pacific*, by the present author (1922).

2. Quoted from *Notes and Queries on Anthropology*, pp. 210 and 211.

References

Malinowski, Bronislaw. 1922. *Argonauts of the Western Pacific*. London: Routledge.

Myres, J. L. and C. S. Burne. 1912. In *Notes and Queries on Anthropology*, ed. Barbara Freire-Mareco and John L. Myres. London: Royal Anthropological Institute.

Seligman, C. G. 1910. *Melanesians of British New Guinea*. Cambridge: Cambridge University Press.

Introductory Lectures on Psycho-analysis

Sigmund Freud

I will now go on to make a survey, starting not from the thing represented, but from the symbol, of the fields from which sexual symbols are most derived, and I will make a few additional remarks, with special reference to the symbols where the common element in the comparison is not understood. The *hat* is an obscure symbol of this kind – perhaps, too, head-coverings in general – with a male significance as a rule, but also capable of a female one. In the same way an *overcoat* or *cloak* means a man, perhaps not always with a genital reference; it is open to you to ask why. Neckties, which hang down and are not worn by women, are definitely a male symbol. *Underclothing* and *linen* in general are female. *Clothes and uniforms*, as we have seen, are a substitute for nakedness of bodily shapes. *Shoes* and *slippers* are female genitals. *Tables* and *wood* have already been mentioned as puzzling but certainly female symbols. *Ladders, steps* and *staircases*, or, more precisely, walking on them, are clear symbols of sexual intercourse. On reflection, it will occur to us that the common element here is the rhythm of walking up them – perhaps, too, the excitement and breathlessness the higher one climbs.

We have earlier referred to *landscapes* as representing the female genitals. *Hills* and *rocks* are symbols of the male organ. *Gardens* are common symbols of the female genitals. *Fruit* stands, not for children, but for the breasts. *Wild animals* mean people in an excited sensual state, and further, evil instincts or passions. *Blossoms* and *flowers* indicate women's genitals, or, in particular, virginity. Do not forget that blossoms are actually the genitals of plants.

We are already acquainted with *rooms* as a symbol. The representation can be carried further, for windows, and doors in and out of rooms, take over the meaning of the orifices in the body. And the question of the room being *open* or *locked* fits with this symbolism, and the *key* that opens it is decidedly a male symbol.

Here, then, is material used for symbolism in dreams. It is not complete and could be carried deeper as well as further. But I fancy it will seem to you more than enough and may even have exasperated you. "Do I really live in the thick of sexual symbols?" you may ask. "Are all the objects around me, all the clothes I put on, all the things I pick up, all of them sexual symbols and nothing else?" There is really ground enough for raising astonished questions, and, as a first one, we may enquire how we in fact come to know the meaning of these dream-symbols, upon which the dreamer himself gives us insufficient information or none at all.

My reply is that we learn it from very different sources – from fairy tales and myths, from buffoonery and jokes, from folklore (that is, from knowledge about popular manners and customs, sayings and songs) and from poetic and colloquial linguistic usage. In all these directions we come upon the same symbolism, and in some of them we can understand it without further instruction. If we go into these sources in detail, we shall find so many parallels to dream-symbolism that we cannot fail to be convinced of our interpretations.

According to Scherner, as we have said [above, ed.], the human body is often represented in dreams by the symbol of a house. Carrying this representation further, we found that windows, doors and gates stood for openings in the body and that facades of houses were either smooth or provided with balconies and projections to hold on to. But the same symbolism is found in our linguistic usage – when we greet an acquaintance familiarly as an "*altes Haus*" ["old house"], when we speak of giving someone "*eins aufs Dach*" [a knock on the head, literally, "one on the roof"], or when we say of someone else that "he's not quite right in the upper storey." In anatomy the orifices of the body are in so many ways termed "*Leibespforten*" [literally, "portals of the body"].

It seems surprising at first to find one's parents in dreams as an imperial or royal couple. But it has its parallel in fairy tales. It begins to draw on us that the many fairy tales which begin "Once upon a time there were a King and a Queen" only mean to say that there were once a father and mother. In a family the children are jokingly called "princes" and the eldest "crown prince." The king himself calls himself the father of his country. We speak of small children jokingly as "*Würmer*" ["worms"] and speak sympathetically of a child as "*der arme Wurm*" ["the poor worm"].

Let us go back to house-symbolism. When in a dream we make use of the projections of houses for catching hold of, we may be reminded of a common vulgar expression for well-developed breasts: "She's got something to catch hold of." There is another popular expression in such cases: "She's got plenty of wood in front of the house," which seems to confirm our interpretation of wood as a female, maternal symbol.

And, speaking of wood, it is hard to understand how that material came to represent what is maternal and female. But here comparative philology may come to our help.

Our German word "*Holz*" seems to come from the same root as the Greek "hulê," meaning "stuff," "raw material." This seems to be an inheritance of the not uncommon event of the general name of a material eventually coming to be reserved for some particular material. Now there is an island in the Atlantic named "Madeira." This name was given to it by the Portuguese when they discovered it, because at that time it was covered all over with woods. For in the Portuguese language "*madeira*" means "wood." You will notice, however, that "*madeira*" is only a slightly modified form of the Latin word "*materia*," which once more means "material" in general. But "*materia*" is derived from "*mater*," "mother": the material out of which anything is made is, as it were, a mother to it. The ancient view of the thing survives, therefore, in the symbolic use of wood for "woman" or "mother."

Birth is regularly expressed in dreams by some connection with water: one falls into the water or one comes out of the water – one gives birth or one is born. We must not forget that this symbol is able to appeal in two ways to evolutionary truth. Not only are all terrestrial mammals, including man's ancestors, descended from aquatic creatures (this is the more remote of the two facts), but every individual mammal, every human being, spent the first phase of its existence in water – namely as an embryo in the amniotic fluid in its mother's uterus, and came out of that water when it was born. I do not say that the dreamer knows this; on the other hand, I maintain that he need not know it. There is something else that the dreamer probably knows from having been told in his childhood; and I even maintain of that too that his knowledge of it contributed nothing to the construction of the symbol. He was told in his nursery that the stork brings the babies. But where does it fetch them from? From the pond, or from the stream – once again, then, from the water. One of my patients after he had been given this information – he was a little Count at the time – disappeared for a whole afternoon. He was found at last lying by the edge of the castle pool, with his little face bending over the surface of the water eagerly peering down to try and see the babies at the bottom.

In myths about the birth of heroes – to which Otto Rank (1909) has devoted a comparative study, the oldest being that of King Sargon of Agade (about 2800 BC) – a predominant part is played by exposure in the water and rescue from the water. Ran has perceived that these are representations of birth, analogous to those that are usual in dreams. If one rescues someone from the water in a dream, one is making oneself into his mother, or simply into *a* mother. In myths a person who rescues a baby from the water is admitting that she is the baby's true mother. There is a well-known comic anecdote according to which an intelligent Jewish boy was asked who the mother of Moses was. He replied without hesitation: "The Princess." "No," he was told, "she only too him out of the water." "That's what *she* says," he replied, and so proved that he had found the correct interpretation of the myth.[1]

Departure in dreams means dying. So, too, if a child asks where someone is who has died and whom he misses, it is common nursery usage to reply that he has gone on a journey. Once more I should like to contradict the belief that the dream-symbol is derived from this evasion. The dramatist is using the same symbolic connection when he speaks of the after-life as "the undiscovered country from whose bourn no *traveller* returns." Even in ordinary life it is common to speak of "the last journey." Everyone acquainted with ancient rituals is aware of how seriously (in the religion of Ancient Egypt, for instance) the idea is taken of a journey to the land of the dead. Many copies have survived of *The Book of the Dead*, which has supplied to the mummy like a Baedeker to take with him on the journey. Ever since burial-places have been separated from dwelling-places the dead person's last journey has indeed become a reality.

It is just as little the case that genital symbolism is something that is found only in dreams. Every one of you has probably at one time or another spoken impolitely of a woman as an *"alte Schachtel"* ["old box"], perhaps without knowing that you were using a genital symbol. In the New Testament we find woman referred to as "the weaker vessel." The Hebrew scriptures, written in a style that comes close to poetry, are full of sexually symbolic expressions, which have not always been correctly understood and whose exegesis (for instance, in the case of the Song of Solomon) has led to some misunderstandings. In the later Hebrew literature it is very common to find a woman represented by a house, whose door stands for the sexual orifice. A man complains, for instance, in a case of lost virginity, that he has "found the door open." So, too, the symbol of a table for a woman in these writings. Thus, a woman says of her husband: "I laid the table for him, but he turned it round." Lame children are said to come about through the man's "turning the table round." I take these examples from a paper by Dr. Levy of Brünn (1914).

The fact that ships, too, in dreams stand for women is made credible by the etymologists, who tell us that "Schiff [ship]" was originally the name of an earthenware vessel and is the same word as *"Schaff"* [a dialect word meaning "tub"]. That ovens represent women and the uterus is confirmed by the Greek legend of Periander of Corinth and his wife Melissa. The tyrant, according to Herodotus, conjured up the shade of his wife, whom he had loved passionately but had murdered out of jealousy, to obtain some information from her. The dead woman proved her identity by saying that he (Periander) had *"pushed his bread into a cold oven,"* as a disguise for an event which no one else could know of. In the periodical *Anthropophyteia*, edited by F. S. Krauss, an invaluable source of knowledge of sexual anthropology,[2] we learn that in a particular part of Germany they say of a woman who has given birth to child that *"her oven has come to pieces."* Kindling fire, and everything to do with it, is intimately interwoven with sexual symbolism. Flame is always a male genital, and the hearth is the female counterpart.

If you may have felt surprise at the frequency with which landscapes are used in dreams to represent the female genitals, you can learn from mythology the part played by *Mother Earth* in the concepts and cults of the peoples of antiquity and how their view of agriculture was determined by this symbolism. You will perhaps be inclined to trace the fact that in dreams a room represents a woman to the common usage in our language by which *"Frau"* is replaced by *"Frauenzimmer"*[3] – the human being is replaced by the apartment allotted to her. Similarly we speak of the "Sublime Porte,"[4] meaning the Sultan and his government. So too the title of the Ancient Egyptian ruler, "Pharaoh," means simply "Great Courtyard." (In the Ancient East the courts between the double gateways of a city were public meeting-places like the market-places of the classical world.) This derivation, however, appears to be too superficial. It seems to me more likely that a room became the symbol of a woman as being the space which encloses human beings. We have already found "house" used in a similar sense; and mythlogy and poetical language enable us to add "city," "citadel," "castle," and "fortress" as further symbols for "woman." The question could easily be settled from the dreams of people who do not speak or understand German. During the last few years I have mainly treated foreign-speaking patients, and I seem to remember that in their dreams too *"Zimmer"* ["room"] meant *"Frauenzimmer,"* though they had no similar usage in their languages. There are other indications that the symbolic relation can go beyond the limits of language – which, incidentally, was asserted long ago by an old investigator of dreams, Schubert (1814). However, none of my dreamers were completely ignorant of German, so the decision must be left to psycho-analysts who can collect data from unilingual people in other countries.

There is scarcely one of the symbolic representations of the male genitals which does not recur in joking, vulgar or poetic usage, especially in the ancient classical dramatists. But here we meet not only the symbols which appear in dreams, but others besides – for instance tools employed in various operations, and particularly the plough. Moreover, the symbolic representation of masculinity leads us to a very extensive and much disputed region, which, on grounds of economy, we shall avoid. I should like, however, to devote a few words to one symbol, which as it were, falls outside this class – the number 3. Whether this number owes its sacred character to this symbolic connection remains undecided. But what seems certain is that the number of tripartite things that occur in nature – the clover leaf, for instance – owe their use for coats of arms and emblems to this symbolic meaning. Similarly, the tripartite lily – the so-called *fleur-de-lis* – and the remarkable heraldic device of two islands so far apart as Sicily and The Isle of Man – the *triskeles* (three bent legs radiating from a centre) – seem to be stylized versions of the male genitals. Likenesses of the male organ were regarded in antiquity as the most powerful *apotropaic* (means of defence) against evil influences, and, in conformity with this, the lucky charms of our own day can all be easily recognized as genital or sexual symbols. Let us consider a collection of such things – as they are worn, for instance, in the form of small silver hanging trinkets: a four-leaved clover, a pig, a horseshoe, a ladder, a chimney-sweep. The four-leaved clover has taken the place of the three-leaved one which is really suited to be a symbol. The mushroom is an undoubted penis-symbol: there are mushrooms [fungi] which owe their systematic name (*Phallus impudicus*) to their unmistakable resemblance to the male organ. The horseshoe copies the outline of the female genital orifice, while the chimney-sweep, who carries the ladder, appears in this company on account of his activities, with which sexual intercourse is vulgarly compared. (Cf. *Anthropophyteia*). We have made acquaintance of his ladder in dreams as a sexual symbol; here German linguistic usage comes to our help and shows us how the word *"steigen"* ["to climb," or "to mount"] is used in what is *par excellence* a sexual sense. We say "*den Frauen nachsteigen*" ["to run" (literally "climb") "after women"], and "*ein alter Steiger*" ["an old rake" (literally "climber")]. In French, in which the word for steps on a staircase is "*marches*," we find a precisely analogous term "*un vieux marcheur.*" The fact that in many languages large animals climbing or "mounting" on the female is a necessary preliminary to sexual intercourse probably fits into this context.

"Pulling off a branch" as a symbolic representation of masturbation is not merely in harmony with vulgar descriptions of the act but has far-reaching mythological parallels. But that masturbation, or rather the punishment for it – castration –, should be represented by the falling out or pulling out of teeth is especially remarkable, since there is a counterpart to it in anthropology which can be known to only a very small number of dreamers. There seems to me no doubt that the circumcision practised by so many peoples is an equivalent and substitute for castration. And we now learn that certain primitive tribes in Australia carry out circumcision as a puberty rite (at the festival to celebrate a boy's attaining sexual maturity), while other tribes, their near neighbours, have replaced this act by the knocking out of a tooth.

Here I bring my account of these specimens to an end. They are only specimens. We know more on the subject; but you may imagine how much richer and more interesting a collection like this could be if it were brought together, not by amateurs like us, but by real professionals in mythology, anthropology, philology and folklore.

A few consequences force themselves on our notice; they cannot be exhaustive, but they offer us food for reflection.

In the first place we are faced by the fact that the dreamer has a symbolic mode of expression at his disposal which he does not know in waking life and does not recognize. This is as extraordinary as if you were to discover that your housemaid understood Sanskrit, though you know that she was born in a Bohemian village and never learnt it. It is not easy to account for this fact by the help of our psychological views. We can only say that the knowledge of symbolism is unconscious to the dreamer, that it belongs to his unconscious mental life. But even with this assumption we do not meet the point. Hitherto it has only been necessary for us to assume the existence of unconscious endeavours – endeavours, that is, of which, temporarily or permanently, we know nothing. Now, however, it is a question of more than this, of unconscious pieces of knowledge, of connections of thought, of comparisons between different objects which result in its being possible for one of them to be regularly put in place of the other. These comparisons are not freshly made on each occasion; they lie ready to hand and are complete, once and for all. This is implied by the fact of their agreeing in the case of different individuals – possibly, indeed, agreeing in spite of differences of language. What can be the origin of these symbolic relations? Linguistic usage covers only a small part of them. The multiplicity of parallels in other spheres of knowledge are mostly unknown to the dreamer; we ourselves have been obliged to collect them laboriously.

Secondly, these symbolic relations are not something peculiar to dreamers or to the dream-work through which they come to expression. This same symbolism, as we have seen, is employed by myths and fairy tales, by the people in their sayings and songs, by colloquial linguistic usage and by the poetic imagination. The field of symbolism is immensely wide, and dream-symbolism is only a small part of it: indeed, it serves no useful purpose to attack the whole problem from the direction of dreams. Many symbols which are commonly used elsewhere appear in dreams very seldom or not at all. Some dream-symbols are not to be found in all other fields but only, as you have seen, here and there. One gets an impression that what we are faced with here is an ancient but extinct mode of expression, of which different pieces have survived in different fields, one piece only here, another only there, a third, perhaps, in slightly modified forms in several fields. And here I shall recall the phantasy of an interesting psychotic patient, who imagined a "basic language" of which all these symbolic relations would be residues.

Thirdly, it must strike you that the symbolism in the other fields I have mentioned is by no means solely sexual symbolism, whereas in dreams symbols are used almost exclusively for the expression of sexual objects and relations. This is not easily explained either. Are we to suppose that symbols which originally had a sexual significance later acquired another application and that, furthermore, the toning-down of representation by symbols into other kinds of representation may be connected with this? The questions can evidently not be answered as long as we have considered dream-symbolism alone. We can only hold firmly to the suspicion that there is a specially intimate relation between true symbols and sexuality.

In this connection we have been given an important hint during the last few years. A philologist, Hans Sperber (1912), of Uppsala, who works independently of psycho-analysis, has put forward the argument that sexual needs have played the biggest part in the origin and development of speech. According to him, the original sounds of speech served for communication, and summoned the speaker's sexual partner; the further development of linguistic roots accompanied the working activities of primal man. These activities, he goes on, were performed in common and were accompanied by rhythmically repeated utterance. In this way a sexual interest became attached to work. Primal man made work acceptable, as it were, by treating it as an equivalent and substitute for sexual activity. The words enunciated during work in common thus had two meanings; they denoted sexual acts as well as the working activity equated with them. As time went on, the words became detached from the sexual meanings and fixed to the work. In later generations the same thing happened with new words, which had a sexual meaning and were applied to new forms of work. In this way a number of verbal roots would have been formed, all of which were of sexual origin and subsequently lost their sexual meaning. If the hypothesis I have sketched out here is correct, it would give us a possibility of understanding dream-symbolism. We should understand why dreams, which preserve something of the earliest conditions, have such an extraordinarily large number of sexual symbols, and why, in general, weapons and tools always stand for what is male while materials and things that are worked upon stand for what is female. The symbolic relation would be the residue of an ancient verbal identity; things which were once called by the same name as the genitals could now serve as symbols for them in dreams.

The parallels we have found to dream-symbolism also allow us to form an estimate of the characteristic of psycho-analysis which enables it to attract general interest in a way in which neither psychology nor psychiatry have succeeded in doing. In the work of psycho-analysis links are formed with numbers of other mental sciences, the investigation of which promises results of the greatest value: links with mythology and philology, with folklore, with social psychology and the theory of religion. You will not be surprised to hear that a periodical has grown up on psycho-analytic soil whose sole aim is to foster these links. This periodical is known as *Imago*, founded in 1912 and edited by Hanns Sachs and Otto Rank.[5] In all these links the share of psycho-analysis is in the first instance that of giver and only to a less extent that of receiver. It is true that this brings it an advantage in the fact that its strange findings become more familiar when they are met with again in other fields; but on the whole it is psycho-analysis which provides the technical methods and the points of view whose application in these other fields should prove fruitful. The mental life of human individuals, when subjected to psycho-analytic investigation, offers us the explanations with the help of which we are able to solve a number of riddles in the life of human communities or at least to set them in a true light.

Incidentally, I have said nothing at all to you yet as to the circumstances in which we can obtain our deepest insight into the hypothetical "primal language" and as to the field in which most of it has survived. Until you know this you cannot form an opinion of its whole significance. For this field is that of the neuroses and its material is the symptoms and other manifestations of neurotic patients, for the explanation and treatment of which psycho-analysis was, indeed, created.

The fourth of my reflections takes us back to the beginning and directs us along our prescribed path. I have said [above, ed.] that even if there were no dream-censorship dreams would still not easily be intelligible to us, for we should still be faced with the task of translating the symbolic language of dreams into that of our waking thought. Thus symbolism is a second and independent factor in the distortion of dreams, alongside of the dream-censorship. It is plausible to suppose, however, that the dream-censorship finds it convenient to make use of symbolism, since it leads towards the same end – the strangeness and incomprehensibility of dreams. It will shortly become clear whether a further study of dreams may not bring us up against yet another factor that contributes to the distortion of dreams. But I should not like to leave the subject of dream-symbolism without once more touching on the problem of why it can meet with such violent resistance in educated people when the wide diffusion of symbolism in myths, religion, art and language is so unquestionable. May it not be that what is responsible is once again its connection with sexuality?

Notes

1. [Freud used this "correct interpretation of the myth" as the basis for of his last work, *Moses and Monotheism* (1939).]
2. [Cf. Freud's appreciative letter to Kraus (in 1910).]
3. [Literally "woman's apartment." The word is very often used in German as a slightly derogatory synonym for "woman."]
4. [Literally, "Gateway," the old diplomatic term for the Ottoman Court at Constantinople before 1923, derived *via* the French from the Turkish title.]
5. [It ceased publication in 1941. A journal with a similar aim, *The American Imago*, was founded by Hanns Sachs in Boston in 1939.]

References

Freud, Sigmund. 1939. *Moses and Monotheism*. London and New York: The Hogarth Press.

Levy, Ludwig 1914. "Die Sexualsymbolik der Bibel und des Talmuds." *Zeitschrift für Sexualwissenschaft* 1: 274.

Sperber, Hans. 1912. "Über den Einfluss sexueller Momente auf Entstehung und Entwicklung der Sprache." *Imago* 1.

Cosmogonic Myth and "Sacred History"*

Mircea Eliade

The Living Myth and the Historian of Religions

It is not without fear and trembling that a historian of religion approaches the problem of myth. This is not only because of that preliminary embarrassing question: what is intended by myth? It is also because the answers given depend for the most part on the documents selected by the scholar. From Plato and Fontenelle to Schelling and Bultmann, philosophers and theologians have proposed innumerable definitions of myth. But all of these have one thing in common: they are based on the analysis of Greek mythology. Now, for a historian of religions this choice is not a very happy one. It is true that only in Greece did myth inspire and guide epic poetry, tragedy, and comedy, as well as the plastic arts; but it is no less true that it is especially in Greek culture that myth was submitted to a long and penetrating analysis, from which it emerged radically "demythicized." If in every European language the word "myth" denotes a "fiction," it is because the Greeks proclaimed it to be such twenty-five centuries ago. What is even more serious for an historian of religion: we do not know a single Greek myth within its ritual context. Of course this is not the case with the paleo-oriental and Asiatic religions; it is especially not the case with the so-called primitive religions. As is well known, a *living myth* is always connected with a cult, inspiring and justifying a religious behavior. None of this of course means that Greek myth should not figure in an investigation of the mythical phenomenon. But it would seem unwise to begin our kind of inquiry by the study of Greek documents, and even more so to restrict it to such documents. The mythology which informs Homer, Hesiod, and the tragic poets represents already a selection and an interpretation of archaic materials, some of which had become almost unintelligible. In short, our best chance of understanding the structure of mythical thought is to study cultures where myth is a "living thing," where it constitutes the very ground of the religious life; in other words, where myth, far from indicating a *fiction*, is considered to reveal the *truth par excellence*.

This is what anthropologists have done, for more than half a century, concentrating on "primitive" societies. We cannot here review the contributions of Andrew Lang, Frazer, Lévy-Bruhl, Malinowski, Leenhardt, or Lévi-Strauss. Some results of ethnological research will have our attention later on. We have to add, however, that the historian of religions is not always happy with the approach of the anthropologists nor with their general conclusions. Reacting against an excessive concern with comparison, most of the authors have neglected to supplement their anthropological research with a rigorous study of other mythologies, for example those of the ancient Near East, in the first place of Mesopotamia and Egypt, those of the Indo-Europeans – especially the grandiose, exuberant mythologies of ancient and medieval India – and those, finally, of the Turco-Mongols, the Tibetans, and the peoples of Southeast Asia. A restriction of the inquiry to "primitive" mythologies risks giving the impression that there is no continuity between archaic thought and the thought of the peoples who played an important role in ancient history. Now, such a solution of continuity does not exist. Moreover, by limiting the research to primitive societies, we are left with no measure of the role of myths in complex and highly developed religions, like those of the ancient Near East and India. To give only one example, it is impossible to understand the religion and, in general, the style of Mesopotamian culture if we ignore the cosmogonic myth and the origin myths preserved in *Enuma elish* and in the Gilgamesh Epic. At every New Year the fabulous events related in *Enuma elish* were ritually reenacted; every New Year the world needed to be re-created – and this necessity reveals a profound dimension of Mesopotamian thought. Moreover, the myth of the origin of man illuminates, at least in part, the tragic world-view and pessimism characteristic of Mesopotamian culture: for man has been molded by Marduk from clay, that is, from the very body of the primordial monster Tiamat, and from the blood of the arch-demon Kingu. And the myth clearly indicates that man has been created by Marduk in order that the gods may be nourished by human labor. Finally, the Gilgamesh Epic presents an equally pessimistic vision by explaining why man did not, and could not, obtain immortality.

This is the reason why the historians of religions prefer the approach of their colleagues – a Raffaele Pettazzoni or a Gerardus van der Leeuw – or even the approach of certain scholars in the field of comparative anthropology, like Adolf Jensen or H. Baumann, who deal with all categories of mythological creativity, those of the "primitives" as well as of the peoples of high cultures. While one may not always agree with the results of their researches, one is at least certain that their documentation is sufficiently broad to permit valid generalizations.

But the divergences resulting from an incomplete documentation do not constitute the only difficulty in the dialogue between the historian of religions and his colleagues from other disciplines. It is his very approach which separates him, for instance, from the anthropologist or the psychologist. The historian of religions is too conscious of the axiological difference of his documents to marshal them on the same level. Aware of nuances and distinctions, he cannot ignore the fact that there exist great myths and myths of less importance; myths which dominate and characterize a religion, and secondary myths, repetitious and parasitical. *Enuma elish*, for example, cannot figure on the same plane with the mythology of the female demon Lamashtu; the Polynesian cosmogonic myth has not the same weight as the myth of the origin of a plant, for it precedes it and serves as a model for it. Such differences may not be important for an anthropologist or a psychologist. For instance, a sociologist concerned to study the French novel in the nineteenth century or a psychologist interested in literary imagination might discuss Balzac and Eugéne Sue, Stendhal or Jules Sandeau indifferently, irrespective of the quality of their art. But for a literary critic such conflation is simply unthinkable, for it annihilates his own hermeneutical principles.

When, in one or two generations, perhaps even earlier, we have historians of religions who are descended from Australian, African, or Melanesian tribal societies, I do not doubt that, among other things, they will reproach Western scholars for their indifference to the scale of values *indigenous* to these societies. Let us imagine a history of Greek culture in which Homer, the tragic poets, and Plato are passed by silently while the *Book of Dreams* of Artemidorus and the novel of Heliodorus from Emessa are laboriously commented on, under the pretext that such works better illuminate the specific traits of the Greek genius and help us to understand its destiny. To come back to our theme, I do not think that we can grasp the structure and function of mythical thought in a society which has myth as its foundation if we do not take into account the *mythology in its totality* and, at the same time, the *scale of values* which such mythology implicitly or explicitly proclaims.

Now in every case where we have access to a still living tradition, and not to an acculturated one, one thing strikes us from the very beginning: the mythology not only constitutes, as it were, the "sacred history" of the tribe, not only does it explain the total reality and justify its contradictions, but it equally reveals a hierarchy in the series of fabulous events that it reports. In general, one can say that any myth tells how something came into being, the world, or man, or an animal species, or a social institution, and so on. But by the very fact that the creation of the world precedes everything else, the cosmogony enjoys a special prestige. In fact, as I have tried to show elsewhere,[1] the cosmogonic myth furnishes the model for all myths of origin. The creation of animals, plants, or man presupposes the existence of a world.

Certainly, the myth of the creation of the world does not always look like a cosmogonic myth *stricto sensu*, like the Indian or Polynesian myth, or the one narrated in *Enuma elish*. In a great part of Australia, for example, such cosmogonic myths are unknown. But there is always a central myth which describes the beginnings of the world, that is, what happened before the world became as it is today. Thus, there is always a *primordial history* and this history has a *beginning*: a cosmogonic myth proper, or a myth that describes the first, germinal stage of the world. This beginning is always implied in the sequence of myths which recounts the fabulous events that took place after the creation or the coming into being of the universe, namely, the myths of the origin of plants, animals, and man, or of the origin of marriage, family, and death, etc. Taken all together, these myths of origin constitute a fairly coherent history. They reveal how the cosmos was shaped and changed, how man became mortal, sexually diversified, and compelled to work in order to live; they equally reveal what the supernatural beings and the mythical ancestors did, and how and why they abandoned the earth and disappeared. We can also say that any mythology that is still accessible in an appropriate form contains not only a beginning but also an end, determined by the last manifestation of the supernatural beings, the cultural heroes, or the ancestors.

Now this primordial, sacred history, brought together by the totality of significant myths, is fundamental because it explains, and by the same token justifies, the existence of the world, of man and of society. This is the reason that a mythology is considered at once a *true history*: it relates how things came into being, providing the exemplary model and also the justifications of man's activities. One understands what one is – mortal and of a certain sex – and how that came about, because the myths tell how death and sexuality made their appearance. One engages in a certain type of hunting or agriculture because the myths report how the cultural heroes taught these techniques to the ancestors. I have insisted on this paradigmatic function of myth in other publications, and consequently I do not need to repeat the point again.

I would like, however, to amplify and complete what I have said, having regard mainly to what I called the sacred history preserved in the great myths. This is easier said than done. The first difficulty which confronts us is a material one. To analyze and interpret a mythology or a mythological theme conveniently, one has to take into consideration all the available documents. But this is impossible in a lecture, or even in a short monograph. Claude Lévi-Strauss has devoted more than 300 pages to the analysis of a group of South American myths, and he had to leave aside the mythologies of the Fuegians and other neighboring peoples in order to concentrate primarily on the origin myths of the Amazonians. I must therefore limit myself to one or two characteristic examples. I will examine primarily those elements that seem essential to the myths of aborigines. Of course even such résumés might appear too long. But since I am dealing with rather unfamiliar mythologies, I cannot be content with mere allusions to them, as I could in the case of *Enuma elish* or the Greek, and even Indian, myths. Moreover, any exegesis is grounded in a philology. It would be pointless to propose an interpretation of the myths I have in mind without providing at least a minimum of documentation.

Meaning and Function of a Cosmogonic Myth

My first example is the mythology of the Ngadju Dayak of Borneo. I have chosen it because there is available a work about it which deserves to become a classic: *Die Gottesidee der Ngadju Dajak in Süd-Borneo* (Leiden, 1946) by Hans Schärer.[2] The author, who unfortunately died prematurely, studied these people for many years. The mythological documents which he collected, if ever printed, would cover 12,000 pages. Hans Schärer not only mastered the language of these people and thoroughly knew their customs, but he also understood the structure of mythology and its role in the life of the Dayak. As for many other archaic peoples, for the Dayak the cosmogonic myth discloses the eventful creation of the world and of man and, at the same time, the principles which govern the cosmic process and human existence. One must read this book to realize how much everything attains consistency in the life of an archaic people, how the myths succeed each other and articulate themselves into a sacred history which is continuously recovered in the life of the community as well as in the existence of each individual. Through the cosmogonic myth and its sequel, the Dayak progressively unveils the structures of reality and of his own proper mode of being. What happened in the beginning describes at once both the original perfection and the destiny of each individual.

At the beginning, so the myth goes, the cosmic totality was still undivided in the mouth of the coiled watersnake. Eventually two mountains arise and from their repeated clashes the cosmic reality comes progressively into existence: the clouds, the hills, the sun and the moon, and so on. The mountains are the seats of the two supreme deities, and they are also these deities themselves. They reveal their human forms, however, only at the end of the first part of the creation. In their anthropomorphic form, the two supreme deities, Mahatala and his wife Putir, pursue the cosmogonic work and create the upperworld and the underworld. But there is still lacking an intermediary world, and mankind to inhabit it. The third phase of the creation is carried out by two hornbills, male and female, who are actually identical with the two supreme deities. Mahatala raises the tree of life in the "Center," the two hornbills fly over toward it, and eventually meet each other in its branches. A furious fight breaks out between the two birds, and as a result the tree of life is extensively damaged. From the knotty excrescences of the tree and from the moss falling out from the throat of the female hornbill, a maiden and a young man come forth, the ancestors of the Dayak. The tree of life is finally destroyed and the two birds end by killing each other.

In sum, during the work of creation the deities reveal themselves under three different forms: cosmic (the two mountains), anthropomorphic (Mahatala and Putir), theriomorphic (the two hornbills). But these polar manifestations represent only one aspect of the divinity. Not less important are the godhead's manifestations as a *totality*: the primordial watersnake, for instance, or the tree of life. This totality – which Schärer calls divine/ambivalent totality – constitutes the fundamental principle of the religious life of the Dayak, and it is proclaimed again and again in different contexts. One can say that, for the Dayaks, every divine form contains its opposite in the same measure as itself: Mahatala is also his own wife and *vice versa*, and the watersnake is also the hornbill and *vice versa.*

The cosmogonic myth enables us to understand the religious life of the Dayaks as well as their culture and their social organization. The world is the result of a combat between two polar principles, during which the tree of life – i.e. their own embodiment – is annihilated. "But from destruction and death spring the cosmos and a new life. The new creation originates in the death of the total godhead" (Schärer 1963, 34). In the most important religious ceremonies – birth, initiation, marriage, death – this creative clash is tirelessly reiterated. As a matter of fact, everything which is significant in the eyes of a Dayak is an imitation of exemplary models and a repetition of the events narrated in the cosmogonic myth. The village as well as the house represent the universe and are supposed to be situated at the Center of the World. The exemplary house is an *imago mundi*: it is erected on the back of the watersnake, its steep roof symbolizes the primeval mountain on which Mahatala is enthroned, and an umbrella represents the tree of life on whose branches one can see the two birds.

During the ceremonies of marriage, the couple return to the mythical primeval time. Such a return is indicated by a replica of the tree of life that is clasped by the bridal pair. Schärer was told that clasping the tree of life means to form a unity with it. "The wedding is the reenactment of the creation, and the reenactment of the creation is the creation of the first human couple from the Tree of Life" (ibid., 85). Birth also is related to the original time. The room in which the child is born is symbolically situated in the primeval waters. Likewise, the room where the young girls are enclosed during initiation ceremonies is imagined to be located in the primordial ocean. The young girl descends to the underworld and after some time assumes the form of a watersnake. She comes back to earth as a new person and begins a new life, both socially and religiously (ibid., 87). Death is equally conceived as a passage to a new and richer life. The deceased person returns to the primeval era, his mystical voyage indicated by the form and decorations of his coffin. In fact, the coffin has the shape of a boat, and on its sides are painted the watersnake, the tree of life, the primordial mountains, that is to say the cosmic/divine totality. In other words, the dead man returns to the divine totality which existed at the beginning.

On the occasion of each decisive crisis and each *rite de passage*, man takes up again *ab initio* the world's drama. The operation is carried out in two times: (1) the return to the primordial totality, and (2) the repetition of the cosmogony, that is to say, the breaking up of the primitive unity. The same operation takes place again during the collective annual ceremonies. Schärer points out that the end of the year signifies the end of an era and also of a world (1963, 94ff.); the ceremonies clearly indicate that there is a return to the precosmic time, the time of the sacred totality embodied in the watersnake and in the tree of life. In fact, during this period, sacred *par excellence*, which is called *helat nyelo*, "the time between the years," a replica of the tree of life is erected in the village and all the population returns to the primeval (i.e., precosmogonic) age. Rules and interdictions are suspended since the world has ceased to exist. While waiting for a new creation the community lives near the godhead, more exactly lives *in* the total primeval godhead. The orgiastic character of the interval between the years ought not to obscure its sacrality. As Schärer puts it, "there is no question of disorder (even if it may appear so to us) but of another order" (1963, 97). The orgy takes place in accordance with the divine commandments, and those who participate in it recover in themselves the total godhead. As is well known, in many other religions, primitive as well as historical, the periodical orgy is considered to be the instrument *par excellence* to achieve the perfect totality. It is from such a totality that a new creation will take place – for the Dayaks as well as for the Mesopotamians.

Primordiality and Totality

Even this imperfect résumé of an immense amount of material has enabled us to grasp the considerable role that the cosmogonic myth plays in an archaic society. The myth unveils the religious thought of the Dayaks in all its depth and complexity. As we have just seen it, the individual and collective life has a cosmological structure: every life constitutes a cycle, whose model is the sempiternal creation, destruction, and re-creation of the world. Such a conception is not restricted to the Dayak, or even to peoples having their type of culture. In other words, the Dayak myth reveals to us a meaning which transcends its ethnographic frontiers. Now, what is striking in this mythology is the great importance bestowed upon the *primordial totality*. One may almost say that the Dayaks are obsessed by two aspects of the sacred: the *primordiality* and the *totality*. This does not mean that they belittle the work of creation. There is nothing of the Indian or gnostic pessimism in the Dayak conception of the cosmos and of life. The world is good and significant because it is sacred, since it came out from the tree of life, that is to say from the total godhead. But only the primordial total godhead is perfect. If the cosmos must be periodically abolished and recreated, it is not because the first creation did not succeed, but because it is only that stage which precedes the creation which represents a plenitude and a beatitude otherwise inaccessible in the created world. On the other hand, the myth points out the necessity of creation, that is, of the breaking up of the primeval unity. The original perfection is periodically reintegrated, but such perfection is always transitory. The Dayak myth proclaims that the creation – with all that it made possible: human existence, society, culture – cannot be definitively abolished. In other words, a "sacred history" has taken place, and this history must be perpetuated by periodical reiteration. It is impossible to freeze the reality in its germinal modality, such as it was in the beginning, immersed as it were in the primordial divine totality.

Now, it is this exceptional value conferred upon the "sacred history," ground and model of all human history, that is significant. Such attribution of value is recognizable in many other primitive mythologies, but it becomes particularly important in the mythologies of the ancient Near East and of Asia. If we examine a mythology in its totality we learn the judgment of the particular people upon its own sacred history. Every mythology presents a successive and coherent series of primordial events, but different peoples judge these fabulous acts in different ways, underlining the importance of some of them, casting aside, or even completely neglecting, others. If we analyze the context of what may be called the myth of the estrangement of the creator god and his progressive transformation into a *deus otiosus*, we notice a similar process, involving an analogous choice and judgment: out of a series of primordial creative events, only some of them are exalted, those in particular which are of consequence for human life. In other words, the coherent series of events which constitute the *sacred history* is incessantly remembered and extolled, while the previous stage, everything which existed *before* that sacred history – first and above all, the majestic and solitary presence of the creator God – fades away. If the High God is still remembered, he is known to have created the world and man, but this is almost all. Such a Supreme God seems to have ended his role by achieving the work of creation. He plays almost no role in the cult, his myths are few and rather banal, and, when he is not completely forgotten, he is invoked only in cases of extreme distress, when all other divine beings have proved utterly ineffectual.

The "Great Father" and the Mythical Ancestors

This lesson of the primitive myths is particularly revealing. It not only shows us that man, turning toward the divinities of life and fecundity, became as it were more and more incarnated. It also shows that early man assumes already, in his way, a history of which he is at once both the center and the victim. What happened to his mythical ancestors became, for him, more important than what happened *before* their appearance. One can illustrate this process with innumerable examples. I have discussed a number of such myths in previous works.[3] But I would like to examine now the mythical traditions of a people who for more than half a century have enjoyed a considerable vogue among anthropologists, sociologists, and psychologists, namely the Aranda tribes of Central Australia. I will draw exclusively from the materials collected by T. G. H. Strehlow,[4] the son of the famous missionary Carl Strehlow, whose writings gave rise to heated controversies in Durkheim's time. I think I choose the best living authority, for Aranda was the first language spoken by T. G. H. Strehlow, and he studied these tribes intensely for more than thirty years.

According to the Aranda, the sky and the earth have always existed and have always been inhabited by supernatural beings. In the sky there is an emu-footed personage, having emu-footed wives and children: it is the Great Father (*knaritja*), called also the Eternal Youth (*altjira nditja*). All these supernatural beings live in a perpetually green land, rich in flowers and fruits, traversed by the Milky Way. All of them are eternally young, the Great Father being in appearance as young as his children. And all of them are as immortal as the stars themselves, for death cannot enter their home.

Strehlow thinks that it would be impossible to regard this emu-footed Great Father as a supernatural being analogous to certain celestial gods of Southeast Australia.

Indeed, he did not create or shape the earth, nor did he bring into existence either plants, animals, man, or the totemic ancestors, nor did he inspire or control the ancestors' activities. The Great Father and the other inhabitants of heaven were never interested in what happened on the earth. Evil-doers had to fear not the celestial Great Father but the wrath of the totemic ancestors and the punishment of the tribal authorities. For, as we shall see in a moment, all the creative and meaningful acts were effected by the earth-born totemic ancestors. In sum, one can see here a drastic transformation of a celestial being into a *deus otiosus*. The next step could only be his falling into total oblivion. This probably did happen outside of the western Aranda territory, where Strehlow could not find any comparable beliefs in sky beings.

Nevertheless, there are some characteristic traits which allow this otiose and transcendent Great Father and Eternal Youth a place in the category of supreme beings. There is, first, his immortality, his youth, and his beatific existence; there is then his ontological anteriority with regard to the totemic heroes; indeed, he had been up there, in the sky, for a long time before the emergence of the totemic ancestors from under the earth. Finally, the religious importance of the sky is repeatedly proclaimed: for example, in the myths of certain heroes who conquered immortality by ascending to heaven, in the mythical traditions of trees or ladders connecting heaven and earth, and especially in the widespread Aranda beliefs that death came into being because the communications with heaven had been violently interrupted. Strehlow recalls the traditions concerning a ladder joining the earth to heaven, and describes the sites where, according to the legend, there grew gigantic trees which certain mythical ancestors were able to climb to heaven. Similar beliefs are to be found in many other archaic traditions, particularly in myths relating that after the interruption of the communications between heaven and earth, the gods retired to the highest sky and became more or less *dei otiosi*. From that moment on, only a few privileged personages – heroes, shamans, medicine men – have been able to ascend to heaven. We do not know how much of this mythical theme was familiar to the Aranda. But the fact is that, despite the reciprocal indifference between the Aranda and the celestial beings, the religious prestige of heaven continues to survive along with the haunting memory of a conquest of immortality by an ascension to heaven. One is tempted to read in these mythical fragments a certain nostalgia for a primordial situation irretrievably lost.

In any case the *primordium* represented by the celestial Great Father does not have any immediate significance for the Aranda. On the contrary, the Aranda seem to be interested exclusively in what happened at a certain moment *on the earth*. Such happenings are supremely significant; that is to say, in our terminology, they have a religious value. Indeed, the events that took place in the mythical times, in the "Dream Time," are religious in the sense that they constitute a paradigmatic history which man has to follow and repeat in order to assure the continuity of the world, of life and society.

While the Great Father and his family lived a sort of paradisiacal existence in the sky, without any responsibility, on the surface of earth there existed even from time immemorial amorphous, semiembryonic masses of half-developed infants. They could not develop into individual men and women, but neither could they grow old or die. Indeed, neither life nor death was known on earth. Life existed fully below the surface of the earth, in the form of thousands of slumbering supernatural beings. They also were uncreated (as a matter of fact they are called "born out of their own eternity," *altijirana nambakala*). Finally they awoke from their sleep and broke through the surface of the earth. Their birthplaces are impregnated with their life and power. One of these supernatural beings is the sun, and when he emerged out of the ground the earth was flooded with light.

The forms of these chthonian beings were varied; some emerged in animal forms, others as men and women. But all of them had something in common: the theriomorphic ones acted and thought like humans, and those in human forms could change at will into a particular species of animal. These chthonian beings, commonly designated totemic ancestors, began to wander on the surface of the earth and to modify the land, giving the Central Australian landscape its actual physical features. Such works constitute properly speaking a cosmogony; the ancestors did not create the earth, but they gave form to a preexistent *materia prima*. And the anthropogony repeats the cosmogony. Some of the totemic ancestors took on the roles of culture heroes, slicing apart the semiembryonic aggregate, then shaping each individual infant by slitting the webs between his fingers and toes and cutting open his ears, eyes, and mouth. Other culture heroes taught men how to make tools and fire and to cook food, and they also revealed social and religious institutions to them.

As a result of all these labors, an extreme fatigue overpowered the ancestors, and they sank into the ground or turned into rocks, trees, or ritual objects (*tjurunga*). The sites which marked their final resting places are, like their birth places, regarded as important sacred centers, and are called by the same name, *pmara kutata*. But the disappearance of the ancestors, which put an end to the primordial age, is not final. Though reimmersed in their initial slumber under the surface of the earth, they watch over the behavior of men. Moreover, the ancestors reincarnate themselves perpetually; as Strehlow has shown (1964, 730), the immortal soul of each individual represents a particle of an ancestor's life.

This fabulous epoch when the ancestors were roaming about the land is for the Aranda tantamount to a paradisiacal age. Not only do they imagine the freshly formed earth as a paradise, where the different animals allowed themselves to be easily captured and water and fruits were in abundance, but the ancestors were free from the multitude of inhibitions and frustrations that inevitably obstruct all human beings who are living together in organized communities.[5] This primordial paradise still haunts the Aranda. In a certain sense, one can interpret the brief intervals of ritual orgy, when all the interdictions are suspended, as ephemeral returns to the freedom and beatitude of the ancestors.

Such a terrestrial and paradisiacal primordiality – which constitutes both a history and a propaedeutic – is the one that interests the Aranda. In this mythical time man became what he is today, not only because he was then shaped and instructed by the ancestors, but also because he has to repeat continuously every thing that the ancestors did *in illo tempore*. The myths disclose this sacred and creative history. Moreover, through initiation, every young Aranda not only learns what happened *in principio*, but ultimately discovers *that he was already there*, that somehow he participated in those glorious events. The initiation brings about an *anamnesis*. At the end of the ceremony, the novice finds out that the hero of the myths just communicated to him is himself. He is shown a sacred and well-guarded ritual object, a *tjurunga*, and one old man tells him: This is your own body! – for that *tjurunga* represents the body of one of the ancestors. This dramatic revelation of the identity between the eternal ancestor and the individual in which he is reincarnated can be compared with *tat tvam asi* of the Upanishads. These beliefs are not exclusively Aranda. In Northeast Australia, for instance, when an Unambal proceeds to repaint the image of a Wondjina on the rock wall (the Wondjina are the equivalent of the Central Australian totemic ancestors), he says: "I am going now to refresh and invigorate myself; I paint myself anew, so that the rain can come" (Eliade 1967, 227).

To the irrevocability of death, as a result of the brutal interruption of the communications between earth and heaven, the Aranda replied with a theory of transmigration thanks to which the ancestors – that is to say, they themselves – are supposed to return perpetually to life. One can distinguish, then, two sorts of *primordiality*, to which two types of nostalgia correspond: (1) the *primordium* represented by the celestial Great Father and by the celestial immortality that is inaccessible to ordinary human beings; (2) the fabulous epoch of the ancestors, when life in general and human life in particular was brought about. The Aranda yearn above all for the terrestrial paradise represented by this second *primordium*.

Two Types of Primordiality

Such a process is also known in other religions, even in the most complex ones. We may refer, for example, to the primordiality of Tiamat and the passage to the creative primordial epoch represented by the victory of Marduk, along with the cosmogony, anthropogony, and the founding of a new divine hierarchy. Or we might compare the primordiality of Ouranos with the establishment of Zeus's supremacy, or point to the passage from the almost forgotten Dyaus to Varuna, and later still to the consecutive supremacies of Indra, Shiva, and Vishnu. In all these cases one may say that the creation of a new world is implied, even when there is no question of a cosmogony properly speaking. But it is always the emergence of a new religious world that appears to be in a more direct relation with the human condition.

What is significant in this substitution of an existential primordiality for a rather speculative one is that this process represents a more radical incarnation of the *sacred* in *life* and in *human existence* as such. Of course, this process is fairly common in the history of religions, and it is not completely foreign to the Judeo-Christian tradition. One may say that we have in Bonhoeffer the most recent example of the incarnation of the sacred in the profane existence of historical man; one may also identify in the most recent American theology, the god-is-dead theology, yet another variant, drastically secularized, of the myth of *deus otiosus*.

Thus, we can distinguish two types of primordialities: (1) a precosmic, unhistorical primordiality, and (2) a cosmogonic or historical one. In effect, the cosmogonic myth opens the *sacred history*; it is an *historical myth*, though not in the Judeo-Christian sense of the word, for the cosmogonic myth has the function of an exemplary model and as such it is periodically reactualized. We can also distinguish two species of *religious nostalgias*: (1) the longing to reintegrate the primordial totality that existed before the creation (the Dayak type of religious nostalgia); and (2) the longing to recover the primordial epoch that began immediately *after* the creation (the Aranda type). In this latter case the nostalgia yearns for the *sacred history* of the tribe. It is with such *myths of the sacred history* – still alive in many traditional societies – that the Judeo-Christian idea of history has to vie.

* This chapter is a revised and expanded version of an article first published in *Religious Studies* 2 (1967): 171–83.

The article in *Religious Studies* represents a slightly modified translation of a public lecture given at the XIII Congress of the "Sociétés de Philosophie de Langue Française," Geneva, September 2–6, 1966. Hence the style of the spoken word.

Notes

1. See especially Eliade 1954 and 1963.
2. The book has recently been translated into English by Rodney Needham (see Schärer 1963).
3. See particularly *Myth and Reality*, pp. 92 ff.
4. Especially his *Aranda Traditions* (Melbourne, 1947) and his recent article (1964, 723–54); cf. also idem 1957, 14–23. See also Eliade 1967, especially pp. 209ff.
5. Strehlow 1964, 729. Cf. also idem (1947, 36ff.), on the "Golden Age" of the totemic ancestors.

References

Eliade, Mircea. 1954. *The Myth of the Eternal Return* (transl. from the French by Willard R. Trask). New York: Harper and Row.

———1963. *Myth and Reality*. New York: Harper and Row.

———1967. "Australian Religion: An Introduction. Part II." *History of Religions* 6: 208–35.

Schärer, Hans. 1963. *Ngaju Religion: The Conception of God among a South Borneo People* (trans. Rodney Needham). The Hague: Mouton.

Strehlow, T. G. H. 1947. *Aranda Traditions*. Melbourne: Melbourne University Press.

_____1957. "La gémellité de l'âme humaine." *La Tour Saint-Jacques* (Paris) Nos. 11–12: 14–23.

_____1964. "Personal Monototemism in a Polytotemic Community." In *Festschrift für Ad. E. Jensen*, 723–54. Munich.

PART III

SOCIOLOGICAL APPROACHES

INTRODUCTION TO PART III

It is easy to present a broad definition of sociological approaches to myths and mythologies as "somehow related to society" whereas it is more difficult to provide a definition in precise terms. Most definitions in the study of myth, religion, and culture are best conceived of as kinds of description or as "generalized interpretation" and as such they inevitably come with some degree of imprecision. So, generally speaking, a sociological approach is one in which myths are considered explainable and understandable primarily in their relation to the social world. Such social relations may be conceived of in two different ways: the first concerns the contents of myth, that is, the subject matters of myths to be explained refer to the social world, and in the second the methods and theories involved in the explaining are of a sociological kind. Thus, (1) either myth explains (perhaps very subtly, concealed or indirectly) what goes on in society or (2) sociological method and theory are judged more appropriate in explaining myth. In the first case, the view of myth is intellectualist as myth is held to explain something about the realities of social world, whereas in the second view the method and theory is predominantly about mythical projections of social matters or about correlations between what goes on in the myth and what goes on in society. It should be noted that contemporary sociologists are generally not much concerned with scholarship on myths and mythologies because the sociologists' fields of inquiry mostly are located in modern societies, which are generally thought of as "post-mythic."[1] However, many anthropologists have applied sociological approaches in their studies of myth in traditional societies. Historians of religions have also employed sociological approaches as they are not the prerogative of any particular discipline. The sociological approaches began to appear in the last decades of the nineteenth century which a turn towards more synchronic studies of human and social phenomena. Earlier scholarship was diachronic, intent on disclosing origins, histories and developments. In contrast, synchronic studies introduced two crucial notions: function and structure. For the study of culture, religion and myth this meant that the emphasis was no longer on origins etc., but on the function, the impact and importance, of, say myth, in a society. Anthropologists took from speculating about origins to going on fieldwork, to find out how cultures and societies function, that is, how they are structured and how the various parts of the cultural and social organism cooperate.

Since their inception, sociological approaches to myth have been important and proved relevant in the study of myth as a social human phenomenon. It is indeed one of the criteria for the definition of myths that they are shared by groups and societies and involved in the making of concerted human action. Myths are inextricably linked to social institutions and conventions; if they were not so linked and had no social authority then they would be something other than "myth," e.g. fairytale or daydreaming. It is therefore the premise of sociological approaches that myths are best explained and understood in their social contexts and that the social references of myths are considered the most important. Sociological theories of myth are often "Correspondence theories" as they focus on the correspondences between social facts and their representations in myths. Correspondence theories also come under that label of "symbolism" but that term is somewhat misleading in that there may not be any specific symbols or symbolizing involved; it is rather the idea that myths reflect, or "symbolize," more basic social forms, such as kinship or legal rules. It must be emphasized that the relations between myth and society are not straightforward and that it may be completely impossible to reason from a myth to the social conditions to which it belongs. To give but one example, here is how R. A. Buxton explains the situation concerning Greek myth: "Sometimes Greek myths reflect social reality, but sometimes they distort or invert it" (1981, xvi). This seems to be a valid observation concerning mythologies of (presumably) all societies in the history of the world. Myths about transgressions, violations, distortions are remarkably frequent. But thereby, they more often than not actually sanction the order of things because the situation presented by the myth is recognizable as an impossible way for the world to be. Chaotic myths go against chaos. If myths are, amongst other things, blueprints and charters for social affairs they are seldom so in any law-like manner – they do not present worldviews in the shapes of highway codes. As we shall see below, myths may "be about" social matters in many different ways.

Myths as Social Representations

No society or group can function without ideas about itself, that is, without some form of ideology. Every social organization produces information about itself, in models of its own reality and in models for its continued existence in the exemplary manner. That information has to be passed on from generation to generation, or else society will lose its collective memory, its ideas and representation, or, in brief, its cohesion and sense of direction. It is therefore logical to see myth straightforwardly as social ideology in narrative form. Already Émile Durkheim noticed this: "But the mythology of a group is the system of beliefs common to this group. The traditions whose memory it perpetuates express the way in which society represents man and the world; it is moral system and a cosmology as well as a history" (1965, 419–20). In myth we find the representations that people have of the world and who they and others are. The stories and representations in them may represent matters hard to believe for the outsider, but that is not an issue because myths are for the insiders. They are, so to speak, produced for "domestic" consumption. Durkheim also said that, "a *représentation* is considered to be true when it is believed to represent reality" (in Lukes 1973, 491). This view obviously gives the impression of an invitation to relativism and seems to lack criteria for determining the epistemic value of myth. The point is, however, that the scholar must proceed from the methodological principle that myths are relevant and *considered* to be true in and by a given group. The social value of a cosmology is not judged by its scientific accuracy. Today scientific representations or explanations of the word are "considered true" and myths not so. However, history shows that many once accepted scientific "truths" have since been relegated to the realm of belief and mythological worldview. The value of differentiating between fact and fiction in the study of myth is often not at all relevant. Distinctions can be made, of course, with reference to the contents of myths. It is evident that unicorns or dragons do not belong in scientific zoological classifications, but that does not make unicorns or dragons uninteresting – nor does it make them go away – because, in spite of their fictitious nature, they can be socially, culturally and religiously very important. Thus, the criteria we employ concerning the truth or validity of myth have nothing to do with the criteria we use for judging e.g. the veracity of scientific statements or the accuracy of payslips. It is worth noting Durkheim's further considerations:

> Now, what led men to consider these mythological propositions or beliefs as true? Was it because they had confronted them with a given reality, with spirits, for example, or with divinities of whom they had had real experience? Not at all: the world of mythical beings is not a real world, and yet men have believed in it. Mythological ideas have not been regarded as true because founded on an objective reality. It is, on the contrary, our ideas, our beliefs which confer on the objects of thought their reality. (in Lukes 1973, 491)

Steven Lukes' comment on Durkheim's view is: "Thus, 'mythical *représentations* are false in relation to things, but they are true in relation to the subjects who think them' and thus they can be said to be true, not in their contents, but in their social roles, and because of their 'functions in relation to the peoples who have believed in them.'" (1973, 493). Humans make their own world and it can hardly be contested that religion and myth are the arenas of social constructionism (Engler 2004). Even in the modern, secular world are humans guided by their collective representations, and much more than they think. Not least because one of the dominant current representations is that modern humankind is *not* guided by representations but by scientific truth. Political and other normative debates over the use and limits of science prove this manifestly. This points to the ways in which myths are involved in politics.

Political Uses of Myth: Myth as Masking

The social and political use of myth, consciously or unconsciously, for the purpose of masking certain social realities is as long as the history of myth itself. Myths have always proven the rights of kings to their throne, the entitlement of hunters of a certain clan to a specific territory etc. The close relations between myth, ideology and politics have a long history. Already in the Babylonian Marduk-cycle do political issues appear as projections on the mythological and religious plane. Where some scholars have approached the myth about the supremacy of the god Marduk as a primordial testimony of archaic mentality and religiosity, others have demonstrated how the same myth is a projection of political conditions (Smith 1982).

Myth is "masking" and most often in the form of unconscious projections. Projection is a psychological mechanism whereby subjective phenomena become treated as real, objective and independent objects. Projections achieve the status of collective, social reality when its propositions become widely accepted; from the time when someone suggests something till the same proposition ends as tacit and accepted knowledge there may be a long way, but that is how "truths" are made as social facts. An illustrative example, and this time from within myth scholarship itself, is the "myth" from and about the Indo-Europeans as a very careful construction (Lincoln 1999, 121–37 and 207–16). Quite a good deal of scholarship about religion and myth may, with the benefit of hindsight, be characterized as "ideological" and to some extent therefore also as "myth-like." McCutcheon argues that

> ...the widespread and virtually normative scholarly assumption that religion is sui generis, autonomous, strictly personal, essential, unique, prior to, and ultimately distinct from, all other facets of human life and interaction, is a highly useful discursive *as well as* political strategy. It makes possible an autonomous discourse, complete with the benefits and the authority of its practitioners, and privileges political claims. (1997, 26)

Likewise, scholarship is a political field and the discursive formations that it bases its legitimacy and authority on are often constructed by the establishment of a "counter-myth." In that perspective, my own analysis cannot lay claim to being any final, authoritative treatment of "what is myth?"

In a historical perspective, some mythological formations have been more enduring than others. Myths in histories is a large subject in itself and one that has been approached from various angles. Traditional historiography has no place for myth in the study of what "really happened"; mythical information obviously could not pass the tests of source criticism and was therefore judged irrelevant. By the middle of the twentieth century, however, new modes of historical research were presented by the French "Annales" school with their emphasis on the history of mentalities, collective representations which have a more enduring character and provide the long lines in cultural and intellectual history. Michel Foucault, whose work is an inspiration for much contemporary critical analysis of myth as discourse (see also Part VI, below), later introduced the notion of "episteme" as a term for modes of thought, which have traits and functions similar to mythologies and worldviews. Mentalities and "epistemes" are interpretive tools with which humans approach their worlds and order them according to political programmes that have most often been clad in mythological garb. Gavin Flood states that mythmaking is something that still totally permeates political discourse and "It is an entirely normal way of making political events intelligible in the light of ideological beliefs" (1996, 275). More often than not, myths make the world not only intelligible, but the only "natural" way for the world to be. Where modern science explains culture on the basis of human nature, myth has always (re-)presented culture as if it were nature. As Roland Barthes once stated: "Myth is what goes without saying," because not only does myth refer to the natural order, it creates it.

Myth as Mediating Worlds: Natural, Mental, Social, Ideal

These relations between the "Lived in" social world and the "Thought of" ideal world can be very complicated indeed. It is the business of worldviews to mediate between the natural physical world, the mental and social worlds and the ideal world. Myths, as well as rituals and classification, play a large part in upholding religious worldviews (Lincoln 1989).[2] Worldviews are related to and constrained by specific social formations and modes of subsistence. What is important materially will mostly be reflected in myths, but again there are no simple cause-and-effects here between the material bases and conditions of human life and ideological or mythical super-structures. The ambition of earlier structural-functionalist anthropological and sociological research was to uncover general sociological laws, so-called "nomothetic" explanations and models of society and the concomitant relations to ideologies, cosmologies and thus also myths. That ambition was not fruitful because the relations certainly are complicated. An example of complex correspondences between social reality and the tales that people tell, including myths, is given by anthropologist Christine Hugh-Jones in her remarks on the anthropological methodology involved in the analysis of cosmology and myth:

> Pira-pirana Indians see themselves as existing within an ordered cosmos created in the ancestral past. The world of their present-day experience is a residue or product of the ancestral doings related in myths, ritual chants, and shamanic spells. From their own point of view, this cosmos and the mythical deeds

associated with it control their contemporary social life and provide a moral framework for present-day action... I work the other way round... I start with the building of basic unit of social structure, families and patrilineal groups, through marriage and procreation. I begin by showing how different phases of the temporal process are associated with different spaces in and around the longhouse and end by showing that the very same 'space-time' principles underlie the structure of the cosmos... The anthropologist must regard the ancestral cosmos as an imaginary projection of present experience, but at the same time it is a projection which both controls the present experience and forms an integral part of it. There is therefore a sense in which each world – the ancestral world and the present-day secular one – regulates the other... (1979, 1, 13)

Edmund Leach notes on the traditional small-scale societies of indigenous peoples that one of their attributes is that they are "mythopoeic":

The state of how things are, as evidenced by who has rights over what and over whom, is justified by 'myth', that is to say by tales which have a sacred or religious quality (after the fashion of the Christian Bible), rather than by legislative enactments or precedence recorded in historical documents.

Furthermore this mythological-cosmological justification of the ordering of the prevailing social system is recurrently exhibited in 'rituals' of various kinds. These may include sacrifices, shamanistic trances, divinations, magical performance, sorcery, and even the curing of the sick. (Leach 1982, 144–5).

As Leach also notes, this range of performances does not amount to "any coherent body of theology." But it shows how myths are integral to both ritual actions and social life in general. That is not least because they sanctify the order of the world and the ways in which humans are to behave in it; myth thereby also expresses a kind of social cybernetics. In the words of Roy Rappaport:

Myths – narratives in which humans are made from earth by words, or the world is sung into its shape by heroes, or first ancestors emerged from the tribal ground – are often intimately related to canon. They are, if not themselves ultimately sacred or the locus of Ultimate Sacred Postulates, highly sanctified, as may be other sanctified expressions which, in their enunciation, select as true particular understandings of the world from the great range of understandings and words the world makes. But sanctification is obviously not limited to discourse guiding thought or representing values. It also invests sentences stipulating specific actions or classes of actions to be undertaken or avoided. (1999, 317)

Features of Sociological Approaches

All sociological approaches to myth focus on myth as a property of groups. Although individuals' renditions of myths are important they are only so if they belong to a social formation and are part of the production and reproduction of ideology, the value system, and worldview of the social group. The sociological approach will concentrate on issues such as social structure, politic hierarchy, and the distribution of authority. Included in this perspective are also economic factors concerning the differences in, e.g., property and wealth and legitimation of access to, and control over, modes of production and the goods produced or procured thereby. In sociological perspectives other central issues regarding myth are social order versus disorder, purity versus impurity, the creation of identities and borders between ethnic groups. Systems of classification are important objects of study as they reveal how the thought-of worlds are composed and what they entail for human practice. Sociological approaches generally highlight the functions of myth in culture and society and not so much on the question of origin, because the sociological approach has as its starting premise that myth originates in society. This may seem circular, but it is not. If it appears idealist to some extent then this is because idealism is inevitably involved in human affairs and therefore methodologically permissible. Groups and individuals do things, and do things in certain ways, because they have ideas, values, representations and traditions that tell them in which ways to be human. And, because they do things in certain ways, they have some ideas and not others.

Contributions

Émile Durkheim and Marcel Mauss

Émile Durkheim (1858–1917) and Marcel Mauss (1872–1950) are generally recognized as founders of the "French school" in anthropology and sociology. Both were born in Epinal in Eastern France, from the same family of French Jews with the younger Mauss being the nephew of Durkheim. Durkheim's father was a rabbi, but he himself remained a secular person all of his life. He entered the École Normale Supérieure in Paris at the age of twenty-one, and among his classmates were Henri Bergson and Jean Jaurès, later very famous figures in French society and intellectual culture. He studied with Fustel de Coulanges and was influenced by the theories of Auguste Comte and Herbert Spencer, which sharpened his ideas about social matters being empirical objects that can be studied rigorously, as what he termed "social facts." He graduated in 1882, but it was very difficult for him, being a Jewish socialist, to find a job in Paris in the nationalist climate after the French defeat in the Prussian war. He then took a new position in Bordeaux in pedagogy and social science. During the 1890s he was creative and productive and published later classics such as *The Division of Labour in Society*, *Rules of the Sociological Method*, and *Suicide*. In 1902 he was appointed to the chair of education at the Sorbonne university, where his lectures were compulsory for all students as the French universities were founded on the training of teachers for the secondary school system. This fact greatly contributed to his influence among students, of whom many worked and published with him and his colleagues, Mauss, Henri

Hubert and Robert Hertz. In 1912 he published his last great work *The Elementary Forms of the Religious Life*, which was to become one of the all time classics in the study of religion across several disciplines. World War I took a high toll on the group of younger scholars; many of them died in the trenches and when Durkheim's own son was killed, he never recovered and died in 1917.

Marcel Mauss, both a sociologist and an anthropologist, is known for his comprehensive studies on the relations between social structures and modes of exchange, not least from his original work *The Gift* from 1925. His interests were broad, comparative, and ranged *wide* as witnessed in his study of Eskimo societies and their patterns of subsistence related activities (1978). Furthermore, with Henri Hubert he published *Sacrifice: Its Nature and Function* in 1899 and *A General Theory of Magic* in 1904.[3] One of the recurrent issues are the links between social arrangements and forms of classification in "primitive societies." Mauss took a great interest in many diverse aspects of religions, their worlds of ideas and the forms of their practice. He never did fieldwork himself but he inspired a large group of younger French anthropologists who went far and wide. It was an axiom in Durkheim and Mauss's theory that social phenomena, "social facts," could not be derived from individual psychological phenomena, but only from other social phenomena. Thus their thesis that the origin of classification is social and not mental, or cognitive, and that the individual lacks the faculty of classification. In other words, theirs is a theory of humanity as born with a *Tabula rasa*, an empty mind which is then "filled" with matters social. This was a corrective to the then prevailing individualistic and psychologistic theories about culture and society, but not tenable today (cf. section "Cognitivist Approaches" below). In his introduction to the little volume from which this contribution is excerpted, the British anthropologist Rodney Needham, translator of the text, notes: "Very few academics have any ideas of their own" (p. xliv), but Durkheim and Mauss certainly did. Their contribution to the study of religion – and many other subjects – has been tremendous. The present piece consists of their final reflections on the subject of primitive classification as it was offered in their essay, originally published in their journal *L'Année Sociologique* published in 1903, when Durkheim was forty-five and Mauss thirty-one. The French subtitle has it as "A contribution to the study of collective representations." The essay contains some very important insights into the subject, but until Needham's translation in 1963 (sixty years later!) it was curiously neglected in the world of Anglophone anthropologists. This little section shows how they argue against empiricism and rationalism as the epistemic foundations of human knowledge. In their view of human knowledge it is social all the way down.

Georges Dumézil

Georges Dumézil (1898–1986) has been a very prominent scholar in the study of Indo-European languages and mythologies. He has also been severely criticized by some, who have found him to entertain an undue fascination with Germanic ideology (e.g. Lincoln 1999, 121–37). There is, however, disagreement among scholars on the extent of his right-wing political involvement or the importance of this issue for the results of his researches or the utility of his methods and perspective in the study of myths and mythologies. There can be no doubt that he was extremely prolific and a highly competent linguist specializing in the Indo-European languages. Among the main achievements of his work is the theory of Indo-European tripartite ideology so that the old myths and cosmologies reflect an ideology about the shape and structure as ideally divided into three realms: sovereignty, warfare and subsistence (fertility). This ideal is reflected in the assembly ("pantheon") of the gods and their respective competencies. It must be emphasized that the tripartite model is not meant as a description of actual historical societies, but of their ideology as reflected in myth and mythology. Dumézil's contribution to this volume demonstrates how a historical type of explanation of a problem in a mythological corpus is not as convincing as one that argues on the basis of the structures of the myths, relate them to social and religious formations and them seek validation in comparative analyses. The issue here is one that for a long time has puzzled and attracted great attention from scholars in the study of Old Norse mythology: the war between the two kinds of gods. Most scholars suggested that this war "of the gods" must reflect or echo historical events, such as battles between two groups of people of perhaps very different origin, for example an indigenous population and an invading one. Dumézil's analysis suggests a very different and quite convincing solution. The contribution also shows why his approach may be classed as proto-structuralist – a kind of structuralism emerging before that formulated by Claude Lévi-Strauss (cf. Part IV, Semiological approaches, below).

Mary Douglas

Mary Douglas (1921–2007) studied at the University of Oxford where E. E. Evans-Pritchard was a major influence. During and after World War II she worked in the British Colonial Service until 1947. She went to do fieldwork in the then Belgian Congo, among the Lele people of the Kasai region. Mary Douglas finished her doctorate in 1950 and then taught and did research at University College, London for about twenty-five years. Among her well-known books, *Purity and Danger* (1966) was the one that especially earned her great reputation. That work abundantly demonstrated the legacy from Durkheim and the French Sociological School and their strong influence on British social anthropology. According to this tradition, cultural institution, such as systems of classification and myths, derive their meaning from their position and function in society and therefore they can be said to be "mirror images" of the social structures, social values and norms. So, for Mary Douglas and other representatives of British Social Anthropology, "the meaning of myth" is to be found on the basis of a theory of "social correspondence" and this is a clear example of a sociological approach to myth. In the contribution chosen here, Mary Douglas concentrates on the issues concerning classification systems. Scholars applying sociological approaches tend to focus less on the narrative aspects of myth as their interpretations and explanations are primarily concerned with elements and functions that refer to the social world. The present contribution here has also been chosen because it provides an overview and discussion of a number of relevant issues in the history of research and the development of theory.

Pierre Clastres

Pierre Clastres (1934–1977) was a French anthropologist of anarchist persuasion as is reflected in his major work *Society against the State* where he addresses the questions of the forms and distribution of power in small-scale ("primitive") societies. A major point in his analysis of the South American Indians and their social formations is the absence of centralized power so they have societies but no state(s). Of course, chiefs and shamans are influential but somehow society and culture "work against" the accumulation of power that could result in the formations of states and social hierarchies with ensuing exploitation of some classes by others. Clastres' ethnography demonstrated that the formation of the state is a particular historical event and not a universal "given." The contribution here has been chosen as a fine example of fieldwork scholarship where it can clearly be seen, as Malinowski declared, what it means when the anthropologist has the native informants "at his elbow" (1977). The contexts of the telling of the myths are of immense importance if we are to understand what they mean when "lived." Clastres' contribution also shows that there is no direct one-to-one relationship between what goes on in the myth and in the context of its declaration, but that the connections are more complex and even more revealing of not only the social roles and rules among the Indians but of salient issues in their entire cosmology. "What makes Indians laugh" are not just silly things. The myths recorded by Clastres during his fieldwork are in themselves very fine examples of the genre and can be read with benefit as an introduction for readers less familiar with myths in small-scale societies.

Notes

1. In the last section in this volume, Part VI, we shall see that this is not really the case. Modern societies are fully saturated with myths but their character and location are transformed.
2. As it has happened to so many other terms, "worldview" has come under suspicion and even attack in fields such as anthropology, apparently because it has come with a hypothesis that it is supposedly a systematic and pre-packaged entity that is "downloaded" and distributed evenly in a population. A similar accusation has been levelled against the

use of the term "culture." In this connection I must admit that I find these criticisms to be exaggerated and I consider the terms quite useful. As long as we remember that all terms are maps or perspectives and avoid reifying them we should be doing well. Thus, "worldview" as an innocuous descriptive term that simply refers to a general outlook on world and life in a given social formation. On an anthropological view of "worldview" see Kearney 1988.

3. Lukes 1973 is a valuable and accessible source on Durkheim's influence, his collaborators and their many achievements. As the group put an emphasis on the importance of "collective representations" and "collective consciousness" in social life, it is interesting to note the great extent to which this also applies to their work together; there is a rare correspondence and theoretical integration to their work.

References

Buxton, R. A. 1981. "Introduction". In *Myth, Religion & Society: Structuralist Essays by M. Detienne, L. Gernet, J.-P. Vernant & P. Vidal-Naquet*, ed. R. L. Gordon, ix–xvii. Cambridge: Cambridge University Press.

Clastres, Pierre. 1977. *Society against the State*. Oxford: Blackwell.

Durkheim, Émile. 1965 (orig. 1915). *The Elementary Forms of the Religious Life*. London: The Free Press.

Durkheim, Émile and Marcel Mauss. 1963 (orig. 1901–02). *Primitive Classification*. (trans. Rodney Needham). Chicago: University of Chicago Press.

Engler, Steven. 2004. "Constructionism versus What?" *Religion* 34: 291–313.

Flood, Gavin. 1996. *Beyond Phenomenology: Rethinking the Study of Religion*. London: Cassell.

Hugh-Jones, Christine. 1979. *From the Milk River: Spatial and Temporal Processes in North West Amazonia*. Cambridge: Cambridge University Press.

Kearney, Michael. 1988. *World View*. Novato, CA: Chandler and Sharp.

Leach, Edmund. 1982. *Social Anthropology*. London: Fontana.

Lincoln, Bruce. 1989. *Discourse and the Construction of Society: Comparative Studies on Myth, Ritual and Classification*. New York: Oxford University Press.

_____1999. *Theorizing Myth: Narrative, Ideology, and Scholarship*. Chicago: University of Chicago Press.

Lukes, Steven. 1973. *Émile Durkheim: His Life and Work: A Historical and Critical Study*. London: Allen Lane.

Mauss, Marcel. 1978 (orig. 1906). *Seasonal Variations of the Eskimo: A Study in Social Morphology*. London: Routledge & Kegan Paul.

McCutcheon, Russell T. 1997. *Manufacturing Religion: The Discourse on* sui generis *Religion and the Politics of Nostalgia*. New York: Oxford University Press.

Rappaport, Roy A. 1999. *Ritual and Religion in the Making of Humankind*. Cambridge: Cambridge University Press.

Smith, Jonathan Z. 1982. *Imagining Religion: From Babylon to Jonestown*. Chicago: University of Chicago Press.

Primitive Classifications: Conclusions

Émile Durkheim and Marcel Mauss

PRIMITIVE CLASSIFICATIONS are therefore not singular or exceptional, having no analogy with those employed by more civilized peoples; on the contrary, they seem to be connected, with no break in continuity, to the first scientific classifications. In fact, however different they may be in certain respects from the latter, they nevertheless have all their essential characteristics. First of all, like all sophisticated classifications, they are systems of hierarchized notions. Things are not simply arranged by them in the form of isolated groups, but these groups stand in fixed relationships to each other and together form a single whole. Moreover, these systems, like those of science, have a purely speculative purpose. Their object is not to facilitate action, but to advance understanding, to make intelligible the relations which exist between things. Given certain concepts which are considered to be fundamental, the mind feels the need to connect to them the ideas which it forms about other things. Such classifications are thus intended, above all, to connect ideas, to unify knowledge; as such, they may be said without inexactitude to be scientific, and to constitute a first philosophy of nature.[1] The Australian does not divide the universe between the totems of his tribe with a view to regulating his conduct or even to justify his practice; it is because, the idea of the totem being cardinal for him, he is under a necessity to place everything else that he knows in relation to it. We may therefore think that the conditions on which these very ancient classifications depend may have played an important part in the genesis of the classificatory function in general.

Now it results from this study that the nature of these conditions is social. Far from it being the case, as Frazer seems to think, that the social relations of men are based on logical relations between things, in reality it is the former which have provided the prototype for the latter. According to him, men were divided into clans by a preexisting classification of things; but, quite on the contrary, they classified things because they were divided by clans.

We have seen, indeed, how these classifications were modelled on the closest and most fundamental form of social organization. This, however, is not going far enough. Society was not simply a model which classificatory thought followed; it was its own divisions which served as divisions for the system of classification. The first logical categories were social categories; the first classes of things were classes of men, into which these things were integrated. It was because men were grouped, and thought of themselves in the form of groups, that in their ideas they grouped other things, and in the beginning the two modes of grouping were merged to the point of being indistinct. Moieties were the first genera; clans, the first species. Things were thought to be integral parts of society, and it was their place in society which determined their place in nature. We may even wonder whether the schematic manner in which genera are ordinarily conceived may not have depended in part on the same influences. It is a fact of current observation that the things which they comprise are generally imagined as situated in a sort of ideational milieu, with a more or less clearly delimited spatial circumscription. It is certainly not without cause that concepts and their interrelations have so often been represented by concentric and eccentric circles, interior and exterior to each other, etc. Might it not be that this tendency to imagine purely logical groupings in a form contrasting so much with their true nature originated in the fact that at first they were conceived in the form of social groups occupying, consequently, definite positions in space? And have we not in fact seen this spatial localization of genus and species in a fairly large number of very different societies?

Not only the external form of classes, but also the relations uniting them to each other, are of social origin. It is because human groups fit one into another – the sub-clan into the clan, the clan into the moiety, the moiety into the tribe – that groups of things are ordered in the same way. Their regular diminution in span, from genus to species, species to variety, and so on, comes from the equally diminishing extent presented by social groups as one leaves the largest and oldest and approaches the more recent and the more derivative. And if the totality of things is conceived as a single system, this is because society itself is seen in the same way. It is a whole, or rather it is *the* unique whole to which everything is related. Thus logical hierarchy is only another aspect of social hierarchy, and the unity of knowledge is nothing else than the very unity of the collectivity, extended to the universe.

Furthermore, the ties which unite things of the same group or different groups to each other are themselves conceived as social ties. We recalled in the beginning that the expressions by which we refer to these relations still have a moral significance; but whereas for us they are hardly more than metaphors, originally they meant what they said. Things of the same class were really considered as relatives of the individuals of the same social group, and consequently of each other. They are of "the same flesh," the same family. Logical relations are thus, in a sense, domestic relations. Sometimes, too, as we have seen, they are comparable at all points with those which exist between a master and an object possessed, between a chief and his subjects. We may even wonder whether the idea of the pre-eminence of genus over species, which is so strange from a positivistic point of view, may not be seen here in its rudimentary form. Just as, for the realist, the general idea dominates the individual, so the clan totem dominates those of the sub-clans and, still more, the personal totems of individuals; and wherever the moiety has retained its original stability it has a sort of primacy over the divisions of which it is composed and the particular things which are included in them. Though he may be essentially Wartwut and partially Moiwiluk, the Wotjobaluk described by Howitt is above all a Krokitch or a Gamutch. Among the Zuñi, the animals symbolizing the six main clans are set in sovereign charge over their respective sub-clans and over creatures of all kinds which are grouped with them.

But if the foregoing has allowed us to understand how the notion of classes, linked to each other in a single system, could have been born, we still do not know what the forces were which induced men to divide things as they did between the classes. From the fact that the external form of the classification was furnished by society, it does not necessarily follow that the way in which the framework was used is due to reasons of the same origin. *A priori* it is very possible that motives of a quite different order should have determined the way in which things were connected and merged, or else, on the contrary, distinguished and opposed.

The particular conception of logical connexions which we now have permits us to reject this hypothesis. We have just seen, in fact, that they are represented in the form of familial connexions, or as relations of economic or political subordination; so that the same sentiments which are the basis of domestic, social, and other kinds of organization have also been effective in this logical division of things. The latter are attracted or opposed to each other in the same way as men are bound by kinship or opposed in the vendetta. They are merged as members of the same family are merged by common sentiment. That some are subordinate to others is analogous in every respect to the fact that an object possessed appears inferior to its owner, and likewise the subject to his master. It is thus states of the collective mind (*âme*) which gave birth to these groupings, and these states moreover are manifestly affective. There are sentimental affinities between things as between individuals, and they are classed according to these affinities.

We thus arrive at this conclusion: it is possible to classify other things than concepts, and otherwise than in accordance with the laws of pure understanding. For in order for it to be possible for ideas to be systematically arranged for reasons of sentiment, it is necessary that they should not be pure ideas, but that they should themselves be products of sentiment. And in fact, for those who are called primitives, a species of things is not a simple object of knowledge but corresponds above all to a certain sentimental attitude. All kinds of affective elements combine in the representation made of it. Religious emotions, notably, not only give it a special tinge, but attribute to it the most essential properties of which it is constituted. Things are above all sacred or profane, pure or impure, friends or enemies, favourable or unfavourable;[2] i.e. their most fundamental characteristics are only expressions of the way in which they affect social sensibility. The differences and resemblances which determine the fashion in which they are grouped are more affective than intellectual. This is how it happens that things change their nature, in a way, from society to society; it is because they affect the sentiments of groups differently. What is conceived in one as perfectly homogeneous is represented elsewhere as essentially heterogeneous. For us, space is formed of similar parts which are substitutable one for the other. We have seen, however, that for many peoples it is profoundly differentiated according to regions. This is because each region has its own affective value. Under the influence of diverse sentiments, it is connected with a special religious principle, and consequently it is endowed with virtues *sui generis* which distinguish it from all others. And it is this emotional value of notions which plays the preponderant part in the manner in which ideas are connected or separated. It is the dominant characteristic in classification.

It has quite often been said that man began to conceive things by relating them to himself. The above allows us to see more precisely what this anthropocentrism, which might better be called *sociocentrism*, consists of. The centre of the first schemes of nature is not the individual; it is society.[3] It is this that is objectified, not man. Nothing shows this more clearly than the way in which the Sioux retain the whole universe, in a way, within the limits of tribal space; and we have seen how universal space itself is nothing else than the site occupied by the tribe, only indefinitely extended beyond its real limits. It is by virtue of the same mental disposition that so many peoples have placed the centre of the world, "the navel of the earth," in their own political or religious capital,[4] i.e. at the place which is the centre of their moral life. Similarly, but in another order of ideas, the creative force of the universe and everything in it was first conceived as a mythical ancestor, the generator of the society.

This is how it is that the idea of a logical classification was so hard to form, as we showed at the beginning of this work. It is because a logical classification is a classification of concepts. Now a concept is the notion of a clearly determined group of things; its limits may be marked precisely. Emotion, on the contrary, is something essentially fluid and inconsistent. Its contagious influence spreads far beyond its point of origin, extending to everything about it, so that it is not possible to say where its power of propagation ends. States of an emotional nature necessarily possess the same characteristic. It is not possible to say where they begin or where they end; they lose themselves in each other, and mingle their properties in such a way that they cannot be rigorously categorized. From another point of view, in order to be able to mark out the limits of a class, it is necessary to have analysed the characteristics by which the things assembled in this class are recognized and by which they are distinguished. Now emotion is naturally refractory to analysis, or at least lends itself uneasily to it, because it is too complex. Above all when it has a collective origin it defies critical and rational examination. The pressure exerted by the group on each of its members does not permit individuals to judge freely the notions which society itself has elaborated and in which it has placed something of its personality. Such constructs are sacred for individuals. Thus the history of scientific classification is, in the last analysis, the history of the stages by which this element of social affectivity has progressively weakened, leaving more and more room for the reflective thought of individuals. But it is not the case that these remote influences which we have just studied have ceased to be felt today. They have left behind them an effect which survives and which is always present; it is the very cadre of all classification, it is the ensemble of mental habits by virtue of which we conceive things and facts in the form of coordinated or hierarchized groups.

This example shows what light sociology throws on the genesis, and consequently the functioning, of logical operations. What we have tried to do for classification might equally be attempted for the other functions or fundamental notions of the understanding. We have already had occasion to mention, in passing, how even ideas so abstract as those of time and space are, at each point in their history, closely connected with the corresponding social organization. The same method could help us likewise to understand the manner in which the ideas of cause, substance, and the different modes of reasoning, etc. were formed. As soon as they are posed in sociological terms, all these questions, so long debated by metaphysicians and psychologists, will at last be liberated from the tautologies in which they have languished. At least, this is a new way which deserves to be tried.

Notes

1. As such they are very clearly distinguished from what might be called technological classifications. It is probable that man has always classified, more or less clearly, the things on which he lived, according to the means he used to get them: for example, animals living in the water, or in the air or on the ground. But at first such groups were not connected with each other or systematized. They were divisions, distinctions of ideas, not schemes of classification. Moreover, it is evident that these distinctions are closely linked to practical concerns, of which they merely express certain aspects. It is for this reason that we have not spoken of them in this work, in which we have tried above all to throw some light on the origins of the logical procedure which is the basis of scientific classifications.

2. For the adherent of many cults, even now, foodstuffs are classified first of all into two main classes, fat and lean, and we know to what extent this classification is subjective.

3. De la Grasserie has developed ideas fairly similar to our own, though rather obscurely and above all without evidence (1899, chap. III).

4. Something understandable enough for the Romans and even the Zuñi, but less so for the inhabitants of Easter Island, called Te Pito-te Henua (navel of the earth); but the idea is perfectly natural everywhere.

Reference

De la Grasserie, Raoul. 1899. *Des Religions comparées au point de vue sociologique*. Paris: V. Girard & E. Brière.

The Gods: Æsir and Vanir

Georges Dumézil

In Scandinavian mythology – the best described, or rather the only one of the Germanic mythologies which is described – the leading roles are divided among two groups, the Æsir (ON *Æsir*, sg. *áss*), and the Vanir (ON *vanir*, sg. *vanr*). Certain other divine types are mentioned, such as the Elves (ON *alfar*, sg. *alfr*), but no important or even specifically named gods are found among such groups. The meaning to be attributed to this coexistence of Æsir and Vanir constitutes our fundamental problem. In the analysis of *altnordische*, and consequently in that of *altgermanische*, *Religionsgeschichte* (see Bibliographical Notes), everything depends on which solution one proposes to this problem. All new attempts at interpretation must immediately come to grips with it, even to establish the very setting of the mythology.

No text provides a general and differentiating definition of the two divine groups. They are easily characterized, however, by examining their principal representatives. The distinction is so clear that, at least with regard to their leading traits, interpreters of all schools are in agreement. The two outstanding Æsir are Odin (Óðinn)[1] and Thor (þórr), along with Tyr (Týr), clearly somewhat faded, while the three most typical Vanir are Njord (Njorðr), Frey (Freyr), and Freya (Freyja). Even if it exceptionally occurs that they must be or do something else, the latter three are first and foremost rich and givers of riches; they are patrons of fecundity and of pleasure (Frey, Freya), also of peace (Frey); and they are associated, topographically and economically, with the earth that produces crops (Njord, Frey), and with the sea that enriches its sailors (Njord). Odin and Thor have other cares. Neither is of course uninterested in riches or in the products of the soil, but, at the time when Scandinavian religion is known to us, they have other centers of gravity. Odin is the supreme magician, master of runes, head of all divine society, patron of heroes, living or dead. Thor is the god of the hammer, enemy of the giants, whom he occasionally resembles in his fury. His name means "the god who thunders," and, if he helps the peasant in his work with the earth, it is in some violent fashion, even according to modern folklore, and as a mere byproduct of his atmospheric battle. In the course of the following chapters, we shall expand these brief descriptions; but they will suffice to show how the homogeneous Vanir stand in opposition to the Æsir, who are much more varied in their vocations.

With regard to their affinities, they are of two kinds, depending on whether one contemplates the cult practice and the divine state of things that maintains it, or the traditions concerning the remote origins of this state of things, what might be called the divine prehistory.

In the religious present, Æsir and Vanir live in perfect accord, without quarrel or jealousy, and this harmony permits men, in prayer and more generally in cult, to associate them without wariness. It also permits poets to forget occasionally that the Vanir indeed *are* Vanir and to designate with the name Æsir a divine community that is noted for its unity. Their association is often expressed in a three-term enumeration that brings out a clear hierarchy, with the Æsir coming first, superior to the Vanir: Odin, Thor, Frey (occasionally, in the third position, Frey and Njord; more rarely the god Frey gives his place to the goddess Freya). This formula so frequently sums up the needs and imaginations of men, in such different circumstances, and in such different parts of the Scandinavian world, that it must be significant.

Here are the principal examples of it. When Adam of Bremen, toward the end of the pagan period, reported on the religion practiced at the temple of Uppsala by the Swedes in Uppland, it was physically symbolized by the three idols standing side by side in the temple, presenting to the believers a semicircle of devotions:

> In this temple, entirely covered with gold, there are the statues of three gods, which the people worship, so arranged that the mightiest of them, Thor, occupies a throne in the middle of the chamber, while Wodan and Fricco have places on either side. The significance of these gods is as follows: Thor, they say, rules in the air, governing the thunder and lightning, the winds and rains, fair weather and crops. The other, Wodan – that is, "Frenzy" (*furor*) – wages war and grants man courage against his enemies. The third is Fricco, who bestows peace and pleasure to mortals. His likeness, too, they fashion with an immense phallus.
>
> For all their gods there are appointed priests to offer sacrifices for the people. If plague and famine threaten, a libation is poured to the idol Thor; if war, to Wodan; if marriages are to be celebrated, to Fricco.[2]

These notices pose problems of detail which we shall examine later, both with regard to the boundaries of divine specialties and to the place of honor accorded to Thor. What is important now is simply that these idols attest to, and excellently describe, a tripartite theological structure.

We know very little about the Scandinavian form of cult and liturgies, but two points of agreement show that the same triad at least presided over the most solemn maledictions. In the saga that bears his name, Egill Skallagrímsson, on the verge of leaving Norway for Iceland, curses the king who has stripped him of his goods and consigned him to this exile. After a general appeal to the gods under the names of *bond* and *goð*, he continues:

... reið sé rogn ok Óðinn!	... may the gods and Odin grow angry (at him)!
... folkmýgi lát flýja,	... may Frey and Njord make the
Freyr ok Njorðr, af jorðum!	oppressor of the people flee his lands!
Leiðisk lofða stríði	May Thor ("God of the land") loathe
landoss, þanns vé grandar![3]	the scourge who defiles the sanctuaries!

In his commentary, Finnur Jónsson analyzes the action of this stanza well: "The poet first invokes the gods in general; then individually the all-powerful Odin, Thor, the vigorous God-of-the-land, then Frey and Njord, as gods of fecundity and dispensers of riches" (Jonsson 1894, 180). In the still earlier Eddic poem *Skírnísmál*, Frey's servant, relinquishing his attempts to convince Gerd, object of his master's love, menaces her in these terms (str. 33):

Reiðr er þér Óðinn,   reiðr er þér ásabragr,
    þik scal Freyr fiásc,
in fyrinilla mÆr, enn þú fengit hefir
    gambanreiði goða.[4]

Angry is Odin at you, angry is the foremost god (=Thor) at you,
    Frey shall hate you,
monstrous maid, and you have won
    the wrath of the gods.[5]

At the beginning of the eleventh century, in the poem about his conversion, Hallfreðr VandrÆðaskáld, before giving himself over to Christ, the Father, and "God," defies the same heathen divinities (str. 9):

mér skyli Freyr ok Freyja,	Let Frey and Freya rage,
fjorð létk af dul Njarðar,	and Thor the thunderer too;
líknisk grom við Grímni	let wretches worship Odin:
gramr ok þórr enn rammi.	I forsook the folly of Njord.
(Kock 1946, I, 86)	

In magic such tripartite formulas against sickness or evil were possibly maintained for a long time: "'In the name of Odin, Thor, and Frigg' alternates there [Norway] with the Christian trinity" (Bang 1901, 21, 127).

Finally, mythology frequently joins the same characters in a triad. Among them alone are divided the three treasures forged by the dwarfs after losing a bet with the malicious Loki: Odin gets the magic ring, Thor the hammer that is to be the instrument of his battles, and Frey the wild boar with the golden bristles (Jónsson 1931, 123).[6] It is they, and only they, whom the *Voluspá* (strs. 53-56) describes as being joined in the supreme duels and deaths of the eschatological battle.[7] More generally, it is they – and the goddess Freya, closely associated with Freyr and Njord – who dominate, who indeed monopolize almost all the mythological material. It is no less significant that the three gods who split the property of the dead – the last two under rather obscure conditions – are Odin, who consigns to himself the nobles or "half the dead" from the battlefield, Thor, to whom go the thralls (more correctly, no doubt, the nonnobles), and Freya, who according to one text[8] takes the other half of those killed in battle and according to another text takes the dead women.[9]

Such is the present situation. But this union and this happy harmony, founded on a clear analysis of human wishes, have not always existed, according to the legend. In a far distant past the two divine groups lived at first separately, as neighbors; then they fought a fierce war, after which the most distinguished Vanir were associated with the Æsir, with the rest of their "people" living somewhere away from the struggle and the cares of their cult. Four strophes from that breathless poem, the *Voluspá*, in which the sibyl relates quite allusively the entire history of the gods; two texts of the erudite Snorri; and finally an unadroit plagiarism by his contemporary Saxo Grammaticus – these inform us of this initial crisis of the gods, which is presupposed also in several passages from other Eddic poems. These documents are not homogeneous: two present the event in mythological terms, two transpose it into historical and geographical terms. The first group includes strophes 21-24 of the *Voluspá* and a passage in Snorri's mythological manual written for the use of poets, the *Skáldskaparmál* (chap. 4); the second includes chapters 1, 2, 4, and 5 of the *Ynglingasaga*, discussing the *Ynglingar*, supposed descendants of Frey, and chapter 7 of the first book of Saxo's *Gesta Danorum*, a fragment of the "saga of Hadingus" which fills chapters 5 through 8 of that book.

a) *Voluspá* 21-24. I have elsewhere (Dumézil 1947) made an extended analysis of this passage, which the hypercritical Eugen Mogk (1924) sought to eliminate from the dossier on the Æsir and Vanir. The order of events – described as "the first war of armies in the world" – seems somewhat confused in these rapid and discontinuous strophes, which do not narrate, but content themselves with evoking episodes already known to the listeners. There is extensive reference to a female being called *Gullveig*, literally, "gold-drink, gold-drunkenness," sent by the Vanir to the Æsir, who, despite metallurgical treatment, cannot rid themselves of her. A sorceress, she sows corruption, particularly among women. There is also reference (24) to a spear, apparently magic, thrown by Odin against an enemy army, which does not prevent that "broken was the wall of the stronghold of the Æsir" and that "the warlike (?) Vanir were able to trample the plains." But nothing decisive results from these contrary movements, because (23) the gods hold an assembly for peace where they discuss eventual compensation.[10]

b) *Skáldskaparmál* (chap. 5, *Prose Edda*) (The response of Bragi to the question "Whence comes the art called poetry?"):

> The beginning of it was that the gods were at war with the people known as the Vanir and they arranged for a peace meeting between them and made a truce in this way: they both went up to a crock and spat into it. When they were going away, the gods took the truce token and would not allow it to be lost, and made of it a man. He was called Kvasir. He is so wise that nobody asks him any question he is unable to answer. He travelled far and wide over the world to teach men wisdom and came once to feast with some dwarfs, Fjalar and Galar. These called him aside for a word in private and killed him, letting his blood run into two crocks and one kettle. The kettle was called Óðrörir, but the crocks were known as Són and Boðn. They mixed his blood with honey, and it became the mead which makes whoever drinks of it a poet or a scholar. The dwarfs told the Æsir that Kvasir had choked with learning, because there was no one sufficiently well-informed to compete with him in knowledge.[11]

(There follows the story of the acquisition of the mead by Odin, who is to be its greatest beneficiary.)

c) *Ynglingasaga* (the beginning of the *Heimskringla*) (chaps. 1, 2, 4, 5):

> 1. Of the Three Continents. – The earth's round, on which mankind lives, is much indented. Great seas cut into the land from the ocean. We know that a sea goes from the Norva Sound (the Strait of Gibraltar) all the way to Jórsalaland ("Jerusalem Land," Palestine). From this sea a long arm extends to the northeast which is called the Black Sea. It separates the three parts of the world. The part to the eastward is called Asia; but that which lies to the west of it is called by some Europe, by others Eneá. North of the Black Sea lies Svíthjóth the Great or the Cold.
>
> Some men consider Svíthjóth the Great not less in size than Serkland the Great ("Saracen Land," North Africa), and some think it is equal in size to Bláland ("Blackman's Land," Africa). The northern part of Svíthjóth is uncultivated on account of frost and cold, just as the southern part of Bláland is a desert because of the heat of the sun. In Svíthjóth there are many large provinces. There are also many tribes and many tongues. There are giants and dwarfs; there are black men and many kinds of strange tribes. Also there are animals and dragons of marvellous size. Out of the north, from the mountains which are beyond all inhabited districts, a river runs through Svíthjóth whose correct name is Tanais (the Don River). In olden times it was called Tana Fork or Vana Fork. Its mouth is in the Black Sea. The land around the Vana Fork was then called Vana Home or the Home of the Vanir. This river divides the three continents. East of it is Asia, west of it Europe.

2. Of Ásgarth and Óthin. – The land east of the Tana Fork was called the Land or Home of the Æsir, and the capital of that country they called Ásgarth. In this capital the chieftain ruled whose name was Óthin. This was a great place for sacrifices. The rule prevailed there that twelve temple priests were highest in rank. They were to have charge of sacrifices and to judge between men. They are called *díar* or chiefs. All the people were to serve them and show them reverence.

Óthin was a great warrior and fared widely, conquering many countries. He was so victorious that he won the upper hand in every battle; as a result, his men believed that it was granted to him to be victorious in every battle. It was his habit that, before sending his men to battle or on other errands, he would lay his hands on their heads and give them a *bjannak* [benediction]. Then they believed they would succeed. It was also noted that wherever his men were sore bestead, on sea or on land, they would call on his name, and they would get help from so doing. They put all their trust in him. Often he was away so long as to be gone for many years.

[note: D. omits # 3 because that is not relevant for the story]

4. The War between the Æsir and the Vanir. – Óthin made war on the Vanir, but they resisted stoutly and defended their land; now the one, now the other was victorious, and both devastated the land of their opponents, doing each other damage. But when both wearied of that, they agreed on a peace meeting and concluded a peace, giving each other hostages. The Vanir gave their most outstanding men, Njorth the Wealthy and his son Frey; but the Æsir, in their turn, furnished one whose name was Hœnir declaring him to be well fitted to be a chieftain. He was a large man and exceedingly handsome. Together with him the Æsir sent one called Mímir, a very wise man; and the Vanir in return sent the one who was the cleverest among them. His name was Kvasir. Now when Hœnir arrived in Vanaheim he was at once made a chieftain. Mímir advised him in all things. But when Hœnir was present at meetings or assemblies without having Mímir at his side and was asked for his opinion on a difficult matter, he would always answer in the same way, saying, "Let others decide." Then the Vanir suspected that the Æsir had defrauded them in the exchange of hostages. Then they seized Mímir and beheaded him and sent the head to the Æsir. Óthin took it and embalmed it with herbs so that it would not rot, and spoke charms over it, giving it magic power so that it would answer him and tell him many occult things.

Óthin appointed Njorth and Frey to be priests for the sacrificial offerings, and they were *díar* [gods] among the Æsir. Freya was the daughter of Njorth. She was the priestess at the sacrifices. It was she who first taught the Æsir magic such as was practiced among the Vanir. While Njorth lived with the Vanir he had his sister as wife, because that was the custom among them. Their children were Frey and Freya. But among the Æsir it was forbidden to marry so near a kin.

5. Gefjon Ploughs Zeeland Out of Lake Mälaren. – A great mountain chain runs from the northeast to the southwest. It divides Svíthjóth the Great from other realms. South of the mountains it is not far to Turkey. There Óthin had large possessions. At that time the generals of the Romans moved about far and wide, subjugating all peoples, and many chieftains fled from their possessions because of these hostilities. And because Óthin had the gift of prophecy and was skilled in magic, he knew that his offspring would inhabit the northern part of the world. Then he set his brothers Vé and Víli over Ásgarth, but he himself and all *díar* and many other people, departed. First he journeyed west to Garthríki [Russia], and then south, to Saxland [northwestern Germany]. He had many sons. He took possession of lands far and wide in Saxland and set his sons to defend these lands. Then he journeyed north to the sea and fixed his abode on an island. That place is now called Óthinsey [Óthin's Island], on the island of Funen.

Thereupon he sent Gefjon north over the sound to seek for land. She came to King Gylfi, and he gave her a ploughland. Then she went to Giantland and there bore four sons to some giant. She transformed them into oxen and attached them to the plough and drew the land westward into the sea, opposite Óthin's Island, and that is [now] called Selund [Zeeland], and there she dwelled afterwards. Skjold, a son of Óthin married her. They lived at Hleithrar. A lake was left [where the land was taken] which is called Logrin. The bays in that lake correspond to the nesses of Selund. Thus says Bragi the Old:

> Gefjon, glad in mind, from
>
> Gylfi drew the good land,
>
> Denmark's increase, from the
>
> oxen so the sweat ran.
>
> Did four beasts of burden –
>
> with brow-moons eight in foreheads –
>
> walk before the wide isle
>
> won by her from Sweden.

But when Óthin learned that there was good land east in Gylfi's kingdom he journeyed there; and Gylfi came to an agreement with him, because he did not consider himself strong enough to withstand the Æsir. Óthin and Gylfi vied much with each other in magic and spells, but the Æsir always had the better of it.

Óthin settled by Lake Logrin, at a place which formerly was called Sigtúnir. There he erected a large temple and made sacrifices according to the custom of the Æsir. He took possession of the land as far as he had called it Sigtúnir. He gave dwelling places to the temple priests. Njorth dwelled at Nóatún, Frey at Uppsala, Heimdall at Himinbjorg, Thór at Thrúthvang, Baldr at Breithablik. To all he gave good estates.[12]

d) Saxo Grammaticus, *Gesta Danorum*, I, 7.[13] This brief passage is clarified by the texts of the *Voluspá* and of Snorri, but in itself clarifies nothing. It gathers and alters radically several features of the legend of the war and of the reconciliation of the Æsir and the Vanir, notably the gold statue (*Voluspá*), the beheading of Mímir (*Ynglingasaga*), and the murder of Kvasir (*Skáldskaparmál*). "Othinus" here too is a king, whose capital is "Byzantium," but who willingly spends time *apud Upsalam* (Dumézil 1953).

I have quoted these texts at length, first to make the reader feel, on the basis of a precise example, in what state, or rather in what diverse states, Scandinavian mythology has been transmitted to us, but also so that he may refer back to them constantly during the discussion that follows.

* * *

In 1903 Bernhard Salin (1861–1931) proposed a literal interpretation of the "invasion of the Æsir" which has remained the model accepted (at least until recently) by most historians of Scandinavian religion. Salin was a great man, as learned as he was modest, and the fine *Nordiska Museet* in Stockholm owes a great deal to him. Salin's theory was that Snorri's narrative, including the episode of the war between the Æsir and the Vanir and their reconciliation, contains in corrupted form the memory of great, historical, authentic events: a long *migration* of a people according to a precise itinerary from north of the Black Sea to Scandinavia, and a *struggle* between two peoples, one worshiping the Æsir and the other the Vanir. This struggle, according to the tradition that transposed men into gods or rather confused the gods with their worshipers, ended in a compromise, a fusion. Certain critics, such as R. Schück and E. Mogk, have thought of a religious war, which in itself is quite improbable. The majority, like H. Güntert and more recently E. A. Philippson, think of a purely ethnic and political war, a war of conquest, a type more assuredly present in the ancient history of Europe. According to some writers, who follow B. Salin closely, these events would have occurred around the fourth century; according to others, they might even represent the Indo-European invasion into the Germanic area, clearly far earlier. It would appear that this second opinion is in greater favor. In archaeological language – for archaeology is often appealed to in such a debate – the combatants in this great duel, first historic, later legendary and mythic, would be the representatives of two cultures that the excavations in northern Europe make it possible to identify: the Megalith people and the Battle Axe people (or *Schnurkeramiker*). Here, for example, is how E. A. Philippson explains it:

> The difference between the religion of the Vanir and the religion of the Æsir is a fundamental one. The religion of the Vanir was older, autochthonous, the product of an agricultural civilization. The religion of the Æsir was younger, the expression of a virile, warlike, but also more spiritual epoch. The gap between these religions, which was missed by Roman observers, was obvious to the pagans:

the legend of the Scandinavians relating to the war of the Vanir confirms it. (1953, 19)

Other interpreters, few in number but growing, such as O. Höfler, J. de Vries, W. Betz, and myself, resist this historicizing view, this idea of transcription, in mythic language, of historical events. We do not deny, of course, the material changes, the invasions, the fusions of peoples, or the duality of civilization which is observable, archaeologically, on Germanic soil, between what was there before the Indo-Europeans and what followed their invasion. Nor do we contest that Germanic religions, especially the Scandinavian, evolved during the course of centuries. But we do believe that the duality of the Æsir and the Vanir is not a reflection of these events, nor an effect of that evolution. We believe rather that it is a question here of two complementary terms in a unitary religious and ideological structure, one of which presupposes the other. These were brought, fully articulated, by those Indo-European invaders who became the Germanic peoples; we believe that the initial war between the Æsir and the Vanir is only a spectacular manifestation, as is the function of a myth, in the form of a violent conflict, of the distinction, the conceptual opposition, which justifies their coexistence. Finally, we suggest that the unbreakable association that follows the war, and which the war only prepares for, signifies that the opposition is also a complementarity, a solidarity, and that the Æsir and Vanir adjust and balance themselves for the greatest good of a human society that feels an equal need for protectors of both kinds.

I propose to show briefly the fragility and the internal contradictions of the historical thesis, and then to indicate the principal positive reasons that support the structural thesis.

1. Among the three principal documents relating to the war between the Æsir and the Vanir just cited (that of Saxo being without interest here), the historical thesis is founded only on the third. Neither the *Voluspá* nor the *Skáldskaparmál* – where Snorri has no other concern than to recount the divine stories – localizes the two groups of adversaries; nor does either imply any migration. On the contrary, they present the divine beings and their actions in the same tone and in the same perspective as, for example, the combats between the gods and giants, that is in the imprecise time and space of myth. Only the beginning of Snorri's second work is expressed in terms of geography and history, multiplying its precisions, going to the point of a Roman synchronization. But these terms, even these precisions, are suspect: Snorri, this time, sees himself as historian and genealogist, and he acts like the Irish monks of the high Middle Ages who joyously historicized information inherited from the druids and the pagan *filid*. They inserted it into their Latin erudition, drawing their principal arguments from word play, from the consonance of indigenous proper names with biblical or classical names, deriving the *Scots* from *Scythia*, supposing a great migration of *Picts* with, naturally, a stop in France, at Poitiers, capital of the *Pictaui*. Snorri proceeds no differently. He not only reduces the gods to kings now dead, who have succeeded one another and who, during their lifetimes, moved, emigrated, and invaded. He also localizes on the map of the known world the divine races thus humanized, and for that, depends on puns, some of them excellent (*Æsir – Asia*),

others less successful (Vanir – * Vana-kvísl-Tanaïs, "River Don"). If he places the Æsir and the Vanir, initially, on the banks of the Black Sea, at the mouth of the Don, it is not from an obscure memory of some migration, Gothic or otherwise, nor even from knowledge of a great commercial route going, from the Crimea to Scandinavia, but simply from the allure of a play of sounds, during an epoch when such quasi-etymological word play was acceptable as a historical argument.

2. Those who, despite this a priori improbability, wish to utilize the chapters from the *Ynglingasaga* to found a historical interpretation of the war between the Æsir and the Vanir, fall – have fallen – now into contradiction, now into arbitrariness. Snorri, in fact, localizes the war before all migration, at the very place of the primitive home which he attributes to the two peoples, that is the frontier of "Asia," at the mouth of the Don. It is only after the postwar reconciliation that Odin, gathering up his new subjects, the three great Vanir, with the same privileges as his older subjects, the Æsir, starts off on the expedition which is finally to lead them to Uppland in Sweden. To credit this text, the formation of a unified religion would have taken place far from Scandinavia, far from Germania, previous to any encounter on Germanic soil between an agricultural culture and a more virile, warlike one, one more spiritual, too, as E. A. Philippson generously suggests. But it is in Scandinavia and northern Germany that archaeological traces of a duality and succession of cultures appear. If one wishes to justify the duality of divine types by the duality of cultures, it is in these Germanic lands that the contact, struggle, and fusion of the two peoples must be located, and not somewhere around the mouth of the Don. If in order to escape contradiction, one retains from Snorri, as is usual, only the *idea* of the conflict and of the reconciliation, reserving the right not to situate everything where Snorri does, on the Black Sea, during the initial period, but on the contrary, near the terminus, at a northern point in the Germanic regions, one is clearly being arbitrary, for what objective criteria permit one to decide that one part of a text is truly remembered, hence useful as a historical document, and that some other part is fantasy?

3. A third criticism of the historicizing thesis leads us directly to our own task. Even in this text of the *Ynglingasaga* which claims to be historical with more reason than the other two purely mythological texts, which contain no attempt whatsoever at spatial or temporal localization, one is struck by an abundance of details of another order. These details concern the phases of the war (*Voluspá*) and the terms of the peace (*Skáldskaparmál, Ynglingasaga*), notably the gods exchanged as security, their characters and their adventures. These minute and picturesque details cannot be even greatly deformed history; they cannot possibly represent any trace of the customs of peoples supposedly in conflict. The historicizers must therefore ignore them completely and consider them only secondary devices to make the text more lively. It is, however, these very details that are the essence of the stories, and which clearly interested the Icelandic writer Snorri most when he was not absorbed in word play, as they did the *Voluspá* poet and no doubt the listeners or readers of both.

An important question of principle is here raised: is it sound, when using a mythological text, thus to abstract away all the rich detail of its contents? In my view, it certainly is not. The historian of religions must, like all historians, treat his documents with respect. Before asking which features, great or small, he can extract from them to support his thesis, he must read and reread them, immerse himself in them passively and receptively, being extremely careful to leave all features in their places, both those that support him and those that resist him. If one submits to this regimen, one soon learns that there is more to be done with such texts than to destroy them in order to insert a few relics drawn from the debris into other constructions. First, one must understand their internal structure, which justifies the ordering of their elements, even the strangest and most bizarre. What might thus be lost from the realm of history is regained in that of theology, in knowledge of the religious thought embedded in the documents.

It is occasionally argued that this structural view also leads to arbitrariness or even to a mirage. What is related by Snorri and suggested by the *Voluspá* is after all picturesque and strange, and does not at first glance have an air of containing or even wishing to express a religious concept. To reject the localization of the Æsir on the threshold of Asia, as some historians do, or to retain the "idea" of the conflict between the two peoples, as the more moderate do, is well and good. But does one not show equal credulity in seeking, indeed discovering, any sense in the mass of details that after all might be just as artificial, literary, or late – in a word, useless – as the onomastic puns?

It is here that comparative considerations may (and must) intervene to assure us that our texts do in fact have meaning, and to determine what that meaning is. Let us be very precise: we are concerned here with comparative Indo-European considerations, implying a common genetic relationship (filiation), not simply typological or universal considerations. The latter are by no means negligible: it may happen that a trait or group of traits which seems strange and meaningless on a page of Snorri may be found in the folklore of peoples far removed from the Scandinavians, and may there be understood, commented on, and justified by these people in terms valid also for the Icelandic documents. But our efforts shall not advance in that direction: we shall employ a more delicate instrument of comparison.

The Scandinavians and all Germanic peoples spoke Indo-European languages, curiously deformed phonetically, but in which the non-Indo-European residue of the vocabulary is negligible compared to what can be observed in certain southern languages within the Indo-European family. If the concepts of language, nation, and race, even of civilization, are not interchangeable, it is no less true, especially for very ancient times, that community of language implies a rather considerable minimum of community in concepts and in their mode of organization, in short "ideology," for which religion has long been the principal expression. It is thus legitimate and even methodologically necessary, before denying significance or antiquity to a "theologeme" or myth among the Scandinavians, to ask if the religions of the most conservative Indo-European peoples, the speakers of Sanskrit, Italic, and Celtic, do not present a similar belief or story. This is sometimes the case, and it happens that in its Indic version for example, which is attested earlier in books written directly by the keepers of divine knowledge, the structure of a formula or the meaning of a story appears more clearly, more obviously linked to religious and social life, than in the literary works of the Christian Snorri. And if this kind of comparative observation is applied to a complex tradition, that is, one articulating a fairly large number of ideological elements, and which is furthermore truly singular, seldom found throughout the world, it becomes less likely that the Scandinavian-Indic concordance should be fortuitous and not to be explained by common prehistoric heritage. It happens that the problems of the Æsir and the Vanir are of the kind that lend themselves to such a method.

* * *

In Vedic religion, in fact in pre-Vedic religion – this we know from the list of Aryan gods by Mitani, preserved in epigraphic documents from the fourteenth century BC – and already in Indo-Iranian religion – this we know from the transplantation of it into the hierarchy of Zoroastrian archangels – a small number of gods were regularly associated in invocations, rituals, and hierarchical lists, in order to sum up the totality of the invisible society. These divinities were distributed, with regard to their functions, into the three levels of an already well-known structure: the one that later, in classical India, gave rise to the rigid social classification of the *varna*, namely *brāhmana* or priests, *ksatriya* or warriors, and *vaiśya* or breeder-farmers – so parallel to that which ancient Ireland exhibited in more supple fashion with its corps of druids, its military class of *flaith*, and its freemen, the cattle-owning *bō airig*. The briefest form of this list, that of Mitani, enumerates first two sovereign gods, *Mitra* and *Varuna*, then the god essentially representing strength and war, *Ind(a)ra*, and then the twin gods who give health, youth, fertility, and happiness, the *Nāsatya* or *Aśvin*. The Zoroastrian transposition rests on the same list with one additional entry, also known in India, a goddess found linked to the twins of the third level. In the mythology, not of the Vedas but of Indian epic, the gods of the first level are quite diminished, and although they have not completely vanished, it is Indra who figures as king of the gods, which no doubt reflects a social evolution favorable to the warrior class. In 1938 it was possible to demonstrate that the pre-Capitoline triad, which presided over the oldest Roman religion, rested on the same analysis of the needs of man and of divine services: the *Jupiter* of the *flamen dialis*, so narrowly associated with the *rex*, brought to the Romans all the forms of sovereign and celestial protection; *Mars* gave them physical force and victory in combat against both visible and invisible enemies; *Quirinus*, judging by the offices of his Flamen, by the ritual of his festival, by the gods regularly associated with him, even by his name, and finally by the definitions conserved down to a late commentary in the *Æneid*, supervised the good harvest and the conservation of grains, the social masses which were the substance of Rome, and civil life (cf. Lat. *quirites*) during a vigilant peace. The historicizing hypotheses that have attempted to explain this triad as a secondary feature, the effect of historical accident, the cooperation of peoples in the founding of Rome, are a priori condemned because among other Italic peoples, the Umbrians of Iguvium – at a time when Roman influence was out of the question – the ritual of the famous *Tables* honors within the same hierarchy a very similar triad composed of a *Juu-*, a *Mart-*, and a *Vofiono-*.

The concordance of Indo-Iranian and Italic religious features guarantees that the tripartite theological structure and the practice of summarizing it in a brief list of gods characteristic of each level dates back to the time of the Indo-European community. The exact parallel of Scandinavian mythology, expressed in the formula Odin-Thor-Frey, may not therefore be an innovation, but a faithfully conserved archaism. No more than that of Jupiter-Mars-Quirinus does the grouping of the three Scandinavian gods justify an explanation through chance or compromise in the prehistory of the great peninsula or in northern Germany. Each has a meaning, the same meaning, and each of the three terms requires its complements. If we recall, furthermore, the precise analogies long noticed between Thor and Indra (red hair; hammer and *vajra*, etc.), if we note that the third level in Scandinavia is sometimes occupied not only by Frey but also by the pair Njord and Frey, who, not being twins but father and son, are no less closely associated than the two Nāsatya, if we recall too that on this same third level the goddess Freya is often honored beside the gods Njord and Frey, just as a goddess is usually associated with the Indo-Iranian Nāsatya, then we begin to discern not only the parallelism of the entire structure but also important correspondences of individual terms which simply could not have been accumulated by chance. Finally, Vedic ideology – and we already have good reasons to call it Indo-Iranian – displayed a firm solidarity between the first two levels in opposition to the third, as occurred later in human society, between the Brahmins and the ksatriya, called the two forces, *ubhe vīrye*, in opposition to the *vaiśya*. Completely parallel is the union of Odin and Thor in Scandinavia in a single divine race, the Æsir, in opposition to the Vanir, Njord, Frey, and Freya.

It has been objected that this comparative procedure takes into account from all Germanic religion only its Scandinavian form, and in the relatively late state in which we know it, that is, that nothing establishes this tripartite division among other Germanic peoples, such as the Goths or those of the West Germanic group. Further, it has been noted that while the name of the Æsir is to be found elsewhere, that of the Vanir is found nowhere outside of Scandinavia, and finally that the oldest archaeological material in Scandinavia seems to show that the god of the hammer and the ithyphallic god preceded the Indo-European invasion.

These objections are not as considerable as they appear at first glance. As for the last one, we admit perfectly willingly that the Indo-European gods of the second and third levels, Thor and Frey, probably annexed to themselves certain conceptions of another origin, already popular among the conquered indigenous population. Again we must not interpret too generously the famous rock carvings of Sweden, where the archaeologists have a tendency to call all the silhouettes armed with hammers Thor and all the obscene silhouettes Frey. As for the objection about the names, I believe that it rests on an unjustified, unreasonable claim, for the proper names are not of such great importance. The name *vanir*, of obscure etymology (of the eight which have been proposed, the best is still that which equates it with Lat. *Venus, venerari,* etc.), may well be limited to Old Norse, but the type, the class of gods which it designates could have existed elsewhere under another name or without any generic name. The Scandinavian Njord (ON *Njorðr ← *Nerþu-*), one of the principal Vanir, must be the one described by Tacitus under the name Nerthus, with feminine sex and clear characteristics of the third function (fecundity, peace, etc.) in northern Germany. Furthermore it is not quite true that the triad or other very similar triads are not attested in other areas of the ancient Germanic world.

One can not argue on this point from the silence of the Goths: we know almost nothing of their mythology. As for the West Germanic peoples, our oldest explicit source, Tacitus,[14] enumerates to the contrary – and in terms that prove that there was a structure – gods who are clearly distributed into the three levels, and in the expected hierarchical order. The most honored god, whom Tacitus calls *Mercurius,* is surely the equivalent of Odin. Then came Hercules and Mars, that is the two warrior gods who are surely the Scandinavian Thor and Tyr (we shall take up the latter in the next chapter). Finally, at least for a part of the Suevians, a goddess is joined to these two gods. Tacitus calls her Isis; there is no reason (especially that which he gives: the cult boat) to consider her of foreign origin, *advectam religionem.* It is even possible that before Tacitus Caesar, in his short and inexact account of the Germanic gods, may have attempted to interpret summarily a comparable triad:

> To the number of the Gods they admit only those whom they see and whose good deeds they enjoy, the *Sun, Vulcan,* and the *Moon;* they have not even heard the others spoken of.[15]

Even if the term "sun" is indeed inadequate to describe a god of the sovereign type such as Odin, in return Vulcan, god of the hammer, may be a translation, certainly functionally improper, but obviously explicable, of the continental counterpart of Thor, and, for a goddess of fertility seen by a Roman, the lunary label would be no more bizarre than for many maternal or nourishing goddesses of the Mediterranean world who have received it too, from Oriental Isis and Semele to that Roman Anna Perenna who figures in the speculations of Ovid. Finally, more recently, among the Saxons, who were converted by Charlemagne even before the Eddic poems we have were composed in Scandinavia, a triad is attested which must, term for term, be the same as that of the Scandinavians. The formula of abjuration imposed on them, which is conserved in the Vatican in a ninth-century manuscript, contains in fact these words: "I renounce all works and words of the devil, *Thunar, Uuōten,* and *Saxnot* and all the demons who are their companions (*hira genōtas*)." The first two of these divine names are the cognates of Thor and Odin. The third name, whose second element corresponds to modern Germanic *(Ge)noss* "companion," means nothing more than "companion of the Saxons." We have to do with a Saxon god who actually appears only in Old English, where it has the form *Seaxnēat.* This reminds us that, just as in Rome Quirinus (probably *co-uirīno-*) was the god of the *quirites* collectivity, so the Scandinavian Frey is distinctly, among the gods, the *folkvaldi* "captain, lit. leader of men or of the folk" (*Skírnismál* 3: *folkvaldi goða*). Also, in the cult he is the *veraldar goð*, that is the god of that complex Germanic notion (Ger. *Welt*, Eng. *world*, Swed. *värld*, etc.), which designates etymologically men (*ver-*) through the ages (*old*). These indications compel us not to interpret silence as absence in other Germanic realms where our information has even more lacunae.

* * *

Indo-European parallels help to explain not only the formula of the composition of the triad, but also the legend of the initial separation and war, as well as the reconciliation and fusion of the Æsir with the Vanir. To be sure, the Vedic hymns say nothing about this, oriented as they are toward eulogy and prayer: they are hardly proper for recalling the delicate episodes of divine history. The later literature, the epic, knows that the gods Indra and the Nāsatya, whose association is so necessary and so close, were nevertheless not always joined in one unified society. By chance an Iranian legend confirms that several essential traits of the material in this story, which probably comes from the "fifth Veda," the oral corpus of legends, were pre-Vedic, indeed Indo-Iranian. Originally the gods of the lower level, the Nāsatya or givers of health and prosperity, were apart from the other gods. The gods, headed by Indra (for such is the state of the divine hierarchy in the epic), whose weapon is the lightning, refused them what is the privilege and practically part of the credentials of divinity, participation in benefits of the oblations, under the pretext that they were not "proper" gods, but rather some kind of artisans or warriors who were too much mixed in with men. On the day when the Nāsatya raised their claims and tried to enter into divine society, a bitter conflict ensued.

We see how this entrance is substantially parallel to the initial separation of the higher Æsir – the masters of magic and lightning – and the lower Vanir – givers of richness and fecundity. In India, let us note without delay, the heterogeneity of the two groups of gods could not be explained by the contact and conflict of religions or of different peoples, as is proposed in Scandinavia for the Æsir and Vanir: Mitra-Varuna and Indra on the one hand, the Nāsatya on the other, grouped together at the same time and with the same hierarchical order, were brought by the Indo-Iranian conquerors to the bend in the Euphrates as well as into the Iranian plateau and the basin of the Indus in the fourteenth century BC. But the correspondences between Snorri and the *Mahābhārata* do not stop there. They extend to a group of rare and complex traits which permit the comparativist to be more positive.

We recall from the *Skáldskaparmál* the birth and death of Kvasir: at the moment when peace is concluded between the divine adversaries, they all spit into the same vessel. Out of this "pledge of peace" the gods fashion a man named Kvasir who has extraordinary, absolutely enormous, wisdom. He travels about the world, but two dwarfs kill him, distributing his blood among three bowls, mixing honey with it and thus concocting the "mead of poetry and wisdom." Then they tell the gods that Kvasir has choked with learning, no one having been able to compete with him in knowledge.

The name *Kvasir* in this legend has long been interpreted: since 1864 K. Simrock, then R. Heinzel 1889, and then E. Mogk (1924) have shown that it is an onomastic personification of an intoxicating drink which recalls the *kvas* of the Slavs.[16] It is natural that the precious intoxication given by the mead of poetry and wisdom should have honey as an ingredient. It is equally natural that a drink fermented from squashed vegetables (Dan. *kvas* "crushed fruits, wort of those fruits") should be made to ferment by spittle. This technique is frequently attested; it is at least conceivable, as we are here dealing with a ceremonial or communal drink, sanctioning the agreement between two social groups, that such fermentation should be caused by the spittle of all concerned. Furthermore, on this point E. Mogk has gathered sufficient ethnographic parallels.

What is less common is that the intoxicating drink prepared with the spittle and called upon to enter as a component of the other intoxicating drink, the mead of poetry, between its two stages as a drink, should take on a completely different form, that of a man or superman, and this by the will of the gods. Furthermore, this theme is not only rare (the "King Soma," and Dionysos-Zagreus, are something else again); it is inserted in a complex and precise whole, which must not be dislocated. It was not under just any circumstance, nor without design, that this man-drink was created. He was created at the conclusion of the war between the Æsir and Vanir, to seal the peace. Then he was put to death, and his blood, spread among the three recipients, served to make another drink, more durable in that it still inebriates Odin, poets, and visionaries.

Let us return now from Scandinavia to India, where we have left the higher gods and the Nāsatya in a great conflict, Indra already brandishing his thunderbolts against the latter. How does this crisis turn out? An ascetic allied with the Nāsatya who, as part of their usual services, have restored his youth to him, creates, through the force of his asceticism – the great weapon of Indian penitents – a gigantic man, who threatens to swallow the world, including the recalcitrant gods. This enormous monster's name is *Mada* "Drunkenness": he is drunkenness personified. Even Indra gives in, peace is made, the Nāsatya definitely join the divine community, and no allusion will ever be made to the distinction among gods or to the initial conflict. But what to do with this character, Drunkenness, whose task is finished and who is now only dangerous? The one who created him, this time with the accord of the gods, cuts him into four pieces and his unitary essence is split up into the four things that, literally or figuratively, are indeed intoxicating: drink, women, gaming, and hunting.

Such is the story to be read in the third book of the *Mahābhārata*, sections 123-125. An Iranian legend that I called attention to in the last section of my *Naissance d'archanges* (Dumézil 1945) and which Professor Jean de Menasce (1947) has further scrutinized, that of the *Hārūt-Mārūt*, confirms the linkage of drunkenness with this affair from the beginning of Indo-Iranian mythology. The reader will not have failed to notice the analogy between the fabrications and the liquidations of Kvasir and

Mada, an analogy that it is easy to delimit and define. Here is how the balance sheet was formulated in my *Loki*:

> Certainly the differences between Germanic and Indic myth are striking, but so is the analogy between their fundamental situations and results. Here are the differences: among the Germanic peoples, the character "Kvas" is formed *after* the peace is concluded, as a *symbol of that peace*, and he is made according to a precise realistic technique, fermentation with spittle, whereas the character "Drunkenness" is made as a *weapon, in order to* force the gods into peace, and he is made *mystically* (we are in India), by the force of ascetism, without reference to a technique of fermentation. Then, when "Kvas" is killed and his blood divided in thirds, *it is not done by the gods* who made him, but by two dwarfs, whereas in India, it is his creator who at the order of the gods dismembers "Drunkenness" into four parts. Further, the dismemberment of "Kvas" is simply *quantitative*, into three homogeneous parts (three vessels receiving the blood, all of the same value, though one happens to be larger than the others), whereas that of "Drunkenness" is *qualitative*, into differentiated parts (four sorts of drunkenness). In Germanic legend, it is simply as a lying explanation that the dwarfs afterwards tell the gods of an intolerable force (of a purely *intellectual* kind), out of proportion with the human world, which *would* have led to the suffocation of "Kvas," whereas in the Indian legend the excess of force (*physical*, brutal) of Drunkenness is *authentically* intolerable, incompatible with the life of the world, and as such leads authentically to his being dismembered. Finally the Germanic legend presents "Kvas" as a *benefactor* from the beginning, well disposed toward men – a sort of martyr – and his blood, properly treated, produces that most valued thing, the mead of poetry and wisdom, whereas in India "Drunkenness" is a *malefactor* from the beginning and his four fractions are the scourge of mankind.

All this is true, but it would only prove, if there were need of it, that India is not Iceland and that the two stories were told in civilizations that in content and form had developed in almost diametrically opposite directions. Notably their ideologies of insobriety had become just about inverse. There exists nevertheless a common pattern. It is at the moment when divine society is with difficulty but definitively joined by the adjunction of the representatives of fecundity and prosperity to those of sovereignty and force, it is at the moment when the two hostile groups make their peace, that a character is artificially created incarnating the force of intoxicating drink or of insobriety and is named after it. When this force proves to be excessive for the conditions of this world – for good or for evil – the person thus made is then killed and divided into three or four intoxicating parts that either aid or threaten man.

This pattern is original. It is not met with anywhere in the world but in these two cases. In addition, its principle is easily understood, if one pays attention to the social conditions and conceptions which must have existed among the Indo-European peoples. In particular, intoxication under various names and shapes would have been of use to all three social functions. On the one hand, it is one of the fundamental stimuli in the life of a sorcerer-priest and of a hunter-warrior in this culture, and, on the other hand, it is procured through plants that the farmer must *cultivate* and *prepare*. It is thus natural that the "birth" of intoxication and all that goes with it should be situated at that moment of mythological history when society is formed through reconciliation and the union of priests and warriors on the one hand with farmers and all the powers of fecundity and nourishment on the other. There is a profound harmony between this sociomythological event and the appearance of intoxication, and it is not superfluous to remark here that neither the poets of the *Mahābhārata* nor Snorri could still have been aware of this, which lends a strange air to their tales. For the poets of the *Mahābhārata*, the Nāsatya are no longer what they were at the time of the Vedic compilation, typical canonized representatives of the third function. However well Snorri in his various treatises portrays the differing characters of Odin, Thor, and Frey, he surely does not understand the reconciliation of the Æsir and the Vanir as a myth concerning the origin of the harmonious collaboration of the diverse social functions. (Dumézil 1948, 102–5)

This correspondence is not the only one. We have also a Roman tradition that presents a new pattern for the events of the war between the Æsir and the Vanir given by the sibyl in the *Voluspá*, one that confirms the meaning of the entire story. In Rome, as we know, there is no more mythology, and the earliest lore is deposited in the epic of origins. Further, the "complete society" whose creation interested the very matter-of-fact Romans could only be their own. It is in fact the tradition about the birth of the city which offers the Germanist the parallel of which we speak. Rome, says the legend, was constituted by the union of two groups of men, the purely masculine companions of the demigod Romulus, maintainers of the *promises of Jupiter* and strong in their *military valor*, and the Sabines of Titus Tatius, *rich farmers* and, through their *women*, the only ones capable of giving fecundity and durability to the nascent society. But the happy union of these two complementary groups, like that of the Æsir and Vanir, was brought about at the conclusion of a difficult and long-contested war, in the course of which each adversary in turn gained the upper hand. The union was affirmed in a scene and by means that would well illustrate its "functional specialty." The Sabines, the "rich ones," nearly won by occupying the capitol, but how did they occupy it? By bribing Tarpeia, a *woman*, with *gold* – or with *love*, according to another version. Later, in the battle of the forum, when his army fled in disorder, Romulus not only restored order, but even drove the Sabine army out of the capitol back to their camp. How did he achieve this result? With his eyes and hands to the sky, he addressed himself to the *sovereign Jupiter*, reminding him of his promises, imploring a miraculous suspension of panic; and Jupiter granted it. It is notable that the two episodes of the war of the two divine clans in the *Voluspá* correspond to these two, with the same functional features. The rich and voluptuous Vanir send among the Æsir as a scourge the woman called Gullveig, "insobriety (or power) of gold," who corrupts their hearts, especially those of the women. Further, Odin *throws his spear* in a gesture that the sagas know well, where it regularly has the effect of throwing the enemy army into a fatal panic. In the conflict of Indra and the Nāsatya, which was treated at some length above, and which does not achieve the dignity of a war of peoples, the conduct of the two parties is no less clearly significant of their functional levels. The Nāsatya have as their ally the ascetic *Cyavana*, whom they obtained by restoring his *youth* and *beauty* and by permitting him to keep his *wife* whom they had first intended to take for themselves. And it is with brandished thunderbolt that Indra responds to their audacity.

Even if all the picturesque details of Snorri's narrative have not found equally striking correspondences outside Scandinavia (I am thinking of the stories of Hœnir and the decapitation of Mímir), those just recited should suffice to establish that the war of the Æsir and the Vanir is indeed a myth that is *older* than the Germanic peoples, *older* than the dispersion of their ancestors and those of the Italic, Indo-Iranian, and other Indo-European peoples. It is a myth whose apparently strange elements still preserve, though not fully understood by its narrators, the complex elements and nuances of a "lesson" on the structure of Indo-European societies.

Notes

1. Old Norse names are anglicized according to the principles usually followed in English and American writings on Scandinavian mythology. If the Old Norse form differs significantly, it will be given in parentheses on its first occurrence.
2. *Gesta Hammaburgensis Ecclesiae Pontificum*, IV, 26–27. In Adam of Bremen 1959, 207–8.
3. *Egils saga Skalla-Grímssonar*, chap. 56 in Nordal 1933, 163.
4. Here and elsewhere the Old Norse text of poems from the *Poetic Edda* is cited from Kuhn 1962.
5. Most of the translations of poems from the *Poetic Edda* are cited from Bellows 1923 (and later).
6. *Edda Snorra Sturlusonar*, Jónsson 1931, 123 (*Skáldskaparmál*, chap. 44). References to Snorri's *Edda* (also known as *The Prose Edda*) are to this edition. *The Prose Edda* is divided into parts with separate chapter numbering: *Gylfaginning*, *Bragarœður*, *Skaldskaparmál*, *Háttatal*.
7. *Edda* (Kuhn 1962, 12–13); *Edda* (Bellows 1923, 22–23). References to individual poems of the *Edda* are frequent in the text and are not separately footnoted except for direct quotations.
8. *Grímnismál*, str. 14: *Edda* (Kuhn 1962, 60); *Edda* (Bellows 1923, 90–91).
9. *Egils saga*, chap. 78.
10. *Edda* (Kuhn 1962, 5); *Edda* (Bellows 1923, 10–11).
11. *The Prose Edda of Snorri Sturluson* (Young 1964, 100). Translations from the *Snorra Edda* are taken from this version.
12. *Heimskringla*, Hollander trans. 1964, 6–10.
13. Cited from the edition of Olrik and Ræder 1931.
14. C. Tacitus, *Germania*, chap. 9.

15. G. Caesar, *The Gallic Wars*, VI, 21, 2.
16. For references see the bibliography in de Vries, 1956–7, ix–xlix.

References

Adam of Bremen. 1959. *History of the Archbishops of Hamburg-Bremen* (trans. Francis J. Tschan). New York: Columbia University Press.

Bang, A. 1901. *Norske hexeformularer og magiske opskrifter*. Christiania: Videnskabernes Selskab.

Bellows, H.A., trans. 1923. *The Poetic Edda*. New York: The American-Scandinavian Foundation.

de Vries, Jan 1956–7. *Altgermanische Religionsgeschichte*. 2nd ed., 2 vols. Berlin: Walter de Gruyter (1st ed. 1935–7).

Dumézil, Georges. 1945. *Naissance d'archanges*. Paris: Gallimard.

_____1947. *Tarpeia*. Paris: Gallimard.

_____1948. *Loki*. Paris: G.-P. Maisonneuve.

_____1953. *La saga de Hadingus*. Paris: Presses Universitaires de France.

Hollander, Lee M., trans. 1964. *Heimskringla: History of the Kings of Norway*. Austin: University of Texas Press.

Jónsson, F. 1894. *Altnordische Sagabibliothek 3*. Halle.

Jónsson, Finnur, ed. 1931. *Edda Snorra Sturlusonar*. Copenhagen: Nordisk Forlag.

Kock, E. A. 1946. *Den norsk-isländska Skaldediktningen*. Lund: Glerup.

Kuhn, Hans, ed. 1962. *Edda: die Lieder des Codex Regius*. Heidelberg: Carl Winter.

Menasce, Jean de. 1947. "Une légende indo-européenne dans la angéologie judéo-musulmane: á propos de Harût et Marût." *Asiatische Studien – Études Asiatiques. Revue de la Société Suisse d'Études Asiatiques* 1: 10–18.

Mogk, Eugen. 1924. *Die Gigantomachie in der Völuspá*. Helsinki: Folklore Fellows Communications 58.

Nordal, S., ed. 1933. *Egils saga Skalla-Grímssonar Islenzk fornrit 2*. Reykjavik: Islenzka Fornritefélag.

Olrik, J. and H. RÆder, eds. 1931. *Saxo Grammaticus: Gesta Danorum*. Copenhagen: Levin og Munksgaard.

Philippson, E. A. 1953. *Die Genealogie der Götter*. Urbana, IL: University of Illinois.

Young, Jean I., trans. 1964. *The Prose Edda of Snorri Sturluson*. Berkeley and Los Angeles: University of California Press.

Primitive Worlds

Mary Douglas

"Now what are the characteristic marks of the sea-anemone," George Eliot muses, "which entitle it to be removed from the hands of the botanist and placed in those of the zoologist?"

For us ambiguous species merely provoke essayists to elegant reflections. For Leviticus the rock badger or Syrian hyrax is unclean and abominable. Certainly it is an anomaly all right. It looks like an earless rabbit, has teeth like a rhino and the small hoofs on its toes seem to relate it to the elephant. But its existence does not threaten to bring the structure of our culture tumbling round our ears. Now that we have recognized and assimilated our common descent with apes nothing can happen in the field of animal taxonomy to rouse our concern. This is one reason why cosmic pollution is more difficult for us to understand than social pollutions of which we have some personal experience.

Another difficulty is our long tradition of playing down the difference between our own point of vantage and that of primitive cultures. The very real differences between "us" and "them" are made little of, and even the word "primitive" is rarely used. Yet it is impossible to make any headway with a study of ritual pollution if we cannot face the question of why primitive culture is pollution-prone and ours is not. With us pollution is a matter of aesthetics, hygiene or etiquette, which only becomes grave in so far as it may create social embarrassment. The sanctions are social sanctions, contempt, ostracism, gossip, perhaps even police action. But in another large group of human societies the effects of pollution are much more wide ranging. A grave pollution is a religious offence. What is the basis of this difference? We cannot avoid the question and must attempt to phrase an objective, verifiable distinction between two types of culture, primitive and modern. Perhaps we Anglo-Saxons are more concerned to emphasize our sense of common humanity. We feel there is something discourteous in the term "primitive" and so we avoid it and the whole subject too. Why else should Professor Herskovits have renamed the second edition of *Primitive Economics* to *Economic Anthropology* if his sophisticated West African friends had not expressed dislike of being lumped together with naked Fuegians and Aborigines under this general sign? Perhaps it is partly also in healthy reaction to early anthropology: "Perhaps nothing so sharply differentiates the savage from the civilised man as the circumstance that the former observes tabus, the latter does not" (Rose 1926, 111). No one can be blamed for wincing at a passage such as the following, though I do not know who would take it seriously:

> We know that the primitive man of today has mental equipment very different from that of the civilised man. It is much more fragmented, much more discontinuous, more "gestalt-free". Professor Jung once told me how, in his travels in the African bush, he had noticed the quivering eye-balls of his native guides: not the steady gaze of the European, but a darting restlessness of vision, due perhaps to the constant expectation of danger. Such eye movements must be coordinated with a mental alertness and a swiftly changing imagery that allows little opportunity for discursive reasoning, for contemplation and comparison. (Read 1955)

If this were written by a professor of psychology it might be significant, but it is not. I suspect that our professional delicacy in avoiding the term "primitive" is the product of secret convictions of superiority. The physical anthropologists have a similar problem. While they attempt to substitute "ethnic group" for the word "race" (see *Current Anthropology*, 1964), their terminological problems do not inhibit them from their task of distinguishing and classifying forms of human variation. But social anthropologists, to the extent that they avoid reflecting on the grand distinctions between human cultures, seriously impede their own work. So it is worth asking why the term "primitive" should imply any denigration.

Part of our difficulty in England is that Lévy-Bruhl, who first posed all the important questions about primitive cultures and their distinctiveness as a class, wrote in deliberate criticism of the English of his day, particularly of Frazer. Furthermore, Lévy-Bruhl laid himself open to powerful counter-attack. Most text-books on comparative religion are emphatic about the mistakes he made, and say nothing about the value of the questions he asked. (For example, Bartlett 1923, 283–4; Radin 1956, 230–1.) In my view he has not deserved such neglect.

Lévy-Bruhl was concerned to document and to explain a peculiar mode of thought. He started (1922) with the problem set by an apparent paradox. On the one hand there were convincing reports of the high level of intelligence of Eskimo or Bushmen (or of other such hunters and gatherers, or primitive cultivators or herdsmen), and on the other hand reports of peculiar leaps made in their reasoning and interpretation of events which suggested that their thought followed very different paths from our own. He insisted that their alleged dislike of discursive reasoning is not due to intellectual incapacity but to highly selective standards of relevance which produce in them an "insuperable indifference to matters bearing no apparent relation to those which interest them." The problem then was to discover the principles of selection and of association which made the primitive culture favour explanation in terms of remote, invisible mystic agencies and to lack curiosity about the intermediate links in a chain of events. Sometimes Lévy-Bruhl seems to be putting his problems in terms of individual psychology, but it is clear that he saw it as a problem of the comparison of cultures first and as a psychological one only in so far as individual psychology is affected by cultural environment. He was interested in analysing "collective representations," that is standardized assumptions and categories, rather than in individual aptitudes. It is precisely on this score that he criticized Tylor and Frazer, who tried to explain primitive beliefs in terms of individual psychology, whereas he followed Durkheim in seeing collective representations as social phenomena, as common patterns of thought which are related to social institutions. In this he was undoubtedly right, but as his strength lay more in massive documentation than in analysis he was unable to apply his own precepts.

What Lévy-Bruhl should have done, Evans-Pritchard has said, was to examine the variations in social structure and relate them to concomitant variations in the patterns of thought. Instead he contented himself with saying that all primitive people present uniform patterns of thought when contrasted with ourselves, and laid himself open to further criticism by seeming to make primitive cultures more mystical than they are and making civilized thought more rational than it is (Evans-Pritchard 1934). It seems that Evans-Pritchard himself was the first person to listen sympathetically to Lévy-Bruhl and to direct his research to carrying Lévy-Bruhl's problems into the more fruitful field which Lévy-Bruhl himself missed. For his analysis of Azande witchcraft beliefs was exactly an exercise of this sort. It was the first study to describe a particular set of collective representations and to relate them intelligibly to social institutions (Evans-Pritchard 1937). Many studies have now ploughed lines parallel to this first furrow, so that from England and America a large body of sociological analysis of religions has vindicated Durkheim's insight. I say Durkheim's insight and not Lévy-Bruhl's advisedly, for in so far as he contributed his own original slant to the matter, so Lévy-Bruhl earned the just criticism of his reviewers. It was his idea to contrast primitive mentality with rational thought instead of sticking to the problem adumbrated by the master. If he had stayed with Durkheim's view of the problem he would not have been led into the confusing contrast of mystical with scientific thought, but would have compared primitive social organization with complex modern social organization and perhaps have done something useful towards elucidating the difference between organic and mechanical solidarity, between two types of social organization which Durkheim saw to underlie differences in beliefs.

Since Lévy-Bruhl the general tendency in England has been to treat each culture studied as wholly *sui generis*, a unique and more or less successful adaptation to a particular environment (see Beattie 1961, 83; 1964, 272). Evans-Pritchard's criticism that Lévy-Bruhl treated primitive cultures as if they were more uniform than they really are has stuck. But it is vital now to take up this matter again. We cannot understand sacred contagion unless we can distinguish a class of cultures in which pollution ideas flourish from another class of cultures, including our own, in which they do not. Old Testament scholars do not hesitate to enliven their interpretations of Israelite culture by comparison with primitive cultures. Psychoanalysts since Freud, and metaphysicians since Cassirer, are not backward in drawing general comparisons between our present civilization and others very different. Nor can anthropologists do without such general distinctions.

The right basis for comparison is to insist on the unity of human experience and at the same time to insist on its variety, on the differences which make comparison worthwhile. The only way to do this is to recognize the nature of historical progress and the nature of primitive and of modern society. Progress means differentiation. Thus primitive means undifferentiated; modern means differentiated. Advance in technology involves differentiation in every sphere, in techniques and materials, in productive and political roles.

We could, theoretically, construct a rough gradient along which different economic systems would lie according to the degree to which they have developed specialized economic institutions. In the most undifferentiated economies roles in the productive system are not allocated by market considerations and there are few specialized labourers or craftsmen. A man does what work he does as part of performing his role as, say, son or brother or head of family. The same goes for the processes of distribution. As there is no labour exchange, so there is no supermarket. Individuals get their share of the community's product in virtue of their membership; their age, sex, seniority, their relationship to others. The patterns of status are etched by grooves of obligatory gift-making, along which rights to wealth are channelled.

Unfortunately for economic comparison there are many societies, small in scale, based on primitive techniques, which are not organized in this way, but rather on principles of market competition (see Pospisil 1963). However, development in the political sphere lends itself very satisfactorily to the pattern I wish to introduce. There are not, in the most small-scale type of society, any specialized political institutions. Historical progress is marked by the development of diverse judicial, military, police, parliamentary and bureaucratic institutions. So it is easy enough to trace what internal differentiation would mean for social institutions.

On the face of it the same process should be traceable in the intellectual sphere. It seems unlikely that institutions should diversify and proliferate without a comparable movement in the realm of ideas. Indeed we know that it does not happen. Great steps separate the historical development of the Hadza in Tanganyikan forests, who still never have occasion to count beyond four, from that of West Africans who for centuries have reckoned fines and taxes in thousands of cowries. Those of us who have not mastered modern techniques of communication such as the language of mathematics or of computers can put ourselves in the Hadza class compared with the ones who have become articulate in these media. We know only too well the educational burden our own civilization carries in the form of specialized compartments of learning. Obviously the demand for special expertise and the education for providing it create cultural environments in which certain kinds of thinking can flourish and others cannot. Differentiation in thought patterns goes along with differentiated social conditions.

From this basis it ought to be straightforward to say that in the realm of ideas there are differentiated thought systems which contrast with undifferentiated ones, and leave it at that. But the trap is just here. What could be more complex, diversified and elaborate than the Dogon cosmology? Or the Australian Murinbata cosmology, or the cosmology of Samoa, or of Western Pueblo Hopi for that matter? The criterion we are looking for is not in elaborateness and sheer complication of ideas.

There is only one kind of differentiation in thought that is relevant, and that provides a criterion that we can apply equally to different cultures and to the history of our own scientific ideas. That criterion is based on the Kantian principle that thought can only advance by freeing itself from the shackles of its own subjective conditions. The first Copernican revolution, the discovery that only man's subjective viewpoint made the sun seem to revolve round the earth, is continually renewed. In our own culture mathematics first and later logic, now history, now language and now thought processes themselves and even knowledge of the self and of society, are fields of knowledge progressively freed from the subjective limitations of the mind. To the extent to which sociology, anthropology and psychology are possible in it, our own type of culture needs to be distinguished from others which lack this self-awareness and conscious reaching for objectivity.

Radin interprets the Trickster myth of the Winnebago Indians on lines which serve to illustrate this point. Here is a primitive parallel to Teilhard de Chardin's theme that the movement of evolution has been towards ever-increasing complexification and self-awareness.

These Indians lived technically, economically and politically in the most simple, undifferentiated conditions. Their myth contains their profound reflections on the whole subject of differentiation. The trickster starts as an unselfconscious, amorphous being. As the story unfolds he gradually discovers his own identity, gradually recognizes and controls his own anatomical parts: he oscillates between female and male, but eventually fixes his own male sexual role; and finally learns to assess his environment for what it is. Radin says in his preface:

> He wills nothing consciously. At all times he is constrained to behave as he does from impulses over which he has no control ... he is at the mercy of his passions and appetites ... possesses no defined and well-fixed form ... primarily an inchoate being of indeterminate proportions, a figure foreshadowing the shape of man. In this version he possesses intestines wrapped around his body and an equally long penis, likewise wrapped round his body with his scrotum on top of it. (1956)

Two examples of his strange adventures will illustrate this theme. Trickster kills a buffalo and is butchering it with a knife in his right hand:

> In the midst of all these operations suddenly his left arm grabbed the buffalo. "Give that back to me, it is mine! Stop that or I will use my knife on you!" So spoke the right arm. "I will cut you to pieces, that is what I will do to you," continued the right arm. Thereupon the left arm released its hold. But shortly after, the left arm again grabbed hold of the right arm ... again and again this was repeated. In this manner did Trickster make both his arms quarrel. That quarrel soon turned into a vicious fight and the left arm was badly cut up... (Radin 1956)

In another story Trickster treats his own anus as if it could act as an independent agent and ally. He had killed some ducks and before going to sleep he tells his anus to keep guard over the meat. While he is asleep some foxes draw near:

> When they came close, much to their surprise however, gas was expelled from somewhere. "Pooh" was the sound made. "Be careful! He must be awake," so they ran back. After a while one of them said "Well, I guess he is asleep now. That was only a bluff. He is always up to some tricks." So again they approached the fire. Again gas was expelled and again they ran back. Three times this happened... Then louder, still louder, was the sound of gas expelled. "Pooh! Pooh! Pooh!" Yet they did not run away. On the contrary they now began to eat the roasted pieces of duck. . . . (Radin 1956)

When Trickster woke up and saw the duck gone:

> "Oh, you too, you despicable object, what about your behaviour? Did I not tell you to watch this fire? You shall remember this! As a punishment for your remissness, I will burn your mouth so that you will not be able to use it!" So he took a piece of burning wood and burned the mouth of his anus...and cried out of pain he was inflicting on himself. (Radin 1956)

Trickster begins, isolated, amoral and unselfconscious, clumsy, ineffectual, an animal-like buffoon. Various episodes prune down and place more correctly his bodily organs so that he ends by looking like a man. At the same time he begins to have a more consistent set of social relations and to learn hard lessons about his physical environment. In one important episode he mistakes a tree for a man and responds to it as he would to a person until eventually he discovers it is a mere inanimate thing. So gradually he learns the functions and limits of his being.

I take this myth as a fine poetic statement of the process that leads from the early stages of culture to contemporary civilization, differentiated in so many ways. The first type of culture is not pre-logical, as Lévy-Bruhl unfortunately dubbed it, but pre-Copernican. Its world revolves round the observer who is trying to interpret his experiences. Gradually he separates himself from his environment and perceives his real limitations and powers. Above all this pre-Copernican world is personal. Trickster speaks to creatures, things and parts of things without discrimination as if they were animate, intelligent beings. This personal universe is the kind of universe that Lévy-Bruhl describes. It is also the primitive culture of Tylor and the animist culture of Marett, and the mythological thought of Cassirer.

In the next few pages I am going to press as hard as I can the analogy between primitive cultures and the early episodes of the Trickster myth. I will try to present the characteristic areas of non-differentiation which define the primitive world-view. I shall develop the impression that the primitive world-view is subjective and personal, that different modes of existence are confused, that the limitations of man's being are not known. This is the view of primitive culture which was accepted by Tylor and Frazer and which posed the problems of primitive mentality. I shall then try to show how this approach distorts the truth.

First, this world-view is man-centred in the sense that explanations of events are couched in notions of good and bad fortune, which are implicitly subjective notions ego-centred in reference. In such a universe the elemental forces are seen as linked so closely to individual human beings that we can hardly speak of an external, physical environment. Each individual carries within himself such close links with the universe that he is like the centre of a magnetic field of force. Events can be explained in terms of his being what he is and doing what he has done. In this world it makes good sense for Thurber's fairy tale king to complain that falling meteors are being hurled at himself, and for Jonah to come forward and confess that he is the cause of a storm. The distinctive point here is not whether the working of the universe is thought to be governed by spiritual beings or by impersonal powers. That is hardly relevant. Even powers which are taken to be thoroughly impersonal are held to be reacting directly to the behaviour of individual humans.

A good example of belief in anthropocentric powers is the !Kung Bushmen belief in *N!ow*, a force thought to be responsible for meteorological conditions at least in the Nyae-Nyae area of Bechuanaland. *N!ow* is an impersonal, amoral force, definitely a thing and not a person. It is released when a hunter who has one kind of physical make-up kills an animal which has the corresponding element in its own make-up. The actual weather at any time is theoretically accounted for by the complex interaction of different hunters with different animals (Marshall 1957). This hypothesis is attractive and one feels it must be intellectually satisfying since it is a view which is theoretically capable of being verified and yet no serious testing would ever be practical.

To illustrate further the man-centred universe I quote from what Father Tempels says of Luba philosophy. He has been criticized for implying that what he says so authoritatively from his intimate knowledge of Luba thought applies to all the Bantu. But I suspect that in its broad lines his view on Bantu ideas of vital force applies not merely to all the Bantu, but much more widely. It probably applies to the whole range of thought which I am seeking to contrast with modern differentiated thought in European and American cultures.

For the Luba, he says, the created universe is centred on man (Tempels 1962, 43–5). The three laws of vital causality are:

1. that a human (living or dead) can directly reinforce or diminish the being (or force) of another human
2. that the vital force of a human can directly influence inferior force-beings (animal, vegetable or mineral)
3. that a rational being (spirit, dead or living human) can act indirectly on another by communicating his vital influence to an intermediary inferior force.

Of course there are very many different forms which the idea of a man-centred universe may take. Inevitably ideas of how men affect other men must reflect political realities. So ultimately we shall find that these beliefs in man-centred control of the environment vary according to the prevailing tendencies in the political system (see Chapter 6 [below, ed.]). But in general we can distinguish beliefs which hold that all men are equally involved with the universe from beliefs in the special cosmic powers of selected individuals. There are beliefs about destiny which are thought to apply universally to all men. In the culture of Homeric literature it was not certain outstanding individuals whose destiny was the concern of the gods, but all and each whose personal fate was spun on the knees of the gods and woven for good or ill with the fates of others. Just to take one contemporary example, Hinduism today teaches, as it has for centuries, that for each individual the precise conjunction of the planets at the time he was born signifies much for his personal good or ill-fortune. Horoscopes are for everybody. In both these instances, though the individual can be warned by diviners about what is in store for him, he cannot change it radically, only soften a little the hard blows, defer or abandon hopeless desires, be alert to the opportunities that will lie in his path.

Other ideas about the way in which the individual's fortune is bound up with the cosmos may be more pliable. In many parts of West Africa today, the individual is held to have a complex personality whose component parts act like separate persons. One part of the personality speaks the life-course of the individual before he is born. After birth, if the individual strives for success in a sphere which has been spoken against, his efforts will always be in vain. A diviner can diagnose this spoken destiny as cause of his failures and can then exorcise his prenatal choice. The nature of his pre-destined failure which a man has to take account of varies from one West African society to another. Among the Tallensi in the Ghana hinterland the conscious personality is thought to be amiable and uncompetitive. His unconscious element which spoke his destiny before birth is liable to be diagnosed as over-aggressive and rivalrous, and so makes him a misfit in a system of controlled statuses. By contrast the Ijo of the Niger Delta, whose social organization is fluid and competitive, take the conscious component of the self to be full of aggression, desire to compete and to excel. In this case it is the unconscious self which may be pre-destined to failure because it chose obscurity and peace. Divination can discover the discrepancy of aims within the person, and ritual can put it right (Fortes 1959; Horton 1961).

These examples point to another lack of differentiation in the personal world-view. We saw above that the physical environment is not clearly thought of in separate terms, but only with reference to the fortunes of human selves. Now we see that the self is not clearly separated as an agent. The extent and limits of its autonomy are not defined. So the universe is part of the self in a complementary sense, seen from the angle of the individual's idea, not this time of nature, but of himself.

The Tallensi and Ijo ideas about the multiple warring personalities in the self seem to be more differentiated than the Homeric Greek idea. In these West African cultures the binding words of destiny are spoken by part of the individual himself. Once he knows what he has done he can repudiate his earlier choice. In Ancient Greece the self was seen as a passive victim of external agents:

> In Homer one is struck by the fact that his heroes with all their magnificent vitality and activity feel themselves at every turn not free agents but passive instruments or victims of other powers ... a man felt that he could not help his own emotions. An idea, an emotion, an impulse came to him; he acted and presently rejoiced or lamented. Some god had inspired him or blinded him. He prospered, then was poor, perhaps enslaved; he wasted away with disease, or died in battle. It was divinely ordained, his portion apportioned long before. The prophet or diviner might discover it in advance; the plain man knew a little about omens and merely seeing his shaft hit its mark or the enemy prevailing, concluded that Zeus had assigned defeat to himself and his comrades. He did not wait to fight further but fled. (Onians 1951, 302)

The pastoral Dinka living in the Sudan similarly are said not to distinguish the self as an independent source of action and of reaction. They do not reflect on the fact that they themselves react with feelings of guilt and anxiety and that these feelings initiate other states of mind. The self acted upon by emotions they portray by external powers, spiritual beings who cause misfortune of various kinds. So in an effort to do justice to the complex reality of the self's interaction within itself the Dinka universe is peopled with dangerous personal extensions to the self. This is almost exactly how Jung described the primitive world-view when he said:

> An unlimited amount of what we now consider an integral part of our own psychic being disports itself merrily for the primitive in projections reaching far and wide.

I give one more example of a world in which all individuals are seen as personally linked with the cosmos to show how varied these linkages can be. Chinese culture is dominated by the idea of harmony in the universe. If an individual can place himself to ensure the most harmonious relationship possible, he can hope for good fortune. Misfortune may be attributed to lack of just such a happy alignment. The influence of the waters and the airs, called Feng Shui, will bring him good fortune if his house and his ancestors' graves are well placed. Professional geomancers can divine the causes of his misfortune and he can then rearrange his home or his parental graves to better effect. Dr. Freedman in his forthcoming book holds that geomancy has an important place in Chinese beliefs alongside ancestor worship. The fortune which a man can manipulate thus by geomantic skills has no moral implications; but ultimately it must be brought to terms with the reward of merit which in the same set of beliefs is meted out by heaven. Finally then, the whole universe is interpreted as tied in its detailed workings to the lives of human persons. Some individuals are more successful in dealing with Feng Shui than others, just as some Greeks have a more splendid fate decreed for them and some West Africans a spoken destiny more committed to success.

Sometimes it is only marked individuals and not all humans who are significant. Such marked individuals draw lesser men in their wake, whether their endowment is for good or evil fortune. For the ordinary man in the street, not endowed himself, the practical problem is to study his fellow men and discover whom among them he ought to avoid or follow.

In all the cosmologies we have mentioned so far, the lot of individual humans is thought to be affected by power inhering in themselves or in other humans. The cosmos is turned in, as it were, on man. Its transforming energy is threaded on to the lives of individuals so that nothing happens in the way of storms, sickness, blights or droughts except in virtue of these personal links. So the universe is man-centred in the sense that it must be interpreted by reference to humans.

But there is a quite other sense in which the primitive undifferentiated world-view may be described as personal. Persons are essentially not things. They have wills and intelligence. With their wills they love, hate and respond emotionally. With their intelligence they interpret signs. But in the kind of universe I am contrasting with our own world-view, things are not clearly distinct from persons. Certain kinds of behaviour characterize person-to-person relations. First, persons communicate with one another by symbols in speech, gesture, rite, gift and so on. Second, they react to moral situations. However impersonally the cosmic forces may be defined, if they seem to respond to a person-to-person style of address their quality of thing is not fully differentiated from their personality. They may not be persons but nor are they entirely things.

Here there is a trap to avoid. Some ways of talking about things might seem to the naïve observer to imply personality. Nothing can necessarily be inferred about beliefs from purely linguistic distinctions or confusions. For instance a Martian anthropologist might come to the wrong conclusion on overhearing an English plumber asking his mate for the male and female parts of plugs. To avoid falling into linguistic pitfalls, I confine my interests to the kind of behaviour which is supposed to produce a response from allegedly impersonal forces.

It may not be at all relevant here that the Nyae-Nyae Bushmen attribute male and female character to clouds, any more than it is relevant that we use "she" for cars and boats. But it may be relevant that the pygmies of the Ituri forest, when misfortune befalls, say that the forest is in a bad mood and go to the trouble of singing to it all night to cheer it up, and that they then expect their affairs to prosper (Turnbull 1961). No European mechanic in his senses would hope to cure engine trouble by serenade or curse.

So here is another way in which the primitive, undifferentiated universe is personal. It is expected to behave as if it was intelligent, responsive to signs, symbols, gestures, gifts, and as if it could discern between social relationships.

The most obvious example of impersonal powers being thought responsive to symbolic communication is the belief in sorcery. The sorcerer is the magician who tries to transform the path of events by symbolic enactment. He may use gestures or plain words in spells or incantations. Now words are the proper mode of communication between persons. If there is an idea that words correctly said are essential to the efficacy of an action, then, although the thing spoken to cannot answer back, there is a belief in a limited kind of one-way verbal communication. And this belief obscures the clear thing-status of the thing being addressed. A good example is the poison used for the oracular detection of witches in Zandeland (Evans-Pritchard 1937). The Azande themselves brew their poison from bark. It is not said to be a person but a thing. They do not suppose there is a little man inside which works the oracle. Yet for the oracle to work the poison must be addressed aloud, the address must convey the question unequivocally and, to eliminate error of interpretation, the same question must be put in reverse form in the second round of consultation. In this case not only does the poison hear and understand the words, but it has limited powers of reply. Either it kills the chicken or it does not. It can only give yes and no answers. It cannot initiate a conversation or conduct an unstructured interview. Yet this limited response to questioning radically modifies its thing-status in the Azande universe. It is not an ordinary poison, but more like a captive interviewee filling in a survey questionnaire with crosses and ticks.

The Golden Bough is full of examples of belief in an impersonal universe which, nevertheless, listens to speech and responds to it one way or another. So are modern field-workers' reports. Stanner says: "Most of the choir and furniture of heaven and earth are regarded by the Aborigines as a vast sign system. Anyone who understandingly has moved in the Australian bush with aborigine associates becomes aware of the fact. He moves, not in a landscape but in a humanised realm saturated with significations" (1965).

Finally there are the beliefs which imply that the impersonal universe has discernment. It may discern between fine nuances in social relations, such as whether the partners in sexual intercourse are related within prohibited degrees, or between less fine ones such as whether a murder has been committed on a fellow-tribesman or on a stranger, or whether a woman is married or not. Or it may discern secret emotions hidden in men's breasts. There are many examples of implied discernment of social status. The hunting Cheyenne thought that the buffaloes who provide their main livelihood were affected by the rotten smell of a man who had murdered a fellow-tribesman and they moved away, thus endangering the survival of the tribe. The buffalo were not supposed to react to the smell of murder of a foreigner. The Australian Aborigines of Arnhemland conclude their fertility and initiation ceremonies with ceremonial copulation, believing that the rite is more efficacious if sexual intercourse takes place between persons who are at other times strictly prohibited (Berndt 1951,

49). The Lele believe that a diviner who has had sexual intercourse with the wife of his patient, or whose patient has had sexual intercourse with his wife, cannot heal him, because the medicine intended to heal would kill. This result is not dependent on any intention or knowledge on the part of the doctor. The medicine itself is thought to react in this discriminating way. Furthermore, the Lele believe that if a cure is effected and the patient omits to pay his healer promptly for his services, early relapse or even a more fatal complication of the illness will result. So Lele medicine, by implication, is credited with discerning debt as well as secret adultery. Even more intelligent is the vengeance magic bought by the Azande which detects unerringly the witch responsible for a given death, and does capital justice on him. So impersonal elements in the universe are credited with discrimination which enables them to intervene in human affairs and uphold the moral code.

In this sense the universe is apparently able to make judgments on the moral value of human relations and to act accordingly. *Malweza*, among the Plateau Tonga in Northern Rhodesia, is a misfortune which afflicts those who commit certain specific offences against the moral code. Those offences are in general of a kind against which ordinary punitive sanctions cannot be applied. For example, homicide within the group of matrilineal kinsmen cannot be avenged because the group is organized to avenge the murder of its members by outsiders (Colson 1958, 107). *Malweza* punishes offences which are inaccessible to ordinary sanctions.

To sum up, a primitive world-view looks out on a universe which is personal in several different senses. Physical forces are thought of as interwoven with the lives of persons. Things are not completely distinguished from persons and persons are not completely distinguished from their external environment. The universe responds to speech and mime. It discerns the social order and intervenes to uphold it.

I have done my best to draw from accounts of primitive cultures a list of beliefs which imply lack of differentiation. The materials I have used are based on modern fieldwork. Yet the general picture closely accords with that accepted by Tylor or Marett in their discussions of primitive animism. They are the kind of beliefs from which Frazer inferred that the primitive mind confused its subjective and objective experiences. They are the same beliefs which provoked Lévy-Bruhl to reflect on the way that collective representations impose a selective principle on interpretation. The whole discussion of these beliefs has been haunted by obscure psychological implications.

If these beliefs are presented as the result of so many failures to discriminate correctly they evoke to a startling degree the fumbling efforts of children to master their environment. Whether we follow Klein or Piaget, the theme is the same: confusion of internal and external, of thing and person, self and environment, sign and instrument, speech and action. Such confusions may be necessary and universal stages in the passage of the individual from the chaotic, undifferentiated experience of infancy to intellectual and moral maturity.

So it is important to point out again, as has often been said before, that these connections between persons and events which characterize the primitive culture do not derive from failure to differentiate. They do not even necessarily express the thoughts of individuals. It is quite possible that individual members of such cultures hold very divergent views on cosmology. Vansina recalls affectionately three very independent thinkers he encountered among the Bushong, who liked to expound their personal philosophies to him. One old man had come to the conclusion that there was no reality, that all experience is a shifting illusion. The second had developed a numerological type of metaphysics, and the last had evolved a cosmological scheme of great complexity which no one understood but himself (1964). It is misleading to think of ideas such as destiny, witchcraft, *mana*, magic as part of philosophies, or as systematically thought out at all. They are not just linked to institutions, as Evans-Pritchard put it, but they are institutions – every bit as much as Habeas Corpus or Halloween. They are all compounded part of belief and part of practice. They would not have been recorded in the ethnography if there were no practices attached to them. Like other institutions they are both resistant to change and sensitive to strong pressure. Individuals can change them by neglect or by taking an interest.

If we remember that it is a practical interest in living and not an academic interest in metaphysics which has produced these beliefs, their whole significance alters. To ask an Azande whether the poison oracle is a person or a thing is to ask a kind of nonsensical question which he would never pause to ask himself. The fact that he addresses the poison oracle in words does not imply any confusion whatever in his mind between things and persons. It merely means that he is not striving for intellectual consistency and that in this field symbolic action seems appropriate. He can express the situation as he sees it by speech and mime, and these ritual elements have become incorporated into a technique which, to many intents and purposes, is like programming a problem through a computer. I think that this is something argued by Radin in 1927 and by Gellner (1962) when he points to the social function of incoherences in doctrines and concepts.

Robertson Smith first tried to draw attention away from beliefs considered as such, to the practices associated with them. And much other testimony has piled up since on the strictly practical limitation on the curiosity of individuals. This is not a peculiarity of primitive culture. It is true of "us" as much as of "them," in so far as "we" are not professional philosophers. As business man, farmer, housewife no one of us has time or inclination to work out a systematic metaphysics. Our view of the world is arrived at piecemeal, in response to particular practical problems.

In discussing Azande ideas about witchcraft Evans-Pritchard insists on this concentration of curiosity on the singularity of an individual event. If an old and rotten granary falls down and kills someone sitting in its shadow, the event is ascribed to witchcraft. Azande freely admit that it is in the nature of old and rotten granaries to collapse, and they admit that if a person sits for several hours under its shadow, day after day, he may be crushed when it falls. The general rule is obvious and not an interesting field for speculation. The question that interests them is the emergence of a unique event out of the meeting point of two separate sequences. There were many hours when no one was sitting under that granary and when it might have collapsed harmlessly, killing no one. There were many hours when other people were seated by it, who might have been victims when it fell, but who happened not to be there. The fascinating problem is why it should have fallen just when it did, just when so-and-so and no one else was sitting there. The general regularities of nature are observed accurately and finely enough for the technical requirements of Azande culture. But when technical information has been exhausted, curiosity turns instead to focus on the involvement of a particular person with the universe. Why did it have to happen to him? What can he do to prevent misfortune? Is it anyone's fault? This applies, of course, to a theistic world-view. As with witchcraft only certain questions are answered by reference to spirits. The regular procession of the seasons, the relation of cloud to rain and rain to harvest, of drought to epidemic and so on, is recognized. They are taken for granted as the back-drop against which more personal and pressing problems can be solved. The vital questions in any theistic world-view are the same as for the Azande: why did this farmer's crops fail and not his neighbour's? Why did this man get gored by a wild buffalo and not another of his hunting party? Why did this man's children or cows die?

Why me? Why today? What can be done about it? These insistent demands for explanation are focussed on an individual's concern for himself and his community. We now know what Durkheim knew, and what Frazer, Tylor and Marett did not. These questions are not phrased primarily to satisfy man's curiosity about the seasons and the rest of the natural environment. They are phrased to satisfy a dominant social concern, the problem of how to organize together in society. They can only be answered, it is true, in terms of man's place in nature. But the metaphysic is a by-product, as it were, of the urgent practical concern. The anthropologist who draws out the whole scheme of the cosmos which is implied in these practices does the primitive culture great violence if he seems to present the cosmology as a systematic philosophy subscribed to consciously by individuals. We can study our own cosmology in a specialized department of astronomy. But primitive cosmologies cannot rightly be pinned out for display like exotic lepidoptera, without distortion to the nature of a primitive culture. In a primitive culture the technical problems have been more or less settled for generations past. The live issue is how to organize other people and oneself in relation to them; how to control turbulent youth, how to soothe disgruntled neighbours, how to gain one's rights, how to prevent usurpation of authority, or how to justify it. To serve these practical social ends all kinds of beliefs in the omniscience and omnipotence of the environment are called into play. If social life in a particular community has settled down into any sort of constant form, social problems tend to crop up in the same areas of tension or strife. And so as part of the machinery for resolving them, these beliefs about automatic punishment, destiny, ghostly vengeance and witchcraft crystallize in the institutions. So the primitive world-view which I have defined above is rarely itself an object of contemplation and speculation in the primitive culture. It has evolved as the appanage of other social institutions. To this extent it is produced indirectly, and to this extent the primitive culture must be taken to be unaware of itself, unconscious of its own conditions.

In the course of social evolution institutions proliferate and specialize. The movement is a double one in which increased social control makes possible greater technical developments and the latter opens the way to increased social control again.

Finally we find ourselves in the modern world where economic interdependence is carried to the highest pitch reached by mankind so far. One inevitable by-product of social differentiation is social awareness, self-consciousness about the processes of communal life. And with differentiation go special forms of social coercion, special monetary incentives to conform, special types of punitive sanctions, specialized police and overseers and progress men scanning our performance, and so on, a whole paraphernalia of social control which would never be conceivable in small-scale undifferentiated economic conditions. This is the experience of organic solidarity which makes it so hard for us to interpret the efforts of men in primitive society to overcome the weakness of their social organization. Without forms filled in triplicate, without licences and passports and radio-police cars they must somehow create a society and commit men and women to its norms. I hope I have now shown why Lévy-Bruhl was mistaken in comparing one type of thought with another instead of comparing social institutions.

We can also see why Christian believers, Moslems and Jews are not to be classed as primitive on account of their beliefs. Nor necessarily Hindus, Buddhists or Mormons, for that matter. It is true that their beliefs are developed to answer the questions "Why did it happen to me: Why now?" and the rest. It is true that their universe is man-centred and personal. Perhaps in entertaining metaphysical questions at all these religions may be counted anomalous institutions in the modern world. For unbelievers may leave such problems aside. But this in itself does not make of believers promontories of primitive culture sticking out strangely in a modern world. For their beliefs have been phrased and rephrased with each century and their intermeshing with social life cut loose. The European history of ecclesiastical withdrawal from secular politics and from secular intellectual problems to specialized religious spheres is the history of this whole movement from primitive to modern.

Finally we should revive the question of whether the word "primitive" should be abandoned. I hope not. It has a defined and respected sense in art. It can be given a valid meaning for technology and possibly for economics. What is the objection to saying that a personal, anthropocentric, undifferentiated world-view characterizes a primitive culture? The only source of objection could be from the notion that it has a pejorative sense in relation to religious beliefs which it does not carry in technology and art. There may be something in this for a certain section of the English-speaking world.

The idea of a primitive economy is slightly romantic. It is true that we are materially and technically incomparably better equipped, but no one would frankly base a cultural distinction on purely materialist grounds. The facts of relative poverty and wealth are not in question. But the idea of the primitive economy is one which handles goods and services without the intervention of money. So the primitives have the advantage over us in that they encounter economic reality direct, while we are always being deflected from our course by the complicated, unpredictable and independent behaviour of money. But on this basis, when it comes to the spiritual economy, we seem to have the advantage. For their relation to their external environment is mediated by demons and ghosts whose behaviour is complicated and unpredictable, while we encounter our environment more simply and directly. This latter advantage we owe to our wealth and material progress which has enabled other developments to take place. So, on this reckoning, the primitive is ultimately at a disadvantage both in the economic and spiritual field. Those who feel this double superiority are naturally inhibited from flaunting it and this is presumably why they prefer not to distinguish primitive culture at all.

Continentals seem to have no such squeamishness. "*Le primitif*" enjoys honour in the pages of Lienhardt, Lévi-Strauss, Ricoeur and Eliade. The only conclusion that I can draw is that they are not secretly convinced of superiority, and are intensely appreciative of forms of culture other than their own.

References

Bartlett, F. C. 1923. *Psychology and Primitive Culture*. Cambridge: Cambridge University Press

Beattie, John. 1961. *Bunyoro: An African Kingdom*. New York: Holt, Rinehart and Winston.

_____1964. *Other Cultures: Aims, Methods and Achievements in Social Anthropology*. London: Routledge & Kegan Paul.

Berndt, Ronald. 1951. *Kunapipi: A Study of an Australian Aboriginal Religious Cult*. Melbourne: International University Press.

Colson, Elizabeth. 1958. *Marriage and the Family among the Plateau Tonga of Northern Rhodesia*. Manchester: Manchester University Press.

Evans-Pritchard, E. E. 1934. "Lévy-Bruhl's Theory of Primitive Mentality." *Bulletin of the Faculty of Arts*, vol. II, part 1. Cairo.

_____1937. *Witchcraft, Oracles and Magic among the Azande*. Oxford: Clarendon.

Fortes, Meyer. 1959. *Oedipus and Job in West African Religion*. Cambridge: Cambridge University Press.

Freedman, Maurice, forthcoming. *Chinese Lineage and Society, Fukien and Kwangtun*. [Published 1966 as a London School of Economics monograph in social anthropology no. 33. Ed.]

Gellner, Ernest. 1962. "Concepts and Society." In *Transactions of the Fifth World Congress of Sociology*, vol. I. Washington DC: International Sociological Association.

Horton, Robin. 1961. "Destiny and the Unconscious in West Africa." *Africa* 31: 110–16.

Levý-Bruhl, Lucien. 1922. *La mentalité primitive*. Paris: PUF.

Marshall, Lorna. 1957. "N!OW." *Africa* 27/3: 232–40.

Onians, Robert B. 1951. *Origins of European Thought about the Body, the Mind etc*. Cambridge: Cambridge University Press.

Pospisil, Leopold. 1963. *Kapauku Papuan Economy*. New Haven: Yale University Press.

Radin, Paul. 1927. *Primitive Man as Philosopher*. New York: Dover.

_____1956. *The Trickster: A Study in American Indian Mythology*. London: Routledge & Kegan Paul.

Read, Herbert. 1955. *Icon and Idea: The Function of Art in the Development of Human Consciousness*. London: Faber & Faber.

Rose, H. J. 1926. *Primitive Culture in Italy*. London: Methuen.

Stanner, W. E. H. 1965. "Religion, Totemism and Symbolism." In *Aboriginal Man in Australia*, ed. Ronald M. Berndt and Catherine M. Berndt, Ch. 8. Sydney: Angus & Robertson.

Tempels, Placide. 1962. *Bantu Philosophy*. Paris: Présence Africaine.

Turnbull, Colin. 1961. *The Forest People*. London: Chatto & Windus.

Vansina, Jan. 1964. "Le Royaume Kuba." *Annales-Sciences Humaines* 49. Musée Royale de l'Afrique Centrale.

WHAT MAKES INDIANS LAUGH

Pierre Clastres

Resolved to take the narratives of "savages" *seriously*, structural analysis has shown for some years that they are in fact quite serious; that they present a system of inquiries which raises mythical thinking to the level of thought as such. They have acquired a new prestige since the *Mythologiques* of Lévi-Strauss taught us that myths are not empty talk. And it is merely giving them their due to endow them with such gravity. Yet, perhaps the renewed interest aroused by myths will lead us this time to take them too "seriously," as it were, and to assess poorly their range of thought. In short, if their less stringent aspects are left obscure, a kind of mythomania may gain currency which ignores a trait a great number of myths have in common: one not incompatible with their gravity: their humor.

Serious both for those who relate them (the Indians, for instance) and those who record or read them, myths can nevertheless exhibit a comic intent. They sometimes perform the express function of amusing their listeners, triggering their mirth. If one cares about preserving the integral truth of myths, the real significance of the laughter they provoke must not be underestimated. The fact must be taken into account that a myth can *simultaneously* speak of serious things and set those who hear it laughing. Despite its harshness, the daily life of "primitives" is not always governed by toil and worry. They too indulge in real moments of relaxation, and their acute sense of the absurd frequently has them making fun of their own fears. Now it is not unusual for these cultures to entrust their myths with the job of entertaining the people by de-dramatizing, as it were, their existence.

The two myths we are about to read belong in that category. They were collected last year among the Chulupi Indians who live in the southern part of the Paraguayan Chaco. These narratives, going from the mock-heroic to the ribald, yet not altogether wanting in lyricism, are well known by all members of the tribe, young and old; but when they really want to laugh, they ask some old man versed in the traditional lore to tell these stories one more time. The effect never fails: the smiles at the beginning become chortles that are barely stifled, then shameless peals of laughter burst out, and finally it is all howls of joy. While these myths were being recorded on tape, the uproar of the dozens of Indians who were listening sometimes blotted out the voice of the narrator, who was himself constantly on the verge of losing his composure. We are not Indians, but perhaps by listening to their myths we will find some reason to rejoice with them.

First Myth
The Man Who Couldn't Be Told Anything[1]

This old man's family possessed just a small quantity of boiled pumpkins, when one day he asked to go find a few friends and invite them to eat these gourds. But instead, he called out to the people of all the houses in the village. He shouted as loudly as he could:

"Everyone come and eat! Everybody must come eat!"

"We're coming! Everyone is going to come!" the people answered. And yet there was scarcely one dish of pumpkins. So the first two or three to arrive ate up everything, and for those who kept showing up there was practically nothing left. Everyone was assembled in the old man's house and there was no longer anything at all to eat. "How can this be possible?" he said with amazement. "Why the devil did they ask me to invite the people to come eat? As for me, I did what I was told. I thought there was a heap of pumpkins. It's not my fault! It's always the others who make me tell lies! And afterwards they are angry with me because I was made to say what wasn't so!" Then his wife explained to him: "You have to speak softly! You need to say very softly, in a low voice: 'Come eat some pumpkin!'" "But why did you tell me to invite the people who are here? I shouted so they could hear me!" The old woman grumbled: "What an old ignoramus that one is to invite all these people."

Some time later, he went around urging his kin to come harvest his watermelon patch. But once again everyone turned up even though there were only three stalks of watermelons. "We're going to gather my watermelon crop! There are a lot of them!" he had proclaimed in a very loud voice. And all the people were there with their sacks, standing over the three stalks of watermelons. I really thought there were a lot of them," the old man said apologetically. "But there are pumpkins and *anda'i*:[2] take them!" The people filled their sacks with pumpkins and *anda'i* instead of watermelons.

After the harvest, the old man returned home. He met his granddaughter there: she was bringing him her sick baby to be treated by the old man, for he was a *tôoie'éh*, a shaman.

"Grandfather! Do something then for your great-grandson who has the fever. Spit!"

"Yes, I will take care of him right away!"

And he commenced to spit on the little boy without stopping, completely covering him with saliva. The child's mother exclaimed:

"Not like that! You must blow! Blow too! Come now, take better care of him, old man!"

"Alright, alright! But why didn't you say that sooner? You asked me to spit on my grandson, but not to blow. So I did; I spat!"

Obeying his granddaughter, the old man then set to blowing on the child, blowing and blowing, without a pause. After a moment, the woman stopped him and reminded him that it was also necessary to search for the spirit of the sick one. The grandfather got up at once and began looking, lifting up the objects in all the nooks and crannies of the house.

"No, no, grandfather! Sit down! Blow! And you have to sing!"

"But why do you wait til now to tell me that? You asked me to look for my great-grandson so I got up in order to look for him!"

He sat back down and sent for the other sorcerers so they could assist him in his cure, help him to find again the spirit of his great-grandson. They all gathered together in his house, and the old man spoke to them thus:

"Our great-grandson is ill. Hence we shall try to discover the cause of his illness."

The old man had a she-ass as the domestic animal of his spirit. The spirits of the shamans undertook the journey. The old man climbed up on his she-ass and started his chant: "*Kuvo' uitaché! kuvo'uitaché! kuvo'uitaché!* ... she-ass! she-ass! she-ass! ..." They walked in this way a fairly long while.

At a certain moment, the she-ass sank a hoof into the soft ground: there were pumpkin seeds there. The she-ass halted. The old man pointed out the fact to his companions: "The she-ass has just come to a halt. There must be something there!" They looked carefully and discovered a large amount of boiled pumpkins: they started eating them. When they were all done, the old man announced: "Well then! Now we can continue on our way."

They started off again, still keeping to the rhythm of the same chant: "*Kuvo'uitaché! kuvo'uitaché! kuvo'uitaché!* ... she-ass! she-ass! she-ass! ..." Suddenly the animal's ear cocked: "Aha!" said the old man. At that moment he remembered that near that very spot was a beehive that he had blocked up so that the bees would come back and make their honey there. The shamans cleared a path to allow the she-ass to reach that place. When they got near to the hive, they positioned the she-ass with its rump against the tree and, with her tail, she began extracting the honey. The old man said, "Suck the honey! Suck all the honey that's in the tail hairs! We're going to draw out some more." The beast repeated the operation and collected a lot more honey. "Go ahead, go ahead!" the old man said, "Eat all the honey, men with the same noses! Do you want more, or have you had your fill?" The other shamans were no longer hungry. "Very well then, let's move on!"

They set out once more, still chanting: "She-ass! she-ass! she-ass! . . ." They went on that way for a while. All at once, the old man cried out: "Aha! There's something up ahead! What can that be? That has to be a *ts'ich'e*, an evil spirit!" They came close to it and the old man declared: "Oh, that is a very swift being! We won't be able to catch up with it." And yet it was only a tortoise. "I'll stay in the middle and grab it," he said, "for I am older and more experienced than you." He arranged them in a circle and, at his signal, they all fell upon the tortoise: "She-ass! she-ass! she-ass! . . ." But the animal didn't make the slightest movement, for it was a tortoise. They got the better of it. The old man exclaimed, "How pretty it is! What a beautiful pattern! It will be my domestic animal." He picked it up and they got under way again, still chanting: "She-ass! . . ."

But before long, "Aha!" and they stopped. "The she-ass will go no further. Something is up ahead." They looked and spied a skunk. "He will be our dog!" the old man affirmed. "He is very pretty, a wild dog!" They encircled it and the old man himself took up a position at the center, declaring, "I am older and more skillful than you." And, to the chant "She-ass! she-ass! she-ass! . . .", they went on the offensive. But the skunk disappeared into its burrow: "He went in there! I'll try to get him out." The old sorcerer stuck his hand through the opening, bent way down, and the skunk pissed in his face.[3] "Aiee!" he screamed. The stench was so great he nearly fainted. The other shamans scattered in confusion, crying: "That stinks! That stinks like hell!"

They took up their journey, all of them chanting in chorus, and soon they felt like having a smoke. The ear of the she-ass dipped and the animal halted once more. "So now we will smoke a little," the old man decided. He was carrying all his smoking gear in a little sack; he started searching for his pipe and tobacco. "Ah, I didn't count on forgetting my pipe!" He searched everywhere, but without finding anything. "Don't budge!" he said to the others. "I'll go as fast as I can to get my pipe and tobacco." And he left, urging himself along with his chanting: "She-ass! she-ass! she-ass!" At the end of the chant, he was already back with them.

"Here I am!"

"So you're back, are you? We'll smoke a little then."

They commenced to smoke.

When they were done smoking, they started out on their way again; they were still chanting. Suddenly the animal's ear pointed and the old man alerted his companions: "Aha! That sounds like dancing over yonder!" As a matter of fact, the beat of a drum could be heard. The shamans arrived at the place of merrymaking and began to dance. Each one of them joined up with a pair of dancers. They danced for a while, then talked the women into going for a little stroll with them. They went out away from the dancing place, and all the shamans made love with the women. Their old chief copulated too. But he had hardly finished when he fainted, for he was very old.

"Houf! houf! houf!" His gasping grew heavier and heavier and finally, completely out of breath, he fell into a swoon. After a minute or two, he regained his senses: "Houf! houf! houf!" he went, heaving great sighs and becoming much calmer. He gradually recuperated, gathered his companions about him, and asked: "Well then? You too are satisfied?"

"Oh, yes! Now we are free! We can get going, and a lot lighter than before!"

And, intoning their chant, they got under way again. After a while, the trail became very narrow: "We'll clear this path so the she-ass won't stick thorns in her feet." It was full of cactuses. So they cleared the path and came to the spot where the trail widened again. They continued chanting: "She-ass! she-ass! she-ass!..." A motion of the animal's ear made them stop: "There is something up ahead! Let's go see what it is." They advanced and the old shaman saw that it was his helper spirits. He had already informed them of what he was looking for. He drew near them and they announced to him: "It is *Faiho'ai*, the spirit of charcoal, who holds the soul of your great-grandson. He has also enlisted the aid of *Op'etsukfai*, the spirit of the cactus."

"Yes, yes! Exactly! That's it! I know them very well, those spirits."

There were others, but those he did not know. Advised of all this by his helper spirits, he now knew where to find his great-grandson: in a storehouse.[4]

Perched on his she-ass, he went ahead chanting and arrived at the place mentioned. But there he remained prisoner of the spiny branches of the structure. He took fright and called to the others for help. But seeing that they remained unconcerned, he gave out a howl. Only then did his shaman friends come to his aid, and thus he was able to retrieve the spirit of the sick boy. He brought it back home and re-inserted it in the body of the child. Thereupon, his granddaughter got up, took her cured child, and went away.

This old shaman had other granddaughters. They liked very much to go gather the fruit of the *algarrobo*. The next day at dawn they came looking for him.

"Our grandfather is already up?"

"Of course; I've been awake for a long time!"

"So! Let's go then!"

And he left to hunt for the black *algarrobo* with one of his granddaughters who was still single. He led her to a place that had a lot of trees and the young woman started gathering the fruit. As for him, he sat down to smoke. But already the desire came to him, little by little, to do something with his granddaughter, for the session the day before, with the women encountered during the journey, had aroused his passions. So he began to consider ways to seduce his granddaughter.

He collected a thorn from the *algarrobo* and stuck it in his foot. Then he pretended to be trying to pull it out. He groaned in a pitiful manner.

"Unh! unh! unh!"

"Oh! My poor grandfather! What on earth has happened to him?"

"An accident! I have a thorn in my foot. And it feels like it's going all the way to my heart!"

The young woman, upset, went over to him and the grandfather said to her – "Take off your belt, for bandaging my wound! Because I can't stand it any longer!" She did as he said, and the grandfather advised her to sit down: "Now then, raise your loincloth a little so I can place my foot on your thighs. Unh! unh! Aiee!" Awful moans! He was really hurting: "Let me put my foot on your thighs! Unh! Unh! How it hurts! I can't bear it any more! Spread your thighs a little bit. Aiee! Aiee!" And the sympathetic young woman obeyed. The old man was all excited, for she was now completely naked: "Hmm! What beautiful legs she has, my little granddaughter! Couldn't you move my foot a little higher, granddaughter?"

That's when he threw himself on her, exclaiming – "Aha! Now we are going to forget about your future husband!"

"Oh! Grandfather!" said the young woman, who didn't want to.

"I am not your grandfather!"

"Grandfather, I'll tell everything!"

"Well then, so will I! I'll tell everything too!"

He threw her down and thrust his penis into her. Once he was on top of her, he exclaimed: "Ho! You see! Now you are benefitting from my leftovers. The very last ones indeed!" Then they returned to the village. She was so ashamed that she didn't tell anything.

The old man had yet another granddaughter, and she was also unmarried. And he would have liked very much to take advantage of her as well. So he invited her to go with him to gather the fruit of the *algarrobo*, and, once there, he repeated the same charade with the thorn. But this time, he was more in a hurry; he showed his granddaughter the thorn and, without further ado, threw her on the ground and stretched out on top of her. He started to penetrate her, but the young woman gave a violent jerk and the old man's penis went and planted itself in a tuft of grass, jamming one blade of the grass inside, wounding him slightly: "Aiee! My granddaughter has stung my nose!"[5] Once again he threw himself on top of her and they wrestled on the ground. At the right moment, the grandfather got it up, but he missed his target a second time, and, in his exertion, went and uprooted the whole tuft of grass with his penis. He started bleeding, covering the granddaughter's stomach with blood.

She made a big effort and managed to get out from under her grandfather. She caught him by the hair, dragged him to the cactus, and set about rubbing his face against the thorns. He pleaded, "Take pity on your grandfather!"

"I don't want to hear a word about my grandfather!"

"You are going to lose your grandfather!"

"That's all the same to me!"

And she continued thrusting his face into the cactus. Next she took him again by the hair and dragged him into the middle of a *caraguata* bush. The old man withstood this for a few moments, then attempted to get back up; but she prevented him from doing so. The *caraguata* thorns scratched his stomach, his testicles, and his penis: "My testicles! My testicles are being torn to shreds!" the grandfather protested. *Krr! Krr!* went the thorns, tearing open his skin. At last, the granddaughter left him sprawled out on the *caraguata* heap. The old man's head was already completely swelled up from all the needles stuck in it. The young woman collected her sack, returned home, and revealed to her grandmother what her grandfather had tried to do. As for the latter, who could barely see any longer because of the needles that covered his eyes, he groped his way back and dragged himself into his house.

There, his wife removed her loincloth and flailed away at his face with it. "Come here for a minute and touch what I have there!" she cried. And, taking his hand, she made him touch her *hlasu*, her vagina. She was in a rage.

"Yes! You like the things that belong to others; but you want nothing to do with what is yours!"

"I don't want any of your *hlasu*! It's too old! Nobody wants to use old things!"

Second Myth
The Adventures of the Jaguar

One morning the jaguar went out walking and came upon a chameleon. As everyone knows, the chameleon can go through fire without being burned. The jaguar exclaimed, "How I would like to play with the fire too!"

"You can play if you want, but you won't be able to bear the heat and you will burn yourself."

"Huh! Hmph. Why couldn't I bear it? I'm fast too, you know!"

"Well then! Let's go over there; the embers are not so hot."

They went there, but actually the embers burned brighter there than anywhere else. The chameleon explained to the jaguar how he had to go about it and passed through the fire once to demonstrate: nothing happened to him. "Good! Get out of the way! I'm going to go too. If you can do it, so can I!" The jaguar jumped into the fire and immediately burned himself: hsss! He managed to get through, but he was already half charred, and he died, reduced to ashes.

In the midst of all this, the *ts'a-ts'i* bird arrived and started crying: "Oh! My poor grandson! I'll never be able to get used to singing in the footsteps of a buck!" He came down from his tree; then, with his wing, he began gathering the jaguar's ashes into a pile. Next he poured water on the ashes and hopped over the pile: the jaguar got back up. "Whew, such heat!" he exclaimed. "Why the devil did I go to sleep out in the bright sun?" He set out walking again.

Before long, he heard someone singing: it was the buck, who was standing in the sweet potato patch. The sweet potatoes were really cactuses. "*At'ona'i! At'ona'i!* I am sleepy for no reason!" And as he sang, he danced over the cactuses: since bucks have very small feet, he could easily avoid the thorns. The jaguar watched his goings on.

"Ah! How I would like to dance there too!"

"I don't think you will be able to walk over the cactuses without getting spines stuck in your paws."

"And why not? If you can go through them, then I can go there just as well!"

"OK! In that case, let's go over there: there are fewer spines."

But there were actually a lot more. The buck went first to show the jaguar how it was done: he danced over the cactuses, then came back, without any spines. "Hee!

Hee! Hee!" went the jaguar. "How much fun all that is!" It was his turn. He entered the cactus patch and at once the spines drove into his paws. Two leaps carried him to the middle of the cactus patch. He suffered great pain and could no longer keep himself standing: he lay down full length, his body riddled with spines.

The *ts'a-ts'i* appeared again, pulled the jaguar out of there, and removed all the spines one by one. Then, using his wing, he pushed him a little further. "Such heat!" exclaimed the jaguar. "Why the devil did I fall asleep in the hot sun?"

He set out again. A few minutes later, he met up with a lizard: lizards can climb up trees all the way to the ends of the branches and come back down very quickly without falling. The jaguar watched him do it and immediately felt like having fun too. So the lizard led him to another tree and showed him first how it had to be done: he went up to the top and came back down full speed. The jaguar dashed off in his turn, but on reaching the top of the tree, he fell and a branch rammed up his anus, coming out through his mouth. "Oh!" said the jaguar, "That feels just like when I have diarrhea." Again *ts'a-ts'i* came to get him out of the jam, nursed his anus, and the jaguar was able to start off once more.

He then encountered a bird who was playing with two branches that the wind was causing to cross one another. The bird was entertaining himself by going between them just as they crossed. The jaguar thought that looked like great fun. "Me too, I want to play too!"

"But you won't be able to do it! You're too big, not little like me."

"Who says I won't be able to?"

So the bird led the jaguar to another tree and passed through once to show him: the branches nearly touched the bird's tail when they came together. "Now it's your turn!" The jaguar sprang, but the branches caught him by the middle of his body, cutting him in two. "Aiee!" cried the jaguar. The two pieces fell and he died.

Ts'a-ts'i reappeared and saw his dead grandson. He started weeping: "I'll never be able to get used to singing in the footsteps of a buck!" He flew down and stitched the two pieces of the jaguar back together. With a snail's shell, he carefully smoothed out the scam; then he walked on the jaguar, who then got back up, alive.

He went on his way again. Then he saw *It'o* the royal vulture, who was amusing himself by flying up and down. That too delighted the jaguar: he announced to *It'o* that he wanted to play like he was doing. "Oh, my friend! How wonderful it would be to play like you!"

"That would be fine indeed, but you have no wings."

"That's true; I don't have any, but you can lend me some."

It'o agreed. He made two wings which he glued to the jaguar's body with some wax. When that was done, he invited his companion to fly. Together they rose to an incredible height and enjoyed themselves the whole morning long. But towards midday the sun was scorching hot and caused the wax to melt: the two wings came loose. The jaguar crashed to the ground with all his weight and died, practically smashed to bits. *Ts'a-ts'i* arrived, mended the jaguar's bones, and set him back on his feet. The jaguar started off again.

It wasn't long until he came upon the skunk, who was playing with his son, breaking pieces of wood. The jaguar came closer to see what was going on: he immediately pounced on the skunk's son, then tried attacking the father. But the latter pissed in his eyes and the jaguar was left blinded.[6] He walked and could no longer see a thing. But *ts'a-ts'i* appeared once more and gave his eyes a good washing; that is why the jaguar's vision is so good. Without the *ts'a-ts'i*, the jaguar would no longer exist.

The value of these two myths is not limited to the intensity of the laughter they produce. It is a matter of thoroughly understanding what it is about these stories that amuses the Indians; it also needs establishing that comic force is not the only property these two myths have in common. On the contrary, they constitute a set of myths on the basis of less external reasons, reasons that enable one to see their being grouped as something other than an arbitrary juxtaposition.

The central character of the first myth is an old shaman. First we see him take everything literally, confuse the letter with the spirit (so that *he can't be told anything*), and, as a result, cover himself with ridicule in the eyes of the Indians. Next we accompany him in the adventures his doctor's "trade" exposes him to. The zany expedition he undertakes with the other shamans, in search of his grandson's soul, is sprinkled with episodes that reveal the doctors' total incompetence and their prodigious capacity to forget the purpose of their mission: they hunt, they eat, they copulate, they seize upon the least pretext for forgetting they are doctors. Their old chief, after having brought about the cure just in time, gives free rein to a frantic debauchery: he takes unfair advantage of the innocence and kindness of his own granddaughters so as to get under their skirts in the forest. In short, he is a grotesque hero, and one laughs at his expense.

The second myth tells us of the jaguar. Although it is a mere outing, his journey is not lacking in the unexpected. This big simpleton, who decidedly meets up with a lot of characters on his way, falls systematically into the traps laid for him by those he holds so haughtily in contempt. The jaguar is big, strong, and stupid; he never understands anything that happens to him, and without the interventions of an insignificant little bird, he would have succumbed a long time ago. Every one of his moves proves his doltishness and demonstrates the ridiculousness of the character. To sum up, these two myths present shamans and jaguars as the victims of their own stupidity and vanity, victims who, accordingly, do not deserve compassion, but rather hearty laughter.

This is the proper place to raise the question: who is being made fun of? The first conjunction shows the jaguar and the shaman brought together through the laughter their misadventures arouse. But when we examine the real status of these two types of beings, the Indians' real-life relationship to them, we find them placed side by side in a second analogy: the fact is, far from being comic figures, both of them are dangerous beings capable of inspiring fear, respect, and hatred, but never the desire to laugh.

In most South American Indian tribes, shamans share prestige and authority with the chiefs, that is, when they themselves do not fill that political function. The shaman is always a very important figure in Indian societies, and, as such, he is at the same time respected, admired, and feared. This is because in reality he is the only one in the group who possesses supernatural powers, the only one with the power to control the dangerous world of the spirits and the dead. Hence the shaman is a man of knowledge who puts what he knows in the service of the group by caring for the sick. But the same powers that make him a doctor, that is, a man capable of bringing life, enables him to rule over death as well. For that reason, he is dangerous, disquieting; one is constantly mistrustful of him. As the master of life and death, he is immediately made responsible for every extraordinary occurrence, and very often he is killed out of fear. This means, consequently, that the shaman moves within a space that is too distant from, too external to that of the group for the group to dream, in real life, of letting its laughter bring it nearer to him.

What of the jaguar? This feline is an effective hunter, for it is powerful and cunning. The prey it attacks most readily (wild hogs, animals of the deer family) are also the game generally preferred by the Indians. The result is that the jaguar is seen by them – and here the myths in which the jaguar appears supply a frequent confirmation of these facts based on observation – more as a competitor to be reckoned with than as a fearsome enemy. However, it would be a mistake to conclude that the jaguar is not dangerous. It is true no doubt that it rarely attacks men; but I know of several cases of Indians being attacked and devoured by this beast, so it is always risky business when one encounters the jaguar. Moreover, its very qualities as a hunter, together with the dominion it exercises over the forest, induce the Indians to accord it the full measure of respect and to refrain from underestimating it: they respect the jaguar as an equal and in no instance do they make light of it.[7] In real life, the jaguar and the laughter of men remain disjoined.

Let us conclude, then, the first phase of this summary investigation by stating that:
1. The two myths considered present the shaman and the jaguar as grotesque beings and objects of laughter;
2. As for the relations between men on one hand, shamans and jaguars on the other hand, insofar as these relations are actually experienced, the position of the shamans and jaguars is just the opposite of that presented by the myths: they are dangerous beings, hence worthy of respect, who by that very fact remain beyond laughter;
3. The contradiction between the imaginary world of the myth and the real world of everyday life is resolved when one recognizes in the myths a derisive intent: *the Chulupi do in mythical life what is forbidden them in real life*. One does not laugh at real shamans or real jaguars, for they are not in the least bit amusing. For the Indians, it is a matter of challenging, of demystifying in their own eyes, the fear and the respect that jaguars and shamans inspire in them. This calling in question can be carried out in two ways: in actual fact, in which case the shaman deemed too dangerous, or the jaguar encountered in the forest, is killed; or symbolically, *through laughter*, in which case the myth invents a variety of shamans

and jaguars of a kind that can be ridiculed, stripped as they are of their real attributes and transformed into village idiots.

Let us consider the first myth, for example. The central part of it is devoted to the description of a shamanistic cure. The doctor's task is a serious matter, since, in order to heal the one who is sick, it is necessary to discover and reintegrate into the patient's body the soul held captive far away. This means that during the expedition undertaken by his spirit, the shaman has to give full attention to his work and cannot allow himself to be distracted by anything. Now what happens to him in the myth? First of all, there are many shamans, while the case to be treated is relatively mild: the child is running a fever. A shaman does not send for his colleagues except in really hopeless cases. Next we see the doctors, like children, taking advantage of the slightest opportunity to play hookey: they eat (first boiled pumpkins, then the honey extracted by the she-ass's tail); they hunt (a tortoise, then a skunk); they dance with women (instead of dancing by themselves, as they should), and waste no time in seducing them, then going off to copulate with them (something a shaman at work must absolutely abstain from). During this time, the old man realizes he has forgotten the one thing a true shaman would never forget, that is, his tobacco. To top it off, he becomes entangled like a fool in a mass of thorns where his companions would leave him to thrash about if he did not howl for assistance. In short, the head shaman does exactly the contrary of what a genuine doctor would do. It is not possible, without overburdening the discussion, to recall all the traits that hold the mythical shaman up to ridicule. A brief word should be said about two of them, however: his "domestic animal" and his chant. Whenever a shaman of the Chaco undertakes a cure, he sends (in his imagination, of course) his pet animal out to explore. Every shaman is the master of such an animal helper spirit: more often than not, these are little birds or snakes, and in any case never animals as ludicrous (for Indians) as a she-ass. By choosing for the shaman a domestic animal so clumsy and stubborn, the myth indicates straight away that it is going to speak of a poor clown. Moreover, the songs of the Chulupi are always wordless. They consist of a slightly modulated chant, repeated indefinitely and punctuated, at infrequent intervals, by a single word: the name of the pet animal. Now the chant of our shaman is made up exclusively of his animal's name: in this manner, he is constantly issuing, like a victory cry, the confession of his shamanistic shenanigans.

Here we see emerge a cathartic function of the myth, so to speak: in its narration it frees one of the Indians' passions, the secret obsession to laugh at what one fears. It devalues on the plane of language a thing that cannot be taken lightly in reality, and, manifesting in laughter an equivalent of death, it instructs us that among the Indians, ridicule kills.

Although superficial thus far, our reading of the myths is nonetheless sufficient to establish that the mythological resemblance of the jaguar and the shaman is the transformation of a real resemblance. But the equivalence between them that we have brought to light remains external, and the characteristics that unite them always refer to a third term: the Indians' real attitude towards shamans and jaguars. Let us probe deeper into the text of the myths to see if the kinship of these two beings is not much closer than it appears.

It will be remarked first of all that the central part of the first myth and the second in its entirety speak of exactly the same thing. Involved in both instances is a *journey strewn with obstacles*: that of the shaman going off in search of the spirit of a sick boy, and that of the jaguar who is simply out for a walk. Now the quixotic or mock-heroic adventures of our two protagonists actually conceal, under the mask of a false innocence, a quite serious project, a very important sort of journey: *the journey that takes the shamans to the Sun*. Here we must invoke the ethnographic context.

The shamans of the Chaco are not merely doctors, but also soothsayers capable of seeing into the future (the outcome of a martial expedition, for example). Sometimes, when they do not feel certain of their knowledge, they go consult the Sun, who is an omniscient being. But the Sun, preferring not to be bothered, has placed a series of very difficult obstacles along the route leading to his abode. That is why only the best shamans, the most cunning and courageous, manage to stand the tests; then the Sun agrees to extinguish its rays and inform those who come before him. Expeditions of this kind, precisely because of their difficulty, are always collective and are always enacted under the direction of the most experienced of the sorcerers. Now, when one compares the ups and downs of a voyage to the Sun to the adventures of the old shaman, one notices that the two myths in question describe, often in precise detail, the stages of the Great Voyage of the shamans. The first myth tells of a cure: the doctor sends his spirit in search of the sick person's spirit. But the fact that the journey is conducted in a group already implies that more than a routine excursion is at stake, that something much more solemn is involved: a voyage to the Sun. Furthermore, certain obstacles encountered by the shamans in the myth correspond to the traps with which the Sun has marked out his road: the different barriers of thorns, for instance, and the episode with the skunk. The latter, by *blinding* the shaman, is repeating one of the moments of the voyage to the Sun: the passage through the darkness where one *does not see anything*.

In the end, what is found in this myth is a burlesque parody of the voyage to the Sun, a parody that takes its pretext from a theme that is more familiar to the Indians (the shamanistic cure) so as to poke fun at their sorcerers twice over. As for the second myth, it takes up, virtually element by element, the scenario of the voyage to the Sun, and the various games where the jaguar loses correspond to the obstacles that the true shaman is able to surmount: the dance in the thorns, the branches that criss-cross, the skunk that plunges the jaguar into darkness, and, finally, the Icarian flight towards the sun in the company of the vulture. There is actually nothing surprising in the fact that the sun melts the wax that holds the jaguar's wings in place, since before the Sun will extinguish its rays the good shaman must have gotten over the previous obstacles.

Our two myths thus make use of the theme of the Great Voyage to caricature shamans and jaguars by showing them to be incapable of completing that voyage. It is not without reason that the indigenous mind chooses the activity most closely tied to the shaman's task, the meeting with the Sun; it tries to introduce a boundless space between the shaman and the jaguar of the myths and their goal, a space that is filled in by the comic. And the fall of the jaguar who loses his wings through recklessness is the metaphor of a demystification intended by the myth.

Hence we find that the two roads on which the shaman and the jaguar, respectively, are made to travel by the myths lead in the same direction; we see the resemblance the myths set out to elicit between the two protagonists gradually become more specific. But are these parallels destined to meet? An objection might be countered to the above observations: while it is perfectly consistent and, one might say predictable even, for the first myth to evoke the setting of the voyage to the Sun in order to make fun of those who accomplish the voyage – the shamans – one fails to understand, on the other hand, the conjunction of the jaguar *qua* jaguar and the theme of the Great Voyage; it is hard to comprehend why the indigenous mind calls upon this aspect of shamanism in order to deride the jaguar. Since the two myths examined do not throw any light on the question, it is again necessary to rely on the ethnography of the Chaco.

As we have seen, various tribes of this region share the conviction that good shamans are capable of reaching the abode of the Sun, which permits them both to demonstrate their talent and enrich their knowledge by questioning the omniscient heavenly body. But for these Indians there exists another test of the power (and malice) of the better sorcerers: the fact that the latter are able to *transform themselves into jaguars*. The points of similarity between these two myths now cease to be arbitrary, and the heretofore external relationship between jaguars and shamans gives place to an identity, since, from a certain viewpoint, *shamans are jaguars*. Our demonstration would be complete if the converse of this proposition could be established: are jaguars shamans?

Now another Chulupi myth (too lengthy to be transcribed here) provides us with the answer: in former times, jaguars were in fact shamans. They were bad shamans, moreover, for, instead of healing their patients, they sought rather to devour them. It would seem that the circle is now closed, since this last piece of information allows us to confirm what went before: *jaguars are shamans*. By the same token, another obscure aspect of the second myth becomes clear: if it makes the jaguar into the protagonist of adventures usually reserved for sorcerers, this is because it is not a matter of the jaguar as a jaguar, but the jaguar as a shaman.

The fact, then, that the shaman and the jaguar are in a sense interchangeable confers a certain homogeneity on our two myths and gives credibility to our initial hypothesis: namely, that they constitute a kind of group such that each of the two components of which it is composed can be understood only by reference to the other. Of course we are now a long way from our point of departure. At the outset, the resemblance of the two myths was external; it was based solely on the necessity for the indigenous mind to bring about a mythical conjunction that was not possible in reality: that of laughter on one hand, the shaman and the jaguar on the other. The preceding commentary (and let me emphasize that it is by no means an analysis, but rather preliminary to such a treatment) attempted to establish that this conjunction concealed beneath its comic intent the identification of the two characters.

When the Indians listen to these stories, their only thought, naturally, is to laugh at them. But the comic element of the myths does not prevent their having a serious side as well. A pedagogical aim can be discerned in the laughter provoked: while the myths amuse those who hear them, at the same time they convey and transmit the culture of the tribe. They thus constitute the gay science of the Indians.

Notes

1. This is the title given to me by the Indians.
2. *Cucurbita moschata*.
3. In actual fact, the skunk projects a foul-smelling liquid contained in an anal gland.
4. A hut made of branches, where the Indians store their provisions.
5. According to the Chulupi social code, it would be coarse to call the penis by its name. Hence it is necessary to say: the nose.
6. See note 3.
7. I have even noted among tribes having very different cultures, as for example the Guayaki, the Guarani, the Chulupi, a tendency to exaggerate the risk of meeting this animal: the Indians *play* at being afraid of the jaguar, because they really do fear it.

PART IV

SEMIOLOGICAL APPROACHES

Introduction to Part IV

As a term, "semiological approaches" refers to the main characteristic of what the contributions in this section have in common, namely the "semiological" perspective concerned with viewing the signification aspects of human socio-cultural products. Other designations could come to mind, such as structuralist, semiotic and narratological, as the four selected contributions could be classed as one or more of these. My main reason for this choice of terminology is that the contributions approach myths and mythologies as complex arrangements of signs, that is, as combinations of signifying elements that may produce meaningful communication and stories when "assembled," put together in narrative chains as stories. To that end the combination of signs ("semeia" in Greek) must obey some rules of reason and logic to make sense to the community in which they belong. There is thus always also a sociological dimension present. As myths are clearly narratives, one might also have called this section "narratological" but although reasonable to a large extent, this would not bring out so clearly the main intention of analysing and disclosing the cultural and cognitive logics of myths and mythologies as combinations of signs. Cultures, in their ideational aspects, can be said to consist of reservoirs and repertoires of meanings, ideas, concepts, values, etc. and these may then be more or less consciously and skilfully employed in the social group whose symbolic property they are. Accordingly, there is a symbol and meaning "system" – they are not always seamless and non-contradictive – that is being put to use and "articulated" in human social practice. This view is generally well known from structuralism and structuralist theory. This is not the place to present a review or history of structuralism, however brief.[1] Below, I wish only to point to a few salient features and their originators that may enhance the benefits of reading the contributions. At this point, some readers may ask why there is not a section on "post-structuralism" for the rumour is out that this is a more recent development than structuralist and semiological approaches. It is normally quite reasonable to choose the most recent tools for scientific practice and scholarly analysis, so why not here? The reason is that as strategies for analysis of cultural "products" in traditional societies, the "post"-theories and methodologies are less fruitful than traditional structural analysis. The explanation of this is that traditional cultures and their products (myths, rituals, cosmologies) are socially shared and (mostly) unconsciously used and reproduced by members of the society or social group. Most cultural products are in that sense "language-like."

It should also be mentioned that "semiology" is the "old," original designation used by the Swiss linguist Ferdinand de Saussure, who started the theoretical turn towards systems and synchronicity, which later resulted in structuralism, semiotics, etc. Saussure predicted that one day there would be sciences of culture modelled on the study of language. Now, myths are expressed in language, but then also, as combinations of motifs, images, metaphors, concepts, etc. in narrative chains, that are akin to "super-sentences." On the analogy with language as a characteristic of structuralism, the classical scholar R. G. Buxton stated that in his view of Greek mythology:

> ...we should be reasonable here. 1) To say that myth is like a language in certain aspects is not to say that it is language in every respect. 2) To speak of Greek myths as constituting a 'system' may err on the side of formality, but it is a vitally important counter to those who regard the stories as a random hotch-potch of the inherited conglomerate. (1981, xiv–xv)

It is the hypothesis of the "analogy to language" and its concomitant methologies that holds together otherwise different areas and subjects in, for example, linguistics, literary analysis, anthropology and the study of religion. A cursory glimpse back in history allows us to see how these developments came about.

The Relations between Semiology and Narratology

Logically as well as chronologically there are some affinities between semiology and narratology. The first scholar normally credited with developing a model and hypothesis about the general characteristics of traditional tales is Vladimir Propp, who in his work "Morphology of the Folktale" (1928) enumerated thirty-one plot elements that go into traditional tales, from fairytales to myth. These include, for example, an initial interdiction that the main character violates, villains appear, so do magical helpers, a situation characterized by lack is discovered, the hero is tested, the hero returns, the villain is punished, etc. – all so well-known from all over the world, that one wonders if there really are universal human structures in narratives. I think there are. The important contribution of Propp was that he demonstrated how the myriads of tales can be formally analysed and he is therefore one of the precursors of modern "Formalism" in narratology – it already in some sense began with Aristotle. Very briefly portrayed, formalism deals with the formal characteristics of narratives, such as their motifs, plots, functions, and structures.[2] One of the main proponents of formalism, the linguist Roman Jakobson, first studied sound systems in languages (phonology) and later took principles of linguistic analysis into the study of literature, poetry and semiotics (the study of signs in general). Thereby he emphasized the importance of linguistic perspectives in the studies not only of language, but also of narratives, such as myths, as well of the structural and semiotic properties of other human cultural products. Many lessons from the study of language may thus also be employed in studies of other kinds of communication.

In a different vein, Claude Bremond laboured on a systematization of the logic in the actions in narratives.[3] He defined the basic narrative chain, in a very simple model, as consisting of three links: An opening situation with a possibility, a virtuality, where things can go well or wrong. Then the occurrence of the possibility or not and finally the achievement or failure of the project of the story. He also developed a complex system of roles in stories; crucial is the distinction between agents and patients: agents start the processes, influence the patients and turn them into either victims or beneficiaries. The characters in the stories meet obstacles which they or may not have the means to overcome; there may be traps and deceit, seduction and threats. The relations between characters may rely on conventions (parents help their children) or they may negotiate and make alliances with others, either in solidarity relations among equals or in unequal relations between debtors and creditors. In Bremond's view one gets an almost economical analysis of the logic of tales. We all know the impression we get when a story appears unfinished because it did not reach an equilibrium that seemed inherent in the plot.

Algirdas J. Greimas, the Lithuanian designer of "structural semantics," theorized about the formal properties of narratives as well as the formal organization of discourse in general. He also employed his theory to the semantics of myth analysis (e.g. in Maranda and Maranda 1971).

In this context one of his most influential achievements is the "actantial model" – a systematization and simplification of Propp's catalogue. The model situates the actants in a systematic and abstract relationship. It is important to note the model does not show actual actors or characters, but the dramatic positions and roles that the actors may play. To the abstract actants' positions, we may add, as an illustration, some typical fairy-tale roles. The story is thus: The King (sender) has a princess to wed (object) to a young man (receiver). The young man (subject) has a project, namely to marry the princess (object). A fairy (helper) assists him in tricking the dangerous Dragon (opponent). Graphically the model looks like this:

It is obvious that most (if not all) of the world's narratives may be plotted on this model. It also works for films, etc. Even whole religions may find their place in this schema as cosmic dramas where there is a precious object (e.g. salvation) to be gained and there are helpers as well as opponents. The model is deliberately simplistic and that is precisely one of its main virtues. Any one of the myths in this volume will easily lend itself to an analysis of this kind. Something suggests that this is a universal model in the sense that as every culture has stories (which one has not?) – then these stories will involve the actantial positions of the model.[4] Greimas' idea is that a narrative must be considered as a whole because it generates the message as a consequence of the structural relations and dynamics between the actantial roles. According to

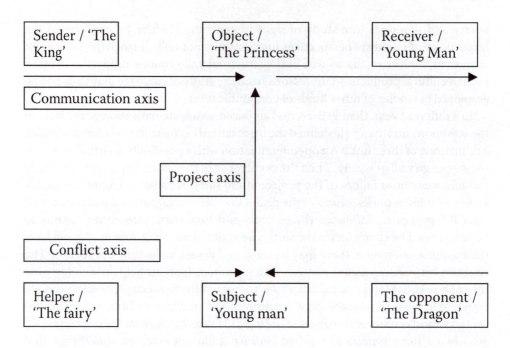

Greimas we may also discriminate between the kind of test that the character, typically a hero, has to pass: first the qualifying test that demonstrates his ability and later the glorifying test, which proves him the victor. With a different inspiration from linguistics, Greimas developed a paradigm for the qualities of the actions of actors. This paradigm is built upon the system of modal verbs and they may be illustrated in a table. The "exotactic" refer to external, translative relations and the "endotactic" are simple modalities. They are also arranged according to the classical philosophical distinction between three modes or levels of existence: "Virtual," "Actual," and "Realized" existence.

Modalities	Virtualizing	Actualizing	Realizing
Exotactic	Ought ('devoir')	Can ('pouvoir')	Do ('faire')
Endotactic	Will ('vouloir')	Know ('savoir')	Be ('être')

For the study of narratives, such as myths, the point of this table is that it facilitates classifications and typologies of who does what, when and why as well as a distribution of duties, possibilities, abilities, etc. in the universe of the narrative. These narrative worlds can be seen as consisting of four modal domains, which constrain and determine the narrative plots and dynamics. Interestingly for the study of religions, these modalities also characterize religious worlds and their patterns. The four modalities of the universes (e.g. fictional or religious) are (1) the "Alethic" about what is possible and impossible, (2) the "Deontic" about what is permissible and not permissible, the norms for actions (permitted, obligatory or prohibited), (3) "Axiological" concerning the vaue system, the valorizations of the universe, and (4) "Epistemic" about the modal system of knowledge, what can be known and not known in a given universe.[5] Using this classification as a grid we may see how a profane universe differs from a religious, how a historical account differs from a work of, say, science fiction. Narratology is a field that has received strong, and renewed interest – still building on the classics but taking the field much farther (e.g., Herman et al. 2005).

On Structuralism – also as a Future Approach

The history of structuralism has been told often enough and it shall not be repeated here, but for a few notes with direct relevance to our set of problems. In Lévi-Strauss' contribution below, some of the features of structuralism and structural analysis will be also presented – other contributions give examples of structuralist theory and method. The analogy to language is the most basic tenet of structuralism. Lévi-Strauss who must be considered *the* founder of structuralism in cultural analysis was inspired by Roman Jakobson. Structuralism, in an incipient form, is also found in the work of Ernst Cassirer (cf. section above). Lévi-Strauss' first large work, *The Elementary Structures of Kinship* (orig. 1949) was on a very classical anthropological topic. Other anthropologists had demonstrated how kinship functions in "primitive society" but Lévi-Strauss demonstrated how kinship could be seen as a system of communication, which had its own grammatical rules. Most of his later works centred on another well-known anthropological topic: systems of classification where he proved that the worldviews of "primitives" were, if not seamless, then to a large degree logical and consistent. Pre-literate cultures express their cosmologies through the use of concrete symbols instead of abstract words and concepts. They use what they have, and this Lévi-Strauss termed "Bricolage" – French for what the handyman does: He takes the bits and pieces available and puts them together. In the same manner, says Lévi-Strauss, is the world *imagined* in myths and cosmologies described through the use of symbols taken from the world *lived in*, the concrete signs available in the classifications of, say, animals and plants, that exhibit certain aspects of the human intentionality, thought and emotion. Thus, the South American Indian myths, to the study of which he dedicated a lifetime, use jaguars, parrots, the sun and moon, plants, etc. as means of signification. Where myths had for many been indications of the primitives' lack of reason, Lévi-Strauss turned the tables and stressed how the myths were logical, thus the title of his four-volume work "Mythologiques" ("Myth-ologics"). The British anthropologist Edmund Leach (1976) took the structuralist inspiration further and applied it to rituals and socio-cultural institutions (such as hierarchy, marriage, purity rules, food and etiquette). In the 1950s Roland Barthes took the principles of Lévi-Strauss' myth analysis and employed them on "modern myths," for instance styles of fashion as signification, or he set out to disclose other hidden codes of bourgeois society (e.g. racism and imperialism).

Other scholars, such as Jean-Paul Vernant and Marcel Detienne, brought structural analysis to the study of Ancient Greek religion and were able to unlock many of the riddles that had puzzled scholars for a long time, especially nineteenth-century scholars who were the custodians of the classical heritage: How could the Greeks, for all their rationality etc., "believe" in such bizarre myths about sodomy, parricide, cannibalism, incest, etc.? They did not perhaps "believe" in the modern sense of the word; more important was it that myths were a part of the total fabric of culture and society which was taken seriously in its own right. The *imagined* assembly of the gods, the "pantheon," is more than a projection of the human society; it is a system of classification with its own rationale, where humans are positioned between gods and beasts, and where the pure and the impure, the proper and the improper are given due attention through the language and imagery of the myths. Vernant also authored a very lucid and comendable account of the history of scholarship on Greek mythology from comparative and historical philology, across psychologizing interpretations, anthropological functionalism to structuralism (1980).

In its earlier phases structuralism was met with some suspicion among more empirically minded scholars and considered another "French academic fashion." Subsequently, it has become an accepted mainstream approach among others (Jensen 2005) and many things point to the fact that structuralism can be considered a very valuable contribution to the human and social sciences. Some maintain that it *is the* philosophy of science for the humanities (Caws 1997). There are also many affinities between structuralism and the developments in the philosophy of language, in that they are holistic in their perspective and stress the importance of understanding as very contextually bound (Peregrin 2001). No single item or element in a meanings system (e.g. language) has meaning in itself, because meanings are constituted by relations. But for this to be possible the systems of relations must be rational – otherwise communication will break down. Just as "snow" makes sense in English and "Schnee" in German, so all other cultural "items" must be located and understood in their proper contexts.

Of further developments from structuralism and semiology was first semiotics, sometimes also called structural semantics, as the more formal analyses of the systems of signs by which humans navigate in this world. Later, structuralism also led to discourse analysis, but this is a topic for the final chapter. And, as the term indicates, "Post-structuralism" is also heir to structuralism, albeit in a form of opposition and criticism. A common criticism of structuralism has been that it is static and a-historical, because structural analysis stresses the simultaneous and synchronic features of a group of conceptual and signifying objects instead of the dynamic or historical. Other critics deemed it a method and theory that posited the existence of structures of meanings were supposedly timeless and universal. The accusation somewhat misses the point, because the structural analysis of myths (our main interest here) will explicitly aim at disclosing the conceptual grammar that underlies or goes into the making of the story, for example the behavioural codes of marital life (Detienne, below), and grammars are, almost per definition, not dynamic, but they indicate what can and may be used in a particular articulation. Returning to de Saussure at this point, he introduced a clear distinction between two aspects of language, the language system ("Langue") and actual speech ("Parole"). In an analogy, we can say that the structuralist's analysis works from mythical "speech" as a first level object to a second level object, i.e., the system behind the articulation, because the object of the analysis is also to find the system and the rules of combinations. The other accusation was more serious, but unfounded, because the structuralist theory of meaning is non-foundationalist because it has as a major premise that signs ("signifiers") do not point to fixed meanings ("signifieds"). That premise was somehow overlooked by some critics, and, admittedly, some analyses labelled "structural" did look as if signs had stable meanings.[6] That they do not and that human knowledge is contingent upon time and place should be evident from the contributions below. In some versions of the criticism it seemed that structuralism and structural analysis was about the search for binary oppositions only. There certainly is more to it, but it really *is* remarkable how human thought and language are full of dichotomies and oppositions – it is probably very difficult to find concepts and terms that do not have opposites.

Contributions

Claude Lévi-Strauss

The work of Claude Lévi-Strauss (b. 1908) is as immense as his influence. He was born in Brussels, moved to Paris to study law and philosophy at the Sorbonne and graduated in 1931. After an interlude of teaching he left for Brazil, where he was visiting professor to the University of São Paulo and also studied the condition of various Indian tribes, primarily the Nambikwara and Tupi. Shortly after his return to France in 1939, he, as a Jew, escaped from France and worked his way to the USA and New York City where he remained during World War II. He taught at the New School for Social Research and met many other European emigrés, prominent among these the structural linguist Roman Jakobson. Lévi-Strauss also became familiar with the legacy of Franz Boas in American anthropology. He returned to France in 1948 to receive his doctorate on the basis of *The Elementary Structures of Kinship*, where he argues that kinship was based on alliances and exchange between families and not on descent as was the common view in anthropology. Lévi-Straus was instrumental in setting up the new anthropological journal *L'Homme* but he also become a public intellectual figure when *Tristes Tropiques*, his impressions from travels in Brazil, were published in 1955. Since then, his career has been one of the most illustrious. Claude Lévi-Strauss is credited with being the author of structuralism in anthropology and influential in many disciplines that since borrowed the ideas, from archaeology to cultural studies, philosophy and the study of religion. The major works were *The Elementary Structures of Kinship*, the two volumes of *Structural Anthropology*, the four volumes in the series *Introduction to Science of Mythology*, *Totemism Today* and *The Savage Mind* – to name but the most famous. For many years running, public opinion polls in France showed that he was the most well-known intellectual. Picking just a score of pages to represent his efforts are difficult, but here it is part of the opening passage from the four-volume work on the mythologies of the South American Indians, in order to demonstrate what he means by a "Science of Mythology." The article is clearly programmatic and not so much a analysis of existing myths.

Marcel Detienne

Marcel Detienne has a background in classics and religious studies and for many years he taught at the École Pratique des Hautes Études in Paris. Detienne has published numerous books on Greek religion since his first work in French came out in 1962, for example *The Gardens of Adonis* and *The Creation of Mythology*. He is now Professor of Classics at the Johns Hopkins University in the United States. Much of his work is novel structural interpretations of classical myths. In the contribution chosen here, he presents a startling analysis of the myths about Orpheus and Euridice. The basic premise of the analysis is that a myth must not be interpreted on its own, but only and always as part of a group of myths. Sometimes myths with apparently completely different motives and stories can be used to cast light on a hard-to-crack myth and that is because – in a mythology such as the Greek – the myths support each other in a holistic "web" and they are transformations of each others, using different codes to say something about one or more topics, as in this example, affection, marriage, matrimony and gender roles. Detienne's contribution amply demonstrates the extent to which structural analysis must necessariy depend on but also may very fruitfully exploit anthropological, ethnographic and historical evidence. When structuralism and structuralist analysis were first developed, primarily by Lévi-Strauss, common criticism was that it was too "theoretical" and speculative. The studies carried out by Detienne and other members of the "Parisian school" (Vidal-Naquet and Vernant primarily) in classical studies refute that criticism by their very examples of erudite scholarship.

Roland Barthes

Roland Barthes (1915–80) was a many-faceted scholar: He was a critic of literature and culture, a semiotician and a linguist. One of his main achievements is his insistence on a science of narrative. This he did with inspiration from de Saussure and subsequent structural linguistics. His publications range widely, and among them is the interesting volume *Mythologies* about "myth today," transformed into many genres of representation, where ideological messages are presented in such self-evident formats that they seem perfectly natural. For Barthes, then, myth is "what goes without saying." As myths and narratives are so ubiquitous, and because narratives come in so many genres, from advertising to courtroom statements, the study of narrative must, in his view, be strongly cross-disciplinary. Narratives have important functions in not only linguistic communication and literary traditions but they also play a major role in organizing cognitive activities. Narratives are implicit in art and in other kinds of symbolic behaviour, for example music and dance or in fashion and car design. In the contribution here, Barthes explicitly sets out to develop a grammar of narratives, where especially the distinction between functions and indices are important for the study of myth. The many references to the Russian formalists, to Bremond and Greimas, place Barthes squarely in that tradition. Important is his note on the deductive turn, the development in linguistics that proved successful in that field. Likewise, the study of narratives must "turn" deductive, because it is impossible to construct a model of narrative based on induction. The study must proceed, instead, from a theory and a model.

Roy Wagner

Roy Wagner is an American anthropologist, who completed his PhD in 1966. Wagner did fieldwork in New Ireland in Melanesia from which developed his prime interests in ritual, myth and worldview, and indigenous conceptual systems. Later he worked on methods of cultural representation in symbolism. Among his well-known works are *The Invention of Culture* and *Symbols that Stand for Themselves*. The contribution chosen for inclusion here (from 1978) is rather extraordinary. So far his theory of "symbolic obviation" has been overlooked in research on myth, but it deserves much more attention than it has received. Part of the reason for its not being so well known is the complexity of the argument. The introduction is challenging reading, and only after some pages do we see the contours of Wagner's theory about what it is that myths do – they "obviate," that is, they make things obvious. It is the "definitive paradigm of semiotic transformation" because "obviation is the discourse or invention that speaks between the lines of a given reality."

Notes

1. See overview with direct reference to the study of religion in Jensen 2000. More comprehensive are Caws 1997 and Peregrin 2001. For the legacy of Saussure, see the expositions by Culler 1976 (easily accessible) and Thibault 1997 (detailed and technical). A now classic demonstration of the structuralist approach to culture and religion, including myth and ritual, is Leach 1976.
2. Some of these characteristics will be treated in more detail in Barthes' contribution in this section.
3. I synthesize Bremond's views very briefly (it was not possible to find a suitable extract for inclusion here).

4. A classic study is Maranda and Maranda (1971). A cognitive semantic analysis would suggest that the model also represents ordinary human action and that its attractiveness stems from its deep correspondence to human activities in general.
5. The presentation here is extremely brief; see Dolezel (1998, 113–32) for a thorough elaboration.
6. Lechte 1994 is very helpful to the student trying to make sense of all the "-isms."

References

Barthes, Roland. 1994. "Introduction to the Structural Analysis of Narratives" (orig. 1966). In idem, *The Semiotic Challenge*, 95–136 (excerpt). Berkeley: University of California Press.

Buxton, R. G. A. 1981. "Introduction." In Gordon 1981: ix–xvii.

Caws, Peter. 1997. *Structuralism: A Philosophy for the Human Sciences*. Atlantic Highlands: Humanities Press.

Culler, Jonathan. 1976. *Saussure*. London: Fontana Press.

Detienne, Marcel. 1981. "The Myth of 'Honeyed Orpheus.'" In Gordon 1981: 95–109.

Dolezel, Lubomir. 1998. *Heterocomisca: Fiction and Possible Worlds*. Baltimore: Johns Hopkins University Press.

Gordon, R. L., ed. 1981. *Myth, Religion and Society: Structuralist Essays by M. Detienne, L. Gernet, J.-P. Vernant & P. Vidal-Naquet*. Cambridge: Cambridge University Press.

Herman, David, Manfred Jahn and Marie-Laure Ryan, eds. 2005. *The Routledge Encyclopedia of Narrative Theory*. London: Routledge.

Jensen, Jeppe Sinding. 2000. "Structure." In *Guide to the Study of Religion*, ed. Willi Braun and Russell N. McCutcheon, 314–33. London: Cassell Academic.

_____2005. "Structuralism – Further Considerations." In *The Encyclopedia of Religion*, rev. ed., vol. 13, 8757–8768. Detroit: Macmillan Reference.

Leach, Edmund. 1976. *Culture and Communication: The Logic by which Symbols are Connected*. Cambridge: Cambridge University Press.

Lechte, John. 1994. *Fifty Key Contemporary Thinkers: From Structuralism to Postmodernity*. London: Routledge.

Lévi-Strauss, Claude. 1969. *The Raw and the Cooked: Introduction to a Science of Mythology*, vol. I (orig. 1964). Harmondsworth: Penguin.

Maranda, Pierre and Elli K. Maranda, eds. 1971. *Structural Analysis of Oral Tradition*. Philadelphia: University of Pennsylvania Press.

Penner, Hans H. 1998. *Teaching Lévi-Strauss*. Atlanta: Scholars Press.

Peregrin, Jaroslav. 2001. *Meaning and Structure: Structuralism and (Post)analytic Philosophers*. Aldershot: Ashgate.

Thibault, Paul J. 1997. *Re-reading Saussure: The Dynamics of Signs in Social Life*. London: Routledge.

Vernant, Jean-Paul. 1980. *Myth and Socety in Ancient Greece*. Sussex: Harvester Press.

Wagner, Roy. 1978. *Lethal Speech: Daribi Myth as Symbolic Obviation*. Ithaca: Cornell University Press.

OVERTURE

Claude Lévi-Strauss

The aim of this book is to show how empirical categories – such as the categories of the raw and the cooked, the fresh and the decayed, the moistened and the burned, etc., which can only be accurately defined by ethnographic observation and, in each instance, by adopting the standpoint of a particular culture – can nonetheless be used as conceptual tools with which to elaborate abstract ideas and combine them in the form of propositions.

The initial hypothesis demands therefore that from the outset we place ourselves at the most concrete level – that is, in the heart of a community or of a group of communities sufficiently alike in regard to their habitat, history, and culture. However, while this is undoubtedly an essential methodological precaution, it cannot mask or restrict my intention. Using a small number of myths taken from native communities which will serve as a laboratory, I intend to carry out an experiment which, should it prove successful, will be of universal significance, since I expect it to prove that there is a kind of logic in tangible qualities, and to demonstrate the operation of that logic and reveal its laws.

I shall take as my starting point one myth, originating from one community, and shall analyze it, referring first of all to the ethnographic context and then to other myths belonging to the same community. Gradually broadening the field of inquiry, I shall then move on to myths from neighboring societies, after previously placing them, too, in their particular ethnographic context. Step by step, I shall proceed to more remote communities but only after authentic links of a historical or a geographic nature have been established with them or can reasonably be assumed to exist. The present work will describe only the initial stages of a long journey through the native mythologies of the New World, starting in the heart of tropical America and leading, as I can already foresee, to the furthermost regions of North America. The connecting thread throughout will be a myth of the Bororo Indians of central Brazil; this is not because this particular myth is more archaic than others that will be examined later, or because I consider it to be simpler or more complete. It attracted my attention in the first place for reasons that are largely contingent. And if I have tried to make the explanation of my synthesis correspond as far as possible to the analytical procedure by which I have arrived at it, this is because I felt that the close link I observe in such matters between their empirical and systematic aspects would be brought out all the more clearly if the method followed exemplified it in the first place.

In fact, the Bororo myth, which I shall refer to from now on as the key myth, is, as I shall try to show, simply a transformation, to a greater or a lesser extent, of other myths originating either in the same society or in neighboring or remote societies. I could, therefore, have legitimately taken as my starting point any one representative myth of the group. From this point of view, the key myth is interesting not because it is typical, but rather because of its irregular position within the group. It so happens that this particular myth raises problems of interpretation that are especially likely to stimulate reflection.

Even though I have thus stated my aims clearly, there is some danger that my project may meet with preliminary objections on the part of mythographers and specialists of tropical America. It cannot be contained within precise territorial limits or within the framework of any one system of classification. However it is approached, it spreads out like a nebula, without ever bringing together in any lasting or systematic way the sum total of the elements from which it blindly derives its substance, being confident that reality will be its guide and show it a surer road than any it might have invented. Starting with a myth chosen not so much arbitrarily as through an intuitive feeling that it was both rich and rewarding, and then, after analyzing it in accordance with rules laid down in previous works (L.-S. 5, 6, 7, and 9),* I establish the group of transformations for each sequence, either within the myth itself, or by elucidation of the isomorphic links between sequences derived from several myths originating in the same community. This itself takes us beyond the study of individual myths to the consideration of certain guiding patterns situated along a single axis. At each point on the axis where there is such a pattern or schema, we then draw, as it were, a vertical line representing another axis established by the same operation but carried out this time not by means of apparently different myths originating from a single community, but by myths that present certain analogies with the first, although they derive from neighboring communities. As a result, the guiding patterns are simplified, made more complex or transformed. Each one becomes a source of new axes, which are perpendicular to the first on different levels, and to which will presently be connected, by a twofold prospective and retrospective movement, sequences derived either from myths originating in more remote communities or from myths initially neglected because they seemed useless or impossible to interpret, even though they belonged to peoples already discussed. It follows that as the nebula gradually spreads, its nucleus condenses and becomes more organized. Loose threads join up with one another, gaps are closed, connections are established, and something resembling order is to be seen emerging from chaos. Sequences arranged in transformation groups, as if around a germinal molecule, join up with the initial group and reproduce its structure and determinative tendencies. Thus is brought into being a multidimensional body, whose central parts disclose a structure, while uncertainty and confusion continue to prevail along its periphery.

But I do not hope to reach a stage at which the subject matter of mythology, after being broken down by analysis, will crystallize again into a whole with the general appearance of a stable and well-defined structure. Apart from the fact that the science of myths is still in its infancy, so that its practitioners must consider themselves fortunate to obtain even a few tentative, preliminary results, we can already be certain that the ultimate state will never be attained, since were it theoretically possible, the fact still remains that there does not exist, nor ever will exist, any community or group of communities whose mythology and ethnography (and without the latter the study of myths is ineffectual) can be known in their entirety. The ambition to achieve such knowledge is meaningless, since we are dealing with a shifting reality, perpetually exposed to the attacks of a past that destroys it and of a future that changes it. For every instance recorded in written form, there are obviously many others unknown to us; and we are only too pleased with the samples and scraps at our disposal. It has already been pointed out that the starting point of the analysis must inevitably be chosen at random, since the organizational principles governing the subject matter of mythology are contained within it and only emerge as the analysis progresses. It is also inevitable that the point of arrival will appear of its own accord, and unexpectedly: this will occur when, a certain stage of the undertaking having been reached, it becomes clear that its ideal object has acquired sufficient consistency and shape for some of its latent properties, and especially its existence as an object, to be definitely placed beyond all doubt. As happens in the case of an optical microscope, which is incapable of revealing the ultimate structure of matter to the observer, we can only choose between various degrees of enlargement: each one reveals a level of organization which has no more than a relative truth and, while it lasts, excludes the perception of other levels.

The above remarks go some way toward explaining the nature of a book which might otherwise be considered paradoxical. While it is complete in itself and leads to conclusions that, I hope, the reader will accept as answers to the problems posed at the beginning, it makes reference to a second volume, beyond which can be glimpsed the outline of yet a third. But if these works ever see the light of day, they will not be so much a continuation as a different handling of the same material, a new attack on the same problems, in the hope that they will bring out hitherto blurred or unnoticed features, by means of different lighting or by a different coloring of histological cross sections. Therefore, if my inquiry proceeds in the way I hope, it will develop not along a linear axis but in a spiral; it will go back over previous findings and incorporate new objects only in so far as their examination can deepen knowledge that had previously existed only in rudimentary form.

Moreover, it must not be considered surprising if this work, which is avowedly devoted to mythology, draws unhesitatingly on material provided by folk tales, legends, and pseudo-historical traditions and frequently refers to ceremonies and rites. I cannot accept overhasty pronouncements about what is mythology and what is not; but rather I claim the right to make use of any manifestation of the mental or social activities of the communities under consideration which seems likely to allow me, as the analysis proceeds, to complete or explain the myth, even though it may not constitute an obbligato accompaniment of the myth in a musician's sense of the term (on this point cf. Lévi.-Strauss 1958, Ch. 12). On another level – and in spite of the fact that my inquiry is centered on the myths of tropical America, which supply most of the examples – the analysis itself, as it progresses, demands that use be made of myths originating in more remote regions, just as primitive organisms, although enclosed within a membrane, still retain the ability to move their protoplasm within this covering and to achieve such extraordinary distention that they put forth pseudopodia; their behavior appears less strange, once we have ascertained that its object is the capture and assimilation of foreign bodies. Finally I have been careful to avoid grouping the myths into preconceived classifications, under such headings as cosmological, seasonal, divine, heroic, technological, etc. Here again the myth itself, on being put to the test of analysis, is left to reveal its nature and to show the type to which it belongs; such an aim is beyond the scope of the mythographer if he relies on external and arbitrarily isolated characteristics.

In short, the peculiarity of this book is that it has no subject: it is restricted in the first place to the study of one myth; yet to achieve even partial success, it must assimilate the subject matter of two hundred others. Anxious though I am to keep within a clearly defined geographic and cultural area, I cannot prevent the book from taking on, from time to time, the appearance of a general treatise on mythology. It has no beginning, since it would have developed along similar lines if it had had a different starting point; and it has no end, since many problems are dealt with in summary fashion, and others are simply mentioned in the hope that they may be treated more fully at some later date. In order to draw my map, I have been obliged to work outward from the center: first I establish the semantic field surrounding a given myth, with the help of ethnography and by means of other myths; and then I repeat the operation in the case of each of these myths. In this way the arbitrarily chosen central zone can be crisscrossed by various intersecting lines, although fewer overlappings occur as we move further out. In order to make the grid or mesh even, one would have to repeat the process several times, by drawing more circles around points situated along the periphery. But at the same time this would increase the size of the original area. And so we see that the analysis of myths is an endless task. Each step forward creates a new hope, realization of which is dependent on the solution of some new difficulty. The evidence is never complete.

I must, however, admit that the curious conception underlying this book, far from alarming me, seems rather to be a sign that I have perhaps succeeded in grasping certain fundamental properties of my subject, thanks to a plan and a method that were not so much chosen by me as forced upon me by the nature of the material.

Durkheim has said (1925, 142) of the study of myths: "It is a difficult problem which should be dealt with in itself, for itself, and according to its own particular method." He also suggested an explanation of this state of affairs when later (190) he referred to the totemic myths, "which no doubt explain nothing and merely shift the difficulty elsewhere, but at least, in so doing, appear to attenuate its crying illogicality." This is a profound definition, which in my opinion can be extended to the entire field of mythological thought, if we give it a fuller meaning than the author himself would have agreed to.

The study of myths raises a methodological problem, in that it cannot be carried out according to the Cartesian principle of breaking down the difficulty into as many parts as may be necessary for finding the solution. There is no real end to mythological analysis, no hidden unity to be grasped once the breaking-down process has been completed. Themes can be split up *ad infinitum*. Just when you think you have disentangled and separated them, you realize that they are knitting together again in response to the operation of unexpected affinities. Consequently the unity of the myth is never more than tendential and projective and cannot reflect a state or a particular moment of the myth. It is a phenomenon of the imagination, resulting from the attempt at interpretation; and its function is to endow the myth with synthetic form and to prevent its disintegration into a confusion of opposites. The science of myths might therefore be termed "anaclastic," if we take this old term in the broader etymological sense which includes the study of both reflected rays and broken rays. But unlike philosophical reflection, which claims to go back to its own source, the reflections we are dealing with here concern rays whose only source is hypothetical. Divergence of sequences and themes is a fundamental characteristic of mythological thought, which manifests itself as an irradiation; by measuring the directions and angles of the rays, we are led to postulate their common origin, as an ideal point on which those deflected by the structure of the myth would have converged had they not started, precisely, from some other point and remained parallel throughout their entire course. As I shall show in my conclusion, this multiplicity is an essential characteristic, since it is connected with the dual nature of mythological thought, which coincides with its object by forming a homologous image of it but never succeeds in blending with it, since thought and object operate on different levels. The constant recurrence of the same themes expresses this mixture of powerlessness and persistence. Since it has no interest in definite beginnings or endings, mythological thought never develops any theme to completion: there is always something left unfinished. Myths, like rites, are "in-terminable." And in seeking to imitate the spontaneous movement of mythological thought, this essay, which is also both too brief and too long, has had to conform to the requirements of that thought and to respect its rhythm. It follows that this book on myths is itself a kind of myth. If it has any unity, that unity will appear only behind or beyond the text and, in the best hypothesis, will become a reality in the mind of the reader.

But I shall probably incur the severest criticism on the ethnographic level. Although the book is carefully documented, I have disregarded certain sources of information, and some others have proved inaccessible.[1] Those I have made use of do not always appear in the final draft. To avoid making the demonstration too unwieldy, I had to decide which myths to use, to opt for certain versions, and in some measure to simplify the variants. Some people will accuse me of having adapted the subject matter of my inquiry to suit my own purposes. If I had selected, from the vast quantity of available myths, only those that were most likely to support my thesis, my argument would have lost much of its force. It might therefore be said that I ought to have gone through all the known myths of tropical America before venturing to embark on a comparison between them.

The objection may seem particularly telling in the light of the circumstances that delayed the appearance of this book. It was almost completed when the publication of the first volume of the *Enciclopédia Boróro* was announced; and I waited until the work had reached France and I had studied it before putting the finishing touches to my text. But, following the same line of reasoning, I ought perhaps to have waited another two or three years for the second volume, which will deal with myths and will include a section on proper names. Actually the study of the volume already to hand suggested a different conclusion, in spite of the wealth of detail it provides. The Salesians, who record their own changes of opinion with great serenity, when they do not simply fail to mention them, can be harshly critical if a piece of information published by some author does not coincide with their own most recent findings. In both cases they are committing the same methodological error. The fact that one item of information contradicts another poses a problem but does not solve it. I have more respect for the informants, whether they are our own or those who were employed in the old days by the missionaries, and whose evidence is consequently of particular value. The merits of the Salesians are so indisputable that, without failing in the debt of gratitude that is owed them, we can voice one slight criticism: they have an unfortunate tendency to believe that the most recent piece of information cancels out everything else.

I do not doubt for a moment that further information already available or as yet unpublished will affect my interpretations. Some that are no more than tentative will perhaps be confirmed; others will be abandoned or modified. No matter; in a subject such as this, scientific knowledge advances haltingly and is stimulated by contention and doubt. Unlike metaphysics, it does not insist on all or nothing. For this book to be worthwhile, it is not necessary in my view that it should be assumed to embody the truth for years to come and with regard to the tiniest details. I shall be satisfied if it is credited with the modest achievement of having left a difficult problem in a rather less unsatisfactory state than it was before. Nor must we forget that in science there are no final truths. The scientific mind does not so much provide the right answers as ask the right questions.

I can go further. If critics reproach me with not having carried out an exhaustive inventory of South American myths before analyzing them, they are making a grave mistake about the nature and function of these documents. The total body of myth belonging to a given community is comparable to its speech. Unless the population dies out physically or morally, this totality is never complete. You might as well criticize a linguist for compiling the grammar of a language without having complete records of the words pronounced since the language came into being, and without knowing what will be said in it during the future part of its existence. Experience proves that a linguist can work out the grammar of a given language from a remarkably small number of sentences, compared to all those he might in theory have collected (not to mention those he cannot be acquainted with because they were uttered before he started on his task, or outside his presence, or will be uttered at some later date). And even a partial grammar or an outline grammar is a precious acquisition when we are dealing with unknown languages. Syntax does not become evident only after a (theoretically limitless) series of events has been recorded and examined, because it is itself the body of rules governing their production. What I have tried to give is an outline of the syntax of South American mythology. Should fresh data come to hand, they will be used to check or modify the formulation of certain grammatical laws, so that some are abandoned and replaced by new ones. But in no instance would I feel constrained to accept the arbitrary demand for a total mythological pattern, since, as has just been shown, such a requirement has no meaning.

Another more serious objection is possible. Someone may question my right to choose myths from various sources, to explain a myth from the Gran Chaco by means of a variant from Guiana, or a Ge myth by a similar one from Colombia. But structural analysis – however respectful it may be of history and however anxious to take advantage of all its teachings – refuses to be confined within the frontiers already established by historical investigation. On the contrary, by demonstrating that myths from widely divergent sources can be seen objectively as a set, it presents history with a problem and invites it to set about finding a solution. I have defined such a set, and I hope I have supplied proof of its being a set. It is the business of ethnographers, historians, and archeologists to explain how and why it exists.

They can rest assured that, as regards the explanation of the group nature of the myths assembled here (and which have been brought together solely for the purposes of my investigation), I do not expect that historical criticism will ever be able to reduce a system of logical affinities to an enormous list of borrowings, either successive or simultaneous, made by contemporary or ancient communities from each other, over distances and intervals of time often so vast as to render any interpretation of this kind implausible, and in any case impossible to verify. From the start then, I ask the historian to look upon Indian America as a kind of Middle Ages which lacked a Rome: a confused mass that emerged from a long-established, doubtless very loosely textured syncretism, which for many centuries had contained at one and the same time centers of advanced civilization and savage peoples, centralizing tendencies and disruptive forces. Although the latter finally prevailed through the working of internal causes and as a result of the arrival of the European conquerors, it is nonetheless certain that a set, such as the one studied here, owes its character to the fact that in a sense it became crystallized in an already established semantic environment, whose elements had been used in all kinds of combinations – not so much, I suppose, in a spirit of imitation but rather to allow small but numerous communities to express their different originalities by manipulating the resources of a dialectical system of contrasts and correlations within the framework of a common conception of the world.

Such an interpretation, which I shall leave in this tentative form, is obviously based on historical conjecture: it supposes that tropical America was inhabited in very early times; that numerous tribes were frequently in movement in various directions; that demographic fluidity and the fusion of populations created the appropriate conditions for a very old-established syncretism, which preceded the differences observable between the groups; and that these differences reflect nothing or almost nothing of the archaic conditions but are in most cases secondary or derivative. Therefore, in spite of its formal approach, structural analysis establishes the validity of ethnographic and historical interpretations that I put forward more than twenty years ago; at the time they were thought to be somewhat rash (1958, 118ff. and Ch. 6), but they have continued to gain ground. If any ethnographic conclusion is to be deduced from the present work, it is that the Ge, far from being the "marginal" people they were supposed to be in 1942, when Volume I of *The Handbook of South American Indians* came out (I protested at the time against this assumption), represent a pivotal element in South America, whose function is comparable to the part played in North America by the old settlements along the Fraser and Columbia rivers, and their survivors. When I extend my inquiry to the northern areas of North America, the basis for the comparison will appear more clearly.

It was necessary to mention at least the concrete results achieved by structural analysis (certain others, relating only to the peoples of tropical America, will be explained in the course of this book) to put the reader on his guard against the charge of formalism, and even of idealism, that has sometimes been leveled against me. It may be said that the present book, even more than my previous works, takes ethnographic research in the direction of psychology, logic, and philosophy, where it has no right to venture. Am I not helping to deflect ethnography from its real task, which should be the study of native communities and the examination, from the social, political, and economic points of view, of problems posed by the relations among individuals and groups within a given community? Such misgivings, which have often been expressed, seem to me to arise from a total misunderstanding of what I am trying to do. And what is more serious, I think, is that they cast doubt on the logical continuity of the program I have been pursuing since I wrote *Les Structures élémentaires de la parenté*, a work about which the same objection cannot reasonably be made.

The fact is, however, that *La Pensée sauvage* represented a kind of pause in the development of my theories: I felt the need for a break between two bursts of effort. It is true that I took advantage of the situation to scan the scene before me, to estimate the ground covered, to map out my future itinerary, and to get a rough idea of the foreign territories I would have to cross, even though I was determined never to deviate for any length of time from my allotted path and – apart from some minor poaching – never to encroach on the only too closely guarded preserves of philosophy. ... Nevertheless, the pause that some people misinterpreted as marking a conclusion was meant to be a merely temporary halt between the first stage that had been covered by *Les Structures* and the second, which the present work is intended to open.

Throughout, my intention remains unchanged. Starting from ethnographic experience, I have always aimed at drawing up an inventory of mental patterns, to reduce apparently arbitrary data to some kind of order, and to attain a level at which a kind of necessity becomes apparent, underlying the illusions of liberty. In *Les Structures*, behind what seemed to be the superficial contingency and incoherent diversity of the laws governing marriage, I discerned a small number of simple principles, thanks to which a very complex mass of customs and practices, at first sight absurd (and generally I held to be so), could be reduced to a meaningful system. However, there was nothing to guarantee that the obligations came from within. Perhaps they were merely the reflection in men's minds of certain social demands that had been objectified in institutions. If so, their effect on the psychological level would be the result of mechanisms about which all that remains to be determined is their mode of operation.

The experiment I am now embarking on with mythology will consequently be more decisive. Mythology has no obvious practical function: unlike the phenomena previously studied, it is not directly linked with a different kind of reality, which is endowed with a higher degree of objectivity than its own and whose injunctions it might therefore transmit to minds that seem perfectly free to indulge their creative spontaneity. And so, if it were possible to prove in this instance, too, that the apparent arbitrariness of the mind, its supposedly spontaneous flow of inspiration, and its seemingly uncontrolled inventiveness imply the existence of laws operating at a deeper level, we would inevitably be forced to conclude that when the mind is left to commune with itself and no longer has to come to terms with objects, it is in a sense reduced to imitating itself as object; and that since the laws governing its operations are not fundamentally different from those it exhibits in its other functions, it shows itself to be of the nature of a thing among things. The argument need not be carried to this point, since it is enough to establish the conviction that if the human mind appears determined even in the realm of mythology, *a fortiori* it must also be determined in all its spheres of activity.[2]

In allowing myself to be guided by the search for the constraining structures of the mind, I am proceeding in the manner of Kantian philosophy, although along different lines leading to different conclusions. The ethnologist, unlike the philosopher, does not feel obliged to take the conditions in which his own thought operates, or the science peculiar to his society and his period, as a fundamental subject of reflection in order to extend these local findings into a form of understanding, the universality of which can never be more than hypothetical and potential. Although concerned with the same problems, he adopts an opposite approach in two respects. Instead of assuming a universal form of human understanding, he prefers to study empirically collective forms of understanding, whose properties have been solidified, as it were, and are revealed to him in countless concrete representational systems. And since for him, belonging as he does to a given social milieu, culture, region, and period of history, these systems represent the whole range of possible variations within a particular type, he chooses those that seem to him to be the most markedly divergent, in the hope that the methodological rules he will have to evolve in order to translate these systems in terms of his own system and vice versa, will reveal a pattern of basic and universal laws: this is a supreme form of mental gymnastics, in which the exercise of thought, carried to its objective limits (since the latter have been previously explored and recorded by ethnographic research), emphasizes every muscle and every joint of the skeleton, thus revealing a general pattern of anatomical structure.

I am perfectly aware that it is this aspect of my work that Ricoeur is referring to when he rightly describes it as "Kantism without a transcendental subject."[3] But far from considering this reservation as indicating sonic deficiency, I see it as the inevitable consequence, on the philosophical level, of the ethnographic approach I have chosen; since, my ambition being to discover the conditions in which systems of truths become mutually convertible and therefore simultaneously acceptable to several different subjects, the pattern of those conditions takes on the character of an autonomous object, independent of any subject.

I believe that mythology, more than anything else, makes it possible to illustrate such objectified thought and to provide empirical proof of its reality. Although the possibility cannot be excluded that the speakers who create and transmit myths may become aware of their structure and mode of operation, this cannot occur as a normal thing, but only partially and intermittently. It is the same with myths as with language: the individual who conscientiously applied phonological and grammatical laws in his speech, supposing he possessed the necessary knowledge and virtuosity to do so, would nevertheless lose the thread of his ideas almost immediately. In the same way the practice and the use of mythological thought demand that its properties remain hidden: otherwise the subject would find himself in the position of the mythologist, who cannot believe in myths because it is his task to take them to pieces. Mythological analysis has not, and cannot have, as its aim to show how men think. In the particular example we are dealing with here, it is doubtful, to say the least, whether the natives of central Brazil, over and above the fact that they are fascinated by mythological stories, have any understanding of the systems of interrelations to which we reduce them. And when by appealing to such myths we justify the existence of certain archaic or colorful expressions in our own popular speech, the same comment can be made, since our awareness is retrospective and is engineered from without and under the pressure of a foreign mythology. I therefore claim to show, not how men think in myths, but how myths operate in men's minds without their being aware of the fact.

And, as I have already suggested, it would perhaps be better to go still further and, disregarding the thinking subject completely, proceed as if the thinking process were taking place in the myths, in their reflection upon themselves and their interrelation.[4] For what I am concerned to clarify is not so much what there is in myths (without, incidentally, being in man's consciousness) as the system of axioms and postulates defining the best possible code, capable of conferring a common significance on unconscious formulations which are the work of minds, societies, and civilizations chosen from among those most remote from each other. As the myths themselves are based on secondary codes (the primary codes being those that provide the substance of language), the present work is put forward as a tentative draft of a tertiary code, which is intended to ensure the reciprocal translatability of several myths. This is why it would not be wrong to consider this book itself as a myth: it is, as it were, the myth of mythology.

However, this code, like the others, has neither been invented nor brought in from without. It is inherent in mythology itself, where we simply discover its presence. One ethnographer working in South America expresses surprise at the way in which the myths were conveyed to him: "The stories are told differently by almost every teller. The amount of variation in important details is enormous." Yet the natives do not seem to worry about this state of affairs: "A Caraja, who traveled with me from village to village, heard all sorts of variants of this kind and accepted them all in almost equal confidence. It was not that he did not see the discrepancies, but they did not matter to him . . ." (Lipkind 1940, 251). A naïve observer from some other planet might more justifiably (since he would be dealing with history, not myths) be amazed that in the mass of works devoted to the French Revolution the same incidents are not always quoted or disregarded, and that the same incidents are presented in different lights by various authors. And yet these variants refer to the same country, the same period, and the same events, the reality of which is scattered throughout the various levels of a complex structure. The criterion of validity is, therefore, not to be found among the elements of history. Each one, if separately pursued, would prove elusive. But some of them at least acquire a certain solidity through being integrated into a series, whose terms can be accorded some degree of credibility because of their overall coherence.

In spite of worthy, and indeed indispensable, attempts to become different, history, as its clearsighted practitioners are obliged to admit, can never completely divest itself of myth. What is true for history is, therefore, *a fortiori* truer still in regard to myth itself. Mythological patterns have to an extreme degree the character of absolute objects, which would neither lose their old elements nor acquire new ones if they were not affected by external influences. The result is that when the pattern undergoes some kind of transformation, all its aspects are affected at once. And so if one aspect of a particular myth seems unintelligible, it can be legitimately dealt with, in the preliminary stage and on the hypothetical level, as a transformation of the homologous aspect of another myth, which has been linked with the same group for the sake of the argument, and which lends itself more readily to interpretation. This I have done on more than one occasion: for instance, by explaining the episode of the jaguar's closed jaws in M7 by the reverse episode of the wide-open jaws in M55; or the episode of the genuine willingness to help shown by the vultures in M1 by their false willingness in M65. The method does not, as one might expect, create a vicious circle. It merely implies that each myth taken separately exists as the limited application of a pattern, which is gradually revealed by the relations of reciprocal intelligibility discerned between several myths.

I shall no doubt be accused of overinterpretation and oversimplification in my use of this method. Let me say again that all the solutions put forward are not presented as being of equal value, since I myself have made a point of emphasizing the uncertainty of some of them; however, it would be hypocritical not to carry my thought to its logical conclusion. I therefore say in advance to possible critics: what does this matter? For if the final aim of anthropology is to contribute to a better knowledge of objectified thought and its mechanisms, it is in the last resort immaterial whether in this book the thought processes of the South American Indians take shape through the medium of my thought, or whether mine take place through the medium of theirs. What matters is that the human mind, regardless of the identity of those who happen to be giving it expression, should display an increasingly intelligible structure as a result of the doubly reflexive forward movement of two thought processes acting one upon the other, either of which can in turn provide the spark or tinder whose conjunction will shed light on both.

And should this light happen to reveal a treasure, there will be no need of an arbitrator to parcel it out, since, as I declared at the outset (L.-S. 9), the heritage is untransferable and cannot be split up.

Notes

* See Bibliography, pages 361-370, for full information on this and other references. [In ed.]

1. Certain works, such as *Die Tacana* by Hissink and Hahn (Stuttgart, 1961) have been only skimmed through, because of their relatively recent publication; while others, which did not reach France until after the completion of this book, have not been consulted at all: e.g., J. Wilbert, *Indios de la región Orinoco-Ventuari* (Caracas, 1963); and *Warao Oral Literature* (Caracas, 1964); and N. Fock, *Waiwai, Religion and Society of an Amazonian Tribe* (Copenhagen, 1963). However, in this last book I have already noted a myth about the opossum which confirms my analyses in the third and fourth parts. This new material will be utilized in a later volume.

2. "If law is anywhere, it is everywhere." Such was the conclusion reached by Tylor in the passage that I used seventeen years ago as an epigraph for *Les Structures élémentaires de la parenté*.

3. Ricoeur (1963, 24). Cf. also: "A Kantian rather than a Freudian unconscious, a combinative, categorizing, unconscious ..." (9); and "a categorizing system unconnected with a thinking subject ... homologous with nature; it may perhaps be nature...."(10)

   With his customary subtlety and insight Roger Bastide (1961, 65–79) anticipated the whole of the preceding argument. The coincidence of our views is a most eloquent indication of his clearsightedness, since I did not see his work (which he himself kindly sent me) until I was busy correcting the proofs of this book.

4. The Ojibwa Indians consider myths as "conscious beings, with powers of thought and action" (Jones 1919, 574, n.1).

References

Bastide, Roger. 1961. "La nature humaine: le point de vue du sociologue et de l'ethnologue." In *La nature humaine, actes du XIe Congrès des Sociétés de Philosophie de langue francaise*. Montpellier, September 4–6, 1961. Paris.

Durkheim, Émile. 1925. *Les formes élémentaires de la vie religieuse*. Paris: Bibliothèque de Philosophie Contemporaine.

Jones, William. 1919. "Ojibwa Texts." In *Publications of the American Ethnological Society*, Vol. III, Part II. New York: G.E. Stechert & Co.

Lévi-Strauss, Claude. 1958. *Anthropologie structurale*. Paris: Plon.

———1986. *The Raw and the Cooked: Introduction to a Science of Mythology*. Harmondsworth: Penguin. (1st. English ed. publ. 1970 by Jonathan Cape, London.)

Lipkind, W. 1940. "Caraja Cosmography." *Journal of American Folklore* 53.

Ricoeur, P. 1963. "Symbole et temporalité." *Archivio di Filosofia*, Nos. 1–2.

THE MYTH OF "HONEYED ORPHEUS"

Marcel Detienne

In the middle of the nineteenth century there started a debate between classical scholars and anthropologists on the nature of mythology. Both sides were agreed that myths rested on a "basis of rude savage ideas" (Lang 1885, 28), but there the agreement ended. The classical scholars, led by Max Müller and full of the recent discovery of comparative linguistics, regarded mythology as an unexpected product of verbal misunderstanding, a sort of "disease of language." The anthropologists, from Tylor to Mannhardt, treated the mythical stories of the Greeks and Romans as evidence of a "savage intellectual condition" through which the civilized races had had to pass and which could still be seen in primitive peoples such as the Australian aborigines, the Bushmen and the Red Indians (Lang 1885, 83).

Then Max Müller died, and the classicists tidied up, here and elsewhere. Since they regarded classical mythology as inseparable from the values of which they, as heirs of Graeco-Roman civilization, were the appointed guardians, they thought it best to check this talk of its "savage basis." They did this by restoring the myths to history. They had a number of methods. They insisted that the stories belonged to a society of which they were the appointed interpreters. Or they detected traces of fact in the myths, but sufficiently obscured to send the mythologists chasing after the mythical narratives, tracking them across Greece from the first cities which could have been their original sites to the last to which waves of migration might have brought them.[1] But most effective of all was their third method, the handing over of mythical narrative to literary history. Ever since, classical scholars have used the written status of classical mythology to justify their prior claim to it, and until quite recently they did no more than select from it the elements compatible with the dominant ideology of the bourgeois society whose interests and aims so-called "classical" philology has always so faithfully served.

A century after Tylor, social anthropology is taking the initiative in re-opening the dialogue with the classical fraternity by proposing that one of the most famous myths of the Graeco-Roman world should be re-examined in the light of data from Latin America. Claude Lévi-Strauss's suggestion (1973, 403, n.17) that the adventures of Orpheus, Eurydice and Aristaeus should be looked at afresh in conjunction with the myths of the "girl mad about honey" was made in full awareness that he was proposing to tackle one of the most vigorous myths of the West, one which had become firmly rooted in history in at least two ways. One of these is the metamorphosis into literature guaranteed to it by its possession of a hero with a voice sweet enough to charm all nature and a love strong enough to conquer death. Long before Virgil's fourth *Georgic*, Orpheus stood for the mythical figure of the poet, the master of the incantation in which words merge with music. And, just as his legend was transformed into musical narrative (cantata, oratorio, opera) so it developed into a major myth of literature, one of the extreme forms of which can be seen in the "aesthetic mysticism" of Valéry and Mallarmé (Desport 1952; Juden et al. 1970). On the other hand, the myth of Orpheus is not merely the vehicle of a succession of literary ideologies; as it appears in the *Georgics* it refers to a factual history explained in detail by Servius in his commentary on the works of Virgil. According to Servius, the episode of Aristeus and the myth of Orpheus and Eurydice was inserted in the second edition of the *Georgics* to replace an original section in honour of Gallus, a poet-friend of Virgil's and prefect of Egypt who was forced to suicide after losing favour with Augustus. It has been quite plausibly deduced from this that, obliged by his position of literary dependence to alter his poem, Virgil chose to tell the story of this myth rather than another, not only because of Aristaeus's affinities with bees, which are the subject of the fourth *Georgic*, but because the adventure of Orpheus gave him an opportunity to make a discreet allusion to his departed friend and, in particular, to Gallus's conviction that passionate love was a central element in human life (Brisson 1966, 305–29). Paradoxically however, with such an eminently "literary" myth, coloured by so many precise references to history, it is the failure of a purely philological and historical approach to account for it satisfactorily which justifies a structural analysis. The first advantage of this approach, banal though it may seem, is that it takes a mythical narrative seriously, takes account of all its episodes and explains even the most unlikely details.

Summary of the Myth of Aristaeus, Orpheus and Eurydice

In the fourth book of the *Georgics*, after describing how bees can be generated from the rotted flesh of an ox, Virgil goes on to tell the story of Aristaeus, from whom men first learnt this technique of *bougonia*.

Aristaeus has lost his bees. He is desolate, and goes to see his mother, the nymph Cyrene, who advises him to consult Proteus, since only he can tell Aristaeus why the bees have deserted his hives. During the dog-days Aristaeus lies in wait. He surprises the sea-god as he is about to take his siesta in the heat of the day, surrounded by his seals. Unable to escape from a grip which holds him in spite of all his changes of shape, Proteus reveals to Aristaeus that his bees have left him to punish him for a serious offence he has committed. Aristaeus had pursued Eurydice, who, in trying to get away from him, had fallen on a monstrous water-serpent. In desperation, her husband Orpheus went to look for her in the underworld. Persephone had given Eurydice back when Orpheus suddenly forgot his instructions, turned round to look at his wife and lost her forever. Orpheus himself then died, torn to pieces by furious women who took his obliviousness to anything except the memory of his wife for contempt of womankind.

After making these revelations Proteus disappears, leaving Aristaeus deeply repentant. Cyrene then tells Aristaeus how he can appease the nymphs, the companions of Eurydice: he is to offer them a sacrifice of four bulls, whose flesh, when rotted, will produce new swarms.

The main element which ancient mythology preserved from the myth of Orpheus and Aristaeus was the death of Eurydice and the tragic passion which drove Orpheus to go down to the underworld. This tradition emphasized the exemplary fate of the lovers precisely because it was incapable of accounting for the relation set up by the myth between the beekeeper Aristaeus and the couple Eurydice – Orpheus. Two series of questions arise immediately from the story in the *Georgics*. In the first place, why did Aristaeus chose to pursue Eurydice rather than another nymph? And why does his action result in the disappearance of bees which, apparently, have no special connection with Orpheus's young wife? Secondly, Orpheus is only brought into the myth because of Eurydice; is not his connection with the bee-keeper purely fortuitous and therefore gratuitous? In a famous study, the German philologist Eduard Norden set out to demonstrate the arbitrary character of the myth told in the *Georgics*. He argued that Virgil had latched on to the insubstantial figure of Aristaeus and simply invented his adventure with Eurydice and his rivalry with Orpheus (Norden 1966, 468–532). The fact that the author of the *Georgics* was apparently the only authority for a connection between two separate myths, at least as far as their mediate significance was concerned, seemed to support his claim. The only objections were from those who attributed Virgil's inspiration to a Greek version of the Hellenistic period,[2] a mere question of "sources" which did nothing to challenge the myth's status as the product of individual imagination. The reason for the persistent failure of ancient myth analysis to understand the meaning of the triangular relationship Aristaeus – Eurydice – Orpheus to which the *Georgics* bear witness is not simply that the method has an implicit tendency to select from the myths values which legitimate a particular ideology of the eternal man. At a deeper level, its own definition of the literary work makes it incapable of recognizing the double context of this story, the mythical context and the ethnographic one. Only the first of these can account for the unexpected presence of Eurydice and Orpheus in the story of the inventor of honey, and the second is essential if any meaning is to be given on the level of myth to Aristaeus's misfortune in losing his bees.[3] Virgil's story begins with the disappearance of Aristaeus's bees. Three reasons are given for the disappearance of the bees, all equally explicit: First, there is a statement which derives from the experience of the peasant bee-keepers to whom book 4 of the *Georgics* is addressed: the bees died of hunger and disease (4.251ff., 318-19). This is followed by two complementary explanations of a mythical character, Orpheus's grudge and the anger of the Nymphs (4.453 and 533-4). Orpheus does not himself exact vengeance for the death of Eurydice; the only ones who have power over the bees are the Nymphs who brought them from their wild state in the oaks to the hive which they placed under the protection of Aristaeus. Conversely, only they can remove them from the half-wild, half-domesticated state in which agriculture has placed them. But the irritation of the Nymphs, as companions of Eurydice, is not enough to account for Aristaeus's misfortune. We must go further back; it is the offence committed by the first bee-keeper himself which compromises his special relationship with the bees.

From Aristotle to the Byzantine treatises such as the *Geoponica* and the *De animalium proprietate* of Philo, the Greek conception of the bee (*melissa*) was based on a model which, in essential features, remained unchanged for over fifteen centuries. The *melissa* was distinguished by a way of life which was pure and chaste and also by a strictly vegetarian diet. In addition to its rejection of hunting and the carnivorous life, and its possession of a "special" food which it helped to prepare and which was part of itself, the bee showed a most scrupulous purity; not only did it avoid rotting substances and keep well away from impure things, but it also had the reputation of extreme abstinence in sexual matters. The same insistence on purity was also visible in the bee's distaste for smells, whether very pleasant or highly rebarbative; in particular it detested the scent of aromatics.[4] This last characteristic seems to have been sufficiently striking to make bee-keepers take various precautions, which are mentioned in Graeco-Roman treatises on bee-keeping; some recommend the bee-keeper to shave his head before going near the bees in order to be absolutely sure of not having any trace of scent or aromatic ointment on him.[5] The extreme olfactory sensitivity of bees is not the only reason for this behaviour; the bees' detestation of perfumes arises out of their hatred of effeminacy and voluptuousness and their particular hostility towards debauchees and seducers, in other words, for those who misuse ointments and aromatics.[6] Plutarch even, in one of his treatises, stresses the infallible discernment with which bees single out for their attacks only those users of perfume who are guilty of illicit sexual relationships.[7] He also emphasizes, in a chapter of the *Coniugalia praecepta* (44, 144d), that bee-keeping requires exemplary marital fidelity of its practitioners: the bee-keeper must approach his bees as a good husband does his lawful wife, that is, in a state of purity, without being polluted by sexual relations with other women. If he does not, he will have to face the hostility of his charges as the husband has to face the anger of his partner. This ethnographic context explains why

Aristaeus lost his bees. While Virgil has no more than a discreet reference to the flight of Eurydice and her nymphs before the Thessalian bee-keeper, other less squeamish writers say plainly that Aristaeus desired Eurydice, that he wanted to seduce her and attempted to assault her (*stuprare, vitiare*).[8] It was because the inventor of honey had the smell of seduction on him that he was deprived of his bees. Orpheus's bitterness and the Nymphs' anger are therefore reactions to a sexual offence. This, by accidentally causing the death of Eurydice – who was bitten by a serpent in her flight – drove to despair a lover passionately devoted to his new wife, and deeply disappointed Aristaeus's protecting powers, the bees, who had chosen him for his exemplary conduct and his good upbringing – for which latter they had also been largely responsible.

The ethnographic context, which reveals a close relation between the conduct of the bees and the sexual behaviour of the bee-keeper, now sends us back to the wider mythical context to which the meeting between Aristaeus and Eurydice belongs. There are two immediate problems here. What can be the significance of the misconduct of a figure whose reputation as a virtuous husband is solidly established by the rest of the mythical tradition? And why does he pick on Orpheus's wife when no other myth puts them in direct connection or makes any reference to their possible affinity? A full answer would require a detailed analysis of the early sections of the myth of Aristaeus, for which there is no room here, but two things can be said. First, all the education given to the "master of honey" was a preparation for a solemn marriage with the eldest daughter of the king of Thebes, and the bridegroom sealed the alliance with his father-in-law with the honey he brought as one of a number of useful presents. Secondly, one of the main results of Aristaeus's activity – in the episode which takes place on Ceos – is the establishment of harmony in conjugal relations; the sweet honey seems to produce a married life untroubled by either adultery or seduction. But what about the madness which came over Aristaeus when he came in contact with Eurydice? To explain this the sociological status of this young woman has to be examined and defined in relation to the mythology of honey, particularly since, as a nymph, Eurydice is one of the powers to which some traditions ascribe the invention of honey. Two myths, which dovetail closely, make an association between two groups in Demeter's entourage, the Nymphs and the Bee-Women, the *Melissai*. According to the first of these stories, it was a nymph called Melissa who discovered the first honeycombs in the forest, ate some and mixed it with water and drank it, and then taught her companions to make the drink and eat the food. This was part of the nymphs' achievement in bringing man out of his wild state; under the guidance of Melissa, Bee, they not only turned men away from eating each other to eating only this product of the forest trees, but also introduced into the world of men the feeling of modesty, *aidōs*, which they established by means of another invention, intended to reinforce the first, the discovery of woven garments. Since then, explains the myth finally, no marriage takes place without the first honours being reserved to the nymphs, the companions of Demeter, in memory of their part in establishing a way of life ruled by piety and approved by the gods. The purpose of the second story is to explain the association of Demeter with the nymphs connected with honey and bees. There is nothing unusual in the presence of Demeter in a myth centred on a "cultivated" form of life consisting of dietary prescriptions and a sexual code, but it is given even greater justification by a ritual feature mentioned explicitly in the second myth. After the kidnapping of Persephone, the sorrowing Demeter entrusted to the Nymphs the basket (kálathos) which had held Persephone's weaving and went to Paros, where she was welcomed by King Melisseus, the king of the bees. When she was leaving the goddess wanted to thank her host, and so she gave Melisseus's sixty daughters the cloth Persephone had been weaving for her wedding, and at the same time told them of her sufferings and revealed to them the secret ceremonies she wished to institute. Ever after, the women who celebrate the Thesmophoria – the feast of Demeter reserved for lawful wives – were known as *Melissai*; their ritual name was *Bees* (Detienne 1977, 79–80; Detienne and Vernant 1979, 211–12).

The emphasis now is no longer on dietary rules, which slip into the background, but on two different female statuses. The daughters of Melisseus move between the two, first receiving the cloth woven by Persephone, which stands for the state of the *numphē*, the young girl thinking of marriage, and then giving their name to the married women, lawful wives, who meet to celebrate the mysteries of Demeter Thesmophoros. Nymph woman, Thesmophorian woman: this duality of the daughters of Melisseus is only fully exposed when placed in the setting of a series of images in which the bee is the animal symbol of certain female virtues. The description given above of various unique features in the behaviour of bees relied on the evidence of Plutarch in a long comparison between the bee and the lawful wife. When Plutarch included in the *Coniugalia praecepta* the advice that the husband should have the same regard for his wife as a bee-keeper for his bees, he was in agreement with a tradition as old as Hesiod, in which the bee stands for the good wife in the same way that the fox symbolizes cunning. In the minds of the Greeks, the *melissa* is the emblem of female domestic virtue; faithful to her husband and the mother of legitimate children, she watches over the private area of the house, taking care of the couple's possessions, always reticent and modest (*sōphrōn* and *aidēmōn*), so adding to the functions of a wife those of a housekeeper never greedy or fond of drink or inclined to doze, who firmly rejects the romantic chatter that women in general enjoy.

It is this model of the bee-woman which determines the distribution of attributes between the two female statuses possessed by the daughters of Melisseus, who are at one stage nymphs and at another *thesmophoroi*. Since only the women who celebrate the Thesmophoria are given the explicit title of *Melissai, Bees*, it is with their rôle that we will start.

The structure of the Thesmophoria is most clearly shown by contrast with the ritual of the Adonia. A comparison of the two rituals (see fig. 1) reveals a series of fundamental oppositions: between Demeter and Adonis, between cereals and aromatics, and between marriage and seduction (Detienne 1977, 60–98). Analysis of the mythology of aromatics has produced two results which are relevant here, the contrast between the legitimate wife and the courtesan and the distance between the former, with her faintly unpleasant smell, and the pungent perfume of the latter.

Whereas the festivals of Adonis display the licence of which women are capable when abandoned to themselves, the Thesmophoria always took place in a serious, almost severe atmosphere. The worshippers of Adonis were often courtesans; the followers of Demeter Thesmophoros were always the legitimate wives of the citizens, and the festival was strictly reserved for them; ceremonies were closed to slave women, the wives of metics and foreigners, and of course courtesans and concubines. The opposition between the *thesmophoros* and the devotee of Adonis was most sharply marked in the sexual behaviour prescribed for the participants in the two rites. In the Adonia men and women behaved as lovers, on the model of the relationship of Aphrodite and Adonis, but in the Thesmophoria not only were men carefully excluded but even the married women were bound to continence for the duration of the festival. The prohibition of sexual activity was reinforced in two ways, by the use of branches of Abraham's balm, chosen for its anti-aphrodisiac reputation, to make litters, and also by the faintly unpleasant smell which accompanied the fast kept by the worshippers of Demeter. In contrast to the perfumed courtesans who took part in the Adonia, the *thesmophoros* gave off a very faint smell of fasting which had the same function as the garlic eaten by the women at the Skiraphoria, namely – according to Philochoros of Athens – to keep their breath from being sweet-smelling and so enable them the more easily to avoid sexual activity. In short, the sexual and dietary abstinence practised by the women taking part in the Thesmophoria marked them out as exaggerated versions of the model of female domestic virtues represented by the bee. Furthermore, in ritual terms the *thesmophoros* is the sociological counterpart of the bees angered by the scent of aromatics.

Determining the status of the Nymph, who in this case is the *numphē*, necessarily involves the definition of her name. In the Greek classification of female ages, *numphē* denotes a status between those of the *korē* and the *mētēr*. A *korē* is often an immature girl, and always an unmarried woman (*agamos*); the *mētēr*, on the other hand, is the

	Adonia	Thesmophoria
Divine powers	Adonis and his mistress Aphrodite	Demeter Thesmophoros and her daughter Persephone
Sociological status of women	Courtesans and concubines	Lawful wives
Status of men	Invited by women	All (including husbands) barred
Sexual attitude	Seduction	Continence
Associated plants	Incense and myrrh	Abraham's balm
Smells	Abuse of perfumes	Slight smell of fasting Hatred of the Bee-women for those who wear perfume
Food	Feasting	Fasting

Figure 1

matron, the woman who has given birth to children. *Numphē* stands at the intersection of these two categories, and applies both to the young woman just before her marriage and to the bride before the birth of her children finally commits her to the alien home of her husband. This ambivalence makes the *numphē* an *ambiguous* bee and so very different from the *thesmophoros*. In her ritual dealings with the nymphs, who are the patrons of marriage, preside at the *Hydrophoria* (one of the marriage-rituals), receive the "pre-nuptial sacrifices" (*proteleia*), and supervise the weaving of the long bridal veil, the *numphē* represents a type of woman who fully deserves the description "bee," not just because she submits to purificatory procedures which qualify her for the most emphatically ritual part of marriage, but also because she displays *aidōs* and *sōphrosunē*, the modesty and reticence which are the mark of her new state. Nevertheless, before emerging as a *thesmophoros*, before becoming a Bee in the ritual sense, the *numphē* must necessarily pass through another state. In the days immediately following the marriage she will lead the life reserved for young married couples, the *numphiōn bios*. Crowned with aphrodisiac plants such as myrtle and mint and gorging themselves with cakes spiced with sesame and poppy seeds, the bridal pair need think of nothing else but leading a "life of pleasure and voluptuousness," a life of *hēdupatheia*. This is a way of life symbolized by honey, for the Greek proverbial tradition makes an equation between the expressions "to sprinkle oneself with honey" and *hēdupatheia*, which is the search for excessive pleasure and satisfaction. At this time of "honeymoon" the young bride, the *numphē*, runs the risk of no longer being a bee but becoming a hornet (*kēphēn*), turning into the reverse of a bee, a carnivorous bee, brutal and at the mercy of excessive desires, driven to gorge without measure on honey and condemned to roll in what Plato describes as "hornet honey," all the pleasures of the belly and the flesh.

So the status of *numphē* is an ambiguous one in a woman's life, since while society, by ritual procedures, invites the *numphē* to behave like a good bee, it nevertheless cannot prevent the new bride, who has access to the pleasures of love (*aphrodisia*), from automatically giving off a scent which makes her desirable and so, momentarily, even dangerous. This detour by way of the honeymoon was necessary to understand how Eurydice, the young girl who had become Orpheus's bride, could, quite involuntarily, have transformed the first bee-keeper into a vulgar seducer. In rushing after Eurydice, Aristaeus gave way for an instant to the seduction exercised by the honeymoon, to the seduction within marriage which threatens most of all someone whose whole life has been passed within the area of marriage. To see that the nymph Eurydice was particularly fitted for the part of the young bride on honeymoon, we need only remember that the mythical figure of Eurydice is entirely swallowed up in her love for Orpheus, the Thracian enchanter. All that remains to complete our analysis is to show that his intrusion into the story of Aristaeus is neither fortuitous nor unmotivated.

Orpheus has a double claim to a place in the mythology of honey, for the excessive love with which he surrounds Eurydice and for the contrast he offers in a number of respects with his ephemeral rival, Aristaeus the bee-keeper. In all the descriptions of their relationship, Eurydice and Orpheus appear as a pair of lovers who cannot bear to be separated, even by death. When Orpheus exploits the charm of his honeyed voice to get permission to leave the underworld with Eurydice, the gods of those regions impose a triple prohibition, oral, visual and tactile (Virgil, *Georgics* 4.487; *Culex* 289-93).[9] He is not to speak to Eurydice, not to look at her, not to embrace her. These are three forms of distance which the gods of the underworld impose on lovers too violently in love with one another to put off the moment of meeting. The "too great love" (Virgil's *tantus furor*, *Georgics* 4.495) which precipitates the destruction of both Eurydice and Orpheus is the sign of their inability to live the relationship of marriage outside the honeymoon. The story of Orpheus and Eurydice is not a story of tragic love or unhappy passion; it is the failure of a couple incapable of establishing a conjugal relationship which allows for the proper distances.

Nevertheless, Orpheus's propensity to "roll in honey" is not the only feature of his which justifies the connection of his story with the mythology of honey and accounts for his involvement with the master of the bees. Honey is connected with the figure of Eurydice's lover in two ways. First metaphorically: from his melodious mouth come honeyed sounds which – according to the whole Greek tradition – enabled him to charm all nature and drew after him fish, birds and the very wildest animals. Secondly in matters of food, where he is the legendary initiator of a particular way of life, a diet of cakes and fruit coated with honey adopted by those who call themselves his followers, who also offer them to the gods in sacrifice in order to avoid shedding the blood of domestic animals. However, to fix more exactly Orpheus's position in the mythology of honey, he must be contrasted, not only with Aristaeus, but also with Orion a savage hunter whose adventures, prefigured in the exploits of Aristaeus's son Actaeon, develop in constant contrast with those of the bee-keeper. A triangular relationship between Orpheus, Aristaeus and Orion is established in three areas, animals, women and honey, three areas in which Orion and Orpheus correspond as two extremes situated on either side of Aristaeus, their mutual mediator. Orion, a brutal, violent, club-wielding figure, appears throughout the mythical tradition as a savage, for ever pursuing fierce animals, which he loves to slaughter, and even going so far as to boast that he will wipe off the face of the earth all the animals which Gaia bears and nurtures. Orpheus is the opposite of Orion. Where Orion shows an excess of savagery in setting no limits to his hunting, Orpheus's distinctive characteristic is a perverse gentleness which makes him gather round him all the animals of the earth, even the fiercest, which like all the rest are drawn by the charm of his voice and the sweetness of his song. Aristaeus is hunter and shepherd, *agreus* and *nomios*, both at once, and his uniqueness lies in his ability to maintain an equal distance from each of these extremes; he tames some animal species (cattle, goats, sheep) and inaugurates their husbandry, but also uses traps to hunt the wild creatures (wolves and bears) which are a direct threat to his activities as a shepherd and a bee-keeper. The same relationships between the three figures reappear in their attitude to women. All that Orion can do is rape them; almost as soon as he sets eyes on his host's daughter on Chios he lusts after her and wants to have her; as soon as he catches sight of the Pleiades he chases after them. His violent desire even tempts him to lay hands on Artemis while she is taking part in one of his extermination hunts. At the opposite extreme from this brute, Orpheus is a young husband passionately attached to his wife; his honeymoon with her is excessive, and prevents him – like Orion – from becoming either a good son-in-law or a perfect husband, but in his case from an excess of attachment rather than violence. Both Orion and Orpheus, by opposite excesses, are excluded from the status attributed by the myth to the bee-keeper Aristaeus, the husband who keeps a proper distance between himself and his wife and who uses honey as an instrument of alliance with his father-in-law.

It is, however, honey which illustrates most clearly the function of Aristaeus as mediator between Orion and Orpheus. Aristaeus is a model bee-keeper. He receives from the nymphs the task of caring for the bees and obtains from his protectors the secret of the process which will establish honey and bees permanently in the world of men. Aristaeus's honey is the basis of a form of civilized life from which both Orion and Orpheus are excluded, though for directly opposite reasons. The giant Orion, because of his excessive brutality and violence, is unable to escape from a state of primitive savagery which he betrays most obviously by trying to violate the Pleiades – the Dove-Women counterparts of the Bees who nurtured Zeus. Orpheus, through an excess of honey, is likewise excluded from a civilized world which bee-keeping has begun, tentatively, to define. It is because he is "all honey" that Orpheus obliterates the boundaries between the wild and the cultivated and mixes marriage and seduction together. In the presence of Orpheus, lions and bears live alongside roe and fallow deer, and the fiercest animals are gentler than lambs. Just as he is all honey for the whole of nature, by his excessive attachment to his young wife Orpheus cannot prevent himself from being the lover and seducer of a woman whose lawful husband he also is.

The tragic death of Orpheus is the final event which confirms his inability to establish himself in the area defined by the action of Aristaeus (fig. 2). Once Eurydice is gone for good, her distraught husband goes from improper closeness to excessive distance. Orpheus cuts himself off from women, who, furious at their rejection, behave towards him like wild beasts, and by so doing seem to take the place left empty by the beasts themselves, whom Orpheus has chosen as his closest companions and friends. This spatial pattern is illustrated in Ovid's *Metamorphoses*. When the women launch the attack which ends in the dismemberment of Orpheus, the man with the honeyed voice is in the middle of a circle of animals, and it is these who are the first victims of the enraged bacchants, who are armed with hoes, sickles, earth-pounders, spits and two-headed axes, all tools belonging to the cultivated life from which they now finally exclude Orpheus.

The hatred of bees for seducers, the social status of the bee-keeper, the social position of the bride, the definition of honey in relation to hunting and not-hunting, all these are aspects and dimensions which fill out the mythical background without which the misfortune of Aristaeus and Orpheus remains shut up inside a literary narrative. In the field of classical mythology the methodological contribution of social anthropology is as much to establish mythical language as an autonomous object as to work out the basic rules for deciphering it. The mythical narrative in Virgil's story only acquires definition when placed within its double context of ethnography and mythology. To identify the different levels of meaning, the different codes, which form the texture of the myth, all the cultural associations of honey must be explored, which involves areas as diverse as techniques of collection and the symbolism of the bee, institutions such as marriage and various ritual practices. Similarly, in order to interpret the Orpheus myth we need to explore its connections with other myths such as those of Aristaeus and Orion which with it form a group within which a number of "transformations" take place. The result of this double analysis is a grid on which levels of meaning are distinguished along the vertical axis and correlations with other myths along the horizontal. All the elements of the myth now have a place, and decipherment can continue until the full richness of the logic of mythical statement is laid open.[10]

It is, of course, possible to interpret the Orpheus myth differently, but alternative interpretations achieve plausibility only by destroying the structure of codes which underpins the honey myths (in this case sociological, dietary and sexual codes). In such approaches Orpheus's glance at Eurydice, isolated from the other prohibitions (oral and tactile) revealed by a structural analysis, becomes pure impatience or, as in Monteverdi's opera, inability to control his urges, or again – this is Rameau's version – a breach of romantic conventions.[11] The climax of this process is humanism's discovery of it as "the most marvellous symbol of love ... which, stronger than death, triumphs over everything, except itself" (Bellessort 1920, 145). All these are fragmentary interpretations, dazzled by the glitter of a single detail, but all still able to find support in the *Georgics*, where Virgil, without breaching the conventions of the myth or engaging in major distortion, gives Orpheus's glance an importance which makes it reveal the ideological bias of his story.

This detail also gives us a preliminary criterion by which to determine the level of mythical thought represented by Virgil's mythology; it is a reminder that, although most of the mythical discourse produced by ancient societies is embedded in literary

	Orion	Aristaeus	Orpheus
Animals	Destroys all by savage hunting	Tames some (goats, sheep, cattle), hunts	Captivates all, even the fiercest
Women	Rapes and assaults. Detested "son-in-law"	Model husband. Perfect son-in-law	Lover-husband. Incapable of becoming a good husband and *a fortiori* a proper son-in-law
Honey	Pursues Dove-Women (=Bee-Women)	Bee-keeper. Protector of bees, protected by Bee-Nymphs	"All honey"

Figure 2

narratives, often influenced by various forms of ideology, this does not necessarily mean that the development of the literary settings has distorted or destroyed the myths. This characteristic may be combined with another, which was recognized as a result of an investigation of a group of myths centred on aromatics and seduction; it was found that the categories and logical relations revealed by structural analysis of mythology are very largely the same as those used by the Greeks in a series of explicitly "rational" works composed at the same time as the literary works which contain the myths. Provisional though they are, these conclusions on the type of mythical thought found in Greece suggest that we should not seek to press the very close connections between the honey myths centred on Aristaeus and the corresponding mythology of Latin America which seem to be indicated at first sight by the affinities between two mythical complexes of clearly unequal dimensions, but both centred on a pathology of marriage in which the mythical operator is honey. Our aim is no longer, as in Tylor's day, to recover the half-vanished traces of a "savage stage of thought" revealed to us by archaic societies. The first, and essential, task is to construct the grammar of the way of thinking expressed in the myths, without prejudging the question whether mythical thought is a privileged expression of an image of the world immanent in the structure of the mind, or whether structural resemblances are to be attributed to a palaeolithic heritage on which both the Old and the New worlds have drawn. More urgent tasks confront the mythologist. The myths have to be grouped by means of an exhaustive analysis of their ethnographic context in ways which go beyond the cycles and classifications of the ancient mythographers. In addition, since the classical myths are deeply embedded in different literary forms, the analysis of the semantic field in which myths operate must be developed, and linguistic structures related to mythological ones (Sperber 1968, 200–6).

All these tasks will help to comprehend a history inseparable from mythical statement throughout Graeco-Roman civilization. Until very recently, isolated myths tempted the hellenist's curiosity with the prospect of an institutional residue or the scarcely discernible lineament of some archaic practice. In future the business of the student of myth will no longer be to extract an institution or a social practice from a mythical narrative like a kernel from its splintered shell. What the mythical statements of a society reveal is its total mental universe, since, as we know, the only possible basis for structural analysis is a thorough acquaintance with the ethnographic context of each group of myths. Ritual practices, economic techniques, forms of marriage, legal institutions, classifications of animals, descriptions of plant species, all are aspects of a society which the mythologist must classify. Only then will he be able to judge the relevance of each term in its sequence and each sequence in its narrative, and go on to place the narrative, by reference to its various codes or levels of meaning, within a major or minor mythical complex. All this whole ethnographic context is nothing other than history, the history whose rhythm, chronology, changes, flux and reflux have been the objects of the historical study of ancient societies since the nineteenth century. The mythologist's structural models cannot do without the analyses of the historian; without them their coherence and logic would have no foundation.

Antiquarians and other believers in a history of "events" wander through mythology with their spikes, triumphantly winkling out of corners a fragment of archaism here or the fossilized memory of some "real" event there. Structural analysis of myth rejects this approach. Its discovery of invariant forms underlying of content enables it to design an alternative total history moving on a slower and more fundamental time-scale (Burguière 1971, v–vii). Structural analysis penetrates below conscious expressions and, beneath the superficial movement of things, traces the deep, slow currents which flow in silence. This is one of its contributions to modern historical technique, but there is also another. By examining the myths in themselves, in their own organizational forms, the historian of the Greek world is enabled in his turn to isolate various general properties of mythical thought, confronted as he is by the problem of coming to grips with a society in which the appearance of a totally new form of thought, philosophy, had a definite effect on the functioning of myths, but did not immediately induce a process of decay.[12]

Notes

1. This approach was used by Gruppe (1906), for example.
2. As suggested by Wilamowitz-Moellendorff (1955, 244 n. 2); see also Wilkinson 1969, 325–6.
3. The analysis presented here in summary form, without full documentation, will be developed in detail in a general study of honey myths in Greece, which will also contain a discussion of purely literary approaches, such as Segal 1966, 307–25.
4. Aristotle, *Historia animalium* 9.40, 626a26 ff.; Theophrastus, *De causis plantarum* 6.5.1 etc.
5. According to Aristophanes of Byzantium (*Anecdota graeca*) this was the practice in Egypt.
6. Aelian, *Historia animalium* 5.11; Cassianus Bassus, *Geoponica* 15.2.19.
7. Plutarch, *Quaestiones naturales* 36 (Loeb ed., vol. 11, 218–20).
8. Servius, *in Verg. Georg.* 4.317; Scholion Bern., *in Verg. Georg.* 4.493.
9. [Ed. note: *Culex* ("Mosquito"): an addition by an unknown author to Virgil's poem.]
10. Claude Lévi-Strauss (1977, 60–7) has described some aspects of this method of analysis.
11. "De ses desirs impetueux / l'amant habile est toujours maître." See Bellas 1970, 234.
12. See further, Detienne 1979.

References

Bellas, Jacqueline. 1970. "'Orphée' au XIXe et au XXe siècle: interférences littéraires et musicales." *Cahiers de l'Association internationale des Études Francaises* 22: 229–46.
Bellessort, André. 1920. *Virgile: Son oeuvre et son temps.* Paris: Perrin.
Brisson, Jean-Paul.1966. *Virgile: Son temps et le nôtre.* Textes à l'appui 17. Paris: Masepro.
Burguière, André. 1971. "Introduction à 'Histoire et structure.'" *Annales: économies, sociétés, civilisations* 26/3: i–vii.

Desport, Marie. 1952. *L'Incantation virgilienne: Virgile et Ophée*. Bordeaux: Imprim. Delmas.

Detienne, Marcel. 1977. *The Gardens of Adonis: Spices in Greek Mythology*. Sussex: Harvester Press.

_____1979. "Repenser a mythologie." In *La function symbolique: Essais d'anthropologie*, ed. M. Izard and P. Smith. Paris: Galimard.

Detienne, Marcel and Jean-Pierre Vernant. 1979. *La cuisine du sacrifice en pays grec*. Paris: Gallimard.

Gruppe, P. Otto. 1906. *Griechische Mythologie und Religionsgeschichte*. München: Beck.

Juden, Brian et al. 1970. "Le Mythe d'Orphée au XIXe et au Xxe sie siècle." (Proceedings of the 21st Congress of the Association internationale des Études francaises, 23–25 July 1969), *Cahiers de l'Association internationale des Études Francaises* 22: 137–246.

Lang, Andrew. 1885. *Custom and Myth*. London: Longmans.

Lévi-Strauss, Claude. 1973. *From Honey to Ashes*. London and New York: Jonathan Cape.

_____1977. "Comparative Religions of Non-literate Peoples." In idem, *Structural Anthropology 2*, 60–67. London: Allen Lane.

Norden, Eduard. 1966. "Orpheus und Eurydike: ein nachträgliches Gedenkblatt, für Vergil." In idem, *Kleine Schriften zum klassischen Altertum*, 468–532. Berlin: Walter de Gruyter.

Segal, Charles P. 1966. "Orpheus and the Fourth Georgic: Virgil on Nature." *American Journal of Philology* 87: 307–25.

Sperber, Dan. 1968. "Le structuralisme en anthropologie." In *Qu'est-ce que le structuralisme?*, ed. Francois Wahl, 167–238. Paris: Seuil.

Wilamowitz-Moellendorff, Ulrich von. 1955. *Der Glaube der Hellenen* (1st ed. 1931). Darmstadt: Wissenschaftliche Buchgesellschaft.

Wilkinson, Lionel P. 1969. *The Georgics of Virgil: A Critical Survey*. Cambridge: Cambridge University Press.

INTRODUCTION TO THE STRUCTURAL ANALYSIS OF NARRATIVES

Roland Barthes

Numberless are the world's narratives. First of all in a prodigious variety of genres, themselves distributed among different substances, as if any material were appropriate for man to entrust his stories to it: narrative can be supported by articulated speech, oral or written, by image, fixed or moving, by gesture, and by the organized mixture of all these substances; it is present in myth, legend, fable, tale, tragedy, comedy, epic, history, pantomime, painting (think of Carpaccio's *Saint Ursula*), stained-glass window, cinema, comic book, news item, conversation. Further, in these almost infinite forms, narrative occurs in all periods, all places, all societies; narrative begins with the very history of humanity; there is not, there has never been, any people anywhere without narrative; all classes, all human groups have their narratives, and very often these are enjoyed by men of different, even opposing culture:[1] narrative never prefers good to bad literature: international, transhistorical, transcultural, narrative is *there*, like life.

Is such universality a reason for us to infer narrative's unimportance? Is narrative so general that we have nothing to say about it, except modestly to describe a few of its extreme varieties, as literary history sometimes does? But how are we to master these very varieties, how are we to establish our right to distinguish them, to recognize them? How are we to set novel against novella, tale against myth, drama against tragedy (as has been done a thousand times) without reference to a common model? This model is implied by all speech concerning the most individual, the most historical of narrative forms. Hence it is legitimate that, far from renouncing all ambition to speak of narrative on the excuse that it is, after all, a universal phenomenon, there should have been periodic concern with narrative form (Aristotle); and it is normal that a nascent structuralism should make this form one of its first preoccupations: is it not a permanent preoccupation of structuralism to master the infinity of words by describing the language by which they are produced and out of which they can be engendered? Confronting the infinity of narratives, the multiplicity of the points of view from which we can speak of them (historical, psychological, sociological, ethnological, esthetic, etc.), the analyst is virtually in the same situation as Saussure, confronting the heteroclite nature of language and attempting to perceive in the apparent anarchy of its messages a principle of classification and a focus of description. To remain within the present period, the Russian Formalists, Propp, and Lévi-Strauss have taught us to recognize the following dilemma: either narrative is a simple chronicling of events, in which case we can discuss it only by relying on the teller's (the author's) art, talent, genius – all mythic forms of chance[2] – or else it shares with other narratives a structure accessible to analysis, whatever patience is necessary in order to articulate that structure; for there is an abyss between the most complex aleatory world and the simplest combinatory one, and no one can combine (produce) a narrative without referring to an implicit system of units and rules.

Where then are we to look for the structure of narrative? In the narratives themselves no doubt. *All* narratives? Many commentators, who accept the notion of a narrative structure, cannot bring themselves to separate literary analysis from the model of the experimental sciences: they intrepidly insist that a purely inductive method be applied to narration and that the first step be to study all the narratives of a genre, of a period, of a society, and then to undertake the sketch of a general model. This commonsense view is utopian. Linguistics itself, which has only some three thousand languages to survey, cannot manage this; wisely, it has remained deductive, and it was moreover from the day of that decision that linguistics actually constituted itself and has advanced with giant strides, managing even to anticipate phenomena which had not yet been discovered.[3] What then are we to say of narrative analysis, confronting millions of narratives? It is necessarily doomed to a deductive program; it is obliged to conceive, first of all, a hypothetical model of description (which the American linguists call a "theory"), and then to descend gradually from this model to the species which, simultaneously, participate in it and depart from it: it is only on the level of these conformities and these departures that narrative analysis will recognize, armed with a unique instrument of description, the plurality of narratives, their historical, geographic, cultural diversity.[4]

In order to describe and classify the infinite number of narratives, we must therefore have a "theory" (in the pragmatic sense just given), and our first task will be to find it and sketch it out. The elaboration of this theory can be greatly facilitated if we begin with a model which provides it with its first terms and its first principles. In the present state of research, it seems reasonable[5] to take linguistics itself as a founding model for the structural analysis of narrative.

I. The Language of Narrative

1. Beyond the Sentence

As we know, linguistics stops at the sentence, which is the last unit it considers itself entitled to deal with; if the sentence, being an order and not a series, cannot be reduced to the sum of words composing it and thereby constitutes an original unit, a larger discourse, on the contrary, is nothing but the sequence of sentences which compose it: from the linguistic point of view, there is nothing in discourse which is not to be found in the sentence: "The sentence," Martinet says, "is the smallest segment which is perfectly and integrally representative of discourse" (1961, 113). Hence linguistics cannot take an object superior to the sentence, because, beyond the sentence, there is never anything but more sentences: having described the flower, the botanist cannot be concerned with describing the bouquet.

And yet, it is obvious that discourse itself (as a group of sentences) is organized and that by this organization it appears as the message of another language, superior to the language of the linguists;[6] discourse has its units, its rules, its "grammar": beyond the sentence and although composed solely of sentences, discourse must naturally be the object of a second linguistics. This linguistics of discourse has for a very long time possessed a celebrated name: Rhetoric; but since Rhetoric, through a complex historical development, had become linked to belles lettres and since belles lettres had been separated from the study of language, it has seemed necessary, in recent years, to take up the question anew: the new linguistics of discourse has not yet developed, but it has at least been postulated, and by the linguists themselves.[7] This fact is significant: though constituting an autonomous object, discourse is to be studied from a linguistic basis; if we must grant a working hypothesis to an analysis whose task is enormous and whose materials are infinite, the most reasonable thing is to postulate a homologous relation between sentence and discourse, insofar as the same formal organization apparently regulates all semiotic systems, whatever their substances and dimensions: discourse would be one huge "sentence" (whose units would not necessarily be sentences), just as the sentence, allowing for certain specifications, is a little "discourse." This hypothesis fits in with certain propositions of contemporary anthropology: Jakobson and Lévi-Strauss have observed that humanity could be defined by the power to create secondary, "multiplying" systems (tools serving to fabricate other tools, the double articulation of language, the incest taboo permitting the proliferation of families), and the Soviet linguist Ivanov speculates that artificial languages can be acquired only after natural language: since what is important for humanity is being able to use several systems of meaning, natural language helps in elaborating artificial languages. Hence it is legitimate to postulate between sentence and discourse a "secondary" relation – which we shall call homological, in order to respect the purely formal character of the correspondences.

The general language of narrative is obviously but one of the idioms available to the linguistics of discourse,[8] and is consequently subject to the homological hypothesis:

structurally, narrative participates in the sentence without ever being reducible to a total of sentences: narrative is a great sentence, just as every constative sentence is, in a way, the sketch of a little narrative. Though afforded there with original (often highly complex) signifiers, we in effect recognize in narrative, enlarged and transformed in proportion the main categories of the verb: tenses, aspects, modes, persons; further the "subjects" themselves set in opposition to the verbal predicates do not fail to submit to the sentence model: the actantial typology Greimas proposes (cf. below, III, 1) acknowledges in the host of characters of narrative the elementary functions of grammatical analysis. The homology we are suggesting here has not only a heuristic value: it implies an identity between language and literature (inasmuch as literature is a kind of privileged vehicle of narrative): it is no longer possible to conceive of literature as an art unconcerned with any relation to language, once it has used language as an instrument to express ideas, passion, or beauty: language does not cease to accompany discourse, holding up to it the mirror of its own structure: does not literature, especially today, make a language out of the very conditions of language?[9]

2. The Levels of Meaning

From the start, linguistics provides the structural analysis of narrative with a decisive concept, because, immediately accounting for what is essential in any system of meaning, i.e., its organization, it permits both the demonstration of how a narrative is not a simple total of propositions and the classification of an enormous mass of elements which participate in the composition of a narrative. This concept is that of the *level of description*.[10]

A sentence, as we know, can be described, linguistically, on several levels (phonetic, phonological, grammatical, contextual); these levels are in a hierarchical relation, for if each has its own units and its own correlations, necessitating for each an independent description, no level can in and of itself produce meaning: every unit which belongs to a certain level assumes meaning only if it can be integrated into a higher level: a phoneme, though perfectly describable, in itself means nothing; it participates in meaning only when integrated into a word; and the word itself must be integrated into the sentence.[11] The theory of levels (as articulated by Benveniste) provides two types of relations: distributional (if the relations are situated on the same level), integrative (if they are apprehended from one level to another). It follows that the distributional levels do not suffice to account for meaning. In order to achieve a structural analysis, we must therefore first distinguish several instances of description and place these instances in a hierarchical (integrative) perspective.

The levels are operations.[12] Hence it is normal that as it proceeds linguistics tends to multiply them. The analysis of discourse can as yet work on only rudimentary levels. In its fashion, rhetoric had assigned to discourse at least two planes of description: *dispositio* and *elocutio*.[13] In our own day, in his analysis of the structure of myth, Lévi-Strauss has already specified that the constitutive units of mythic discourse (mythemes) acquire meaning only because they are grouped in bundles and because these bundles themselves are combined (1963, 213); and Tzvetan Todorov, adopting the distinction of the Russian formalists, has proposed to work on two main levels, themselves subdivided: *story* (the argument), including a logic of actions and a "syntax" of characters, and *discourse*, including tenses, aspects, and modes of narrative (1966). Whatever the numbers of levels proposed and whatever definition given of them, there can be no doubt that narrative is a hierarchy of instances. To understand a narrative is not only to follow the process of the story, it is also to recognize in it certain "stages," to project the horizontal concatenations of the narrative "thread" on an implicitly vertical axis; to read (to hear) a narrative is not only to pass from one word to the next, but also to pass from one level to the next. Let me offer a kind of fable here: in his *Purloined Letter*, Poe acutely analyzed the failure of the Paris police chief, who was unable to find the letter: his investigations were perfect, Poe says, "so far as his labors extended": the police chief omitted no location, he entirely "saturated" the level of "search"; but in order to find the letter – protected by its conspicuousness – it was essential to pass to another level, to substitute the concealer's pertinence for that of the policeman. In the same way, complete as the "search" performed on a horizontal group of narrative relations may be, in order to be effective it must also be oriented "vertically": meaning is not "at the end" of narrative, it traverses it; quite as conspicuous as the *purloined letter*, it similarly escapes any unilateral exploration.

Much groping will still be necessary before we can determine the levels of narrative. Those which we are going to propose here constitute a temporary outline, whose advantage is still almost exclusively didactic: they permit locating and grouping the problems, without disagreeing, it would appear, with the various analyses made so far. We propose to distinguish in the narrative work three levels of description: the level of "*functions*" (in the meaning this word is given by Propp and Bremond), the level of "*actions*" (in the meaning this word is given by Greimas when he speaks of characters as actants), and the level of "*narration*" (which is, by and large, the level of "discourse" in Todorov). It must be recalled that these three levels are linked together according to a mode of progressive integration: a function has meaning only insofar as it occurs in the general action of an actant; and this action itself receives its ultimate meaning from the fact that it is narrated, entrusted to a discourse which has its own code.

II. Functions

1. The Determination of Units

Every system being the combination of units whose classes are known, we must first segment the narrative and determine the segments of the narrative discourse which can be distributed into a small number of classes; in a word, we must define the smallest narrative units.

According to the integrative perspective defined here, the analysis cannot be limited to a purely distributional definition of the units: meaning must from the first be the criterion of the unit: it is the functional character of certain segments of the story which makes them units: whence the name "functions," immediately given to these first units. Since the Russian Formalists,[14] any segment of the story is constituted as a unit which is presented as the term of a correlation. The soul of any function is, so to speak, its seed, what allows it to sow the narrative with an element which will ripen later, on the same level, or elsewhere, on another level: if, in *Un Coeur simple*, Flaubert tells us at a certain point, apparently without insisting on it, that the daughters of the sub-prefect of Pont-l'Éveque owned a parrot, it is because this parrot will later have a great importance in Félicité's life: the statement of this detail (whatever its linguistic form) therefore constitutes a function, or narrative unit.

Is everything, in a narrative, functional? Does everything, down to the least detail, have a meaning? Can the narrative be entirely segmented into functional units? As we shall shortly see, there are doubtless several types of functions, for there are several types of correlations. Nonetheless a narrative always consists of nothing but functions: everything in it, to varying degrees, signifies. This is not a question of art (of the narrator's share), it is a question of structure: in the order of discourse, what is noted is, by definition, notable: even when a detail seems irreducibly insignificant, refractory to any function, it will nonetheless ultimately have the very meaning of absurdity or uselessness: everything has a meaning or nothing has. We might say in other words that art does not acknowledge "noise" (in the meaning that word has in information theory):[15] it is a pure system, there is never a "wasted" unit,[16] however long, loose, and tenuous the thread linking it to the levels of the story.[17]

Function is obviously, from the linguistic point of view, a unit of content: it is what a statement "means" which constitutes it as a functional unit,[18] not the way in which it is said. This constitutive signified can have different signifiers, often very complicated ones: if I am told (in *Goldfinger*) that *"James Bond saw a man of about fifty,"* etc., the information simultaneously harbors two functions, of unequal pressure: on the one hand, the age of the character is integrated into a certain portrayal (whose "usefulness" for the rest of the story is not nil, but diffused, delayed), and on the other, the immediate signified of the statement is that Bond does not know his future interlocutor: the unit therefore implies a very strong correlation (initiation of a threat and obligation to identify the character). In order to determine the first narrative units, it is therefore necessary never to lose sight of the functional character of the segments being examined, and to admit in advance that they will not inevitably coincide with the forms traditionally identified with the different parts of narrative discourse (actions, scenes, paragraphs, dialogues, interior monologues, etc.), and still less with the "psychological" classes (kinds of behavior, feelings, intentions, motivations, rationalizations of characters).

In the same way, since the language of narrative is not that of articulated speech – though often supported by it – the narrative units will be substantially independent of the linguistic units: they may of course coincide, but occasionally, not systematically; the functions will be represented sometimes by units superior to the sentence (groups of sentences of various dimension, up to the work in its entirety), sometimes by units inferior to it (the syntagm, the word, and even, within the word, only certain literary elements);[19] when we are told that – while he is on duty in his office at Secret Service headquarters – "*Bond picked up one of the four receivers*," the moneme *four* constitutes by itself a functional unit, for it refers to a concept necessary to the whole of the story (that of an elaborate bureaucratic technique); as a matter of fact, the narrative unit here is not the linguistic unit (the word), but only its connoted value (linguistically, the word /*four*/ never means "*four*"); this explains how certain functional units can be inferior to the sentence, without ceasing to belong to the discourse: they then overflow not the sentence, to which they remain materially inferior, but the level of denotation, which belongs, like the sentence, to linguistics properly speaking.

2. Classes of Units

These functional units must be distributed within a small number of formal classes. If we want to determine these classes without resorting to the substance of the content (a psychological substance, for example), we must again consider the different levels of meaning: certain units have for correlates units on the same level; on the contrary, in order to saturate the others, we must pass to another level. Hence, at the start, two major classes of functions, some distributional, others integrative. The former correspond to Propp's functions, adopted notably by Bremond, but which we are considering here in an infinitely more detailed fashion than these authors; it is to them that we shall apply the name "functions" (though the other units, too, are functional); the model for them has been classical since Tomashevsky's analysis: the purchase of a revolver has for its correlate the moment when it will be used (and if it is not used, the notation is reversed as a sign of indecision, etc.); to pick up the telephone has for its correlate the moment when it will be hung up again; the intrusion of the parrot into Félicité's house has for its correlate the episode of the parrot's being stuffed, worshiped, etc. The second major class of units, of an integrative nature, includes all the "*indices*" (in the very general sense of the word),[20] when the unit refers not to a complementary and consequential action, but to a more or less diffused concept, though one necessary to the meaning of the story: characterial indices concerning the characters, information relative to their identity, notations of "atmosphere," etc.; the relation of the unit and its correlate is then no longer distributional (frequently several indices refer to the same signified and their order of appearance in the discourse is not necessarily pertinent), but integrative; in order to understand the "use" of an indicial notation, we must pass to a higher level (actions of the characters or narration), for it is only here that the index is explained; the administrative power which is behind Bond, indexed by the number of telephones, has no bearing on the sequence of actions in which Bond is engaged by answering the call; it assumes its meaning only on the level of a general typology of actants (Bond is on the side of order); the indices, by the more or less vertical nature of their relations, are truly semantic units, for contrary to the true "functions," they refer to a signified, not to an "operation"; the sanction of the indices is "higher up," sometimes even virtual, outside the explicit syntagm (the "character" of a character can never be named, though ceaselessly indexed), it is a paradigmatic sanction; on the contrary, the sanction of the "functions" is always "farther on," it is a syntagmatic sanction.[21] *Functions* and *indices* thus cover another classical distinction: the functions imply metonymic *relata*, the indices imply metaphoric *relata*; the former correspond to a functionality of doing, the latter to a functionality of being.[22]

These two major classes of units, Functions and Indices, should already permit a certain classification of narratives. Certain narratives are powerfully functional (such as folktales), and on the other hand others are powerfully indicial (such as "psychological" novels); between these two poles, a whole series of intermediary forms, dependent on history, society, genre. But this is not all: within each of these two major classes, it is immediately possible to determine two subclasses of narrative units. With regard to the class of Functions, its units do not all have the same "importance"; some constitute veritable hinges of the narrative (or of a narrative fragment); others merely "fill" the narrative space separating the hinge-functions: let us call the former *cardinal functions* (or *nuclei*) and the latter, given their completive nature, *catalyses*. For a function to be cardinal, it suffices that the action to which it refers opens (or sustains, or closes) an alternative consequential for the rest of the story, in short, that it inaugurate or conclude an uncertainty; if, in a narrative fragment, *the telephone rings*, it is equally possible that it will or will not be answered, which will not fail to lead the story in two different directions. On the other hand, between two cardinal functions, it is always possible to arrange subsidiary notations, which agglomerate around one nucleus or another without modifying their alternative nature: the space which separates "*the telephone rang*" and "*Bond answered*" can be saturated by a host of tiny incidents or tiny descriptions: "*Bond went over to the desk, picked up a receiver, put down his cigarette,*" etc. Such catalyses remain functional, insofar as they enter into correlation with a nucleus, but their functionality is attenuated, unilateral, parasitic: we are concerned here with a purely chronological functionality (what is being described is what separates two moments of the story), while, in the link which unites two cardinal functions, is invested a double functionality, both chronological and logical: the catalyses are merely consecutive units, the cardinal functions are both consecutive and consequential. There is every reason to believe, as a matter of fact, that the mainspring of narrative activity is the very confusion of consecution and consequentiality, what comes *after* being read in the narrative as *caused* by; the narrative would in this case be a systematic application of the logical error condemned by Scholasticism in the formula *post hoc, ergo propter hoc*, which might well be the motto of Fate, of which the narrative is in fact merely the "language"; and this "squeezing together" of logic and temporality is achieved by the armature of the cardinal functions. These functions may seem at first glance quite insignificant; what constitutes them is not spectacle (the importance, volume, rarity, or power of the action articulated), it is, so to speak, risk: the cardinal functions are the moments of risk of the narrative; between these points of alternative, between these "dispatchers," the catalyses set up zones of security, rests, luxuries; these "luxuries" are not, however, useless: from the story's point of view, let us repeat, the functionality of the catalysis may be weak but not nil: were it purely redundant (in relation to its nucleus), it would participate no less in the message's economy; but this is not the case: a notation, apparently expletive, always has a discursive function: it accelerates, delays, resumes the discourse, it summarizes, anticipates, sometimes even misleads or baffles:[23] what is noted always appearing as notable, catalysis constantly wakens the semantic tension of the discourse, constantly says: there has been, there is going to be meaning; the constant function of catalysis is therefore, ultimately, a phatic one (to adopt Jakobson's word): it sustains the contact between the narrator and the receiver of the narrative. Let us say that we cannot suppress a nucleus without altering the story, but that we also cannot suppress a catalysis without altering the discourse. As for the second major class of narrative units (the Indices), an integrative class, the units which occur here have in common the fact that they can be saturated (completed) only on the level of the characters or of the narration; they therefore belong to a *parametric* relation[24] whose second, implicit term is continuous, extensive to an episode, a character or an entire work; yet we can distinguish here certain *indices*, strictly speaking, referring to a character, to a feeling, to an atmosphere (for instance, one of suspicion), to a philosophy, from items of *information*, which serve to identify, to situate in time and in space. To say that Bond is on duty in an office whose open window reveals the moon between huge, rolling clouds is to index a stormy summer night, and this deduction itself forms an atmospheric index which refers to the heavy, oppressive climate of an action which is not yet known. The indices therefore always have implicit signifieds; the items of information, on the contrary, do not, at least on the level of the story: they are pure data, immediately signifying. The indices imply an activity of decipherment: the reader must learn to know a character, an atmosphere; the items of information supply a ready-made knowledge; their functionality, like that of the catalyses, is therefore weak, but it too is not nil: whatever its "matte" nature in relation to the story, the item of information (for instance, the exact age of a character) serves to authenticate the reality of the referent, to implant the fiction in reality: it is a realist operator, and thus possesses an incontestable functionality, not on the level of the story but on the level of the discourse.[25]

Nuclei and catalyses, indices and items of information (once again, the names are of little importance) – such are, it would seem, the first classes among which the units of the functional level can be distributed. We must complete this classification by two remarks. First of all, a unit can belong at the same time to two different classes: to drink a whisky (in an airport lounge) is an action which may serve as a catalysis to the (cardinal) notation of *waiting*, but it is also and at the same time the index of a certain atmosphere (modernity, relaxation, memories, etc.): in other words, certain units can be mixed. Thus a whole play of possibilities arises in the narrative economy; in the novel *Goldfinger*, Bond, having to search his adversary's bedroom, receives a skeleton key from his partner: the notation is a pure (cardinal) function; in the film, this detail is altered: Bond manages to relieve an unprotesting chambermaid of her keys; the notation is not only functional now, but also indicial, it refers to Bond's character (his offhandedness and his success with women). Secondly, we must remark (what will moreover be taken up again later on) that the other classes we have just mentioned can be subject to another distribution, one more in accord, moreover, with the linguistic model. The catalyses, the indices and the items of information have a common character: they are all expansions, in relation to the nuclei: the nuclei (as we shall soon see) form finite groups of a small number of terms, they are governed by a logic, they are at once necessary and sufficient; given this armature, the other units fill it out according to a mode of proliferation which is in principle infinite; as we know, this is what happens in the case of the sentence, consisting of simple propositions, complicated to infinity by duplications, by paddings, insertions, etc.: like the sentence, the narrative is infinitely catalyzable. Mallarmé attached such importance to this type of structure that he used it to construct his poem *Un Coup de dès* which we may well consider, with its "nodes" and its "loops," its "node-words" and its "lace-words," as the emblem of all narrative – of all language.

3. Functional Syntax

How – according to what "grammar" – do these different units link up with each other throughout the narrative syntagm? What are the rules of the functional combinatory system? The items of information and the indices can freely combine among themselves: for example in the character sketch, which unconstrainedly juxtaposes data of civil status and character traits. A relation of simple implication unites the catalyses and the nuclei: a catalysis necessarily implies the existence of a cardinal function to which it is attached, but not vice versa. As for the cardinal functions, they are united by a relation of solidarity: a function of this kind requires another of the same kind, and vice versa. It is this last relation which we must attend to briefly: first of all because it defines the very armature of the narrative (the expansions can be suppressed, but not the nuclei), then because it chiefly concerns those who are seeking to structure narrative.

We have already observed that, by its very structure, narrative instituted a confusion between consecution and consequentiality, time and logic. It is this ambiguity which forms the central problem of narrative syntax. Is there behind narrative time an atemporal logic? This point divided investigators quite recently. Propp, whose analysis as we know opened the way to contemporary studies, insists on the irreducibility of the chronological order: time in his eyes is reality, and for this reason it seems necessary to root the tale in time. Yet Aristotle himself, setting tragedy (defined by the unity of action) in opposition to history (defined by the plurality of actions and the unity of time), already attributed primacy to logic over chronology (*Poetics*, 1459a). As do all contemporary researchers (Lévi-Strauss, Greimas, Bremond, Todorov), all of whom might subscribe (though diverging on other points) to Lévi-Strauss's proposition: "The order of chronological succession is reabsorbed into an atemporal matrix structure."[26] Contemporary analysis tends, as a matter of fact, to "dechronologize" narrative content and to "relogicize" it, to subject it to what Mallarmé called, apropos of the French language, "the primitive thunderbolts of logic" (1961, 386). Or more exactly – at least, so we hope – the task is to produce a structural description of the chronological illusion; it is up to narrative logic to account for narrative time. We might say in another fashion that temporality is only a structural class of narrative (of discourse), just as, in language, time exists only in a systematic form; from the point of view of narrative, what we call time does not exist, or at least exists only functionally, as an element of a semiotic system: time does not belong to discourse properly speaking, but to the referent; narrative and language know only a semiologic time; "real" time is a referential, "realist" illusion, as Propp's commentary shows, and it is as such that structural description must treat it.[27]

What then is this logic which governs the chief functions of narrative? This is what current investigation is attempting to establish, and what has hitherto been most widely debated. Hence we shall refer to the contributions of Greimas, Bremond, and Todorov in *Communications* (#8, 1966), all of which deal with the logic of the functions. Three main directions of investigation are notable, set forth by Todorov. The first (Bremond) is more strictly logical: it seeks to reconstruct the syntax of human behavior utilized in narrative, to retrace the trajectory of the "choices" which, at each point of the story, a character is inevitably compelled to make,[28] and thus to reveal what we might call an energetic logic,[29] since it apprehends the characters at the moment when they choose to act. The second model is linguistic (Lévi-Strauss, Greimas): the essential concern of this investigation is to identify in the functions certain paradigmatic oppositions, these oppositions, according to the Jakobsonian principle of "poetics," being "extended" throughout the narrative (yet we shall see the new developments by which Greimas corrects or completes the paradigmatism of the functions). The third way, sketched by Todorov, is somewhat different, for it establishes the analysis on the level of the "actions" (i.e., of the characters), by attempting to establish the rules by which the narrative combines, varies, and transforms a certain number of basic predicates.

There is no question of choosing among these working hypotheses; they are not competitive but concurrent, and moreover they are still being elaborated. The only addition we shall attempt to make here regards the dimensions of the analysis. Even if we set aside the indices, the items of information, and the catalyses, there still remains in a narrative (particularly in speaking of the novel rather than the tale) a very great number of cardinal functions; many cannot be mastered by the analyses we have just cited, which have so far been concerned with major articulations of narrative. Yet we must anticipate a sufficiently dense description to account for all the narrative units, for its smallest segments; the cardinal functions, we recall, cannot be determined by their "importance," but only by the (doubly implicative) nature of their relations: a "telephone call," however trivial it may appear on the one hand, involves in itself several cardinal functions (ringing, picking up the receiver, speaking, hanging up), and moreover, taking these all together, we must be able to attach them as closely as possible to the major articulations of the anecdote. The functional covering of narrative compels an organization of relays, whose basic unit can only be a small group of functions, which we shall here call (following Bremond) a *sequence*.

A sequence is a logical succession of nuclei, linked together by a relation of solidarity:[30] the sequence opens when one of its terms has no solidary antecedent and it closes when another of its terms has no consequent. To take a deliberately trivial example, to order a drink, to receive it, to drink it, to pay for it – these various functions constitute an evidently closed sequence, for it is not possible to put something before the ordering of the drink or to put something after the payment without leaving the homogeneous group "Having a drink." The sequence is in fact always nameable. Determining the major functions of the folktale, Propp, then Bremond, have already been led to name them (*Fraud, Betrayal, Struggle, Contract, Seduction*, etc.); the nominative operation is just as inevitable for trivial sequences, which one might call "microsequences," those which frequently form the finest texture of the narrative fabric. Are these nominations solely the province of the analyst? In other words, are they purely metalinguistic? No doubt they are, since they deal with the narrative code, but we can suppose that they belong to a metalanguage internal to the reader (to the auditor) himself, who apprehends any logical succession of actions as a nominal whole: to read is to name; to hear is not only to perceive a language, it is also to construct it. The titles of sequences are rather analogous to those cover-words of translation machines, which more or less adequately cover a wide variety of meanings and nuances. The language of narrative, which is in ourselves, initially involves these essential rubrics: the closed logic which structures a sequence is indissolubly linked to its name: any function which inaugurates a *seduction*, say, prescribes upon its appearance, in the name which it produces, the whole process of seduction that we have learned from all the narratives which have formed in us the language of narrative.

Whatever its lack of importance, being composed of a small number of nuclei (i.e., actually, of "dispatchers"), the sequence always involves moments of risk, and this is what justifies our analysis of it: it might seem absurd to constitute as a sequence the logical succession of tiny actions which compose the offer of a cigarette (*to offer, to accept, to light, to smoke*); but the fact is that precisely at each of these points an alternative, hence a freedom of meaning, is possible: Du Pont, James Bond's partner, offers him a light from his lighter, but Bond refuses; the meaning of this bifurcation is that Bond instinctively fears a booby-trapped device.[31] Hence the sequence is, so to speak, a *threatened logical unit*: that is its justification *a minimo*. It is also founded *a maximo*: closed over its functions, subsumed under a name, the sequence itself constitutes a new unit, ready to function as the simple term of another, larger sequence. Here is a micro-sequence: *hold out a hand, shake the hand, release the hand*; this greeting becomes a simple function: on the one side, it takes the part of an index (Du

Pont's slackness, Bond's distaste), and on the other, it forms *in toto* the term of a larger sequence called *Meeting*, whose other terms (*approach halt, interpellation, greeting, sitting down*) can themselves be micro-sequences. A whole network of subrogations thus structures the narrative, from the tiniest matrices to the largest functions. We are here concerned, of course, with a hierarchy which remains internal to the functional level: it is only when it has been possible to enlarge the narrative, step by step, from Du Pont's cigarette to Bond's battle against Goldfinger, that the functional analysis is concluded: the pyramid of functions then touches the following level (that of Actions). There is both a syntax internal to the sequences and a (subrogating) syntax of the sequences among themselves. The first episode of *Goldfinger* thus assumes a "stemmatic" aspect (see figure).

This representation is obviously analytical. The reader perceives a linear succession of terms. But what must be noted is that the terms of several sequences can very well be imbricated one within the other: a sequence is not finished when, already, inset, the initial term of a new sequence can appear: the sequences move in counterpoint;[32] functionally the narrative structure is "fugued": this is how narrative simultaneously "holds" and "aspires." The imbrication of the sequences can only be allowed to cease, within a single work, by a phenomenon of radical rupture if the several closed blocks (or "stemmas") which then compose it are somehow recuperated at the higher level of Actions (of characters): *Goldfinger* is composed of three functionally independent episodes, for their functional stemmas twice cease to communicate: there is no sequential relation between the episode of the swimming pool and that of Fort Knox; but there remains an actantial relation, for the characters (and consequently the structure of their relations) are the same. Here we recognize the epic ("group of several fables"): the epic is a narrative broken on the functional level but unitary on the actantial level (as can be verified in the *Odyssey* or in Brecht's "epic theater"). Hence we must crown the level of functions (which furnishes the main part of the narrative syntagm) by a higher level, from which, step by step, the units of the first level draw their meaning, and which is the level of Actions.

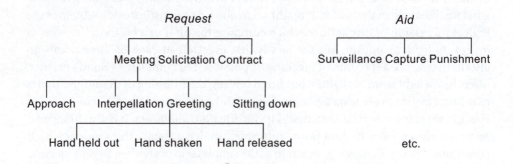

III. Actions

1. Toward a Structural Status of Characters

In Aristotelian poetics, the notion of character is secondary, entirely subsidiary to the notion of action: there can be stories without "characters," Aristotle says; there cannot be characters without a story. This view was adopted by the classical theoreticians (Vossius).[33] Later, the character, who hitherto was merely a name, the agent of an action,[34] assumed a psychological consistency, became an individual, a "person," in short a fully constituted being, even when he performed no action, and of course, even before acting,[35] the character ceased to be subordinate to the action, embodying from the start a psychological essence; such essences could be subject to an inventory, whose purest form was the bourgeois theater's list of "roles" (the coquette, the noble father, etc.). From its first appearance, structural analysis has shown the greatest reluctance to treat the character as an essence, even to classify it; as Todorov observes, Tomashevsky went so far as to deny the character any narrative importance whatever, a point of view which he subsequently modified. Without going so far as to withdraw characters from his analysis, Propp reduced them to a simple typology, based not on psychology but on the unity of the actions the narrative imparted to them (Giver of a magical object, Helper, Villain, etc.).

Since Propp, the character continues to raise the same problem for the structural analysis of narrative: on one hand, the characters (whatever they are called: *dramatis personae* or *actants*) form a necessary plan of description, outside which the trivial "actions" reported cease to be intelligible, so that we might say that there does not exist a single narrative the world over without "characters,"[36] or at least without "agents"; but on the other hand, these very numerous "agents" can be neither described nor classified in terms of "persons," whether because we consider the "person" as a purely historical form limited to certain genres (though the best known ones), so that we must set aside the enormous case of all the narratives (folktales, contemporary texts) which involve agents but not persons; or because we regard the "person" as nothing but a critical rationalization imposed by our period on pure narrative agents. Structural analysis, scrupulous not to define character in terms of psychological essences, has sought till now, through various hypotheses, to define character not as a "being" but as a "participant." For Claude Bremond, each character can be the agent of sequences of actions which are proper to it (*Fraud*, *Seduction*); when the same sequence implicates two characters (as is usually the case), the sequence involves two perspectives or, one might say, two names (what is *Fraud* for one is *Gullibility* for the other); in short, each character, even a secondary one, is the hero of his own sequence. Todorov, analyzing a "psychological" novel (*Les Liaisons dangereuses*), starts not from character-persons but from three main relations in which they can engage and which he calls basic predicates (love, communication, help); these relations are subjected by the analysis to two kinds of rules: of *derivation* when it is a matter of accounting for other relations and of *action* when it is a matter of describing the transformation of these relations in the course of the story: there are many characters in *Les Liaisons dangereuses*, but "what is said of them" (their predicates) can be classified (Todorov 1967). Finally, Greimas has proposed describing and classifying the characters of narrative not according to what they are but according to what they do (whence their name, *actants*), insofar as they participate in three main semantic axes, which we identify moreover in the sentence (subject, object, indirect object, adjunct) and which are communication, desire (or quest) and ordeal (Greimas 1966); since this participation is organized in pairs, the infinite world of characters is also subject to a paradigmatic structure (*Subject/Object, Giver/Receiver, Helper/Opponent*), projected throughout the narrative; and since the actant defines a class, it can be filled with different actors, mobilized according to the rules of multiplication, substitution, or deficiency.

These three conceptions have many points in common. The main one, we repeat, is to define the character by its participation in a sphere of actions, such spheres being few in number, typical, classifiable; this is why we have here called the second level of description, though that of the characters, the level of Actions: this word must therefore not be understood here in the sense of the trivial actions which form the fabric of the first level, but in the sense of the major articulations of *praxis* (to desire, to communicate, to struggle).

[Barthes continues on the role of the subject, a theory of narration and "The system of narrative", ed.]

Notes

1. This is not the case, it will be recalled, with poetry nor with the essay, dependent on the cultural level of their consumers.
2. The storyteller's "art" exists, of course: it is the power to engender narratives (messages) from the structure (code); this art corresponds to Chomsky's notion of performance and this notion is quite remote from an author's "genius," romantically conceived as a scarcely explicable individual secret.
3. See the history of Hittite *a*, postulated by Saussure and actually discovered fifty years later, in Emile Benveniste (1971, 32).
4. We may note the present conditions of linguistic description: ". . . linguistic 'structure' is always relative not just to the data or corpus but also to the grammatical theory describing the data" (Bach 1964, 29); "it has been recognized that language must be described as a formal structure, but that the description first of all necessitates specification of adequate procedures and criteria and that, finally, the reality of the object is inseparable from the method given for its description" (Benveniste 1971, 101).
5. But not imperative (see Claude Bremond 1966, more logical than linguistic).
6. It follows, as Jakobson has observed, that there are transitions from the sentence to what lies beyond it: coordination, for example, can function beyond the sentence.
7. See especially: Benveniste 1971, Ch. 10; Harris 1952; Ruwet 1972, 151–75.
8. It would be, specifically, one of the tasks of the linguistics of discourse to establish a typology of discourses. For the time being, we can recognize three major types of

discourse: metonymic (narrative), metaphoric (lyric poetry, sapiential discourse), enthymematic (intellectual discourse).

9. Here is the place to recall Mallarmé's intuition, formed just when he was planning a work of linguistics: "Language appeared to him the instrument of fiction: he will follow the method of language (determine this method). Language reflecting itself. Finally fiction seems to him the very process of the human mind – it is fiction which brings every method into play, and man is reduced to will" (1961, 851).

10. "Linguistic descriptions are not, so to speak, monovalent. A description is not simply 'right' or 'wrong' in itself . . . it is better thought of as more useful or less" (Halliday 1966, 8).

11. The levels of integration were postulated by the Prague School (Vachek 1964, 468) and subsequently adopted by many linguists. It is Benveniste, it seems to me, who has produced their most enlightening analysis (1971, Ch. 10).

12. "In somewhat vague terms, a level may be considered as a system of symbols, rules, and so on, to be used for representing utterances" (Bach 1964, 57).

13. The third part of rhetoric, *inventio*, did not concern language: it dealt with *res*, not with *verba*.

14. See especially B. Tomashevsky, "Thématique" (orig. 1925), in Todorov 1965. Somewhat later, Propp defined function as "the action of a character, defined from the point of view of its signification in the course of the Plot" (1969, 21). See also Todorov's definition. "The meaning (or the function) of an element of the work is its possibility of entering into correlation with other elements of this work and with the work as a whole" (1966) and the clarifications provided by Greimas, who has just defined the unit by its paradigmatic correlation, but also by its place within the syntagmatic unit of which it constitutes a part.

15. It is this that makes art different from "life," which acknowledges only "blurred" communications. "Blurring" (what one cannot see beyond) can exist in art, but then as a coded element (Watteau, for instance) [French rococo painter 1684–1721, ed.]; again, this "blurring" is unknown to the written code: writing is fatally distinct.

16. At least in literature, where the freedom of notation (consequent upon the abstract character of articulated language) involves a stronger responsibility than in the "analogical" arts, such as the cinema.

17. The functionality of the narrative unit is more or less immediate (hence apparent), according to the level where it functions: when the units are placed on the same level (in the case of suspense, for instance), functionality is very sensitive; much less so when the function is saturated on the narrational level: a modern text, weakly signifying on the anecdotal plane, recovers a great strength of meaning only on the plane of writing.

18. "Syntactical units (beyond the sentence) are actually units of content" (Greimas 1966, VI, 5). – Hence the exploration of the functional level is part of general semantics.

19. "We must not treat the word as if it were an indivisible element of literary art, the brick with which the building is constructed. It can be decomposed into much finer 'verbal elements'" (J. Tynyanov, quoted by Todorov in 1966, 18).

20. These designations, like those that follow, may all be provisional.

21. Which does not keep the syntagmatic display of functions from finally being able to cover paradigmatic relations between separate functions as has been acknowledged since Lévi-Strauss and Greimas.

22. We cannot reduce the functions to actions (verbs) and the indices to qualities (adjectives), for there are actions which are indicial, being "signs" of a character, of an atmosphere, etc.

23. Valéry used to speak of "dilatory signs." The detective story makes great use of these "baffling" signs.

24. Nicolas Ruwet calls a parametric element one which is constant throughout an entire piece of music (for example, the tempo of an allegro by Bach, or the monodic character of a solo).

25. Gérard Genette distinguishes two kinds of descriptions: ornamental and significant (1969). The significant description must obviously be attached to the level of the story and the ornamental description to the level of the discourse, which explains why for so long it formed a perfectly coded rhetorical "piece": *descriptio* or *ekphrasis*, a highly prized exercise of neo-rhetoric.

26. Quoted by Claude Bremond, "Le message narratif," in Bremond 1973.

27. In his fashion, as always perspicacious though undeveloped, Valéry has well expressed the status of narrative time: "Belief in time as agent and guiding thread is based on the mechanism of memory and on that of combined discourse" (1957, 348): the illusion is actually produced by the discourse itself.

28. This conception recalls an Aristotelian view: *proairesis*, rational choice of the actions to be made, establishes *praxis*, a practical science which produces no distinct work of the agent, contrary to *poeisis*. In these terms, we shall say that the analyst tries to reconstitute the *praxis* inherent in narrative.

29. This logic, based on an alternative (*to do this or that*), has the merit of accounting for the process of dramatization of which narrative is ordinarily the seat.

30. In the Hjelmslevian sense of double implication: two terms presuppose each other. [Louis Hjemslev, Danish linguist 1899–1965, ed.]

31. It is quite possible to identify, even at this infinitesimal level, an opposition of the paradigmatic type, if not between two terms, at least between two poles of the sequence: the sequence *Offer of a cigarette* displays, while suspending it, the paradigm *Danger/Safety* (shown by Shcheglov in his analysis of the Sherlock Holmes cycle), *Suspicion/Protection, Aggressiveness/Friendliness*.

32. This counterpoint was anticipated by the Russian Formalists, who outlined its typology; it suggests the main "intricate" structures of the sentence.

33. G. J. Vossius (1649–1677), Dutch-German professor of rhetoric, classics and theology [ed.].

34. Let us not forget that classical tragedy still knows only "actors," not "characters."

35. The "character-person" prevails in the bourgeois novel: in *War and Peace*, Nicholas Rostov is from the start a good boy, loyal, courageous, ardent; Prince Andrew is a disillusioned man of noble birth, etc.: what happens to them illustrates them, it does not constitute them.

36. If one part of contemporary literature has attacked the "character," it has done so not in order to destroy it (an impossibility) but to depersonalize it, a very different affair. A novel apparently without characters, such as Philippe Sollers's *Drame*, entirely subjugates the person to language, but nonetheless retains a fundamental play of actants, confronting the very action of speech. Such literature still knows a "subject," but this "subject" is henceforth that of language.

References

Bach, Emmon. 1964. *An Introduction to Transformational Grammars*. New York: Holt, Rinehart and Winston.

Benveniste, Émile. 1971. *Problems of General Linguistics*. Coral Gables: University of Florida Press. (Orig., *Problèmes de linguistique générale*. Paris: Gallimard, 1966.)

Bremond, Claude. 1966. "La logique des possibles narratifs." *Communications* #8.

_____1973. "Le message narrative." In *Logique du récit*. Paris: Éditions du Seuil.

Genette, Gérard. 1969. *Figures*, vol. II. Paris: Éditions du Seuil.

Greimas, A. J. 1966. *Sémantique structurale*. Paris: Larousse.

Halliday, M. A. K. 1966. "General Linguistics and its Application to Language Teaching." In M. A. K. Halliday and Angus McIntosh, *Patterns of Language*. London: Longmans.

Harris, Zelig. 1952. "Discourse Analysis." *Language* 28/18-23: 474–94.

Lévi-Strauss, Claude. 1963. *Structural Anthropology*. New York: Basic Books.

Mallarmé, Stéphane. 1961. *Oeuvres completes*. Paris: Bibliothèque de la Pléiade.

Martinet, André. 1961. "Réflexions sur la phrase." In *Language and Society: Essays presented to Arthur M. Jensen*. Copenhagen: Det Berlingske Bogtrykkeri.

Propp, Vladimir. 1969. *Morphology of the Folktale*. Austin: Texas University Press.

Ruwet, Nicolas. 1972. *Language, Musique, Poésie*. Paris: Éditions du Seuil.

Todorov, Tzvetan. 1965. *Théorie de la littérature. Textes des formalistes russes réunis*. (transl. and ed., T. Todorov). Paris: Éditions du Seuil.

_____1966. "Les catégories du récit littéraire." *Communications* #8.

_____1967. *Littérature et Signification*. Paris: Larousse.

Tomashevsky, B. 1925. "Thématique." In Todorov 1965.

Vachek, J. 1964. *A Prague School Reader in Linguistics*. Bloomington: Indiania University Press.

Valéry, Paul. 1957. *Tel Quel*. In *Oeuvres*, vol. II. Paris: Bibliothèque de la Pléiade.

The Theory of Symbolic Obviation

Roy Wagner

Anthropology, the "science of culture," has traditionally been oriented to the comparison and analysis of modes of action and conceptualization found among the various peoples of the world. "Culture" is the term used by anthropologists to phenomenalize and differentiate these modes into discrete entities, so that we speak of "our culture and their culture," of "members of a culture," or "the cultures of the world." We can lump all of these modes together into something called "human culture," or split this aggregate into as many individual entities as our comparison and analysis requires.

Symbols and Realities

But the science of culture itself is a part of something we might call the "culture of science." Like its sister sciences, including those that pertain to biological and physical, as well as social, phenomena, anthropology is part of a vast rationalistic enterprise aimed at the analysis of the phenomenal world. Ultimately, science itself as a collective, rationalistic enterprise is part of a larger undertaking that deals in manifold ways with a phenomenal "reality" of incident and situation. The culture of science is merely a specialized aspect of that larger undertaking that we call our "culture" or our "civilization," including our artistic, literary, political and legal, and practical traditions, our heritage, material and nonmaterial, and our technology. This culture is in all its diverse aspects an enterprise of deliberately building collective and conventional orders, reducing or deciphering a world of phenomena, unique natural and historical event, to a rational and utilitarian pattern. Our culture is systematic, and we use it to systematize the world around us. Our selves, situations, and surroundings – the individuality of moment, event, and place – are by contrast unique; they are the things that culture systematizes.

Thus for the purposes of our inquiry, the term "culture" has two distinct sets of meanings attached to it. One of these has to do with the phenomenalizing of different modes of human thought and action. The other has to do with our own rational and collective effort to systematize a world of unique situations, incidents, and phenomena. But these two sets of meanings, different as they may be, cannot be completely distinct, for they are both associations of the same word. Moreover, since all of these associations are fairly conventional ones, we cannot hope to ignore or cancel out one set of them by narrowing our definition; if we explicitly include only one set, the other will be present by implication and will merely have eluded our attempts at precision. "Culture," then, means both "one or all of a number of different modes of action and conception" and "a collective effort at systematizing a world of unique phenomenal incidents." This compound definition implies very strongly that all human cultures are like our own in that they deliberately set out to systematize a world of unique incident, and it implies that all human cultures (or "human culture" itself) deal with the same phenomenal "reality." These are extremely ethnocentric implications. When evoked and brought to the fore by anthropologists with a strong commitment to scientism and the methodologies of science, they have the effect of turning the science of culture into the culture of science. They re-create and justify our cultural order, instead of questioning and analyzing it.

Yet the dual range of associations that anthropology gives to the term "culture" has another, and opposite, implication. It implies that cultures themselves are phenomena, as well as (or rather than) organizers of phenomena, and it implies that Western rationalist culture and the Western conception of reality represent merely one among a number of ways of experiencing and creating the world. When followed conscientiously by anthropologists, these implications have the effect of laying bare our own assumptions for the purposes of analysis, of turning the culture of science into the science of culture.

But this relativistic reading of the concept has another, and even more intriguing, implication, one that has only recently come to the attention of anthropologists, though few of them are willing to follow it through to its conclusions. If our "reality" of unique incident, time, and situation, of nature and history, is not universal, but depends very largely on a particular cultural viewpoint, then no culture's idea of reality can be taken as absolute. Man does not deal with "the world" or "the environment," he cannot know and does not touch upon an "absolute reality" at any point. He deals with semiotic constructions that are experienced as, or, if you will, confused with, reality or the world, and he deals with these through the medium of other semiotic constructions.

Hence an anthropology based on the culture of science and formulated in terms of the interplay of symbols (or any other heuristic constructs) with the "world" ("nature," "reality," "the environment") can only replicate our own cultural conceptions in everything it studies. What we need is not a model of how symbols interact with "reality," but a model of how symbols interact with other symbols. And clearly, since a commitment to "reality" is so persistent and insidious among anthropologists as well as their subjects, such a model must account for the fact that some symbolic expressions are perceived as "reality" whereas others are not. It must show how and why people use symbols in relation to other symbols, what motivates them to do so, and how symbolic constructions persist and change in the course of construction.

The phenomenal order upon which the culture of science is based, and which forms its rationale, is, like all phenomenal orders, articulated through a set of names. The denominators of this world of objects, actions, passions, and so forth, whether verbal or not, have traditionally been called "symbols," and the traditional sense of "symbol" has been of that which "stands for" its referents without having any sort of intrinsic connection with them. Thus a symbol is said to be "arbitrary," in the way in which the sight and sound of the word "cow" is only one of a myriad possible ways of designating its bovine referent.

But of course there is one way in which "cow" is *not* arbitrary, and that is with regard to English linguistic convention. When "cow" is used, in an appropriate way, in reference to its conventionally appropriate referents, its effect is to invoke and emphasize *convention*. Verbal denominators are but a part of a vast range of ordering elements, lexical, grammatical, syntactic, linguistic, cultural, institutional, among others, whose primary associations are conventional. Some of these are very general, pertaining to language, law, family, personal demeanor, and so on, whereas others are peculiar to certain regions, professions, time periods, subcultures ("the culture of science"), and other categories. However much the conventional spheres may overlap or flow together, it is possible to speak of them as distinct conventional orders, or cultures.

The meaningful and affective significance of convention, whenever invoked in an appropriate manner, is that of a moral covenant, or "membership." Thus there are many "moralities," weak and strong, diffuse and intense, and each corresponds to a matrix of convention. Each corresponds to a set of symbols whose reference or ordering effect is largely arbitrary *except with regard to convention*. (The culture of science, for example, is one such "morality," dedicated to the articulation of a conventional body of knowledge.) And because the symbols themselves are thus *contrasted* with their referents, they form an ideal "set" or "family" among themselves, one that must necessarily separate and distinguish itself from the phenomenal world. (Any abrogation of this ideal separation would compromise the purely conventional emphasis of the symbolizing function.) Conventional symbolization defines and precipitates a sharp distinction between its own symbols and orders on one hand and the world of their reference and ordering on the other. I have argued that this distinction discriminates, for every human culture, between the realm of the culturally recognized "innate," or "given," and the realm of legitimate human action and artifice.[1]

This is not to argue, however, that the conventional, for instance, carries the same identification in every culture. Although conventional symbolization is necessary to and definitive of every human culture, comparatively few traditions identify it as the legitimate realm of human action. The idea of collective responsibility for knowledge and human government, and of the "innateness" of the individual and the incidental, is characteristic largely of the rationalist movements that sponsor and emulate the culture of science. A majority of anthropology's research subjects, however, invert this order and regard the conventional order as innate.

A tradition that takes responsibility for the deliberate ordering of knowledge and human affairs will obviously approach the issue of "meaning" very differently from a tradition dedicated to the indirect elicitation of an innate knowledge. Conventional symbolization aims at the precise, orderly classification and replication (as scientific "law" replicates natural "law") of the natural world; it negotiates an orderly universe through the fabrication of a heuristic theoretical order. And this obsession with the artifice of order carries over into epistemology also. The study of verbal denotation and connotation that we call semantics is concerned with the ways in which the elicitation of meaning can be brought within the compass of conventional order. Thus Stephen Ullman (1963) classifies three kinds of lexical "motivation" (that is, nonarbitrary relation between a word and its referents beyond that of mere convention) as, respectively, semantic, morphological, and phonological. But the first of these is concerned with polysemy (multiple referents) by way of broadening the word's range of conventional reference, whereas the last two deal with regular word-combination ("agglutination") and sound-imitation. Generations of lexicographers and philologists have demonstrated the value of such semantic solutions, particularly in linguistic studies. I would emphasize, however, that they belong to a particular, and limited, approach to meaning, one that subordinates the properties of meaningful construction to those of static systematics. I shall use the term "semantic" in reference to this epistemological stance.

If we can persuade ourselves to put by the semantic orientation as an attempt to relegate meaning to the province of lexical plurality and consider instead the radical implications of polysemy, an alternative approach is implied. For any nonarbitrary symbolization, any "motivation," that is not of a conventional character threatens to subvert and supplant the conventional symbolization with a "nonarbitrariness" of a much more piquant and individual variety. The "trope," or "turning," of the symbol from its conventional application directly confutes or denies the latter. The conventional (or, in the case of a well-worn trope, *a* conventional) sense "dies," and is fragmented or "differentiated" into something "new." This confutation of the conventional is an effect of what is generally called "metaphor," and is germinal to what I shall call, in its broadest implications, *obviation*. If the semantic approach fosters the de-emphasis of polysemy into mere connotation, then a tropic ("trope-ic," from "trope") orientation must emphasize the contrastive effect of metaphor, even in cases where the metaphor is a worn or a tired one. Thus a dynamic comprehension of meaning, and of cultural domain, is won at the expense of a static one, and even the forms of slack rhetoric rehearse the continual invention and reinvention of culture out of itself.

Since we have undertaken an inquiry into symbolic usage, it is appropriate to consider tropic usage from a symbolic standpoint. Since tropic usage sets one symbol (or denominate entity) into some relatively nonconventional relation to another such symbol (or entity), replacing the "nonarbitrariness" of conventional usage with some more specific motivation, it is obvious that a notion of simple (literal) reference no longer applies. The nonconventional relation introduces a new symbolization simultaneously with a "new" referent, *and the symbolization and its referent are identical*. We might say that a metaphor or other tropic usage assimilates symbol and referent into one expression, that a metaphor is a *symbol that stands for itself* – it is self-contained. Thus the symbolic effect of tropic usage opposes or counteracts that of conventional usage in two ways: it assimilates that which it "symbolizes" within a distinct, unitary expression (collapsing the distinction between symbol and symbolized), and it differentiates that expression from other expressions (rather than articulating it with them).

If it makes sense to describe a trope as a kind of symbol, then it might be suggested that symbols, even in their conventional role, are a kind of trope. This proposition exemplifies yet another effect of tropic usage: reflexivity. The "vehicle," or signifying element of a metaphor, and the "tenor," or signified element, actually exist in a relation of mutuality – each metaphorizes the other, transforming and being transformed. Every trope depends upon the conventional significances of its constituent elements for communicability, but conventional usage is in turn dependent upon tropic variation as a foil for its own generalizing effect. There is in fact an ever-present tension between the conventionalizing potentialities and the tropic potentialities of all symbolic elements in use – a tension that threatens to erode and counteract the intentionality of the user. As tropic usage proceeds by "metaphorizing" the conventional, so conventional nonarbitrariness often threatens to displace the tropic variety and reiterate itself dialectically through the metaphorization of metaphor.[2] The complementary relationship of convention and tropic usage sets them into a dialectical opposition, such that each kind of usage can be encompassed, for purposes of analysis, wholly within the other.

From this standpoint it is not too difficult to imagine how conventional usage and tropic usage can be opposed to each other as equivalent, although complementary, modalities. I have suggested, furthermore, that the two modalities embody the realms of human responsibility and of the innate, differentially in particular cultural traditions. I do not mean to imply, however, that the distinction is one of substantive symbolic content; it is primarily a contrast of symbolic usage (other-signification versus self-signification), and only incidentally an opposition between sacred and secular, or between village and bush. In a semiotic sense each realm is the *referent*, or the object, or the context of the other. This can be seen clearly in the case of our own phenomenal, particulate "reality" ("nature"). Every object, incident, disposition, or set that we might choose to exemplify the referent of one of our conventional symbols, is, arguably, a self-contained symbolic expression. Any cow, for instance, that we might wish to exemplify our notion of "cow," will be *some particular cow*, and hence she will be, in Korzybski's felicitous phrasing, "a cow, *et cetera*": a thing in herself, and, for all her organic charm, a *metaphor* of the ideal notion of cowness. And a first-edition score of Beethoven's *Hammerklavier* Sonata, though it "belongs" to "culture," is, however privileged, an exemplification of a referential symbol, and hence, no less than the cow, a self-contained aspect of particulate "reality." The cow and the score are referents of the particular symbols, but, as a self-contained expression, each assimilates its conventional denominator within its makeup. All that which tells us what a cow is in relation to a sonata, or to this particular sonata, belongs to the realm of conventional symbol; that which expresses the uniqueness of a particular cow, or a particular musical manuscript, is an effect of tropic construction.

For the tradition that I have called the culture of science, of course, such a conclusion would appear overdrawn, or simply wrong. The conventional perspective that dominates our semantics and that parses our phenomenal world for us insists that trope and metaphor are literary forms, mere human contrivances adequate to express its "reality" of incident and particularity, but certainly not to constitute it. The transition from this ethnocentric perspective to the relativity of the science of culture becomes a possibility when the reflexivity of tropic usage is seen as a viable alternative to the "taxonomy" and "coding" of the semantic approach. If symbols can be shown to function both as signifier and signified, to embody one or both of these functions, then any particular cultural arbitration of the "innate" versus the "artificial" is obviated.

Tribal peoples like the Daribi and their counterparts the world over, as well as the mature[3] civilizations of Asia and the Near East, orient their actions and interpretations around ideologies that are in every respect semiotic inversions of our own. They are based on the deliberate articulation of tropic, differentiating constructions, identifying these constructions as the proper and legitimate subject of human action and assigning man's conventions to the realm of that which is innate. The rules, laws, traditions, and other conventional regularities of society, the grammars and orders of language, are for them part of a "flow" of immanent sociality, conceived as an essential "humanity" that is part of the nature of things. Man's work is to extend its subliminal definitions, to infuse the flow with contrasts and distinctions that can contain it and give it immediacy and force.

Although it calls forth analogies to certain activities in our own society, such as advertising, showmanship, and leadership, this style of living and acting generally appears irresponsible (if not "prelogical" or "primitive") to Westerners. Its responsibilities (which are quite formidable, in fact) are those of appropriate "spirit" or "style." Although a tropic expression appears as a distinct "thing-in-itself," it owes its intelligibility to the conventions it incorporates. Such an expression is always constituted as an "innovation" upon some conventionally recognized usage, and therefore, in Louis Dumont's terms, it *encompasses* the conventional. One of my

Daribi friends, for whom pigs were the definitive domestic food animal, exemplified the form very nicely once in conversation: "a goat is not a very good pig; the best pig is a cow."

Differentiating acts take the form of competitive improvisations, substituting an unconventional element for that which one might literally expect. The result is a novel expression that intentionally "deconventionalizes" the conventional (and unintentionally conventionalizes the unconventional): a new meaning has been formed (and an old meaning has been extended). The novel expression both amplifies and controverts the significance of the convention upon which it innovates. The force and color that it embodies is a measure of its differentiation of the conventional; the test of its appropriateness is the degree to which it amplifies or "interprets" convention strategically. (Both goats and cows make provocatively different kinds of "pigs," but a cow amplifies the traditional sense of "pig" much better than a goat does.)

Order, consistency, and relational paradigm do not "model" knowledge and understanding for the Daribi, as they do for the culture of science. It is not that the Daribi are incapable of "abstract" thinking, or that they have some predisposition to or preference for the irrational; their logic and "common sense," when the occasion demands it, is as good as anyone's. It is rather that Daribi tradition allocates human responsibility to the realm of the incidental and the tropic, and Daribi do not build themselves orders of knowledge. Indeed, in a world where convention and relational order are held to be innate, such articulation would be a bit silly: shall man replicate the work of the creator,[4] like a foolish younger brother, a *peraberabidi*? [a Daribi mythic fool, ed.] Instead of pooling their knowledge as "culture" and drawing from the pool, instead of linking fact to fact and making understanding part of a collective effort, Daribi articulate and prize their flashes of understanding as things-in-themselves, frozen lightning bolts to be thawed out in nightly sessions by the firepit.

The life of a tribal people is carried on through a continuing series of innovations, motivated and guided by the conventional flow that it elicits reflexively. The lifestyles of men and women are realized as innovations upon one another, constrained by the contingencies of tropic construction. "Magical" procedures lend force and potency to human undertakings through their own (quite incidental) amplification of conventional qualities. Rituals replicate immanent cosmological order through human means, resolving its crises via communion with its powers.

Of course, the ritual replication of the cosmos by tribal peoples is as much a collectivizing act as the replication of "natural law" in science. Such are the constraints of ideology, however, that tribal collectivization is fitted into the conceptual format of differentiation, just as differentiating acts in Western society (such as those of advertising) are justified in conventional terms (advertising "brings us news about products"). Ritual and advertising are techniques of sustaining the respective ideologies by inverting their characteristic modes of symbolic construction – they "recharge" the resources of ordinary activity reflexively, but they also pose the danger of working against the moral expectations of one's tradition.[5]

Reflexivity, the key to the science of culture and its hallmark of relativity, is the means by which symbol can interact (as signifier or signified) with symbol so as to constitute cultural significance and cultural domain. As such, this effect of tropic usage is self-demonstrating: as the "internal" criterion of my argument it is the "means," and as the adduced model of semiotic construction it is the "end," of this theoretical inquiry. Because the arena in which reflexivity and its kindred effects operate is a symbolic one, I speak primarily of "ideologies" and "traditions," and mention culture and society as derivative phenomena. Just as my definitions of the ethical realms of a tradition are as kinds of usage and only incidentally as substantive things, or places, so the substantive contents of symbolic construction – the textural and experiential dimensions of a symbolized "world" – are incidental to my formal argument. I understand perfectly well that symbols can no more exist "in the abstract" than people can; the knowledge that every symbol must be a particular symbol is an implication of the insight that every symbol is a trope. But the particularity of a symbol, the significance of its content, is a function of its context, or environment: it evokes, and belongs to, a particular cultural "reality." I shall consider the Daribi world in this light, through the medium of its myths and tales, in the ensuing chapters.

The genre of tradition and invention that we call "myth" corresponds to a regime of tropic construction, however much outsiders may appreciate and emulate its styles and products. Like the other aspects of tribal life, myth has been approached and illuminated from many angles. Myths have been traced from place to place, dissected into motifs and catalogued, interpreted as historical fact, psychological fantasy, or legitimating charter; they have been understood as illogical, prelogical, and as examples of a fine, particularizing logic. In general these approaches have paralleled the concerns of a rationalistic and knowledge-oriented culture of science, anxious to find explanation (and justification) in the heuristic application of its own orders. My intent here is to use myth as a "self-demonstration" of the workings of an ideology based on tropic construction. And this requires that we turn our attention to the general effect that I have called "obviation."

Obviation

Obviation is the effect of supplanting a conventional semiotic relation with an innovative and self-contained relation; it is the definitive paradigm of semiotic transformation. When applied on the scale of individual words or other symbolic elements, obviation takes the form of a trope, or metaphor; when applied on the scale of semiotic modality (the realms of human responsibility and of the innate), obviation assumes the force of a major cultural derivation or demonstration. Because the reflexivity of tropic usage allows us to consider conventional usage as a kind of trope (the metaphor, as it were, of a metaphor), obviation could be described as the process by which the artificial comes to metaphorize the innate (and the reverse process). Or it might be said – since these realms correspond to kinds of semiotic usage and not to substantive things – that obviation is the process by which the realm of human responsibility must forever be created out of the innate, and the realm of the innate must be constituted out of that of the artificial.

Why "obviation"? The common Latin root, *obvius* (from *obviam*, "in the way"), which "obviate" ("to anticipate and dispose of") shares with "obvious" ("apparent, easily perceived"), suggests a complex analogy. A metaphor is mediative, inserting an unconventional element "in the way of" conventional reference, so that the new relation comes to supplant, to "anticipate and dispose of" conventional effect. And by constituting "its own" relation in the process, becoming an "icon" of itself, a symbol that shows its own meaning, the trope renders itself "apparent." Stated etymologically in this way, the "obviation" metaphor appears awkward and fortuitous. Like all tropes, however, it deserves a sympathetic hearing. Understood in their own terms, "to anticipate and dispose of" and "to render apparent" become a single operation, that of circumventing the arbitrariness of some expression or situation by discovering and making "obvious" an analogy that motivates it. Somewhat less precisely, to obviate a symbol is to dissolve it into something else in an illuminating way; to obviate the realm of human responsibility or that of the innate is to derive the other from it in a demonstrably meaningful way. In the latter respect, obviation corresponds to the revelatory aspect of ritual.[6]

Obviation, then, is a metaphor for metaphor, "naming" it by substituting its effect. But if we liken the effect to trope or metaphor, it must be with the provision that obviation is not limited to the "atomism" of individual words or single elements. The transformation that takes place in a myth is as surely an instance of obviation as the transformation that occurs in a metaphor, and the meaning elicited as unitary. Though we may not be used to considering an entire "work" on the same terms as a single word, this is one of the implications of the concept of obviation. The processual form of tropic construction, a myth or ritual, amounts to what we might call a "meta-trope," figuring one aspect of the total cosmos in terms of the other. Processually, of course, the sequence is one of individual elements or episodes succeeding one another. Semiotically, the conventional effect of separating signifier and signified and the tropic effect of assimilating them into a unitary expression succeed each other in a kind of mutually constrained interplay. As this continues, the effects of the tropic assimilations become cumulative; eventually the distinction between the modalities, recast into ever more liminal form, is eroded away, and the initial construction, pushed to the point of paradox, collapses into its modal opposite. The metaphorizing of one element or episode by another leads, progressively and cumulatively, to the metaphorizing of one modality by the other. The effect suggests the closing of the traditional hermeneutical circle, for, in the final metaphorization, the reflexive component of construction, normally "out of awareness," becomes apparent *as a consequence of the construction.*

Myth, as obviation sequence, shares with metaphor the power of brilliant, concerted expression. As a self-contained construction, however, it also shares the limiting particularity of metaphor. As much an event (like a scientific experiment) as it is an explanation, a myth accounts for very little indeed, and what it does explicate often enough appears naive, especially when approached literally. Its power (and wisdom) only becomes evident when the transformation is regarded as exemplary, the demonstration or dramatization of the general through some especially compelling particular. The facility of the myth or tale is not that of replicating the world, but of setting up its own world in contradistinction.

Myth "remakes" the realms of morality and fact in its own terms, but it touches those realms only briefly, in the act of attainment. Whereas Westerners confine the bulk of their serious effort within one realm or the other, considering, articulating, and implementing law, theory, and the social order, or testing and describing phenomenal "nature," myth constructs its understandings across these realms. The action of myth spends most of its time in a space liminal to them, in what Victor Turner calls the "subjunctive mood" of culture; its objects and characters are demiphenomena, woven "of the light and the half-light." Analytically, these characters and objects are relations within the larger relation of the myth itself. For the peoples who create myth, however, they are perhaps a kind of power (as speech itself is a power), having the facility to elicit and compel the moral and the factual without being *of* them.

Westerners, committed to the building and preservation of a "culture" of deliberately articulated convention, tend to view obviation in a negative sense – as uncanny and potentially erosive. Insight is an accidental thing for us, creeping up on our scholastic efforts to build the structures of knowledge. We call it "invention" or "discovery" and attribute innate powers of genius to those who happen upon it. But invention and obviation, and the insight and understanding they entail, are deliberate modes of procedure for a regime of tropic construction. They facilitate, and to some extent presuppose, a world of deliberate obfuscation and startling, highly particular revelation. Just as the study of "phenomena" belongs to the culture of science, whose semantic symbology presupposes a "phenomenal" world, so mythic orientation corresponds to an epistemology of "dephenomenalization." Obviation as a regular style of action amounts to the reduction and working out, the collapsing, of one existential modality (the "innate" or the "artificial") to produce the other. Liminal to any system or schema (including, or course, those presented here), obviation is the discourse or invention that speaks between the lines of a given reality, as, to use Rilke's image, the tongue lives between the hammers of the teeth.

What myth analysis can offer anthropology is a demythologizing of an insidious presupposition: that of the innateness and impenetrability of obviation. This can be facilitated by presenting and analyzing examples of obviation in traditions where tropic symbolization is ideologically stressed, for deliberate obviation is the processual manifestation of figurative symbolization as a mode of thought and action. Myth, as a subject of inquiry, is in other words a most appropriate vehicle for demythologizing; but myth is merely one aspect of a thoroughgoing culture of obviation.

Mythic expression, in contrast to "literature," is based on a deliberately tropic and transformational means of articulation. Rather than providing linear exposition, building up Aristotelian lexicons of knowledge or Lévi-Straussian relational paradigms, myth emphasizes substitutions and transformations openly – hence its "primitive" or "prelogical" appearance. But since the conventional aspect of symbolization is necessarily a part of any meaningful expression, the flow of figurative substitution that we call "plot" is by no means unconstrained – a thing of "free association." Every myth or tale is intrinsically bound up with the cultural realms of the innate and the artificial, with what is "given" and perhaps sacred, and what man can and should morally do. It is indeed the very essence of myth, and of the obviation through which myth exists, to transform one of these realms into the other.

Thus the plot of a myth is not simply a succession of substitutions or transformations, but a transformational dialectic that embodies the interplay between contextual separation and its obviation. The episodes and situations of a plot are linked together by the implications of successive transformations in terms of that interplay. Effectively, the transformations take the form of alternating constructions of a social (collectivizing) nature and an individual (differentiating) nature. Keeping in mind that the conventional mode, that of social construction, also embodies the property of contextual separation, and that the inventive mode, that of innovation, embodies the tropic properties of contextual assimilation, we can see that this is a special kind of dialectic. Whereas its "open," bipolar form as a dialogue between opposed principles, or semiotic modes, is maintained by one of these modes, a cumulative movement toward closure and resolution, toward figurative self-continence, is maintained by the other mode. The result is an obviation sequence, a self-containing and self-closing dialectic – or better, perhaps, a dialectic that *becomes* something.

To put it somewhat differently, the diachronic interrelation between the social and the individual is never simply oppositional; it is also constitutive of events. It is, to use a concept that Lévi-Strauss has very successfully introduced to the study of myth, mediative. The notion of mediation or synthesis, originated by Hegel (and applied by Marx), added the dimension of historicity to what had originally been, among the Greek philosophers, a mere polarity of opposed speakers, or principles. As dialectic, in fact, the ternary Hegelian form of thesis-antithesis-synthesis quickly resolves itself into a bipolar dialogue, for the "synthesis" of each successive closure becomes the "thesis" of the following one. (The scheme becomes: thesis-antithesis-synthesis-antithesis-synthesis-antithesis-synthesis and so on.) Depending upon his interests and point of view, the analyst may regard such a schema as either ternary or binary. An obviation sequence, however, carries mediation to its ultimate conclusion by the very continuity that makes its closing term a mediation of the original dialectical polarity. Thus the overall "shape" of such a sequence might best be visualized as ternary, an encompassing mediational triangle (Figure 1). Indeed the notion of a self-closing dialectic was almost (but not quite) developed by Lévi-Strauss in his penetrating analysis of the myth of Asdiwal.

When we consider the semantic framework within which Lévi-Strauss couched his analysis, it becomes apparent why this should be so. A dialectic that mediates its own oppositions, moving inexorably toward a nondialectical expression, can scarcely be analyzed in clear-cut lexical terms. It becomes, rather, a kind of "calculus" of semiotic approximation, in which the "oppositions" like above and below, male and female are gradually reduced and finally summed together. Viewed from the standpoint of tropic construction, a sequence of constructive substitutions is simply a series of metaphors, one that tends, through successive assimilations of the foregoing material as "context," to the formation of a final, consummate figurative expression. The error of "decoding" such a series (translating it into a message) is one of reducing meaningful expressions to their primitive lexical terms.

Hence the problem of exegesis resolves itself into that of sympathetic figurative construction, metaphorizing the figurative construction of myth (making "myth" of the myth, as Lévi-Strauss would have it), rather than dissecting the expressions into their component lexical parts. It is the figurative, rather than the literal, aspect that must be "translated." But precisely because substitution is substitution, and not identity, because the thing that is substituted must be different from that which it replaces, this approach (like myth itself) carries certain implications that differentiate it from the expectations of semantic science. Because the range of potential differences and similarities between the thing substituted and that for which it is substituted is so great, even within the compass of a tribal culture, and because different selections of these differences and similarities may be evoked by the makers, successive tellers, and analysts of a myth, every myth, when it is told, remembered, translated, or analyzed, is a "myth" about itself. Because substitution invariably changes, extends, and relocates the recognized differences and similarities, displacing through its own creative action any possible lexical guides, every myth is a unique experiental world. A myth is "another

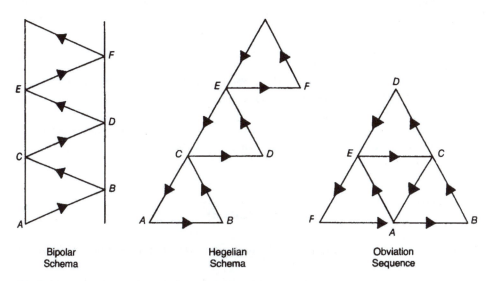

Bipolar
Schema

Hegelian
Schema

Obviation
Sequence

Figure 1. Visual representations of three dialectical schemata (the latters are homologous in each diagram).

culture," even for those of its own culture, just as "another culture" is something of a myth for the anthropologist. As much as it tells one what "its" culture is like, a myth demonstrates also what that culture is not like. Finally, since languages themselves are different, every act of translation is likewise a substitutive metaphorization, and for that reason there can be no "exact" or "correct" translation.

Saying something "in" (or more precisely, "with") a particular language always amounts to an act of analysis. It amounts to an (usually inadvertent) analysis of the "said" in terms of a particular set of linguistic conventions and paradigms, what we might call the "imagery of saying" of a language. Speaking and writing English amounts to analysis in terms of person, gender, number, a variety of nominal and pronominal paradigms, verbal and clausal modalities, tense, mood, lexical association, and the like. Speaking itself can be understood as a kind of obviation, substituting sound (or silence) for sound, word for word, phrase for phrase, in a discursive sequence. Each newly spoken or perceived element supplants previous ones and adds them to its context.[7]

Notes

1. Wagner 1975, chap. 4.
2. In *The Invention of Culture*, I suggest that human motivation, in a number of its normal as well as pathological dispositions, might be understood as the consequence of the actors' identification of the "self" and its various intentionalities with certain of these tendencies.
3. By "mature" I mean societies that have passed through an evolutionary transition, based on their own semiotic self creation, from classless "tribal" situations to a regime incorporating the mutual creativity of dialectically opposed classes. I would suggest that contemporary Western culture is presently in the final stages of such a transition, corresponding to Spengler's notion of the development of a "high culture" into a "civilization." See Wagner 1975.
4. The Daribi *tq nigare bidi* ("man who made the land"), or creator, Souw, is generally associated with the arrangement of the cosmos.
5. See Wagner 1975, 46–50.
6. Compare the Ndembu verb *ku-solola*, "to reveal," "to make visible," and the associated cluster of terms discussed by Victor Turner (1975, 180).
7. Michael Meeker, personal communication, 1975.

References

Turner, Victor W. 1975. *Revelation and Divination in Ndembu Ritual*. Ithaca, NY: Cornell University Press.

Ullman, S. 1963. "Semantic Universals." In *Universals of Language*, ed. J. Greenburg. Cambridge, MA: MIT Press.

Wagner, Roy. 1975. *The Invention of Culture*. Chicago: University of Chicago Press.

PART V

COGNITIVIST APPROACHES

INTRODUCTION TO PART V

Despite the impression one may get from reading the current literature on cognitive approaches to religion these approaches are not purely a discovery of late twentieth-century scholars and scientists. Any approach that focuses on cognition also focuses on issues and problems that have for long been known in psychology and even in philosophy before that. Cognition is a term that covers a very wide array of phenomena, objects, subjects and issues, such as memory, representation, language, thought, perception, projection and imagination. And, not to forget the most complicated issue of them all: human consciousness. These are matters that have occupied philosophers, psychologists, and anthropologists, to just name those disciplines that are of greater relevance to our topic. As we already have sections in this volume that cover approaches to myth in those fields of scholarship, the choice of having a separate section of "cognitive approaches" may need a few words of explanation and justification. The rationale behind this choice is that there is a growing interest and literature on religion and cognition and it is my prediction that this "movement" will also concern myth and mythology in a larger measure than already acknowledged. Where most of the materials chosen for the other sections represent established scholarship, in some respects mainly historical and even retrospective, the contributions here should be treated as indicators of how findings in a range of subjects in cognitive studies may present new and different perspectives and ideas for the analyses of myths and mythologies. Most of the contributions do not display the term "myth" (or any derivative) in the title and some do not even tackle it in the text. However, it is the intention to demonstrate, through these contributions, that cognitive

323

theories and methods are relevant to the study of myths and mythologies and that they may even provide answers to some of the enduring and puzzling questions in previous scholarship on myth. The major distinction between current cognitive studies and earlier investigations is that recent methodologies are backed not only by empirical data but also based on experimental research. It should be noted, however, that the cognitive sciences are no uniform nor unified discipline and that competing theories abound. The "field" is extremely complex and so are its many objects of research. There is also a history about how all this developed (Bechtel et al. 1998, 1–104).[1]

Earlier cognitive psychology and anthropology operated at levels different from the later developments and they were clearly more oriented towards culture and society, as for example in the "Culture and Personality" school of anthropology or as in social psychologies, exemplified for example by the pioneering work of George Herbert Mead (1863–1931). Of the presentations above, some of them clearly display cognitive orientations and interests, for example Cassirer, Searle, Malinowski, Douglas, Lévi-Strauss and Wagner. Anyone with an interest in human cognition (i.e. the many subjects listed above) could qualify as cognitively oriented, but here the dividing line is whether or not the contributions explicitly address cognitive science perspectives as they have been developed over the last half-century.

The "new" standard modular and information processing approach to cognition dates back to the 1950s with the emergence of Artificial Intelligence and the demise of behaviourism in psychology. In linguistics Noam Chomsky revolutionized the field with his invention of "Generative" or "Transformative" grammar, which clearly located the human language faculty inside the brain. Thus, to some extent, linguistics became a "brain science."[2] Most of the subsequent researchers and scholars in the cognitive sciences can be classified as "hardliners" in so far as they proceeded from the "Identity hypothesis" which states that mind is "nothing but" the physical or material brain. That something is "nothing but" natural or physical is the reductionists' favourite slogan. But there is a wide range of theories, as some scientists and philosophers opine that the mind simply is identical to the brain while others endorse versions where cognition and consciousness are non-material, mental epiphenomena produced by, but not reducible to, the brain. All of these positions are in principle familiar from the history of philosophy: dualists posit a dichotomy between consciousness as non-material and the brain as material whereas others are materialists, naturalists, or physicalists depending on their theories of human consciousness and cognition. The latter allow into their worldview or ontology only matters that can be treated by the methods of the natural sciences. Moreover, there is the question of whether to include consciousness in cognition, which some do not as they focus only on subconscious processes, such as those of vision and tactile perception. There is also the distinction between those who address only mental functions that we are born with while others take into account the ontogenesis and socialization of the individual. The scope is, as this indicates, immense. However diverse, from a scientific perspective the cognitive sciences often seem themselves as the "new humanities," studying not so much the end products of human mental activities, but the cognitive properties and mechanisms that are responsible for all of this being produced.

As for the relevance to the study of myths and mythologies it is clear that an exposition and explanation of how and why myths are as they are and how they attract human attention, that is, they are reproduced and remain "alive" as parts of cultural traditions, must be considered a noteworthy achievement. Many proponents of the cognitive study of religion have been busy exploring and explaining the characteristics of religious representations and their production by the individual mind. Most scientist operating on these premises have tended to disregard culture and in some cases, this amounts to "cultural eliminativism," i.e. eliminating culture as part of the project. Thus, they have been less, and perhaps not at all, occupied with investigations of what those products of the mind, *in casu* myths, can do when they feed back into minds – when the symbolic, linguistic, cultural, etc. representations are internalized by minds. There is no doubt that minds produce culture but to what extend does culture produce minds? The question is relevant and crucial, but it has not yet been sufficiently explored.[3]

One of the main proponents of the cognitive approaches to the study of religion is Pascal Boyer. He started out by working on a strong theory about memory and its relation to cultural reproduction and found that one way of making matters (stories, tradition, representations) memorable could be achieved by breaking certain intuitive expectations that humans universally seem to have about the world – but just in adequate proportions. If the stories were too ordinary, they were forgotten and if they were too "wild" they would be difficult to transmit. The right balance, the "cognitive optimum" is when our default assumptions about the inventory of world are being violated to a fitting degree, for example when trees are said to remember or statues to weep. There had to be a measure of counter-intuitivity, and such blending of the ordinary with the impossible is what myths very often do. If one would systematically begin to look for violation when reading myths, the results would be revealing. Blending and violation explain, at least in part, why surviving myths are so "strange," the boring stories presumably just faded away. What the old evolutionists saw as childishness is rather, to put it metaphorically, a "strategy of myth," depending on the preferences of those who tell them but unconsciously so. Myths are not romantic versions of childhood experiences, as the psychoanalytic analysis would claim. Rather we can see how myths are organized thoughts, along and against templates and schemata; they display the imaginative productivity of the human mind. The idea of the counter-intuitive is highly applicable to the study of all forms of religious narrative. In fact Edmund Leach once proposed something similar about religious symbolism: "The non-logicality of religious statements is itself 'part of the code', it is an index of what such statements are about, it tells us that we are concerned with metaphysical rather than physical reality, with belief rather than knowledge" (1976, 70).

Yet another approach with cognitive features is the Metaphor theory proposed by George Lakoff and Mark Johnson (1980). Against the prevailing idea that metaphors are but stylistic and literary embellishment, they demonstrated how metaphors are tied to basic linguistic and cognitive operations. In metaphors we blend representations from two (or more) source domains into a target domain and we may then say things like "life is a journey," "I am boiling with anger," "This surgeon is a butcher," etc. so as to furnish thoughts, imaginations and expressions with something "other" – that attracts attention and produces images and complex representations. Myths contain plenty of such constructions. Because myths are as much analogical as metaphoric and as analogical thought is often considered unverifiable and illogical, so does myth become relegated to the realm of fantasy. Then again, that may be a skewed and unproductive view, for analogical thought is fundamental to the workings of the human mind, also those considered more rational than myth (Shelley and Thagard 1996). Minds and myths are places where many things become "blended" – in such ways as to produce new and "attention-grabbing" mental and linguistic constructions, startling and memorable, fictive and counterfactual, but not boring or easy to forget.[4]

Another major question in cognitive studies concerns the relations between thought and language. To make a very long story very short: No one has (so far) the final answer to that. We do not yet know, in the sense of general scientific agreement, how thought and language connect. Perhaps our language makes us think that because we have two labels then there are also just two entities that somehow combine or that there may even be causal relations between them. In all probability, there are many more entities and the metaphor should not be one of two-way connection or causality but one of a web. Thus, on links between brain and language, no one knows for certain, but there are numerous competing theories. One line of thought that I would press in this connection concerns the way in which myths are collective, objectively available narratives with organized contents of representations and thoughts. That is, myths provide their audience with sets, scripts and programmes for making the world (be it physical, social, mental and supernatural) understandable and manageable. By telling improbable stories we organize our thoughts about our lived-in realities – just remember Clastres' analysis of what made the Indians laugh (see Part III). The key question is, however, to what extent and on which levels of the cognitive faculties and mechanisms may the narrative materials condition the way we think? How deep does narrative go? The cultural eliminativist position, as it is often espoused by materialists, will assert that narratives and other cultural product are non-material, so-called "epiphenomenal" products of the material brain, and that they, for the same reason, cannot influence the processes of and in the material brain. One representative of this orientation is Pascal Boyer and that clearly comes out in his work on the composition of religious representations (e.g. 2001). He has very usefully systematized the ways in which religious representations go against our everyday, intuitive ideas about the properties of things that surround us, such as persons, animals, plants, natural objects, and tools (artefacts). These common ideas are our "intuitive ontology" and religious (we may substitute "mythical" here) representations are characterized by going against these intuitive expectations that are supposedly the results of the workings of an innate mechanism that humans are born with.[5] Thus, religions (and myths) abound with strange subjects and objects: artefacts that can cure illness or mountains that can bring salvation, zombies, saints that fly or live forever – the list of such "counter-intuitive" notions is long. On Boyer's theory of religious representations, these are quite "natural," as evolutionary by-products, that is, results of the evolution of the flexibility of the brain. Religious counter-intuitive notions are so ordinary that one may talk about "The religious brain" as a common phenomenon that also accounts for the proliferation of beliefs in miracles and magic (Pyysiäinen 2004).

It was Boyer's original intention to find out what makes things memorable in oral traditions, and as noted, it turns out that *just* the right combination of ordinary story-telling, with the *appropriate* amount of counter-intuitive notions seem to secure memorability, the "cognitive optimum." These fieldwork based observations and hypotheses have later been supported by experimental psychological evidence. This obviously has interesting consequences for the study of myth because it does contribute to an explanation of the range of "oddities" of mythical discourse. But one thing is to show how the mind, the brain and all the cognitive properties and mechanisms contribute to the production and reproduction of socio-cultural materials, such as interesting narratives; quite another is the influence of socio-cultural materials on the brain.[6] We see how Boyer and other materialist and naturalist approaches (see e.g. Sperber 1996) are at a loss here, because as a consequence of their individualist methodology and their materialist ontology there can be no such "influences" that cause anything.

However, not only as students and scholars, but also as just human beings we have a quite robust intuition that cultural differences, socialization and the environments that we grow up in must "mean" something. There are other trends in the cognitive sciences and studies that ensue, for example, from developmental and social psychology, focus on the impact of the social and cultural (language, norms, roles, values, etc.) upon the cognitive. These trends are more interesting for our purpose, because they furnish myths and narrative with some authority and control over how we *learn* to think and feel. The question is how to combine the two types of approaches, those that cover the "inside out" and those that concentrate on "outside in" (Jensen 2002; Herman 2003).

The questions concerning the appropriation of culture, for example language, norms, roles, values, etc., are many. How is it possible to describe and explain the transmission of representations, beliefs, or, say the understanding of symbols from brain to culture and back again? In previous interactionist sociological and psychological theories these alternations were simply termed "externalization" and "internalization." However, the terms do not explain themselves, nor do their references, so a new field of investigation is forming around a cluster of theories and methods, including psychologies of language, discourse, culture and development as well as cognitive semantics and semiotics. To this may be added advances in the study of primates, evolutionary biology and neuroscience – and this all indicates the complexities of studying what comes so naturally to us: being human (Deacon 1997).

There are, however, many ways of becoming human in specific societies and cultures and these ways are not given biologically but through imitation, instruction, and training, directly or indirectly. One could easily imagine how different manuals for bringing up children in different societies could be (DeLoache and Gottlieb 2002). In order to be able to perform according to the expectations in any society, children must develop sensitivity to "sign-decoding," from simple signs of, say, danger, to complex symbols of authority. They have to become "symbol-minded" (DeLoache 2004). That is no simple feat and humans are the only animals that have developed such a capacity. It is the basis of all the world's cultures and the acquisition of language and all that follows from that. It is the basis for human cooperation. It allows us to do things together, to act, to think – and most relevant to an understanding of myths and mythologies – it even allows us to *imagine* things in the past, in the future or in "strange spaces." As noted by Kevin Oatley in a study on the role of inference in narrative and science:

> The success of our human adaptation is that humans, more than any other vertebrate species, can join together to do things that are too difficult to do alone. A great deal of thinking is of this kind. It includes thinking the thought prompted by reading a novel in a writerly way, and it includes scientific thinking. It is not so much that certain kinds of thinking are difficult in themselves. Rather, some of the overall patterns of thinking are too difficult for individuals: therefore we do them together, each of us taking on from time to time a different role in a larger, distributed, inferential process. (Oatley 1996, 139)

The ontogenesis of the individual is crucial here, not only physically and psychologically as an individual with biological properties, but ontogenesis in the wider perspective of "becoming a person," a normal human being, able to interact with others and understand their intentions. That is: a person able to function in a given culture.

Michael Tomasello, primatologist and developmental psychologist, has a clear-cut conception of the role of cultural cognition in ontogenesis. Language is of crucial importance for any individual. As a symbolic medium built upon the foundations of the capability of joint attention it allows us to proceed from the sharing of intentions to the understanding of very complex symbolic structures. As he says:

> My own view is that social and cultural processes – of a type that is common across all cultures – are an integral and essential part of the normal ontogenetic pathways of many of the most fundamental and universal skills of humans, especially those that are unique to the species. Some of these socio-cultural processes are so obvious that they are rarely commented upon by any theorist, for example, the "transmission" of knowledge and information from adults to children via language and other symbolic media. (1999, 162)

Extending the argument on the importance of symbolic knowledge, Tomasello adds (with a direct bearing on our subject):

> ...even nonliterate cultures have important domains of knowledge that are almost exclusively in symbolic format, and so they can be only be transmitted

symbolically – most clearly knowledge concerning things removed in space and time such as characteristics of distant relatives and ancestors, myths and some religious rituals, some knowledge of local flora and fauna. (1999, 165)

Natural language, of course, contains information but that is not all, because learning a natural language also involves socialization, learning to structure thought and action along the lines of one's culture. In a philosophy of language perspective it should be remembered that language and language use is always a normative affair that involves judgments and attitudes. Children thus also learn to attend to and conceptualize other aspects than those of their immediate world. This is because language presents conceptual categories and the perspectives of others that the child may use. One of the very important social skills is meta-cognitive self-monitoring and self-regulation. This is also learned via language: "...there is some evidence that these kinds of self-regulatory and metacognitive skills are related to adults using reflective meta-discourse with children – with the children then internalizing this discourse for use in regulating their own behaviour independently" (Tomasello 1999, 192). Children talk to themselves when they try to learn difficult tasks and the cognitive representation of the task is not simply instruction but dialogical, it is intersubjective. Such dialogues are a way of internalizing, through virtual imitation, the designs and procedures offered by others and available in the formats that prevail locally. Thus, it is not only our own intuition, but there is also concrete scientific evidence that individual minds are (at least partly) constituted through inter-subjectivity, symbolic activities and discourse. This happens predominantly in early life, but it does not stop there. In Rom Harré's and Grant Gillet's theory of discursive psychology the human mind continues to be moulded by experience.

> Throughout life, the brain stores 'experience in terms of the meanings' that have structured that experience and the responses made by the individual to aspects of the events experienced. We have argued that the meanings used to structure the responses of an individual draw on rules that have been shaped in human discourse. This implies there must be a deep relation between the language that a community speaks and the categorizations or significations that members of the community use to unify stimulus presentations and group them into meaningful patterns. (1994, 81–82)[8]

Again, we may keep in mind Clastres' account of what made the Indians laugh. It is also an indication of how and why religions "work" as symbolic structures. Not only are our stories arranged in the form of narrative, but our interpretive apparatus, our epistemic faculties may be much more dependent on getting or arranging information in narrative formats than otherwise conceived. Mark Turner, literary scholar and cognitive scientist, demonstrates how narrative and grammatical structures are related and what they confer to cognitive development. Children's acquisition of grammatical competence "could reinforce the learning of story structure." The acquisition of language has tremendous consequences in Turner's view:

The learning of a language may quite literally change the neurobiology of the infant in ways that are influential over cognition. This creates the intriguing possibility that speech and writing could be ways for the brain of one person to exert biological influence upon the brain of another person: thinking may be affected abidingly by experience with language.

If we use the old metaphoric conception of the brain as an agent who "deals with" language or as a container that for a moment "holds" language while examining it for storage or discard, then it is natural to think of the biology of the brain as unchanged by its dealings with language. But if we use instead the conception of the brain as an active and plastic biological system, we are led to consider a rather different range of hypotheses: The brain is changed importantly by experience with language; language is an instrument used by separate brains to exert influence on each other, creating through biological action at a distance a *virtual* brain distributed in the individual brains of all the participants in the culture; early experience with language affects cognitive operations that go beyond language. (1996, 159–60)

Consider myths again. In the course of cultural evolution they may have been very active, "hardworking forces," for they survived. For the most part evolution does not discard something that works and that principle probably also applies to the products of cultural evolution. Merlin Donald, neuroscientist and developmental psychologist, has set forward a complex hypothesis on the origin and function of cultural institutions in a phylogenetic perspective, that is, how the development of culture has co-evolved with the development of the mind. As Donald says, and it is hard to disagree with this: "the cognitive tools that we use to do much of our thinking seem to be dependent on our cultural institutions, and all our symbolic tools are imported from the outside – that is, from culture" (2001, xiii). In this way, cultural artefacts such as symbols, myths and religious representations cease to be evolutionary by-products but become, instead, co-responsive for the development of the human mind as a complex consisting of both brains and the symbolic materials they handle, "The human mind is thus a 'hybrid' product of biology and culture." According to Donald:

> The key to understanding the human intellect is not so much the design of the individual brain as the synergy of many brains. We have evolved an adaptation for living in culture, and our exceptional powers as a species derive from the curious fact that we have broken out of one of the most critical limitations of traditional nervous systems – their loneliness, or solipsism. From our earliest birth as a species, humanity has relied upon creating "distributed" systems of thought and memory, in which intellectual work is shared across many nervous systems. (2001, xiii)

As a consequence, for humans with "hybrid minds," "…any given culture is a gigantic cognitive web, defining and constraining the parameters of memory, knowledge, and thoughts in its members, both as individuals and as a group" (xiv). It is obvious to see myths and mythologies as part and parcel of such cultural forms of memory, knowledge, and thoughts. Among the roles performed by myth is that of preserving shared cultural memory and so reproducing the "collectivity of mind." Like other external symbol entities and structures ("exograms") they are a great aid to memory of what is significant, because they give us "stable, permanent, virtually unlimited memory records that are infinitely reformattable and more easily displayed to awareness" (2001, 309). The sum total of these external cultural devices makes up "symbolic technologies" – to which myths and mythologies belong. Although so far relatively unchartered territory, cognitive approaches to myths and mythologies appear to hold promising potentials, especially when sensitive to language and culture.

In a previous work, Donald contemplated the possible lines of cultural evolution and suggested the term "mythic culture" for a phase of early language development with language as a social device, useful for social organization and cooperation but also for metaphorical thought and conceptual modelling. It is fitting to let Donald have the last word here in this section – with what seems a plausible hypothesis about the place of myth in human evolution:

> The myth is the prototypal, fundamental, integrative mind tool. It tries to integrate a variety of events in a temporal and causal framework. It is inherently a modeling device, whose *primary* level of representation is thematic. The pre-eminence of myth in early human society is testimony that humans were using language for a totally new kind of integrative thought. Therefore, the possibility must be entertained that the primary human adaptation was not language *qua* language but rather integrative, initially mythical, thought. Modern humans developed language in response to pressure to improve their conceptual apparatus, not vice versa. (1991, 215; original italics)

Contributions

Edwin Hutchins

Edwin Hutchins is Professor of Cognitive Science at the University of California, San Diego, where he earned his PhD in Anthropology in 1978. He worked extensively on the conceptual structures underlying Melanesian practices of land litigation and of the native Micronesian navigation systems used by local sailors to find islands in the vast Pacific Ocean. He also studied Melanesian culture and myth. He later coined the term "cognition in the wild" in his study of navigation practices on the bridge of a large navy ship, where he demonstrates how the attention and information processed by a group of persons interact as joint cognitive products (1995). This also led to later work on the problems of designing airplane cockpits. Hutchins' primary research is on human cognitive activity in "real-life" situations, where cognition processes are not only about what goes on in heads, but among individual minds in what is called "Distributed," or "Social" cognition. The current contribution links psychoanalytic and cognitive reflections on the relations between socio-cultural patterns, individual psychology and the function of myth. In its own interesting ways it also links to the studies that Malinowski did in the same location – among the Trobrianders. The original publication, an anthology (1987), was the result of the work of a group of scholars, anthropologists, linguists and psychologists, with a common interest in "cultural models" – the models by which humans conceive of themselves, their actions and their worlds. Hutchins' contribution comes from the section on "Negotiating social and psychological realities." In his formulation, "we can see why it is that the sacred myths are so adamantly defended. They are formulations that from the Trobriander's perspective *must be true*. Were they not true, then experience would be exceedingly threatening." That is because myth is "an interpretive resource" that provides understanding of troubling aspects of human life and experience.

Bradd Shore

Bradd Shore is Professor of Anthropology at Emory University in Georgia, USA. He did fieldwork in Western Samoa on kinship and social control. He also published the work *Sala'ilua: A Samoan Mystery* about ethnopsychology of Polynesia. Shore's major recent work is *Culture in Mind: Cognition, Culture, and the Problem of Meaning* from 1996. To Shore, culture is an intrinsic component of the human mind and in his work about cultural models and their cognitive aspects and functions he distinguishes sharply between information processing and cultural meaning construction as a form of "explanatory understanding" where cognitive processes play a crucial role:

> *Cultural meaning construction* is a kind of assimilation, requiring two distinct cognitive processes. First, a conventional form of cognitive model is derived from instituted models present in the social environment. Second, a novel experience is organized for an individual in relation to this conventional cognitive model, providing a significant degree of sharing in the way individuals within a community experience the world. Cultural cognition is a special kind of meaning-seeking activity closely related to more general processes of meaning construction. (1996, 319)

It is obvious how myths provide cultural models and patterns as part of such meaning-seeking activities. This takes place in all kinds of societies and generally in a state of flux, in history. Thus, cultures are not fixed entities but "historically contingent artefacts": "At any given time in the life of a community, however, the stock of models is usually sufficiently stable to produce among its members the sense of living in a 'natural' universe with a shared stock of common resources for making sense out of things" (371).

Shore has also developed the research project "MARIAL" on "Myth and Ritual and American Life." The project is intended to demonstrate how ritual, myths, and mythologies are still important in modern society, for, although the formats and the media may change, "invisible" myths in more or less structured clusters of representations, bits of narratives and scraps of motifs are as important for human thought and behaviour as they ever were. The contribution chosen here amply demonstrates Shore's points about myth and it role in the creation and maintenance of knowledge in culture and in cognition. The analysis is complicated but its results are rewarding.

Jerome Bruner

Jerome Bruner was born in New York City in 1915 and educated at Duke University. He served in US Army intelligence work during World War II, completed his PhD (psychology) at Harvard where he also helped to set up the well-known Center for Cognitive Studies there. For a while he was professor at the University of Oxford, before returning to New York City. His contribution to psychology has been vast in a number of areas, especially in developmental and cognitive areas. Bruner's publications are numerous and his influence outside psychology is also remarkable, not least in the field of education theory. Not least of interest in this connection: he has worked consistently to bring culture and cultural products (myth could be one) into developmental psychology. His theorizing owes much to inspiration from the psychologist Lev Vygotsky (1896–1934) who regarded language an important "tool" for the developing child. From early on, Bruner began studies on the effects of emotion and needs on infant perception as well as the factors in experiences and environments that are formative for the development patterns of individuals. Important here are the effects of language and other forms of representation, because humans are capable not just of representing experience, but also of transforming it through the use of symbolic media. One important aspect of his more socially oriented psychology to us here is his later interest in the internalization and use of narrative (1986). According to Bruner, all human cognitive activity involves the use of categories in order to make sense of the world. Often, in such processes, we need to make inferences and guesses, and go beyond the information at hand and what we already know in order to deal with experiences. The inferences are driven by our previous experience, but this experience may also be vicarious, that is, something we have been informed about by others, orally, literally or other means of representation. Cultures are symbolic constructs that include repertoires and reservoirs of inference potentials. For the same reason, the use of narrative, for example myth, enables us to make our lived-in reality sensible because narratives provide frameworks for organizing experience and contextualizing information and thereby calibrating our worlds, even those that are imagined. Bruner's cultural psychology is slightly relativist (at the descriptive level) in that he sees different cultures as having different patterns of behaviour and thought as *their* relevant media for meaning making. His cultural psychology includes views from anthropology, linguistics, sociology, and philosophy. Bruner thus succeeds in weaving together many of the strands that have been of concern throughout this volume.

Andy Clark

Andy Clark, Professor of Philosophy at the University of Edinburgh, did his PhD in philosophy at the University of Stirling in 1984, and has also held the position of director of the Philosophy/Neuroscience/Psychology Program at Washington University in St. Louis. Clark is a philosopher with strong cross-disciplinary interests, in psychology, the cognitive sciences and particularly in theories of "distributed cognition" which hold that human cognition involves processes that go beyond the individual brain, much like Donald's idea of the "hybrid mind." Thus, the "special kind of smartness" of human beings, says Clark, may not only be due to features of the biological brain, but to the "architecture of a kind of extended hybrid system incorporating biological and non-biological elements, each performing different (but closely matched and complementary) kinds of operation." The main resource for such properties of human cognitive interaction is language, but many other media may be involved as well. In this contribution Clark (1997) describes language as the ultimate artefact, for example, because: "Language stands revealed as a key resource by which we effectively redescribe our own thoughts in a format that makes them available for a variety of new operations and manipulation." He adds: "Much of what we commonly identify as our mental capacities may likewise, I suspect, turn out to be properties of the wider, environmentally extended systems of which human brains are just one (important) part." If Clark is right in so imagining, we may see very different prospects for myths and the study of them: they are symbolic and mental environments to be taken seriously and although products of the imagination, and sometime even of *wild* imagination, they are instantiations of an imagination that makes a difference – a "world making" difference.

Notes

1. A good historical and thematic overview of relevance to the study of religion (and myth) is Geertz 2005. Bechtel et al. 1998 contains an exposition from a cognitive science perspective. Roy D'Andrade 1995 is to be recommended for its overview of the development in anthropology.
2. See very critical views of Chomsky in Donald 2001 and Tomasello 1999.
3. One main reason for this has been the lack of methods suited to investigate this in controlled experimental settings. New technologies, e.g. brain scanning, may provide possibilities for such research.
4. See Fauconnier 1997 on blending theory.
5. Thus this position is often referred to as "nativism."

6. It should be noted that there are massive disagreements about most of the issues pertaining to the cognitive studies, also of religion. See e.g. Donald 2001 for a critique of the "hardliner" (materialist, nativist, etc.) position.

7. The idea of becoming "normal" is of course a normative judgment which to some extent is relative to culture, but there are many more human universals involved here than often imagined, and all cultures have ideas about "normal" behaviour. It is a thorny anthropological issue and this is not the place to discuss it. However, both Tomasello and Donald address these issues.

8. Most of this also seems to relate to what happens in education – even at higher levels. This is probably why education works at all.

References

Bechtel, William, Adele Abrahamsen and George Graham. 1998. "The Life of Cognitive Science." In *A Companion to Cognitive Science*, 1–104. Oxford: Blackwell.

Boyer, Pascal. 2001. *Religion Explained: The Evolutionary Origins of Religious Thought*. New York: Basic Books.

Bruner, Jerome. 1986. *Actual Minds, Possible Worlds*. Cambridge, MA: Harvard University Press.

Clark, Andy. 1997. *Being There: Putting Brain, Body, and the World Together Again*. Cambridge, MA: MIT Press.

D'Andrade, Roy. 1995. *The Development of Cognitive Anthropology*. Cambridge: Cambridge University Press.

Deacon, Terrence. 1997. *The Symbolic Species: The Co-evolution of Language and the Human Brain*. Harmondsworth: Penguin.

DeLoache, Judy S. 2004. "Becoming Symbol-minded." *Trends in Cognitive Science* 8/2: 66–70.

DeLoache, Judy S. and Alma Gottlieb, eds. 2002. *A World of Babies: Imagined Childcare Guides for Seven Societies*. Cambridge: Cambridge University Press.

Donald, Merlin. 1991. *Origins of the Modern Mind: Three Stages in the Evolution of Culture and Cognition*. Cambridge, MA: Harvard University Press.

_____2001. *A Mind So Rare: The Evolution of Human Consciousness*. New York: Norton.

Fauconnier, Gilles. 1997. *Mappings in Thought and Language*. Cambridge: Cambridge University Press.

Geertz, Armin W. 2005. "Cognitive Approaches to the Study of Religion." In *New Approaches to the Study of Religion*, ed. Peter Antes, Armin W. Geertz and Randi Warne, 347–99. Berlin: Walter de Gruyter.

Harré, Rom and Grant Gillet. 1994. *The Discursive Mind*. Thousand Oaks, CA and London: Sage Publications.

Herman, David, ed. 2003. *Narrative Theory and the Cognitive Sciences*. Stanford: Center for the Study of Language and Information.

Hutchins, Edwin. 1995. *Cognition in the Wild*. Cambridge, MA: MIT Press.

Jensen, Jeppe Sinding. 2002. "The Complex World of Religion: Connecting Cultural and Cognitive Analysis." In *Religion, Cognition and Cultural Context*, ed. Ilkka Pyysiäinen and Veikko Anttonen, 203–25. London: Continuum.

Lakoff, George and Mark Johnson. 1980. *Metaphors We Live By*. Chicago: University of Chicago Press.

Leach, Edmund. 1976. *Culture and Communication: The Logic by which Symbols are Connected*. Cambridge: Cambridge University Press.

Oatley, Keith. 1996. "Inference in Narrative and Science." In *Modes of Thought: Explorations in Culture and Cognition*, ed. David R. Olson and Nancy Torrance, 123–40. Cambridge: Cambridge University Press.

Pyysiäinen, Ilkka. 2004. *Magic, Miracles, and Religion: A Scientist's Perspective*. Walnut Creek, CA: Altamira Press.

Shelley, Cameron and Paul Thagard. 1996. "Mythology and Analogy." In *Modes of Thought: Explorations in Culture and Cognition*, ed. David R. Olson and Nancy Torrance, 152–83. Cambridge: Cambridge University Press.

Shore, Bradd. 1996. *Culture in Mind: Cognition, Culture, and the Problem of Meaning*. New York: Oxford University Press.

Sperber, Dan. 1996. *Explaining Culture: A Naturalistic Approach*. Oxford: Blackwell.

Tomasello, Michael. 1999. *The Cultural Origins of Human Cognition*. Cambridge, MA: Harvard University Press.

Turner, Mark. 1996. *The Literary Mind: The Origins of Thought and Language*. New York: Oxford University Press.

Myth and Experience in the Trobriand Islands[1]

Edwin Hutchins

This chapter examines how the knowledge of a myth is brought to bear on the interpretation of experience. This topic requires an eclectic approach since the issues it raises are simultaneously part of a venerable tradition in anthropology concerning the role of myth in society and part of a new research area in cognitive science concerning the nature of the processes by which people interpret and understand their world.

The experiences to be interpreted are those surrounding an encounter between a Trobriand Island village and the spirit of one of its recently deceased members. I begin with a brief ethnographic sketch of the nature of spirits of the dead in the Trobriand Islands, which will enable the reader to make sense of the events reported. The next section describes an actual case of a spirit haunting a village. This haunting set the stage for the phenomenon we wish to understand – that is, an old woman's account of how she saw a cosmological question in these events and how a sacred myth provided her with an answer to her question. The heart of the paper is an examination of the relationship between the myth itself and the phenomena it is marshaled to explain. I argue that the myth has two kinds of connections to experience. One is an explicit link based on a belief in the power of mythic events as historical precedents. The events in the myth are seen as causes of important aspects of the experience. The second kind of connection is an implicit and unadmitted link based on a similarity of organization between the events of the myth and the experience of events of life. Although the historical link is emphasized by Trobrianders, an examination of the implicit link based on shared structure shows the myth to be a transformed description of repressed thoughts about contemporary relations between the living and spirits of the dead. That is, the myth is shown to be a cultural defence mechanism. I conclude with a discussion of how this role of myth bears on two otherwise anomalous properties of myths: the tenacity of native belief and the radical disjunction between historical time and mythic time.

The Ways of the Spirits

The class of beings that are spirits of the dead in the Trobriands all fall under the generic term *baloma*. In some contexts, including the recitation of myth, the archaic term *yaluwa* may be used instead. Within the category of spirits of the dead are several subcategories that partition the world of spirits on the basis of some of their salient attributes (see figure). Each category has a specific term associated with it. It is important to note that *baloma* occurs both as a generic term for all spirits of the dead and as an unmarked specific term that can stand in contrast to other specific types of spirits.

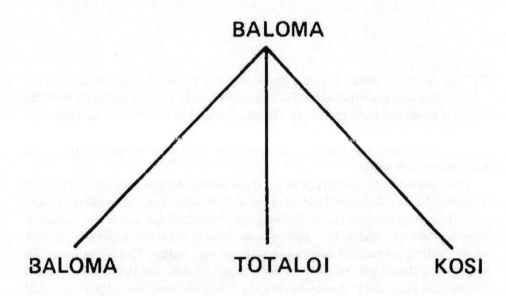

Fig 1.

Baloma

Before the marked terms can be discussed, more needs to be said about the nature of the unmarked specific category of *baloma*.[2] When a person dies, his or her *baloma* leaves the body and goes to reside on the island of Tuma, a real island located about 10 miles northwest of the main island in the Trobriand group. Arriving at Tuma, the *baloma* meets a spirit named Topileta, who "acts as a kind of Cerberus or St. Peter in so far as he admits the spirit into the nether world, and is even supposed to be able to refuse admission" (Malinowski 1954, 156).

The *baloma* "live" normal lives on Tuma and return to their natal villages during the harvest season each year to partake of the spiritual goodness of harvested yams and valuables placed for them on special platforms out of doors. While they are in the village, the *baloma* sometimes indulge in mildly annoying pranks, such as making noises and moving things, but people do not find them eerie nor do they fear them the way Europeans fear ghosts. At the end of the harvest feast, the *baloma* are unceremoniously driven from the village by gangs of children who shout and swing sticks. This driving-out is called *yoba*. The *baloma* then return to Tuma, where they remain until the next year's harvest feast.

At any time of the year, *baloma* may intercede invisibly in human affairs by bringing bad luck to people who have behaved badly. For example, a village that is constantly embroiled in petty squabbles may find a poor harvest because the *baloma* of the village feel that the people have not comported themselves with dignity.

Baloma frequently appear in dreams or even to people who are awake to announce to a woman that she will become pregnant or to suggest a course of action to an important person. In such cases, the *baloma* is seen and recognized as a person who once lived. The only other circumstances in which *baloma* are visible to the living are those near the boundary of life and death. A person on a deathbed may see into the spirit world while speaking to those in the world of the living who are keeping the death vigil. Also, the spirits of the recently deceased may appear to the living. In the latter case, the terminology of spirits of the dead is elaborated in reference to the behavior of the spirits.

Totaloi

The spirits of the recently dead sometimes linger for a day or two after death to say goodbye to loved-ones. They may present themselves to persons either in dream or awake. These spirits are called *totaloi*, from the root *-taloi*, referring to the minor rituals of leave-taking performed by socially engaged persons when they part company. Such encounters are sad, but not at all frightening. For example, the spirit of a young girl appeared to her mother the day after her death to request that her favorite hymn be sung in church.

Kosi

Other spirits called *kosi* stay around the village longer and frighten people. They are much more malevolent than *baloma*. When a *kosi* is in a village at night, villagers say that it "rounds the village." The verb "round" describes the movement of the spirit from house to house through the roughly circular layout of the village. The literalness of this usage was not apparent to me until, on the nights of the encounter described below, I could actually follow the progress of the *kosi* as the screams of those visited emanated first from one part of the village, then from another.

The unpleasantness and the duration of visits from *kosi* are said to be related to the social character of the deceased while he or she was alive. If the deceased was a sorcerer, an adulterer, or a thief, for example, the *kosi* is expected to be malicious and will remain in the village for a long time. Some of my informants speculated, in contradiction to Malinowski (1954, 156), that the reason the *kosi* of evil people stay in the village for a long time is that Topileta refuses them entry at Tuma and they then have no place to go.[3]

According to Malinowski (1954, 154), *kosi* are only encountered out of doors. In the days following the death of a villager, the sound of footfall in darkness on a jungle path at night or the otherwise unexplained rustling of vegetation in the deceased's garden enclosure may be taken as evidence of the presence of a *kosi*. In the village, a *kosi* might call out a person's name or throw a stone or slap the thatched wall of a house much as a *baloma* might do during the harvest season. Summing up the reaction of Trobrianders in his times, Malinowski called *kosi*, "the frivolous and meek ghost of the deceased who vanishes after a few days of irrelevant existence" (1954, 154). Modern-day Trobrianders agree that Malinowski's description is an accurate depiction of the behavior of *kosi* in the past, but times have changed. In more recent times, in addition to frightening people with their poltergeistlike activities out of doors, *kosi* have taken to confronting people in a visible form in their homes as they lie in what we would call hypnagogic sleep. The Trobrianders call this state *kilisala* and describe it as resting with the eyes closed, but with the ears open and the mind awake. They are adamant that it is not sleep, and the events experienced in that state are real events of this world, not dreams or hallucinations. The assertion that these events are real is supported by items of evidence such as the fact that *kosi* knock things off of shelves and throw stones on the roof when everyone is wide awake. In those contexts though, the *kosi* is not seen.

Encounter with a Kosi

In March 1976, Toigisasopa (a pseudonym), a prominent and feared citizen of a large Trobriand village, died. For more than a month following his death, the village was plagued by almost nightly visits from his *kosi*. Occasionally, the *kosi* appeared as the ghoulish figure of the rotting corpse of the deceased. As time went on, his reported appearance became increasingly revolting.

The following is a translation of an excerpt of an interview with a woman who had twice been visited by this *kosi*.

He was out walking about and he came to our place. I woke and saw him come in. His face was awful – completely black, his arms and legs were like those of an undernourished child and his belly was bloated. He just came in and grabbed my legs. I lay there. My body was completely numb and paralysed. Then I kicked and the old man [her husband] felt me kicking. He roused me and I grabbed him and cried out. He asked, "What was it?" "Toigisasopa's ghost!" By then my body was recovering from numbness a bit. The stench was awful. The first time he just looked black, but this second time, you know, it was as if there were holes in his body as well. It gave the house a terrible odor.

Myth Interprets Life

For nearly a month, I heard reports of the activities of the ghost. Many villagers reported evidence of the *kosi*'s presence, and the village as a whole was quite disturbed by the length of the stay of the *kosi*.[4] Near the end of Toigisasopa's stay in the village, an old woman came to me with the following account.

One night as she lay in her house, she heard banging on the side of her neighbor's house and heard her neighbor's yelling to drive the *kosi* away. She later reported:

I had gotten up and was sitting there. I thought, "perhaps that was a *kosi*." This one will not soon disappear because when he went to Tuma, Topileta closed [the way in]. Because he was a thief. He stole seed yams in the garden, and whatever he saw unattended in the village he would put in his basket as well. Everyone saw him do it. You see, this was his one bad habit. It was nothing of consequence; he seemed a good man except for this. Now he has died. Who knows, perhaps he was a sorcerer, perhaps... Anyway, I thought to myself, "Why is it that the *kosi* and *baloma* see us, but we do not see them?"

She said that in considering this question, she remembered that it had not always been so. Long ago, the *baloma* would come into the village and sit with their kin, chewing betel nut and conversing in a pleasant way. They were generally amicable and even helpful. This old woman remembered the myth of Baroweni, and it, she claimed, provided the answers to her questions.

Myths form one of several classes of oral tradition in the Trobriands. The major distinction of importance here is between sacred myths, called *liliu* or *libogwa* and folk tales, *kukwanebu*. Both *liliu* and *kukwanebu* are sometimes performed in the story-telling sessions that occupy many idle hours in the rainy season. The events that are depicted in both genres are placed in time long, long ago beyond the stretch of ordinary historical time. *Kukwanebu* are told largely for their entertainment value, and tend to be a bit bawdy, whereas *liliu* are thought to have a message and the events they describe are often taken as historical precedents for the states of affairs in the contemporary world. Some myths establish sociocultural precedents concerning the ownership of land and the ranking of descent groups. Others concern fundamental states of existence, such as the inevitability of aging and death or, in the myth of Baroweni, the invisibility of the spirits of the dead.

The Myth of Baroweni

A full translation of the telling of the myth as I recorded it is given below. I have included some additional commentary on a paragraph-by-paragraph basis where the telling of the myth assumes listener knowledge that is particular to Trobriand culture. By and large, these are things that from the Trobriand perspective go without saying.

> Hey, Baroweni's mother had died. She had died and Baroweni was already pregnant. When she was due to give birth, another woman in the village was dying. She was on the verge of death – they had already made the mortuary preparations for her. Baroweni went to her and said, "Go to my mother. Tell my mother, 'Hey, your child is pregnant and will soon give birth. Take food to her.'"

This section establishes the relationships of the major actors in the myth to each other. The mother/daughter relationship cited is important because Trobriand mothers have a special obligation to care for their pregnant daughters. In fact, the female matrilineal kin of the pregnant woman are responsible for feeding and caring for both the new mother and the infant for several months after birth. Asking a dying person to take messages to Tuma is a common occurrence. Trobrianders make no effort to conceal their assessment of an ailing person's chances of survival from that person, and those who are about to die provide an obvious communications link between the world of the living and the world of the dead.

> So the dying woman died and went [to Tuma]. She told her companion there [Baroweni's mother], "Your child is pregnant and close to giving birth, but what shall she eat?" She said, "She told me to come and tell you, 'You should take food to her.'"
> So the spirit [Baroweni's mother] got up and began cutting taro shoots. She raised the taro shoots onto her head and rose up (as a spirit rises when it leaves the corporal body). She came. She continued on, what's it, at Tuma on the main beach at Kuruvitu, on their beach at Tuma. She came ashore and continued on there to Libutuma.

There is an interesting mixing of attributes here. The spirit carries her load on her head as all Trobriand women do, yet the verb used to describe her rising is not one used for a woman, but one used to describe the rising of a spirit from a corporeal body.

> [directed to me] Shall I sing the song that you might hear it?

> "Baroweni, Baroweni, Baroweniweni. I will set it down, I will set it down. Oh, my neck. Oh, my neck ... Oh, my neck. We [inclusive dual form] suppose a girl is standing with us whose name is *yaluwa*."

As we shall see, variants of this ditty are sung at several points in the story. Baroweni's mother whines her daughter's name and complains of her desire to set down her load and the pain it causes in her weak spirit neck. The last phrase in the ditty suggests a dual persona for the mother. She supposes or assumes a girl is standing with her, but her name is just *yaluwa* or spirit.

> So she walked and cried, and in that way she entered a village. She just cried, she was crying for her child. Because she was a spirit she couldn't touch anything or hold it. She had already died, and there was nothing she could hold.

This makes clear the source of the mother's discomfort. She is carrying real taro, but as a spirit, she is known to be unable to carry anything. The explanation of this comes in the next sentence of the telling of the myth.

> However, this is a *liliu*. This happened long long ago and for that reason [it is as it is].

Here is the first of several indications that inferences based on present-day understandings of the world are not always applicable to myth. That it happened long, long ago is sufficient explanation of events that violate common-sense knowledge. I return to this point later.

> [She just continued on to – what's its name – Yalaka ... Buduwelaka. Yes at Buduwelaka she was just the same, crying, crying for her child.

> "Baroweni, Baroweni, Baroweniweni. I will set it down, I will set it down. Oh, my neck Ya! Oh, my neck. She just scoops it up the girl that stands with us [inclusive dual]. Her name is *yaluwa*. We are surely overloaded."
> This because she had already died.

The ditty Baroweni's mother sings is a magic spell she uses to cause the taro to be carried. Since she is dead, she cannot carry things in a normal fashion. Notice that the mother's persona is completely confounded with that of the spirit girl whose presence she invokes. She says she herself would like to put the basket down, it is her neck that hurts, yet she refers to herself and the spirit girl using the inclusive dual form of the first person pronoun.

> She just brought it and continued on to Okupukopu. At Okupukopu she chanted just the same as she was crying, crying for her child.

> "Baroweni, Baroweni, Baroweniweni. I will set it down, I will set it down. Oh, my neck. Oh, my neck. Oh, my neck Ya! Oh, my neck. What is her name? What is she? Girl or person? But her name is *yaluwa*."
> Because she was already dead there was nothing she could touch or carry on her head. And this: she was of the time long ago, our [exclusive plural] ancestor's time. [*then, directed to me*] I shall take it to its conclusion that you should grasp it?

The use of the exclusive plural possessive form here in referring to the ancestors makes it clear that these asides about the time of the ancestors and the special nature of events that happened then are directed at me as an outsider to the culture. I suspect she uses this form in order to say, "This is how it was with Trobriand ancestors. How it was with your European ancestors is irrelevant."

> She continued on from Okupukopu to Ilalima. At Ilalima it was just the same. She went then to Osapoula.
> It was night when she arrived and everyone was sleeping. She knocked on the coconut fronds [the wall of the house]. Her child woke up and said, "Who are you?"

Having the spirit mother arrive in the village at night is plausible since spirits are most active at night. It also simplifies the story because even though the mother is at this point in time a visible spirit, it is possible for her to go unseen in the darkness while the village sleeps.

> She said, "I am your mother. I have brought your food. Open the house."

> Her child opened up her house. She went to her and saw her mother putting down the food basket she had been carrying on her head. In the night there she [mother] told her, she said, "Hey, go prepare the area behind the house as if, wa, as if you were to plant flowers there."
> She said, "Take these (the taro stalks) and bury them. They will be yours to eat with your child. When the seed root has sprouted, cut off the side roots. Cut off the side roots and replant the seed. The side roots alone you shall eat with your son. You prepare behind the house. I shall go, beside the house and sit. I shall be watching you."

This is interesting since a family metaphor is commonly applied to the form of taro propagation referred to here. The seed corm is called *inala*, mother, and the side roots are referred to as *litula*, her children (Malinowski 1965, vol. 2, 105–6). Given the traditional importance of yams in the maintenance of descent group identity in the Trobriands, it is surprising that the mother brought taro rather than yams to feed her daughter. It is possible that the existence of this metaphor for taro propagation, which has no parallel in the cultivation of yams, made taro a more felicitous symbolic choice than yams.

> Her mother spoke well. She told her she would sit beside the house and watch, but Baroweni by herself was already going on with her things. She forgot. She boiled her food and ate. Her mother was sitting there watching her. She [Baroweni] picked up that container, a coconut shell bowl, a soup bowl. Like those containers that the Lukwasisiga clan drank from. She just picked it up, drank her fill and threw it out beside the house. She threw it out and it drenched her mother's body. Her mother felt it.

> She said, "Hey! Why did you dump that on me?"

She said, "Oh my! Mother mine, chieftan's wife. Mother no . . . I just forgot. I forgot about you. [Don't be angry] because it can't be a killing since you are already a *baloma*."

This event is outrageous in the Trobriand view of things. Remember that Baroweni's mother had gone to great effort and borne great pain to meet her responsibilities to her daughter. Trobriand children have a like set of responsibilities to their parents. Meeting these obligations is called *velina*, and failing to meet them has moral as well as jural consequences. When children are young and need support, parents supply what is needed. When parents grow old, the roles are reversed. Children must care for their parents in their old age. This role reversal is sometimes marked by a mother addressing her grown daughter as *inagu*, "my mother." When parents become infirm and require constant care, this job falls largely on the grown children. It is they who must feed their aged parents, bathe them, and, if necessary, carry them on their backs away from the village so that they can defecate in the privacy of the forest. These responsibilities, burdensome though they may be, are taken very seriously by all. It is understandable, however, that parents sometimes complain about not being well treated by their children, and children sometimes come to resent the imposition of a parent's needs on their lives. Here in the myth, Baroweni has failed to meet her obligations to her mother and she has done so in a particularly offensive way. Her mother brought food, and Baroweni has thrown food on her mother. Worse yet, she has done so, she says, because she has forgotten about her mother.

She said, "You have thrown out my soup. I shall return [to Tuma]. I shall return, I shall go. You will stay here. I will split our [inclusive dual consumable] coconut. The lower half is yours. The half with the eyes is mine. [*Directed to me*] Where is that coconut? [*I produce a coconut and she demonstrates*].

She split the coconut. "This half is yours. The end with eyes we shall drink, and it will be my coconut. I will go. I will go and then I will come back and see you. You shall not see me."

This ritual performance concludes the actual telling of the myth itself. The symbolism of the eyes in the coconut is not as transparent as it seems. The end of the coconut without eyes is called *kwesibuna*, which means literally the "cold" part. So the mother has not only taken the eyes, she has taken the "hot" end of the coconut in a world where hot is potent and powerful.

Commentary on the Myth

The remainder of the text is the old woman's commentary on the myth and her attempts to show the connection of the myth to the world of experience.

[*Commentary*] Look, now-a-days people die and go [to Tuma] and their *kosi* come around, but we can't see them. He [Toigisasopa's *kosi*] sees us and wakes us

345

up, but we do not see him, and this is the reason. Our ancestors have changed things. They come and see us. Our fathers and mothers die and go away and then they come back and are watching us. We see them not. But this old woman in times long ago started this. This particular *liliu* here. Some think it is just a fairy tale [*kukwanebu*], but it is real *liliu*.

However, if that woman, Baroweni had not done that, had not thrown out the soup, our mothers would be with us now. We would die. Later we would come back and stay and be seen. But here she made her mistake. She grabbed that soup cup, drank from it and threw it out, hitting her mother who was beside the house. The old woman cast an appropriate spell. She said, "Why did you throw soup on my body?"

Notice the inference here: had Baroweni not made her mistake, our parents would be with us, that is, visible to us, now. This is a direct connection between the myth and the situation of life as it is experienced.

She said, "Oh, mother, I forgot about you."

She said, "You yourself have banished me. You have injured me. I will go back [to Tuma]."

Here, the terms of the mother's interpretation of Baroweni's act has escalated. The mother has no sympathy for Baroweni's excuse. She has equated Baroweni's mistake with a grievous form of social punishment, *yoba*, banishment from one's village.

She got a coconut and told her child, she said, "I will split it in half you see. The lower end is yours. The end with eyes is mine. I will go away. When I come back, I will see you. You will not see me." So she went back and stayed.

You see, the other day when Toigisasopa was going around the village as a spirit. We did not see him. Except those who saw him all blackened. Look, [*makes empty circles around her eyes with index fingers and thumbs*] with his eye sockets empty. His whole body was black and when he went to someone, that's what they would see. This was just sleepers, in *kilisala* of course, who saw him thus. The other day I was listening to them screaming in the village. I thought to myself, "What is the source of this? Oh, this thing from long ago." My mind went to these words [this myth].

This is what the old woman had to say by way of explanation for the perceived invisibility of the spirits of the dead. By her account, she has used her knowledge of a myth to find an interpretation of an important and puzzling aspect of life. That in itself is perhaps interesting, but not entirely surprising. It is a confirmation of Malinowski's claim that "myth is not an idle tale, but a hard worked active force" (1954, 101). However, more remains to be said about how the force of myth is brought to bear on life.

The Historical Connection

In her commentary on the story, the old woman emphasizes the fact that the story of Baroweni is the reason for the invisibility of the spirits of the dead. Baroweni's mother declared that Baroweni would no longer see her. The relevance of this myth to the events surrounding the poltergeist behavior of the *kosi* in the village is based on the perception of the *kosi* as an (usually) invisible spirit of the dead. The connection is purported to be historical and causal, where the causality of the connection is based in the cosmological status of *liliu*, sacred myths. The actions of Baroweni's mother (as a spirit) with respect to Baroweni (as a living person) set a precedent for all subsequent relations between spirits and living persons. This causal connection appears in discourse in the form of a pervasive Trobriand metaphor. The myth is the *uula*, root or cause of the current state of affairs, which is, in turn, the *dogina*, extremity or result of the myth. According to the old woman's account, it was this causal connection that led her from her question about the invisibleness of spirits of the dead to the myth of Baroweni. On this view, the events described in the myth were identified as the cause of the salient aspect of the experience.

This connection is also the one emphasized by Malinowski in his analysis of the role of myth in primitive psychology. In considering several related myths including another version of myth of Baroweni, which he had collected, he notes that such myths provide mundane precedents for some very unpleasant facts of life.

> What it actually does is to transform an emotionally overwhelming foreboding, behind which, even for a native, there lurks the idea of an inevitable and ruthless fatality. Myth presents, first of all, a clear realization of this idea. In the second place, it brings down a vague, but great apprehension to the compass of a trivial, domestic reality.... The separation from the beloved ones after death is conceived as due to the careless handling of a coconut cup and to a small altercation. (1954, 137)

There are two loose ends to be attended to here. First, this tantalizing quote raises the question of the source of the great apprehension experienced in connection with the invisibility of the beloved ones after death. Malinowski is surely right that when Trobrianders consider the invisibility of the spirits of the dead they do so with apprehension. If this myth permits that invisibility to be conceived as due to a small altercation, what might it have been conceived as due to that provokes apprehension? That is, if it provides a substitute conception of the invisibility of the spirits, for what is it a substitute? What was the terrifying conception of the cause of the invisibility of the spirits that it replaces?

Second, there is something paradoxical about this historical relation of myth to the nature of life as it is experienced in the present. Things happen in myths that all Trobrianders agree could not happen in life today. The carrying of the taro by the spirit woman in the myth of Baroweni is an example, and in the telling of the myth, the old woman repeatedly reminds us in that context that this is a *liliu*; that it happened long ago. Even though the events of the myth have direct causal relations to states of affairs in the present, the time of myth is not historical time. As Malinowski puts it, ". . . the distinction between the *liliu* and actual or historical reality is drawn firmly, and there is a definite cleavage between the two" (1922, 303). Myth must be closely linked to life so that the events of myth can serve as precedents and causes for the events of life; yet myth must also be kept distant from life to protect it from mundane inferences, about what might and what might not be possible by present standards.

A Mythic Schema

When we look more closely at the myth itself and at how it is applied to the interpretation of the behavior of the spirits of the dead, we find other connections between the myth and experience. These connections have to do with similarities in organization between the concepts encountered in the myth and concepts encountered in life.

The myth of Baroweni contains a structure of relationships among things and actors and actions. If we ignore the specific identities of the things and actors and actions and concentrate instead on the organization of the relationships among them, we see a structure I call a *schema*.[5] When particular instances are plugged into the slots in the schema, we say the schema is instantiated, and the result is a proposition that is an assertion about the world. The schema underlying this myth encodes cultural knowledge about relations between the living and the dead. It is based on a set of implicit cultural theories about human motivation and human psychology. It implicitly attributes abilities, failings, behaviors, and reactions to deceased persons and to their survivors.

The basic points of the myth can be summarized in the following simple three-term propositions.

M1. Baroweni	threw soup on	Baroweni's mother
M2. Baroweni's mother	became invisible to	Baroweni

These two propositions are related to each other in that the event described in proposition *M1* led to the event described in *M2*. Baroweni's mother's action in *M2* somehow "caused" present-day spirits of the dead to be invisible to the living.

M3. Baloma	are invisible to	the living

Since each event uniquely precipitated its successor, the negations of these propositions also form a plausible sequence. That is, if Baroweni had not thrown soup on her mother, then her mother would not have been angry at her and would not have made herself invisible and, so argues the old woman who told the myth, present-day spirits of the dead would still be visible to the living. It is clear how these propositions are connected to each other and how the old woman can use the connections to make inferences about how things might have been different than they are. It is less clear how this is connected to the world of contemporary experience.

The Structural Connection

The question really is how one gets from the notion of contemporary spirits of the dead being invisible (proposition *M3*) to the idea of Baroweni's mother becoming invisible to Baroweni (proposition *M2*). No historical mechanism is offered in the telling of the myth or in its commentary, but both of these propositions are instantiations of the same structure, "x is invisible to y." This suggests that the relation might be analogical rather than historical. Support for the analogical interpretation requires a single schema that, when instantiated in different ways, generates the propositions of the myth as well as the propositions describing the conditions of life. Such a schema would be a structure composed of more general terms than those found in the instances to be accounted for. To discover the underlying schema, we examine the terms in the propositions of the myth and of the description of the relevant bit of life and find for them the most specific category that is general enough to contain the set of terms. For example, Baroweni's mother, the *kosi*, and our dead parents are all instances of deceased persons, whereas the living and Baroweni are instances of survivors.

Interpreting Actions

Finding the appropriate general terms for the actions in the schema is more difficult. Baroweni's mother leaves her and becomes invisible, the *baloma* are invisible to the living, yet the *kosi* is occasionally visible while frightening people. Fortunately, there are other instances at hand and other ethnographic evidence that can help determine the more general categories of action of which the throwing of soup and the coconut ritual are instances. Within the myth itself, the throwing of the soup and the splitting of the coconut are given metaphorical interpretations. Baroweni's mother says that her daughter has injured her and has banished her by throwing the soup on her. So Baroweni's act is an instance of injury and one of banishment as well. The mention of banishment here is interesting because in one version of the myth of Baroweni collected by Malinowski (1954, 133–4), the same soup-throwing incident and subsequent coconut-splitting ritual were posed as being both the cause of the invisibility of the *baloma* and the origin of the banishment of the *baloma* to the island of Tuma. In that version of the myth, prior to Baroweni's mistake, the spirits of the dead were visible to the living and resided in their natal villages after their deaths. Before Baroweni's mistake, it seems, dying was not really much of an inconvenience. In fact, being dead looks quite a lot like being alive, with the possible exception that one gains considerable magical power by dying. Seen in this light, Baroweni's mistake is an enormously important event. It is as a result of her action that death acquires its most salient and distressing features: exile to Tuma and invisibility. Because of Baroweni's actions, death comes to mean removal of the spirit from the sphere of social intercourse.

Now, in the telling of the myth and in providing commentary on it, my old informant gave several paraphrases of the conversation that took place between Baroweni and her mother. In one of those, she attributes the following words to Baroweni, "*Gala bisimamatila, pela bogwa baloma*" – "It is not a killing because (you are) already a *baloma*." Baroweni protests to her mother that she could not have killed her because she is already a spirit. Where does this talk of killing come from? After all, Baroweni might have harmed her mother by throwing hot soup on her, but killing seems out of proportion to the nature of the mistake. It is, however, in perfect proportion to the consequences of that mistake. In spite of Baroweni's urgent denial, her act is a killing in the sense that before this act, there is no death as Trobrianders now know it. True, her mother had previously died, but her spirit was visible and interacted with her daughter as a living mother would. Death to Baroweni's mother did not mean what death means now. And, in fact, in terms of the Trobrianders' current understanding of death, Baroweni's mother did not "die" until this altercation had taken place. It is as a result of Baroweni's actions that death becomes the horrible state of separation from the living. In this light, the soup-throwing incident can be seen as a metaphor for killing, accidental to be sure, but killing nevertheless. The mother's reactions to this are the ritual splitting of the coconut and the pronouncements about how things will be henceforth. The old woman telling the myth called this a just punishment for Baroweni, but it is also the mother's act of dying. With this act, Baroweni's mother declares she will leave, that is, not help Baroweni with her child soon to be born, and when she returns she will be invisible.

Remember also that Baroweni's action occurs in the context of mother meeting her responsibilities to her daughter, but daughter, Baroweni, reciprocates by negligently failing to meet her obligations to her mother. Thus, while the story is in one sense about a trivial mistake, it is also about a daughter's inadvertently ending her mother's life through negligence. This is a theme that is probably universal. Freud, writing about his European patients, says:

> When a wife loses her husband, or a daughter her mother, it not infrequently happens that the survivor is afflicted with tormenting scruples, called "obsessive reproaches" which raise the question whether she herself has not been guilty through carelessness or neglect of the death of the beloved person. (1918, 80)

Freud describes the source of these thoughts as follows:

> Not that the mourner has really been guilty of the death or that she has really been careless, as the obsessive reproach asserts; but still there was something in her, a wish of which she herself was not aware, which was not displeased with the fact that death came, and which would have brought it about sooner had it been strong enough. The reproach now reacts against this unconscious wish after the death of the beloved person. Such hostility, hidden in the unconscious behind

tender love, exists in almost all cases of intensive emotional allegiance to a particular person, indeed it represents the classic case, the prototype of the ambivalence of human emotions. (1918, 80)

This ambivalence resonates perfectly with the Trobrianders' feelings about *velina*. We know that children often feel anxiety about meeting their obligations to their parents, and we know that in the Trobriands (as in our own culture) elderly parents often complain that they are not properly treated by their children. If the historical causal link were indeed the only link between the myth and the experience it is marshaled to explain, then there are many scenarios that could arrange events in which spirits become invisible here ever after. Yet, this mythic structure mirrors the thoughts and fears that are experienced by Trobriand children (whether in childhood or as adults) on the death of a parent. In a world in which there are no natural deaths and in which elderly parents depend on their children for their very existence, a fleeting secret wish that one's burdensome parent were dead or doubts about having met one's filial obligations can easily lead to self-reproach on the death of one's parent. In the earlier discussion of Malinowski's account of the connection of myth to life, we asked, "What could have been the original terrible conception of the cause of the invisibility of the spirits of the dead that must be replaced?" The answer for the survivors is that the dead are invisible because we killed them. This is the source of the Trobrianders' great apprehension over the separation from the beloved ones to which Malinowski referred.

Reading the throwing of soup as a gloss for wishing death on and inadvertently killing the deceased makes the dynamics of the retaliatory nature of the myth clear. According to Freud, the defence against the hostility that was felt toward the deceased

... is accomplished by displacement upon the object of hostility, namely, the dead. We call this defence process, projection. The survivor will deny that he has ever entertained hostile impulses toward the beloved dead; but now the soul of the deceased entertains them and will try to give vent to them... (1918, 81)

The anger of the deceased at the survivor, then, is a projection of the survivor's hostility toward the deceased.

Transforming the Mythic Schema

The parallelism of these schemas is easy to show. The psychodynamic schema described in the paragraphs from Freud is as follows:

P1. survivor   wished death to   deceased
P2. deceased   punishes   survivor

Here, *P2* arises from *P1* when the survivor projects to the deceased the hostility that the survivor felt toward the deceased.

The myth mirrors this structure, although it is not a direct instantiation of it. The structure of the myth was:

| *M1.* Baroweni | threw soup on | Baroweni's mother |
| *M2.* Baroweni's mother | became invisible to | Baroweni |

where the mother's act can be seen both as dying and as punishing Baroweni. The myth is reputed to explain the facts of life. The claimed connection is that Baroweni's mother's act somehow "caused" the observable phenomenon that the spirits of the dead are not visible to the living. In particular, it was claimed that dead parents are not visible to their living children. This is experienced by all surviving children. Furthermore, had Baroweni not made her mistake, the dead parents would be visible. Instantiating the psychodynamic schema in the first person (as experienced by the survivor) yields the propositions:

| *T1.* I | wished death to | my dead parent |
| *T2.* my dead parent | punishes | me |

Obsessive scruples turn this active hostility, wishing death, into a passive animosity, negligent killing, and turn the punishment into a passive projected retaliation, becoming invisible and going into self-imposed exile.

| *L1.* I | negligently killed | my dead parent |
| *L2.* my dead parent | is invisible to and leaves | me |

The first proposition here is one that elderly parents sometimes voice in their complaints about the way their children neglect them. The second is a statement of the phenomenon the myth is supposed to explain. This transformation of the mythic schema, then, provides a simple explanation of the invisibility of the spirits of the deceased, which is, after all, what is in need of explanation here, but it is a very painful explanation indeed.

This is the schema that underlies the myth. It arises in the minds of the survivors following the death of a person with whom they have been involved in life. To this point, we have considered evidence about the myth and its telling as well as psychodynamic theory in order to discover the schema underlying the myth. Suppose this is the schema underlying the myth, how could the myth come to be structured the way it is?

We have already seen that the defence process of projection operates in the composition of the internal structure of the schema. It is the source of the retributive nature of the myth. The defence process of projection and two others, intellectualization and displacement, also operate in the transformation of the propositions that represent the experienced relations between the living and the dead into the myth of Baroweni. Suppes and Warren (1975) propose a scheme for the generation and classification of defence mechanisms that is directly applicable to sets of propositions such as those discussed. In their model, defence mechanisms are created by transforming propositions of the form, "self + action + object." The classification of the defence mechanism is based on the nature of the transformations applied. Among the transformations they describe are putting another in the place of self, projection; changing the nature of the act performed, intellectualization; and changing the identity of the object, displacement. The myth of Baroweni is produced by applying all three of these transformations to the original repressed propositions *L1* and *L2* as follows. Let us begin with the underlying propositions:

L1. I	negligently killed	my dead parent
L2. my dead parent	is invisible to and leaves	me

Projection changes the identity of the self, and displacement changes the identity of the object. In the case of the myth, Baroweni takes the place of self and Baroweni's mother takes the place of one's own dead parent.

1. Baroweni	negligently killed	Baroweni's mother
2. Baroweni's mother	punishes	Baroweni

Intellectualization changes the nature of the act performed. In the case of the myth, negligent killing becomes negligent handling of food, and the punishment is the experienced invisibility of the dead. This brings us back to the propositions that summarize the myth.

M1. Baroweni	threw soup on	Baroweni's mother
M2. Baroweni's mother	became invisible to	Baroweni

Having arrived at the schema underlying the myth, we are ready to return to the phenomenon that brought these issues to light in the first place – the terrifying visits of the *kosi* of Toigisasopa. By placing Toigisasopa in the role of decedent and those villagers who experienced the presence of his *kosi* in the role of survivors, substitution into the psychodynamic schema produces the following set of propositions:

K1. Villagers	wished death to	Toigisasopa
K2. Toigisasopa	punishes	villagers

These propositions, like those involving the parents, are likely to be repressed. Given that this may be an important structure for the organization of ideas about the nature of relations between the living and the dead, it is easy to see the mechanism underlying Trobrianders' assertions that if a person is bad in life, his or her *kosi* will haunt the village for a long time and will be malevolent. Those who are sorcerers, adulterers, or thieves are likely to evoke hostility in their neighbors. Those who are none of these things are less likely to be hated and/or wished dead by their companions in life. Thus, the deaths of powerful and evil persons may evoke many reactions of this sort from the community, whereas the deaths of more sociable people are likely to evoke few such reactions.

I have argued that the way the myth accounts for the invisibility of the spirits of the dead is not through the historical connection claimed by the Trobrianders, but through the fact that the myth is a disguised version of the inadmissible cognitive and affective structure experienced on the death of a loved one. We find also that a different instantiation of the same schema underlies the interpretation of the haunting of the village by the *kosi*. In each case, there is independent sociological evidence concerning the reality of the repressed propositions.

What Do They Know?

The application of schemas across sets of instances is a ubiquitous cognitive activity. Instantiation in conventional ways is involved in understanding, reasoning, and predicting (Hutchins 1980). Unexpected insights often seem to arise from unconventional instantiations. Metaphors and some types of humor are also based on the assignment of new instances to familiar schemas (cf. Lakoff and Kövecses this volume). This same process is also apparently at work in the creation and use of myths. This myth is both a charter or a precedent for an unpleasant fact of life and a cultural model of relationships between the living and the dead. The schema it embodies is as applicable to contemporary personal relationships as it is to those of the ancestors with each other.

If what I have said is true, then there is an important problem for those of us interested in the role of cultural knowledge and belief in everyday cognition. When we turn to the complexities of cognition in real-life settings, distinctions between the realm of the cognitive and the realm of the affective begin to melt away.[6] It is clear that a great deal of knowledge used in the interpretation of everyday events is never explicitly stated. The sort of knowledge that resides in these unpleasant and unstated instantiations of the mythic schema cannot be ignored. To the extent that they may influence memory, judgments, inferences, and other cognitive processes, they are things that are "known." Yet, in a sense, they are things that are too painful to be known. Trobrianders (or anyone, for that matter) need cultural knowledge to understand the myth, and they use the schema of the myth to understand, perhaps in a more profound sense than they can admit, the events of their everyday lives.

Why Sacred Myths are Sacred

In the telling of the myth, the old woman went to some pains to assert the truth of the myth and to impress on me that the events in myth cannot always be made sense of in terms of what we know about the present-day world. Having examined the use of the *liliu* of Baroweni in the interpretation of these modern events, we can see why it is that the sacred myths are so adamantly defended. They are formulations that from the Trobriander's perspective *must be true*. Were they not true, then experience could be exceedingly threatening. Remembering the myth must be a very rewarding experience since it allows the myth to perform its role as a defence mechanism. It allows the believer to confront the ugly subjective realities of deceased parents who can no longer be seen or a visit from a *kosi* with the sense that these are explicable phenomena. Not only can they be explained explicitly in terms of historical causality, but the process of remembering the mythic schema that explains the events also binds the dangerous, unstated, unconscious propositions to a conscious and innocuous isomorph. The situation is explained, and the disruptive propositions in the unconscious are transformed into acceptable elements of a description of an event that happened to someone else, long, long ago.

Malinowski documented the reasons that the Trobriand people gave for the legitimacy of myth and interpreted their insistence on the truth of myth as deriving from the necessity to maintain the historical connection to the precedents of the past. That is part of the reason the *liliu* are sacred; as we have seen, however, there is more to it than that. The myth as a defence mechanism must be both legitimized and protected from challenge. If the myth must be literally true to have its historical/causal effects and if, given what we all accept about how the world works now, the myth cannot be literally true, then what we all accept about how the world works now cannot be applicable to myth. The gulf between the present and the distant past (*omitibogwa*), the larger-than-life quality of the characters and their actions in myth, the unquestioned justice of their decisions, the insistence that in the past things were of a different sort than they are now, the denial that the inferences we would make today are applicable to the events in myth, in short, the whole collection of reasons people give for the legitimacy of myth, are a secondary defence structure erected to protect the primary defence of the myth.[7]

The sacred *liliu* must be true because the putative historical/causal connection of myth to life depends on the myth's being literally true, and that connection is the only connection between myth and life that can be explicitly recognized. If the myth is to be recalled and used as an interpretive resource in understanding some troubling real-world event, there has to be some connection between it and the event other than the inadmissible fact that it shares a common schema with the unconscious propositions evoked by the event. The historico-causal link provides that connection.

Conclusion

We began with a description of an actual encounter between a Trobriand village and the spirit of one of its deceased members. For one villager, at least, this raised the question of why the spirits of the dead are nearly always invisible. We saw how myth was marshaled as an interpretive resource to provide an understanding of this troubling aspect of the experience. The story of Baroweni's clumsiness and her mother's retribution are taken as an historical precedent for all subsequent interactions between the living and the dead. An examination of the myth itself, and of the putative historical-causal connection of the myth to experience, has shown that there is another, more compelling connection. That is that the myth is a disguised representation of repressed thoughts and fears concerning relations between self as survivor and the deceased. We cannot say by which link the myth was retrieved from the old woman's memory. But we can say that the way it accounts for the invisibility of the spirits of the dead is via the structural connection rather than the historical connection.

The schema instantiated by the myth is the same schema unconsciously instantiated by survivors following the death of someone important to them. It embodies the anxiety about possible responsibility for the death and the projection onto the deceased of the repressed hostility of the survivor toward the deceased. But the mythic version is a safe version. It is not about self. It is about someone else – a special someone else whose actions long ago caused all spirits to be invisible. The myth, as a transformed instantiation of this schema, is a culturally constituted defence mechanism. Furthermore, even though the *kosi* is sometimes visible, the underlying schema also describes the relationship of living villagers to *kosi*. We expect the hostility that is projected onto the deceased, and therefore the severity of the deceased's punishment of survivors, to be all the more intense when the deceased was hated in life. This appears from the Trobriand perspective as the observation that the *kosi* of evil people haunt the village for a long time. So, the schema that underlies the myth of Baroweni and explains the invisibility of the spirits also appears to be the schema that causes villagers to experience the *kosi* as well.

This chapter shows that there is a living connection between myth and experience in the Trobriand Islands. By its structural connection to life, the myth provides a way of thinking about things that are too painful or too threatening to address directly. By way of its historical connection to life, it is both a causal precedent for the current state of affairs and a story that exonerates the living from culpability in the disappearance of the dead.

Notes

1. Earlier versions of this paper were presented at the Conference on Folk Models held in 1983 at the Institute for Advanced Study, Princeton, New Jersey, and in the symposium organized by Dorothy Holland and Naomi Quinn for the 80th Annual Meeting of the American Anthropological Association and entitled "Folk Theories in Everyday Cognition." Field research during which the data reported here were collected was supported by a grant from the Social Science Research Council. Text processing facilities were provided by the Navy Personnel Research and Development Center, San Diego. I am grateful to Roy D'Andrade and Laurie Price for reading and commenting on an earlier draft of this chapter. Whatever errors it contains are my own. My greatest debt is to Bomtavau, who told me the myth and provided her own rich commentary on it.

2. See Malinowski's paper, "*Baloma*: Spirits of the Dead in the Trobriand Islands," for a more detailed discussion of the nature of *baloma* and *kosi* and of their relationships to the living.

3. I also collected a supposedly historical story in which a woman encounters a more horrible fate. The woman converted to Christianity and married a native pastor. After a few years of marriage, she fatally poisoned her husband, moved to a different village, and remarried. When her second husband died, she moved back to her own natal

village, where she eventually died. Her *kosi* plagued the village for months, and it was finally determined that Topileta had closed the doors of Tuma to her, and God had closed the doors of heaven as well.

4. Unfortunately, I do not know just who (or even how many) among the villagers actually claimed to have seen the *kosi*, nor do I know what relationship those few I talked to bore to the deceased.

5. Current approaches to implementing cultural knowledge representations include schemas, frames, scripts, and more. For our purposes, it is not important which approach is used so long as it captures the structural relationships of the terms of the propositions.

6. D'Andrade (1981, 190–3) argues the importance of cognitive scientists' looking at cognition and affect together as related parts of meaning systems.

7. This device is not unique to technologically primitive societies. Consider, for example, the following testimony given by a creation scientist in a recent court hearing:

> We cannot discover by scientific investigation, anything about the creative process used by the creator because He used processes which are not now operating anywhere in the natural universe. (Lewin 1982, 144)

In order to assert the literal truth of accounts which, by our present criteria of truth and falsehood, cannot be literally true, the claim of the special nature of that time must be made.

References

D'Andrade, Roy G. 1981. "The Cultural Part of Cognition." *Cognitive Science* 5/3: 175–95.

Freud, Sigmund. 1918. *Totem and Taboo*. New York: Vintage Books.

Hutchins, E. 1980. *Culture and Inference: A Trobriand Case Study*. Cambridge, MA: Harvard University Press.

Lewin, R. 1982. "Where is the Science in Creation Science?" *Science* 215(4529): 142–6.

Malinowski, Bronislaw K. 1922. *Argonauts of the Western Pacific*. London: Routledge and Kegan Paul.

_____1954. *Magic, Science, and Religion and Other Essays*. New York: Doubleday and Co. (First published in 1948: contains "*Baloma*: The Spirits of the Dead in the Trobriand Islands," first published in 1916; and "Myth in Primitive Psychology," first published in 1926.)

_____1965 (orig. 1935). *Coral Gardens and their Magic*. 2 vols. Bloomington: Indiana University Press.

Suppes, P. and H. Warren. 1975. "On the Generation and Classification of Defence Mechanisms." *International Journal of Psycho-Analysis* 56: 405–14.

Dreamtime Learning, Inside-Out: The Narrative of the Wawilak Sisters

Bradd Shore

There is ... a sort of fundamental antipathy between history and systems of classification. – Claude Lévi-Strauss

The Totemic Illusion

The "illusion" of totemism was not to be found in the mystical "participation" Lévy-Bruhl recognized in the totemic equations between humans and animals. What was illusory were the false dichotomies perpetuated by generations of observers, dichotomies that artificially distinguished the mystical principles of "primitive thought" from those informing Western logic. These principles were used to construct our own classifications, dividing "primitive" from "civilized" forms of humanity.

Totemic beliefs and practices model in various ways the complex relations and exchanges between human groups and other forms on which humans depend for their continuity and regeneration. Traditionally, those other life forms have been plant and animal species that figured as alimentary and generative images of continuity. In industrial societies, however, the same problems cluster around machine-human relations, producing a distinctive techno-totemism.

By attempting to reduce totemism to either the mystical participations between species or the logical categorizations mapped by totemic emblems, anthropologists have often bypassed the real richness and complexity of totemism. Close analyses of Kwakiutl animal symbolism as well as cyborg images from contemporary science fiction suggest a far more interesting set of models, models that represent a wide range of relations linking animals, machines, humans, and spirits.

From a semiotic perspective, the totemistic complex is not reducible to a single symbolic or cognitive modality. In fact, totemism derives much of its philosophical and symbolic power from its capacity to model the multiple relations humans bear with other forms of life, *and the transformations of those relationships over time.* Not surprisingly, these multiple representations exploit several distinct semiotic and cognitive modes.

The reason that different observers were able to find the essence of totemism in both rationalism and mysticism is that totemism always implies a complex relation between classification and participation. To the extent that human life depends materially on various kinds of exchange with other forms of life (or technology), humans tend to reflect these "participations" symbolically in complex metonymies that model (sometimes "mystically") hybrid forms of life. These metonymies model humanity compromised in its categorical purity by its necessary intercourse with the non-human.

Such is the power of these material connections among forms of life that they may also serve metaphorically as classifiers of difference. As metaphors, animal, plant, or machine emblems propose parallel worlds to humans and engage the human as symbols of classification, modeling difference rather than participation between forms of life. This is what I called totemism's *classificatory moment*, a manifestation of what we identify as the classifying function of mind. But totemism can be reduced to this function only by abstracting it from its rich and complex unity. In its wholeness, totemism proposes a dialectical relationship between the physical reproduction of life through participation and the intellectual regeneration of life forms through categorization.

Australian Totemism

Chapters 9 and 10 are grouped together under the title "Dreamtime Learning." The complex Australian ethnography has been organized here to explore an important problem in cognitive anthropology: the "outside-in" fate of cultural models – the way in which cultural "texts" or "practices" become internalized as experiences. A central problem for cognitive anthropology is how to connect the two lives of any cultural model. All human institutions are necessarily human creations, the projection of someone's feelings and thoughts into publicly accessible forms (Obeyesekere 1981, especially part 5). So from the perspective of objectivist history, human culture might be said to be produced inside-out – from the mind into the world. Yet for any individual born into a community, cultural forms have their first life as instituted models. These external models become experiences only to the extent that they can be translated "outside-in" into mental models – from the social world to the mind.

These "two births" of culture, inside-out and outside-in, present a serious challenge to an adequate cognitive theory of culture. This analysis of Dreamtime learning in an aboriginal setting will provide one ethnographic answer to the question of how culture is brought from the world to the mind. But we will first examine, by way of an astonishingly subtle and rich origin myth, how a group of aborigines conceive of the origin of their cultural forms. The myth recounts a set of primal beings whose actions establish a set of foundational patterns, or models, that comprise what modern Murngin consider their "law." So while Chapter 10 deals with the question of the second birth of culture – outside-in, as mind – this chapter considers how these people represent culture's first birth – inside-out, as external institutions.

A Distributive View of Cultural Knowledge

As anthropologists have come to better understand the social life of everyday knowledge, they have increasingly adopted a "distributive" view of culture. Culture is not accurately conceived of as a neat packaging of traditions possessed equally by all members of a community. A distributive view of culture sees culture as a complex knowledge system unevenly appropriated in social and political time and space. The clearest statement of this distributive view of cultural knowledge has come from Fredrik Barth. In a recent work on New Guinea, Barth refers to his object of analysis not as a culture or even a culture area but rather as an "aggregate tradition of knowledge." His goal, he says, is to examine "the (variety of) ideas it contains, and how they are expressed, the pattern of their distribution, within communities and between communities; the processes of (re)production in this tradition of knowledge, and how they may explain its content and pattern of distribution; thus the processes of creativity, transmission and change" (Barth 1987, 1).[1]

Distributive studies of cultural knowledge often stress the "sociology of knowledge," an observer's account of the functional implications of the social allocation of knowledge. The present analysis is a little different. It emphasizes the "culture of knowledge" and its acquisition over time by Murngin youth. The "culture of knowledge" implies a sort of "ethno-epistemology," the folk theory and social practice of knowledge acquisition of a particular community.

The Murngin

Arnhem Land is a vast territory on the northern coast of Australia, bordered by the Arafura Sea to the north and west and the Gulf of Carpentaria to the east. This sprawling coastal region of northern Australia is tropical in climate; with marked alternation between wet and dry seasons. Acacia, ti, and eucalyptus trees provide green respite in an otherwise barren landscape. The vegetation is largely of the savannah variety, and during the rainy season spear grass covers much of the otherwise arid plains. With the coming of the rains, the land is dotted with temporary lakes. Numerous bays and tidal rivers punctuate the coastal regions. The coastal waters abound in edible sea life. Scattered along coastal sites and along the numerous islands lying just offshore is dense mangrove jungle.

The northeast and central regions of Arnhem Land are home to approximately four thousand aborigines who are well known to anthropologists as the Murngin and now tend to be called Yolngu.[2] It is hardly surprising that the problem of the discreteness of cultural units should become apparent in Arnhem Land. Here are populations that until the 1960s wandered their vast and relatively bountiful savannah in "bands" of flexible size, gathering plant foods, hunting small land animals (marsupials and lizards), and fishing the tidal rivers and the sea.

Traditionally the societies of aboriginal Australia were made up of patrilocal bands of foragers lacking clear political or ethnic borders. Australian social organization comprises fission-fusion societies where the size of foraging groups swells or contracts from season to season. Before their total resettlement in government and mission camps, local groups varied from tiny foraging units of up to ten individuals to larger aggregates of a hundred or more for religious celebrations. Typically, these variations were seasonal and depended on the availability of food. Warner's 1936 account underscores the significance of these seasonal changes in rainfall:

> In the rainy season great torrents of tropical rain fall daily, making large portions of the mainland south of the Arafura Sea, for weeks and sometimes months at a time, a series of islands in a shallow sea of mud and water. Then, with rare interruptions there is continuous drought for six or seven months.... The water recedes, the water holes become drier and drier, and a large number disappear entirely; birds and fish are gone and the many varieties of lilies and yams disappear. It is then that the native appreciates the value of water, just as before he realized the harm it could do him.... It is small wonder that with the food and drink of life dependent on the water holes, and possible death resulting from the great floods, the native has made water his chief symbol of the clan's spiritual life. (Warner 1936/1958, 20)

Starting with European penetration into the northern territories of the subcontinent in the 1920s, the aborigines of Arnhem Land were gradually settled into several mission stations. But since the 1970s, many groups have once again dispersed, to their traditional homelands, living at what are now called "outstations," where they feel less vulnerable to European intrusion.

While Murngin elders serve as local leaders and wield an often considerable degree of ritual and political authority, there are no specialized political institutions above the local group, though Murngin elders have since the 1960s effectively lobbied the Australian government on behalf of their land claims (Williams 1986).[3] Kinship and marriage relations, and the complex obligations they entail among individuals and groups, are the basis of Murngin "politics."

In this kind of setting, local groups, moieties, clans, clan aggregates, dialect groups, and traditional networks through marriage ties all define a complex skein of related groups and categories, with many variations in language and tradition. Here the local "culture" can only be accurately described in Barth's terms as an "aggregate tradition," differentially distributed among numerous groups and individuals. Nonetheless, many of the local groups in northeast Arnhem Land appear to share several important cultural schemas that give them a degree of cultural unity despite this diversity. Still, variations in virtually every important cultural practice are not merely recognized by local groups but are prized as markers of ethnic distinctiveness.

The uneven diffusion of cultural knowledge in this region is not limited to regional variations in understandings. Even within any local group there is a deliberate segregation of men's and women's knowledge traditions. The most sacred rituals and beliefs are largely controlled by men and are (at least in theory) withheld from women. In recent years, however, many of the "inside" or sacred forms of knowledge have been opened up both to Murngin women and to Europeans through the commercialization of Murngin culture. Morphy, however, suggests that what has really happened has been merely the intensification of processes that have always characterized Murngin knowledge creation. Formerly sacred (inside) knowledge has been selectively released, while new forms of inside knowledge have been created to take their place (Morphy 1991, chap. 5; especially pp. 78ff).

The distinctions between knowledge appropriate for initiated men and that appropriate for all others remains a powerful force in contemporary Murngin life. The origins and significance of the separation of men's and women's knowledge are important subjects of Murngin ritual and myth. There is also an important allocation of knowledge over social time. Murngin initiation practices control the transmission of knowledge from (certain) elders to (certain) youths at privileged moments. Murngin "religion"[4] is a complex of beliefs and practices that regulates and directs the reproduction of cultural knowledge in such a way as to maximize the power inequalities between men and women and between old and young.

An Economy of Religious Knowledge

Keen has written of "an economy of religious knowledge" among the Murngin through which Murngin men maintain control over vital resources, not the least of which is Murngin women (Keen 1978, 2). These same practices also underwrite the domination of the old over the young. In this context, religion becomes an economy of vital knowledge focusing on the control of reproduction and the regeneration of all forms of life. For the Murngin, as for the Kwakiutl, "reproduction" refers to interrelated processes that are at once physiological, psychological, social, ecological, and cosmic. This concern with reproduction as a total social and cosmic issue is expressed in sacred rites and narratives as well as in an elaborate set of social categories and processes that anthropologists term "social structure."

While anthropologists usually distinguish the study of religion from that of social structure, this distinction is not viable in every society. There appears to be no clear distinction between social structure and religion for the Murngin. Moreover, separating the study of social organization from that of religion and cosmology has unnecessarily encumbered our insight into these people.

An Epistemology Embedded in Social Practice

What interests me about the Murngin is the centrality of processes of knowledge acquisition to their conception of social and biological reproduction. Murngin social organization and religion comprise a set of intricate models of how the emergence of knowledge is connected to the regeneration of people, plants, animals, society, and the cosmos itself. From a cognitive perspective, it is notable that in their rituals and stories the Murngin simultaneously *propose* a theory about knowledge and *enact* that theory in the ritual transmission of knowledge from elders to the young. *What* the young men learn in the initiation rituals is intimately linked with *how* it is learned. An epistemology is embedded and transmitted in social practice. The Murngin vision of how an initiate's understanding unfolds in a sacred education is linked to their vision of creation as a dialectic integrating what philosophers would call analytic and synthetic modes of knowledge.

Each Murngin clan derives its identity, its own particular law (*rom*), from its local stories (Keen 1978, 41). These narrative models link a clan with a collection of particular songs, designs, dances, and power beings. These are their *madayin*, their "religious law" (Keen 1978, 41; Morphy 1991, 48–49). The Murngin landscape, which may appear rather empty and even forbidding to outsiders, is filled with objects and places of great significance for the Murngin. To the Murngin clans whose "countries" these are, these sacred places and objects are *mali* (shadows or emblems) of the power beings who left them behind. A group's *ranga*, its totemic sacra, are the emblems of its specific ancestral power beings. A clan's sacred *ranga*, which include a wide variety of objects – ranging from rocks, feather strings, and particular animal species to constructed ritual artifacts – all are signs of the continued efficacy of the ancestors' original creative acts, acts that took place in the *bamun* or primal creative epoch.[5]

In addition to the numerous local tales, the Murngin also have several key narratives that serve as foundational schemes for the entire northeast region of Arnhem Land. The events revealed in these narratives underlie important regional rituals. Two of them, the chronicle of the wanderings of the Wawilak sisters and the Djunkgao sisters' journey, belong jointly to all the clans of the Dua moiety, though the associated rituals necessarily involve the Yiritja moiety as well.[6] A third narrative, the Laindjung story, is the Yiritja clan's equivalent of the Djunkgao narrative. It deals with a male stranger,

Laindjung, who visits the Yiritja clans and brings them their religious "law" (Allen 1975, 59ff).

The two Dua moiety narratives are creation stories and share a similar structure. Both recount how women (two sisters, ancestral power beings) originally possessed all the creative potency needed by their people but came to lose part of their power to the men through a series of misfortunes. The narratives are charters that underwrite the current unequal distribution of knowledge, and the transfer of ritual power and know-how from women to men.

Each of these narratives is linked with a complex set of rites. The Djunkgao[7] narrative provides the imagery for Murngin Narra ceremonies, in which clans reveal their most sacred *ranga* to young men who are deemed ready to see them and understand their significance.[8] The Wawilak narrative is linked with the most important rites of male initiation in the region. Marndiella and Djungguan are important rites commonly associated with circumcision. Gunabibi[9] celebrates fertility, marriage, and the interdependence of moieties. Ulmark is a dry-season ceremony in which, according to Warner's somewhat vague description, "a boy ... is placed definitely in the men's age grade" (Warner 1936/1958, 301).[10]

While the Djunkgao and the Wawilak tales are important throughout much of northeast and central Arnhem Land, there is considerable local variation in the details of both narratives. This is because all sacred narratives involve clan claims of rights over certain land and associated resources. Thus the specific "map" defining the narrative journey as well as which events will be highlighted will vary depending upon which clan is telling the story. Clans tend to place the central episode of a story in their own clan country, since the telling of the story is always a claim of ownership to both countries and associated ceremonies (Keen 1978, 75).

Different clans also tend to substitute their own totemic snakes as the central figures in the Wawilak story, thereby focusing the story on their own country and its *ranga*. These local recreations of the foundational tale are especially useful when one clan is in the process of taking over the country of another (Keen 1978, 75–76). Local variations in the narratives will be emphasized when claims are being pressed or when clans with competing versions are not present. However, Keen suggests that the Murngin also have rhetorical strategies for suppressing the perception of incongruity among variations of a story when the appearance of consensus and harmony is important. Individuals will generally not challenge a "foreign" version of a story unless it is taken as a direct challenge to their own clan's specific claims. Even the fact that some clans stress the Djunkgao version of creation while others stress the Wawilak version can be rhetorically masked, if necessary, by the allusion to the story of "those two sisters," a reference that encompasses both narratives.

The Wawilak story provides a narrative foundation for Murngin age grading. Its central focus is the distribution and reproduction of sacred cultural knowledge. The Wawilak narrative and its associated rites deal directly with epistemological issues and so will provide the ethnographic focus for Chapters 9 and 10.

What Kind of Narrative is Warner's Wawilak Myth?

Because the Wawilak narrative is crucial to an understanding of knowledge emergence in initiation, I will paraphrase Warner's version at length.[11] The matter of which version of the story is used is far from trivial. Catherine Berndt has written on the great range of variation in any such narrative between different regions, between men's and women's versions, and between different individuals' renderings of the myth. Variations include not only specifics of content but also amount and complexity of detail and the sequencing and ordering of the elements of the story (Berndt and Berndt 1970, 13–17). Nonetheless the story has the same basic form throughout the region.

Warner's text version of the story is probably a fairly faithful translation of a narrative told to him by an informant at Milingimbi.[12] It is important to remember that a story of this sort would only rarely have been related as a coherent oral text. The Wawilak narrative is among the most sacred ("inside") of all Murngin stories. As such, it would hardly ever be presented to anyone in the fashion in which Warner has recorded it. First of all, only a few senior men would know the myth well enough to recite it in detail (Jeffrey Heath, personal communication). It is not even clear that the story has any reality as a "text" except in the publications of anthropologists. Howard Morphy, who studied Murngin paintings at Yirrkala, claims:

> Neither I nor any anthropologist I know has heard the Wawilag myth told as an oral story in any indigenous contexts, though I have seen it painted, danced and sung – or rather paintings, dances and songs performed that are part of its presentation. Yolngu certainly do have formal story-myth telling speech forms....
> *But* the Wawilag myth would not be told in this way. (Morphy, personal communication)

In Chapter 10, we will take up the important question of how a narrative model such as the Wawilak story is "known" to initiates when its reality is not a narrated text but rather an emergent product of various configurations of dances, songs, and painting performed at different points in an individual's ritual life cycle.

In this chapter we begin with Warner's text and leave to Chapter 10 the questions of the actual form in which the narrative is transmitted from old men to young men during initiation.

The Narrative

The story takes place in the *Bamun* (mythological) period, a time of *Wongar* (mythological) power beings, when, according to Warner's informant, "everything was different" and "animals were like men" (Warner 1936/1958, 240). The informant begins by announcing that two Wawilak sisters had walked from the "far interior" of

Wawilak Kardao Kardao country to the Arafura Sea. One of the sisters carried her infant son in a paper-bark cradle, while the other was pregnant with her first child.

The sisters also carried bush cotton, hawks' down, and stone spears. On the way, they killed various food animals, and gathered bush yams. As they killed each food species, they gave it the name it currently bears. To each species they killed and named, the sisters said "You will be *maraiin* [sacred] by and by" (241).[13] They moved on in their journey, naming all the countries through which they passed. They also moved from language to language, clan to clan. They spoke Djaun, Rainbarngo, Djimba, Wawilak, and finally Liaalaomir, a language of the northern part of Arnhem Land.

In Wawilak country the sisters had cohabited with their own clan brothers, who, like them, belonged to the Dua moiety. "This was very wrong and asocial." Feeling her baby starting to move within her, the younger sister stopped to rest. Labor began. Soon her child was born. Before this birth there was only the Dua moiety. But now, the mother being Dua, the child belonged to the Yiritja moiety. In this first birth, social difference is created.

The older sister gathered more bush food. Then both sisters and their children resumed their journey toward the sea. Passing through all the territories of the Dua clans, the sisters continued to name the lands and all the localities within them. But in all their travels, they never left Dua country. They did not stop until they arrived at the great Mirrirmina ("rock python's back") water hole in the country of the Liaalaomir clan, on the upper Woolen River. At the bottom of this well lived Yurlunggur, the great copper snake and python totem of the Dua moiety. For the first time they called the name of the country Mirrirmina.

The elder sister made a fire and began to cook the animals, yams, and other bush foods they had brought with them. After each plant and animal was cooked, it came back to life. Leaping from the fire, each species jumped into the Mirrirmina water hole:

> They all went into this Djungguan and Gunabibi well. The crab ran in first. When he did this, the two women talked Liaalaomir for the first time; before this they had talked Wawilak. The other plants and animals followed the crab. The yams ran like men, as did the iguanas, frilled-neck lizard, darpa, ovarku snake, rock python, sea gull, sea eagles, native companions and crocodiles. Each ran and dived into the clans' totemic well and disappeared from sight. (242)

The older sister made a paper-bark bed for her sister's new baby. Turning to her sister, she proposed that they soon circumcise their two sons. As the elder sister walked near the water hole to gather bark for the cradle, some of her menstrual blood spilled accidentally into the well where Yurlunggur, "the Big Father," lived.

Yurlunggur, asleep on the bottom of the pool, smelled the blood in the water and raised his head several times to trace the scent. Throwing a stone which covered the well's bottom onto the land (where it can be seen today), Yurlunggur opened the well and crawled out slowly "like a snake does." Emerging from the well to see who had dripped blood into his well water, Yurlunggur produced a flood of well water which began to inundate the land.

A black cloud swelled overhead. The rain began to fall. Unaware of where the rains had come from, the sisters quickly built a small house and hurried in for shelter. Confused by the lone black cloud in an otherwise cloudless sky, the sisters feared that something terrible was about to happen. The younger sister stayed in the house and sang. The older sister went outside and beat the ground with her yam stick. "She knew now that Yurlunggur was going to swallow her, and she wanted to stop the rain." She sang and danced around the house, and uttered the taboo names of the Mirrirmina well, hoping that Yurlunggur would spare them. But the singing was for nought. Soon the sisters found themselves surrounded by all the Dua totem snakes in the land, who had heard the call of their father Yurlunggur.

The older sister tried to sing away the snakes and the rain. She began by singing all the "outside" songs that are now sung in the general camp (i.e., the less secret songs). When that did not work, she sang the less powerful general camp songs of the Gunabibi rites. But that too was futile. "She was afraid of this rain, for it came out of a cloud she could not understand, because this cloud had come from nowhere" (244–5). In desperation, she began singing the sacred "inside" songs of the Djungguan ceremony, singing first the Dua subsection songs, then the Yiritja subsection songs. The younger sister led the singing, much as the male ritual leader does today. But the deluge only intensified.

When the women started to sing of Yurlunggur and of menstrual blood, the great python heard the songs. He rose from out of the well. He found the women and their sons asleep. He licked them, bit their noses to make blood come. Then he swallowed all four of them in order of age. The old sister went first. At dawn, Yurlunggur lifted himself skyward, standing straight like a tree. "His head reached as high as a cloud. When he raised himself to the sky, the flood waters came up as he did. They flooded and covered the entire earth" (244). While thus erect, and with the sisters and their sons inside him, Yurlunggur proceeded to sing all the songs of the Marndiella Djungguan, Ulmark, and Gunabibi ceremonies, thus completing what the sisters had started.

The Dua moiety totemic snakes gathered together to talk. They discovered that they all spoke different languages. Lamenting that they did not speak one tongue, the totemic snakes agreed that they would hold their ceremonies together. After all, they shared the same totemic emblems. They then sang together, their voices echoing throughout the skies, like thunder.

Yurlunggur inquired of various Dua snakes what they had eaten. The snakes replied that they had consumed various fish and animals. But the Wessel Island snake was reluctant to admit that he had eaten the wrong kind of food – a blue parrot fish with white teeth. Yurlunggur berated his *yukiyuko* (younger brother), the Wessel Island snake, for having eaten the wrong sort of food. But when the Wessel Island snake turned to Yurlunggur and inquired what sort of food *he* had eaten, the great rock python was ashamed to admit the truth. After much prodding from the angry Wessel

Island snake, Yurlunggur admitted that he had ingested two sisters and a small boy and girl.[14]

Once Yurlunggur confessed to eating the sisters and their children, the winds began to roar and the southeastern monsoon started blowing from off of the land. The Wessel Island snake withdrew into his own well. Yurlunggur let out a roar, and at the same moment fell to the ground with a thud. The impact split open the earth, creating the present dance ground at the Liaalaomir ceremonial place. Sure that his fall had killed the women and children inside him, he spit, regurgitating the two women and their children into an ant nest.[15] The Wessel Island snake, Yurlunggur's younger brother, was disgusted when he realized that Yurlunggur had eaten his own sisters (*yeppas*) and his sisters' children (*wakus*).

Yurlunggur slowly made his way back into his water hole. Without warning, the Yurlunggur totemic trumpet suddenly appeared next to the python. It sang out on its own, blowing over the two women and their sons, all of whom appeared to be dead. Green ants came and bit them, and the sisters and their children suddenly jumped up. Surprised to see that the sisters and their babies weren't dead after all, Yurlunggur picked up two sticks. He called his sons – snakes, lizards, snails – and draped them all on his head. Then Yurlunggur proceeded to beat the sisters and their sons on the head with the two sticks. Then, once again, he swallowed all four of them. But realizing that he had again swallowed his own Dua people, Yurlunggur felt sick.

Mandelpui snake asked him what he had eaten, but Yurlunggur lied that he had eaten bandicoot. Not believing him, Mandelpui snake insisted that Yurlunggur confess the truth. When he did, admitting that he had eaten "two Dua women and two Yiritja boys," Yurlunggur fell once again, and the impact of his body created the Gunabibi and Ulmark dancing grounds.

Yurlunggur returned to the deep subterranean waters of the Liaalaomir well, placed a stone over its entrance, and stopped the water which had been flooding the land. He then swam underground to the Wawilak country. He wanted to take the two women and their sons back to their own country. Arriving in Wawilak country, Yurlunggur spat out his sisters one last time. The two sisters turned to stone, and can be seen as such in Wawilak country today. But the women's sons, Yurlunggur's own *wakus*, he kept inside of him "for they were Yiritja and he was Dua. The two women did not circumcise their sons as they intended because Yurlunggur had interfered before they were ready. It was because they so intended, and said for other people to perform this act, that people cut their sons today" (248).

While these great events were taking place, two Wawilak *wongar* men had seen the sky filled with lightning and had heard the thunder voice of the great python. Realizing that something was amiss, they followed the sisters' tracks for many days until they came upon the tracks of the great snake. Immediately, one of the men guessed that the sisters had fallen prey to something terrible, like a python. When they arrived at Mirrirmina well, and saw the ants all over the place, and saw the well water shining like a rainbow, they knew there was a great snake below in the waters of the well. Then they discovered the dancing grounds that Yurlunggur had made in his falls to the earth. The men realized that a *wongar* python had been there. They also found the blood of the women and the boys on some stones. The *wongar* men made a basket of paper bark and collected two baskets full of blood. At the dance ground the men erected a bush house on the part of the ground that was made by the snake's tail.

One man took hawk feathers and bush cotton and stuck them onto his body with the blood from the sisters. The other made a Yurlunggur trumpet out of a hollow log. The men then fell into a deep sleep, and while asleep they dreamed what the two sisters saw and sang and danced while they were trying to stop the rain. The Wawilak sisters came to the men in their dreams. They taught them all the ceremonies they knew, all the songs and all the dances, both general and "inside." The sisters warned the men that they were to use this knowledge every year, painting their bodies with the blood feathers, and dancing out the things that the women saw and named on their journey. "After the men danced the new dances and ceremonies for the first time, they went back to their own country. We dance these things now because our Wongar ancestors learned them from the two Wawilak sisters" (249).

Epistemogenesis: Creation as Externalization[16]

This extraordinary narrative is an odd kind of creation story. It is not clear what sort of creation the two sisters achieve. In the biblical Genesis, God creates the world ex nihilo and then proceeds to order his creation by separating out the basic elements of the cosmos. By naming the animals, Adam continues this act of creation through a generative logos. The Wawilak sisters possess no powers of primal creation. Their story begins at a time and place when everything already exists, albeit in a kind of indistinct wholeness. As Stanner has argued, "Nowhere in the [aboriginal] myths was there a suggestion, of that extraordinary idea of creation ex nihilo. To Aborigines, something always was" (Stanner 1976, 24). The role of creation in these myths is that of reordering and structuring that which was already present. What the sisters actually accomplish is much like Adam's creative work of naming the animals. This kind of creative activity is the creation of a knowable world by imposing form and difference on a primal undifferentiated wholeness. The primary act of knowledge creation is to give things names and thus distinct identities. Categories are created by drawing boundaries.

The sisters' generative acts involve them in many kinds of *separation*. In the narrative, this separation is represented as what we might call *externalization*.[17] The sisters' initial journey moves them from "deep" inside Wawilak country outward toward the shore. At the same time the younger sister gives birth, her child moving from within her womb out into the world. The two sisters taken together (as two images superimposed) suggest the sequence or process of giving birth, the elder sister having recently given birth, the younger just about to.

They move from possessing what Murngin call "inside" or "deep" knowledge of creation to having merely "outside" camp knowledge, which is what contemporary

Murngin women are supposed to know of sacred matters. This transformation in the sisters' knowledge of the world is linked with a kind of externalization of their knowledge onto the surfaces of things. They lose their grasp of "inner" or "deep" understandings, understandings that we would term symbolic or metaphorical.

This externalization of women's knowledge is marked by the sisters being spit out from the belly of the python totem. In an inversion of their own birthing of their sons, the sisters are expelled from the totemic womb. At the same time their sons are retained within Yurlunggur. In this inverted birth, the women's children are separated from their mothers, both physically and as types. In the case of any wrong marriages, Murngin always calculate a child's identity in (negative) relation to its mother rather than its father. A child's initial social identity is achieved by a separation from its mother(s) rather than by identification with its father(s). For example, membership in social categories that organize marriage relations among local groups, categories that anthropologists call subsections, is always calculated by *opposing* a child to its mother. This is merely a more elaborate version of discovering a child's moiety membership in (negative) relation to its mother's.

Up to now everything has been classified as Dua, of the same nature. But now the sons are understood to be Other in relation to their mothers. They introduce the category of Yiritja into a Dua world. This initial separateness is won out of primal identification. Separation is the initial phase of knowledge creation, or what I call *epistemogenesis.* Just as the organization of professional baseball in America is based on the fundamental sorting of teams into National and American Leagues, everything in the Murngin world takes on its fundamental meaning in relation to the division of Dua and Yiritja moieties. Not only people but land, objects, and sacred symbols are, according to their natures, either Dua or Yiritja.

We have already noted the ambiguity over the sex of the sisters' offspring that Warner and others have reported for this narrative. Some accounts relate that both children were sons, others that they were a son and a daughter, and still others seem to move between the two alternatives. This ambiguity is not a "flaw" in the narration or even a matter of local variation. It is a crucial part of the story. The gender ambiguity derives from the fact that the sons have not yet been circumcised. During the Djungguan ceremony, which is linked to Murngin rites of circumcision, the boys are initially identified with the two sisters as females rather than males. Dressed in feather-string breast girdles, the initiates are closely identified with the Wawilak sisters rather than with any of the male figures in the story. Moreover, the sacred posts erected during the rites represent both the sisters and their sons (Morphy 1991, 91, 130). Since the initiates' foreskins, what Murngin consider the female part of male infants, have not yet been separated from the infants, they are, strictly speaking, not yet fully male but still retain part of their original female identity (see Warner 1936/1958, 120). The sisters' offspring, when taken together (as images superimposed), represent maleness as a process of transformation rather than a biological fact.

Creation is initially portrayed as externalization. The sisters produce from themselves not just children but children who gradually become thoroughly "Other" to the sisters. While their "brothers" and their "father" (Yurlunggur) were males, they were Dua males, at once different and the same as the sisters. Only in their sons do mothers create a being that becomes so completely Other in relation to her. Females create males; Dua produces Yiritja. This externalization is gradual. To bring it about requires not simply biological transformation but ritual work as well. Little wonder that the offspring of the sisters are said sometimes to be two males and sometimes a male and a female. Within the limits of the story, this transformation of the offspring into the sisters' Other remains incomplete. The sisters never do circumcise their sons as they had planned.

The sisters externalize a male from out of their own bodies. They also come to externalize male forms of work from out of their own labors. Initially, the sisters hunt *and* gather food. They perform all the work that is now divided between men and women. Similarly, they attempt to control both physical birth and ritual rebirth. Not only do the sisters bear their sons, but they carry with them the hawks' down and bush cotton that will come to be used for the initiation ritual. Just as the sisters externalize male offspring from a female body, they eventually externalize certain parts of their labor to men.

There is another form of externalization evident in the myth. This is what becomes socially correct marriage. The sisters learn that they must separate from their clan brothers and have relations with men who are outside their own moiety and thus "other" than themselves. This prohibition of incest is another form of externalization. The sorting out of right relations dominates not only the sisters' sexual relations but the "eating" relations of the Dua totemic snakes. You do not, they learn, eat your own.

Initially, the sisters appear as self-sufficient.[18] In fact, it is not at all clear whether they need men at all.[19] The narrative reveals them to be pregnant even before it reveals that they sleep with their own moiety brothers. Eventually, they copulate, but with Wongar Dua men, their own brothers. But it remains unclear who the fathers of these children are. This incestuous mating is a kind of half step to recognition of interdependence, and otherness. Once kinship is gradually established by the snakes, the sisters recognize that they must unite with "other" men in order to give birth to "other" children. Cycles of externalization and identification are established, and society as we know it commences.

Blood Bonds

In the Wawilak story as in life, men never overcome their reliance on women to reproduce themselves. The narrative suggests that men must forever wrest their sons from their wives and complete their birth by forms of symbolic creation. Symbolic transformation upstages organic transformation but never really overcomes it. The very forms of men's rituals call to mind physiological processes at the same moment as they seek to deny them. Male symbols of ritual potency are transformations of female symbols of fecundity. As such, they point to the centrality of women's physiological processes at the same time as they attempt to cancel them.

The key symbol of such a compromised transformation in the Wawilak story is blood. For the Murngin, blood is a potent symbol of life (Berndt 1976, 28). As Morphy suggests, blood is a multivocal symbol that proposes the transformational relations between death and life (Morphy 1991, 281ff). The other life-giving liquid is water, often associated by Murngin with semen. The Murngin recognize four stages in the conception of a child (Keen 1978, 304–5): (1) menstruation begins with an act of intercourse, which opens up the vagina and allows the menstrual blood to flow out; (2) repeated entry of the penis into the vagina blocks up the flow of blood, forcing it back up to the uterus and causing it to clot (Berndt 1953, 271; Keen 1978, 304–5; Munn 1969, 184–5); (3) while clotted menstrual blood makes up the fetus's blood and soft parts, deposits of semen are responsible for the bone, the body, and especially the limbs; (4) but a child is not formed until a "spirit child," often in the form of a freshwater fish or an animal, enters the women and makes the connection between her uterus and her heart (Keen 1978, 304).

Spirit children (or conception totems) are often said to live in fresh water and are commonly linked with seafood. Often the spirit child is first glimpsed in a dream by the child's father (pater). It may enter the woman through her vagina. Women are particularly likely to conceive spirit children when they are washing near wells or near water associated with wells. Morphy describes spirit conception in terms of a kind of water cycle, in which the spirits of the dead rise skyward as clouds and fall again to earth in the form of rain, where they enter the wells and thence into women as regenerated humans (Morphy 1991, 255). Alternately, a spirit gains entry orally, through certain "strong" foods, particularly honey and fish, given to a woman by her husband (Munn 1969, 184–5).

The Wawilak narrative is full of indirect symbolic allusions to conception. In the narrative, the sister's menstrual blood falls from the sister's body and accidentally enters the watery pool of her "brother" Yurlunggur. The image employs many of the elements of conception but inverts them (Munn 1969, 185). Blood flows freely into the snake's water. It forces the snake to the surface. This is an inverted image of a phallus entering a vagina, depositing semen, and forcing the menstrual blood up into the uterus to clot (see Morphy 1991, 255ff).[20]

Later in the narrative, the Dua snakes discuss how they have eaten and spewed up various freshwater fish and game animals. Again, an inverted image of conception is proposed whereby the phallic snakes ingest the "strong" foods and thus the spirit children. But Yurlunggur's ingested spirit children are his two nephews (*waku*). The image is complex and subject to numerous readings. In one reading, that exploited by the Djungguan ceremony, this image of a gestating male constitutes a grotesque inversion of normal conception. It is part of what Munn calls "a distorted sexual cycle" (Munn 1969, 185) and symbolically recapitulates the sisters' incestuous copulation with their clan brother.

When the Wongar Wawilak men retrace the sisters' steps and immediately recognize what has happened, they mimic their sister's childbirth by making a bark cradle and gathering up the blood left behind from the heads of their sisters and their sons. In the narrative, the Wongar men collect two baskets of blood which they use to perform their rituals. Note their use of the blood. The men allow the blood to coagulate overnight. When it is sticky, it is used to attach the hawks' down and cotton to their bodies, implicitly transforming them into totemic ancestors and thereby reclaiming the wholeness that was left behind in the initial stages of creation.[21]

For women, the act of gashing the head is a form of ritual mourning, so the blood associated specifically with the head is linked to mortuary rites (Morphy 1991, Ch. 12). The complex symbol of blood in this story thus calls upon understandings of the various symbolic associations of head blood, menstrual blood, and the men's arm blood used in ritual body painting and decoration. The narrative, like conception beliefs, suggests that coagulated blood is life-producing. Without the work of men in reproduction, menstrual blood spills freely from the body and produces no life. The Murngin at Yirrkala, studied by Berndt, call a menstruating woman a "spring woman." They explicitly compared menstrual flow to the flowing waters of the spring (Berndt 1951, 26; Munn 1969, 185). The unstoppable flow of blood calls forth an unstoppable flow of water. The image of the uncontrolled flow of vital fluid bringing destruction rather than life is one of the central images of the Wawilak story. It is in this context that coagulated blood takes on such significance as an image of transformation.

For the Murngin, it is the role of men to transform the flow of blood into a coagulated form that can be channeled into the production of life. In physical birth, male penetration forces menstrual blood into the uterus, where it can clot and form a fetus. In the second birth, initiation, men's own "arm blood" is allowed to coagulate and is then stuck back on novices to transform them into totemic Wongar creatures. Such ritually "bound" blood is held to be especially potent and especially dangerous to women (Warner 1936/1958, 237).

As with blood, so with knowledge. The outflow of blood from the women is paralleled by their uncontrolled loss of knowledge. With both of these losses, the women are deprived of self-sufficiency in reproduction. Ritual "stops up" the flow of knowledge in forms that are contained and controllable. The Wongar men, in discovering the powers of coagulated blood, simultaneously find a way to "memorialize" the transient events of the narrative and transform them into permanent forms of ritual reproduction (Munn 1969, 182–3).

Sacred Dialectic: Creation as Killing

Initially, the sisters carry out two kinds of creation. They bear children and bestow names and languages on the world. They also intend to circumcise their children but never accomplish that act. With each generative act, an individual is separated and externalized by degrees from a prior wholeness. In giving birth, women give physical life and autonomy to their sons. In giving names, they bring forth types and individuals, making things knowable and communicable. Williams has argued that, for the Murngin, words, and especially names, constitute the most important noncorporeal property for any group (Williams 1986, 42). Naming is essentially an act of asserting ownership. For men, the correct knowledge and use of the "power names" for ritual dances and songs is a kind of identification with the spirit creatures associated with the rituals (Williams 1986, 44).

But though naming, especially in ritual contexts, appears to have deeply religious associations for the Murngin, in the myth the significance of naming is far more complex. For as the sisters name the animals and plants, giving them life as knowable life forms, they also kill them. The plants and animals achieve articulateness but at the cost of their lives.

Each life form is killed repeatedly, with the name, with the spear, with the fire, and finally by jumping into the totemic well. The final "death" (in the well) appears to transcend the other forms of destruction and shows them to have been false deaths. As they name and kill each creature, the sisters assure it that it will be *maraain* (sacred/powerful) "by and by." In one hand, the sisters carry a spear, the instrument of the totemic animals' death. Yet in the other hand they carry bush cotton and hawks' down – the (ritual) instruments of the resurrection of the totemic species in the dances of the initiation ceremonies and in the paintings that will cover their bodies.

With the aid of coagulated blood, the down and cotton will effect an identification between people and totems, transforming dancers back into Wongar forms. Separation is overcome by identification. The distinction between animals and humans is bridged. Once again, human and animal and plant are indistinguishable, as in the Bamun.

This is a remarkable formulation. The Murngin seem to refute the Durkheimian (and the Jewish) equation of the sacred as separate (that which is set apart). As with the Kwakiutl, distinctness is not the soul of the sacred. The kind of distinctness suggested by name giving and all other forms of externalization is presented as a kind of death, a loss of an original wholeness. This "death" is a limited form of life. It is *life-in-the-world* and defines the logic of "outside" existence. So it approximates what we usually mean by secular existence rather than sacredness. Sacredness in this view comes eventually ("by and by"). But it is achieved only when the life forms reenter the well and thereby return to the "Dreamtime" or *Bamun* state.[22] Here separation is overcome and the lost wholeness is recovered.

The process traces out a general foundational schema for the Murngin. The schema proposes that separation is overcome by a reunion of divided parts after a journey through a complex landscape of organized categories. It is a kind of "walkabout," a dialectical model of social process (Figure 1). The walkabout schema is a particularly good example of what, in Chapter 2, I termed a foundational schema. In itself it is very abstract, but it serves as a common organizing template for a large number of specific Murngin cultural models.

The myth enacts this foundational schema in four ways:

- The food species are named, killed, and cooked. Then they are "reborn" twice, once as they leap out of the fire, and again as they return to the *Bamun* or *Wongar* state by jumping into the totemic well. In their final destruction they overcome the opposition between life and death.
- The children are separated from their mothers in birth only to be swallowed up again by Yurlunggur. To the boys, the python is both a father (*bapa*) and a maternal uncle (*gawel* or *ngapipi*). This act of incorporation generates several distinct images that will be exploited in initiation ceremonies.
- The ambiguously male infant sons will be ritually killed and cooked (steamed) before they are reborn as males to their clan fathers in both Djungguan or Marndiella circumcision rituals and in Ulmark.
- Even the separation of the Dua moiety into distinct clans with distinct names and countries is overcome by the Dua Wawilak myth itself and its associated age-grading rites. The myth recounts the necessity to order the cosmos by making distinctions and getting the relations right among the parts. But it also celebrates the ultimate ("inside") unity of all that had been externalized and rendered distinct.

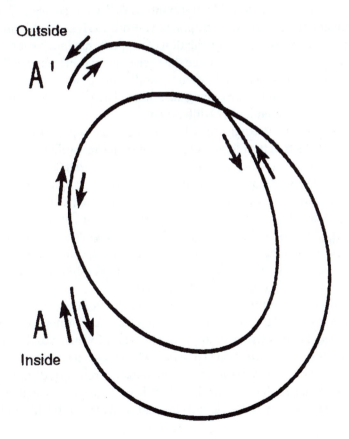

Figure 1: The Walkabout: A Murngin Foundational Schema

The two visions are mediated by the ambiguous status of Yurlunggur. He is not just a multivocal symbol but a true polytrope, suggesting in a single ambiguous image various kinds of relationship. The python is presented as at once a symbol of the separateness of clans, the unity of the moiety, and the interdependence of opposing moieties.[23] As "older brother" (*wawa*) to the other snakes, Yurlunggur is an emblem of clan distinctness (as the central totem of the Liaalaomir clan). As "father" (*bapa*) of all Dua snakes, Yurlunggur embodies their unity and identification. As moiety emblem, Yurlunggur is the image of the great python with all his "sons" draped around his neck. And as *gawel*[24] (mother's brother/wife's father) to the boys within his belly, Yurlunggur proposes the interdependence and reunification of opposites (Dua and Yiritja) through marriage. He also reconciles the opposition between male and female, not simply in being a male representative of a maternal line but also in the image of a phallic womb.

The swallowing/spitting action is at once a phallic, ejaculatory image and a uterine birth image. As with the Kwakiutl cannibal poles, the images of ingestion and expulsion are inextricably linked in a kind of visual and generative oxymoron. Just as the sisters' offspring are ambiguously male, their maternal uncle, Yurlunggur, merges male and female roles in conception. Berndt's informants at Yirrkala often referred to the snake as female but nonetheless as explicitly phallic (Berndt 1951, 21, 25; Munn 1969, 181). As a totalizing social model, a reconciliation of normally distinct kinship and gender statuses, Yurlunggur represents at once the social distinctions between brother and father, father and maternal uncle, female and male, and also the possibility of overcoming these distinctions by being all at once. The key emblem of difference is also the key to the transcendence of difference.

In their rituals, the Murngin seek to overcome the separation of the distinct languages and dialects in the region. As the Wawilak narrative illustrates, clan groups and moiety differences are often associated with distinct *matha* (languages or tongues) (Warner 1936/1958, 16, 36–9; Williams 1986, 40). Murngin theorize that the distinction between Dua and Yiritja is, at heart, linguistic (Keen 1978, 30; Warner 1936/1958, 38). Keen reports that the songs of the Gunabibi rite are sung in a special ritual language. "Songs are in no Yolngu [Murngin] language, indeed they are in no language at all. Some song-words resemble Yolngu words, some are names of objects used in ceremony whose meaning varies in any case. The songs are all capable of a multiplicity of interpretations" (Keen 1978, 168).

Warner also refers to the use during the Ulmark ceremony of Ki-jin, a kind of pidgin, a composite of languages like Millikin, Djaun, and other tongues from the south of Arnhem Land (Warner 1936/1958, 312). His informants told him that Ki-jin was the "language" used by the Wawilak sisters when they sang to try and stop the rain (313). While secular language creates social divisions and semantic distinctions, sacred language transcends such divisions. It unites distinct groups through a composite "language" and unites disparate referents through semantic ambiguity and polysemy.

The Emergence of Symbolism: From *"Inside"* to *"Outside"* Knowledge

The Wawilak sisters and their generative powers dominate the first part of the myth. Then, one of the sisters accidentally lets some of her menstrual blood drip into a sacred totem well. At the bottom of the well sleeps the great python Yurlunggur. He is their own brother, and also their father. The blood mingles with the water of the well. The snake is aroused. The sisters' understanding of their world, as well as their power to create with words, begin to wane. As the great carpet snake emerges from the well to see where the blood came from, he floods the world with well water and a great rainstorm ensues.[25] Here is (with emphases added) how Warner's informant described this episode.

> When he came out he sucked some of the well *water into his mouth*. He *spat* it into the sky. Soon a cloud about the *size of a man's hand* appeared from nowhere in the center of the sky. As Yurlunggur slowly rose from out of the bottom of the pool the *totemic well-water rose* too and flooded the earth. He pulled himself up on the stone which he had thrown, and laid his head there. *He saw* the women and their babies. . . .
>
> Yurlunggur continued to look at them. *He hissed. This was to call out for rain.* There was no cloud in the sky until then, but soon the two sisters saw a small, a very small black cloud appear in the heavens. *They did not see* the great python lying there watching them. (Warner 1936/1958, 242–3)

In this complex narrative Yurlunggur's emergence from the well is described not once but several times. Each retelling of the event involves a subtle change in the "interpretation" of the event. This transformation in knowledge is signaled in the narrative by a gradual shift in how the rainfall is understood. Several times the action seems to be stopped and replayed.

- Initially, the flooding is described as Yurlunggur spitting into the sky.
- Then the physical act of producing the water is repeated, but as the splash resulting from Yurlunggur's physical emergence from the well.
- In the third version, Yurlunggur only hisses, halfway between spitting and speaking.
- Then, fully articulate, he calls for rain.
- And finally, the great python's role is completely obscured by a small cloud "die size of a man's hand" that seems to come from nowhere.

The sisters can see only the cloud-darkened sky. Clouds for Murngin symbolize death. With their knowledge thus "clouded over," the sisters have no further understanding of the true source of the flooding. The passage seems to be an account of the "inside" (or underlying) meaning behind the annual rains that flood Arnhem Land. It is also the pivotal moment in the myth, the appropriation of some of the sisters' generative powers by the men.

Like the heavens, the sisters' understanding of their world becomes clouded, as the python emerges from his rest. The cause of the rain shifts from direct and physical to indirect and symbolic. More specifically, the change is from efficient cause (the python's body, or spitting), to metonymy (clouds), to metaphor (rain as a symbolic evocation of the mythic event).

But to the sisters, this shift in causality is experienced as a beclouding of their understanding. In the end, the material source of the rain (Yurlunggur) becomes unknowable to the sisters. This inside knowledge has now become abstracted, mediated by all sorts of symbols. The sisters' literal vision cannot penetrate the cloud or the emergent symbolism that it precipitates.[26] With Yurlunggur's emergence, the inner cause of the rain (the python) is now understandable only through interpretation. Physical causality does not disappear. But now it is mediated by a world of abstract signs.

The "inside" meaning of the rain remains the python and its semantic chain of associated meanings. But to the sisters, the meaning of the rain is limited to the cloud which Yurlunggur precipitated. What the sisters perceive as the real causes of the rain are merely indications of something deeper, but something to which they have no interpretive access. The sisters' knowledge has been fully externalized. Inside meanings have been replaced by outside ones. But these meanings are viewed as literal facts of nature rather than as an index of deeper meanings.

As the women's understanding becomes externalized and impoverished, the men seem to gain in insight. The Wongar men know intuitively what has happened to the sisters. They can read the signs left behind. Only those with powers over symbols can achieve an inside understanding. Those who have left the Bamun behind, and thus are deprived of initiation, have no access to symbolic knowledge. They are equipped to know the world in a limited and literal way. In a world now mediated by symbols, the second creation of humans through ritual requires men's (interpretive) power rather than women's (procreative) power.

Initially, the sisters' own relation to life processes was both material and symbolic. They created by naming species as they journeyed outward, from their home country. And at the same time, they gave birth to sons. But with the python's emergence, they lose access to symbolic (ritual) potency, which becomes the prerogative of the men. The myth represents this transfer of powers, *both* as the men (through Yurlunggur) appropriate it *and* as the women voluntarily pass on their secrets. Though the sisters bear their sons, it remains for the men to complete the creation of the boys through ritual initiation.

Narrative Anomalies

The Wawilak story unfolds in space and action, but it does so in a peculiar way. Two alternative models of space and action appear to be superimposed upon one another, giving the narrative an "illogical" spatial and temporal framework. The narrative recounts the sisters' journey as a linear track from inside (south) to outside (north), "from the far interior to the Arafura Sea" (Warner 1936/1958, 240). Specifically, this outbound journey ends at the Mirrirmina well, near the Woolen River in Liaalaomir country.

Yet when the narrative specifies the languages the sisters spoke, presumably an indication of the countries through which they traveled, it does not suggest a linear track at all, but rather a kind of circle – a walkabout. In fact, the narrative insists that the sisters began their trip in Wawilak country. If we equate language with country, then they spoke in sequence the following "languages": Wawilak, Djaun, Rainbarngo, Djimba, Wawilak, and Liaalaomir. I have reproduced this journey on a map taken from Warner's book (Figure 2). There is no reference on Warner's map to Djaun country, but Murphy (personal communication) identifies it as Djawany. One can see that the trip described is no simple south-north journey, but rather something more circular.[27]

Particularly strange is the reference to the sisters speaking Wawilak just before they spoke the language of Liaalaomir. This apparent return to their own home language underscores the circularity of their journey. At a later point in the narrative, the sisters cook a crab they caught, and he jumps into the well. The narrator comments, "When he did this, the two women talked Liaalaomir for the first time; before this they had talked Wawilak." Again, the sisters are said to move on from speaking Wawilak, but at the same time they never seem to really move beyond their first language. As with their incestuous intercourse, they seem to recognize social differentiation at the same moment as they deny it. In the end, Yurlunggur does take the sisters on the return track back to their own home country, where they are immobilized as stone. The sense of the sisters making a linear journey is canceled. Only their son(s) end up continuing the journey, but this time through ritual.

The journey of the Wawilak sisters moves simultaneously forward and back upon itself. The same structural paradox characterizes the narrative, which proposes a set of primal events that turn out (on second thought) not to have been events at all. Every creative act of the sisters – whether the individuating of the plants and the animals, the birth of their sons, or the separating of Dua languages and territories – is also *undone* in the course of the story. Animals are made separate, only to return to a primal wholeness. Sons are externalized into the world from a maternal womb, only to be reincorporated into an avuncular one. The snakes sort out their separate Dua identities, only to be reincorporated in the head of their father Yurlunggur.

The point is *not* that Murngin myth proposes an absence of change or linear time. Much has been written about the presumed circularity of aboriginal time concepts (Stanner 1966; Williams 1986). Yet Eliade's notion of the *eternal return*, a denial of historical change (Eliade 1965), is somewhat misleading in reference to the Murngin. The Murngin view superimposes such a return upon a linear change. It suggests *transformation within repetition*. Von Sturmer put it well when he characterized the aboriginal conception of time as "Still and moving all at once – like days and seasons in a regular sequence, a sequence (or a change) of sameness" (quoted in Williams 1986, 35, n. 16).

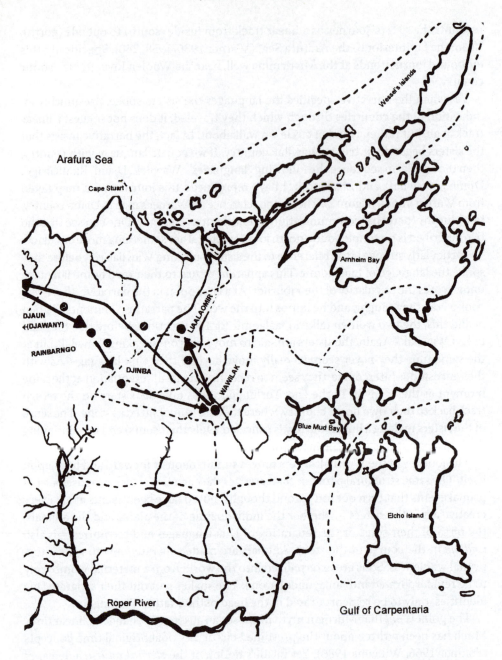

Figure 2: The Wawilak Sisters' Track (after Warner 1936/1958)

Morphy has written, "Because of the nature of the Yolngu conception of time, mythological events are not simply located in the distant past but are also in some sense seen to be part of the continuous present" (Morphy 1991, 45). This view of time is dialectical. Time is at once acknowledged and transcended. This transcendence evokes Hegel's notion of *Aufhebung*. This is the idea that what is canceled in a dialectic is also encompassed in (literally "lifted up into") the return. But in the Murngin schema the process is a kind of downward penetration rather than a lifting up. *Aufheben* combines the sense of canceling or erasing something with the notion of incorporating it at a higher (or, in Murngin conception, more inside) level. This Hegelian notion of "transcendence" approximates the Murngin view of time and action.[28] Time and events may be overcome by a cycling back, but they are also acknowledged and incorporated. The traveler bears the marks of the journey taken (see Figure 1).

While the Murngin suggest that the individual emerges from a dreamtime *Wongar* state into a differentiated world, the course of life will ultimately return that individual back to the well, the source of all that is sacred. But a *return* to the Dreamtime is quite different from the condition of never having left. Time is at once acknowledged and transcended. The fate of humans is to journey, whether through the reproductive history that marks Murngin women's status throughout life or the initiation history by which males are socially marked.[29]

As with the totemic plants and animals that eventually return to the well, sacredness for humans is achieved not by *being* a Dreamtime creature but by *becoming* one again, through a return. In terms of the life cycle, Murngin mortuary rites aim at reincorporating one of the two spirits of the deceased back into the ancestral well so it can be recycled back into life as a new cycle of generation. From the individual's perspective in the course of initiation, what is gained on the journey – both for the Murngin males who are allowed to undergo the sacred rites and for the older females who may be shown the most sacred objects in the *narra* rites – is self-knowledge and consciousness of one's true identity.

In the Wawilak narrative these paradoxes of temporal and spatial representation are repeated in relation to action. While it appears to be a creation tale, it is far from clear whether the sisters actually create anything de novo. To name animals, to speak languages, to label countries is not the same thing as creating them. The narrative suggests that the sisters simply give voice to names, languages, and labels that had always been there. This is also true of the songs and dances the sisters perform for the first time. They do not compose these songs, they appropriate them, singing them as if they had always been there for the performing.

So just as the narrative proposes an outward journey that in the end goes nowhere at the same time as it proceeds on its outward track, it also describes a set of primal events that are also nonevents or preexisting facts. They are foundational models of reality that have no origin in the external world but do have a history in the consciousness of each initiate. These anomalies which appear in the narrative structure of the myth are thus central to the theory of knowledge that the story is proposing. They suggest that this narrative presents a story simultaneously from two perspectives:

an "outer" perspective of a fixed and timeless set of laws and an "inner" perspective of a young boy's coming into awareness of those laws. The Murngin have, in a most remarkable way, represented in a single complex narrative form the two births of culture.

Transformation of Knowledge: Murngin Theory and Practice

These narrative anomalies suggest that the Wawilak tale is not a straightforward creation story. The cosmogony of the Wawilak narrative is logocentric. It operates through language: through naming, language differentiation, and sung narrative. The notion that the origin of the cosmos involves the imposition of linguistic form on an otherwise undifferentiated world is a common feature of creation stories. This logocentric conception of creation conforms to the general emphasis of the Murngin on the importance of controlling names and sacred words as powerful identifications both with land and with spiritual entities.

In the Wawilak narrative, the first stage of creation is analytical and logical, the drawing of boundaries and the creation of difference where there was indistinction. Creatures are given names and groups are given distinct languages and territorial boundaries.

The second stage involves the establishment of relations between the differentiated parts. Once categories are demarcated, then orderly relations of exchange among them can be constituted. The sisters together with the totemic snakes authorize an ordered universe in which words and categories enter into complex relations of exchange and avoidance. Kinship, the syntax of social reproduction, is established.

Yet we might also ask what the *experiential basis* of such a logocentric view of creation might be. In everyday experience, we know of no physical world that is created simply by speech. The logocentric view of creation appears irrational in that it is empirically false. Yet there *is* one kind of world creation that is, in fact, always mediated by language. This is the origin of one's *consciousness of the world*. The Wawilak story, like our own Genesis, embeds its ontology in the ontogeny of consciousness, collapsing the origin of the world into the origin of the world's *knowability*.[30] This is genesis as epistemogenesis.

The emergence of a child into a self-conscious and world-conscious adult is a kind of creation that has some of the peculiar narrative anomalies we have seen in the Wawilak tale. The emerging consciousness of the child is the preexisting world of the adult. It is a journey which is at once linear and static, in which everything that is being "created" also already exists. It is simultaneously a becoming and a being.

The Wawilak narrative is not just a creation story. It is specifically the narrative that is used to "structure" the age-grading rites of Murngin boys. It employs the imagery of world creation to shape the course of consciousness creation for Murngin males. While Murngin myth surely proposes an ontology of the world, the Wawilak narrative is more clearly about the origin of knowledge than it is about the physical world per se. These epistemological biases are evident *both* in the myth's content and in its very narrative structure.

In its content, the Wawilak myth recounts the transfer of sacred knowledge from the hands of women into the hands of men. It also proposes a general dialectical schema for the creation of knowledge. At first things are all one, but they are indistinct and inaccessible to humans. Then knowledge unfolds by distinctions of all kinds: things get distinct names, groups distinct languages and countries, and individuals distinct kinship statuses and relations. Once things are distinct, they can be reconnected. But the first kind of connectedness is not through relations of identity but through syntactic relations of difference – relations of rule-governed exchange. These are the very relations that so absorbed generations of anthropologists who called them "social structure" and at times despaired of ever figuring them out. The myth proposes that such complex exchange relations tend toward both organic increase and systemic complexity. The notorious complexity of Murngin social arrangements is not simply a peripheral characteristic of their social life. It represents at the level of mind and of abstract system the same increase and vitality that progeny represent at the level of organic life.

"One Small Dot, Too Many Meanings"

To conclude our characterization in terms of such syntactic complexity would be to miss the significance of the Murngin dialectic. Such complexity represents for the Murngin a transitional kind of understanding, knowledge-in-the world, a knowing that is essential for being a member of a human society. The myth also proposes that all such analytical knowledge is also a kind of death, for it gains knowledge of the parts by sacrificing a direct apprehension of the wholeness of things.

So in the end, the Wawilak story proposes an ultimate transcendence of this kind of partialness by suggesting that what was known through externalization and relations of exchange may eventually be "re-cognized" as unification, a return to the wholeness of things, a jumping back into the well. In terms of Murngin symbology, it proposes that the extraordinary fan of meanings of any given symbol or symbol complex in myth, painting, or song will eventually be understood to be a coherent and unitary picture of reality. As the Murngin say "It's all the same ..." even when things sometimes appear to be a profusion of disparate images.[31]

Morphy's informant, himself a distinguished Murngin artist, commented, while trying to explicate the multiple meanings of his red dots: "One small dot, too many meanings" (Morphy 1991, 143). Yet, ultimately, the meanings converge. This kind of knowledge, the return to a former wholeness, is the "sacred" (*maraiin*) quality that the totemic animals and plants have when they are killed, cooked, and returned to the well. And it is equally the sacred character of humans who are permitted to take the parallel journey from undifferentiated fetus to differentiated adult to sacred elder. For the totemic species, the journey is mediated by myth; for the humans, it is mediated by initiation rites.

The Murngin theory of knowledge is thus built into both the myth's content and its narrative textures. The narrative is recounted in this manner to propose that in its very forms a kind of knowledge is mirrored that proceeds by differentiation and forward movement but which simultaneously overcomes that differentiation by turning back upon itself, turning a trip outward bound into a kind of walkabout.

The rhetorical power of this narrative does not reside so much in its status as text as in its narrative structure, which replicates the life course through which initiates must pass. The myth comes to be known only through its diverse instantiations in ritual acts and representations. The theory of knowledge as creation contained in the Wawilak myth, what Morphy calls "a continual process of semiosis" (Morphy 1991, 144), is never simply proposed to Murngin youth directly. Instead, the myth itself is deconstructed by Murngin elders and revealed to the novices piecemeal, in conjunction with the central age-grading rites of Murngin society. It is to the practices of knowledge creation, the outside-in perspective on Dreamtime learning, that we turn in the following chapter.

Notes

1. This change from viewing cultures as bounded entities within which knowledge is fully shared to a view of cultures as open and dynamic knowledge systems in which competence is distributed unevenly parallels the biologist's change from the taxonomic approach to viewing "races" as discrete biological populations to a more "populational approach" in which distributions of gene frequencies define populations only in terms of statistical frequencies of traits within a gene pool. Yet it is interesting that in both cases, the ideologies of ethnicity continue to insist on viewing populations both as bounded "races" and as discrete "cultures."

2. There is no agreed-upon collective name for the aborigines living on the northeast coast of Arnhem Land and the islands between Arnhem Bay (to the east) and Cape Steward to the west. This is mainly due to the fact that, lacking a sense of themselves as a distinct political unit, the four thousand or so "Murngin" that were the basis of Warner's ethnography have no collective name for themselves. The name Murngin has become famous in anthropology because it is the name that W. Lloyd Warner used for the population around Milingimbi, a Methodist mission station in central Arnhem Land, which was the basis of his 1936 classic ethnography *A Black Civilization*.

   There has never been any agreement among anthropologists about the appropriate collective name for the people of northeast and central Arnhem Land or even about the significance of the name Murngin. Warner himself claimed that the name Murngin actually referred to the largest of the eight local groups he called "tribes," which were the basis of his ethnography (Warner 1936/1958, 15). Warner claimed that Murngin (meaning "fire sparks") was the name of the tribe whose country bordered Arnhem Bay.

   Yet the issue remains in doubt. Ian Keen, whose fieldwork in the region was carried out in the 1970s, identifies the "Murrungun" as a "semi-moiety name" from the Roper

River area (Keen 1977). Berndt, however, suggests that "Murungun," meaning "red ochre," is the name of "a small *dua* moiety clan . . . associated with two or more dialect units" (Berndt 1976, 19). The name Murngin became something of a household name among anthropologists because of the famous "Murngin problem" (the problem of sorting out the relations between the subsection terminology and the Murngin marriage norms), which generated an entire literature of its own in anthropology.

More recent ethnographies have coined a variety of new collective names for these people, further confusing the issue. Shapiro calls them Miwuyt (Shapiro 1981). Berndt, whose fieldwork was centered at the mission station of Yirrkala on the northeast coast of Arnhem Land, referred to the people collectively as Wulamba in his early work (Berndt 1955). More recently he has suggested the term Malag, the term used for these people by their neighbors in western Arnhem Land, or else Miwoidj, that which refers to the different dialects linked with the clan (Berndt 1976, 19–20). Most recently, the name Yolngu has become a popular collective appellation for these people (Keen 1978; Williams 1986). Yolngu means "human being" or "black person," as opposed to Europeans or Asians.

Were this book intended for mainly specialists on Australia, I would probably follow the current practice of using the term Yolngu for this population. However, at the risk of anachronism and continuing to perpetrate a kind of part-for-whole error, I have decided to use Warner's term Murngin because it is by far the most widely recognized name among anthropologists at large. The same goes for spellings, which have never been standardized and therefore are slightly different in virtually every publication on the Murngin. Though they are probably not quite as phonetically accurate as some of the more recent transcriptions, I shall stick with Warner's spellings.

3. The issue of verb tense is important and problematical in this context. For some thirty years now, no aboriginal populations have lived an exclusively nomadic life as foragers. All have been settled into government and mission camps and reservations, though many have moved in recent years to more isolated and dispersed outstations. In many ways all references to "traditional" subsistence belong in the past tense and not in any misleading "ethnographic present." On the other hand, from all published reports, social organization and religious practices remain largely in place for these populations, though how much longer the traditional sacred knowledge will be passed onto succeeding generations is clearly in question. Because these traditions and social practices are still vital for the Murngin population, I shall use the present tense when writing about them and the past tense when writing about events and practices that are clearly defunct.

4. The term "religion" is somewhat misleading for the Murngin, since they appear to recognize no clear boundaries between religious and secular matters. Their "religious" beliefs and practices pervade almost every important aspect of their lives.

5. The Murngin terms *"Bamun"* and *"Wongar"* suggest a common aboriginal concept of a foundational set of events and power beings who once and for all laid down the patterns for all life, and whose work is carried on by contemporary aborigines through stories, and ritual. This notion has frequently been translated as The Dreamtime or The Dreaming (but see Williams 1986, appendix I).

6. A moiety system is a kind of dual organization in which any social group or unit is divided into two halves, which are then related to each other by some sort of exchange relationship. British "house" systems in public schools or the National and American Leagues in North American baseball are familiar examples of moiety organization.

Moieties are a common feature of Australian aboriginal social organization. Their significance for the Murngin will be discussed further on in this chapter.

7. Berndt calls this myth and its associated song cycle and *Narra rites* Djanggawul (Berndt 1953).

8. Detailed accounts of the Djunkgao story may be found in Allen 1975, 43–58; Berndt 1953; Warner 1936/1958, chap. 10; and Keen 1978, chap. 4. For analyses of the associated Narra rites, see Warner 1936/1958, chap. 10; and Keen 1978, chap. 6. Berndt, whose ethnography comes from Yirrkala and Milingimbi mission settlements, claims that the Djunkgao "cult" is really the oldest and most sacred of the religious cults on northeastern Arnhem Land. The Djunkgao myth is centrally concerned with origins, while the Wawilak complex focuses more on the ordering of social relations and the transmission of sacred knowledge by daughters of the original Djunkgao sisters (Berndt 1953, 14).

9. Compare Berndt's *kunapipi* (Berndt 1951).

10. Warner (1936/1958, 301) reported that Ulmark was a fairly recent innovation in central Arnhem Land and had not yet been fully learned by all the old men at Milingimbi. Yet Keen (1978, 156) reports that Ulmark appears to be no longer practiced in the Woolen River area, which suggests that it never was fully incorporated into the Murngin age-grading complex.

11. Warner calls his version of the narrative "The Myth of the Wawilak Women" (Warner 1936/1958, 240ff). Other published versions of this myth are found in Allen 1975 and Berndt 1951.

12. Milingimbi, where Warner collected most of his ethnographic material, was the earliest Murngin settlement, founded in 1922. The other two settlements are Yirrkala (1935) and the Elcho Island settlement (1942). Some of the variations among ethnographic reports of Murngin culture stem from local variations from settlement to settlement.

13. The term *maraiin* comes from *mar*, a Murngin term for spiritual power.

14. Warner notes that his informants could not agree whether the Wawilak sisters had two sons or a son and a daughter. We shall discuss this ambiguity, which I suspect is not coincidental, below.

15. For an analysis of the significance of ants in the narrative and in the Djungguan ceremony, see Munn 1969.

16. This analysis has benefited from Nancy Munn's profoundly insightful analysis of the sources of the psychological effectiveness of the symbols of the Wawilak myth and the associated age-grading rites (Munn 1969).

17. Munn refers to these processes as "memorialization" and "symbolic objectifications" (Munn 1969, 183).

18. This same suggestion of a primal reproductive self-sufficiency is also present in the story of the two Nyapililingu from Djarrakpi analyzed by Morphy 1991 (see especially ch. 12).

19. In Berndt's analysis of the Djunkgao (Djangguwul) sisters myth, the two creator sisters and their brother are described as having abnormally long genitalia. One of Berndt's informants suggested that the women's long clitorises meant that they were hermaphroditic possessing both male and female reproductive organs. By way of clarification, the informant told Berndt of a man who had been born in historic times who had the sexual attributes of both male and female and was thus able to reproduce by self-impregnation (Berndt 1953, 11).

20. Morphy recounts another Murngin narrative from Yirrkala dealing with the Nyapililngu woman (or women) from Djarrakpi, whose menstrual blood creates an entire lake. The image, suggests Morphy, is linked to the idea of women's menstrual blood being the medium of regenerating human spirits. Thus it is clear that for Murngin menstrual blood is a multivalent symbol which, in different contexts, conveys images of creation, destruction, and their mutual transformations (Morphy 1991, 282–3).

21 Nancy Munn has analyzed the transformations in blood symbolism within the myth as it relates to the sisters and then to their male counterparts:

> ...the women's blood is detached from their bodies and painted on the bodies of the men in order to "play back" the original events. Although ostensibly this blood is from the snake's bites ... it is also identified with the women's menstrual blood. The blood is thus translated from the interior of the women's bodies to the external world, where, separated from its biological matrix, it enters the realm of the symbolic, social things. (Munn 1969, 183–4)

22. While Warner uses the term "Bamun," other works on the Murngin/Yolngu suggest the more common term of "Wangarr" or (in Warner) "Wongar" for the mythological period. See Williams 1986, 28. Williams discusses at length the somewhat misleading use of the English words "dreaming" or "dreamtime" as a translation for the aboriginal concept of a mythological period (Williams 1986, 234ff).

23. On the importance of the multivocality of Murngin symbols and the continuous process of interpretation by which symbolic forms are renewed, see Morphy 1991.

24. Keen (1978) and Shapiro (1981) use the term *ngapipi* for mother's brother/wife's father, a term which seems to be in more common usage than *gawel*.

25. Warner interprets this pivotal episode as suggesting the Murngin belief that women are profane and particularly so when they are menstruating (Warner 1936/1958, 65). Both Berndt and Keen attempt to refute this assertion. Keen argues that while women are not made sacred (*duyu*) in ceremonies, as men are, they are not considered ordinary or profane. "On the contrary," Keen argues, "men are inclined to say that 'women are the real bosses'" (Keen 1978, 370; see also Berndt 1953, 14). Berndt goes even further. He argues that women actually have a sacred status, and that this is enhanced during their menstrual periods (Berndt 1976, 28). This is because all blood is assumed to have life-enhancing powers:

> There is...positive value accorded to blood (whether menstrual or afterbirth, or from ritual defloration, or from penis incision). Not only is blood sacred, symbolizing as it does life-giving attributes; it also has a sexual connotation, which in turn emphasizes the social significance of coitus. Contrary to Warner's view...women's physiological functions were not regarded as "unclean" or as profaning sacred ritual... Also, while a menstruating woman was subject to certain tabus and ideally should not have intercourse at that time, there is evidence to suggest that this physical condition was seen as enhancing her sexual attractiveness.

Berndt's refutation of Warner's claims about female pollution are remarkably similar to an argument proposed by Hanson on the status of Maori women in relation to menstruation (Hanson 1982).

Morphy also stresses the centrality of female powers at the heart of all Murngin ideas of power. Morphy's informant, Narritjin, frequently told him that in relation to all generative power, "really, women are the inside" (Morphy 1991, 97). As for the distribution of ritual knowledge, Morphy argues that women actually know much of what goes on in the most sacred rites, and this fact is central to the power of the ideology of secrecy of Murngin epistemology (Morphy 1991).

26. The narrative transformation in the Wawilak story of literal action into abstract symbol has its parallel in the Murngin conception of the gradual penetration of symbols involved in understanding the meaning of paintings. In his fascinating study of Yolngu art and knowledge, Howard Morphy describes an interpretive system whereby the relatively figurative and literal "outside" representations in art are gradually transformed into "inside" forms that are more general, abstract, and comprise geometrical motifs rather than directly iconic figures. This "movement" from specific figurative forms to more general geometric representations distinguishes more open and outside paintings from more restricted and inside ones. The same semiotic shift also characterizes an individual's changing understanding of a sacred painting through sacred education (Morphy 1991, especially ch. 10).

27. On page 241 [of Warner 1936/1958] the narrative makes additional references to numerous place names where the sisters stopped, but since these localities are not included on any maps of Arnhem Land I could find, there is no way for me to check whether this section of the narrative reproduces the same anomaly as the one just discussed.

28. I am grateful to Professors Donald Verene and Rudolph Makreel of Emory University's philosophy department for clarifying the Hegelian notion of *Aufhebung*.

29. Murngin girls and women are generally known by terms that indicate their reproductive status, while boys and men are classified by their state of ritual knowledge as indicated by the sequence of initiation rites.

30. On Genesis as a story of the emergence of consciousness, see Paul 1977.

31. It is important to note that the same walkabout schema that governs Murngin notions of knowledge creation and transmission also structures many of the extraordinarily complex models governing kinship and marriage relations. The Murngin have numerous cultural models governing marriage. They are alternate phrasings of a single general schema. Marriage models range from simple moiety exogamy, to "Mother's Brother's Daughter's" marriage, to subsection rules, to very complex long cycles of exchange between alternate generations and distant lines. These latter attenuated models include a form of mother-in-law bestowal, where a man and his sister arrange for his daughter to produce a wife for their own kutara "Mother's Mother's Brother's Daughter's Son." The common schema for all of these models is one proposing that one must separate in order eventually to overcome the separation and reunite. This is true not only for marriage but also for kinship personalities as manifested in kin terms. Kin terms tend to disappear, only to cycle back again in extraordinarily complex but persistent patterns (Morphy 1991; Keen 1978; Warner 1936/1958). These kin models are linked by a "walkabout" schema, proposing that one leaves home only to effect an eventual return, having been transformed by the journey.

References

Allen, Louis A. 1975. *Time Before Morning: Art and Myth of the Australian Aborigines.* New York: Crowell.

Barth, Fredrik. 1987. *Cosmologies in the Making: A Generative Approach to Cultural Variation in Inner New Guinea.* New York: Cambridge University Press.

Berndt, Ronald M. 1951. *Kunapipi: A Study of an Australian Aboriginal Fertility Cult.* Melbourne: Cheshire.

_____1953. *Djanggawul: An Aboriginal Religious Cult of North-Eastern Arnhem Land.* New York: The Philosophical Society.

_____1955. "Murngin (Wulamba) social organization." *American Anthropologist* 57/1: 84–106.

_____1976. *Love Songs of Arnhem Land.* Chicago: University of Chicago Press.

Berndt, Ronald M. and Catherine Berndt. 1970. *Man, Land and Myth in North Australia: The Guwinggu People.* East Lansing, MI: Michigan State University Press.

Eliade, Mircea. 1965. *The Myth of Eternal Return or Cosmos and History.* Rev. ed. Princeton, NJ: Princeton University Press.

Hanson, F. Allan. 1982. "Female Pollution in Polynesia." *Journal of the Polynesian Society* 91: 335–81.

Keen, Ian. 1977. "Ambiguity in Yolngu Religious Language." *Canberra Anthropology* 1: 33–50.

_____1978. "One Country, One Song." Doctoral dissertation. Canberra: Department of Anthropology, Australian National University.

Morphy, Howard. 1991. *Ancestral Connections: Art and an Aboriginal System of Knowledge.* Chicago: University of Chicago Press.

Munn, Nancy. 1969. "The Effectiveness of Symbols in Murngin Myth and Rite." In *Forms of Symbolic Action*, ed. Robert Spencer. Seattle: University of Washington Press.

Obeyesekere, Gananath. 1981. *Medusa's Hair: An Essay on Personal Symbols and Religious Experience.* Chicago: University of Chicago Press.

Paul, Robert A. 1977. "The First Speech Events: "Genesis" as the Nursery for Consciousness." *Psychocultural Review*, Spring: 179–94.

Shapiro, Warren. 1981. *Miwuyit Marriage: The Cultural Anthropology of Affinity in Northeast Arnhem Land.* Philadelphia: Institute for the Study of Human Issues (ISHI).

Stanner, W. E. H. 1966. *On Aboriginal Religion.* Oceania Monograph No. 11. Sydney: Oceania Publications.

_____1976. "Some Aspects of Aboriginal Liffe." *Colloquium* 9/1: 19–35.

Warner, W. Lloyd. 1936/1958. *A Black Civilization.* New York: Harper & Row.

Williams, Nancy. 1986. *The Yolngu and Their Land: A System of Land Tenure and Its Fight for Recognition.* Dissertation. Canberra: Australian Institute of Aboriginal Studies. (Published by Stanford University Press, 1987.)

THE TRANSACTIONAL SELF

Jerome Bruner

I f you engage for long in the study of how human beings relate to one another, especially through the use of language, you are bound to be struck by the importance of "transactions." This is not an easy word to define. I want to signify those dealings which are premised on a mutual sharing of assumptions and beliefs about how the world is, how mind works, what we are up to, and how communication should proceed. It is an idea captured to some extent by Paul Grice's maxims about how to proceed in conversation, by Deirdre Wilson and Dan Sperber's notion that we always assume that what others have said must make *some* sense, by Hilary Putnam's recognition that we usually assign the right level of ignorance or cleverness to our interlocutors. Beyond these specifics, there remains a shady but important area of sharing – Colwyn Trevarthen calls it "intersubjectivity" – that makes the philosopher's query about how we know Other Minds seem more practical than the philosopher ever intended it to be.

One knows intuitively as a psychologist (or simply as a human being) that the easy access we have into each other's minds, not so much in the particulars of what we are thinking but in general about what minds are like, cannot be explained away by invoking singular concepts like "empathy." Nor does it seem sufficient to perform a miracle of phenomenology, as did the German philosopher Max Scheler, and subdivide *Einfuhlung* into a half-dozen "feelable" classes. Or to take the route of nineteenth-century psychologists and elevate "sympathy" to the status of an instinct. More typically, the contemporary student [58] of mind will try to unravel the mystery by exploring how we develop this sense of what other minds are about, or by examining its pathologies, as in autistic children and in young schizophrenics. Or he will try to unravel the details of interpersonal knowledge among adults by conducting experiments on facets of this knowledge, as have Fritz Heider and his students. Or, yet another alternative, he will dismiss the issue of intersubjective knowledge as "nothing but" projection, for whatever smug satisfaction that may give him.

I first became caught up in this issue through work I did in collaboration with Renato Tagiuri, and we ended up writing a chapter on "person perception" in one of the standard Handbooks – treating it as a perceptual problem. Along the way to that chapter we did some of those little experiments which are the craft of psychology. We asked people who were parts of small groups or cliques and who knew each other well two very simple questions: who in the group would they (each individual) most like to spend more time with, and who in the group did they think would most like to spend more time with them. I should say at the outset that this is a procedure fraught with statistical problems, particularly if one wants to study the "accuracy" of interpersonal perceptions or to determine whether people's choices are "transparent" to others. But the statistical hurdles can be jumped by using what are called "Monte Carlo procedures," which consist of allocating each person's choices and guesses of others' choices with the aid of a roulette wheel. One can then compare the subjects' real performance with the wheel's allocation of choices and guesses by chance. Yes, on average people are more accurate and more transparent than would be expected by chance – a not very startling finding. They know better than chance who likes them, or to put it inversely, people's preferences are transparent.

But there is something very curious about how people operate in such situations that is not so obvious after all. For one thing, a person who chooses another will (in excess of chance) believe that the other person chooses him back. Or, since the direction of cause is never clear in human affairs, if we *feel* chosen by somebody, we will choose that person in return whether our feeling is correct or not. There is simply a human bias: feeling liked by somebody begets liking him back. To this add the fact that we know better than chance who likes us. Now, is this a matter of "accuracy" or of "vanity"? Are we "victims" of vanity or [59] beneficiaries of our sensitivity? If we bias our Monte Carlo wheels with these same "human" tendencies, they will perform indistinguishably from humans. Does that mean that humans are simply biased robots? Is that a meaningful question, really? It smacks altogether too much of those early Cartesian questions about man as a machine with a human soul added to it, perhaps making its will known through the pineal gland just as we can make "humanness" available to the Monte Carlo robot by rigging the wheel.

The model we had been using seemed wrong – or at least it led us down dead ends where we did not want to travel. What it told us – and it was not trivial – was that shared sensitivities and biases can produce some strikingly social consequences. For one thing, they produce astonishing stability within groups. People act in accordance with their perceptions and their choices, and they reciprocate accordingly. We created a little discussion group of seven members, to discuss "psychology and life" (they were all undergraduates). And we administered our test four or five times over a term. Some interesting things happened to the dyads or pairs that composed that group.

Certain patterns virtually disappeared over time or occurred eventually at levels *below* chance. Instances of pairs in which each chose the other with neither feeling chosen in return were gone by the end of the term. So too were cases where both felt chosen by the other but did not choose in return. The transactional process seemed to intensify over time. We left it at that and went off to pursue other matters.

But the problem was to return, and it did so, more than a decade later, when I began a series of studies on growth in human infancy and particularly on the development of human language and its precursors. My first brush with it was in studying the development of exchange games in infancy, when I was struck with how quickly and easily a child, once having mastered the manipulation of objects, could enter into "handing back and forth," handing objects around a circle, exchanging objects for each other. The competence seemed there, as if *ab ovum*; the performance was what needed some smoothing out. Very young children had something clearly in mind about what others had in mind, and organized their actions accordingly. I thought of it as the child achieving mastery of one of the precursors of language use: a sense of mutuality in action.

So too in a second study (which I shall tell about more fully later) in [60] which we were interested in how the child came to manage his attention jointly with others – a prerequisite of linguistic reference. We found that by their first birthday children are already adept at following another's line of regard to search for an object that is engaging their partner's attention. That surely requires a sophisticated conception of a partner's mind.

Yet why should we have been surprised? The child has such conceptions "in mind" in approaching language. Children show virtually no difficulty in mastering pronouns and certain demonstratives, for example, even though these constitute that confusing class of referring expressions called deictic shifters. A deictic shifter is an expression whose meaning one can grasp only through appreciating the interpersonal context in which it is uttered and by whom it is uttered. That is to say, when I use the pronoun *I*, it means me; when my partner uses it, it refers to him. A spatial shifter pair like *here* and *there* poses the same problem: *here* used by me is close to me; *here* used by you is close to you. The shifter ought to be hard to solve for the child, and yet it isn't.

It ought to be, that is, if the child were as "self-centered" as he is initially made out to be by current theories of child development. For our current theories (with notable exceptions carried over from the past, like the views of George Herbert Mead) picture the child as starting his career in infancy and continuing it for some years after, locked in his own perspective, unable to take the perspective of another with whom he is in interaction. And, indeed, there are even experimental "demonstrations" to prove the point. But *what* point? Surely not that we can take any perspective of anybody in any plight at any time. We would not have been so slow in achieving the Copernican revolution if that were the case, or in understanding that to the Indians North America must have seemed like *their* homeland. To show that a child (or an adult) cannot, for example, figure out what three mountains he sees before him might look like to somebody viewing them from their "back" sides (to take as our whipping boy one of the classic experiments demonstrating egocentrism), does not mean he cannot take another's perspective into account *in general.*

It is curious, in view of the kinds of considerations I have raised, that psychological theories of development have pictured the young child as so lacking in the skills of transaction. The prevailing view of initial [61] (and slowly waning) egocentrism is, in certain respects, so grossly, almost incongruously wrong and yet so durable, that it deserves to be looked at with care. Then we can get back to the main issue – what it is that readies the child so early for transacting his life with others on the basis of some workable intuitions about Other Minds and, perhaps, about Human Situations as well. The standard view seems to have four principal tenets:

1. *Egocentric perspective.* That initially young children are incapable of taking the perspective of others, have no conception of Other Minds, and must be brought to sociality or allocentrism through development and learning. In its baldest form, this is the doctrine of initial primary process in terms of which even the first perceptions of the child are said to be little more than hallucinatory wish-fulfillments.

2. *Privacy.* That there is some inherently individualistic Self that develops, determined by the universal nature of man, and that it is beyond culture. In some deep sense, this Self is assumed to be ineffable, private. It is socialized, finally, by such processes as identification and internalization: the outer, public world becoming represented in the inner, private one.

3. *Unmediated conceptualism.* That the child's growing knowledge of the world is achieved principally by direct encounters with that world rather than mediated through vicarious encounters with it in interacting and negotiating with others. This is the doctrine of the child going it alone in mastering his knowledge of the world.

4. *Tripartism.* That cognition, affect, and action are represented by separate processes that, with time and socialization, come to interact with one another. Or the opposite view: that the three stem from a common process and that, with growth, they differentiate into autonomous systems. In either case, cognition is the late bloomer, the weak vessel, and is socially blind.

I do not want to argue that these four premises are "wrong," only that they are arbitrary, partial, and deeply rooted in the morality of our own culture. They are true under certain conditions, false under others, and their "universalization" reflects cultural bias. Their acceptance as universals, moreover, inhibits the development of a workable theory of the nature of social transaction and, indeed, even of the concept of Self. One could argue against the tenet of privacy, for example (inspired by anthropologists), that the distinction between [62] "private self" and "public self" is a function of the culture's conventions about when one talks and negotiates the meanings of events and when one keeps silent, and of the ontological status given to that which is kept silent and that which is made public. Cultures and subcultures differ in this regard; so even do families.

*

But let us return now to the main point: to the nature of transaction and the "executive processes" necessary to effect it, to those transactional selves hinted at in the title of this chapter. Consider in more detail now what the mastery of language entails with respect to these ideas.

Take *syntax* first. We need not pause long over it. The main point that needs making is that the possession of language gives us rules for generating well-formed utterances, whether they depend on the genome, upon experience, or upon some interaction of the two. Syntax provides a highly abstract system for accomplishing communicative functions that are crucial for regulating joint attention and joint action, for creating topics and commenting upon them in a fashion that segments "reality," for forefronting and imposing perspectives on events, for indicating our stance toward the world to which we refer and toward our interlocutors, for triggering presuppositions, and so on. We may not "know" all these things about our language in any explicit way (unless we happen to have that special form of consciousness which linguists develop), but what we do know from the earliest entry into language is that others can be counted upon to use the same rules of syntax for forming and for comprehending utterances as we use. It is so pervasive a system of calibration that we take it for granted. It entails not just the formulas of Grice, or of Sperber and Wilson, or of Putnam to which I referred, but the assurance that mind is being used by others as we use it. Syntax indeed entails a particular use of mind, and however much one may argue (as Joseph Greenberg in his way and Noam Chomsky in his have argued) that we cannot even conceive of alternative ways of using our minds, that language expresses our natural "organs of thought," it is still the case that the joint and mutual use of language gives us a huge step in the direction of understanding other minds. For it is not simply that we all *have* forms of mental organization that are akin, but that we *express* these forms constantly in our transactions with one another. We can count on constant [63] transactional calibration in language, and we have ways of calling for repairs in one another's utterances to assure such calibration. And when we encounter those who do not share the means for this mutual calibration (as with foreigners), we regress, become suspicious, border on the paranoid, shout.

Language is also our principal means of *referring*. In doing so, it uses cues to the context in which utterances are being made and triggers presuppositions that situate the referent (matters discussed in Chapter 2). Indeed, reference plays upon the shared presuppositions and shared contexts of speakers. It is to the credit of Gareth Evans that he recognized the profound extent to which referring involves the mapping of speakers' subjective spheres on one another. He reminds us, for example, that even a failed effort to refer is not just a failure, but rather that it is an offer, an invitation to another to search possible contexts with us for a possible referent. In this sense, referring to something with the intent of directing another's attention to it requires even at its simplest some form of negotiation, some hermeneutic process. And it becomes the more so when the reference is not present or accessible to pointing or to some other ostensive maneuver. Achieving joint reference is achieving a kind of solidarity with somebody. The achievement by the child of such "intersubjective" reference comes so easily, so naturally, that it raises puzzling questions.

The evidence from early pointing (usually achieved before the first birthday) and from the infant's early following of another's line of regard suggests that there must be something preadapted and prelinguistic that aids us in achieving initial linguistic reference. I do not doubt the importance of such a biological assist. But this early assist is so paltry in comparison to the finished achievement of reference that it cannot be the whole of the story. The capacity of the average speaker to handle the subtleties of ellipsis, of anaphora – to know that, in the locution "Yesterday I saw *a* bird; *the* bird was singing," the shift from indefinite to definite article signals that the same bird is referred to in the second phrase as in the first – is too far removed from its prelinguistic beginnings to be accounted for by them. One has to conclude that the subtle and systematic basis upon which linguistic reference itself rests must reflect a natural organization of mind, one into which we *grow* through experience rather than one we achieve by learning.

If this is the case – and I find it difficult to resist – then human [64] beings must come equipped with the means not only to calibrate the workings of their minds against one another, but to calibrate the worlds in which they live through the subtle means of reference. In effect, then, this is the means whereby we know Other Minds and their possible worlds.

The relation of words or expressions to other words or expressions constitutes, along with reference, the sphere of *meaning*. Because reference rarely achieves the abstract punctiliousness of a "singular, definite referring expression," is always subject to *polysemy* and because there is no limit on the ways in which expressions can relate to one another, meaning is always underdetermined, ambiguous. To "make sense" in language, as David Olson argued persuasively some years ago, always requires an act of "disambiguation." Young children are not expert at such disambiguation, but procedures for effecting it are there from the earliest speech. They negotiate – even at two years of age – not only what is being referred to by an expression, but what other expressions the present one relates to. And children's early monologues, reported by Ruth Weir a generation ago and more recently by Katherine Nelson and her colleagues in the New York Language Acquisition Group, all point to a drive to explore and to overcome ambiguities in the meaning of utterances. The young child seems not only to negotiate sense in his exchanges with others but to carry the problems raised by such ambiguities back into the privacy of his own monologues. The realm of meaning, curiously, is not one in which we ever live with total comfort. Perhaps it is this discomfort that drives us finally to construct those larger-scale products of language – drama and science and the disciplines of understanding – where we can construct new forms in which to transact and negotiate this effort after meaning.

To create hypothetical entities and fictions, whether in science or in narrative, requires yet another power of language that, again, is early within reach of the language user. This is the capacity of language to create and stipulate realities of its own, its *constitutiveness*. We create realities by warning, by encouraging, by dubbing with titles, by naming, and by the manner in which words invite us to create "realities" in the world to correspond with them. Constitutiveness gives an externality and an apparent ontological status to the concepts words embody: for example, the law, gross national product, antimatter, the Renaissance. It is what makes us construct proscenia in our theater and still be [65] tempted to stone the villain. At our most unguarded, we are all Naive Realists who believe not only that we know what is "out there," but also that it is out there for *others* as well. Carol Feldman calls it "ontic dumping," converting our mental processes into products and endowing them with a reality in some world. The private is rendered public. And thereby, once again, we locate ourselves in a world of shared reality. The constitutiveness of language, as more than one anthropologist has insisted, creates and transmits culture and locates our place in it – a matter to which I turn next.

Language, as we know, consists not only of a locution, of what is actually said, but of an illocutionary force – a conventional means of indicating what is intended by making that locution under those circumstances. These together constitute the speech acts of ordinary language, and they might be considered as much the business of the anthropologist as of the linguist. I will revisit the psychological implications of speech acts in a later chapter; here we need only take them for granted as a phenomenon. As a phenomenon, they imply that learning how to use language involves both teaming the culture and learning how to express intentions in congruence with the culture. This brings us to the question of how we may conceive of "culture" and in what way it provides means not only for transacting with others but for conceiving of ourselves in such transactions.

*

It would not be an exaggeration to say that in the last decade there has been a revolution in the definition of human culture. It takes the form of a move away from the strict structuralism that held that culture was a set of interconnected rules from which people derive particular behaviors to fit particular situations, to the idea of culture as implicit and only semiconnected knowledge of the world from which, through negotiation, people arrive at satisfactory ways of acting in given contexts. The anthropologist Clifford Geertz likens the process of acting in a culture to that of interpreting an ambiguous text. Let me quote a paragraph written by one of his students, Michelle Rosaldo:

> In anthropology, I would suggest, the key development...is a view of culture...wherein meaning is proclaimed a public fact – or better yet, where culture and meaning are described as processes of interpretive apprehension by individuals of symbolic models. These models are both [66] "of" the world in which we live and "for" the organization of activities, responses, perceptions and experiences by the conscious self. For present purposes, what is important here is first of all the claim that meaning is a fact of public life, and secondly, that

cultural patterns – social facts – provide the template for all human action, growth and understanding. Culture so construed is, furthermore, a matter less of artifacts and propositions, rules, schematic programs, or beliefs, than of associative chains and images that tell what can be reasonably linked up with what; we come to know it through collective stories that suggest the nature of coherence, probability and sense within the actor's world. Culture is, then, always richer than the traits recorded in the ethnographer's accounts because its truth resides not in explicit formulations of the rituals of daily life but in the daily practices of persons who in acting take for granted an account of who they are and how to understand their fellows' moves.

I have already discussed the linguistics, so to speak, by which this is accomplished. What of the "cultural" side of the picture? *How* we decide to enter into transaction with others linguistically and by what exchanges, how *much* we wish to do so (in contrast to remaining "detached" or "silent" or otherwise "private"), will shape our sense of what constitutes culturally acceptable transactions and our definition of our own scope and possibility in doing so – our "selfhood." As Rosaldo reminds us (using the Ilongot people as contrast) our Western concern with "individuals and with their inner hidden selves may well be features of *our* world of action and belief – itself to be explained and not assumed as the foundation of cross-cultural study." Indeed, the images and stories that we provide for guidance to speakers with respect to when they may speak and what they may say in what situations may indeed be a first constraint on the nature of selfhood. It may be one of the many reasons why anthropologists (in contrast to psychologists) have always been attentive not only to the content but to the form of the myths and stories they encounter among their "subjects."

For stories define the range of canonical characters, the settings in which they operate, the actions that are permissible and comprehensible. And thereby they provide, so to speak, a map of possible roles and of possible worlds in which action, thought, and self-definition are permissible (or desirable). As we enter more actively into the life of a culture around us, as Victor Turner remarks, we come increasingly to [67] play parts defined by the "dramas" of that culture. Indeed, in time the young entrant into the culture comes to define his own intentions and even his own history in terms of the characteristic cultural dramas in which he plays a part – at first family dramas, but later the ones that shape the expanding circle of his activities outside the family.

It can never be the case that there is a "self" independent of one's cultural-historical existence. It is usually claimed, in classical philosophical texts at least, that Self rises out of our capacity to reflect upon our own acts, by the operation of "metacognition." But what is strikingly plain in the promising research on metacognition that has appeared in recent years – work by Ann Brown, by J. R. Hayes, by David Perkins, and others – is that metacognitive activity (self-monitoring and self-correction) is very unevenly distributed, varies according to cultural background, and, perhaps most important, can be taught successfully as a skill. Indeed, the available research on "linguistic repairs," self-corrections in utterances either to bring one's utterances into line with one's intent or to make them comprehensible to an interlocutor, suggests that an *Anlage* of metacognition is present as early as the eighteenth month of life. How much and in what form it develops will, it seems reasonable to suppose, depend upon the demands of the culture in which one lives – represented by particular others one encounters and by some notion of a "generalized other" that one forms (in the manner so brilliantly suggested by writers as various and as separated in time as St. Augustine in the *Confessions* and George Herbert Mead in *Mind, Self, and Society*).

It would seem a warranted conclusion, then, that our "smooth" and easy transactions and the regulatory self that executes them, starting as a biological readiness based on a primitive appreciation of other minds, is then reinforced and enriched by the calibrational powers that language bestows, is given a larger-scale map on which to operate by the culture in which transactions take place, and ends by being a reflection of the history of that culture as that history is contained in the culture's images, narratives, and tool kit.

In the light of the foregoing, we would do well to reexamine the tenets of the classical position on egocentrism with which we began:

Egocentric perspective. Michael Scaife and I discovered, as I mentioned in passing, that by the end of the first year of life, normal children habitually follow another's line of regard to see what the other is [68] looking at, and when they can find no target out there, they turn back to the looker to check gaze direction again. At that age the children can perform none of the classic Piagetian tasks indicating that they have passed beyond egocentrism. This finding led me to take very seriously the proposals of both Katherine Nelson and Margaret Donaldson that when the child understands the event structure in which he is operating he is not that different from an adult. He simply does not have as grand a collection of scripts and scenarios and event schemas as adults do. The child's mastery of deictic shifters suggests, moreover, that egocentrism per se is not the problem. It is when the child fails to grasp the structure of events that he adopts an egocentric framework. The problem is not with competence but with performance. It is not that the child does not have the capacity to take another's perspective, but rather that he cannot do so without understanding the situation in which he is operating.

Privacy. The notion of the "private" Self free of cultural definition is part of the stance inherent in our Western conception of Self. The nature of the "untold" and the "untellable" and our attitudes toward them are deeply cultural in character. Private impulses are defined as such by the culture. Obviously, the divide between "private" and "public" meanings prescribed by a given culture makes a great difference in the way people in that culture view such meanings. In our culture, for example, a good deal of heavy emotional weather is made out of the distinction, and there is (at least among the educated) a push to get the private into the public domain – whether through confession or psychoanalysis. To revert to Rosaldo's Ilongot, the pressures are quite different for them, and so is the divide. How a culture defines privacy plays an enormous part in what people feel private *about* and when and how – as we have already seen in Amélie Rorty's account of personhood in Chapter 2.

Unmediated conceptualism. In the main, we do not construct a reality solely on the basis of private encounters with exemplars of natural states. Most of our approaches to the world are mediated through negotiation with others. It is this truth that gives such extraordinary force to Vygotsky's theory of the zone of proximal development, to which I shall turn in the next chapter. We know far too little about learning from vicarious experience, from interaction, from media, even from tutors. [69]

Tripartism. I hope that all of the foregoing underlines the poverty that is bred by making too sharp a distinction between cognition, affect, and action, with cognition as the late-blooming stepsister. David Krech used to urge that people "perfink" – perceive, feel, and think at once. They also act within the constraints of what they "perfink." We can abstract each of these functions from the unified whole, but if we do so too rigidly we lose sight of the fact that it is one of the functions of a culture to keep them related and together in those images, stories, and the like by which our experience is given coherence and cultural relevance. The scripts and stories and "loose associative chains" that Rosaldo spoke of are templates for canonical ways of fusing the three into self-directing patterns – ways of being a Self in transaction. In Chapter 8, on the relation of thought and emotion, I shall take up this matter in more detail.

Finally, I want briefly to relate what I have said in this chapter to the discussions of narrative in the chapters of Part One. Insofar as we account for our own actions and for the human events that occur around us principally in terms of narrative, story, drama, it is conceivable that our sensitivity to narrative provides the major link between our own sense of self and our sense of others in the social world around us. The common coin may be provided by the forms of narrative that the culture offers us. Again, life could be said to imitate art.

References

(p. 57 [of original text])
Grice, H. P. 1976. "Logic and Conversation." In *Syntax and Semantics 3: Speech Acts*, ed. P. Cole and J. L. Morgan. New York: Academic Press.

Sperber, Dan and Deirdre Wilson. 1982. "Mutual Knowledge and Relevance in Theories of Comprehension." In *Mutual Knowledge*, ed. N. V. Smith. London: Academic Press.

Putnam, Hilary. 1975. *Mind, Language and Reality*, vol. 2. Cambridge: Cambridge University Press.

Trevarthen, Colwyn. 1979. "Instincts for Human Understanding and for Cultural Cooperation: Their Development in Infancy." In *Human Ethology: Claims and Limits of a New Discipline*, ed. M. von Cranach, K. Foppa, W. Lepenies and D. Ploog. Cambridge: Cambridge University Press.

Scheler, Max. 1954. *The Nature of Sympathy*. London: Routledge and Kegan Paul.

(p. 58 [of original text])
For a fuller discussion of the impact of Fritz Heider's work, see Jones, E. E. 1985. "Major Developments in Social Psychology during the Last Five Decades." In *Handbook of*

Social Psycology, 3rd ed., vol. 1, ed. G. Lindzey and E. Aronson. New York: Random House.

Bruner, Jerome and Renato Tagiuri. 1954. "The Perception of People." In *Handbook of Social Psychology*, ed. Gardner Lindzey. Reading, MA: Addison-Wesley.

(p. 60 [of original text])

Bruner, Jerome. 1976. "Learning How to Do Things with Words." In *Human Growth and Development*, ed. J. Bruner and A. Garton. Wolfson College Lectures. Oxford: Oxford University Press.

Scaife, Michael and Jerome Bruner. 1975. "The Capacity for Joint Visual Attention in the Infant." *Nature* 253: 265–6.

The two classical discussions of "shifters" are Lyons, John. 1977. *Semantics*, vols. 1 and 2. Cambridge: Cambridge University Press and Benveniste, Emile. 1971. *Problems in General Linguistics*. Coral Gables, FL: University of Miami Press, chs. 18–23. For a more psychological discussion see Clark, Eve. 1976. "From Gesture to Word: On the Natural History of Deixis in Language Acquisition." In Bruner and Garton, eds, *Human Growth and Development* (re. Bruner 1976).

For Mead's views see particularly Mead, George Herbert. 1934. *Mind, Self, and Society*. Chicago: University of Chicago Press.

The "whipping boy" in this case is Piaget, Jean. 1956. *The Child's Conception of Space*. London: Routledge and Kegan Paul.

(p. 62 [of original text])

Greenberg, Joseph, ed. 1963. *Universals of Language*. Cambridge, MA: MIT Press. See also Greenberg, Joseph. 1957. *Essays in Linguistics*. Chicago: University of Chicago Press.

Chomsky, Noam. 1976. *Reflections on Language*. London: Temple Smith.

(p. 63 [of original text])

Evans, Gareth. 1982. *The Varieties of Reference*, ed. J. McDowell. Oxford: Oxford University Press; see also Charles Taylor's interesting review, "Dwellers in Egocentric Space." *Times Literary Supplement*, March 11, 1983.

(p. 64 [of original text])

Olson, David. 1970. "Language and Thought: Aspects of a Cognitive Theory of Semantics." *Psychological Review* 77: 257–73.

Weir, Ruth. 1962. *Language in the Crib*. The Hague: Mouton.

The work of the New York Language Acquisition Group has not yet been published. It was presented in preliminary reports at the New York Child Language Group, November 1983, in papers delivered by Jerome Bruner, John Dore, Carol Feldman, Katherine Nelson, Daniel Stern, and Rita Watson.

For a discussion of constitutiveness as a "design feature" of language see Charles Hockett. 1977. *The View from Language: Selected Essays*. Athens, GA: University of Georgia Press. But of course the principal source for the idea of constitutiveness is John Austin's discussion of performatives in *How to Do Things with Words*. Oxford: Oxford University Press, 1962.

(p. 65 [of original text])

Feldman, Carol. 1983. "Epistemology and Ontology in Current Psychological Theory" (American Psychological Association Address, Sept. 1983); see also her "Thought from Language: The Linguistic Construction of Cognitive Representations." In *Making Sense: The Child's Construction of the World*, ed. Jerome Bruner and Helen Weinreich-Haste. London: Methuen (in press) [published 1987, ed.].

Geertz, Clifford. 1973. *The Interpretation of Cultures*. New York: Basic Books.

Rosaldo, Michelle. 1984. "Toward an Anthropology of Self and Feeling." In *Culture Theory: Essays on Mind, Self, and Emotion*, ed. R. Shweder and R. LeVine, 137–58. Cambridge: Cambridge University Press. Quotations from p. 140.

(p. 66 [of original text])

Turner, Victor. 1982. *From Ritual to Theatre*. New York: Performing Arts Journal Publications.

(p. 67 [of original text])

For an account of the work of Ann Brown, J. R. Hayes, and David Perkins on metacognition, see Chipman, S. F., J. W. Segal and R. Glaser. 1985. *Thinking and Learning Skills*, vol. 2. Hillsdale, NJ: Erlbaum. Esp. chs. 14, 15, and 17.

For a review of studies on "repair" in child language, see Clark, Eve. 1978. "Awareness of language: Some evidence from what children say and do." In *The Child's Conception of Language*, ed. A. Sinclair, R. J. Jarvella and W. J. M. Levelt. Berlin and New York: Springer-Verlag. For a particularly striking example of early repair, see chapter by Mary Louise Kasermann and Klaus Foppa, in Werner Deutsch, ed., *The Child's Construction of Language*. London: Academic Press, 1981.

(p. 68 [of original text])

Katherine Nelson and J. Grundel, "At Morning it's Lunchtime: A Scriptal View of Children's Dialogue" (paper presented at the Conference on Dialogue, Language Development and Dialectical Research, University of Michigan, December 1977).

Donaldson, Margaret. 1978. *Children's Minds*. New York: Norton.

Rosaldo, Michelle. 1980. *Knowledge and Passion*. Stanford: Stanford University Press.

LANGUAGE: THE ULTIMATE ARTIFACT

Andy Clark

10.1 Word Power

What does public language do for us? There is a common, easy answer which, though not incorrect, is subtly misleading. The easy answer is that language helps us to communicate ideas. It lets other human beings profit from what we know, and it enables us to profit from what they know. This is surely true, and it locates one major wellspring of our rather unique kind of cognitive success. However, the emphasis on language as a medium of communication tends to blind us to a subtler but equally potent role: the role of language as a tool[1] that alters the nature of the computational tasks involved in various kinds of problem solving.

The basic idea is simple enough. Consider a familiar tool or artifact, say a pair of scissors.[2] Such an artifact typically exhibits a kind of double adaptation – a two-way fit, both to the user and to the task. On the one hand, the shape of the scissors is remarkably well fitted to the form and the manipulative capacities of the human hand. On the other hand (so to speak), the artifact, when it is in use, confers on the agent some characteristic powers or capacities which humans do not naturally possess: the ability to make neat straight cuts in certain papers and fabrics, the ability to open bubble packs, and so forth. This is obvious enough; why else would we value the artifact at all?

Public language is in many ways the ultimate artifact. Not only does it confer on us added powers of communication; it also enables us to reshape a variety of difficult but important tasks into formats better suited to the basic computational capacities of the human brain. Just as scissors enable us to exploit our basic manipulative capacities to fulfill new ends, language enables us to exploit our basic cognitive capacities of pattern recognition and transformation in ways that reach out to new behavioral and intellectual horizons. Moreover, public language may even exhibit the kind of double adaptation described above, and may hence constitute a body of linguistic artifacts whose form is itself in part evolved so as to exploit the contingencies and biases of human learning and recall. (This reverse adaptation – of the artifact to the user – suggests a possible angle on the controversy concerning innate mechanisms for language acquisition and understanding.) Finally, the sheer intimacy of the relations between human thought and the tools of public language bequeaths an interesting puzzle. For in this case, especially, it is a delicate matter to determine where the user ends and the tool begins!

10.2 Beyond Communication

The idea that language may do far more than merely serve as a vehicle for communication is not new. It is clearly present in the work of developmentalists such as Lev Vygotsky (1986 [1962]) and Laura Berk (see, e.g., Diaz and Berk 1992). It figures in the philosophical conjectures and arguments of, e.g., Peter Carruthers (to appear) and Ray Jackendoff (to appear). And it surfaces in the more cognitive-science-oriented speculations of Daniel Dennett (1991, 1995). It will be helpful to review some of the central ideas in this literature before pursuing our preferred version – viz., the idea of language as a computational transformer that allows pattern-completing brains to tackle otherwise intractable classes of cognitive problems.

In the 1930s, Vygotsky, a psychologist, pioneered the idea that the use of public language had profound effects on cognitive development. He posited powerful links among speech, social experience, and learning. Two Vygotskian ideas that are especially pertinent for present purposes concern private speech and scaffolded action (action within the "zone of proximal development" – see Vygotsky 1986 and chapter 3 above). We have called an action "scaffolded" to the extent that it relies on some kind of external support. Such support could come from the use of tools or from exploitation of the knowledge and skills of others; that is to say, scaffolding (as I shall use the term[3]) denotes a broad class of physical, cognitive, and social augmentations – augmentations that allow us to achieve some goal that would otherwise be beyond us. Simple examples include the use of a compass and a pencil to draw a perfect circle, the role of other crew members in enabling a ship's pilot to steer a course, and an infant's ability to take its first steps only while suspended in the enabling grip of its parents. Vygotsky's focus on the "zone of proximal development" was concerned with cases in which a child is temporarily able to succeed at designated tasks only by courtesy of the guidance or help provided by another human being (usually a parent or a teacher), but the idea dovetails with Vygotsky's interest in private speech in the following way: When a child is "talked through" a tricky challenge by a more experienced agent, the child can often succeed at a task that would otherwise prove impossible. (Think of learning to tie your shoelaces.) Later, when the adult is absent, the child can conduct a similar dialogue, but this time with herself. But even in this latter case, it is argued, the speech (be it vocal or "internalized") functions so as to guide behavior, to focus attention, and to guard against common errors. In such cases, the role of language is to guide and shape our own behavior – it is a tool for structuring and controlling action, not merely a medium of information transfer between agents.

This Vygotskian image is supported by more recent bodies of developmental research. Berk and Garvin (1984) observed and recorded the ongoing speech of a group of children between the ages of 5 and 10 years. They found that most of the children's private speech (speech not addressed to some other listener) seemed keyed to the direction and control of the child's own actions, and that the incidence of such speech increased when the child was alone and trying to perform some difficult task. In subsequent studies (Bivens and Berk 1990; Berk 1994) it was found that the children who made the greatest numbers of self-directed comments were the ones who subsequently mastered the tasks best. Berk concluded, from these and other studies, that self-directed speech (be it vocal or silent inner rehearsal) is a crucial cognitive tool that allows us to highlight the most puzzling features of new situations and to better direct and control our own problem-solving actions.

The theme of language as a tool has also been developed by the philosopher Christopher Gauker. Gauker's concern, however, is to rethink the intra-individual role of language in terms of what he calls a "cause-effect analysis." The idea here is to depict public language "not as a tool for representing the world or expressing one's thoughts but a tool for effecting changes in one's environment" (Gauker 1990, 31). To get the flavor of this, consider the use of a symbol by a chimpanzee to request a banana. The chimp touches a specific key on a keypad (the precise physical location of the key can be varied between trials) and learns that making *that* symbol light tends to promote the arrival of bananas. The chimp's quasi-linguistic understanding is explicable, Gauker suggests, in terms of the chimp's appreciation of a cause-effect relationship between the symbol production and changes in its local environment. Gauker looks at a variety of symbol-using behaviors and concludes that they all succumb to this kind of analysis. This leads him to hypothesize that, although clearly more complex, human beings' linguistic understanding likewise "consists in a grasp of the causal relations into which linguistic signs may enter" (ibid., 44).

Gauker tends to see the role of language as, if you like, directly causal: as a way of getting things done, much like reaching out your hand and grabbing a cake. However, the idea that we learn, by experience, of the peculiar causal potencies of specific signs and symbols is, in principle, much broader. We might even, as in the Vygotskian examples, discover that the self-directed utterance of words and phrases has certain effects on our own behavior.[4] We might also learn to exploit language as a tool in a variety of even less direct ways, as a means of altering the shape of computational problem spaces (see section 10.3).

One obvious question raised by the putative role of language as a self-directed tool is "How does it work?" What is it about, for example, self-directed speech that fits it to play a guiding role? After all, it is not at all clear how we can tell ourselves anything we don't already know! Surely all public language can ever be is a medium for expressing ideas already formulated and understood in some other, more basic inner code. This is precisely the view that a supra-communicative account of language ultimately has to reject. One way to reject it is to depict public language as itself the medium of a special kind of thought. Another (by no means exclusive, and not altogether distinct) way is to depict linguaform inputs as having distinctive *effects* on some inner computational device. Carruthers (to appear) champions the first of these; Dennett (1991) offers a version of the second.[5] Carruthers argues that, in this case at least, we should take very seriously the evidence of our own introspection. It certainly often seems as if our very thoughts are composed of the words and sentences of public language. And the reason we have this impression, Carruthers argues, is because it is true: "inner thinking is literally done in inner speech."[6] By extension, Carruthers is able to view many uses of language as less a matter of simple communication than a matter of what he nicely terms *public thinking*. This perspective fits satisfyingly with the Vygotskian view championed by Berk and is also applicable to the interesting case of writing down our ideas. Carruthers (ibid., 56) suggests that "one does not *first* entertain a private thought and *then* write it down: rather, the thinking is the writing." I shall return to this point later (see section 10.3 and the epilogue), since I believe that what Carruthers says is almost right but that we can better understand the kind of case he has in mind by treating the writing as an environmental manipulation that transforms the problem space for human brains.

A further way to unpack a supra-communicative view of language, as has been noted, is to suppose that the linguistic inputs actually reprogram or otherwise alter the high-level computational structure of the brain itself. The exegesis is delicate (and therefore tentative), but Dennett (1991, 278) seems to hold such a view when he suggests that "conscious human minds are more-or-less serial virtual machines implemented-inefficiently-on the parallel hardware that evolution has provided for us." In this and other passages of the same work, the idea seems to be that the bombardment of (something like) parallel-processing, connectionist, pattern-completing brains by (among other things) public-language texts and sentences (reminders, plans, exhortations, questions, etc.) results in a kind of cognitive reorganization akin to that which occurs when one computer system simulates another. In such cases, the installation of a new program allows the user to treat a serial LISP machine (for example) as if it were a massively parallel connectionist device. What Dennett is proposing is, he tells us (ibid., 218), the same trick in reverse – the simulation of something like a serial logic engine using the altogether different resources of the massively parallel neural networks that biological evolution rightly favors for real-world, real-time survival and action.

Strikingly, Dennett (1995, 370–3) suggests that it is this subtle reprogramming of the brain by (primarily) linguistic bombardment that yields the phenomena of human consciousness (our sense of self) and enables us to far surpass the behavioral and cognitive achievements of most other animals. Dennett thus depicts our advanced cognitive skills as attributable in large part not to our innate hardware (which may differ only in small, though important, ways from that of other animals) but to the special way that various plastic (programmable) features of the brain are modified by the effects of culture and language. As Dennett (1991, 219) puts it, the serial machine is installed by courtesy of "myriad microsettings in the plasticity of the brain." Of course, mere exposure to culture and language is not sufficient to ensure human-like cognition. You can expose a cockroach to all the language you like and get no trace of the cognitive transformations Dennett sees in us. Dennett's claim is not that there are no initial hardware-level differences. Rather it is that some relatively small hardware differences (e.g. between humans and chimpanzees) allow us to both create and benefit from public language and other cultural developments in ways that lead to a great snowball of cognitive change and augmentation – including, perhaps, the literal installation of a new kind of computational device inside the brain.

Dennett's vision is complex and not altogether unambiguous. The view I want to develop is clearly deeply related to it, but it differs (I think) in one crucial respect. Whereas Dennett sees public language as both a cognitive tool and a source of some profound but subtle reorganization of the brain, I am inclined to see it as in essence just a tool – an external resource that complements but does not profoundly alter the brain's own basic modes of representation and computation. That is to say, I see the changes as relatively superficial ones geared to allowing us to use and exploit various *external* resources to the full. The positions are not, of course, wholly distinct. The mere fact that we often mentally rehearse sentences in our heads and use these to guide and alter our behavior means that one cannot and should not treat language and culture as wholly external resources. Nonetheless, it remains possible that such rehearsal does not involve the use of any fundamentally different kind of computational device in the brain so much as the use of the same old (essentially pattern-completing) resources to model the special kinds of behavior observed in the world of public language. And, as Paul Churchland (1995, 264–9) points out, there is indeed a class of connectionist networks ("recurrent networks" – see chapter 7 above, Elman 1994, and further discussion in Clark 1993) that seem well suited to modeling and supporting such linguistic behavior.

This view of inner rehearsal is nicely developed by the connectionists David Rumelhart, Paul Smolensky, James McClelland, and Geoffrey Hinton, who argue that the general strategy of "mentally modeling" the behavior of selected aspects of our environment is especially important insofar as it allows us to imagine external resources with which we have previously physically interacted, and to replay the dynamics of such interactions in our heads. Thus experience with drawing and using Venn diagrams allows us to train a neural network which subsequently allows us to manipulate imagined Venn diagrams in our heads. Such imaginative manipulations require a specially trained neural resource, to be sure, but there is no reason to suppose that such training results in the installation of a different *kind* of computational device. It is the same old process of pattern completion in high-dimensional representational spaces, but applied to the special domain of a specific kind of *external* representation. Rumelhart et al., who note the clear link with a Vygotskian image, summarize their view as follows (1986, 47):

> We can be instructed to behave in a particular way. Responding to instructions in this way can be viewed simply as responding to some environmental event. We can also remember such an instruction and "tell ourselves" what to do. We have, in this way, internalized the instruction. We believe that the process of following instructions is essentially the same whether we have told ourselves or have been told what to do. Thus even here we have a kind of internalization of an external representational format.

The larger passage (44–48) from which the above is extracted is remarkably rich and touches on several of our major themes. Rumelhart et al. note that such external formalisms are especially hard to invent and slow to develop and are themselves the kinds of product that (in an innocently bootstrapping kind of way) can evolve only thanks to the linguistically mediated processes of cultural storage and gradual refinement over many lifetimes. They also note that by using real external representations we put ourselves in a position to use our basic perceptual and motor skills to separate problems into parts and to attend to a series of sub-problems, storing intermediate results along the way – an important property to which we shall return in section 10.3.

The tack I am about to pursue likewise depicts language as an external artifact designed to complement rather than transfigure the basic processing profile we share with other animals. It does not depict experience with language as a source of profound inner reprogramming. Whether it depicts inner linguistic rehearsal as at times literally constitutive of specific human cognizings (as Carruthers claims) is moot. What matters, I think, is not to try to confront the elusive question "Do we actually think in words?" (to which the answer is surely "In a sense yes and in a sense no!"), but to try to see just what computational benefits the pattern-completing brain may press from the rich environment of manipulable external symbolic structures. Time, then, to beard language in its den.

10.3 Trading Spaces

How might linguistic artifacts complement the activity of the pattern-completing brain? One key role, I suggest, is captured by the image of *trading spaces*: the agent who exploits external symbol structures is trading culturally achieved *representation* against what would otherwise be (at best) time-intensive and labor-intensive internal *computation*. This is, in fact, the very same tradeoff we often make purely internally when we stop short of actually manipulating external symbols but instead use our internal models of those very symbols to cast a problem in a notational form that makes it easier to solve. And, as has often been remarked, it is surely our prior experiences with the manipulations of real external symbols that prepares the way for these more self-contained episodes of symbolically simplified problem solving.

Examples are legion, and they include the use of the Arabic numeral system (rather than, e.g., roman numerals) as a notation for arithmetic problem solving; the use of Venn diagrams for solving problems of set theory; the use of the specialized languages of biology, physics, and so on to set up and solve complex problems; and the use of lists and schedules as aides to individual planning and group coordination. All these cases share an underlying rationale which is to build some of the knowledge you need to solve a problem directly into the resources you use to represent the problem in the first place. But the precise details of how the tradeoff is achieved and in what ways it expands our cognitive potential vary from case to case. It is useful, then, to distinguish a variety of ways in which we may trade culturally transmitted representation against individual computational effort.

The very simplest cases are those that involve the use of external symbolic media to offload memory onto the world. Here we simply use the artifactual world of texts, diaries, notebooks, and the like as a means of systematically storing large and often complex bodies of data. We may also use simple external manipulations (such as leaving a note on the mirror) to prompt the recall, from onboard biological memory, of appropriate information and intentions at the right time. Thus, this use of linguistic artifacts is perfectly continuous with a variety of simpler environmental manipulations, such as leaving an empty olive oil bottle by the door so that you cannot help but run across it (and hence recall the need for olive oil) as you set out for the shops.

A slightly more complex case (Dennett 1994) concerns the use of labels as a source of environmental simplification. One idea here is that we use signs and labels to provide perceptually simple clues to help us negotiate complex environments. Signs for cloakrooms, for nightclubs, and for city centers all fulfill this role. They allow a little individual learning to go a very long way, helping others to find their targets in new locales without knowing in advance what, in detail, to seek or even where exactly to seek it. McClamrock (1995, 88) nicely describes this strategy as one in which we "enforce on the environment certain kinds of stable properties that will lessen our computational burdens and the demands on us for inference."

Closely related, but perhaps less obvious, is the provision, by the use of linguistic labels, of a greatly simplified *learning* environment for important concepts – a role already exemplified and discussed in the treatment of the Hutchins's "moon and tide" simulation in chapter 9. The use of simple labels, it seems, provides a hefty clue for the learning device, allowing it to shrink enormous search spaces to manageable size.[7]

More sophisticated benefits of the use of linguistic representation cluster around the use of language in coordinating action. We say to others that we will be at a certain place at a certain time. We even play this game with ourselves, perhaps by writing down a list of what we will do on what days. One effect of such explicit planning is to facilitate the *coordination* of actions. Thus, if another person knows you have said you'll be at the station at 9:00 A.M., they can time their taxi ride accordingly. Or, in the solo case, if you have to buy paint before touching up your car, and if you have to go to the shops to buy other items anyway, you can minimize your efforts and enforce proper sequencing by following an explicit plan. As the space of demands and opportunities grows, it often becomes necessary to use pencil and paper to collect and repeatedly reorganize the options, and then to preserve the result as a kind of external control structure available to guide your subsequent actions.

Such coordinative functions, though important, do not exhaust the benefits of explicit (usually language-based) planning. As Michael Bratman (1987) has pointed out, the creation of explicit plans may play a special role in reducing the on-line cognitive load on resource-limited agents like ourselves. The idea here is that our plans have a kind of stability that pays dividends by reducing the amount of on-line deliberation in which we engage as we go about much of our daily business. Of course, new information can, and often does, cause us to revise our plans. But we do not let every slight change prompt a reassessment of our plans – even when, other things being equal, we might now choose slightly differently. Such stability, Bratman suggests, plays the role of blocking a wasteful process of continual reassessment and choice (except, of course, in cases where there is some quite major payoff for the disruption).[8] Linguistic exchange and formulation thus plays a key role in coordinating activities (at both inter-personal and intra-personal levels) *and* in reducing the amount of daily on-line deliberation in which we engage.

Closely related to these functions of control and coordination is the fascinating but ill-understood role of inner rehearsal of speech in manipulating our own attention and guiding our allocation of cognitive resources. The developmental results mentioned in section 10.2 (concerning the way self-directed speech enhances problem solving) suggest an image of inner speech as an extra *control loop* capable of modulating the brain's use of its own basic cognitive resources. We see such a phenomenon in inter-personal exchange when we follow written instructions, or when we respond to someone else's vocal prompts in learning to drive or to windsurf. When we practice on our own, the mental rehearsal of these same sentences acts as a controlling signal that somehow helps us to monitor and correct our own behaviors.

Dreyfus and Dreyfus (1990) have argued that inner rehearsal plays this role only in novice performance and that real experts leave behind such linguistic props and supports. But although it is clearly true that, for example, expert drivers no longer mentally rehearse such prompts as "mirror-signal-maneuver," this does not show that language-based reason plays no role at all at the expert level. An interesting recent study by Kirsh and Maglio (1991; see chapter 3 above) concerns the roles of reaction and linguaform reflection in expert performance at the computer game Tetris. Tetris, recall, is a game in which the player attempts to accumulate a high score by the compact placement of geometric objects (zoids) which fall down from the top of the screen. As a zoid descends, the player can manipulate its fall by rotating it at the resting point of its current trajectory. When a zoid comes to rest, a new one appears at the top of the screen. The speed of fall increases with score. But (the saving grace) a full row (one in which each screen location is filled by a zoid) disappears entirely. When the player falls behind in zoid placement and the screen fills up so that new zoids cannot enter it, the game ends. Advanced play thus depends crucially on fast decision making. Hence, Tetris provides a clear case of domain in which connectiontist, pattern-completion style reasoning looks required for expert performance. If the model of Dreyfus and Dreyfus is correct, moreover, such parallel, pattern-completion-style reasoning should exhaustively explain expert skill. But, interestingly, this does not seem to be so. Instead, expert play seems to depend on a delicate and non-obvious interaction between a fast, pattern-completion module and a set of explicit higher-level concerns or normative policies. The results are preliminary, and it would be inappropriate to report them in detail, but the key observation is that true Tetris experts report that they rely not solely on a set of fast adaptive responses produced by (as it were) a trained-up network but also on a set of high-level concerns or policies, which they use to monitor the outputs of the skilled network so as to "discover trends or deviations from...normative policy" (Kirsh and Maglio 1991, 10). Examples of such policies include "don't cluster in the center, but try to keep the contour flat" and "avoid piece dependencies" (ibid., 8–9). Now, on the face of it, these are just the kind of rough and ready maxims we might (following Dreyfus and Dreyfus) associate with novice players only. Yet attention to these normative policies seems to mark especially the play of real experts. Still, we must wonder how such policies can help at the level of expert play, given the time constraints on responses. There is just no time for reflection on such policies to override on-line output for a given falling zoid.

It is here that Kirsh and Maglio make a suggestive conjecture. The role of the high-level policies, they suggest, is probably indirect. Instead of using the policy to override the output of a trained-up network, the effect may be to alter the focus of attention for subsequent inputs. The idea is that the trained-up network (or "reactive module," as Kirsh and Maglio put it) will sometimes make moves that lead to dangerous situations in which the higher-level policies are not reflected. The remedy is not to override the reactive module, but to thereafter manipulate the inputs it receives so as to present feature vectors that, when processed by the reactive model in the usual way, will yield outputs in line with policy. As Kirsh and Maglio describe it, the normative policies are thus the business of a distinct and highly "language-infected" resource that indirectly modulates the behavior of a more basic, fast and fluent reactive agency. Just how this indirect modulation is accomplished is, alas, left uncomfortably vague, but Kirsh and Maglio speculate that it might work by biasing perceptual attention toward certain danger regions or by increasing the resolution of specific visual routines.

The most obvious benefit of the linguistic encoding of thoughts and ideas, is, of course, that such encoding formats our ideas into compact and easily transmitted signals that enable other human beings to refine them, to critique them, and to exploit them. This is the *communicative* role, which, I have suggested, tends to dominate our intuitive ideas about the role and function of language. But our conception even of this familiar role remains impoverished until we see that role in the specific computational context provided by broadly connectionist models of the biological brain, for one notable feature of such models is the extreme *path dependence* of their learning routines. For example, a compelling series of experiments by Jeff Elman (1994) and others showed that connectionist learning is heavily dependent on the sequence of training cases. If the early training goes wrong, the network is often unable to recover. A specific network proved able to learn complex grammatical rules from a corpus of example sentences only if it had previously been trained on a more basic subset of the examples highlighting (e.g.) verb-subject number agreement. Early exposure to the other, more complex grammatical cases (such as long-distance dependences) would lead it into bad early "solutions" (local minima) from which it was then unable to escape.[9] Human learning, like learning in artificial neural networks, appears to be hostage to at least some degree of path dependence. Certain ideas can be understood only once others are in place. The training received by one mind fits it to grasp and expand upon ideas which gain no foothold of comprehension in another. The processes of formal education, indeed, are geared to take young (and not-so-young) minds along a genuine intellectual journey, which may even begin with ideas which are now known to be incorrect but which alone seem able to prime the system to later appreciate finer-grained truth. Such mundane facts reflect cognitive path dependence – you can't get everywhere from anywhere, and where you are now strongly constrains your potential future intellectual trajectories. In fact, such path dependence is nicely explained by treating intellectual progress as involving something like a process of computational search in a large and complex space. Previous learning inclines the system to try out certain locations in the space and not others. When the prior learning is appropriate, the job of learning some new regularity is made tractable: the prior learning acts as a filter on the space of options to be explored. Artificial neural networks that employ gradient-descent learning (see chapter 3) are especially highly constrained insofar as the learning routine forces the network always to explore at the edges of its current weight assignments. Since these constitute its current knowledge, it means that such networks cannot "jump around" in hypothesis space. The network's current location in weight space (its current knowledge) is thus a major constraint on what new "ideas" it can next explore (Elman 1994, 94).

In confronting devices that exhibit some degree of path dependence, the mundane observation that language allows ideas to be packaged and to migrate between individuals takes on a new force. We can now appreciate how such migrations may allow the communal construction of extremely delicate and difficult intellectual trajectories and progressions. An idea that only Joe's prior experience could make available, but that can flourish only in the intellectual niche currently provided by the brain of Mary, can now realize its full potential by journeying between Joe and Mary as and when required. The path to a good idea can now criss-cross individual learning histories so that one agent's local minimum becomes another's potent building block. Moreover, the sheer number of intellectual niches available within a linguistically linked community provides a stunning matrix of possible inter-agent trajectories. The observation that public language allows human cognition to be collective (Churchland 1995, 270) thus takes on new depth once we recognize the role of such collective endeavor in transcending the path-dependent nature of individual human cognition. Even a blind and unintelligent search for productive recodings of stored data will now and again yield a powerful result. By allowing such results to migrate between individuals, culturally scaffolded reason is able to incrementally explore spaces which path-dependent individual reason could never hope to penetrate. (For a detailed, statistically based investigation of this claim, see Clark and Thornton, to appear.)

This general picture fits neatly with Merlin Donald's (1991) exploratory work on the evolution of culture and cognition. Donald recognizes very clearly the crucial role of forms of external scaffolding (particularly, of external memory systems) in human thought. But he distinguishes two major types of scaffolding, which he terms the *mythic* and the *theoretic*. Before the Greeks, Donald claims, various external formalisms were in use but were deployed only in the service of myths and narratives. The key innovation of the Greeks was to begin to use the written medium to record the *processes* of thought and argument. Whereas previous written records contained only myths or finished theories (which were to be learned wholesale and passed down relatively unaltered), the Greeks began to record partial ideas, speculations with evidence for and against them, and the like. This new practice allowed partial solutions and conjectures to be passed around, amended, completed by others, and so on. According to Donald (ibid., 343), what was thus created was "much more than a symbolic invention, like the alphabet, or a specific external memory medium, such as improved paper or printing"; it was "the *process* of externally encoded cognitive change and discovery."

To complete our initial inventory of the cognitive virtues of linguistically scaffolded thought, consider the physical properties of certain external media. As I construct this chapter, for example, I am continually creating, putting aside, and reorganizing chunks of text. I have files (both paper and on-line) which contain all kinds of hints and fragments, stored up over a long period of time, which may be germane to the discussion. I have source texts and papers full of notes and annotations. As I (literally, physically) move these things about, interacting first with one and then another and making new notes, annotations, and plans, the intellectual shape of the chapter grows and solidifies. It is a shape that does not spring fully developed from inner cogitations. Instead, it is the product of a sustained and iterated sequence of interactions between my brain and a variety of external props. In these cases, I am willing to say, a good deal of actual thinking involves loops and circuits that run outside the head and through the local environment. Extended intellectual arguments and theses are almost always the products of brains acting in concert with multiple external resources. These resources enable us to pursue manipulations and juxtapositions of ideas and data that would quickly baffle the unaugmented brain.[10] In all these cases, the real physical environment of printed words and symbols allows us to search, store, sequence, and reorganize data in ways alien to the onboard repertoire of the biological brain.[11]

The moral is clear. Public speech, inner rehearsal, and the use of written and on-line texts are all potent tools that reconfigure the shape of computational space.

Again and again we trade culturally achieved representation against individual computation. Again and again we use words to focus, clarify, transform, offload, and control our own thinkings. Thus understood, language is not the mere imperfect mirror of our intuitive knowledge.[12] Rather, it is part and parcel of the mechanism of reason itself.

10.4 Thoughts about Thoughts: The Mangrove Effect

If a tree is seen growing on an island, which do you suppose came first? It is natural (and usually correct) to assume that the island provided the fertile soil in which a lucky seed came to rest. Mangrove forests,[13] however, constitute a revealing exception to this general rule. The mangrove grows from a floating seed which establishes itself in the water, rooting in shallow mud flats. The seedling sends complex vertical roots through the surface of the water, culminating in what looks to all intents and purposes like a small tree posing on stilts. The complex system of aerial roots, however, soon traps floating soil, weeds, and debris. After a time, the accumulation of trapped matter forms a small island. As more time passes, the island grows larger and larger. A growing mass of such islands can eventually merge, effectively extending the shoreline out to the trees. Throughout this process, and despite our prior intuitions, it is the land that is progressively built by the trees.

Something like the "mangrove effect," I suspect, is operative in some species of human thought. It is natural to suppose that words are always rooted in the fertile soil of preexisting thoughts. But sometimes, at least, the influence seems to run in the other direction. A simple example is poetry. In constructing a poem, we do not simply use words to express thoughts. Rather, it is often the properties of the words (their structure and cadence) that determine the thoughts that the poem comes to express. A similar partial reversal can occur during the construction of complex texts and arguments. By writing down our ideas, we generate a trace in a format that opens up a range of new possibilities. We can then inspect and reinspect the same ideas, coming at them from many different angles and in many different frames of mind. We can hold the original ideas steady so that we may judge them, and safely experiment with subtle alterations. We can store them in ways that allow us to compare and combine them with other complexes of ideas in ways that would quickly defeat the unaugmented imagination. In these ways, and as was remarked in the previous section, the real properties of physical text transform the space of possible thoughts.

Such observations lead me to the following conjecture: Perhaps it is public language that is responsible for a complex of rather distinctive features of human thought – viz., the ability to display *second-order cognitive dynamics*. By second-order cognitive dynamics I mean a cluster of powerful capacities involving self-evaluation, self-criticism, and finely honed remedial responses.[14] Examples would include recognizing a flaw in our own plan or argument and dedicating further cognitive efforts to fixing it, reflecting on the unreliability of our own initial judgements in certain types of situations and proceeding with special caution as a result, coming to see why we reached a particular conclusion by appreciating the logical transitions in our own thought, and thinking about the conditions under which we think best and trying to bring them about. The list could be continued, but the pattern should be clear. In all these cases, we are effectively thinking about our own cognitive profiles or about specific thoughts. This "thinking about thinking" is a good candidate for a distinctively human capacity – one not evidently shared by the non-language-using animals that share our planet. Thus, it is natural to wonder whether this might be an entire species of thought in which language plays the generative role – a species of thought that is not just reflected in (or extended by) our use of words but is directly dependent upon language for its very existence. Public language and the inner rehearsal of sentences would, on this model, act like the aerial roots of the mangrove tree – the words would serve as fixed points capable of attracting and positioning additional intellectual matter, creating the islands of second-order thought so characteristic of the cognitive landscape of *Homo sapiens*.

It is easy to see, in broad outline, how this might come about. As soon as we formulate a thought in words (or on paper), it becomes an object for ourselves and for others. As an object, it is the kind of thing we can have thoughts about. In creating the object, we need have no thoughts about thoughts – but once it is there, the opportunity immediately exists to attend to it as an object in its own right. The process of linguistic formulation thus creates the stable structure to which subsequent thinkings attach.

Just such a twist on the potential role of the inner rehearsal of sentences has been suggested by the linguist Ray Jackendoff. Jackendoff (to appear) suggests that the mental rehearsal of sentences may be the primary means by which our own thoughts are able to become objects of further attention and reflection. The key claim is that linguistic formulation makes complex thoughts available to processes of mental attention, and that this, in turn, opens them up to a range of further mental operations. It enables us, for example, to pick out different elements of complex thoughts and to scrutinize each in turn. It enables us to "stabilize" very abstract ideas in working memory. And it enables us to inspect and criticize our own reasoning in ways that no other representational modality allows.

What fits internal sentence-based rehearsal to play such an unusual role? The answer, I suggest, must lie in the more mundane (and temporally antecedent) role of language as an instrument of communication. In order to function as an efficient instrument of communication, public language will have been molded into a code well suited to the kinds of interpersonal exchange in which ideas are presented, inspected, and subsequently criticized. And this, in turn, involves the development of a type of code that minimizes contextuality (most words retain essentially the same meanings in the different sentences in which they occur), is effectively modality-neutral (an idea may be prompted by visual, auditory, or tactile input and yet be preserved using the same verbal formula), and allows easy rote memorization of simple strings.[15] By "freezing" our own thoughts in the memorable, context-resistant, modality-transcending format of a sentence, we thus create a special kind of mental object – an object that is amenable to scrutiny from multiple cognitive angles, is not doomed to alter or change every time we are exposed to new inputs or information, and fixes the ideas at a high level of abstraction from the idiosyncratic details of their proximal origins in sensory input. Such a mental object is, I suggest, ideally suited to figure in the evaluative, critical, and tightly focused operations distinctive of second-order cognition. It is an object fit for the close and repeated inspections highlighted by Jackendoff under the rubric of attending to our own thoughts. The coding system of public language is thus especially apt to be coopted for more private purposes of inner display, self-inspection, and self-criticism, exactly as predicted by the Vygotskian treatments mentioned in section 10.2 above. Language stands revealed as a key resource by which we effectively redescribe[16] our own thoughts in a format that makes them available for a variety of new operations and manipulations.

The emergence of such second-order cognitive dynamics is plausibly seen as one root of the veritable explosion of types and varieties of external scaffolding structures in human cultural evolution. It is because we can think about our own thinking that we can actively structure our world in ways designed to promote, support, and extend our own cognitive achievements. This process also feeds itself, as when the arrival of written text and notation allowed us to begin to fix ever more complex and extended sequences of thought and reason as objects for further scrutiny and attention. (Recall Merlin Donald's conjectures from the preceding section.)

Once the apparatus (internal and external) of sentential and text-based reflection is in place, we may expect the development of new types of non-linguistic thought and encoding – types dedicated to managing and interacting with the sentences and texts in more powerful and efficient ways.[17] The linguistic constructions, thus viewed, are a new class of objects which invite us to develop new (non-language-based) skills of use, recognition, and manipulation. Sentential and nonsentential modes of thought thus coevolve so as to complement, but not replicate, each other's special cognitive virtues.

It is a failure to appreciate this deep complementarity that, I suspect, leads Paul Churchland (one of the best and most imaginative neurophilosophers around) to dismiss linguaform expression as just a shallow reflection of our "real" knowledge. Churchland fears that without such marginalization we might mistakenly depict all thought and cognition as involving the unconscious rehearsal of sentence-like symbol strings, and thus be blinded to the powerful pattern-and-prototype-based encodings that appear to be biologically and evolutionarily fundamental. But we have now scouted much fertile intermediate territory.[18] In combining an array of biologically basic pattern-recognition skills with the special "cognitive fixatives" of word and text, we (like the mangroves) create new landscapes – new fixed points in the sea of thoughts. Viewed as a complementary cognitive artifact, language can genuinely extend our cognitive horizons – and without the impossible burden of recapitulating the detailed contents of nonlinguistic thought.

10.5 The Fit of Language to Brain

Consider an ill-designed artifact – for example, an early word-processing program that required extraordinary efforts to learn and was clumsy and frustrating to use. An imaginary mutant prodigy who found such a program easy would surely have needed neural resources especially pre-tuned to promote the speedy acquisition of such competence!

Now consider a superbly designed artifact: the paper clip.[19] The person who shows great speed and skill at learning to use paper clips need not be a mutant with a specially tuned brain, for the paper clip is *itself* adapted so as to facilitate easy use by beings like us (but not by rats or pigeons) in our office environment.

Suppose (just suppose) that language is like that. That is, it is an artifact that has in part evolved so as to be easily acquired and used by beings like us. It may, for instance, exhibit types of phonetic or grammatical structure that exploit particular natural biases of the human brain and perceptual system. If that were the case, it would look for all the world as if our brains were especially adapted to acquire natural language, but in fact it would be natural language that was especially adapted so as to be acquired by us, cognitive warts and all.

No doubt the truth lies somewhere in between. Recent conjectures by cognitive scientists (see e.g. Newport 1990) do suggest that certain aspects of natural languages (such as morphological structure) may be geared to exploiting windowing effects provided by the specific limitations of memory and attention found in young humans. And Christiansen (1994) has explicitly argued, from the standpoint of connectionist research, that language acquisition is empowered by a kind of symbiotic relationship between the users and the language, such that a language can persist and prosper only if it is easily learned and used by its human hosts. This symbiotic relationship forces languages to change and adapt in ways that promote learning.

Such reverse adaptation, in which natural language is to some extent adapted to the human brain, may be important in assessing the extent to which our capacity to learn and to use public language should *itself* be taken as evidence that we are cognitively very dissimilar to other animals. For humans *are*, it seems, the only animals capable of acquiring and fully exploiting the complex, abstract, open-ended symbol systems of public language.[20] Nonetheless, we need not suppose that this requires major and sweeping computational and neurological differences between us and other animals.[21] Instead, relatively minor neural changes may have made basic language learning possible for our ancestors, with the process of reverse adaptation thereafter leading to linguistic forms that more fully exploit pre-existing, language-independent cognitive biases (especially those of young humans).[22] The human brain, on this model, need not differ profoundly from the brains of higher animals. Instead, normal humans benefit from some small neurological innovation that, paired with the fantastically empowering environment of increasingly reverse-adapted public language, led to the cognitive explosions of human science, culture, and learning.

The vague and suggestive notion of reverse adaptation can even be given some (admittedly simplistic) quantitative and computational flesh. Hare and Elman (1995) used a "cultural phylogeny" of connectionist networks to model, in some detail, the series of changes that characterized the progression from the past-tense system of Old English (circa 870) to the modern system. They showed that the historical progression can be modeled, in some detail, by a series of neural networks in which the output from one generation is used as the training data for the next. This process yields changes in the language itself as the language alters to reflect the learning profiles of its users. Briefly, this is what happens: An original network is trained on the Old English forms. A second network is then trained (though not to perfection) on the forms produced by the first. This output is then used to train a further network, and so on. Crucially, any errors one network makes in learning to perform the mappings become parts of the next network's data set. Patterns that are hard to learn and items that are close in form to other, differently inflected items tend to disappear. As Hare and Elman (ibid., 61) put it:

> At the onset, the classes [of verbs] differ in terms of their phonological coherence and their class size. Those patterns that are initially less common or less well defined are the hardest to learn. And these tend to be lost over several generations of learning. This process snowballs as the dominant class gathers in new members and this combined class becomes an ever more powerful attractor.

By thus studying the interplay between the external data set and the processes of individual learning, Hare and Elman were able to make some quite fine-grained predictions (borne out by the linguistic facts) about the historical progression from Old English to Modern English. The important moral, for our purposes, is that in such cases the external scaffoldings of cognition *themselves* adapt so as to better prosper in the niche provided by human brains. The complementarity between the biological brain and its artifactual props and supports is thus enforced by coevolutionary forces uniting user and artifact in a virtuous circle of mutual modulation.

10.6 Where Does the Mind Stop and the Rest of the World Begin?[23]

The complexities of user-artifact dynamics invite reflection on a more general topic: how to conceive the boundary between the intelligent system and the world. This boundary, as we saw in previous chapters, looks to be rather more plastic than had previously been supposed – in many cases, selected extra-bodily resources constitute important parts of extended computational and cognitive processes. Taken to extremes, this seepage of the mind into the world threatens to reconfigure our fundamental self-image by broadening our view of persons to include, at times, aspects of the local environment. This kind of broadening is probably most plausible in cases involving the external props of written text and spoken words, for interactions with these external media are ubiquitous (in educated modern cultures), reliable, and developmentally basic. Human brains, in such cultures, come to expect the surrounding media of text and speech as surely as they expect to function in a world of weight, force, friction, and gravity. Language is a constant, and as such it can be safely relied upon as the backdrop against which on-line processes of neural computation develop. Just as a neural-network controller for moving an arm to a target in space will define its commands to factor in the spring of muscles and the effects of gravity, so the processes of onboard reason may learn to factor in the potential contributions of textual offloading and reorganization, and vocal rehearsal and exchange. The mature cognitive competencies which we identify as mind and intellect may thus be more like ship navigation (see chapter 3) than capacities of the bare biological brain. Ship navigation emerges from the well-orchestrated adaptation of an extended complex system comprising individuals, instruments, and practices. Much of what we commonly identify as our mental capacities may likewise, I suspect, turn out to be properties of the wider, environmentally extended systems of which human brains are just one (important) part.

This is a big claim, and I do not expect to convince the skeptics here. But it is not, I think, quite as wild as it may at first appear. There is, after all, a quite general difficulty in drawing a firm line between a user and a tool.[24] A stone held in one's hand and used to crack a nut is clearly a tool. But if a bird drops a nut from the air so that it will break on contact with the ground, is the ground a tool? Some birds swallow small stones to aid digestion – are the stones tools, or, once ingested, simply parts of the bird? Is a tree, once climbed to escape a predator, a tool? What about a spider's web?

Public language and the props of text and symbolic notation are, I suggest, not unlike the stones swallowed by birds. The question "Where does the user end and the tool begin?" invites, in both cases, a delicate call. In the light of the larger body of our previous discussions, I am at a minimum persuaded of two claims. The first is that some human actions are more like thoughts than they at first appear. These are the actions whose true goal is to alter the computational tasks that confront the brain as we try to solve a problem – what Kirsh and Maglio called "epistemic actions." The second is that certain harms to the environment may have the kind of moral significance we normally associate with harm to the person – I am thinking here especially of the cases, described in chapter 3 above, of neurologically impaired humans who get along by adding especially dense layers of external prompts and supports to their daily surroundings. Tampering with these supports, it seems to me, would be more akin to a crime against the person than to a crime against property. In a similar vein, Clark and Chalmers (1995) describe the case of a neurologically impaired agent who relies heavily on a constantly carried notebook deferring to its contents on numerous daily occasions. Wanton destruction of the notebook, in such a case, has an especially worrying moral aspect: it is surely harm to the person, in about as literal a sense as can be imagined.

In the light of these concerns and the apparent methodological value (see chapters 3, 4, 6, and 8 above) of studying systems as integrated computational and dynamic wholes, I am convinced that it is valuable to (at times) treat cognitive processes as extending beyond the narrow confines of skin and skull. And I am led to wonder whether the intuitive notion of mind itself should not be broadened so as to encompass a variety of external props and aids – whether, that is, the system we often refer to as "mind" is in fact much wider than the one we call "brain." Such a more general conclusion may at first seem unpalatable. One reason, I think, is that we are prone to confuse the mental with the conscious. And I assuredly do not seek to claim that individual consciousness extends outside the head. It seems clear, however, that not everything that occurs in the brain and constitutes (in current scientific usage) a mental or cognitive process is tied up with *conscious* processing.[25] More plausibly, it may be suggested that what keeps real mental and cognitive processes in the head is some consideration of portability. That is to say, we are moved by a vision of what might be called the Naked Mind: a vision of the resources and operations we can *always* bring to bear on a cognitive task, regardless of whatever further opportunities the local environment may or may not afford us.

I am sympathetic to this objection. It seems clear that the brain (or perhaps, on this view, the brain and body) is a proper and distinct object of study and interest. And what makes it such is precisely the fact that it comprises some such set of core, basic, portable cognitive resources. These resources may incorporate bodily actions as integral parts of some cognitive processes (as when we use our fingers to offload working memory in the context of a tricky calculation). But they will not encompass the more contingent aspects of our external environment – the ones that may come and go, such as a pocket calculator. Nonetheless, I do not think that the portability consideration can ultimately bear sufficient conceptual weight, and for two reasons. First, there is a risk of begging the question. If we ask *why* portability should matter to the constitution of specific mental or cognitive processes, the only answer seems to be that we want such processes to come in a distinct, individually mobile package. But this, of course, is just to invoke the boundary of skin and/or skull all over again – and it is the legitimacy of this very boundary that is in question.

Second, it would be easy (albeit a little tedious for the reader) to construct a variety of troublesome cases. What if some people *always* carried a pocket calculator; what if we one day have such devices implanted in our brains? What if we have "body docks" for a variety of such devices and "dress" each day by adding on devices appropriate for that day's prescribed problem-solving activity? Nor can the vulnerability of such additional devices to discrete damage or malfunction serve to distinguish them, for the biological brain likewise is at risk of losing specific problem-solving capacities through lesion or trauma.

The most compelling source of our anxieties, however, probably concerns that most puzzling entity, the *self*.[26] Does the putative spread of mental and cognitive processes out into the world imply some correlative (and surely unsettling) leakage of the self into the local surroundings? The answer now looks to be (sorry!) "Yes and No."

No, because (as has already been conceded) conscious contents supervene on individual brains. But Yes, because such conscious episodes are at best snapshots of the self considered as an evolving psychological profile. Thoughts, considered only as snapshots of our conscious mental activity, are fully explained, I am willing to say, by the current state of the brain. But the flow of reason and thoughts, and the temporal evolution of ideas and attitudes, are determined and explained by the intimate, complex, continued interplay of brain, body, and world. It is, if you like, a genuine aspect of my psychological profile to be the kind of person who writes a book like this – despite the fact that the flow and shape of the ideas expressed depended profoundly on a variety of iterated interactions between my biological brain and a small army of external encodings, recodings, and structuring resources.

Such liberality about cognitive processes and cognitive profiles must, of course, be balanced by a good helping of common sense. Mind cannot usefully be extended willy-nilly into the world. There would be little value in an analysis that credited me with knowing all the facts in the *Encyclopedia Britannica* just because I paid the monthly installments and found space for it in my garage. Nor should the distinction between my mind and yours be allowed to collapse just because we are found chatting on the bus. What, then, distinguishes the more plausible cases of robust cognitive extension from the rest?

Some important features of the more plausible cases (such as the neurologically impaired agent's notebook) can be isolated quickly. The notebook is always there – it is not locked in the garage, or rarely consulted. The information it contains is easy to access and use. The information is automatically endorsed – not subject to critical scrutiny, unlike the musings of a companion on a bus. Finally, the information was originally gathered and endorsed by the current user (unlike the entries in the encyclopedia). These conditions may not all be essential. And there may be others I have missed. But the overall picture is of a rather special kind of user/artifact relationship – one in which the artifact is reliable, present, frequently used, personally "tailored," and deeply trusted. Human agents, as we saw on numerous occasions in previous chapters, may press all kinds of crucial cognitive and computational benefits from interactions with artifacts that lack one or all of these features. But it is probably only when something like these conditions are met that we can plausibly argue for an extension of the morally resonant notions of self, mind, and agenthood to include aspects of the world beyond the skin. It is thus only when the relationship between user and artifact is about as close and intimate as that between the spider and the web[27] that the bounds of the self – and not just those of computation and broadly cognitive process – threaten to push out into the world.

The crucial point in the case of the agent and the notebook is that the entries in the notebook play the same explanatory role,[28] with respect to the agent's behavior, as would a piece of information encoded in long-term memory. The special conditions (accessibility, automatic endorsement, etc.) are necessary to ensure this kind of functional isomorphism. However, even if one grants (as many will not) that such an isomorphism obtains, it may be possible to avoid the radical conclusion concerning distributed agenthood. An alternative (and, I think, equally acceptable) conclusion would be that the agent remains locked within the envelope of skin and skull, but that beliefs, knowledge, and perhaps other mental states now depend on physical vehicles that can (at times) spread out to include select aspects of the local environment. Such a picture preserves the idea of the agent as the combination of body and biological brain, and hence allows us to speak – as we surely should – of the agent's sometimes manipulating and structuring those same external resources in ways designed to further extend, offload, or transform her own basic problem-solving activities. But it allows also that in this "reaching out" to the world we sometimes create wider cognitive and computational webs: webs whose understanding and analysis requires the application of the tools and concepts of cognitive science to larger, hybrid entities comprising brains, bodies, and a wide variety of external structures and processes.

In sum, I am content to let the notions of self and agency fall where they will. In the final analysis, I assert only that we have, at a minimum, good explanatory and methodological reasons to (at times) embrace a quite liberal notion of the scope of computation and cognitive processes – one that explicitly allows the spread of such processes across brain, body, world, and artifact. Paramount among such artifacts are the various manifestations of public language. Language is in many ways the ultimate artifact: so ubiquitous it is almost invisible, so intimate it is not clear whether it is a kind of tool or a dimension of the user. Whatever the boundaries, we confront at the very least a tightly linked economy in which the biological brain is fantastically empowered by some of its strangest and most recent creations: words in the air, symbols on the printed page.

Notes

1. Recent authors who subscribe to some version of such a view of language include Dennett (1991, 1995), Carruthers (to appear), and possibly Gauker (1990). Carruthers, in particular, distinguishes very carefully between "communicative" and "cognitive" concerns with language (44 and 52). In section 10.2 I attempt to clarify some of the similarities and differences between these treatments and the view of language as a computational transformer. In a related vein, McClamrock (1995) offers an interesting account of "embedded language" in which he stresses facts about the external (physical and social) context in which language is used. However, McClamrock's discussion (see e.g. ibid., 116–31) is centered on the debate concerning "internalist" vs. "externalist" theories of meaning. Several of McClamrock's observations nonetheless bear directly on my concerns, and I discuss them in section 10.3. The view I develop owes most to Hutchins's (1995) treatment of the role of external media in constructing extended cognitive systems (see also chapters 4 and 9 above).

2. Richard Gregory (1981) discusses the role of artifacts (including scissors) as means of reducing individual computational load and expanding our behavioral horizons. Daniel Dennett (1995, 375–8) has pursued the same theme, depicting a class of animals as "Gregorian" creatures (named after Richard Gregory) – creatures that exploit designed

artifacts as amplifiers of intelligence and repositories of achieved knowledge and wisdom. See also Norman 1988.

3 This, as I noted in chapter 3, is a somewhat broader use than is customary. Much of the Soviet-inspired literature treats scaffolding as intrinsically social. I extend the notion to include all cases in which external structures are coopted to aid problem solving.

4. This idea originates, I think, in Dennett's (1991, chapters 7 and 8) powerful discussion of the role of words as a means of self-stimulation. The discussion of this theme continues in chapter 13 of Dennett 1995.

5. A major focus of both Carruthers's and Dennett's treatments is the relation between language and consciousness. I will not discuss these issues here, save to say that my sympathies lie more with Churchland (1995, chapter 10), who depicts basic consciousness as the common property of humans and many nonlinguistic animals. Language fantastically augments the power of human cognition. But it does not, I believe, bring into being the basic apprehensions of pleasure, pain, and the sensory world in which the true mystery of consciousness inheres.

6. See chapter 2 of Carruthers (to appear) for an extensive discussion.

7. See Clark (1993, 97–8) and Clark and Thornton (to appear) for further discussion of this phenomenon, especially as it arises in connectionist learning.

8. See Bratman 1987 for a full discussion.

9. For a detailed treatment of this case, including Elman's other main way of solving the problem (by restricting early memory), see Clark 1994.

10. The simple case of physically manipulating Scrabble tiles to present new potential word fragments to a pattern-completing brain (see Kirsh 1995 and chapter 3 above) is a micro version of the same strategy.

11. For example, Bechtel (1996, 128) comments that "linguistic representations possess features that may not be found in our internal cognitive representations. For example, written records can endure unchanged for extended periods of time, whereas our internal 'memory' appears to rely on reconstruction, not retrieval of stored records. Moreover, through the various syntactical devices provided by language, relations between pieces of information can be kept straight (e.g., that a tree fell and a person jumped) that might otherwise become confused (e.g., when linked only in an associative structure such as a simple connectionist network)."

12. It is, I believe, a failure to fully appreciate the multiple roles of public language that sometimes leads the neurophilosopher Paul Churchland to dismiss linguaform expression as just a shallow reflection of our "real" knowledge (see e.g. Churchland 1989, 18). For discussion see Clark 1996 and section 10.4 below.

13. A particularly stunning example is the large mangrove forest extending north from Key West to the Everglades region known as Ten Thousand Islands. The black mangroves of this region can reach heights of 80 feet (Landi 1982, 361–3).

14. Two very recent treatments that emphasize these themes have been brought to my attention. Jean-Pierre Changeux (a neuroscientist and molecular biologist) and Alain Connes (a mathematician) suggest that self-evaluation is the mark of true intelligence – see Changeux and Connes 1995. Derek Bickerton (a linguist) celebrates "off-line thinking" and notes that no other species seems to isolate problems in their own performance and take pointed action to rectify them – see Bickerton 1995.

15. Annette Karmiloff-Smith stresses the modality-neutral dimensions of public language in her closely related work on representational redescription. On the relative context

independence of the signs and symbols of public language see Kirsh 1991 and chapter 6 of Clark 1993.

16. The idea that advanced cognition involves repeated processes in which achieved knowledge and representation is redescribed in new formats (which then support new kinds of cognitive operation and access) is pursued in much more detail in Karmiloff-Smith 1992, Clark 1993, Clark and Karmiloff-Smith 1994, and Dennett 1994. The original hypothesis of representational redescription was developed by Karmiloff-Smith (1979).

17. See e.g. Bechtel 1996, 125–31; Clark 1996, 120–5.

18. Dennett (1991) explores just such an intermediate territory. I discuss Churchland's downplaying of language in detail in Clark 1996. For examples of such downplaying see p. 18 of Churchland 1989 and 265–70 of Churchland and Churchland 1996.

19. For an extensive discussion of the paper clip see Petroski 1992.

20. In what follows I gloss over some very large debates about animal language in general and chimpanzee language in particular. See chapter 13 of Dennett 1995 and chapter 10 of Churchland 1995 for well-balanced discussions.

21. For critical discussion see Pinker 1994, Christiansen 1994, chapter 10 of Churchland 1995, and chapter 13 of Dennett 1995.

22. Any attempt to argue the maximally strong case that human language learning involves no special-purpose language-acquisition device in the brain must, however, contend with a rich variety of detailed linguistic argument and evidence. In particular it must address the "poverty of the stimulus" argument (Pinker 1994), which claims that it is simply not possible to acquire the detailed grammatical competence we do on the basis of the training data to which we are exposed, and assuming only unbiased, general mechanisms of learning. Since my claim is only that reverse adaptation my play some role in downgrading the amount of "native endowment" we must posit, I make no attempt to address these issued here. For a detailed defense of the strong claim see Christiansen 1994.

23. In the philosophical literature this question invites two standard replies. Either we go with the intuitive demarcations of skin and skull, or we assume that the question is really about the analysis of meaning and proceed to debate the pros and cons of the (broadly) Putnamesque doctrine that "meanings just ain't in the head" (Putnam 1975). I propose, however, to pursue a third position: that cognitive processes are no respecters of the boundaries of the skin or skull. That is to say, I claim (1) that the intuitive notion of the mind ought to be purged of its internalist leanings and (2) that the reasons for so doing do not depend on the (debatable) role of truth-condition and real-world reference in fixing the meaning of mental or linguistic tokens. For a full discussion see Clark and Chalmers 1995.

24. I owe the following examples to Beth Preston (1995). See also Beck 1980 and Gibson and Ingold 1993.

25. The vestibulo-ocular reflex (VOR), to take just one example from dozens, stabilizes the image of the world on the retina so as to offset head movement (see e.g. Churchland and Sejnowski 1992, 353–65). This operation is, of course, crucial for human vision. And human consciousness apprehends the world in a way that depends on the correct operation of the VOR. But the computational steps performed by the VOR circuitry do not figure among our conscious contents. If the computational transformations on which the VOR depends were sometimes carried out using some external device (a

neural version of an iron lung or a kidney machine), the interplay between conscious states and VOR computations could remain unaltered. So whatever role is played by the presence of consciousness (whatever exactly that means) somewhere in the loop, that role cannot *itself* afford grounds for rejecting the characterization of some external data transformations as part of our cognitive processing. Rather, it could do so only if we bite the bullet and reject as cognitive all processes which are not themselves consciously introspectable. (If the VOR strikes you as too low-level to count as an example of a nonconscious but genuinely cognitive process, replace it with one you like better – e.g., the processes of content-addressable recall, or whatever introspectively invisible acumen underlies your ability to know which rule to apply next in a logical derivation.)

26. For a valuable but very different discussion of issues concerning the implications of an embodied, embedded approach for conceptions of the self, see Varela et al. 1991.
27. See Dawkins 1982 for an especially biologically astute treatment of this kind of case.
28. For an extended discussion of this claim see Clark and Chalmers 1995.

References

Bechtel, William 1996. "What Knowledge Must be in the Head in Order to Acquire Language?" In *Communicating Meaning: The Evolution and Development of Language*, ed. B. Velichkovsky and D. M. Rumbaugh. Hillsdale, NJ: Lawrence Erlbaum Associates.

Beck, B. 1980. *Animal Tool Behavior: The Use and Manufacture of Tools by Animals*. New York: Garland.

Berk, Laura. 1994. "Why Children Talk to Themselves." *Scientific American* 271/5: 73–83.

Berk, L. and R. Garvin. 1984. "Development of Private Speech Among Low-income Appalachian Children." *Developmental Psychology* 20/2: 271–86.

Bickerton, Derek. 1995. *Language and Human Behavior*. Seattle: University of Washington Press.

Bivens, J. and L. Berk 1990. "A Longitudinal Study of the Development of Elementary School Children's Private Speech." *Merrill-Palmer Quarterly* 36/4: 443–63.

Bratman, M. 1987. *Intentions, Plans and Practical Reason*. Cambridge, MA: Harvard University Press.

Carruthers, P. (to appear). *Language, Thought and Consciousness: An Essay in Philosophical Psychology*. Cambridge: Cambridge University Press. [published 1998, Ed.]

Changeux, J.-P. and A. Connes. 1995. *Conversations and Mind, Matter and Mathematics*. Princeton: Princeton University Press.

Christiansen, M. 1994. *The Evolution and Acquisition of Language*. PNP Research Report, Washington University, St. Louis.

Churchland, Paul M. 1989. *A Neurocomputational Perspective*. Cambridge, MA: MIT Press.
_____1995. *The Engine of Reason, the Seat of the Soul*. Cambridge, MA: MIT Press.

Churchland, P. M. and P. S. Churchland. 1996. "Replies." In *The Churchlands and their Critics*, ed. R. N. McCauley. Oxford: Blackwell.

Churchland, P. S. and T. Sejnowski. 1992. *The Computational Brain*. Cambridge, MA: MIT Press.

Clark, Andy. 1993. *Associative Engines: Connectionism, Concepts and Representational Change*. Cambridge, MA: MIT Press.

_____1994. "Representational Trajectories in Connectionist Learning." *Minds and Machines* 4: 317–32.

_____1996. "Connectionism, Moral Cognition and Collaborative Problem Solving." In *Mind and Morals: Essays on Ethics and Cognitive Science*, ed. L. May et al. Cambridge, MA: MIT Press.

Clark, Andy and D. Chalmers. 1995. "The Extended Mind." Philosophy-Neuroscience-Psychology Research Report, Washington University, St. Louis.

Clark, Andy and A. Karmiloff-Smith. 1994. "The Cognizer's Innards: A Psychological and Philosophical Perspective on the Development of Thought." *Mind and Language* 8: 487–519.

Clark, Andy and C. Thornton (to appear). "Trading spaces: Connectionism and the Limits of Learning." *Behavioral and Brain Sciences*. [published 1997, 20/1, 57–92, ed.]

Dawkins, R. 1982. *The Extended Phenotype*. Oxford: Oxford University Press.

Dennett, Daniel. 1991. *Consciousness Explained*. Boston: Little, Brown.

_____1994. "Labeling and Learning." *Mind and Language* 8: 540–7.

_____1995. *Darwin's Dangerous Idea: Evolution and the Meanings of Life*. New York: Simon & Schuster.

Diaz, R. and L. Berk 1992. *Private Speech: From Social Interaction to Self-Regulation*. Hillsale, NJ: Erlbaum.

Donald, Merlin. 1991. *Origins of the Modern Mind*. Cambridge, MA: Harvard University Press.

Dreyfus, H. and S. Dreyfus. 1990. "What is Morality? A Phenomenological Account of the Development of Ethical Experience." In *Universalism vs. Communitarianism*, ed. D. Rasmussen. Cambridge, MA: MIT Press.

Elman, G. 1994. "Learning and Development in Neural Networks." In *Mind as Motion*, ed. R. Port and T. van Gelder. Cambridge, MA: MIT Press.

Gauker, C. 1990. "How to Learn a Language Like a Chimpanzee." *Philosophical Psychology* 3/1: 31–53.

Gibson, K. and T. Ingold, eds. 1993. *Tools, Language and Cognition in Human Evolution*. Cambridge: Cambridge University Press.

Gregory, Richard. 1981. *Mind in Science*. Cambridge: Cambridge University Press.

Hare, M. and J. Elman. 1995. "Learning and Morphological Change." *Cognition* 56: 61–98.

Hutchins, Edwin. 1995. *Cognition in the Wild*. Cambridge, MA: MIT Press.

Jackendoff, R. (to appear). "How Language Helps us Think." *Pragmatics and Cognition*. [published 1997, 4, 1–34, Ed.]

Karmiloff-Smith, A. 1979. *A Functional Approach to Child Language*. Cambridge: Cambridge University Press.

_____1992. *Beyond Modularity: A Developmental Perspective on Cognitive Science*. Cambridge, MA: MIT Press.

Kirsch, D. 1991. "When is Information Explicitly Represented?". In *Information Thought and Content*, ed. P. Hanson. Vancouver: UBC Press.

_____1995. "The Intelligent Use of Space." *Artificial Intelligence* 72: 1–52.

Kirsch, D. and P. Maglio 1991. "Reaction and Reflection in Tetris." Research report D-015, Cognitive Science Department, University of California, San Diego.

Landi, V. 1982. *The Great American Countryside*. New York: Collier Macmillan.

McClamrock, R. 1995. *Existential Cognition*. Chicago: University of Chicago Press.

Newport, E. 1990. "Maturational Constraints on Language Learning." *Cognitive Science* 14: 11–28.

Norman, D. 1988. *The Psychology of Everyday Things*. New York: Basic Books.

Petroski, H. 1992. "The Evolution of Artefacts." *American Scientist* 80: 416–20.

Pinker, S. 1994. *The Language Instinct*. New York: Morrow.

Preston, Beth. 1995. "Cognition and Tool Use" (draft paper).

Putnam, H. 1975. "The Meaning of 'Meaning'." In *Mind, Language and Reality*, ed. H. Putnam. Cambridge: Cambridge University Press.

Rumelhart, D. et al. 1986. "Schemata and Sequential Thought Processes in PDP Models." In *Parallel Distributed Processing: Explorations in the Microstructure of Cognition*, ed. D. Rumelhart et al. Cambridge, MA: MIT Press.

Varela, F. et al. 1991. *The Embodied Mind: Cognitive Science and Human Experience*. Cambridge, MA: MIT Press.

Vygotsky, Lev S. 1986 (1962). *Thought and Language*. (translation of 1962 edition). Cambridge, MA: MIT Press.

PART VI

CONCLUSION

MODERN MYTHS AND MYTHOLOGIES

In this final chapter I round up some ideas on the fate of myths and mythologies in the contemporary world as well as the possibilities for the study of them. It is relevant to ask "what happened" to the myths with the coming of the modern world, one that has in many places become quite secularized and strongly oriented towards scientific worldviews. If ancient sceptics did not always believe in myth – so much less do the moderns, because they want historical fact and not "idle tale."[1] With the French philosopher of history Michel de Certeau we may say that "Historical discourse becomes the only possible myth of a scientific society that rejects myth" (1986, 220). Then again, that is a very strong version of "myth-rejection" that is not universal, for "modern society" is no uniform category. Although many nations have undergone various modes of secularization in many sectors of society, many have retained their religious and also mythical traditions alongside such changes. Thus, "modern" society does not by necessity imply a totally de-traditionalized or secular society, but may be one in which the many fields, sub-systems or sectors are more or less traditional and driven by conventional religious values and symbols. Closer investigations and new methods, as discussed below, will show that myth and mythmaking has not disappeared, but assumed different forms because myths do not just belong to the past. We are all soaked in them, and they are embedded in everything from art to ideology, from advertising to politics; and there is even an "entertainment" industry that is as much mythmaking as it is entertaining. However, the myths are as "invisible" as they always were; also today they "think themselves in humans" – and without their knowledge of it.[2] The transparency of current myth only becomes discernible through that which is different and at a distance. Thus, the myths of "here and now" will only be disclosed and relinquish their transparency through an intimate acquaintance with the myths of "then and there." This collection has focused on how that can be done. Ideally, we should be able to do fieldwork on our own thoughts and worlds and the study of strange stories may lead to a reflective enlightenment that enables us to do that. This may sound too philosophical or "lyrical" to some, but I think it is important and it is something I tell my students, not least because they seldom realize that they are also "soaked in myths." So, myths have not disappeared in the modern world but changed their appearances and the first part of this chapter addresses the question: "What happened to myth?" That is, if they survived, what do they "look like" today?

The second part concerns new ways in methodology and theory in the study of myths and mythologies. Among recent inspirations some derive from the study of narrative and discourse and thus are also directly applicable to the study of myth. Several of these are being developed in disciplines where (religious) myths are not normally a subject of inquiry so a certain degree of transposition is required. The cognitivist theories, approaches and methods, as introduced above, may also inspire further developments. There seems to be a rich and yet unexploited potential.[3]

If the research history had demonstrated only one thing, it would be that narrow and biased approaches are unproductive. "Myth" is a concept which denotes a multi-tiered cluster of phenomena and such a concept should evoke multiple connotations and associations in the minds of those who work with myths and hence enrich the study of "it." Anyone who wants to become acquainted with the fictionalizing capacities of humankind will benefit from an insight into "myth."

What Happened to the Myths?

With changing theories and new methods of analysis the question about "what happened to myths" in modern society can be answered more adequately.[4] There is no doubt that the forms and formats of myths have changed in the modern world. In modernity, gods and other superhuman agents are no longer the acting subjects in narrated myths that function as the foundation of societies. The narrations of long and complex stories and the production of fiction have been left to literature and other industries. Therefore, apparently the myths "as we knew them" have gone, they are no longer with us. Alternatively, perhaps they are. If we do not find myths in the form of coherent, edited narratives, then we do find them as bits and pieces, as metaphors, tropes, images, schemas in many other features of thought and practice. It is my contention that we find these bits and pieces, the elements of myth, what the structuralists dubbed "mythemes," in lifestyles, identities, ethnicities, imagined communities, fictive kin. It seems that we find myth everywhere, from the most personal and intimate ideas about who we are, to the most communal, social and political representations. The critical voice will say that all these mythemes are not myths *as such*, because they are not organized the way myths should be, i.e. in narrative sequences, and they are not replicated as such in their socio-cultural contexts, say, as in the story of the Wawilak sisters (Shore, above). My point on this argument is that, even if the "mythemes" are like scattered elements, then it is precisely their paradigmatic status, their compositionality that allows them to function in the syntagmatic arrangement into which both the mythmakers and the myth analysts may put them. This means that it is the analysis that will *provide* the arrangements of mythemes with coherence by (re-)constructing the hidden grammar of a modern myth or mythology. The resulting "narrative" can be anything from the myth of the American Dream to the myth of the Individual as a free agent. In the 1950s, the "glory days" of structuralism, Roland Barthes analysed examples of mythmaking in the modern world. The inspirations from such analysis spread to other approaches to "civilizational trivia," for example, to deconstructionist theory and in cultural studies where the critical analyses of socio-cultural representations often proceed along lines that may also apply to the study of mythemes, myths and mythologies.

To the question of "where the myths have gone" it is quite obvious that much of the traditional mythical material survives as collections of motifs, sequences and plots in what is called, somewhat condescending, "trivial myths" in literary terminology. Not least do we find the trivial mythemes in music, films, TV, electronic games, etc.[5] In a consumer society it is to be expected that the fictional, mythological representational realms of imagination are linked closely to consumption and consumerism. Not only the entertainment industries, but also practically all industries, from those that manufacture cars, to clothing, recreational apparel of all kinds – including the toy industry – tap into the mythological reservoirs and repertoires of the modern world. These are no less trivial – and that is how they work: By their very redundancy they become evident truths, they become "what goes without saying." If we wish to analyse "myth today" we find them repeatedly as episodes of "Bricolage," in films etc. and the modern mythemes primarily function as "indices" in the sense introduced by Roland Barthes (in Part IV above). The indices of the modern reservoirs and repertoires are seldom paradigmatically ordered, that is, they materialize as a fussy and messy heap of available signification that may make up some more organized syntagmatic chain of meaning production. The resulting combinations of mythemes may function as hidden "subtexts"; say in advertising, or as utopian space in political discourse or as a transcendent realm of truth and inspiration in Jungian thought and New Age ideology.[6]

Looking to advertising, we easily notice how the text and images reflect sets of representations about "the good life," "the happy family," "health," "youth," "beauty," and all the rest of the stereotypical images that circulate in consumer society. Now, these representations, as "mythemes," are rarely articulated in narrative sequences, but they may be, and often in conjunction or relation to many others. And that is a most salient feature of these representations.[7]

The anthropologist Marc Augé has analysed some of the mechanisms behind the construction of modern myths and the functions of the fictionalizing media (Augé

1999). He put forward an idea for a schematic history of how cosmological truths transform into fiction. An example could be how the important cosmologies of Latin American Indians were turned into "heathen" myth by the European conquerors until today when they figure as fiction and imagination. According to Augé, the common imaginaries of tradition have eroded and the individual's link to and dependence upon these imaginaries disappear. Our modern world becomes increasingly fictionalized and the role of an easily recognizable common "collective imagination and memory" and what was before mythic now becomes fiction as the modern discourse "is bent on occupying the place of the collective memory.... The fact is that, in the name of progress, the ideal of modernity tends to relegate the entire corpus of religious affiliations to the axis of fiction by a movement analogous to the one which ordained the confrontation between religions" (1999, 85). TV (with derivations) is probably the single most important medium for the transformations from the narrative character of the common imaginary to the "all-fictional" and "fictionalization," and, as Augé adds, "...of turning the real into fiction, in which television has been an essential tool from the moment when television stopped imitating real-life and real-life began reproducing fiction" (108). As the fictional equivalents of cosmologies we now have "bubbles of immanence," created, designed, fictionalized environments, that are like "non-places," that is, places with signification that simply refers to their own mythology, their own fictional universe.

An example of myth analysis on a contemporary fictionalizing formation is offered by Thomas Ryba in his acute observations on the complex narrative significations of Disney's "Magic Kingdom":

> The Magic Kingdom is the crystallization of Walt Disney's middle-American values. These values existed, in history, in much greater particularity, and, in myth, with much greater ambiguity. What Walt Disney has done is accomplish a reading of American history and myth that enshrines his interpretation as though it were the one and only American narrative. However, Disney was as much a product of a segment of American culture as he was its producer. The genius of Disney is thus as a *filter* of American values and hopes. His greatest talent was his narrow grasp of what Americans wanted to believe. His greatest creation was to realize this in a new kind of narrative and aesthetic artifact designed to meet those wants. (Ryba 1999–2000, 219)

Further, as Ryba emphasizes on Walt Disney's "work on myth": "It was he who oversaw the *concretization* of the mythic narratives as well as the *abstraction* of its historical narratives so as to create exceedingly simplistic but exceptionally consoling representations of the American *muthos*" (219–20; original italics).

One of the conspicuous features of the contemporary manifestations of the survival of the mythical aspects of human culture is their decidedly ludic features and roles. Myths, mythemes and fragments of myths and mythologies are the materials out of which a vast array of entertainment products are manufactured. What would the electronic games industry be without constant recycling of all kinds of more or less mythological materials? Each game comes with a set of stories, has its own narratively constructed world or cosmology. Most of these are highly dualistic, replicate known religious and mythological scenarios and many of them have (quasi-)ritual features. To a student of religion of mythology, all this is obvious.

On the "Not So Obvious Myths..."

Where mythmaking modes in many popular media, for example of the Hollywood and Disneyland varieties, are readily detectable and do not require critical academic training for their disclosure, other contemporary mythmaking modes are quite elusive. One could say that the less we consciously notice them "at work" the more dangerous they may be – depending of course on their contents and references. In this age of incessant incredulity I venture the opinion (at the risk of being judged naïve) that we should perhaps not forget that there may also be "good myths," myths that provide us with positive imaginaries of being human.[8] At any rate, the method and theories that may provide the tools to unlock the sinister myths also work for the exposure of the benevolent ones. However, we need better methodological tools to disclose these forms of myth. Some of those tools are more recent and have not yet been applied to the study of more "traditional" myths on a larger scale. Primary among these tools are various forms of discourse analysis, narrative theory, and cognitive semantics. Nevertheless, the "old" approaches are still going strong and deserve continued attention. Their basis is constituted by historical-critical research with due awareness to the functions and structures of myths and mythologies. The salient features of the methods of analysis have been aptly summarized in the seven points of Lincoln's "protocol designed for students of myth":

1. Establish the categories of issues in the mythic text on which the inquiry is focused. Note also the relations between these categories (including the ways different categorical sets and subsets are brought into alignment), as well as their ranking relative to one another and the logic used to justify that ranking.

2. Note whether there are any changes in the ranking of categories between the beginning of the narrative and its conclusion. Ascertain the logic used to justify any such shifts.

3. Assemble a set of related materials from the same culture area: other variants of the same story, other closely related stories (on the basis of characters, actions, themes, etc.), and other texts in which the same categories are at issue. Establish any differences that exist between the categories and rankings that appear in the focal text and those in the other materials.

4. Establish any connections that exist between the categories that figure in these texts and those which condition the relations of the social groups among whom the texts circulate.

5. Establish the date and authorship of all texts considered and the circumstances of their appearance, circulation, and reception.

6. Try to draw reasonable inferences about the interests that are advanced, defended, or negotiated through each act of narration. Pay particular attention to the way the categories constituting the social order are defined and recalibrated such that certain groups move up and others move down within the extant hierarchy.
7. Remember that to treat pointed issues, even in the most manipulative form, is to acknowledge them and to open up possibilities for those with other interests to advance alternate interpretations and thematizations. The enunciation of any mythic variant opens up an arena of struggle and maneuver that can be pursued by those who produce other variants of the myth and other interpretations of the variant. (1999, 150–1)

In the twentieth century structuralism became the major shift in the study of traditional cosmologies, and that includes myths and mythologies. Structuralism proved not to be a short-lived "French fad" but an appropriate methodology for the study of all kinds of socio-cultural products. Certainly, as a contender for all-encompassing philosophy of mind and culture, structuralism has been challenged and succeeded by deconstructivist and pragmatist criticisms but as a methodology for the human sciences structuralist modes of explanation and interpretation have become mainstream and a part of normal scholarly practice (Jensen 2005). One of the benefits of structuralist methodology derives from its insistence on the importance of comparative perspectives, which have otherwise been disputed or condemned by the proponents of particularist theories and methods who have disapproved of comparative or generalizing approaches.[9] If the study of anything socio-cultural is to survive, then that "anything" must necessarily be an object that is comparable, for otherwise it cannot be part of any scholarly project. It is not possible to have a science of things that are unique, incomparable or beyond criticism, and in my view the study of myth is inherently comparative. That view is further warranted by the grounding of comparison and comparability in a range of levels of matters generally human and therefore comparable. Viewed from the "bottom-up," there are universal human cognitive properties and mechanisms, there are widespread patterns in social formations, narrativity and narratives are ubiquitous and at a more abstract level, semantic holism in the philosophy of language deem the translatability of all language and speech a basic fact (cf. introduction to Part V above). On this note of the importance of the comparative perspective I shall briefly turn to a few recent approaches and look into their possible contribution to the study of myths and mythologies.

Discourse and Myth

Discourse analysis is a rather recent term but one that also covers a well-known activity: the interpretation of linguistic utterances and of linguistic practice.[10] As practised by most of its proponents, discourse analysis is not a neutral analysis of discourse as articulated in speech or writing (and perhaps other media), but also the practice of a critical social theory that aspires to disclose and unveil hidden agendas, implicit power relations and other instances when humans do things with words that have social consequences (e.g. McCutcheon 2005). Discourse analysis is a term that covers a broad range of methods, some are very technical and punctilious and others are very broad and general concerning a "spirit of the age" or an "episteme." Original inspirations come from the philosophy of Friedrich Nietzsche and later Michel Foucault and his analyses of hidden power structures not only in discourse, for instance about what is normal and abnormal, but also in behaviour, institutions, architecture and the many other forms of politics and technologies that humans engage in.[11] Discourse analysis can be quite a powerful tool in the dismantling of given truths, of those "what-goes-without-saying" constructions, which have gained such currency that they are felt to exist and be self-evidently true. Some of the most persistent myths, accepted by believers as true history and rejected by disbelievers as false history, but nevertheless as history, are those of the births of the "historical religions," Christianity and Islam. Neither religion is normally considered "mythological," but rather discursive formations that assert to be historically founded and developed. Sceptics and agnostics may (and do) question the veracity of transcendent or super-human claims to divine intervention in the world but seldom question the contentions of the religious traditions' claim to being historical. And yet, there may be much more "mythmaking" involved in the advancement of those powerful discourses, and for Christianity this has been investigated over many decades.[12] Further, it should be recognized that large portions of the narrative materials of these religious traditions *function* as myths and mythologies, and very much so in the traditional forms, explained for example by Malinowski (above). The numerous stories about, say, Jesus Christ or Muhammad are used exactly as myths are used, as the building blocks of cosmologies and social formations, and their articulations and pragmatic aspects may thus be studied with the same tools as other myths and mythologies. As they are very often involved in issues of strong social or political concerns, discourse analysis lends itself as a fitting approach. A discourse analysis perspective would view any myth as a space of representations – not necessarily articulated in one consistent narrative – that functions as a guiding principle for evaluating situations, actions and utterances. They are "floating" signifiers which refer to specific orders, hierarchies, systems of values and perceptions. The structurations of the social realities are continuously in flux and determined by the discourses in which they are narrated and signified. "Fictive" entities such as identity, ethnicity and nationality are discursive constructions and formations that depend upon local and temporal social and cultural consensus for their existence; they are constituent for "what counts as" what (see Searle above). Thus, "myths" are in a sense "false" and skewed representations of reality but they are also necessary for our constructions and deconstructions of our "lived-in" world. They set the parameters for what it is possible, sensible and, perhaps even, allowed to talk about. Any discourse is always a reduction of the scopes of potential possibilities – so discourses, like myths in general, function as closures and complexity reduction: The contingencies of the world are overcome by the construction of specific universes of meaning.

Related to discourse theory is "discourse psychology" – a quite radical version of social constructionism which basically explains how narrativity shapes the "soul": Everything that goes into the construction of a human is mediated through and constructed by the means of language, narrativity and myth. Individual and group identity is created and maintained through discourse. Primary spokesmen for this approach are Derek Edwards and Jonathan Potter (1992; Potter 1996). The importance of discourse, narrative, and in the end, myth, is noticeable, as our identities, individually or collectively, are shaped both by the stories told to us and the ones we tell ourselves about us and others. The construction of identity is, more often than not, a matter of pointing out what *we* are *not*. Negative mirror images have always been a convenient way of marking difference. One could talk about "Narrative management" in the production of representations – and that certainly is what happens in myth.

"Deconstruction" is one more addition to the vocabulary of the humanities and the social sciences. Although it may some times be expressed with great philosophical finesse and at others with some obscurity, deconstruction can simply be said to be a practice that de-constructs the conditions (political, economic, socio-cultural, etc.) under which concepts and ideas were constructed in the first place. In that sense deconstruction is basically heir to historical-critical analysis. So, without further mystification, it could be said that many of the analyses presented in this volume qualify as "deconstructive." Discourse analysis certainly is so – also in the study of myth. It further comes with its own reflexive self-critical awareness: "For to look at discourse means to look at both the object of analysis, the text, culture, speech under study, as well as the way in which the scholarly analysis itself is put into discourse. Discourse theory, then, opens the question of the very foundations of its own enterprise" (Murphy 2000, 396).

Final Remarks

This also means that scholars must be relentlessly self-critical. That, of course, is not only difficult, something to learn or acquire through an intimate knowledge of a field of inquiry, but too much self-criticism may well paralyse the author, stall, halt and bring everything to a standstill. One way to avoid that is by freely admitting to considering that what we publish are our best bets, our most informed opinion and insights – and should we miss something there will certainly be others to remedy the state of affairs. The intersubjective nature of the scholarly world will take care of that.

An example of a debate with a direct bearing on our subject is presented by Robert A. Segal's small, but perceptive article about the functions of myths and meta-myths – i.e. the scholars' use of "myth" as a category used to characterize the works and points of view of other scholars (Segal 2005). The category or concept of myth can be used for many purposes; some of these uses may in themselves serve ideological or mythic purposes. But, as Robert Segal has noted on the discussion about the construction and use of the category "religion": "… even an irrefutable demonstration of the ideological use of the category religion would not invalidate the category itself" (2005, 213). The same goes for "myth." As a final methodological remark we could do well to heed some of Segal's admonitions concerning the status and use of terms. The terms "Religion" and "Myth" have come under attack as valid denominators (as has been the case with "Magic" for a long time) for three reasons – or, because of three fallacies – mainly. Segal does not furnish a term for the first problem or fallacy, namely that which says that because the "natives" do not have the term or concept it is then illegitimate to apply it to the study of their culture, but we could call it the "insider correctness fallacy."[13] The second has a name, it is the "genetic fallacy," to be applied when discovery is collapsed into invention or vice versa. In the case of the concept of myth this can be stated thus: "A second form of refutation of the legitimacy of a concept is the invocation of its origin: if one can identify the time and place of the origin of a concept, then the concept automatically ceases to apply any time or anywhere else" (211). This kind of criticism pops up now and then, but the recognition of the fact of invention of a category or a concept does not mean that it is vacuous or inoperative. The third fallacy is the "functionalist fallacy," for instance in "appealing to the function of something as an argument against its propriety" (212). More comprehensively formulated by Segal: "The third form of refutation of the legitimacy of a concept is the invocation of its function: if one can identify the use to which a concept is put, then the concept automatically becomes suspect" (211). Our conclusion is not, then, that all forms of criticism are fallacies, but it does mean that we should not always let criticism have the silencing effect that the critic intends. It could even be that the critic promotes an agenda of silencing critical approaches to the study of myths and mythologies. The critical student of myths and mythologies will soon notice...

*

What we should now have learned – as I do hope – is that the current study of myth is as fascinating as it always was and that we discern the contours of a revived and revised study of myth that also takes into account the forms and functions that "myths and mythologies" have in current modes of conceptualizing and expressing human existence in the world. That is for better or for worse, some myths are good news and some are bad news. On the one hand myths articulate hopes, fears, and desires and on the other they may deceive, cheat and lie. In my opinion, a critical study does not involve an indiscriminate attempt to debunk myth, but rather an informed view and perhaps even an appreciation of some of the many facets of myth.

There has been a strong myth about the disappearance of myth, but now it seems that it is time that that myth itself disappears. For myths simply won't go away.

Notes

1. Not many discuss, in earnest, the issue of the truth, or metaphysics, of myth. However, see Schilbrack 2000 for an interesting view from the philosophy of religion. Schilbrack urges "that the metaphysical interpretation be added to the methodological tool kit used by interpreters of myth... Insofar as myths involve metaphysics, any study of myth that excludes metaphysics distorts and truncates its object" (75). See the collection of essays in Frankenberry 2002 for radical, critical views on the "truth" of religious discourse.

2. As was Lévi-Strauss' dictum (cf. above). On structuralism generally, see discussions and references in the introduction to "Semiological Approaches" above.

3. Interesting that very little is (so far) noted among cognitive scientists about narrative or myth; the comprehensive MIT Encyclopedia of the Cognitive Sciences (1999) has no entry on either. In my view, the field of "cognitive semantics" may become an interesting approach in the study of myth, but its theoretical capabilities have not yet been worked out in easily applicable forms.

4. In this connection defining "modern" society is rather complex. As the level of theoretical model, a modern society is one which is severed from tradition, in the sense that it does not rely upon traditional forms of legitimating authorities such as religion, royalty, nobility, etc., but only on the political rule legitimated by individuals with equal rights. As far as cosmology goes, modern society relies on science and does not answer to transcendent authority, because on a modernist view gods do not intervene in the world of humans. At the individual level this means that the individual is liberated from tradition.

5. Interesting discussions of the changing role and function of narrative in relation to developing types of media can be found in Ryan 2003.

6. This could be the place to mention the impact of the work of Joseph Campbell (1904–1987). Although to some extent a scholar on myth, he was also broker and caretaker of myth and mythology. A whole industry (e.g. "The Joseph Campbell Foundation") has resulted from and around his writings, most of which are stereotypically centred around a few, but existentially potent, themes. See Segal 1999.

7. I have asked student to do this in class, and after a bit of hesitation, because they do not normally think of advertising as mythology, they delve into the task with great enthusiasm. It is detective work and it is fun to construct a coherent (normative and cosmological) narrative from scraps of advertising. Some of the major brands known worldwide could be suspected of employing mythmakers.

8. If this appears a morally normative judgement, I agree. Conversely, critical analysts are also outright normative (what many somehow seem to overlook) but just with a negative "prefix."

9. The criticism or scepticism towards generalizing and comparison has been persistent in the study of religion over many decades, and in anthropology from the 1980s onwards the emphasis has been on local, small-scale and empathic studies true to indigenous self-understandings and often presented in almost literary formats.

10. Among the earliest proponents of "discourse analysis" or "discourse theory" from the 1980s are Norman Fairclough (e.g. 1995) and Ernesto Laclau and Chantal Mouffe (1985). The term "discourse analysis" is also used e.g. in linguistics with a very different meaning: the recording and analysing of conversations.

11. See e.g. Martin et al. (1988) on Foucault and the technologies of self as a good example of a study of a "modern myth."
12. Burton L. Mack (1993) is a radical example of this kind of research of the early stages of the formation of what later became known as Christianity: "Mythmaking in the Jesus movement…was an act of creative borrowing and the clever rearrangement of fascinating figures from several other vibrant mythologies of the time" (1993, 149). Mythmaking-hypotheses do not figure prominently in the research on early Islam. The conditions (i.e. the absence) of source materials would seem to prevent similar investigations of the early phases of the formation of Islam, and the few scholars who have presented source-critical studies have not done so in the perspective of "mythmaking."
13. As Segal notes: "This argument…confuses the object of study – believers – with the ones doing the studying – scholars. That, to use an analogy, a patient is the one with the disease hardly makes the patient the authority on it" (2005, 211).

References

Augé, Marc. 1999. *The War of Dreams: Studies in Ethno Fiction*. London: Pluto Press.

Certeau, Michel de. 1986. *Heterologies: Discourses on the Other*. Minneapolis: University of Minnesota Press.

Edwards, Derek and Jonathan Potter. 1992. *Discursive Psychology*. London: Sage.

Fairclough, Norman. 1995. *Critical Discourse Analysis: The Critical Study of Language*. London: Longman.

Frankenberry, Nancy K., ed. 2002. *Radical Interpretation in Religion*. Cambridge: Cambridge University Press.

Jensen, Jeppe Sinding. 2005. "Structuralism: Further Considerations." In *The Encyclopedia of Religion*, rev. ed., vol. 13, 8757–60. Detroit: Macmillan Reference.

Laclau, Ernesto and Chantal Mouffe. 1985. *Hegemony and Socialist Strategy: Towards a Radical Democratic Politics*. London: Verso.

Lincoln, Bruce. 1999. *Theorizing Myth: Narrative, Ideology, and Scholarship*. Chicago: University of Chicago Press.

Mack, Burton L. 1993. *The Lost Gospel: The Book of Q and Christian Origins*. New York: HarperCollins.

Martin, Luther H., Huck Gutman, Patrick H. Hutton, eds. 1988. *Technologies of the Self: A Seminar with Michel Foucault*. Amherst, MA: University of Massachusetts Press.

McCutcheon, Russell T. 2005. *Religion and the Domestication of Dissent: Or, How to Live in a Less than Perfect Nation*. London: Equinox.

Murphy, Tim. 2000. "Discourse." In *Guide to the Study of Religion*, ed. Willi Braun and R. T. McCutcheon, 396–408. London: Cassell.

Potter, Jonathan. 1996. *Representing Reality: Discourse, Rhetoric and Social Construction*. London: Sage.

Ryan, Marie-Laure. 2003. *Narrative as Virtual Reality*. Baltimore: Johns Hopkins University Press.

Ryba, Thomas. 1999–2000. "The Utopics of Disney World's Magic Kingdom: A Stroll through a Realized American Eschatology." *Temenos* 35-36: 183–223.

Schilbrack, Kevin. 2000. "Myth and Metaphysics." *International Journal for the Philosophy of Religion* 48: 65–80.

Segal, Robert A. 1999. "The Romantic Appeal of Joseph Campbell." In idem, *Theorizing about Myth*, 135–41. Amherst, MA: University of Massachusetts Press.

_____2005. "The Function of "Religion" and "Myth": A response to Russell McCutcheon." *Journal of the American Academy of Religion*, March 2005, vol. 73, no. 1: 209–13.

Index of Names

INDEX OF SUBJECTS